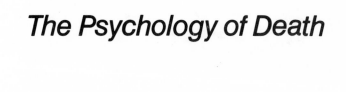

The Psychology of Death

The Psychology of Death

ROBERT KASTENBAUM
and
RUTH AISENBERG

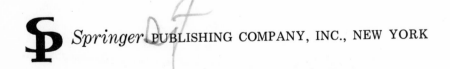 *Springer* PUBLISHING COMPANY, INC., NEW YORK

Copyright ©1972

SPRINGER Publishing Company, Inc.

200 Park Avenue South, New York, 10003

International Standard Book Number: 0-8261-1161-0

Library of Congress Catalog Card Number: 76-130822

Current printing (last digit)

10   9   8   7   6   5   4   3   2

Printed in U.S.A.

To the memory of
Bernhard J. Springer,
artist, publisher, friend

Acknowledgments

The authors wish to thank the following authors and publishers for permission to use material quoted in this book: *American Journal of Psychiatry; Boston Sunday Globe;* Columbia University Press; Giraudoux Estate; Grosset & Dunlap, Inc.; Grove Press, Inc.; Harper & Row, Publishers; Harvard University Press; C. G. Herbert; R. C. A. Hunter; Ninon Tallon Karlweis; Austin H. Kutscher; Little, Brown and Company; Adah Maurer; W. W. Norton & Company, Inc.; Murray Projector; Random House, Inc.; Joseph C. Rheingold; Routledge & Kegan Paul Ltd.; Alexander Simon; Philip Slater.

Permission to use the two poems by Edna St. Vincent Millay was granted by Norma Millay Ellis. They are from *Collected Poems*, Harper & Row, © 1934, 1962.

why this book?

It is not that easy to think about death. Often the mind recoils or skitters away. Even a highly disciplined mind may falter during its encounter (close or distant) with death. All the academic degrees and professional certifications in the world do not guarantee that one will be able to contemplate death in an open, sensitive, and balanced manner. How tempting it is to take refuge in cliche, simplification, or superscientism!

The length of this book is warning enough that we are not dealing in the quick and ready answer. *The Psychology of Death* is an attempt to examine and integrate what has been learned about man's relationship to death. Emphasis is placed upon research, and clinical and theoretical contributions by behavioral and social scientists. However, we also reach back for historical sources and direct attention to current and future patterns in our society.

Is this book, then, for psychologists or for people? The question is relevant, but not as troublesome as it might be if we were concerned with a more conventional topic. Death tends to level the distinctions between specialists and everybody else.

There is also less distinction between an "introductory" and an "advanced" approach. Essentially, we have attempted to begin from the beginning with every problem that is explored here—and to go just as far as available knowledge and the authors' own limitations will allow.

We envision three types of readers. The research-oriented reader will find here a critical review of findings and concepts, along with some new contributions by the authors. No "compleat" scholar would be entirely content with our treatment; as a matter of fact, the authors have not hesitated to share their own discontent about the present state of knowledge. If we are successful in this regard, however, we will have provided a useful resource book for those who are motivated to advance current levels of understanding in both quality and scope. It is the book that we would have liked to have had on hand several years ago when first entering into intensive contacts with the dying and death-concerned.

The next type of reader is more difficult to label. This is the person who always seems to find himself in the role of helper, counselor, or protector. He may have professional responsibilities that formalize this relationship: minister, teacher, social worker, physician, funeral director, etc. Or he may be the neighbor or colleague that people naturally seek out when problems seem to get overwhelming. For the "helping person," then, this book is intended to provide a dependable guide through the thickets of scientific and semi-scientific approaches to the psychology of death. A "how-to-make-people-feel-good-about-death" tract, it is not. Rather, we hope to have provided enough well-selected and sifted material to enable the "helping person" to draw his own conclusions in an enlightened way as he finds himself in death-related situations.

Some people are just curious about death. One does not have to be a trained researcher or mental health specialist in order to have death-related experiences and questions. Apart from the prospect of that death which is our very own, we may be concerned about other people's thoughts, feelings, and experiences. Not every curiosity will survive from the first page through the last page of this book. There is no law against browsing and dabbling for those who do not feel ready for systematic reading on this topic. Yet even the faintest curiosity about death will soon lead one to discover the strands of interrelatedness—how ideas, attitudes, and actions in many spheres of our lives exercise an influence upon our relationship to death—including determination of the date that will be recorded on our own death certificates. For the general reader

we hope to have provided a variety of "handles" by which he can obtain a grasp on the psychology of death.

But is it necessary for curiosity, helpfulness, and knowledge-seeking to be parceled out among three "types" of readers? Can we not approach the psychology of death from each of these standpoints, no matter who we are? Consider, for example, one major theme that is developed in this book. We contend that much can be done to prevent premature death in our society. This challenge is conceived as being an intrinsic part of the psychology of death. The goal, then, is action-oriented. Life-saving actions, however, require a basis in fact. Broad-ranging, even "naive" curiosity has an important role in the identification of relevant factors. What we see with our own eyes and what we learn through media ought to stimulate our curiosity about the place of death in our lives. Curiosity is not sufficient, however. There must be a knack for obtaining, or at least recognizing, what can be accepted as "admissible evidence." Respect for authentic inquiry and high standards of evidence can be joined both to an adventuresome curiosity and the motivation to protect the quality and duration of human life.

Neither the first nor the last word on the subject, this book is an invitation to *continue* the dialogue—with our best minds forward.

R.K.
R.A.

Contents

Introduction

". . . for is not philosophy the study of death?"

—Socrates

A "psychology of death" is both premature and overdue. The prematurity will quickly become evident as the limitations of present knowledge, methodology, and conceptualization are exposed on these pages. No topic in psychology has been more neglected through the years—yet one might contend that psychology *originated* in thoughts about death.

Preliterate man achieved his closet approximation to a definition of mental life when he considered death. The "soul" or "spirit" was regarded as that-which-departs from the corpse. Man's inner life was pictured as an object or creature that is likely to venture away from its bodily residence either temporarily (as in dreams and sneezes) or permanently (as in death). The more sophisticated Greek concept of *psyche* was in large measure an elaboration of that-which-departs. Perhaps the best illustration of this may be found in Socrates' discussion of psyche within the context of his own impending death (1). The anticipated loss of one's most intimate and treasured possession—his own "psyche" or "soul"—seems to have generated not only the discipline of philosophy, but also its offspring, psychology. Were death unknown to man, then presumably we would not have become so

aware of our own mental life, so self-conscious.

Psychology, however, has ignored the implicit mandate from Socrates. It is true that perception, cognition, motivation, instrumental and expressive behavior, and interpersonal relations have been subjected to increasingly refined investigation. But the relationship of these processes and of "the whole person" to death has seldom been considered. How, for example, do perceptions and cognitions of death influence our daily life? Our total development over the life-span? Our value judgments and ambitions? Perhaps this line of questioning, so relevant in the eyes of the ancients, is not truly relevant in "modern psychology." Because death was a significant point of departure for both philosophy and psychology does not necessarily mean that these disciplines should remain preoccupied with death. Nevertheless, we are struck by how little our own field, psychology, has contributed to the understanding of death in proportion to its more general contributions to human knowledge. We would not care to argue that all psychology should be reducible to a psychology of death, but we do wish to suggest that we have been overlong in developing that particular kind of knowledge and understanding that was so prized by Socrates.

Although we lack an organized body of knowledge that might be termed "the psychology of death," we are not completely without materials. Numerous observations on death have been made since the execution of Socrates some 25 centuries ago. Even an incomplete classification of death observations by source reveals a great diversity of materials:

1. Death observations made within the context of psychological research;

2. Death observations made within the context of research in the other social sciences and psychiatry;

3. Death observations made within the context of psychological, psychiatric, or social work services;

4. Death observations made within the context of medical or quasi-medical services;

5. Death observations made by "participant-observers," (e.g., diaries and other documents of daily life);

6. Death observations embodied within artistic productions;

7. Death observations and regulations made within the context of governmental, legal, and other institutions of social control;

8. Death observations made within the context of religious practices and theological formulations;

9. Death observations made within philosophical or other speculative contexts;

10. Death observations made with reference to subhuman phenomena (e.g., animal behavior, biochemistry of death).

This book naturally concentrates upon information that is available from the first source, but draws samples from the other sources as appears relevant. While in no way constituting a substitute for a "biochemistry of death," "anthropology of death," or "cultural history of death," the present work must delve into these fields

to some extent to achieve any sort of perspective.

In attempting to formulate a *psychology* of death we have not only the problem of deciding how far to pursue the topic in other disciplines, but also the problem of how far to pursue the subject in psychology itself. The relative neglect of death *per se* as a research topic does not mean that psychology has nothing to contribute. Concepts, methods, and findings pertaining to a variety of problem areas in psychology may be seen to have considerable bearing upon death once we become sensitized to this possibility. We have a little direct information, for example, concerning children's thoughts of death. But the cognitive processes of the child in general have been examined in hundreds of scientific investigations, as well as by millions of intelligence and achievement tests. Clearly, we could not deal adequately with the child's thoughts of death if we did not also consider the general nature of thought processes in children—but this latter topic in itself requires (and has several times received) book-length consideration. So it is that we have decided to draw upon a number of resources in psychology that were developed without specific reference to death, but not in an exhaustive manner. We hope simply to provide some useful illustrations of ways in which the present strengths of psychology can be applied to this new-old subject matter.

The Psychology of Death is organized around questions that appear to be worth asking, even if satisfactory answers have not yet been forthcoming. Often these queries were developed simply by appending a question-mark to assumptions and cliches that many of us carry about with us. It is frequently assumed, for example, that we know what death *is* (although our knowledge of its antecedents, correlates, and consequences may be imperfect). Instead of sharing this assumption, we prefer to ask, "What is death?" This question unites the chapters from 2 through 7, although each has its own specific content.

In exploring the nature of death we consider not only "Death as a Thought" (Chapter 2), but also the ways in which we go about "Facing the Thought of Death" (Chapter 3). This latter chapter includes the kinds of problems usually considered under the rubric of "attitudes toward death" or "fear of death." In Chapter 4 we step out of psychology *per se* to seek a broader perspective "On the Logic and Methodologic of Death." Then the next three chapters trace—and challenge—our understanding of death as it appears in different contexts.

From this emphasis upon the individual's understanding of and relationship to death, we move next to a consideration of dying and death as phenomena that occur within a cultural milieu. How do societies organize themselves to cope with death? After offering an interpretation of "death systems" in past societies (Chapter 8), we examine these systems in today's society (Chapter 9).

Sometimes it is assumed that how a person lives has something to do with how long he lives. From this general assumption we have attempted to generate a set of more specific questions pertaining to the relationship between psychosocial variables and longevity. The six chapters (9 through 15) devoted to this topic comprise most of the second part of this book. We conclude by "Looking Ahead".

Is a well-balanced "psychology of death" offered in these pages? Probably not. There is no available standard by which to determine what to include or exclude, or how extensively to treat a given topic. Perhaps we give too much attention to topics that are central to the research interests of the authors; perhaps we have unwittingly omitted material of great pertinence and worth; perhaps, in spite of our intentions, we have perpetuated assumptions and stereotypes that deserve to be challenged. The reader is urged to protect himself at all times, while not closing his mind to the questions and challenges that abound here.

REFERENCE

1. Plato. Phaedrus. In *The dialogues of Plato.* (Translated into English with analyses and introduction by B. Jowett.) London: Macmillan & Co. 1875, Vol. 2, pp. 75-160.

Death as a Thought

D-e-a-t-h. This sequence of five letters is fixed and familiar. It is easy to assume that the *meaning* of this term is also fixed (unvarying) and familiar (truly known to us). Furthermore, one is tempted to assume that d-e-a-t-h refers to a "real something" (or a "real nothing") *out there*.

These assumptions will not be honored in the present chapter. For the moment we are setting aside most of what we know or think we know about "real death." Instead we will try to become aware of those mental operations through which we develop and utilize concepts of death. The elementary logic we are invoking here might be stated as follows:

1. Terms such as "dying," "dead," and "death" generally are *intended* by us to *refer* to phenomena that are outside of or beyond our minds. For example, I *think* of Socrates as dead—but the important point is that Socrates *really is* dead.

2. But we never "really" know what is *out there*. We never even know (beyond the possibility of plausible counter-argument) that there *is* an *out there* out there. We live within and by our own psychological processes. The correspondence between our personal thoughts and feelings and anything else in the universe is a matter for conjecture (as it has been for centuries).

3. We do know that concepts of death have a particular form of existence that is amenable to analysis and under-standing. It is even amenable to controlled empirical investigations. Concepts of death are: *concepts*. We can study the development and structure of death concepts in the individual. We can learn how death concepts get along within the individual's entire community of concepts. We can attempt to discover relationships between concepts of death and such covert states as anxiety or resignation. We can attempt to discover relationships with overt behaviors, such as risk-taking actions or the purchase of "life" insurance. We can examine cultures and subcultures with respect to their concepts of death and their implications for social structure and function.

4. This level of analysis is highly relevant because it is clearly within the realm of psychology. Throughout this book, the reader will find that we often delve into topics that are on the other side of the garden wall (especially if he is the kind of psychologist who prefers to labor in a small, well-manicured yard). It is appropriate, then, to make what we can out of that material which does fall within the field of psychology per se. Even if our present knowledge is quite limited, there is some security perhaps in the feeling that we are looking at death from a perspective that is germane to our scientific background.

In short, we are attending to death first as a psychological concept. It is at least a psychological concept, even if it is more. At later points in this book we will attempt to integrate this approach with other viewpoints.

A FEW GENERAL PROPOSITIONS

Perhaps we should expose some of our conclusions ahead of time. In this way the reader may be better prepared to dispute or agree with the materials to come.

1. *The concept of death is always relative.* We will emphasize its relativity to *developmental level*, although a case could be made for other frameworks of relativity. By developmental level we do not necessarily mean the individual's chronological age. It is obvious that chronological age provides important clues to the person's mode of thinking. But we are concerned with developmental level in a structural sense that will already be familiar to those acquainted with the writings of Heinz Werner (1), Jean Piaget (2), and some others. The point, in any event, is that the concept of death should be interpreted within its organismic context.

2. *The concept of death is exceedingly complex.* In most instances it is not sufficient to express the death concept in one or two propositions. Along with the sheer complexity of the death concept we find it does not invariably hold together as a unified, internally-consistent structure. In short, we must be cautious in thinking about somebody having a concept of death in the same way that he has a Social Security number or a big toe.

3. *Concepts of death change.* This proposition is implied by those already mentioned. When we characterize a person's concept of death at a particular point in time we should not suppose that this description will continue to hold true for him indefinitely.

4. *The developmental "goal" of death concepts is obscure, ambiguous, or still being evolved.* It is customary to trace growth curves from starting point to apex. To mention one of the clearest examples, we expect the child's height to increase until it attains its "goal": adult height. (One might also persevere to trace the decline of the growth curve after a period of relative stability during the early and middle years of adulthood.)

Conceptions of death cannot be graphed with the same degree of confidence. Technical reasons for this limitation include difficulties in assessing conceptions of death, and in establishing appropriate quantitative units by which progress or lack of progress can be demonstrated. But the more crucial problem has to do with content, not method: we just do not know what constitutes the most mature or ideal conception of death. There are opinions, of course (too often passed off as though established facts). These opinions represent value orientations rather than inexorable conclusions derived from systematic theory or research. Seldom are attitudinal components distinguished from the more purely cognitive aspects of the conception. Is there, in fact, one and only one mature conception of death? And how can we be certain that the individual does not achieve a mature conception of death relatively early in life, but then retreat to a socially sanctioned position that is less adequate from a developmental standpoint? These questions are merely illustrative. We are suggesting that too little is known at the present time to assume that there is an obvious developmental goal toward which early conceptions of death advance inch by inevitable inch.

5. *Death concepts are influenced by the situational context.* How we conceptualize death at a particular moment is likely to be influenced by many situational factors. Is there a dying person in the room with us? A corpse? Does the situation contain a possible threat to our own life? Are we alone or with friends? Is it bright noon, or black midnight? The situa-

tion may selectively draw out one type of death cognition among the several we possess. Or, the situation may even stimulate us to develop new or modified death conceptions.

6. *Death concepts are related to behavior.* Most immediately, perhaps, we think of a person engaging in an action that is directly and positively related to his death cognition. He comes to the conclusion, for example, that death is the gateway to eternal bliss. Suicide follows as his relevant behavior. But the relationship is seldom, if ever, that simple. Similar death cognitions can lead to different behaviors, just as similar behaviors can be preceded by different sequences of psychologic. Another person with the "eternal bliss" conception of death stays alive so that he can bring his message of hope and comfort to others. Still another person commits suicide without giving much thought to the prospect of an afterlife; he is totally absorbed in his need to escape from unbearable life stress.

One's concept of death can influence behavior in remote and complex ways. Behavior patterns that do not seem to have anything in particular to do with death may nevertheless be influenced by these cognitions. Insomnia, for example, or panic upon temporary separation from a loved one, sometimes can be traced to death concerns. Clinicians Hattie Rosenthal (3) and Herman Feifel (4) are among the experienced observers who have discovered death thoughts to be closely interwoven with many types of behavior.

KNOWING AND RELATING

It is difficult, in practice, to maintain a clear distinction between concepts and attitudes. In this chapter, we concentrate upon the ways in which we explain or interpret death to ourselves. In a later chapter we concentrate upon our attitudes or orientations toward death.

Illustration: We ask a child what a shaggle-toothed boondoggler would look like, were there such an animal. He provides us with a vivid drawing or verbal description. He has, in effect, conveyed his understanding of the boondoggler. Now we inquire what he would do if he saw one of them coming down the street. Here he has the opportunity to express his attitude or orientation ("I would run away—fast!" or "I'd say, 'Here snaggletooth, here's some nice milk for you. Will you give me a ride on your back'?")

Our total relationship with any object involves both conceptual and attitudinal components. The mere fact that we know, or think we know something about this object, is sufficient to guarantee some kind of relationship. We are related to this object *through our own cognitive activity.* Similarly, the existence of an orientation (e.g., approach or avoidance) presumes some cognitive component. At the least, we have performed the mental operation of classifying the object as something-to-be-avoided.

We shall not insist upon an artificial separation of death concepts from our total organismic relationship to death. But it will be useful to begin with an emphasis upon death as a psychological concept. Taken by itself, the topic is complex enough. And consideration of this specific problem will provide helpful perspective for the variety of other problems that lie ahead.

"YOU ARE DEAD"

At least two forms of the death conception should be clearly distinguished at the outset. The first of these is death-of-the-other. There is reason to believe that the cognition, "You are dead" develops more rapidly than the inward-looking, "I will die." Later, both types of death conception will be considered in some detail from a developmental viewpoint. At the moment, we are interested only in sketching some of their implications.

"You are dead" is a proposition that is related to the following considerations:

1. You are *absent*. But what does it mean to be absent? We must appreciate the observer's frame of reference. For a young child, the frame of reference is largely perceptual. Absence means *not* here-and-now. The child is not yet equipped to distinguish adequately between spatial and temporal distance. Suppose that you are "away," in another city. From an adult frame of reference, you have a spatial existence at the present time. But the child experiences your absence (5). You are not in *his* perceptual space at this time, therefore, you are *not*. (There will be an important amendment to this statement later.)

2. I am *abandoned*. This statement is almost a reciprocal of the preceding proposition. Your disappearance from my perceptual frame of reference has an effect upon my sense of security. As a parent or other crucial person, you constitute a significant aspect of the universe that is known to the child. As the child, I am not merely aware of *your absence*, but of the *presence of discomfort feelings within myself.*

3. Your absence plus my sense of abandonment contributes to the general sense of *separation*. I have been alienated from one of my most important sources of contact and support. If this separation is sufficiently critical to me, then I may experience a pervasive sense of losing contact with the environment, not just with you. Furthermore, I may also have the impression of being wrenched away from you. This trauma could intensify the already bleak picture of absence and abandonment.

4. The separation has *no limits*. The young child does not grasp the concept of futurity, or of time in general, in the way that most adults have come to develop these concepts. This is a multidimensional

problem. It may be sufficient at this point to say that the child's immediate sense of separation is not modulated by future expectations. He cannot tell himself, "Mother has gone away . . . but she will return in five days." He cannot distinguish among short-term, long-term, and final (irreversible) separations. Once the separation experience has been induced, he has no dependable way of planning, estimating, or anticipating its conclusion. What the outsider may regard as a brief separation (based upon consensual clock or calendar time) may be indistinguishable in the child's mind from the prospect of prolonged separation.

5. The child's involvement in *recurring psychobiological rhythms* complicates his relationship to separation and death. He is not fully a knowing participant in the world of "objective" time that moves unit by standard unit from the past, through the present, to the future (6). His time begins each morning when he awakes. His midday nap signals a "time out." External rhythms of night and day and internal rhythms of hunger-satiation, sleep-activation, etc., exert a strong influence over his appreciation of time.

How does this relationship to time affect his conception of death-of-the-other? The four preceding points emphasize, in various ways, the child's vulnerability to separation. He cannot, for example, distinguish well between the prospect of moderate-length and long-term or final separation. Now we must add a factor that might seem contradictory. Bear in mind these two points: a) the child's time experience is conditioned by cyclical rhythms, and b) he is apt to experience sensations of absence, abandonment, and separation in situations where adults would argue that the child has not "really" been abandoned.

We see that the sense of *limitless* separation or the *endlessness* of any experience conflicts with the periodic nature of his experiences. It is a bit difficult to express this relationship. As a child who feels abandoned, I have no way of establishing a future limit upon my present experience. In fact, one of the reasons I am so distressed is that this unpleasant experience shows no signs of being self-limiting. Nevertheless, my psychobiological state is always in transition. I am becoming hungry or sleepy. And the environment in which I am embedded is also in transition. The sun is coming up or it is going down. Various periodic household routines are being started or completed. Concretely, as a cyclical creature in a cyclical environment, I am not likely to maintain a constant frame of reference over a protracted period of (clock or calendar) time. There are breaks and interruptions in even my most steadfast thought and behavior patterns. In other words, despite my inability to posit *limits* to the separation experience, I do not actually have a continuous experience. Periodic changes in my inner state and my external environment distract and rest me. There will be more to say later about the relationship we have been proposing here.

What is relevant now is the connection between periodicity and the child's vulnerability to separation experiences. Again, as a child I may "misinterpret" your temporary departure as being a consequential separation. By this same token, however, I may underestimate a consequential separation—even your death. My cyclical patterns of functioning lead me to anticipate that every end has a fresh beginning, just as every beginning has an end. You have been away a long time now (by clock-calendar as well as subjective time). But I do not "know" how long this has been. And I have deeply rooted within me the expectation that the familiar pattern of separation-reunion will be completed. This is another point that we will want to keep in mind when we attempt to trace the entire developmental sequence of death conceptions. The proposition, for now, is that the child is more vulnerable to the death-implications of trivial separations,

and more protected from the death-implications of substantial separations than what might appear to be the case from the viewpoint of an observing adult.

2 "I WILL DIE"

This proposition assumes that one has developed quite a constellation of abstract concepts. The set we offer below is not intended to be exhaustive. The statement, "I will die", implies such related concepts as the following:

1. *I* am an individual with a life of my own, a personal existence.
2. I belong to a *class* of beings one of whose attributes is mortality.
3. Using the intellectual process of logical deduction, I arrive at the conclusion that my personal death is a *certainty*.
4. There are *many possible causes* of my death, and these causes might operate in many different combinations. Although I might evade or escape one particular cause, *I cannot evade all causes.*
5. My death will occur in the *future*. By future, I mean a time-to-live that has not yet elapsed.
6. But I do not know *when* in the future my death will occur. The event is certain; the timing is uncertain.
7. Death is a *final* event. My life ceases. This means that I will never again experience, think, or act, at least as a human being on this earth.
8. Accordingly death is the *ultimate separation* of myself from the world (7).

"I will die" thus implies self-awareness, logical thought operations, conceptions of probability, necessity, and causation, of personal and physical time, of finality and separation. It also seems to require the bridging of a tremendous gap: from what I have experienced of life to the formulation of a death concept. It is a good deal easier to develop a concept of a shaggle-toothed boondoggler; I have had contact with many different animals, so it is just a matter of selecting and combining attributes. Death, however, essentially is a non-experience. I have not been dead (the state). I have not experienced death (the process of life coming to a final halt). The very mental operations I use in my efforts to fathom death falsify as they proceed. The mind's own modus operandi equips it for interpreting life or life-like processes better than the alien void. Perhaps now and then I permit myself to believe that I have actually perceived or formed a concept *of* death. Closer to the truth, however, is the realization that I have simply observed my mind as it scurries about in the dark.

Having seen a dead person, animal, or plant is likely to contribute to my conception of death. Yet these perceptions do not truly bridge the gap. The deadness is perceived from the outside only. What it feels like not to feel eludes me. Furthermore, under some circumstances I am liable to misinterpret my perceptions, seeing the living as dead, or vice versa (Chapter 5). Experiences with the dead, however, is another one of those topics we will keep in mind as we attempt to understand the development of death conceptions.

DEATH CONCEPTIONS IN INFANCY AND EARLY CHILDHOOD

Most developmental psychologists believe that the very young child (from birth to about two years) has no understanding of death (8). This opinion is consistent with the more general contention that young children lack the ability to grasp *any* abstract conception. Jean Piaget, for an important example, has offered a fine-grained analysis of mental development from early infancy through adolescence (9). He identifies many stages of development that seem to have been overlooked by previous observers. Within the period of infancy alone, Piaget recog-

nizes six different stages of mental development. But he does not consider that genuine "formal operations" (abstract conceptualization) enter into the picture until many years have passed. Even the ten-year-old, with all the intellectual resources he now has at his disposal, has only just reached the stage of "concrete operations." He can deal adequately with the "actual," but is just beginning to take proper account of that which is "potential" or "possible." Finally, in adolescence, one is able to think about thought and, thus, bring to bear the full intellectual resources that seem to be required for comprehension of death.

Nevertheless, we believe there is much yet to be learned about conceptions of death in early childhood. It may be true enough that highly abstract and well-verbalized conceptions are beyond the toddler's range. But we do not share the frequent assumption of developmental psychologists that very young children do not have any understanding of death (or, for that matter, that they are incapable of powers of abstraction and generalization). Between the extremes of "no understanding" and explicit, integrated abstract thought there are many ways by which the young mind can enter into relationship with death. This topic deserves more attention than can be provided here. We cannot, for example, examine all the ways in which conceptions of death are relevant to stages of mental development even in one psychologist's (Piaget's) system. And empirical data on death concepts is sparse in this age range. But we can at least attempt to reopen this area that seems to have been so prematurely sealed off. (Psychoanalytically-oriented observers have been more alert than most "straight" developmentalists to early conceptions of death, as we shall see.)

Early Exposure to Death-of-Others

Let us first consider the young child's response to the death of a significant person in his life. This exploration is intended chiefly to provide some clues as to how death registers itself on the minds of the very young. It will not tell us precisely how the infant or small child thinks of death, but it will tell us something about the nature and extent of his response to that event to which we adults give the term, "death."

One of the earliest researches into the psychology of death touched upon this question. G. Stanley Hall and Colin Scott (10) of Clark University obtained responses to death questionnaires. The respondents were adults, but part of their task was to recall their earliest experiences with death. Hall later wrote that ". . . the first impression of death often comes from a sensation of coldness in touching the corpse of a relative and the reaction is a nervous start at the contrast with the warmth that the contact of cuddling and hugging was wont to bring. The child's exquisite temperature sense feels a chill where it formerly felt heat. Then comes the immobility of face and body where it used to find prompt movements of response. There is no answering kiss, pat, or smile. In this respect sleep seems strange but its brother, death, only a little more so. Often the half-opened eyes are noticed with awe. The silence and tearfulness of friends are also impressive to the infant, who often weeps reflexly or sympathetically" (11).

He continues: "Children of from two to five are very prone to fixate certain accessories of death, often remembering the corpse but nothing else of a dead member of the family. But funerals and burials are far more often and more vividly remembered. Such scenes are sometimes the earliest recollections of adults" (12).

It is worth adding here that recent investigations of adults' earliest memories also have turned up death experiences such as those to which Hall has alluded (13, 14).

Funeral customs have changed since the childhood of Hall's respondents (most of whom were born in the middle third of the nineteenth century). Perhaps children tend to be more insulated from funerary proceedings today. But it is interesting to read what Hall has to say about children's cognitive reactions to death when they did have the opportunity to be on the scene: "Little children often focus on some minute detail (thanatic fetishm) and ever after remember, for example, the bright pretty handles or the silver nails of the coffin, the plate, the cloth binding, their own or others' articles of apparel, the shroud, flowers, and wreaths on or near the coffin or thrown into the grave, countless stray phrases of the preacher, the fear lest the bottom of the coffin should drop out or the straps with which it is lowered into the ground should slip or break, a stone in the first handful or shovelful of earth thrown upon the coffin, etc. The hearse is almost always prominent in such memories and children often want to ride in one" (15).

And Hall even has an explanation to offer for the latter observation: "This, of course, conforms to the well-known laws of erotic fetishism by which the single item in a constellation of them that alone can find room in the narrow field of consciousness is over-determined and exaggerated in importance because *the affectivity that belongs to items that are repressed and cannot get into consciousness is transferred to those that can do so*" (16). [Italics ours.]

The observations we have been considering so far were made retrospectively. There are formidable difficulties involved in attempting to determine how accurately these adult-looking-backward reports convey what actually took place in early childhood. The same problem holds true for memories reported within the context of psychoanalytic therapy. This does not mean that we are free to neglect these observations, but that additional sources of information should be obtained.

Retrospective studies are a bit less hazardous when we limit our concern to "objective" or "factual" information. One especially relevant fact is the death of a parent. In many (but not all) instances it can be established that a person had lost one of his parents by death at a particular age. Let us turn to one of the most carefully performed studies available on this topic, with special reference to parental bereavement very early in childhood. (We cannot remain strictly within the birth-to-two-years range, because investigators have tended to make larger grouping of years in their data analysis.) Felix Brown, a British psychiatrist, examined the relationship between childhood bereavement and the development of depressive illness in later life (17). He obtained his basic data from the records of 216 unselected depressive patients who were receiving psychiatric services at the time. Brown made use of two control groups: orphanhood tables from the 1921 census, and the records of 267 medical patients who were receiving treatment at the same time as those suffering from depression. His results are closely tied to a series of statistical comparisons which we do not have space to report in detail. We would like to call attention, however, to some of the findings which are most relevant to our present focus.

Approximately two out of every five adult depressive patients had lost at least one parent by death before the age of 15. This compares with 1-in-8 and 1-in-5 figures for the control groups. One of the more striking findings (from our viewpoint) was that the death of the father had occurred by the age of four in approximately *twice* the number of cases of boys who later experienced depressive pathology (as compared with both control groups). Paternal bereavement was probably higher than usual among very young children during this period in history because of the high death rate of young men in World War I. This unfortunate fact may account for the relatively large number of paternal bereavements, but it

does not account for the differences in adult depression that seem to be related to childhood bereavement.

Brown concludes from his total findings that "bereavement in childhood is one of the most significant factors in the development of depressive illness in later life" (18). However, he does not attempt to oversimplify the etiology of depression, and recognizes the role played by several other factors. This British psychiatrist considers that the effects of bereavement may be long delayed, or at least, their manifestations in clearly psychopathological behavior.

Brown's findings give us some reason to believe that exposure to death in the early years of life can exert an important influence upon the child's subsequent development. Three of his case illustrations involve people whose bereavement had occurred prior to age two.

With all of its limitations, the clinical case method still remains a valuable source of observations and hypotheses. David M. Moriarty, M.D., director of psychiatry at Worcester State Hospital, believes that his psychotherapeutic work has revealed a connection between early bereavement and a girl's later fear of mothering. One of his patients was a woman in her thirties who was more than depressed: she was also in a state of fear that she might kill her own child. "This woman. . . had a brother who died at the age of one year, when she was three years old. The patient's illness coincided in time with the birth of a nephew who was given the same name as the brother who had died" (19).

This case suggests that bereavement as early as the third year of life can have its implications for death-related behavior several decades later. It also attests to the frequent occurrence, as Brown has also noted, of precipitating factors in the current life situation that seem to activate the early trauma. Most of Moriarty's cases seem to have involved bereavement that took place a little later in childhood than the case we selected for mention. Our aim was to indicate the *possibility* that very early exposure to death is registered forcefully upon the child's mind.

Moriarty reports another interesting and relevant case in more detail (20). Here the focus is upon the effect of bereavement on total development, rather than mothering behavior alone. "Mrs. Q." had undergone severe depressive episodes for over a decade. She attempted to take her life on three occasions, and twice was treated with electroshock therapy (but not successfully). Her personality disturbance was obviously of major proportions.

Mrs. Q's mother had died of appendicitis when the patient was a child of three. She recalled standing beside her uncle at the graveside, her arm around his leg. According to Moriarty, "During her treatment, she used to call me in a panic and would say she felt 'the world is coming in on me.' The thought behind this fear was traced to this graveyard scene when they threw a shovel full of dirt on the lowered coffin" (21). The psychotherapist concluded from his work with this patient that "Mrs. Q. lived most of her life afraid that she would lose other people she loved. . . . She felt her children had *no* mother and that someone ought to take her place and do a better job. She felt dead, non-existent, wanted to die, and feared dying. . . . The most impressive fact was that she talked and thought about the death of her mother as much as if it had just happened. This tragic event of forty years ago was still uppermost in her mind" (22).

Such observations as these provide circumstantial evidence for the proposition that the very young child can be impressed by his exposure to death. He may not have high level thought operations at his disposal, but death-related *perceptions* can make a strong and enduring impact. Note that both Hall and Moriarty (years apart in their observations and employing different methods of obtaining their data) have called attention to vivid recollections

of perceptual details. This is not surprising. The very young child cannot label and classify his experiences the way an older and more verbal person can. How is he able to register and maintain the memory of significant experiences? The camera of his mind seems to be equipped for this purpose. He records the perceived scene. This perceptual recording then serves as an organizing point for the inner feelings and thoughts which could not find verbal expression at the time. *Perceptions* of death thus may be important predecessors of subsequent *concepts*.

Actual observations of children's behavior in death situations (as contrasted with adult memories of the same) have been made. However, these observations are none too plentiful or detailed. Information is particularly scarce concerning the response of very young children. At least two factors are probably responsible for the scarcity of such reports: a) often it is *assumed* that very young children do not know enough about death to respond in a way that is worth studying; and b) the limited verbal capacity of the very young child stands as a formidable barrier to exploring his inner response. Systematic research should be possible on this topic if one is prepared to devote sufficient time to the development of appropriate procedures. Exploratory work by psychiatrist Gregory Rochlin, for example, has indicated that a series of fantasy-play sessions can reveal important aspects of the child's interpretation of death (23). Illustrations from his observations will be given a little later.

Consider the "death-exposure" responses of these two very young boys. These responses afford us opportunities to glimpse something of the young child's mind as it tries to come to terms with death, and something of the difficulties adults encounter in attempting to interpret the child's interpretations.

David, at 18 months, was toddling around the back yard. He pointed at something on the ground. Daddy looked.

It was a dead bird. The boy labeled what he saw, "buh . . . buh" (his approximation, at the time, for bird). But he appeared uncertain and puzzled. Furthermore, he made no effort to touch the bird. This was unusual caution for a child who characteristically tried to touch or pick up everything he could reach. David then crouched over and moved slightly closer to the bird. His face changed expression. From its initial expression of excited discovery it had moved to puzzlement: now it took on the aspect of a grief mask. To his parent's surprise, the child's face was set in a frozen, ritualized expression resembling nothing so much as the stylized Greek dramatic mask for tragedy. Daddy only said, "Yes, bird . . . dead bird." In typically adult conflict, the parent thought of adding, "Don't touch," but then decided against applying this injunction. In any event, David made no effort to touch.

Every morning for the next few days, David would begin his morning explorations by toddling over to the dead-bird-place. He no longer assumed the ritual-mask expression, but he still restrained spontaneously, from touching. The bird was allowed to remain there until greatly reduced by decomposition. The parents reasoned that he might as well have the opportunity to see the natural processes at work. This had been, to the best of the parents' knowledge, David's first exposure to death. No general change in his behavior was noted (nor had any been expected). The small first chapter had concluded.

But a few weeks later there was a second dead bird to be discovered (this fatality was clearly the work of a local and well-known cat). David had quite a different orientation toward death #2. He picked up the bird and gestured with it. What was on his mind? Something— because he was also "speaking" with insistence. When his parents did not seem to comprehend his wishes, the boy reached up toward a tree, holding the bird above

his head. He repeated the gesture several times. Finally (perhaps) comprehending, Daddy tried to explain that being placed back on the tree would not help the bird. David continued to insist, accompanying his command now with gestures that could be interpreted as a bird flying.

All too predictably, the bird did not fly when returned to the tree. David insisted that the effort be repeated several times. Then he lost interest altogether.

But there was a sequel a few weeks later (by now, autumn). David and Daddy were walking in the woods. There were many little discoveries to be made. After a while, however, the boy's attention became thoroughly engaged by a single fallen leaf. He tried to place it back on the tree himself. Failure. He gave the leaf to his father with "instructions" that the leaf be restored to its rightful place. Failure again. When Daddy started to try again, David shook his head, "no." He looked both sober and convinced. Although leaves repeatedly were seen to fall and dead animals were encountered every now and then, little David made no further efforts to reverse their fortunes.

These observations illustrate some of the reporter's difficulties: a) He does not know *when* the death-exposure will occur. b) Although his "reading" of the child's emotional response may be accurate, there is no way to confirm his impressions directly, and he may be either attributing too much or not enough to the child's mind. c) It is possible that the observer either does not see or fails to recognize other incidents that belong in the sequence: d) A trained observer who is not related to the child would likely be more "objective," but also would lack sufficient context to interpret specific behaviors.

Recognizing these and other limitations attendant upon the parent-child "generation gap," it is still worthwhile to keep in mind some of the implications of what has been observed: a) The exposure to death did seem to call forth unprecedented and unusual behavior in this child (that is, behavior *he* had not shown before). b) It is not entirely out of question that there may be a disposition to behave toward death in a certain way that is available even to the very young; we hesitate to speak of an "instinctual" reaction, but there is insufficient evidence to dismiss the possibility altogether. c) Responses generated from one death-situation may be capable of generalization to related situations even when the child is quite young (as a matter of fact, limited verbal and conceptual development might serve to facilitate *increased* generalization as one is less able to identify similarities and dissimilarities). d) *Learning* about the properties of death may take place at an early age.

Complexity of the child's relationship to death increases rapidly within the first few years of life. Consider Michael, whose known encounters with death began when he was about two-and-a-quarter years of age. For the following information we are grateful to his father, psychologist Szandor Brent. A more extended account and analysis will be offered elsewhere (24).

Michael had not drunk from a bottle in more than a year. But now, for a period of about six weeks, he had been waking up several times during the night screaming hysterically for a bottle. He could not be satisfied unless the ingredients included both warm water and sugar. Attempts to talk him out of it were useless. He would tearfully insist, "But I *have* to have it!"

One evening his father comforted the boy for a while, and then asked, "What will happen if you don't get your bottle?" Michael replied, "Then I won't (or can't) make contact!" What did that reply mean? Michael explained, sobbing: "If I run out of gas, I can't make contact—my engine won't go. You know!" This statement was punctuated by sobs. The elder Brent reports that at this point "the pieces suddenly began to fall together. During the first two weeks in August we had gone to a country cottage for vacation. At the cottage, we *ran out of gas*

three times. . . . The second time, in a motorboat, far out in the center of a large lake, at high noon, with a strong off-shore wind, and no one else visible out on the lake. At that time I had become anxious. . ." (25).

Michael was asked, "What are you afraid will happen if you run out of gas?" "My motor won't run and then I'll die," he announced, still tearful.

The psychologist then remembered how he and a student had spoken in the boy's presence about how their motor had "died" while they had been puttering with an old car some weeks previously. One of them had also said, "The battery's dead." Dr. Brent asked his boy, "Is that what you are afraid of . . . that your bottle is like gasoline, and like, when the car runs out of gas, the car dies, so if you run out of food, you die?" Michael shook his head, "Yes." But this first attempt at a reassuring explanation did not come across. It was only when he provided the following explanation that Michael understood and relaxed.

"But a car has a key, right? (Michael nods.) And we can turn it on and off anytime we like, right? (I feel him relaxing now.) But where's *your* key? (I lift his shirt playfully and look at his belly button.) Is this your key? (He laughs.) Lemme see. Can I turn your motor on and off? (He laughs again.) See. You are really nothing like a car. Nobody can turn you on and off. Once your motor's on, you don't have to worry about it dying. You can sleep through the whole night, and your motor will keep running without you ever having to fill it up with gas. Do you know what I mean? (He answers, 'Yes,' and I feel his body relax.)" That night, Michael slept through—without a bottle.

Yet even at this early age, Michael's "death history" was more complex than what has already been reported. Upon further thought, his father could piece together a series of incidents that began as far back as his 21st month, when a pet parakeet died. Subsequent incidents included observing his baby sister's umbilical cord fall off during a bath, and his seemingly endless questions about the status of a dead relative whose photograph he had seen.

With this second "case history" before us it would be possible to illustrate a number of additional points. We will concentrate, however, upon three implications that are worth keeping in mind:

1. Exposure to death can contribute, directly or indirectly, to emotional and behavioral disturbances in early childhood. This supplements the material reported previously to the effect that early bereavement experiences may be related to disturbances many years later.

2. Ambiguities in adult language and thought are apt to confuse the young child as he attempts to make sense out of death. At the same time, however, these ambiguities help to introduce him to symbolic usages. Death has more than one meaning; context is important. It is difficult to comprehend how both a battery and a person can be "dead," but in different ways. As he matures, he will be even more versatile in his application of the death concept (e.g., "dead" center, "dying for a cigarette," "aborted" campaign, "deathly silence," etc.). Right from the beginning, then, the infant has the complicated task of learning what is meant by death both in the basic physical sense of the term, and in its varied metaphoric applications.

3. Michael's questioning, so difficult to satisfy, and David's look of puzzlement and uncertainty attest to the fact that death already is providing an intellectual challenge. As we have noted, developmental psychologists and educators tend to emphasize the young child's lack of conceptual ability. He is not yet mentally equipped to understand death (even to the limited extent that his elders are equipped). But the corollary too often is neglected: the young child *tries* to understand. He is able to recognize that a problem has risen before his eyes. And he may persist in his efforts to solve the problem. We err if we simply compare the child's conceptual structure with our own. Such a comparison does little except to confirm the obvious. Would it not be more instructive if we observed the young child's mental operations for their own sake? Patient, unbiased research might be rewarded in many ways. Most relevantly, perhaps, we might discover that the problem of death is the first vital intellectual challenge to engage the child's mind and, as such, is a prime stimulus to his continued mental development. How can we have ignored this possibility so long?

Intimations of Self-Mortality

Observing a young child's response to death (whether of a bird or a motor) has some advantages. Much remains to guesswork. But at least we can establish that a death stimulus was present; therefore, the child's response has some relationship to the stimulus. However, it is exceptionally difficult to ascertain when and how a very young child is concerned about death in the absence of any stimulus that can be perceived by us. An older child can tell us that he is thinking about death. But we are unlikely to hear this from even an unusually verbal sub-two-year-old.

At one extreme it could be argued that "out of sight, out of mind" applies completely in the case of the very young child. We should not allow ourselves to imagine that he has any thoughts or feelings oriented toward death when no relevant stimuli are present (a large assumption is made in this argument; namely, that adults are capable of judging what is a relevant stimulus for what kind of mental activity in a young child). The advocate of this position is also likely to contend that, even in the presence of obvious death stimuli, the very young child does not begin to approach the adult conception. This is a persuasive argument when we recall our previous analysis of the proposition, "I will die." We do not expect the very young to possess *any*, let alone *all* of the intellectual resources that are implied by the statement of personal mortality.

At the other extreme, however, it has been proposed that the infant is already tuning himself in to the d-e-a-t-h wavelength. Adah Maurer is a spokesman for this challenging view (26). She begins by calling attention to the periodic alternation of experiences in the newborn. This is a phenomenon that was mentioned earlier in this chapter and upon which a number of other observers have commented. No controversy so far.

Next, Maurer suggests that periodic alternations such as the sleep-waking cycle endow the infant with a basic appreciation of the dichotomy between *being* and *non-being*. This leads to the additional proposition that the infant is capable of *experimentation*. In fact, Maurer seems to be proposing that experimentation with the states of being and non-being is involved in some of the infant's very earliest behavior patterns:

By the time he is three months old, the healthy baby is secure enough in his self feelings to be ready to experiment with these contrasting states. In the game of peek-a-boo, he replays in safe circumstances the alternate terror and delight, confirming his sense of self by risking and regaining complete consciousness. A light cloth spread over his face and body will elicit an immediate and forceful reaction. Short, sharp intakes of breath, vigorous thrashing of arms and legs removes the erstwhile shroud to reveal widely staring eyes that scan the scene with frantic alertness until they lock glances with the smiling mother, whereupon he will wriggle and laugh with joy. . . . To the empathetic observer, it is obvious that he enjoyed the temporary dimming of the light, the blotting out of the reassuring face and the suggestion of a lack of air which his own efforts enabled him to restore, his aliveness additionally confirmed by the glad greeting implicit in the eye-to-eye oneness with another human" (27).

Maurer claims that the term, "peek-a-boo" derives from an Old English phrase meaning, "alive or dead?" In her view, the infant and toddler's first "games" are not to be dismissed as irrelevant to subsequent development. She believes these activities should be regarded as a crucial part of the long-term process of developing a self identity. Beyond "peek-a-boo," the very young child is likely to engage in a variety of disappearance-and-return games. These are little experiments with non-being or death.

"During the high-chair age, babies persist in tossing away a toy and fretting for someone to return it. If one has patience to replace the toy on the tray a dozen or twenty times, the reward is a child in ecstasy" (28). Gradually, the child learns that some things do not return. "All-gone" becomes one of his earliest and most useful expressions. The child's next line of research may focus upon all-goneness. Three examples are cited by Maurer: "Offer a two-year-old a lighted match and watch his face light up with demonic glee as he blows it out. Notice the willingness with which he helps his mother if the errand is to step on the pedal and bury his banana peel in the covered garbage can. The toilet makes a still better sarcophagus until he must watch in awed dismay while the plumber fishes out the Tinkertoy from the overflowing bowl" (29).

No doubt, these statements by Maurer will be received skeptically (if not incredulously) by some readers, and enthusiastically by others. She has left herself open to the criticism of reading much too much into infant behavior. Those who do not object too strenuously to Maurer's approach may nevertheless object to her specific interpretations. How can she be so sure, for example, that the infant experiences "terror" during the blackout phase of his periodic alternations? Sleep is natural and basic. There is no good reason why a healthy baby should experience sleep as an unpleasant state, or become apprehensive as sleep approaches. Is it not more likely that "terror" and other dysphoric affects develop as *learned* associations to darkness or sleep? In our own observations, uneasiness about being in a dark room usually is absent in infancy and early childhood, appearing toward the end of the preschool period. And if Maurer is using terms such as "terror" in a literary rather than a precise sense, then what *is* she actually saying about the infant's mental life vis-a-vis being and non-being? The foregoing is just one example of how one might object to Maurer's views.

Nevertheless, we believe it is important for improved understanding of human development (including, but not limited to conceptions of death) that some investigators take very seriously the possibility that significant processes are in operation very early. We would direct your attention to such factors as the following:

1. It is all too easy for us, even the developmental specialists among us, to become entangled in theoretical fashions of the day. Whether we insist that the infant already is in possession of enormous psychological resources, or that he is simply a noisy tabula rasa, our contentions are likely to be based upon the general social climate as much as upon scientific considerations per se. Historian Philippe Aries, for example, has shown how conceptions of infancy and childhood have changed markedly over the centuries (30). Even closer to home, psychiatrist Martha Wolfenstein has provided an amusing (if disconcerting) analysis of how the all-American baby has altered his basic personality makeup several times during the course of the present century alone (31). Her material is drawn from "official" pronouncements about infant development and care. One has to conclude, of course, that it is the doctrine rather than the infant who changes so radically every few years. The

lesson for us should be one of readiness to consider any potentially useful approach to understanding human development, free from the blinders of contemporary (and temporary) "establishment" orientations.

2. "How does a person ever come to understand that he will die, when he has never died before?" Questions such as these appear especially formidable if we ignore early clues because they are subtle and ambiguous. Careful exploration of *possibly* death-related experiences right from the beginnings of postnatal life would provide us with a long series of clues. We would not be forced to shrug our shoulders philosophically or maintain that the adult *suddenly* grasps the essence of personal mortality without any relevant preparation. Whether or not Maurer is correct in her specific observations and interpretations, it seems quite sensible to consider the *possibility* that very early behavior patterns have some relevance to subsequent conceptions of life and death.

3. For us, one of the most persuasive or promising aspects of Maurer's viewpoint is her description of the infant's total involvement in his (assumed) being/non-being games. The three-month-old baby is by no means aloof from his little experiments. He is *organismically* involved ("Short, sharp intakes of breath, vigorous thrashing of arms and legs...."). This description appears to be consistent with several of the most astute theoretical models available in the area of human development, notably, those of Kurt Goldstein (32), Kurt Lewin (33), and Heinz Werner (34). From all these models we would expect the infant to respond in a general, undifferentiated mode. In current jargon, we might say he is really "turned on," not holding anything back from his present moment of experiencing. It makes sense that subsequent *concepts* of death gradually would be differentiated out of preconceptual experiences. Although neither Maurer nor the above theoreticians seem to make this point

explicitly, it does seem in keeping with their approaches. And this leads us to a further elaboration of our account of death experiences in early childhood.

4. Earlier we proposed that death *perceptions* probably are forerunners of death conceptions. Now we move back a step in the hypothetical series: First, there may be the infant's experiences of the alternations in his own internal states. Then, if Maurer is correct, he actively seeks out experiences of coming-and-going, appearing-and-disappearing. This is a stage of organismic participation. Later (but still in childhood), he is able to stand a little apart from what he observes. He *perceives* death or death-like attributes in the situation. Still later (beyond early childhood, perhaps) he develops the type of cognitive structures to which the term, "conceptions" ordinarily is applied.

5. Those developmentalists whose primary interest is in understanding the emergence of the sense of self-integrity may also find these considerations relevant. Perhaps we should not expect to find evidences of self-mortality awareness until the sense of self has itself been fairly well established. But it is also possible that the sense of self develops with an intimate relationship to the dynamics of being/non-being or presence/absence. If this is the case, then subsequent threatened dissolution of the self (e.g., impending death in old age) can be understood partially in relationship to the coordinated development of self and death concepts years before.

In general, we are taking the position here that much experiencing and behavior relevant to death takes place during infancy and early childhood. Some fairly specific suggestions have been made, all of which require systematic investigation if they are to be confirmed or disconfirmed. Although we have made reference to the work of several other researchers and observers, the reader should not blame them for the way in which we have used

their materials in offering our own formulations.

Now we can proceed further along the developmental trail with the amiable prospect before us of having more data available from which tentative interpretations might be advanced.

DEATH CONCEPTIONS IN MIDDLE AND LATE CHILDHOOD

A four-year-old girl is conversing with her 84-year-old-great-grandmother: "You are old. That means you will die. I am young, so I won't die, you know." This excerpt from the conversation suggests that the little girl knows what it means to die, even if she has not entirely grasped the relationship between age and death. However, a moment later, she adds: "But it's all right, Gran'mother. Just make sure you wear your *white* dress. Then, after you die, you can marry Nomo (great-grandfather) again, and have babies" (35).

Words such as "dead" and "die" are fairly common in children's conversation. Often enough, as in the above example, they are used with some sense of appropriateness. Yet an additional spontaneous comment ("Then, after you die, you can marry Nomo again, and have babies") or a little questioning by the adult is likely to reveal that the child's understanding of death is quite different from our own. In the following discussion we will be concerned chiefly with the development of the concept of personal mortality, but related topics will also be touched upon.

The most important research contribution in this field was made by psychologist Maria Nagy two decades ago (36). Although her investigation involved Hungarian children, there have been no subsequent indications that her findings require significant modifications when applied to children in the United States. We will consider her study in some detail.

Her respondents ranged in age from

three to ten years. They all lived in or around Budapest. Nagy spoke with each of the 378 children to elicit their thoughts and feelings regarding death. The older children (six to ten) also made drawings to represent their ideas of death. In some cases these children were able to write their own explanations of the drawings. Children aged seven and above were asked to "Write down everything that comes to your mind about death." Nagy's sample was almost equally divided between girls and boys, and she made an effort to include children with various social and religious backgrounds, and with a broad spectrum of intellectual functioning.

Nagy found that her results could be categorized into three major developmental phases. Overlapping does occur, she reported, but it remains possible to identify three fairly discrete states of thought which occur in a particular sequence:

Stage one: present until about age five. The preschool child usually does not recognize that death is *final.* This is probably the most significant characteristic of the first stage. However, he also looks upon death as being continuous with life, that is, deadness is a diminution of aliveness. Nagy's youngest subjects gave two variations on the theme that the dead are still, in a sense, alive: "a) death is a departure, a sleep—this denies death entirely; and b) the child recognizes the fact of physical death but cannot separate it from life—he considers death as gradual or temporary" (37).

A close relationship is seen between death and departure. The person who has gone away is sort of dead. And the dead person has sort of gone away. "To die . . . means the same as living on but under changed circumstances. If someone dies no change takes place in him, but rather our lives change since we can no longer see the dead person as he no longer lives with us" (38). Given this interpreta-

tion of death, the child is most likely to be distressed by its aspect of *separation.*

Most children, however, are not satisfied when someone dies that he should merely disappear, but want to know where and how he continues to live. Most of the children connected the facts of absence and funerals. In the cemetery one lives on. Movement is to a certain degree limited by the coffin, but for all that the dead are still capable of growth. They take nourishment, they breathe. They know what is happening on earth. They feel it if someone thinks of them and they even feel sorry for themselves. Thus the dead live in the grave. However, the children realize—with a resulting aversion for death—that this life is limited, not so complete as our life. Some of them consider this diminished life exclusively restricted to sleep (39).

A number of Nagy's illustrative cases resemble the example we used to open this section. The child first speaks of death in what seems to be realistic terms, but subsequent remarks reveal that death is seen as partial or reversible. In particular, Nagy's children typically seem to begin their remarks with the description of a death *perception.* The perception appears authentic and accurate enough. It is the mental elaboration upon the perception that goes astray (according to adult standards). This characteristic of Nagy's protocols, then, tends to support our suggestion that clear perceptions of death-related phenomena are possible early in life even if the child does not yet possess a mature framework within which to interpret and contain them.

Stage two: between the ages of five and nine. The distinguishing characteristic of this stage is that the child now tends to *personify* death. Although images of death in the form of a person occurred at all ages Nagy studied, this was the dominant view for the five-to-nine age range. She found two general forms of the personification: death is seen as a separate person, or death is himself a dead person.

A number of her respondents spoke about a "death-man" who goes about principally at night. He is difficult to see, although one might get a glimpse of him just before he carries you away. But death may also be a skeleton-man, an angel, or someone who looks like a circus clown, among other variations.

The child now seems to comprehend that death is final. This is obviously an important shift in his thinking. (Unfortunately, Nagy does not report those facets of her data which she interprets as establishing the child's grasp of death as definitive; it might be worthwhile to investigate this point again.) But the second or middle stage view of death retains another protective feature: personal death can be avoided. Run faster than the deathman, lock the door, trick him, somehow elude Mr. Death and you will not die. As Nagy puts it "Death is still outside us and is also not general" (40).

Personifications of death are not limited to childhood's hour. As we will see in Chapter 6, adult personifications of death are fairly common, and their study can be instructive. For now, however, we maintain our focus on childhood.

Stage three, ages nine and ten (and, presumably, thereafter). The oldest children in Nagy's study tended to have a clear recognition that death is not only final but *inevitable*. It will happen to them, too. The nine-or ten-year-old child knows that everybody in the world will die. Death is universal as well as inevitable. "It is a thing from which our bodies cannot be resurrected. It is like the withering of flowers" (41), one of her ten-year-old girls explained to Nagy.

With Nagy's three stages still in mind as an organizing structure, let us branch out to consider some other observations. First we will touch upon other reports of children's death conceptions, then we will briefly explore some closely related aspects of mental development.

One of the most interesting contributions to this topic was made by psycholo-gist Sylvia Anthony with the guidance of psychoanalyst J. C. Flugel. Her explorations into *The Child's Discovery of Death* (42) were made in Great Britain during 1937-39. A study in mental development, it also "gained deeper topical significance from events occurring as its last words are written. In this and other countries millions of young children have been separated from their parents and taken away to other billets. As the imminence of danger fluctuates, families in each country are separated or re-united. In many countries of Europe now, young children's fathers are under arms, and the shadow of death hangs over the families they come from" (43). Anthony could not have known at the time that the shadow of death hovered not only over the men-at-arms, but also over women and children to an extent that people were not prepared to expect in warfare among "civilized" nations. Today we still do not know precisely what is to be attributed to war and other social conditions, and what is to be considered as "intrinsic" to the child's conception of death. This question will be touched upon again later.

Because Anthony reported her observations in a somewhat discursive fashion, subsequent authors have tended merely to note that she performed a "classic" or "pioneering" study without summarizing her specific results. We will consider her work in enough detail to convey the gist of her contribution.

Part of her study was concentrated upon a small number of children whose families agreed to maintain Home Records of questions, remarks, or responses on the subject of death. The observations were to be recorded as soon as possible, following their occurrence. Thirteen children from five families were involved in this aspect of the study.

The other part of her study involved an additional 117 children. Most of these were "normals," but she also included 11 from a school for mental defectives, and 26 who were being treated for behavioral or emotional problems at a child guidance clinic. Most (but not all) of the children were given both a story completion test and the 1937 revision of the Stanford-Binet test of intelligence. The particular story completion test selected for this purpose had been devised by M. Thomas at the Institut Jean Jacques Rousseau, in Geneva (44). Previous use of this procedure had indicated that a high proportion of children made reference to death in their responses—even though the story openings themselves did not mention death. Anthony made a few modifications in the Vocabulary section of the Stanford-Binet test, the most relevant of which was the addition of the word, "dead" between the fourth and fifth items on the standard list. (We are reminded by Anthony that the Binet includes a number of death-stimulus items: e.g., "In an old graveyard in Spain they have discovered a small skull which they believe to be that of Christopher Columbus when he was about ten years old." This is one of the Verbal Absurdity items. The original Binet test had an even more salient presentation of death stimuli, i.e., a girl cut up into 18 pieces who was supposed to have killed herself in this way. Anthony used the revised form from which this item had been deleted.)

Perhaps the clearest and most pervasive finding throughout the total range of materials was that normal children often think of death. Depending upon the method of scoring employed, Anthony found between 46 and 60 percent of the children making some reference to death in their test responses or in spontaneous remarks made to her. Anthony adds that "Obviously it is impossible that children should think about death *less* than they speak about it. And since these story openings present the children with situations which they can and do immediately envisage in terms of their own daily life, the results certainly suggest that the thought of death comes readily to their minds" (45).

The investigator also points out that the specific nature of the answer varied quite a bit from one child to another (she offers many examples of these responses throughout her book). Furthermore, although some story openings elicited more death themes than did others, the children also varied considerably in terms of which cues stimulated their own particular thoughts of death. "Normal" and "problem" children did not differ from each other in the number of death-oriented responses given.

Can anything be deduced from Anthony's data about the types of themes that are most likely to elicit death ideas from children? She finds two themes to be dominant: ". . . death as sorrowful separation and. . . death as the ultimate result of aggression stand out as the main typical connotations of the idea by whatever method we have studied it. We trace them not so much through the direct word-response of the children, as by the context in which they produce a response that has reference to death" (46). The *sorrow* theme often was associated with the loss of a child by a parent, or the loss of a parent by a child. Death was seen primarily as separation and loneliness. The *fear of aggression* theme involved death as the ultimate outcome of violent actions (*e.g.*, a burglar breaking into the house, and then starting to attack its occupants).

The observations that have been mentioned up to this point are not linked to any particular theoretical approach. Let us now sample a few of the psychoanalytic interpretations that Anthony offers from her inspection of the children's fantasy-responses. She notes that, on an *unconscious* level of the child's thought, death by drowning may be identified with prenatal life in the womb. One of her subjects, for example, said that mother was sad because "the child was paddling in the water, and a great big fish came up and ate her." In a later response, the girl's mother was said to have "heard someone crying in the bedroom, and it was a lovely new baby for her, and the same name as the other little girl." Anthony suggests that "here we see clearly the association of death with natal life, and the logical conclusion of that identification in the rebirth of the same person. Occasionally the association of death with drowning, and the suggestions of womb symbolism, occur in another context: For instance, Freddie feared that the burglar who killed him would put his body in a sack and throw it in the river" (47).

Another common fantasy centered around the "bird's-nesting" theme. We will just mention the following typical elements from this complex material: a) the child fantasies that a boy has "accidentally" broken eggs that he discovered in a nest; b) later, he feels guilty about this action; c) fears that he will be punished for this aggression, *e.g.*, by being taken away and destroyed by a giant; and d) he then turns to his mother for protection, wishing to remain snug and safe in his own "nest."

Interpretation of this type of response is difficult to follow because Anthony (probably with Flugel's collaboration) attempts to explore its ramifications at several different levels at the same time. It seems to us that these interpretations can be sorted into three levels:

Psychosexual developmental stage. Anthony proposes that the bird's-nest theme is intimately associated with the oedipal complex. The boy wants mother all for himself (*e.g.*, destroying sibling eggs and taking on the characteristics of a powerful father who can destroy competitors). But this daring act exposes him to the wrath of father-giant. The boy is sent scurrying back to his uncompetitive role as a baby bird under mother's wing.

Moral law. The child is a firm believer in the "law of the talion." This, of course, is the time-honored "eye-for-an-eye" principle. His own aggressive behavior is bound to result in aggressive actions being carried out upon him. (From both a psychoanalytic and a developmental-organismic viewpoint, we would expect the child to be somewhat vague in his distinction between thought and action. Therefore, even if he has merely played with the idea of doing something violent, he may feel that he has marked himself for retaliation.)

Primitive organization of thought. The talion dynamics involve oscillation. One is the aggressor; then one is aggressed-upon. However, Anthony suggests that there is a type of mental oscillation that is more basic, perhaps even more primitive than the law of the talion itself (which is usually considered to be about as "primitive" as any law related to psychic functioning). "The impression is given that the idea of retaliation itself, primitive as it is, develops from a manner of thought still more general and primitive. This manner of thought is an oscillation of attention, by which a whole fantasy or thought-complex is alternately seen in primary and then in reversed aspect, and then again in primary. Thus, a mother loses her child by death, and then the mother herself dies; and then the child (or a substitute) is alive again; and then the mother comes back, too" (48).

Anthony continues this line of reasoning by suggesting that oscillation of attention in *fantasy* has a parallel with oscillation or fluctuation of attention in *perception*:

In the laboratory we find that if we fix our eyes on a pattern of dots or a figure in ambiguous perspective, after a time the pattern changes before our eyes, independently of our volition, and after going through one or more such changes, returns to the original phase; and this process will continue so long as we maintain our attention on the same object. In the oscillations of fantasy, however, the phenomenon is complicated by the fact that each phase is to some extent affected by the experiences that precede it. Thus, if a mother loses her child by death (primary phase), there is a suggestion of remorse associated with her own death (secondary phase); the birth of another child or of some substitute involves reparation and forgiveness, so that we revert to the primary phase but with richer connotations; and the mother, or her motherhood, can now return to make everything just and right (secondary phase) (49).

Complicated? Yes, but what actually takes place is probably a good bit more complicated than what has been described above, as Anthony herself points out. At least two of the additional factors should be mentioned here. One factor concerns the *origin* of the oscillation tendency. Anthony suggests that this might be traced back to very early infancy, specifically to the feeding situation. First in fantasy, then in overt behavior, the infant may exchange places (oscillate) with his mother with respect to who is feeding and who is being fed. "Infants barely weaned, long before they can walk or talk, may be seen spontaneously to offer their biscuit to their mother to eat. . ." (50).

The second factor concerns more directly the relationship between mental oscillation and the development of the death conception. The tendency for the child's cognitive pendulum to swing back and forth makes it natural for him to replace "He is dead" with "I am dead," and vice versa. In other words, the implication is that the child does not have two completely independent lines of development for personal mortality and death-of-the-other. Whenever the thought of death enters his mind he is likely to put it through both orientations. Furthermore, the continuing shifts between self-and-other do not end where they began. The child's thoughts and feelings on this subject become refined and enriched as he proceeds. Retaliation, for example, tends to give way to fantasies of reparation, which is a more complex and sophisticated concept.

There is much more in Anthony's materials and interpretations than can be presented here. But at least brief mention should be made of several of her other observations:

1. The idea of death in children seems to draw much of its emotional component from its links with birth anxiety, and with aggressive impulses.

2. A "magical" quality pervades much of children's thought about death. By "magic," Anthony means the child tends to believe that events *happen* in a certain way because he *thinks* about them in a certain way. There are many "magical" ways of thinking about death. Of particular interest is the notion that an angry thought or intention directed toward somebody makes the child, in effect, a murderer.

3. The example of magical thinking mentioned above is probably related to the sense of *guilt* that children often seem to experience when a person (or animal) in their lives actually dies. Guilt is a psychological condition that has strong cognitive and affective components. In the child, at least, the cognitive component of guilt ("I am really responsible for his death") can be understood by what has already been described about magical thinking. There is also an important practical implication here: adults may fail to recognize that guilt *is* one of the child's typical reactions to death. The child thus may be given no opportunity to relieve himself of this painful frame of mind. He may even, inadvertently, be made to feel more guilty by what adults say and do.

The studies we have considered so far have used the following general types of methodology: retrospective-questionnaire (Hall-Scott), retrospective-demographic (Brown), retrospective-clinical (Moriarty), contemporaneous-interview/testing (Nagy, Anthony), and short-term longitudinal diaries (Anthony). Two additional types of methodology have been applied directly to the study of death conceptions in childhood.

Many child psychotherapists have had the opportunity to make direct observations of childrens' death-oriented conversation and behavior while conducting or viewing "play" sessions. One will encounter occasional references to "death play" in many clinical case reports. The work of Gregory Rochlin is of particular interest here, because he has been conducting such sessions with "normal" or "undisturbed" children for the express purpose of understanding their interpretations of death. He has studied children between the ages of three and five. Rochlin and the child would play together on several occasions while a hidden microphone recorded the proceedings. The method appears to be a successful one, although the therapist-investigator has to be patient enough to devote between three and five sessions before sufficient material is obtained. Because this method combines a measure of control and standardization along with a sense of naturalness and the opportunity for direct observation, it obviously has important advantages.

Considering the difference in methodology from what has been reported previously, it is interesting to note that Rochlin's playmates behaved in ways that were quite consistent with the data reported by Nagy and Anthony. A three-and-a-half-year-old boy, for example, knocks a whole family of dolls out of their chairs. First, the victims are to be taken to the hospital. But then they are moved to a sink with running water. The boy indicates the doll-people are scared because they will die: "No more. He'll be all-gone. He died. He goes down the pipe." "Not really." "Yup. Down the sewer. He gets died. The pipe and the sewer is where he goes down." (He eats candy and then says) "They have to have some food." "But they're dead. Food for the dead ones?" "Yes, they're hungry." (He puts another doll down the drain.) "If you're dead, don't you stay dead?" "No, you grow again. You don't stay dead" (51).

The perceptive reader will see that this brief excerpt from one of Rochlin's sessions confirms many of the observations that have been made by less direct means. Perhaps we can be fairly confident that some of the major aspects of the child's view of death have, indeed, been discovered.

Among Rochlin's other observations, we would like to call attention to the following:

1. When somebody in his own life has died, the child is apt to become fearful that others will also leave him by death. Increased fears of separation and questioning about where people have gone may be expected as typical responses to death (even if the deceased person was not very well known to the child).

2. Death play may serve an important denial function for the young child. Rochlin describes, for example, how a four-year-old boy reacted, in his play, to the impact of two actual deaths (grandfather, and a friend of his father's). "His play emphasized dolls who became ill and had nothing further happen to them. Planes would crash with no effect on the passengers. Operations on tonsils, being boiled in a tub or being burned, led to no harm. He did not want to talk about people being killed. It was, he admitted, too sad" (52). Apparently, this young boy was attempting to master or neutralize death through these play maneuvers.

3. In general, Rochlin's observations lead him to the conclusion that "at a very early age well-developed mental faculties are functioning to defend oneself against the realization that life may end. An elaborate system of psychological defenses may be observed" (53).

Unlike those writers whose views are conditioned by academic or psychometric studies of mental development, Rochlin believes that the young child *does* realize that death is inevitable. He contends that the child brings all of his resources to bear upon this threatening realization. He does not claim that the young child entertains adult conceptions of dying or death, but he does argue that the child understands *enough* to organize his thoughts and feelings protectively against these threats.

The controlled *experimental* method has also been employed in this area of inquiry, although sparingly. Irving E. Alexander and Arthur M. Adlerstein demonstrated that laboratory-type procedures could be employed to investigate at least certain parameters of death sensitivity (54). Although their experiment was chiefly concerned with the child's affective (or emotional) response to death, it has implications for understanding his cognitive response as well.

The subjects for this study were 108 boys between the ages of five and sixteen (but only one at each of the age-extremes). Most of the children were summer campers from low-income families. None of the children were known to have psychiatric histories.

In contrast to the preceding studies, Alexander and Adlerstein concentrated upon objective, quantitative methods. The reader who refers back to their original article will see that the investigators were at pains to avoid any possible intrusion of subjective or other uncontrolled factors. These precautions seem to exceed those which were exercised in any of the other investigations. It is fairly typical, of course, for early, exploratory studies in a particular area to be qualitative and semi-controlled, giving way eventually to "tighter" research designs.

The boys were given individual testing sessions during which time they were asked to say the first word that came into their minds when a stimulus word was presented (word association task). The time lag between presentation and response was recorded. In addition, a psychophysiological measurement was taken. Changes in skin resistance (galvanic skin responses, GSR) were obtained from the palm and dorsal surface of the boys' right hands. The stimulus words consisted of three sets, each of which was equivalent to the others with respect to frequency of usuage in the language, length, and number of syllables. One set was comprised of "neutral" or base-level words. Another set was made up of words that were likely to arouse emotions in children (e.g., mama, papa, child, love, kiss). The critical set consisted of three "death" words: buried, kill, and dead. These words were separated from each other during the presentation sequences.

For all the boys, taken as a group, the death words seemed to make a difference. They were slower in giving a verbal association to the death words, and their skin resistance decreased. The interpretation was that death words led to heightened emotional arousal.

But there also were age differences in response. Although the youngest (five through eight years) and oldest (thirteen through sixteen years) children in this sample showed decreased skin resistance to death words, the middle group had the same skin resistance response to both death and non-death words. How might this pattern be explained? Alexander and Adlerstein suggest that "death has a greater emotional significance for people with less stable ego self-pictures than people with an adequate concept of the self. . . . The interval from the ninth through the twelfth year has been labeled the preadolescent period, a time of latency . . . . No great new demands calling for marked change in response patterns are introduced" (55).

In other words, if ever a child has a "breathing space" in his life to consolidate his gains and develop his skills, it is in this period immediately preceding the adolescent quest for individual identity. The work of Alexander and Adlerstein will be considered again when we turn to the emotional and attitudinal relationship to death. Important here from the cognitive standpoint is that the *saliency* of the death concept may be regarded as a function of amount of pyschosocial stress upon the individual. More specifically, we are referring to forms of stress which challenge or complicate the individual's sense of selfhood. Perhaps the sense of uncertainty or disorganization in "who-I-am" brings to mind the concern that "I-may-be-not." There is the implication that latency-age and adolescent boys may differ not so much in the *content* of their death conceptions, but rather in how *significant* a role these conceptions play in their total mental life.

SOME CONCEPTS RELATED TO DEATH

Animism

Now let us consider a few of the other concepts whose developmental careers intertwine with the concept of death. One of the most relevant concepts is *animism*, or the tendency to impute life to nonliving entities. This, of course, is not identical with the idea of death per se. It is the distinction between living and nonliving that concerns us at the moment.

Perhaps we should begin by recognizing that the term most typically is meant to imply immature or deviant thinking. If the child declares that the squirrel running across the lawn is alive, we would not ordinarily describe this as an "animistic" concept; it is simply being "accurate." But we would consider him to be animistic if he attributed life to a mechanical squirrel, the lawn mower, a squirrel-tailed cap, etc.

The observations and theoretical formulations of Jean Piaget are important with respect to this as with respect to so many other topics in mental development. Piaget maintains that animism is one of the earliest characteristics of the child's thought (56). It is, in fact, based on a "primitive mental structure." The young child does not differentiate between mental and physical realms as clearly as he will when he becomes an adult. Among other implications, this means that he is likely to see external objects in his own image, that is, as live and conscious beings. There is a converse side to this animism: the child is also likely to treat mental phenomena as though they were physical. (We have already touched upon a related phenomenon: the child's tendency to respond as though his angry thoughts had *caused* somebody to die.)

Piaget views animism as undergoing a developmental transformation that is very much in keeping with the general pattern of mental growth. We move, in other words, from the relatively diffuse and undifferentiated to the specific and differentiated. In broad outline, this is also the position of the other premier mental developmentalist of our day, Heinz Werner (57). The young child is said to interpret most activity as the activity of living creatures. Almost everything is alive, or could be alive under the right conditions (water, when it flows; clouds, when they move, etc.). Gradually, the child learns to restrict this category. He progressively excludes certain phenomena from the ranks of the living. He also reduces the amount of consciousness and purpose he is willing to attribute to the non-alive objects he still regards as living. For example, no longer does he regard a table as being alive in any sense of the word, but the moon may retain a more limited kind of "aliveness" because it floats up in the sky "on its own."

Research stimulated by Piaget's ideas has been conducted on Chinese (58) and Swedish (59) as well as American (60) children. The results confirm at least part of Piaget's thesis, namely, that children, especially young children, do have difficulty in distinguishing living from nonliving objects. However, Piaget, as we have seen, had more than this limited proposition in mind. It would appear that his broader formulations have not been as clearly confirmed, at least not in the opinions of some of the independent investigators. A Swedish researcher, Gote Klingberg (61), has offered an alternative explanation of findings in this area. Instead of assuming that the child fundamentally thinks differently and more "primitively" than the adult, why not simply say that the child begins in ignorance and must learn gradually how to make the distinction between living and nonliving? In other words, we should not exaggerate the difference between the basic mental structure of child and adult. It is more a question of learning and experience.

Klingberg's view does seem consistent with some of the findings obtained both by herself and by other investigators. The data indicate that the younger the child, the more likely he is to make errors of over-inclusion. The data do not show precisely that children *think* that much differently from adults. There are also some indications that children abandon their "animistic" thinking somewhat earlier than Piaget reckoned. (But Piaget himself was more interested in establishing the basic stages through which animistic thought passes than in pinning down a standard timetable by which one traverses the stages.) Another interesting trend is the apparent close similarity between children of different nations (as different as the Swedes and the Chinese) in their designation of particular objects as living or nonliving.

We suggest that theories and research on the topic of "animistic" thinking in children may have the following implications for our understanding of the concept of death:

1. By adult standards, the child begins with "inaccurate" interpretations of both life (or perhaps we should say "livingness") and death. These interpretations become increasingly more "accurate" with age, i.e., they come to resemble the concepts of the parental generations.

2. The directionality of the "error" in both instances may possibly reflect the same underlying bias in the child's mind. It is a bias in favor of life. All that is active pertains to life, or is not distinguishable from "livingness." And all that is alive now will continue to be alive (even though subject to disappearances and interruptions).

3. With both concepts, it remains unclear how much of the discernible change reflects an intrinsic, more-or-less built-in developmental program, and how much is a function of learning experiences within a particular psychosocial milieu. Those who emphasize the intrinsic developmental-stages approach tend to regard the young child as fundamentally more different from his elders than do those who attribute the changes to learning and experience. One's position on this question is likely to affect both the nature and the extent of educational or other efforts to influence the child's conceptions of life and death.

4. Surprisingly, there do not seem to have been any developmental studies directed at examining the relationship between concepts of life and death in the same children. Therefore, we do not know, for example, if those children who lag in their tendency to differentiate between the living and the nonliving also are slower or otherwise idiosyncratic in their attainment of death concepts. We have very little information on the general relationship between these two sets of concepts during the early years of life— only separate studies that cannot really be combined.

5. Theoretically, we should expect the relationship between the two concepts to change with age. The child "should" at first be unable to differentiate between the question: living or nonliving? and the question: what is it for living to become dead? The more specific distinction between nonliving and dead should take even longer to become clear to the child (e.g., the stone is not alive, but is not

dead; the bird is dead). The discrimination between nonliving and dead is another problem that seems to lack for research attention. And the general theoretical expectation we have suggested here remains in limbo because of the neglect of research into the relationship between the development of life and death concepts, already mentioned.

6. Data regarding both concepts (and general theory on mental development) suggest that the adult versions usually are attained by the preadolescent or early adolescent years. It is taken for granted that there are individual differences. It would appear that the "mature" or adult concepts for both life and death occur at about the same time.

7. There is evidence of various kinds to suggest that the concept of death is quite important both in the child's daily life and in his future personality. But we know very little about the significance of the living/nonliving ("animistic") distinction for the child's current adjustment and subsequent maturation.

Object and Self Constancy

We continue our sampling of death-related concepts with one of the most elusive ideas in both philosophy and individual experience. This mystery has been given many names (none of which, however, truly provide a solution). By speaking here of *self constancy* we mean only to make it a little easier to relate this concept to material that is more familiar to specialists in developmental psychology. *Object constancy* or "conservation" is, of course, a household, or laboratory word among developmentalists these days. There is abundant theory and research on this topic (again, much of it derived from Piaget). Much less attention in the form of systematic theory and controlled research has been given to the development of *self* constancy.

Let us first have a word or two about

object constancy. For thousands and thousands of words on this topic, the reader will have no difficulty in finding expert treatises (62, 63). The moon is a traditional example here. Silver, crescent, half, or full, no matter how this object in the sky presents itself to our eyes we recognize it as moon. To update this example a little, we are also capable of identifying the lunarity of the lunar body whether it is viewed in its customary guise as a relatively small object displayed within the larger visual field of the evening sky, or in its new aspect: a television-screen-filling expanse of detailed bleakness. Whether we see the "full" moon as a discrete object within its celestial context or a bit of the moon displayed over our entire visual field, moon it remains.

But it was not always thus. As children, presumably we had to learn to identify those varying shapes in the sky as all being the same. Even earlier in our development, we had to recognize that yesterday's moon and tonight's are the same. A number of observers have pointed out that some children tend to speak of "moons" even at a time when they have already begun to apply the singular/plural distinction correctly in regard to other objects. In any event, a period of development or learning experience is required before we appreciate the constancy of an object through its various transformations. Some objects are trickier than others. Piaget-type experiments often are designed to learn if a child can see his way through the visual manipulations and distractions that are presented to him, and demonstrate his command of the true constancy of the object or object-dimension in question.

Now here is what we wish to say on the topic of object constancy:

1. Disappearance or destruction of the object—"death of the object," if you will permit this phrase—cannot be conceived or appreciated unless the constancy

of the object has already been established. We cannot experience the disappearance of an object unless we have already acknowledged its existence as a relatively enduring entity.

2. But constancy of the object itself has little or no meaning if the child has not already come to appreciate the phenomena of change, destruction, and disappearance. The basic notion of constancy implies the possibility of non-constancy.

3. In other words, we are suggesting that the child must develop the concepts of constancy and change in tandem. Each concept is in a sense, "prior" to the other. Right from the start, the concept of enduring qualities is intimately related to the concept of transient or oscillating qualities. This proposition links research and theory on object constancy with much of what has already been said regarding the child's early experience of time as periodical and circular. It is also related to what will be said later regarding our interrelated thoughts of birth and death, and our tendencies to "kill the thing we love." *We are proposing that "the death-of-the-object" is one of the earliest and most fundamental proto-concepts in the child's long progression toward mature cognitive functioning; it is not really to be separated from development of object constancy.*

4. The distinction between death-of-the-object, and death-of-the-object-that-was-once-alive probably requires developmental and learning preconditions. The general theoretical expectations that applied to the concepts of "livingness" and of death should apply here as well. We would expect, for example, that all three concepts are fused together in a very general cognitive orientation, and only gradually differentiated from each other.

5. In infancy and early childhood, the disappearance or destruction of objects probably is experienced as a partial loss of the individual himself. In a sense, he disappears, too, when his mother leaves the room. We do not intend to exaggerate the significance of all object losses. Many of these "losses" are trivial, and are replaced by other objects that are fully as satisfying to the child. In principle, however, the child experiences some sense of self-loss whether it is a crucial or trivial object that has disappeared. That facet of the child (or that quanta of "libidinal energy") that he invested in the object has become stranded. This cognitive and affective investment in the world—in a real sense, this investment of his *self*—is defunct until reinvested elsewhere. He may even "feel dead" when the object has become dead within his own perceptual and phenomenological field.

6. Suppose that a visual field were to be presented in a perfectly stable or static array. Would it be perceived or experienced as unchanging? The answer probably is in the negative, especially if we are concerned with the human eye and the human mind. Our eyes move to traverse the visual field, therefore we bring change and movement to the static array. Furthermore, what we have in mind by "mind" is mental *activity*, events, processes, currents of perception and thought. To the extent, then, that we do perceive and think, to that extent we introduce a certain level of activity and change into even a hypothetically static external world.

But there is another step to be taken here. We ourselves change over time. The changes are especially rapid and profound during precisely those years of early development that have been our concern in this chapter. Our perceptual, cognitive, and affective orientations are in transition—how, then, can *object* constancy be achieved or maintained? We raise this conundrum only to emphasize the intimate relationship between development of *self* constancy or identity and *object* constancy. A comprehensive account of human development must, we think, give full attention to both aspects, and with appreciation for their mutual influences.

Even if we liked to believe that we were interested only in object constancy, we would be unlikely to develop a profound understanding of this topic without also concerning ourselves with what is happening to the self that is achieving or failing to achieve object constancy.

We turn now to a brief consideration of self constancy as this relates to the development of death concepts. (If at this point, the wary reader is expecting another of those apparently obsessive little lists to which he has been exposed so far in this book, his expectation is all too well justified.)

1. It seems unlikely to us that object constancy can run very far ahead of self constancy. There are two related but not identical implications. One implication pertains to the constancy of objects. The other implication is concerned with the constancy of the concepts themselves—but we are going to ignore that problem here. Whatever interferes with the development of a firm sense of self constancy will make it difficult for the child to comprehend constancy external to himself. More accurately, perhaps, he will be too preoccupied with his unsettled internal state to make adequate distinctions between the enduring and transient qualities in his perceptual field. We might expect such a child to have more than the usual difficulty in achieving clear distinctions between living and nonliving objects, and in moving toward the adult concept of death.

2. The previously cited suggestion of Alexander and Adlerstein (64) also seems relevant here. These researchers reasoned that death becomes a more significant or salient concept when the individual's identity is challenged by psychosocial stress. They noted that, in American culture at least, certain periods of early development are more likely to be stressful than others. Threat to the child's self constancy might well arouse more salient thoughts of death. Yet, as we have

proposed, problems in achieving or maintaining self constancy might be expected to make it more difficult for the child to understand death and related matters. There is the possibility of a "vicious circle" here: Formidable losses, challenges, or demands shake up the child's sense of identity. This turbulence tends to bring thoughts of death and destruction to mind. But the cognitive effects of this shaky self constancy may be such as to increase his difficulties with death and related concepts.

3. It is likely that difficulties could *begin* from the death-loss-separation axis. In the present discussion, we have been regarding death concepts as the function of self constancy, which itself is influenced by role expectations, psychosocial stress, developmental level, and physical condition. But the child who has experienced painful separations from important people may develop a kind of death concern that interferes with the development of both self and object constancy. Some earlier material in this chapter is consistent with this proposition. Moriarty's motherless mothers (65), for example, may have difficulty in deciding whether they are themselves, their dead mothers, or their own children.

4. We move deeper into the thicket. Forget the child and his vulnerabilities for the moment. Consider the adolescent or the young adult. The adolescent's *individuality* is likely to be a salient aspect of his total identity. It has taken him a long time to become as individual as he now feels himself to be, and he may be aware that he still has a way to go. But what does it mean to experience oneself as an individual, especially when the experience is of recent vintage? It means to experience oneself as *alone*.

To be individual and to be alone is also to be in a new kind of relationship to death. One is likely to feel more vulnerable to death, or so we believe. And the death to which he is vulnerable is itself more threatening in some respects. More will be said in Chapters 4 and 16 about the relationship between death and individuality. The point for now is that the acute perception of individuality-aloneness seems to invite a sharpened sense of personal mortality. Although he has achieved a higher level of integration than he possessed as a child, the adolescent or young adult has not eluded the relationship between self constancy and the prospect of death. The relationship has changed, however, and it will continue to be subject to change throughout his life.

Futurity

What remains of our lives is "in" the future. But death is "there," too. Small wonder, then, that we may, at times, have mixed feelings about futurity.

Thoughts of time and death have a natural affinity for each other. It is difficult to imagine how we could form any conception of death without some conception of time. To keep this section within limits, we will concentrate upon *futurity*, referring to other aspects of time only for background and context. The interested reader will find an extensive literature on the more general topic of the meaning of time in human experience (66, 67, 68). Here, our purpose is simply to explore a few mutual implications of futurity and death concepts in cognitive development.

The young child's relationship to time and death has been touched upon several times in this chapter. We will not repeat what has already been ventured, especially under the rubrics of "You are dead," and "I will die." Let us move ahead to that station in his developmental career which marks the child's attainment of culturally mature time concepts.

As one might expect, there is a lack of agreement among researchers concerning the precise age at which it is customary for a child to achieve a solid grasp on time. In their pioneering investigation of

this topic, E. C. Oakden and Mary Sturt (69) concluded that the adult's conception of time is not achieved until about age 13 or 15. This estimate is probably close to the mark. Futurity and other basic time concepts probably are attained by most boys and girls somewhere between late childhood and early adolescence. We are assuming approximately normal intellectual endowment, and a reasonably adequate psychosocial environment. There are reasons for believing that intellectual level and social milieu are related to concepts of futurity (70, 71).

We are considering now the older child who knows that future time is *qualitatively* different from past and present time. Things that have already happened have happened in one particular way. They will never re-happen or un-happen. What is *yet* to happen? That is a different story. The future is indeterminate, a zone of possibility, of contingency. This is an exciting discovery for the child. The future is really different from what one has already experienced, from what one already *is*. We leave this discovery for a moment, but place an identification tag on it: both "hope" and "dread" begin with the appreciation of futurity as qualitatively distinct from "used" time.

Our sophisticated child also appreciates the existence of world or "objective" time. There is a constant pulse and flow of time apart from his own personal experiences. His thoughts neither initiate nor terminate external time. If this were not true, then he would never be "late," "early," "impulsive," or "dawdling": his own phenomenological world would justify any tempo at which he cared to function. He knows that he cannot truly take "time out." This insight perhaps bestows special meaning on certain organized games in which one legitimately can suspend time. Even in the game situation, however, he comes to realize that the "time out" must be taken in accordance with concensual rules that govern the total situation.

The discovery of objective time may be one of the major psychic events that force magical thinking into the mind's darker and more remote crevices. If external time is impervious to his control, then how is he to influence events in the world simply by doing things inside his head?

From this point on, it becomes difficult (and perhaps arbitrary) to distinguish between what the individual *knows* about futurity and how he *uses* what he knows. Unlike the younger child, he does not seem limited by lack of basic comprehension. The adolescent is quite capable of engaging in high level mental operations, of "thinking about thought" (72). How he orients himself to time is as much a matter of attitudes and personality structure as it is of cognitive development *per se*. Consider, for example, the results of a multi-dimensional study of time perspective in normal adolescents (73). Three findings are of particular relevance:

1. Typically, these young people directed their thoughts to the future—but only to the near future. Almost everything important in life was "just up the road a piece." The second half of their life-span was almost barren. It was uncommon for these people to express any thoughts regarding the fourth or fifth decades of their own lives, let alone the seventh, eighth, or ninth decades.

2. The past was neglected or "blanked out" as well. Not only was scant attention given to one's personal past, but there was the strong impression that these adolescents felt uneasy when asked to turn their thoughts toward where they had been, in contrast to where they were going.

3. There was a prevailing sense of rapid movement from the present to the future. The adolescents felt they were moving somewhere, and in a hurry. However, there was *not* a strong relationship between the sense of forward motion and the extent to which the individual actually was thinking ahead into the future. It will be recalled that for this population in general there was a disinclination to conceptualize the later years of life. One hurtled from "now" to "next" with all possible speed—but what comes after "next?" Few ideas were expressed on this subject.

All of these adolescents could conceive of futurity. But why did they, as a group, limit themselves to the immediate future? Why did they tend to exclude the past? And why were there important individual differences within this group, as well as within other groups that have been studied? Possible explanations are offered both in the study cited above, and in related investigations (74, 75). The most relevant point here is that any explanation must take motivational and socioemotional factors into account. It is not enough that the adolescent can think about the future. He must also develop a personal orientation toward his future.

Mention has already been made of the likelihood that heightened awareness of one's self as an individual also tends to heighten one's concern about death (an hypothesis that is amost begging for empirical investigation). Studies such as the one summarized above suggest that the adolescent's identity is closely linked to who-he-will-be in the near future. Seen from this viewpoint, death becomes much more than an abstract logical concept. The prospect of death is a threat to who - the - adolescent - is - now because it clouds the possibility that he will ever become the self that he values and is moving toward. Threatened loss of futurity (premature death) confronts the adolescent with an implicit denial of his basic identity. He cannot look back upon a full lifetime to bolster his sense of individual identity, nor is he at a relatively stable point in his present existence. He is emerging. But what is the point of emerging if one is never to attain his full development?

From this line of reasoning we should

expect that the adolescent and the elderly adult would differ markedly in their conceptions of death even though both appreciate the same basic conceptual dimensions (e.g., death is inevitable, final, personal). They would be expected to differ because, among other circumstances, they stand in different relationships to futurity. We will touch upon the older person's view of death and futurity in a moment. Let us remain a little longer with the adolescent—just how concerned is he with the prospect of a foreshortened life? What has been learned about the relationship between conceptions of futurity and conceptions of death?

Psychologists Louis Dickstein and Sidney Blatt studied the relationship between preoccupation with death and two measures of future-time perspective or anticipation (76). The death questions were quite straightforward, for example: "I think about my own death . . . more than once a week, once a week, once a month, once every few months." One of the futurity measures was a set of four story roots from which the subject is requested to construct a story. A sample story root: "Joe is having a cup of coffee in a restaurant. He is thinking of the time to come when. . ." (77). The subjects, all of them Yale undergraduates, were also given the Picture Arrangement subtest of the Wechsler Adult Intelligence Scale, which is regarded by some psychologists as a measure of the capacity to anticipate future events.

Students who scored very high or very low on the death questionnaire were compared with respect to their futurity scores. It was found that young men with *low* manifest death concern showed significantly *greater* extention into the future. Putting it the other way around, high manifest concern over death was associated with a more limited tendency to project into the future.

This finding is based upon correlational techniques, thus it does not tell us much about the processes involved. Nevertheless, it does allow us to ponder a bit further. Is it possible that apprehension about death is one of the main factors in the (apparently typical) adolescent tendency to rein in his thoughts of futurity? Perhaps one does not care to gaze too far down the road because he just might see something (i.e., *nothing*) there. If death concern does serve to restrain one's view of the future, then it may also impair the ability to plan ahead, to anticipate both hazards and opportunities. One might appear from the outside to be impulsive or short-sighted—even blundering or stupid—when there is in fact no actual cognitive impairment involved. It is just that one has averted his attention from an important source of information (futurity) in consequence of an emotionally aversive reaction to one component of the future (annihilation of the self).

This argument can also be put into reverse. It is possible that the individual's general strategy for organizing his temporal experience is the most relevant factor. The person who organizes his life around one hour or one day at a time may, as a result, be more easily dismayed by the prospect of death. He does not have as much insulation from death as does the person who projects many events, goals, and experiences between his present situation and the remote prospect of his own gravestone.

It is pertinent to remind ourselves that while both of these alternatives seem especially germane to adolescence, the dynamics that are involved can also occur at later points in the life-span. Perhaps the adolescent has more built-in reason for fearing death than does his elder. The young person has the task of conceptualizing a longer future, and must do so, of course, from the base of a shorter past. It is likely that he has not had as much occasion to exercise his ability to schedule and organize events in time—this will come later as he moves into occupational, parental, and other social obligatory realms. At any adult age, however, there is probably an important relationship between ability to conceptualize futurity and one's orientation toward death, and the reverse. Again, more research is needed if we are to evaluate the relative significance of the directions: a) death concern affecting futurity, and b) futurity affecting death concern.

For another window on the adolescent's relationship to futurity and death, let us consider an investigation by Neil McLaughlin and Robert Kastenbaum (78). The subjects in this study were also college students, in this case all were co-eds. Each subject was asked to write six personal essays. The conditions included: a pleasant future event, pleasant past event, unpleasant future event, unpleasant past event, your earliest memory, and the day of your death. The young women were also asked to rate each of their essays on a 5-point scale of engrossment or self-involvement. Those who felt objective and detached, as though they were writing about somebody else, would have a low engrossment score. Those who felt so involved with themselves as depicted in their essay that they were vicariously reliving or pre-living the situation would have a high engrossment score. The remainder of the experimental design need not concern us here.

The most relevant point is that the subjects tended to describe their own deaths in a rather tranquil—and distant—manner. The day of death was seen as being a long way off, into their sixties. Not much emotional conflict was expressed, in fact, not much emotion at all. Graceful, peaceful acceptance and resignation were the general themes. The reported engrossment for the death projections was the lowest of all the essays written.

It would seem that college-age women are not nearly as concerned with death as we might have expected from the preceding discussion. In contrast with a number of other studies that might be mentioned, they did tend to project ahead into the fairly remote future (setting their own deaths in the sixth decade of life). But there was more to this piece of research.

After completing the above procedures, the subjects were then asked to imagine the day of their death in a *different* way. Having obtained and, in a sense removed, the image that came most readily to their minds, the investigators attempted to learn what alternate image, if any, was available to them.

The second projected day of death was markedly different from the first. Death was now viewed as a much more proximate event. Many of the young women described deaths that would occur within the next few years. For the total group, the distance between one's present situation and death *decreased* by more than 20 years.

The specific form taken by death also changed. Accidents and acts of violence became much more frequent. The death situations were described more vividly, in greater detail, with more use of emotion-laden words. The writing style became less restrained and proper—apparently, the subjects were now expressing themselves more spontaneously and idiosyncratically. Emotions and emotional conflicts were much in evidence. Judges who read both sets of stories ("blind") had no trouble in determining that the second set conveyed more emotional impact and seemed to represent a greater sense of involvement on the part of the authors.

Yet the subjects themselves reported, through their self-ratings, that they were even *less* engrossed in these essays than they had been in the first set! There was thus a major contradiction between the form and content of the essays as they appeared to outsiders, and as the subjects themselves evaluated them. At the same time that these young women were depicting their deaths as being closer to them in time and in raw affective impact, they were reporting that they felt very little involvement in the situation.

Methodologically, this study underscores the importance of going beyond the subject's first or most accessible response. The subjects' total orientation toward death and futurity would have been badly and incompletely represented had the inquiry been limited to their first responses only.

What does this study suggest about the relationship between concepts of death and futurity in young adults? Futurity is stretched out when the topic of personal death is first introduced. Time serves as an insulation between one's present self and eventual death. The reasonable success of this insulation may be judged by the fact that other aspects of the personal death essay were neutral and tranquil. The subject could rely upon readily available stereotyped expressions. But the requirement to deal twice with the same question forced the respondents to find an alternative organization of thought and feeling within themselves. This turned out to be a more personal kind of response. It was especially interesting to see that as the future shrank, the subject simultaneously introduced a greater *psychological* distance between herself and death. The day of death was seen as much closer at hand, but who was dying? A character on a piece of paper, somebody with whom the writer preferred not to identify.

Which conception of futurity and death was the "real" or "basic" one for these subjects? Perhaps it is more appropriate to inquire: how are these two types of conception related within the same individual? Do adolescents and young adults (and the rest of us) understand our own internal complexity? Is there a clear gap between the conceptions of death and futurity that we have developed on a social expectation level, and our more personal, less often communicated thoughts? It would be useful to know more about this topic.

Let us take up one further point regarding death and futurity in adolescence. One's expectation of personal longevity is an aspect of his future perspective. A series of interrelated studies (79) has been looking into both personal expectations of longevity and their correlates. One of the more interesting findings thus far concerns the relationship between expectations and *preferences*. In all of the adolescent/young adult populations studied to date, there have been an appreciable number of subjects who expect to live longer than they care to live. The (projected) value of being alive seems to run out sooner than life itself. There is some further evidence that people who have this pattern of expectation and preference are relatively less likely to come to the aid of other people who are in life-endangering situations (80).

We see once again that conceptions of time and death are difficult to separate from attitudes or preferences, especially after we leave the early years of childhood. (It is not that easy to differentiate cognitions from attitudes in children, but there, at least, we have the developmental progression of thought to use as a guideline.) We also see that the relationship between futurity and death can be complex within the same individual, let alone from one individual to another. For example, the same young person may a) feel himself moving rapidly into the future, b) look forward to this future self as being the "real me," yet c) think very little about the second half of his life-span, and d) even be convinced that he has more future ahead that he cares to use. Additionally, his #1 expectation that he has a long life-span ahead may alternate with a strong secondary expectation that sudden, violent death will snuff out his life in the near future.

We move now to a brief exploration of futurity and death conceptions in elderly adults. It is true that some aged people are afflicted by chronic brain syndrome or senility. Suffering from organic impairments or deficits, they are not able to think very clearly about the future, or about other matters that require high-level cognitive activity. Some observers may prefer to interpret the deterioration of future-oriented thought as a "natural" accompaniment of the aging process. There is no hard evidence for such an interpretation. It is based upon an inclination to regard the pathology of later life as identical with normal aging.

This is not an idle point. If loss of futurity is part of an inevitable and intrinsic biological process, then it may be as "natural" for the elder to turn away from the future realm as it is for the child to discover this same realm. We prefer to distinguish between a) a general syndrome of age-related decline in which futurity is but one of the psychological casualties, and b) the thought and behavior of individuals who are not incapacitated by massive organic changes as they move into their later years of life. In the former situation, the impaired elderly person is likely to show obvious difficulty in recalling the recent past and registering the present. He may not even be able to distinguish reliably among past, present, and future. In the latter situation, the "normal" aging person may perhaps think and speak less of futurity, but he does not exhibit a general pattern of deterioration.

There is the implication that reduction in future orientation in later life, when it does occur, may be related as much to socioemotional as to cognitive factors. One study has found that mentally alert geriatric patients could use futurity successfully as a category for organizing experience—providing it was not their personal experience at stake (81). But this same study revealed that the elders in question could not (or, at least, did not) offer much about futurity within a personal framework.

If an elder can "work with the future" (as shown by his performances on story construction tasks), why, then, does he not show a propensity to "live in the future?" The investigator proposed two alternative explanations:

A particular elderly person happens to be depressed, institutionalized or fearful of death. This quasi-Aristotelian application of the term "accident" is intended to suggest that elderly people do not *necessarily* have to be limited in their future outlook. . . .Specific conditions have occurred in the particular individual's total life situation which have brought about the observed restriction. That such a restriction might be rather common would be no argument for its necessity. By analogy, even when all oak trees in a given area are blighted with the same disease, no one suggests that this affliction is a necessary and intrinsic characteristic of being an oak tree. This view has practical implications: There would be the prospect that "something could be done" to prevent or remedy this "unfortunate accident" of restriction of future outlook.

An alternative explanation is that there is a certain "necessity" involved in the observed restriction of personal futurity. This might be an individual matter, i.e., not every elderly person would "necessarily" possess this "necessity"— but for those who did, its structuring power would be great. What we mean to suggest here is that certain life-styles imply rather definite self-contained limits. Some elderly people consider that they have lived out their life plan, and thus exist on a sort of "surplus time" that is not part of their lifelong system of values (82).

With respect to the latter point, we are reminded of those young adults who believe they are doomed to an undesired longevity. There are some elders who also seem to feel that they are somewhere between a completed life and a delayed death. (But these orientations are subject to change in both young and old as the conditions of present life change—health, finances, and interpersonal relationships, for example.)

The scarcity of objective future time is likely to confront the elderly person with a problem as fundamental, though qualitatively different, as that which he faced as an identity-conscious adolescent. Should he "write off" the future because so little remains to it? Or should he value the future all the more for precisely the same reason? Again, perhaps he should alter his scale of values and meanings so that *small futures* (tomorrow, not ten years from now) become the relevant frame of reference? Should he retreat into the past? Project himself into a vicarious future through the lives of younger relatives or personally significant endeavors? Bury himself in the present moment, denying both past and future? Whatever solution a particular individual may adopt, it must be acknowledged that the whole pattern of his life is operating within the lengthening shadow of death.

OUR ORGANISMIC RELATIONSHIP TO DEATH

In the preceding pages we have attempted to explore the concept of death within the context of general psychological development. Studies of cognitive development offer one relevant approach to the question, *what is death?* Death is what we gradually come to understand by the word, d-e-a-t-h. It is also what we come to understand as overtones to such words as "future," "myself," "separation," and so forth.

But our relationship to death is not purely cognitive. It is not going too far to say that each of us has an *organismic* relationship to death. We have both transient and relatively enduring attitudes that help to define our position with respect to death—and these attitudes may be found at more than one level within our psyches. Perceptions and cognitions of death arouse feeling-states within us; again, we may or may not have direct awareness of the stimulus-response relationships. I feel a vague sense of sorrow, or an inexplicable chill along my spine. Is this part of my total orientation toward death? Perhaps. The response seems "death-appropriate," but where is the stimulus? Or I bring my car to a halt to permit a funeral procession to pass by. There is an obvious death stimulus. My own reaction? I do not seem to have any. But is it possible that such a stimulus should have no response?

We are talking more directly now about the full range of our attitudes, feelings, and behaviors as these bring us into certain relationships to death. This discussion is pursued in the following chapter.

REFERENCES

1. Werner, H. *Comparative psychology of mental development.* New York: International University Press, 1957.
2. Piaget, J. *The psychology of intelligence.* New York: Littlefield, 1960.
3. Rosenthal, H. R. The fear of death as an indispensable factor in psychotherapy. *American Journal of Psychotherapy,* 1963, *17,* 619-630.
4. Feifel, H. Symposium comments, Gerontological Society, Oct., 1965. Cited by R. Kastenbaum: Death as a research variable in social gerontology: An overview. *Gerontologist,* 1966, 7, 67-69.
5. Kastenbaum, R. Engrossment and perspective in later life. In R. Kastenbaum (Ed.), *Contributions to the psychobiology of aging.* New York: Springer, 1965. Pp. 3-18.
6. Schecter, D. E., Symonds, M., & Bernstein, I. Development of the concept of time in children. *Journal of Nervous and Mental Diseases,* 1955, *21,* 301-310.
7. Kastenbaum, R. The child's understanding of death: How does it develop? In E. Grollman (Ed.), *Explaining death to children.* Boston: Beacon Press, 1967. Pp. 89-110.
8. Gesell, Arnold & Ilg. F. L. *The child from five to ten.* New York: Harper & Bros., 1946.
9. Piaget, J. & Inhelder, B. *The growth of logical thinking from childhood to adolescence.* New York: Basic Books, 1958.
10. Hall, G. S. *Senescence.* New York: Appleton, 1922.
11. *Ibid.,* p. 440.
12. *Ibid.*
13. Tobin, S. The earliest memory as data for research in aging. In D. P. Kent, R. Kastenbaum, & S. Sherwood (Eds.), *Research, planning, and action for the elderly.* New York: Behavioral Publications, 1972, Pp. 252-278.
14. Kastenbaum, R. & Sherwood, S. Unpublished data. Detroit: Wayne State University; Boston: Hebrew Center for Rehabilitation of the Aged.

15. Hall, *op. cit.*, p. 440.

16. Hall, *op. cit.*, p. 441.

17. Brown, F. Depression and childhood bereavement. *Journal of Mental Science.*, 1961, *107*, 754-777.

18. *Ibid.*, p. 775.

19. Moriarty, D. *The loss of loved ones.* Springfield, Ill.: Charles C Thomas, 1967. P. 63.

20. *Ibid.*, pp. 67-89.

21. *Ibid.*, p. 67.

22. *Ibid.*, p. 88.

23. Rochlin, G. How younger children view death and themselves. In E. A. Grollman (Ed.), *Explaining death to children.* Boston: Beacon Press, 1967. Pp. 51-88.

24. Brent, S. Untitled manuscript, being prepared for publication. Detroit: Wayne State University.

25. *Ibid.*

26. Maurer, A. Maturation of concepts of death. *British Journal of Medicine and Psychology*, 1966, *39*, 35-41.

27. *Ibid.*, p. 36.

28. *Ibid.*, p. 37.

29. *Ibid.*

30. Aries, P. *Centuries of childhood.* New York: Knopf, 1962.

31. Wolfenstein, M. The emergence of fun morality. *Journal of Social Issues*, 7, *4*, 1951, 15-25.

32. Goldstein, K. *The organism.* New York: American Book, 1939.

33. Lewin, K. *Principles of topological psychology.* New York: McGraw-Hill, 1936.

34. Werner, *op. cit.*

35. Conversation overheard on the ward of a geriatric hospital.

36. Nagy, M. The child's view of death. *Journal of Genetic Psychology*, 1948, *73*, 3-27. Reprinted in H. Feifel (Ed.), *The meaning of death.* New York: McGraw-Hill, 1959. Pp. 79-98 (page citations are to the more accessible reprinted version).

37. *Ibid.*, p. 81.

38. *Ibid.*, p. 83.

39. *Ibid.*, p. 83.

40. *Ibid.*, p. 96.

41. *Ibid.*, p. 96.

42. Anthony, S. *The child's discovery of death.* New York: Harcourt, Brace, & World, 1940.

43. *Ibid.*, p. 1.

44. Thomas, M. Cited by Anthony, *Ibid.*, p. 36.

45. Anthony, *op. cit.*, pp. 36-37.

46. *Ibid.*, p. 45.

47. *Ibid.*, p. 46.

48. *Ibid.*, p. 46.

49. *Ibid.*, p. 50.

50. *Ibid.*, p. 51.

51. Rochlin, *op. cit.*, p. 74.

52. *Ibid.*, p. 60.

53. *Ibid.*, p. 61.

54. Alexander, I. & Adlerstein, A. M. Affective responses to the concept of death in a population of children and early adolescents. *Journal of Genetic Psychology*, 1958, *93*, 167-177.

55. *Ibid.*, p. 176.

56. Piaget, J. *The construction of reality in the child.* New York: Basic Books, 1954.

57. Werner, *op. cit.*

58. Huang, I., & Lee, H. W. Experimental analysis of child animism. *Journal of Genetic Psychology*, 1945, *66*, 69-74.

59. Klingberg, G. The distinction between living and not living among 7-10 year-old children with some remarks concerning the so-called animism controversy. *Journal of Genetic Psychology*, 1957, *105*, 227-238.

60. Russell, R. W. Studies in animism: II. The development of animism. *Journal of Genetic Psychology*, 1940, *56*, 353-366.

61. Klingberg, *op. cit.*

62. Piaget, *op. cit.*

63. Smedslun, J. The acquisition of conservation of substance and weight in children. I. Introduction. *Scandanavian Journal of Psychology*, 1960, *1*, 49-54.

64. Alexander & Adlerstein, *op. cit.*

65. Moriarty, *op. cit.*

66. Fraisse, P. *The psychology of time.* (Translated by Jennifer Lieth.) New York: Harper & Row, 1963.

67. Poulet, G. *Studies in human time.* (Translated by Elliott Coleman.) New York: Harper Torchbooks, 1959.

68. Campbell, J. (Ed.), *Man and time.* New York: Pantheon, 1957.

69. Sturt, M. *The psychology of time.* New York: Harcourt, Brace, 1925.

70. LeShan, L. Time orientation and social class. *Journal of Abnormal and Social Psychology*, 1952, *47*, 589-592.

71. Schneider, L., & Lysgaard, S. The deferred gratification pattern: A preliminary study. *American Sociological Review*, 1953, *18*, 142-149.

72. Piaget & Inhelder, *op. cit.*

73. Kastenbaum, R. Time and death in adolescence. In H. Feifel (Ed.), *The meaning of death.* New York: McGraw-Hill, 1959. Pp. 99-113.

74. Kastenbaum, R. The dimensions of future time perspective, an experimental analysis. *Journal of Genetic Psychology*, 1961, *65*, 203-218.

75. McLaughlin, N., & Kastenbaum, R. Engrossment in personal past, future and death. Presented at annual meeting, American Psychological Association, New York City, September, 1966.

76. Dickstein, L., & Blatt, S. Death concern, futurity, and anticipation. *Journal of Con-*

sulting Psychology, 1966, *31*, 11-17.

77. Wallace, M. Future time perspective in schizophrenia. *Journal of Abnormal and Social Psychology*, 1956. *52*, 240-245.

78. McLaughlin & Kastenbaum, *op. cit.*

79. Center for Psychological Studies of Dying, Death and Lethal Behavior. Research in progress. Detroit: Wayne State University.

80. Branscomb, A., & Kastenbaum, R. Orientations toward protecting, extending and foreshortening the lifespan: A preliminary study. Center for Psychological Studies of Dying, Death, and Lethal Behavior. Detroit: Wayne State University, 1969, unpublished manuscript.

81. Kastenbaum, R. Cognitive and personal futurity in later life. *Journal of Individual Psychology*, 1963, *19*, 216-222.

82. *Ibid.*

3

Facing the Thought of Death

In writing about man's relationship to death we may have only two choices before us: to simplify, or to oversimplify. Let us begin with an oversimplification.

Death is the *stimulus*. It is "out there" some place. What we are concerned with here is our *response* to this stimulus. There is a descriptive component to this task: How many responses do we have to the death stimulus? Which responses are the strongest, or have the highest probability of occurrence? And there is the *process* component: how does our death-response system function? One might also be concerned about "why" the response to death takes a certain form, even though this kind of question is not very respectable in contemporary behavioral science.

Our inquiry begins within this over-simplified stimulus-response (S-R) framework. The charming simplicity of S-R psychology offers itself as both a tool and a foil as we move into the complexity of man's organismic relationship to death. In the preceding chapter we viewed death as a facet of mental life, death as perception or cognition. We develop certain basic ideas of death as an intrinsic part of our general cognitive growth. Now these ideas and assumptions can be treated as themselves constituting the stimulus configura-

tion of death. We have made ourselves images of death—how do we relate to these images? Burrowing down beneath the bed covers is a death response if the child has formulated a concept that identifies death with that scary monster-man who just might be in the closet. A physician's altered respiration and heightened muscular tension is a death response if one of his definitions of death unexpectedly materializes before his eyes in the form of a "bad news" x-ray film.

As will be seen in the following paragraphs, much of the difficulty in attempting to research man's relationship to death derives from our frequent inability to identify both the stimulus and the response. We could say very little about the behavior of either the boy or the physician if we did not know the nature of the stimulus configuration to which he was responding. And, of course, the stimulus configuration itself must be understood in terms of the individual's own psychology—his developmental level, knowledge, needs, and conflicts. All too often, even the most perceptive clinician or most thorough researcher may be unable to establish that a given response either was or was not elicited by a death stimulus. This is one of the practical drawbacks of applying the S-R approach here. But the *effort* to distinguish and clarify the S-R relationship can spur us on to more adequate methods of investigation—and discourage the tendency to reach hasty conclusions.

FEAR OF DEATH

A Stimulus-Response Approach

Fear is the psychological state that is most often mentioned when clinicians or researchers discuss responses or attitudes toward death. Evidently, there must be something to this association between "fear" (response) and "death" (stimulus). But there is more than one possible relationship. Let us consider some of the logical possibilities before plunging into the clinical and research literature.

1. It is possible that fear is the most typical or the most important psychological response to death. This proposition can be expressed in several ways:
 • "Everybody is afraid of death."
 • "*If* there is anything in common among different people on the subject of death, then it must be fear."
 • "Fear is the response that most deserves our consideration because of the effect it is likely to exert upon the individual's ability to cope with life problems, or because death fear is the psychological state that has the most significant social implications."
These formulations all refer to the basic proposition stated above, and they all differ from each other. For example, the same set of empirical facts might support one of these formulations, undermine another formulation, and have no direct bearing on some of the others. Yet these differences often are unrecognized or slurred over in death discourse and research. Careful investigation of the assumed fear-death relationship would seem to require precise formulation of the hypothesis. It is unfortunate that the precise formulation of the hypothesized *relationship* between fear and death often has been neglected, just as the precise nature of the "stimulus" and the "response" per se have been neglected.

2. Having recognized that the basic "fear of death" proposition is far from simple, let us now suspend this observation for a moment. Let us concentrate upon whatever might be *in common* among the various formulations that were suggested above. It seems appropriate to derive the general definition that death is an aversive or noxious stimulus. Death is "that-which-is-feared." This is a somewhat less than stupendous conclusion. But classifying death explicitly as an aversive or noxious stimulus opens several potentially useful paths:

 a. Death is linked with the vast corpus of psychological research that has been conducted with unpleasant, stressful, or downright nasty stimulus conditions. "Fear of death" thus can be seen in relationship to a mighty collection of theory and research, instead of standing alone as a freakish or "special interest" topic. Is death, for example, the *most* aversive or noxious stimulus available? It is possible that fear might indeed be the basic response to death stimuli, yet that death fear is no greater in its intensity than a number of other types of fear. Whatever we wish to learn about fear of death in particular, it is likely that we can improve our understanding by considering this phenomenon within the more general context of aversive stimuli.

 b. The study of death fear, especially in an experimental-manipulative vein, could be enriched by application of some of the research techniques that have been developed in the broader area of aversive stimuli. We are not recommending that death fear should be laid on a procrustean laboratory table to fit available experimental techniques, but it is likely that many appropriate applications could be found.

c. It is also likely that serious attention to death fear would add something worthwhile to the general topic of man's relationship to aversive/noxious stimuli. We would suggest, for example, that the aversive properties of some stimuli used in psychological research derive, in part, from the implicit "death signals" they emit. It is possible, in other words, that experimental studies of death fear might lead to important reinterpretations of findings obtained on variables that supposedly have nothing to do with death.

3. Stimuli pertaining to death can be regarded as a subset within the larger set of stimuli that elicit avoidance or distress responses. This approach is perhaps the most obvious one. However, it is possible to argue that the relationship goes the other way (as implied in point 2c). All fear responses might derive from the same basic threat: the threat to survival. In some instances, the threat to life is so direct and "unmediated" that we can recognize the stimulus for what it is. In other instances, the threat is indirect. The stimulus means "death" only because it has taken on this association through a complex and idiosyncratic social learning process for this particular person or this special group of people.

It may be that a stimulus which originally drew its menacing qualities from close association with death can take on the power to confer threat qualities to other stimuli whose own "objective" relationship with death is tenuous and remote. The hypothetical basic fear of death would thus spread itself around so much that one could not easily recognize the origins of our daily fears. According to this view, then, fear of *anything* is, at root, a death-related fear. The relationship

just happens to differ in its visibility and directness from fear to fear.

This alternative approach should be kept in the running, we think. It may strike some readers as being farfetched. However, both experimental studies of learning and performance, and psychoanalytic explorations of mental-emotional life have provided us with many examples of how "farfetched" relationships can and do develop. Watch any Russian wolfhound who has learned to increase his salivation at the sight of the light which precedes the bell-ringing that precedes the food! Whether or not this alternative is "truer," or more useful than the original approach is another question. But we have seen that within the stimulus-response framework it is possible to come up with alternative hypotheses and alternative ways of organizing the material. This is a strength. The existence of plausible alternatives often is a stimulant to the development of more adequate formulations of research questions and to more adequate methodologies. The existentialist thinker who sees death and "nothingness" everywhere may have a potential colleague in the experimental psychologist who is interested in testing the proposition that all aversive stimuli have a common origin.

4. Whether or not thanatophobia is the basic or ultimate human fear, followers of both approaches agree that death is that-which-is-feared. But what is to be said about the prevailing social attitude toward fear of death? It seems to us that this fear is *unacceptable*. The unacceptability of death fear can be expressed through the ambiguous statement: "The mature (strong, healthy) person does not fear death." In one sense, this is a statement of (assumed) fact, i.e., if we make ourselves well acquainted with mature people we will find that they harbor no fear of death or, at least, no important fear of death. The factual status of this proposition is in some doubt. But for the moment we are interested chiefly in the *assumption* that mature

(strong or healthy) people do not fear death.

In its second sense, this statement is the equivalent of a cautionary kick underneath the table. "You are not afraid of death—now, *are* you?" It is improper to fear death, not done in the best circles. Whatever we really feel, we are advised to behave as though death fear is behind or beneath us. Admission or exposure of our thanatophobia marks us as immature, weak, or morbid. It is childish. It is unmanly. How many articles in social science, mental health, or popular publications recognize death fear as legitimate, normal, or, perhaps, even desirable? Do we not, by contrast, find the overwhelming number of exhortations moving in the opposite direction? Depending upon one's frame of reference, death fear is seen as a manifestation of spiritual unworthiness, psychopathology, "poor will power," and so forth. Death fear is not to be cultivated or tolerated: it is to be overcome.

There are some exceptions to this rule. However, in general it appears that death is not only that-which-is feared, but also that-which-should-*not*-be-feared. This latter point sets thanatophobia apart from those fears which are regarded as more or less "legitimate" in our society. At this point, we are not attempting to argue in favor of death fear, merely to indicate that many of us approach this topic with a negative bias which itself requires explanation. We seem to fear the fear of death.

Throughout this chapter, we shall call upon the stimulus-response approach in an effort to clarify murky problems. But S-R psychology is unlikely to solve all the problems for us, or to provide a satisfactory basic framework. For one thing, this approach is essentially methodological. It assumes an environment that is comprised of more or less discrete stimuli which impinge upon an empty or interchangeable robot organism that "emits" a "response" which is in some way proportional to the stimulus. While the freedom

from concern with *content* gives this approach a certain "pure" quality, we cannot go very far in understanding man's relationship to death without having immersed ourselves in concrete experiences and observations. It is also questionable whether S-R formulations can cope adequately with complex configurations (gestalten) as contrasted with "pure stimulus/pure response" relationships. The effort required to modify and enrich S-R formulations to accommodate subtle, complex, and shifting phenomena could be better invested in approaches that begin with a greater receptivity to these phenomena.

Let us consider one significant example. How is the "death stimulus" to be defined? We could say that this stimulus is to be defined entirely in terms of the response it elicits. But this assumes that a) fear is the only response to death, b) fear is the response only to death, or c) there is an independent way of ascertaining which fears are related to death and which are not. Each of these alternatives has serious drawbacks. The S-R approach loses much of its "pure and simple" appeal if we have to hem and haw about one of the major terms in the equation.

Another difficulty arises when the death stimulus is regarded as external, independent, and uniform. The S-R approach often seems most effective when the stimulus is physical or quasi-physical, something that can be measured with respect to mass, intensity, speed, etc. But the death stimulus cannot really be located external to the perceiver (the same logic probably applies to the so-called "physical" stimulus as well, but the likelihood of going far astray is greater with less tangible stimuli).

We have seen that the individual's definition of death undergoes developmental transformations throughout his life. As pointed out earlier, the child and the physician receive "death signals" from different stimulus configurations. The individual differences that are to be found in conceptions of death are not limited to chronological age alone. Personality structure, socioeconomic class, and the situational context are among the types of variables that influence our interpretation of stimuli as being death-related. In a way of speaking, then, the death stimulus is always in the mind of the perceiver as much as it is in the outside world. Furthermore, it is likely that many death stimuli are generated *within* the individual's own psychobiological processes. There may be few if any overt indices of the fact that the individual is responding to death signals stirred up by his own bodily state, memories, or "stray" thoughts.

These considerations limit the extent to which we can attribute "deathness" to any set of objective or external stimuli. It follows that we are not in a position to determine the relationship between two sets of independent phenomena. Stimulus and response share a common factor: us.

In this discussion we have not succeeded in avoiding a certain back-to-where-we-started motion. But the side trip to S-R psychology may have prepared us to advance more resourcefully in the difficult terrain ahead.

Death as an Object of Fear

What do we fear? There is reason to believe that important differences exist in the "object" or "stimulus" of death fear. Philosopher Jacques Choron has offered a particularly cogent analysis of death fear and related topics (1). As part of this analysis, he distinguishes three types of death fear. One may be afraid of a) what comes after death, b) the "event" of dying, or c) "ceasing to be." Of course, one does not really have to choose among these fears; we can have them all, or in any combination. Choron also reminds us that fear of the *dead* also is experienced by some people, but he treats this latter concern as being somewhat removed from the three major types of death fear.

These are helpful distinctions. It is quite possible that the various fears differ in their origins, their effects on individual behavior, their function in society, and so forth. By respecting these differences we will probably reduce rather than encourage confusion. Three people who are equally afraid of death may turn out to be afraid of three rather different conditions when we become better acquainted with their mental contents.

In this chapter, we regard the fear of extinction, annihilation, obliteration, or "ceasing to be" as the basic fear of death. This is not to say that we prejudge empirical questions that can be raised about the objects of death fear. It simply means that "ceasing to be" is the most distinctive variety of death fear. We may fear the dead for the mischief they could perform on us—but sometimes we also fear mischief from the living. We may fear what will transpire at the next moment after death. But it is routine enough to fear what may happen to us at the next moment on this side of the grave. Tortured visions of the afterlife must compete with tortured visions of our future on earth. Fear of dying often involves apprehension about prolonged suffering, weakness, dependency, and loss of control; but we have these same apprehensions when death is not in prospect as a certainty.

Extinction is a different matter, is it not? It is difficult to feel, think, or speak of our potential nonexistence. How can we feel ourselves into a state of "nothingness"? There are altered states of consciousness that may move us toward the psychological void. However, the extent to which these states strip us of sensation and mentation determines the extent to which we are deprived of the ability to perceive, interpret, and express the condition. How can we truly "see ourselves dead" when the implicit "we" hovers about as the depository of perception and experience? Death in the sense of not-being or being-not has a way of undercutting our mental and emotional processes. The other feelings are fears *about* death. Fear *of* death is a term that we will reserve for the prospect of extinction.

One distinction leads to another, even in this area of inquiry. The set of death-related fears distinguished by Choron might prove even more useful if allied with a distinction made in Chapter 2. It was shown there that the death-of-self and death-of-the-other concepts undergo somewhat different, although related, developmental transformations. Let us now see what happens when the death-related fields are differentiated according to the self/other distinction.

Figure A offers some conjectures concerning the relatively more *specific* fears that are likely to be engendered within us depending upon whose death is in focus: ours or another's.

Fear of my own process of dying includes the unwelcome prospect of suffering. To put it the other way around, it is the possibility that I will suffer physical distress that makes dying such an aversive event. But I also fear that my integrity might "crack" during the process. I will probably become dependent on others for meeting all my needs. Fear of dependency is thus one of the even more specific subfears within the general fear of indignity. Perhaps I fear physical pain less than the possibility that I might prove "weak"

and "come apart" (i.e., violate the self-concept that has been bred into me by a culture that would prefer people in anguish to "cool it.") These are just a few of the relatively specific fears that the prospect of dying might arouse in me.

Suppose, however, that it is someone else who is on a terminal course, someone who is close to me. It is not unreasonable to speak of *vicarious suffering*. As the condition of my friend deteriorates, my own spirits become more distressed, and I fear the continuation and intensification of this vicarious suffering. Perhaps this fear will be strong enough to deter me from visiting him, although I will manufacture a more acceptable rationalization if this does prove to be the case. But there may also be a fear of something that goes beyond vicarious suffering. Because of my involvement in the life of the "other," his dying process has the effect of *vicarious disintegration* upon me. In a sense, I, too, am falling apart. This vicarious participation in his decline serves as a foretaste of my own future. I can't help but feel that his disintegration also serves as a medium through which I experience intimation of my own demise.

Let us take this paired example just a little further. Fears aroused through experiencing the dying of the other person may have the effect of increasing the fear of my own dying. Yet if the other person dies in such a manner as to relieve my fears, then I might approach my final

FIGURE A
DEATH-RELATED FEARS: SELF AND OTHER

Fear	My Death	Death of the Other
Dying	Personal suffering Personal indignity	Vicarious suffering Vicarious disintegration
Afterlife	Punishment Rejection	Retaliation Loss of relationship
Extinction	Basic death fear Attached fears	Abandonment Vulnerability

days in a more tranquil state. Still again, I may turn out to be one of those people who can bear personal suffering more easily than the vicarious sort. (This may not be so rare a characteristic; many a parent has been frantic because he or she could not bear the pain a child was suffering.) The fear of personal indignity may or may not have a true parallel in the vicarious situation. What we are suggesting, in general, is that self/other dynamics are neither interchangeable nor mutually independent. We stand to learn more about specific fears, as well as other matters, if this distinction is kept in mind.

Fears of what may happen after death often embody the threat of punishment. We will be made to pay for our personal sins and transgressions—perhaps even for the very fact that we are members of such a notorious species. Fear of punishment can be intense enough to provide all the fear that anyone requires of the afterlife (or afterdeath). But, for all its publicity, fear of punishment may be the lesser of the two we have suggested in Figure A. Eternal alienation from God is a form of rejection that trivializes all others. For the believer, fear of this rejection can be a central concern throughout his life. The "moment" after death (or the "instant" of death itself) may be thought to reveal one's ultimate fate. The fear of disgraced existence in the void can be a potent rival to the fear of nonexistence.

Do we fear what happens to the *other* person in his afterlife? This is probably the least thought-about of the six sectors presented in Figure A. It is probably also the least important, yet doubtlessly would reward close attention. There are at least two ways in which the postmortem vicissitudes of another person might be fearful to the living. Guilt-bred fear may arise. This type of fear may even be *expected* of the mourner in some ethnic groups. If I have not done right by the deceased, and if I am not wholehearted in fulfilling my ritualistic obligations as a mourner, then I may be subject to retaliation. The

form of retaliation may remain vague and uncertain (but no less anxiety-provoking for all that). I may, however, fear that the maligned spirit will intervene in my life in unpleasant ways—either by being just pesky enough to make his point, or by major vindicative actions. This fear attached to the behavior of a person on the other side of the grave is, of course, tantamount to fear of the dead. We see that fear of what comes after death and fear of the dead are not entirely independent. Many "ghost stories" and "uncanny experiences," including contemporary as well as historical accounts, involve the sense of being in contact with restless spirits of the dead.

Another form of retaliation may also arouse fear. My failure to safeguard the deceased spirit's passage through his postmortem trials and ordeals might adversely affect my own experiences after death. If I do not pray for my father's spirit, then how can I expect my son to pray for mine? This is one of the ways in which the retaliation dynamics *may* be expressed.

I may also fear loss of an important personal relationship with the departed. Belief in survival after death can insulate the mourner from the full impact of loss. But how can I be sure that the departed spirit will remain faithful, or even remember me? Reassurance may be sought by attempting to communicate with the deceased through a seance. "Do you still care for me? Are you still watching over me?"

Fear of extinction (of "ceasing to be") also has its self/other aspects. It may be that the self/other distinction is greatest here. For the child, death often seems to loom most formidably as threat of abandonment (2). To be separated from nourishing and protective people is also to be made vulnerable. One becomes more vulnerable to everything: to overwhelming dependency needs and anxiety, and to external threats. The death of a parent, for example, may increase the child's fear of further deaths around him: anybody might die at any time, leaving him even more helpless and alone.

Apprehension about one's own extinction is what we have singled out as the basic death fear. This designation by itself does not enlighten us about the fear of death; it simply helps us to avoid confounding this distinctive fear with the other fears and negative reactions that may be stirred up by death.

Let us take this opportunity to comment briefly on what has been mentioned in Figure A as "attached fears." A particular kind of traumatic event may elicit a particular kind of reaction from us. Yet *any* threat may also have the power to enlist or increase other fears. A woman in her first pregnancy may have some fairly specific fears (Will it hurt very much? Will my baby be normal?). At the same time, she may also be more troubled than usual by other background fears, some of which had been relatively "inactive" for a long time (Am I really worth anything? Am I really an attractive person?). It is even possible that complex feelings associated with separation and self-identity are aroused by both the prospect of giving birth and the prospect of death.

Basic death fear possibly functions as a *retriever* and a *multiplier* of other fears. Psychoanalyst Felix Deutsch, for example, has reported cases in which fear of one's own death was compounded by the intrusion of fears stemming from childhood days which, in themselves, had nothing in particular to do with death (3). From both a therapeutic and a theoretical standpoint, it may be important to distinguish between fear of extinction and numerous other fears that may be exacerbated by thoughts of "ceasing to be."

Death as an object of fear may be centered around specific circumstances. One person may dread the possibility of death by suffocation. For the next person, death by fire, by drowning, or by some other mode may have an especially terrifying aspect. Fears of this kind are related more to the process of dying than to extinction. The same might possibly be said of the person who dreads a "dishonorable death" or a protracted period of "waiting for death." Although the particular mode of death (e.g., suffocation) is not salient in these two latter examples, the individual nevertheless concentrates his distress upon the circumstances under which death occurs, rather than the ultimate "ceasing to be." Why do some people develop such "specialized" fears? Is it possible that extreme fear of one possible circumstance of death might serve a protective function?

One object of fear is interesting enough to mark for special consideration. What a person may seem to fear most is the possibility that he will *know* of his impending death, or that he will actually *experience* the moment of death. Knowing and experiencing are inseparably involved in our state of being alive psychologically. When we fear knowing and experiencing, are we not in a sense fearing our own existence? Edwin S. Shneidman, for example, has written eloquently about "the undiluted and enduring love affair that each of us has with his own consciousness. . . . The great threat of death is that, like a cruel stepmother shouting to the excited children at the end of a full day's adventure, it orders a stop to this fascinating conversation-within-the-self"(4).

What Shneidman does not take into account (in this particular context) is the insistence on the part of some of us to ourselves order a stop to this conversation-within-the-self. We do not wish to be alive when we die. Fear of being cognizant of our own death is interesting in terms of its antecedents: Is this also the person who could not bear to experience earlier separations, crises, turning points? Or is death a very special case? This fear is also interesting in terms of its functional implications for the present and future: Does the attempt to block out the image of the final scene influence other behaviors and decisions as well? Is it conceivable that premature death or premature fading-away-before-death might result from this aversive reaction? It is interesting further in terms of the person's inner relationship to himself: Can the wish not to experience the end point of one's own life constitute part of an implicit "deal"? I will commit a sort of psychic suicide before physical death occurs. I have this "understanding" with Death. I fashion myself after Death little by little, and invite him to call earlier than is absolutely necessary—so long as I can avoid looking him (myself) in the face. Fear of experiencing one's death may thus be a stronger self-generated stimulus than fear of extinction per se.

There is one other object of fear which should be mentioned in this discussion, although it is not customarily regarded as part of the "death fear" constellation. A person may fear the loss or destruction of something outside himself that has come to represent his own identity. William James donated the phrase "generic self" to denote possessions, attachments, and other extensions of ourselves in the outside world (5). Paddy Chayefsky has created in John Morley a protagonist who so literally *becomes* his corporation that, as Dr. Klune patiently explains:

He responds . . . only to stimuli affecting his corporation. That's the thing, you see. He has totally identified with his corporation. I'm sure if you talk to him about his corporation, he'll hear and understand you and might even talk to you. Otherwise he has no sensory faculties at all (6).

The fate of the personal Mr. John Morley is ultimately determined by his identification with "Morley House." His attorney explains:

Do you understand what I am saying? You would make a hell of a tax saving if you were to die, John. Can you hear me John? It would be of great benefit to your corporation if you were to die (7).

The present authors have known real-life Mr. Morleys whose lives seemed almost totally invested in corporations or other out-of-the-body entities. Fear of personal extinction seemed almost irrelevant to them. But if something should happen to the *corporation*—if *that* should grow feeble and die!

Although not all of us carry this tendency to the extreme illustrated here, it may not be uncommon to fear the loss of a part of ourselves through the loss of some external object, whether physical or symbolic. And is this not the other side of the coin from "striving for social immortality?" Some of us believe that we "live on" either in our works or the memories of others. Destruction of our works or obliteration of our fame may be dreaded as though it represented a doubling of the death to be inflicted upon us.

The Situational Context of Death Fear

In the foregoing paragraphs we have considered some of the fears that may be aroused by thoughts of death, what has been termed the "basic death fear" (extinction), and several other fears. But nobody experiences these fears in a vacuum. There is always a situational context. Let us sketch in a few of the most salient situational dimensions.

Choron (8) has called attention to a pair of factors that are of obvious importance, although there is much to learn about their precise relationship to death fear. He distinguishes between "the situations where there is a real possibility of one's life coming to an end—the fear of death 'in the face of death'—and the occasions when one thinks about this possibility or about the inevitability of death in general—in short, the fear of death 'in anticipation of death'" (9). His second distinction is less obvious: "In the death fear in the face of death we must further distinguish between occasions a) when there is imminent danger of death by an outside event or act; b) when an 'inside' disturbance in the organism is threatening the individual; and finally c) when one is actually dying" (10).

These two distinctions actually seem to involve three sets of dimensions: time, space, and probability. By formulating each of these dimensions independently we will improve our ability to examine phenomena in this area.

1. *Time.* The time factor in general may be equated with the question: *When will I die?*

a. Death may seem to be only moments away, or it may seem to lie far down the road of time. Between the sense of immediacy and the sense of "over the horizon" there are probably a number of intermediate points. These points should be determined by research rather than conjecture. For the present, let us just think of a primary time dimension that stretches in a continuum from "immediate" to "remote."

b. A slightly less obvious time factor that also should be given formal recognition is the sense of acceleration, of motion-toward. Theory and research on the psychology of time perspective has indicated that the acceleration variable is distinct from other aspects of one's relationship to time (11). Two people who see themselves as being at the same temporal distance from death may differ markedly in their sense of rate-of-approach. One person may feel that he has just started to move toward death at a rapidly accelerated rate. The other person, perhaps afflicted with the same disease process, may have learned that his condition has been brought under partial control so that he is now approaching death at a *slower* tempo. We propose, then, a secondary time dimension concerned with perceived rate-of-movement toward death.

2. *Space.* The question here is not:

Where will I die? The question is: *Where is death?* Choron has proposed the distinction that seems most relevant to us. Death is "inside me" or it is "out there." Let us take a few examples.

Psychiatrist Robert Jay Lifton studied survivors of the atomic bombing of Hiroshima. These people have become known as the *hibakusha*, a group identity. He found that many of the *hibakusha* *"seem not only to have experienced the atomic disaster, but to have imbibed it and incorporated it into their beings, including all of its elements of horror, evil, and particularly of death"* (12). For these people, death is very much an internal threat. This may be one of the reasons why the A-bomb survivors feel themselves to be psychologically isolated from those who did not go through this experience. It is only the *hibakusha* who have the keen awareness of carrying death within them. It is difficult to avoid the stray thought of being "pregnant with death."

In the United States, we may not have a specific subpopulation who experience death as part of themselves in the way that has been reported for the *hibakusha.* But the man who expects to die of the same condition that struck down his father and grandfather before him is likely to locate death within himself. The person who has actually contracted a fatal illness, who is on the brink of starvation, or who is terrified of his own suicidal impulses—is he not contending with an indwelling threat of death? Regarding death as an *external* threat seems to be a natural direction of thought in some situational contexts (e.g., in riot or battle conditions). This tendency may also be a pervasive characteristic of our society (e.g., the possibly exaggerated attention given to death by "accident" (see Chapter 14). Looking around for death may be related to developmental level (e.g., Nagy's child who has not yet attained the idea that all humans are mortal) (13). But it may also be related to personality structure (e.g., the individual who characteristically projects his anxieties and tensions upon his environment, who cannot bear any internal build-up of pressure).

The locus of death is thus of interest from situational, social, developmental, and personality standpoints. We may also ask how a person has *learned* to regard death as "in" or "out." Students of *attitudes* may wish to determine what other beliefs and orientations tend to cluster around this dimension. And we are all likely to wonder precisely what behavior is affected in what way by the tendency to experience death as an internal or an external threat.

3. *Probability.* It is all too obvious to note that death has a probability of 100 percent. This statement does not preclude an examination of the individual's probability of surviving beyond a certain period of time. What is my probability of death within the next hour? Day? Month? Year? Decade? There is no reason to expect identical answers (or for the answers themselves to remain stable over time). Probability is also a dimension of space: What are the relative likelihoods of death coming upon me from the "inside" or the "outside"?

There may be a tendency to equate high probability of death with immediacy (an extreme point on the primary time dimension). With a moment's reflection, however, we see that this is not necessarily the case. A firm medical diagnosis may force the recognition that death is highly probable within approximately two years. This is quite a different psychological situation than being confronted with a high probability of death right now. And it is also different from having even a moderate threat of death facing us today or tomorrow. Let us illustrate this point.

The mere possibility that one might be exposed to a noxious stimulus is likely to heighten inner tension. Another way to describe this effect would be to say that perception of the *possibility* of a noxious

stimulus itself constitutes a noxious or aversive event: one increases his own response tendency to move away from the direction of the threat. If the probability of coming into contact with the noxious stimulus (read "death" here) continues to increase, then we might also expect the aversive response tendency to increase. The individual may not have actually moved at all—he may be powerless to move away, unable to locate the source of the threat, or unable to remove the threat by his own actions. But he does experience an increase in *fearful tension*. He is more fearful because the dreaded event is more probable; he is more tense because his own unfulfilled response tendency to "do something" in face of this danger has reached uncomfortable proportions.

There is some parallel here with what seems to take place when the dreaded prospect is brought closer in time. Fearful tension increases because one has less temporal insulation from the threatening event, and because the "fight or flight" readiness is also stimulated by this circumstance. If death becomes both more probable and more imminent, we would expect an even stronger fear or avoidance response.

But the parallel is far from perfect. The individual with a high probability of death is not necessarily relieved of his fearful tension if the threat remains fairly remote in time. He now has to wait for the sentence to be executed. Fear and other negative affects have more time to build within him; he has longer to live with the prospect of death. Which condition is more fear-provoking—remote or imminent death, with high probability either way? This question requires an empirical answer. It will probably also require identification of sources of significant intra- and interindividual variations. Perhaps, ultimately, this question requires a very personal answer from each of us to ourselves: Is it death we truly fear, or the fear of the fear of death?

The situational dimensions can be illustrated by four hypothetical cases. Mr. A. has accepted the medical verdict that his illness is almost certain to be fatal, and that death is close at hand. Mr. B is convinced that he is the victim of an international plot. He has been marked for immediate assassination. These two men share the perception that death is both highly probable and imminent; they differ in the direction or locus of the threat. Mr. C. expects to succumb to a condition that has claimed the lives of several others in his family, but he figures he has at least another ten years to live. Mr. D. is a rookie police officer on a field assignment in a high-violence area. He feels the odds are against a lethal physical attack upon him. But the danger does exist, and it exists right now.

Theoretically, any of us could be charted in this manner at any hour of our lives. The nature and magnitude of our response to the thought of death could be viewed within the context of the probability, timing, and locus of the threat.

However, we have assumed something in this discussion that should be made explicit. We have assumed that a consistent viewpoint has operated. But whose? The discussion has implied that it is the individual's own viewpoint we should be considering. This probably is the most important frame of reference. Mr. B., for example, is in a state of fearful tension because *he* sees a powerful threat to his life. There will be circumstances, however, in which it would be useful to examine the individual's orientation to death from one or more external perspectives. Perhaps Mr. A. has misinterpreted the clues he received from his physician—he is burying himself prematurely. And perhaps, just perhaps, Mr. B. is not as paranoid as he appears to be; he does have dangerous enemies. The extent of the discrepancy between the individual's assessment of his situation and the assessment of others in his environment is a relevant variable. We suggest that explorations into death fear should always be explicit about the frame of reference that is being used and, when possible, should consider multiple frames of reference.

Deathly Fear

Up to this point, we have been considering death primarily as an object of fear, or an aversive stimulus. But what about the quality of the response itself? What is the nature of the fear? Theory and research often have regarded death fear as one fear among many. This particular fear is distinguished from others by its object. One is afraid of snakes, crowded rooms, essay tests, death, small men with moustaches, for example. The fears may differ in magnitude, but it is assumed that the quality is identical. My fear response will increase in accordance with some mathematical law if a small man with a moustache forces me to take an essay test on snakes in a crowded room. Add a death stimulus to this situation and my fear will again show the predicted increment.

We have already seen that this approach can be misleading if it is assumed that death is a standard and monolithic object of fear. Even the categories proposed above (e.g., fear of the dead, afterlife, dying, and extinction) are not always sufficiently precise to guarantee that we are correctly identifying the stimulus properties that have elicited the individual's fear. Exploration of the fear response itself is important both for methodological and substantive reasons. Let us touch upon one methodological problem. In planning a controlled study in this area one might decide to present both "death" and "non-death" stimuli to the subject. (The stimuli might take the form of photographs flashed on a screen, thematic apperception type cards, or words on a memory drum.) The purpose of the study might be to determine the relative strength of death fear in younger and older adults, or to discover whether individual differences in death fear will predict to differences in some other type of behavior. This kind of research design may be "clean" enough. However, the results could prove difficult to interpret, especially if one is attuned to the subtle ways in which fears may be related to their objects.

Feifel has observed that "anxiety concerning mortality can wrap itself in varying counterfeit cloaks. Death fears can dissemble in insomnia, overconsideration for one's family, fears of loss, the depressed mood, schizophrenic symptomatology, and in diverse psychosomatic disturbances" (14). These remarks should give us pause. As a skilled clinician and a pioneer in the psychology of death, Feifel speaks from ample personal experience. He is arguing here that death fear may express itself *nonverbally* (e.g., insomnia, psychosomatic disturbances). This phenomenon might limit or distort what we think we are learning about death fear if we are basing our conclusions solely upon what people speak or write. But he also is stating that death fear may find its expression in *displaced objects* (e.g., overconsideration for one's family, when it is one's own death that is feared). Therefore, the strong fear response that is elicited by a supposedly "non-death" stimulus might in fact be more closely connected to death for a particular person than many of the obvious "death stimuli." And is it not possible—or probable—that obvious "death stimuli" run up against the respondent's first line of defenses? His "basic" or "real" fear of death may not express itself clearly; instead, what emerges as the overt response is his well-practiced maneuver for neutralizing the noxious stimulus.

Mr. E. evidences greater fear than Mr. F. to the same "death stimulus." Does this mean that Mr. E. "really" is more fearful of death? Perhaps Mr. F. is resorting to exaggerated defenses of selective inattention or repression just because he is so much more afraid of death. But it is not easy to argue that both strong and weak responses to death stimuli constitute evidence of fear. Perhaps, again, Mr. E. seems so fearful of this stimulus because *to him it represents something else that he fears more than death*. Feifel has suggested that death fear may dissemble in other guises. But in our clinical experience we have also seen the reverse process at work, other fears finding their expression around death-related objects. It is not always a matter of dissembling, either. We are thinking, for example, of an elderly woman whose lifelong fear of poverty and dependency could be brought to the surface by certain kinds of "death stimuli." The picture of a rural graveyard brought to mind the deaths of her father and oldest brother many years before, accompanied by behavioral signs of anxiety. The distress was related to her concern about being left unprovided for, having to accept the charity of others. She did not seem to associate the graveyard scene with the prospect of her own death. (If we were bound to the requirements of a preset experimental design, however, we would have had no alternative but to classify her response as death fear.)

The clinician who is focusing his attention upon the psychodynamics of one particular individual may be able to discern his client's idiosyncratic patterns of death fear. In systematic research, however, it is seldom deemed proper to develop different "rules of the game" for each subject in the study. We are accustomed to questing for general relationships, and this seems to require a certain uniformity of procedure. If I wish to define death fear exclusively in terms of its object, then it is, at the least, very inconvenient to have this object shift from case to case.

Those who are not clinicians might find something objectionable in the comments that have been offered above. Let us all "pick on" Feifel for a moment (as he is one of the strongest clinicians). How can he say—despite all his experience and erudition—that such phenomena as schizophrenic symptomatology, depressive mood, and so forth can represent death fear? And why would the same schizophrenic behavior be death-related in one case, but not in another? In essence, how does he have access to the "real" fear of death, while non-clinicians must content themselves with imperfect definitions that are tied down to specific research procedures?

We have here the implication that death fear somehow can be discerned and defined without being entirely dependent upon the object. There is the further implication that only people gifted with special powers of observation and analysis can speak to us about death fear. We will put that latter point aside for the moment. More relevant for now is the possibility that there is something special about the fear itself, rather than its object. This is moving from the treacherous footing of externalistic behaviorism to the even more perilous quicksands of phenomenology, but move there we must.

Let us explore a few of the qualities which may set the fear of death apart from other fears. We speak now of *deathly fear*.

Imagine yourself in a thoroughly familiar and secure environment. Perhaps you are at home. Comfortable reality surrounds you on all sides as you sit in your favorite chair, reading your favorite section of the newspaper. You are at ease, even though you happen to be alone at the moment. Fearful? Not at all: everything is in order.

Suddenly you sense something—or is it someone? There is an alien presence in the room. It is right behind you. A chill runs along your spine. Whether or not you turn around does not matter. Whether or not you see anything unusual does not matter (what does Nothing look like, anyway?). Whether or not you immediately dismiss this sensation as though it never existed does not matter. What does matter is that you have had the literally chilling experience of "uncanny" fear in the midst of the familiar.

Especially significant here is the sensation of being confronted with an almost incredibly alien force while the world retains its superficially familiar veneer. Things look the same. But, for a moment at least, things do not *feel* the same. This intrusion of the alien into the familiar, the menacing into the reassuring, the irrational into the orderly—this perceived intrusion may constitute the core of deathly fear.

A sophisticated analysis of bodily response during such an episode might well reveal an internal state that differs from the conditions we usually label as "fear." Analysis of imagery and other subjective experiences might also disclose differences between being in deathly fear and having a fear *of* something else. The sensation of spinal chill could prove to be one of the more dependable indices. It probably will be very difficult to improve our knowledge in this area. A sort of phenomenological psychophysiology may be required, including the ability to identify and report fairly subtle bodily and psychic changes.

Beyond the perception of an alien intrusion, the mental contents of deathly fear may include such shadings as, *"Life is not what it seems to be,"* or, *"What I have intuited and suspected but could not name, why! it is true."* There is the apprehension, in other words, that what we might term *a second reality* co-exists within us. The gratifyingly commonplace substance of everyday life—including our personal sense of being alive and viable—is accompanied by its own negation. The chair, the newspaper, and the reader all exist. But a fleeting, chilling intuition is enough to remind us that the nonexistence of these realities is also real. We have described a variety of the deathly fear experience as though it were irrational. Perhaps one can be more precise here. We are not up against distortions or contradictions in rational thinking; we are simply up against a phenomenon that seems prior or irrelevant to logical thought operations. The implication of nonexistence, of nothingness has come across to us. We may try to do something "rational" with this perception, but the perception itself is just there.

Consider a second possible form of deathly fear. *Trapped in reality* is one way of expressing the mental representation of this fear. On the psychophysiological side, it is likely to be experienced as a "heavier," "darker," more "massive" state of bodily distress. This is in contrast to the sharp, chilling touch of the state we have described above. Imagine yourself, if you will, in a situation that seems completely complete. *Everything will be the way it is.* The future, in a sense, has already happened. All significant future experiences have been determined or locked into place. You have no further choice about who you will become or what will become of you. The actual weighs you down. The possible no longer exists.

Does not life involve a sense of ongoingness? There is change as well as stability, elements of surprise as well as certainty. To feel that one's life has come to a standstill is perhaps to fear that one's death has begun. This form of deathly fear can be precipitated by either external or internal events. An old man sits in a geriatric institution. He does little. His thoughts and feelings have become highly routinized, almost static. What is the trouble?

A psychological observer might venture the opinion that the environment has exerted a *deadening effect* upon the thoughts and experiences of a vulnerable person (perhaps not so different from the way in which a meretricious educational system can induce "death at an early age" to its students) (15). From the old man's point of view, however, the trouble may be seen as internal. "I can't do anything. I am becoming dead inside" (16). However, it is likely that both internal and external processes have contributed to this man's death-tinged quality of fear. The pulse of

life with which he has identified his own existence is becoming ever more feeble, ever more difficult to detect. In this sense, deathly fear is the perception of one's own phenomenological life "closing up shop." *It is at the same time a partial identification with death, and the alarm one is still capable of experiencing as he intuits what is happening to him.*

Some readers may reject this approach quickly and vehemently (just as some may have rejected our earlier introduction of stimulus-response psychology into the area of death). But wait. Ask yourself a few questions. Is the death-as-object-of fear approach completely adequate by itself? Has psychology given enough attention to the experiential status of fear in general? Of death fear in particular? Do we know for sure that such a phenomenon as deathly fear is out of the question? (And where is the evidence for drawing such a conclusion?) Is it wise to limit ourselves to the impoverished language of behavioristic psychology when we are attempting to capture and describe these elusive phenomena? Do we have an impulse to turn away from the deathly-fear approach because we are scientifically underprepared to investigate and conceptualize inner states? If so, does this mean that such states cannot be allowed to exist, or merely that we have some challenging work ahead of us? Finally, even should the status of deathly fear as an absolutely "real" phenomenon be indeterminate, might it not be useful to "invent" the deathly-fear construct for its heuristic potential?

Suppose that one or more forms of deathly fear could be distinguished from other fears. This distinction would be on the basis of the fear *experience* rather than the object of the fear. There might be an important methodological advantage here. We would be in a better position to learn under what conditions this internal state originates and varies, and to learn how deathly fear "seeks" its objects. Instead of being forced to treat external stimuli as somehow containing or comprising the death fear, we would focus directly upon the individual's own experience. In other words, our own process of inquiry would be free enough to follow the subtle transformations that go on in the lives of real people, rather than being restricted to a set of stimulus-bound definitions.

An example or two might be helpful here. Mr. G. is unremarkable in his response to conventional "death stimuli." What is curious about Mr. G., however, is his enormous difficulty in *completing* anything. His life is a trail of almost-completed endeavors. Why? There are a number of possible answers to this question. But let us say that, for Mr. G., the relevant variable is deathly fear (of the second type described above). He may explain his difficulty in this way or that way. But what he *feels* is a heavy sort of dread as he approaches completion of a project or action. Completion of a task has come to represent the stopping of life, the end of psychological motion. In his form of deathly fearing, it is the perception of his own phenomenological life becoming more static and death-like that is the greatest and most distinctive concern. Mr. G. could be distinguished from another person with the incompletion tendency by the presence or absence of this particular sense of dread. We need not *assume* that everybody with a certain kind of behavior pattern or certain kind of aversion is experiencing the same inner state. We are free to *explore* rather than assume.

Take another example. Mr. H. has his television or radio blaring constantly (yet he does not often seem to be attentive to them). He is seldom in solitary repose. There must be people around. There must be noise, movement, action. "Something going on" fills not only those hours of the day when he has occupational or other responsibilities to perform, but also overflows into hours that could be passed at a different tempo, in a different style. People who know Mr. H. well can predict that he will treat every "extra" hour that comes his way as an empty bag that must promptly be stuffed with something, perhaps anything.

Again, there is more than one possible explanation for this behavior pattern. But again, we will select the most relevant possibility. Mr. H. has an unsettling relationship with deathly fear of the first type described. The shiver of negation is very much with him. Silence, repose, and solitude would leave him too vulnerable to the sensation of deathly fear. He cannot give this experiential state an opportunity to manifest itself fully. Lights, action, companionship, and noise serve as quasi-magical devices to forbid an opening to the alien intrusion of death awareness. How well this life style actually protects him from the experience of deathly fear is another question. What happens when circumstances conspire to leave him alone with himself and his fear of deathly fear?

Deathly *fear* may be a new and unfamiliar concept, but it does have a relative that is better known—death *anxiety*.

Death Anxiety

"Anxiety" and "fear" are sometimes used as interchangeable terms. However, a number of attempts have been made to assign more specific connotations to each of them. We will consider here just a few of the most pertinent approaches to the differentiation of these terms.

There is only one area of common ground. Several major theorists have interpreted anxiety as a negative emotional state that lacks a specific object. In Rollo May's lucid book on this subject, he cites Kurt Goldstein, Sven Kierkegaard, and Sigmund Freud as among those who have expressed this view (17). It is fear that we are experiencing if we can locate and describe the source of our concern. It is anxiety if we have a vague apprehension that something terrible is going to happen—without knowing what, where, when, why, or how.

An adequate treatment of death anxiety would require a much more comprehensive and searching examination of the general topic of anxiety than what can be carried out within the scope of this book. Two decades after its publication, May's treatment of *The Meaning of Anxiety* (18) remains a choice starting place for those who wish to move further into this complex and fascinating area.

Fear of death, as described earlier in this chapter, should not be confused with an anxiety state. There is a tendency to regard anxiety as a more intense or threatening condition than fear. But even a very strong fear of death-related stimuli is not equivalent to anxiety, if we wish to use these terms precisely.

My strongest death fear, let us say, is the prospect of succumbing on the operating table. One can identify a cluster of specific aversive behaviors that I manifest around this central fear. I am afraid of hospitals, surgeons, the odor of antiseptics. Given the opportunity, I will avoid contact with these objects of fear, even when there is no direct threat of going under the knife myself. The fear is specific; my behavior with respect to the fear is directional and organized. And so it goes with other possible objects of death fear.

Now we come to a real puzzler. Can I—or anyone else—experience a state of agitated dysphoria that warrants being designated as *death* anxiety? Or is it the case that anxiety has no coloring? If I have had one anxiety, I have had them all. Precisely because anxiety is characterized as a diffuse, unfocused psychological condition, perhaps it cannot usefully be divided into types (e.g., death-anxiety, identity-anxiety, castration-anxiety). This is another of those questions that will not be answered satisfactorily here. But we might do well to keep the problem of anxiety-specificity in mind as we proceed.

Freud came around to a theoretical position which emphasized the *function* of anxiety in survival and adaptation.* It is important that we have a mechanism for becoming aware of possible dangers. The discomfort we call anxiety serves an alerting function—we cannot rest at ease until we have discovered the source of the threat. Having identified the threat, we have several further options. We may find that the threat is not really so formidable once we have faced up to it. We may indeed identify the source of our discomfort as an authentic threat and take the necessary steps to remove it. Or we may have to live with the continued threat—which is now termed a "fear." In all of these instances, the initial state of anxiety was preparatory to adaptive behavior, and the anxiety dissipated upon our specific response. But it is also possible that we may fall victims to a neurotic, unrealistic, or unadaptive form of anxiety. We become *so* aroused by the as-yet-undefined threat that our state of arousal itself interferes with adaptation. We become paralyzed or disorganized. We react as though threatened when the skies are blue. We are so accustomed to feeling threatened that we fail to discern the valid and substantial threat from among all the murky and diffuse concerns that surround us.

At this point, there is nothing to distinguish between death anxiety and non-death anxiety. Our anxieties are adaptive or non-adaptive depending upon their magnitudes and their relevance to the reality situations before us. Yes, it might turn out that the stimulus triggering our discomfort was an objective threat to our lives. Once identified, this threat either is alleviated, or remains as a specific fear. But the initial state of anxiety itself was

---

*Freud's conception of anxiety underwent significant changes. He also wrote of anxiety within a variety of clinical and theoretical contexts. For these reasons it is not appropriate to offer a simple and static summary of his views. The works of Freud specifically cited in this chapter contain some of his most important statements on anxiety, but his complete collected papers invite further delving.

not necessarily any different from what it would have been were the threat of a different kind.

It might be possible to argue that what Freud describes as *neurotic anxiety* has some special kinship with death. This generalized dread may actually increase our probabilities of premature death because of its adverse effect upon our survival capacities. But this may not be what Freud had in mind. Furthermore, one could also argue in the opposite direction: *normal anxiety* is attuned to the prospect of death, as it represents our basic scanning device to identify survival threats. Again, however, it is doubtful that this view represents Freud's position accurately. But to characterize an internal state as death-related because of its functional implications (increases or decreases the objective probability of death) is an approach that might prove useful in another context. It is different from basing the definition upon the object (fear *of* death), or the quality of the psychological state (*deathly* fear).

Should man's aversion to death then be characterized as fear or anxiety? Does it really make any difference? Let us press on a little further. Freud's labyrinthian explorations of fear and anxiety are perilous to summarize. Even the most astute resume is unlikely to convey both the character and the content of his approach. One can also go astray by attempting to evaluate his theory of anxiety apart from its systematic connections with other psychoanalytic propositions. Somewhat fearfully (or should we say anxiously?), we venture the following interpretations:

1. As already mentioned, anxiety is to be regarded as a diffuse, objectless experiential state of decidedly unpleasant or painful character. The fearful state, by contrast, possesses an object, a direction.

2. Anxiety is the more primitive state. This is so not only because it is less articulated and boundaried, but because it is primal—first. We achieve or learn fears.

But the vulnerability to anxiety is with us right from the start. In the process of being evicted from the womb we are overburdened by the enormous increase in stimulation. This excessive input is experienced as extremely unpleasurable or painful. We are initiated into postnatal life through the experience of what Freud has termed, *the traumatic moment* (19).

3. Anxiety is poison. This aspect of Freud's interpretation often is overlooked. The traumatic moment is thought to be accompanied by a forceful psychobiologic process; it is not just a matter of the newborn "experiencing" an "emotion" that he will later "remember" in some way. But birth anxiety is a *necessary* poison: "at the time . . . the effects upon the heart's action and upon respiration characteristic of anxiety were expedient ones. The very first anxiety would thus have been a toxic one" (20). The traumatic moment might possibly be regarded then as a massive conditioning trial that is almost certain to result in "one-shot learning."

4. The traumatic moment might be inevitable and it might be expedient or even essential in stimulating the infant. He is now ready to do battle with life. But the experience itself does not bear repeating. Having once partaken of this toxic tonic, we are evermore on the alert against the possibility of a second dose. Primal anxiety is the most aversive of all aversive conditions. And important for this discussion is the contention that this dread condition has been known to every person. In attempting to avoid a return to the traumatic moment (or its equivalent in adult life) we are not merely fleeing from a phantom. The undesired encounter with another traumatic moment would take place in the future, of course. But it is a future that has been shaped and projected by our past.

5. When we are functioning properly, the perception of a threat makes us feel uncomfortable enough to do something about it. We act upon the vague

stirrings of anxiety because our nervous system has been "primed" for this task. Even a slight twinge has the effect of reminding us how turbulent and chaotic our lives might become if we failed to heed the warning. As mentioned earlier, this "sentinel" activity (21) should lead to the identification and evaluation of the threat, along with any further coping activities that might be required. This is normal anxiety. It leads us to develop normal fears (i.e., to be wary of realistic dangers with just the right degree of concern).

6. Neurotic anxiety has already been touched upon. Fears that are neurotic owe their derivation to neurotic anxiety. We attempt to inhibit the burgeoning sense of anxiety by maneuvers that seemingly are directed to the external world. We fear this, that, and the next thing. But the fears are not adaptive, not realistic—they are part of our symptomatology. The actual threat in these instances is likely to be within ourselves. We sense trouble, perhaps impending diaster. The threat is misinterpreted as external. It is falsely specified. To contain the incipient state of anxiety we must continue to inhibit or defend. One thinks of the insecure despot who persuades his people that their essential problem is the malice of external powers, not the seething, unresolved problems within.

7. Now we can return to death. In one of his better known formulations, Freud moves from the primal anxiety experience to the fear of death (22). But there is an intermediary point, perhaps two. Anxiety is cued in by excessive stimulation. The young boy's sexualized affection toward his mother fills him with dread; it is "hot stuff" that threatens to get out of control. At the same time, it is "wrong" and "dangerous" to have these feelings because Mother, after all, belongs to Father. The lad tries to put on the controls. Through "superego" processes he develops a fear of castration. As a less noticeable aspect of this formulation, it

would seem that he also regulates his feelings by the fear of over-excitement (or, perhaps, it is the latter fear that spurs on the development of castration fear?)

Fear of death makes its appearance as a second-order phenomenon. The concern about becoming too excited (orgiastic) connects with various childhood experiences and perceptions. The first-order fear (over-excitement) translates itself into death fear (losing complete control of one's self by losing one's self). Castration fear translates itself as massive retaliation from the powers-that-be. The boy dreads the loss of his total self, not merely the offending member.

From this standpoint, then, aversion to death is better regarded as fear rather than anxiety. The aversion evolves from anxiety, and it takes some time to reach identifiable status. It is not even a fear of the first order.

8. Does this derivation of death fear from primal anxiety apply equally well to both sexes? Fear of castration as an intermediary station for the development of death concern seems to be more appropriate for the boy. One might venture either that girls do not develop a fear of death, or that the pathway is different. Freud takes the latter alternative: Fear of castration "finds no place in women, for though they have a castration complex they cannot have a fear of being castrated. Its place is taken in their sex by a fear of loss of love, which is evidently a later prolongation of the infant's anxiety if it minds its mother's absence. You will realize how real a situation of danger is indicated by this anxiety. If a mother is absent or has withdrawn her love from her child, it is no longer sure of the satisfaction of its needs and is perhaps exposed to the most distressing feelings of tension. Do not reject the idea that these determinants of anxiety may at bottom repeat the situation of the original anxiety at birth, which, to be sure, also represented a separation from the mother" (23).

There we have it. Both sexes move from the traumatic moment of birth to fear of death via a more basic, first-order fear. In the case of the boy, it is an elaboration or implication of castration fear. With the girl, fear of death is an outcome of separation fear. In other contexts, Freud also speaks of this as the fear of loneliness. By implication, the boy is also exposed to the fear of loneliness, separation, or loss of love. Therefore his development of death fear proceeds from two sources. Should this mean that men grow up to be more fearful of death? Or should we expect differences in modes of expressing or coping with death fear rather than in magnitude? Freud may not have addressed himself explicitly to these questions, but it should be of interest to relate empirical findings on sex differences to his general formulations.

9. For both sexes, then, it would seem that death concern should be regarded as a second-order fear rather than a basic anxiety. This view is supported by Freud's general position on the cognition of death (24). He believed that one could not conceive of personal mortality. Why not? Because no living person has ever experienced his own death. When we fear death, then, we fear something-we-know-not. It must be the case, Freud averred, that death fear receives its cognitive content from other sources. In a sense, death fear is a thrown-together sentiment, borrowing from a variety of other ideas. Many of these ideas are probably unconscious and prior to adult conceptualizations. This rejection of death as an authentic cognitive content is associated with Freud's efforts to derive death fear in the manner described above. (In the present context we are concentrating upon Freud's approach to death fear and thus may be inadvertently overemphasizing the place of this concept in his general system. In point of fact, Freud's remarks about death fear often were embedded in discussions that were moving toward some other goal, such as explication of the

relationship between anxiety and symptom-formation.)

Freud's disinclination to regard death fear as a basic or authentic condition in its own right has an important implication: fear of death is neurotic. We do not know if Freud ever expressed himself with absolute certainty on this question. But he did indicate that he had serious doubts as to whether there is such a phenomenon as a normal fear of death. This orientation seemed to set a pattern to be followed by many subsequent psychoanalysts. When the sophisticated psychiatrist encounters fear of death in one of his patients he is to turn all his sleuthing talents to the discovery of the "real" fear that underlies the manifest thanatophobia. Some of the most ingenious pages in psychoanalytic case presentations have involved the uncovering of death fear or anxiety as a secondary formation related to other (more "legitimate") trauma and conflicts.

It is not our purpose here to evaluate Freud's views as "true" or "false." Such an effort would be highly premature in light of our own state of knowledge at this time and would also demand its own book. Let us simply attempt to relate Freud's approach to death fear/anxiety to what has already been presented in this chapter. We are still engaged in the task of trying to determine what all of us have been talking about when we use these terms.

Explicit discussion of death dynamics by Freud and the Freudians typically centers around the notion: fear *of* (i.e., death as an object). Attention often is directed to specific objects of fear, that is, to specific modes of death. Why does this person have such a marked fear of death by suffocation, while that person is terrified by the prospect of falling from a high place? In delving into such questions, psychoanalysts have applied their powers of subtle observation and interpretation. However, their general approach can be subsumed under the death-as-an-object-of-fear rubric that was proposed earlier in this chapter. There is no particular need to invoke the additional term, death *anxiety*, unless one wishes to have a synonym. But we are not yet finished with this matter.

As pointed out earlier, objects of death fear can be grouped roughly into concerns about afterlife, dying, and extinction (see Figure A, p. 45). Psychoanalysts sometimes specify the type of fear they have in mind, but not invariably. Fear of what might come after death is not an integral element in the Freudian approach. This fear seems to be excluded from the formulations which derive fear of death from birth anxiety. We have two comments on this point. First, if we cannot have a normal fear of death because the condition is beyond our experience, then the same reasoning should apply as well to fear of the afterlife. Never having experienced the afterlife, we could fashion our fears of same only upon the model of unpleasant conditions already experienced. Secondly, however, the superego aspects of death fear should be of special relevance. Castration fear, it will be recalled, is said to have an important role in the development of death fear. Junior becomes a "good boy" because he is afraid of massive punishment from father—retaliation for the juvenile designs he has on mother. Later on, junior is kept in line by his trusty superego. Instead of the naked fear of castration he has the more socialized dread of disapproval by others and by his own conscience. This generalizing fear of loss is still his connection to fear of death: loss of everything.

In Figure A we suggested that punishment and rejection were among the more specific fears involved in aversion to the afterlife on the personal level, while retaliation and loss of relationship were fears related to death-of-the-other. This is quite consistent with the Freudian view, or so it would appear. While the self-other distinction is not explicit in Freud's paradigm, one should not encounter much difficulty in translating his observations into the categories suggested here. We see that Freudian insights can enrich the understanding of specific objects of death fear at the same time that an explicit general model can help to clarify and organize the Freudian interpretation of death.

The fear of extinction seems to be the most crucial element in Freud's approach. It is the state of non-being that is held to be unthinkable and, therefore, an improper subject for normal fear. Although Freud and his disciples do not always distinguish between fear of dying and fear of extinction, it would appear that this distinction should be made henceforth. It makes more sense to apply Freud's notions to fear of extinction than to fear of the dying process. Extinction can be regarded as an all-or-none affair (but see alternative views, Chapter 4). Dying, however, is a state of progressive failure and incapacitation. Many people have experienced such states, short of death. It is far from inconceivable that a person can form a realistic fear of dying as an extrapolation of his own experiences: "It is something like the way I felt before the medication took hold and my strength came back—dying might be something like that, only more so." In the service of clarity, then, we propose that the basic Freudian concepts about death fear *not* be applied indiscriminately to the fear of dying.

And what about Freud's observations on the fear of extinction? Guided again by Figure A and its context, we see that the focus of his central observations can be even more precisely delimited. Freud's derivation of death fear is not primarily applicable to extinction of the other. This variety of fear is not specifically included within the anxiety-castration/loneliness-extinction paradigm. It would be interesting to speculate on what he might have said had the problem intrigued him, but we shall resist that detour. Perhaps the most relevant point is that in the absence of any formulations to the contrary, we see no evidence that would cause us to believe that his ideas about extinction of the other should be classified as death *anxiety*.

Fear of personal extinction is what we have previously defined as the basic death fear. We attempted to distinguish this from the variety of "attached fears" that can accompany the previewing of one's death. Freud seems to be contending that the basic death fear is somehow superficial, displaced, and neurotic. It does not really exist. At the most, perhaps, fear of personal extinction enjoys a sort of borrowed existence. In terms of our classificatory model, then, Freud would reduce the basic death fear to the status of an "attached fear." We are vulnerable to many fears, some more basic than others. Under certain circumstances one or more of these fears may become transformed in such a way that they find expression in, or masquerade through, the apparent fear of personal extinction. Freud and his disciples do not deny that we might encounter what appears to be a fear of personal extinction. They would just consider us to be naive for taking such fears at face value.

The full weight of the Freudian approach, then—its formidable account of the origin and function of anxiety, fears, defenses, etc.—comes down hard on only one aspect of our topic. It is concerned with death as *object* of fear, and with only one of the six types of fear-objects that have been differentiated here. If you would like, we could say that it deals with two of the six, as basic death fear is considered and rejected. This judgment, however, is not as complete as it might sound. We will need to complicate it a bit in a moment.

It seems appropriate here to issue the reminder that Freud worked out these formulations from the "inside." Exploring the intricacies of intrapsychic dynamics, he came upon fear of death as a product of prior psychic events and experiences. Although much different in detail, there is a certain parallel with the approach we took in the preceding chapter wherein

death was treated as a concept, and as a concept that developed from and in the company of other concepts (which are, of course, intrapsychic inhabitants, too). The big difference is as follows: Freud remained with the inner processes, continuing his stance as their explicator and critic. From this standpoint, there is no real encounter with death per se. Personal extinction as a reality problem is somehow more obscure and less relevant than internal dynamics that occasionally become caught up with thoughts and feelings about death. Freud's modus operandi naturally leads to a rather distinctive set of formulations.

We selected an alternate approach. After exploring concepts of death *as* concepts, we then accepted man's ideas about death as valid or effective on their own terms. We think that we think there is such a thing as our own nonexistence. We think about the afterlife, and about dying. Whatever is "really out there" (the ultimate physical nature of death) and whatever is "really in us" (unfathomable feelings and experiences that give rise to our concepts) are topics that have been set aside at least temporarily. For methodological purposes, if no other, it is useful to regard our conceptions of death as being effective parts of our environment. It is always seasonable to argue that we may not know what we think we know. But it is equally seasonable to proceed on the assumption that our self-generated stimuli (in this case, death concepts) are related to the rest of our phenomenological life and to overt behavior in ways that are worth understanding.

An important implication of this approach lies in the problems which come to be seen as relevant or even urgent. How do people feel and behave when they believe themselves to be this close to death, and when they believe themselves to be even closer? In other words, the situational dimensions of death fear become more salient (as sketched in an earlier section), and the threat of death as a reality problem takes its place alongside the vicissitudes of death fear as an intrapsychic passenger.

Three general types of death orientation have been explored. All of them are characterized by dysphoric, unpleasant, or threatening qualities. While it has been possible to formulate fear of death and deathly fear with some degree of differentiation and clarity, the notion of death anxiety remains elusive. The typical psychoanalytic usage seems to regard death anxiety as a synonym for fear of death, even though in Freud's systematic thinking there are important distinctions made between anxiety and fear. Perhaps a few provisional conclusions may be offered at this point.

The following comments could be regarded as a misdirected attempt to make distinctions beyond the point of diminishing returns. It is true enough that one can go too far in this direction. However, it seems to us that theory and research in this area has suffered more from ambiguity and shifting meanings than it has from over-precision. Indeed, we could only generously be accused of "overprecision" in what we offer here:

1. Most discussions of orientations toward death emphasize dysphoric qualities. In particular, these discussions tend to be concerned with fear of death. From our standpoint, a person who responds with aversive behavior to death-related stimuli may be said to manifest fear of death. What is important here is that the stimuli have come to be associated with the individual's own definition or understanding of death. Whether this fear is to be regarded as "normal" or "neurotic," "authentic" or "displaced," "basic" or "derived," is another matter.

2. Deathly fear may be regarded as a phenomenological experience with important and perhaps distinctive somatic components. With better understanding of this state we would be able to recognize it independent of the particular external stimulus configuration. The suggestion is that this form of fear differs from others chiefly on the response or experiential side—it is different to experience deathly fear than it is to be afraid of one or another object, even death-related objects.

3. Freud and others have referred to a rather awesome state variously designated as "primary anxiety," "the traumatic moment," and the "catastrophic reaction." It has already been implied that this state does not seem to fit the criterion for either fear of death or death anxiety. The person who is afflicted with primary anxiety (*urangst*) does not *have* a fear—his experience is too chaotic, his psychic structures too overwhelmed to "have" anything. There is no delineation of a specific threat. Neither does this state seem classifiable as death anxiety because it is too diffuse a psychic experience to be associated with any particular content: anxiety is anxiety. Furthermore, *urangst* is said to be experienced by neonates, who are unlikely to have any ideas about death. It is also improbable that primal anxiety is equivalent to what we have described as deathly fear. The experience of deathly fear requires a fairly advanced level of psychological development. One has to know something about constancy, the expected, the routine. And one has to know something about striving, fulfillment, possibility, and finality. The sense of "alien intrusion," "second reality," or "trapped in reality" requires both an ample personal history and the existence of a structured frame of mind at the present moment. No, deathly fear and *urangst* cannot be used interchangeably.

4. Yet it would be hasty to declare that primary anxiety has nothing to do with death. The psychophysiological state of turbulence that accompanies birth (or which has at least acquired this reputation) serves as the prototype for *any* subsequent psychic calamity. Death is not the only calamity that may befall us. But death is one of the confrontations that can force us back along the final common

pathway that leads to the traumatic moment. This interpretation seems to be consistent enough with Freud's own formulations; it would portray primary anxiety as a privately-experienced Hell that is universal for our species. We pass through this phase of torment on our way to postnatal life, and we may pass through it again. It would still remain inappropriate to equate primal anxiety with anxiety about death. Death is just one of the circumstances that can threaten us with a return to the traumatic moment. Once we are actually reexperiencing that moment (or even approximating it) we have lost the level of psychic structure at which it is possible to discriminate among different "brands" of terror.

5. The careful reader will be uneasy at this point. Something has been left out, has it not? We seem to have neglected the distinction between death as a physical reality and death as a thought or symbol. We now attempt to correct this omission which is part of our method of successive approximations. We have already seen that fear of death is treated as a second-order, derived phenomenon in traditional psychoanalytic theory. Heightened fear of death presumably would reinstate the traumatic moment, as would sufficiently heightened fear of anything else. But under what conditions would fear of death be so greatly heightened? The most relevant answer for us is that death fear probably would be exacerbated by the arousal of neurotic insecurities. The individual's instinctual conflicts threaten to get out of control. Characteristically, he intensifies his concerns and defenses on some front other than where the real battle is waging. It will be recalled that Freud doubted there was any such thing as a "normal" fear of death on the grounds that we are not able to conceptualize our own lack of existence.

These considerations are introduced here because otherwise it might be natural for us to confuse the role of death fear in psychodynamic systems with the actual death encounter. It has already been mentioned that the prospect of physical death per se was seldom the focus of psychoanalytic observation and interpretation. Furthermore, it is helpful to view the realistic death threat along the situational dimensions previously described in this chapter. Let us concentrate for now upon the time dimensions. One's distance from his private Hell of *urangst* may be related to his perceived distance from physical death. And the relationship may be anything but simple.

The intuitive awareness of impending death is a subject that is poorly understood at present. But it is reasonably clear that some people do seem to be alerted to the prospect of personal death before the indices are clear to others around them, including physicians (25, 26, 27). When death is still fairly remote in time and the cues are still meager and ambiguous, the individual may respond with "secondary anxiety." This is not the overwhelming trauma of which we have been speaking previously, but the unsettled, apprehensive feelings that are aroused in us on a day-by-day basis. It is the anxiety which alerts us to potential dangers that require better identification—and it is the anxiety that "reminds" us how much worse we might feel if we choose to ignore this warning signal.

What happens when the vague cues become more specific—when, in fact, the individual's intensified secondary anxiety is replaced by *knowledge* that a death threat does exist? We have ourselves seen instances in which anxiety diminishes. The person now has a more or less definite object toward which he can direct his thoughts and feelings. He learns what it is that has been troubling him (prospect of death), where it is (inside him, in a particular form to which a name has been attached), when it is likely to occur, and how much probability he may have of turning back this threat to his life. Anxiety may thus be replaced by fear (or, as we shall see later, by other affects). The realistic threat of death does not necessarily cue off *urangst*, either immediately or subsequently. But here we are beginning to infiltrate this background discussion with some empirical propositions. So, back to theory.

6. Follow this threatened person to the bed on which he lies dying. The situation has been transformed from expectation to direct experience. To the extent that he feared dying, he now has the experience itself. The prospect of extinction and the afterlife remain as possible objects of fearful tension. We do not mean to probe the intricacies of his phenomenological situation. We simply call attention to the fact that whatever relationships may exist between primary anxiety and death-concern should not be presumed to remain unchanged as the individual moves from remote expectation through proximal expectation to direct experiencing.

7. Linger here another moment, if you will. The threat to this man's life is intensifying, his time running out. Does this mean that he is destined to pass through the traumatic moment again? Is he to be engulfed by anxiety? If the empirical answer to this question were in the affirmative, then the association between primal anxiety and death would indeed be intimate (and harrowing). But this is an empirical question. The answer is not contained in psychoanalytic theory, or in any other theory. And so we emphasize again that "death anxiety" remains a term whose referents are almost wholly intrapsychic, not clearly related by either theory or fact to our responses to actual death experiences.

Since the question has been raised in this context, we add our own impression that life's end is not invariably or even typically experienced as a traumatic moment. By this time, however, we are just as eager to move into the available research findings as the reader must be.

We pause only long enough to array some of the questions before us.

What Do We Want to Know?

Many empirical questions could be asked concerning fear of death, deathly fear, and, if you still like the term, death anxiety. The groups of questions which follow appear to us to be relevant and to deserve priority.

Genesis. How does aversion to death develop? What states does it pass through? Is there a peak? If so, when? What are the critical factors that influence its scope, particularity and intensity? How does the development of this fear interweave with the other aspects of personality growth?

Manifestation. How does the death fear express itself in thought, feeling, and behavior? By what characteristics are we to differentiate death fear from other responses? To what extent and in what particular forms can death fear be "read" from somatic symptoms? How does this constellation of fears reveal itself in the interpersonal as well as the intrapsychic context? How, for example, can we recognize an especially death-fearing group?

Pathology. Under what conditions is death fear "normal,", "neurotic," or perhaps even "psychotic?" Do individuals classified as suffering from psychiatric syndromes show death fears that are distinctive in quality or magnitude? Are these individuals' death orientations the "cause" or "effect" of their difficulties?

Individual differences. What "kinds" of people show what "kinds" of death fear, and why?

Function. What is the primary role of death fears in our lives? What are some of the more important secondary roles (e.g., do we find it useful to frighten and thus control others with our own fears?).

Behavior. How do our feelings of death show up in the decisions we make and the actions we execute? Under what conditions, for example, does a strong death fear enhance our chances of survival, and under what conditions does it have the opposite effect?

Analysis. Despite all that has been discussed previously in this chapter, we still have the analytic question: Precisely what is it we fear when we have a "fear of death," and what is going on inside us when it is "deathly fear" we are experiencing?

These are among the questions that require answers based upon controlled observation and experimentation. Untutored observation is unlikely to provide adequate answers, which is one of the main reasons we have devoted so much attention to problems of theory and terminology. "Armchair" answers are not adequate either, so we now turn to some of the most relevant empirical forays. At the same time that we inquire specifically into death fears we will also survey responses to the more general question: how *salient* is death concern? This issue often is treated along with (or as an intrinsic component) of death fear.

DEATH FEARS: THE DATA

Types of Information Available

At the present writing, there are well over a hundred reports in our language that present data relevant to death fears. One could easily enlarge or diminish this total by altering the criteria for inclusion. We have chosen to include some clinical reports which are fairly specific about the people who were studied.

These reports vary in many ways. Sociologist Jack Riley, for example, has published partial data based upon a survey of 1,500 adults (28), while psychologist

Joseph Zinker has offered an intensive analysis of a single case (29). The clinical case method has been as popular as one might expect, but so has the questionnaire. Needless to say, there is not a great deal of uniformity within either the clinical or the questionnaire approaches. It is not uncommon for the reader to remain uncertain about precisely how the investigator obtained and analyzed his data. Interview-type studies seem to be more popular than those which call upon objective or projective tests, and experimental manipulations have been decidedly rare. Surprisingly little use has been made of the personal diary technique (30). The psychological autopsy method and other multidisciplinary approaches have also been applied, but not extensively (31).

The studies show a healthy diversity in the variety of populations investigated. The entire human life-span has been encompassed. Not so incidentally, this is one of the few psychological topics for which we have obtained more information on elderly persons than on other age groups. Subjects have also varied greatly on the dimension of physical health. The fatally ill and the "sound as a dollar" have both been studied, as well as those who may be placed between these extremes. "Mentally ill" and "normal" people have both been represented in the research and clinical literature, although not invariably in the same study.

There seems to be a reasonably broad range of educational and occupational backgrounds collectively represented in the available literature. However, the coverage of disadvantaged and minority groups appears to be on the meager side. We have had no success in trying to determine how many non-whites (if any) were included in most of the studies that came to our attention. For that matter, we have yet to find an empirical study directed specifically to death fears of black Americans, although Herbert Hendin has contributed a relevant study of suicidal tendencies in young black men (32).

Some initiative has been shown in the investigation of specific populations. Psychiatrists Harvey Bluestone and Carl L. McGahee, for example, interviewed prisoners awaiting execution (33), and a team of psychologists headed by Paul Ekman looked into divergent reactions to the threat of war in two groups of people with strongly opposing philosophies (34). There have also been studies of death fears in people who suffer from nightmares (35, 36), and psychiatrically-oriented anthropological observations of death concern in American Indian tribes (37).

Most of the research has been of the "one-shot" variety. This imposes a serious limitation on conclusions that can be drawn from the available results. Fortunately, a few investigations have incorporated periodic monitoring or, at least, the single follow-up technique (38, 39). Clinical case reports often seem to have been based upon a series of observations over time, but we have seldom been provided with precise information about the chronology of the death fears.

Most studies have also been of the "one-perspective" variety as well. Rarely have the subjects' orientations toward death been derived from a set of multiple perspectives (e.g., self/other, behavioral/projective, manifest/latent, multi-situational). One might, for example, make effective use of a research design incorporating sociometric procedures along with self-report, projective indices of fantasy life, biographical materials, interview, and direct observation in a variety of relevant behavioral settings. Lacking this kind of investigation, we should keep in mind that many of the available findings were obtained with the use of a single instrument at a single point in time. It follows that we do not yet have a solid empirical grasp of the "construct validity" of death fear. Little direct attention has been given to the relationship between death fear and other possibly relevant variables. Richard Kalish appears to be the

only researcher who has made use of factor-analysis in an attempt to clarify this area (40).

Method of This Review

The authors originally intended to present a review of the literature in a formal and detailed style. Studies were to have been cross-classified in terms of such major variables as age, sex, social class, and mental and physical health status of the subjects, type of procedures used by the investigators, and the varieties of death fear involved. These cross-classifications were to be further organized in accordance with the type of question being asked (e.g., clarification of the nature of death fear, its developmental history or "cause," its behavioral effects, etc.).

However, we have come to the reluctant conclusion that it would be premature to weave such a tapestry at this time. The studies array themselves rather thinly in many areas. Differences in research method (extending to data analysis procedures) sharply reduce the number of points at which it is meaningful to "add" results together. Furthermore, in many instances the studies did not offer sufficient detail to permit unambiguous classification. The usefulness of a detailed classification scheme would be doubtful if many entries had to be qualified with question marks or assigned to categories on an ad hoc basis.

At the moment we simply do not possess a systematic body of empirical knowledge on this topic. There is little to be gained by belaboring this point, or concentrating upon the inadequacies and flaws in what research is available. Let us just see what has been learned about death fears—what has emerged from some of the more adequate research efforts. As far as the data permit, we will group the results around the questions raised earlier. (What Do We Want to Know?). For another view of research literature in this area, the reader is invited to consult the survey article prepared by David Lester (41), who has also made a number of empirical contributions to the topic.

Fear of the Dying

Three types of death-related fears were distinguished earlier, each having its *self* and *other* aspects (Figure A). Perhaps the most convincing research to date has been conducted on the topic of our reaction to the dying process in others. There is reasonably abundant evidence that the dying person constitutes an aversive stimulus for us. We fear contact with him.

Sociologists Barney G. Glaser and Anselm L. Strauss observed patterns of interaction in six San Francisco-area hospitals (42). Employing a naturalistic, flexible research method, Glaser and Strauss eventually came to a focus on the communications which surround the dying person. They introduced the concept of *awareness contexts:* "what *each* interacting person knows of the patient's defined status, along with his recognition of the others' awareness of his own definition" (43). Four awareness contexts were delineated. a) *Closed awareness* exists whenever a patient fails to recognize that others have defined him as a terminal case. b) *Suspicion awareness* sometimes follows the preceding state. Patient and staff test each other out, trying to discover what the other person knows or thinks he knows about the patient's status. c) The *mutual pretense* is another pattern that evades direct communication and confrontation. In a ritualistic manner, patient and staff (sometimes staff and staff) attempt to conceal from each other the fact that each really "knows the score." d) An *open awareness* context was observed on occasion.

But even when all the people involved acknowledged that the patient was on a downhill course, there was sometimes an emotional wall between them. The staff might, for example, become perturbed because the patient was not taking the "proper" attitude while dying. The general impression yielded by the work of Glaser and Strauss is that dying persons arouse strong fears in those who are charged with their care. This point is not made explicitly because the investigators were approaching their material on a different level. But they provide many examples of aversive behavior in the form of distorted communications, elaborate "game-playing," and other defensive maneuvers. The authors observed, for example:

Nurses can also find ways to delegate the death watch, usually to someone who is not quite aware of the task he is being asked to perform (another use of 'role switching'). If the dying patient is in a room with an alert patient, the nurse may leave the room with a 'pressing work' excuse, asking the alert patient to call her immediately if he notices a change in the other patient. Nurses will also ask an ever-present family member, or perhaps a chaplain, to sit with the patient. If no one is available, a patient may be left to die alone, between periodic checks, though nurses find this outcome most disturbing unless he is already comatose (44).

Other in-the-field studies reporting aversive responses to being in the life-space of a dying person are discussed in Chapter 9.

There is also some attitudinal evidence that many of us have the generalized inclination to maintain a large "social distance" between ourselves and the dying person. Kalish added "a dying person" to the standard list of personages included in a well-known measure of social distance (45). This questionnaire-type approach yielded results which tend to support the field studies: We shrink from the prospect of intimate contact with a dying person.

Perhaps the point should be made in another way: The fact that a person is dying (or that we believe he is dying) is an extremely salient piece of information. Our attitudes and behavior seem to become fixed to this one dimension. Something about his new status overshadows almost everything else we know about him. We "out-group" him. But why?

Research has not yet answered this question. However, it appears to us that there are three major sources of our tendency to distanciate oursleves from the dying person:

1. *Social inferiority*. In our culture, dying tends to be interpreted within the context of *failure*. We expose our stupidity, inadequacies, and moral inferiority when we fail . . . fail to achieve at school, on the job, or with the opposite sex. The dying person reveals himself to be inferior to us simply because he is dying. Naturally, we do not care to associate with our inferiors.

2. *Lack of a response repertoire*. We do not know what to do when we are with a dying person. Nobody has given us adequate instruction. We do not like to find ourselves in a situation—especially an important situation—for which we lack adaptive or instrumental responses (46).

3. *Inner perturbation*. We are frightened off from the dying person because his situation arouses our own fears and insecurities. Perhaps we are apprehensive about the possibility of experiencing *vicarious suffering* and *vicarious disintegration* (Figure A and accompanying discussion), or perhaps our fears have a different character. In any event, it is our own rising sense of discomfort that spurs our retreat.

We believe that all these factors are involved. Their relative contribution to distanciation from the dying person remains to be determined. Inner perturbation is of particular interest because this is more or less equivalent to *fear* of the dying. Social inferiority refers to an *ostracism* dimension rather than fearful aversion. Lack of a response repertoire can serve to magnify our fearfulness and also to increase our need to perceive the dying person as inferior. But it also might be the factor that is most amenable to modification. Obviously, there are both theoretical and practical reasons for seeking to

determine the specific sources of our aversion toward the dying person.

Fears of and During the Dying Process

A healthy 34-year-old nurse almost died as the result of her unsuspected allergy to penicillin (administered to clear up an abscess forming at the root of one of her teeth). Fortunately, she made a quick recovery and, also fortunately, she happened to be in treatment with a psychoanalyst who recognized this unusual opportunity to increase our knowledge of psychological responses in the dying process. Although R.C.A. Hunter has provided us with only a single case study, it is worth close attention here (47).

While still in dense traffic, some 20 minutes after taking the penicillin, she began to become aware of difficulty in breathing. Her ability to respire became rapidly more compromised and she had the thought that she was choking to death. She became cyanosed and in a few minutes became unconscious. Fortunately a nearby doctor reached her in time to give her adrenaline subcutaneously, an ambulance was summoned, and she was taken to the nearest hospital. There she was put on oxygen, more adrenaline, and cortical steroids. Preparations were made for a tracheotomy, but the latter did not prove necessary. . . . Within 22 hours of this incident she was able to talk about her experience in an analytic session (48).

From her background as a nurse, this woman realized what was happening to her. She was aware that she was dying. As her breathing became very difficult, she experienced "frantic fear." This experience would seem to confirm the impression that fear is the dominant affect during the dying process. But her fear passed quickly. The nurse's description suggests that she moved through at least four distinct psychological stages—and in very short order:

1. A feeling of intense sympathy for her husband, followed by other thoughts

and feelings about her relationship to him.

2. A "last violent reaction" in which she fought desperately against death, but then ceased to struggle. She now felt that she wanted death to come. This phase was *not* accompanied by a sense of fear.

3. A visual review of scenes from her childhood. The colors were vivid, the accompanying effect was "ecstatically happy." (She saw, for example, a favorite doll she once had, and was struck by how bright blue the glass eyes were; she also saw herself riding her bright red bicycle on a bright green lawn.)

4. A state of bliss, symbolized by a picture of the Taj Mahal. She felt "deeply, idyllically engrossed."

In retrospect, this woman declared that she would never fear dying again.

Her psychoanalyst had a number of comments to make about this experience. We will focus upon the implications he drew for understanding the dying process in general. Hunter suggested that "If we differentiate between the experience of dying and death as a state, it seems that the latter has many idiosyncratic or personal meanings to as many people, but that the process of suddenly, unexpectedly, and painlessly dying may move through certain crudely definable and predictable stages, even though they bear perhaps the stamp of established personality patterns and contemporary conflicts. When the patient began to respond to resuscitation, she did not want to awaken and was enjoying a markedly wish-fulfilling 'dream' of hypnopompic hallucination which was idiosyncratically appropriate to her affective response to her life situation and took into account the sudden threat to her life" (49).

Hunter did not believe that his patient's experiences could be attributable specifically to the mode of (almost) dying, asphyxia. He referred to an earlier report by Otto Pfister, a German psychiatrist (50). Pfister obtained material from several people who had come close to death through other modalities. The quality and sequence of their subjective experiences seemed quite similar to those of Hunter's patient, although her perception of vivid colors was not shared by the others.

The nurse's reactions during her quasi-dying process are explained by Hunter largely in terms of denial/negation and regression. The initial recognition of impending death and the experience of dying was negated and replaced by other thoughts and effects. She then regressed quickly to joyful memories. The psychiatrist viewed these as "screen memories. . . I would guess that what is remembered as pleasurable serves a defensive purpose and conceals behind it a related but unpleasant memory. . . ." But he also raised the possibility that "the letting go, the giving in, with the abandonment of striving to maintain object relationships and acceptance of passivity is intrinsically a joyous or pleasurable state" (51).

This case history parallels several observations that have been made independently by other clinicians and researchers. For some people at some points in time, fear is a salient aspect of the dying experience. At a given moment fear may indeed be extreme. But most people are not overwhelmed by fear throughout the course of their preterminal and terminal phases. Furthermore, not all of the fears experienced during the dying process pertain directly either to dying or death. The phenomenological life of the dying person is complex, and it changes over time. Hunter was inclined to believe that there are "certain crudely definable and predictable stages" through which people pass, at least when the dying process is sudden, unexpected, and relatively painless.

Avery D. Weisman and Robert Kastenbaum have delved into the possibility that the dying process comprises a distinct phase of human development, their observations emerging from the intensive multidisciplinary study of 125 geriatric patients by the psychological autopsy method

(52). Very recently, psychiatrist Elizabeth Kubler-Ross reported on her interviews with approximately 400 terminally ill patients (53). She has offered a specific outline of the psychological phases through which people move as death approaches. It is not relevant here to present and evaluate what Weisman and Kastenbaum, and Kubler-Ross, have suggested about the dying process. Our focus is upon the role of fear. The relevant point is that other investigators agree with Hunter's observation that it is plausible to conceive of dying as a sequence of orderly, definable experiences and behaviors, not necessarily the disorganized "coming apart" of personality, nor a period of captivity within one's own walls of fear. It is encouraging when independent investigators come to similar conclusions, especially in such a complex area of human concern.

Let us now consider some of the studies which support, extend, or modify the statements made above.

Social psychologist Richard A. Kalish appears to be the only researcher who has attempted to obtain a large sampling of responses from people who have been "reprieved" from death (54). With the help of his students, Kalish was able to acquire reports concerning 323 incidents in which a person had a "close call." The most common modalities of threatened death were physical illness, motor vehicle accidents, and drowning, but other types of experience were also reported (including one instance of being locked in a freezer, and another instance of having been pronounced dead). Kalish clearly acknowledges that there are some problems with these data and that the "close calls" did not always involve the experiencer actually having entered the dying or quasi-dying process. Nevertheless, this exploratory study remains of considerable value until Kalish or others are able to conduct further research under more favorable conditions.

Were people in a state of fear or panic during their encounters with possible death? Kalish concluded that "It strikes us as less remarkable that 23 percent of the sample were fearful or in a state of panic than that 77 percent did not mention fear. Just under 25 percent stated that they were unafraid, resigned, anxious to die and get it over with, fatalistic, or 'warm, light, and happy' " (55). In other words, fear is part of the picture, but only a part. Many of his respondents did not even seem to be focused on their own feelings at the time. They were fully occupied in trying to evade death, or were more concerned with the fate of other people. As a matter of fact, the most frequent *first* reaction to finding oneself in peril was reported to have been that of concern for the family and other survivors. Although 27 percent of the interviewees mentioned physical illness as the death threat, only 12 percent of those mentioning fear or panic were among the physically ill group. Kalish found that drowning accounted for nearly one-half of the panic reactions. He comments:

Fear and panic are apparently produced by helplessness, such as occurs in drowning, having to force land in an airplane, being lost, in a bombing raid, or locked in a freezer. . . . We may speculate that fear and panic arise out of situations in which the person facing death feels helpless and has time, albeit fairly little time in some instances, for dwelling upon his circumstances (56).

He also found a few respondents (about 12 percent) who reported the classic "flashback" or life review experience noted by Hunter for his patient.

In the study cited above we cannot distinguish between fear of dying and fear of death. This is true of many other studies as well. But it does suggest that the likelihood of experiencing any form of fear when death is in prospect may depend on the situational context (e.g., the availability of *time* to reflect upon one's predicament). The situational dimensions described earlier in this chapter might well be incorporated explicitly in subsequent research into the psychological responses of "the reprieved." As we will see below, more attention has usually been given to personality or demographic characteristics of the individual than to the nature of the situation in which he finds himself.

Most research concerned with fear of dying has centered around people who were terminally ill at the time of the study. British psychiatrist John M. Hinton has conducted a most careful clinical study in this area (57). He interviewed 102 patients who were expected to die within six months. Unlike many other clinical ventures, Hinton's study included a matched control group. A "non-dying" patient in the same ward and under the care of the same physician was seen on the same day that a particular terminally ill patient was interviewed. The sessions themselves were brief, not exceeding 30 minutes. Each patient's condition was followed on a weekly basis, although it is not clear precisely how this was done. The results, however, are presented in admirable detail. Although the study has its limitations (a number of which are discussed by Hinton), it is, on the whole, one of the most adequate investigations completed in this area.

Hinton found that at least three-fourths of his dying patients knew their prognosis. Physically, they were in more distress than the matched control patients, whose conditions were serious but not fatal. He notes that "In spite of the attempt to choose somewhat comparable physical disorders in the control group, the dying patients were much more likely to have unrelieved physical distress, and much less likely to have none" (58). The reader will appreciate that consideration of a person's fear of dying or death should take into account the intensity of physical suffering he may be experiencing. Hinton's study is one of the few to obtain careful information on this point.

Both sets of patients were suffering mental distress to an extent one would not expect to find in a random adult population (although this is difficult to be sure about). The dying patients were more depressed and more anxious than the controls. These differences were significant and, in fact, were large enough in some instances to make the statistical tests almost superfluous.

It is useful that Hinton included the assessment of depression as well as anxiety. Otherwise we might be led to conclude that dying patients differ from other patients only or essentially in their susceptibility to anxiety. In actuality, the data indicate that *depression* was the more salient differential. Converting Hinton's data into scale scores, we found that the dying patients were more depressed than anxious, and that the same could be said for the controls. Differences between the groups were greater for depression than for anxiety. Again, we have seen that manifestations of anxiety or fear can be found in those who are in jeopardy for their lives, but that typically the intensity is not overwhelming. Furthermore, another form of dysphoric response to one's plight—depression—appears to be more common and more intense than overt fear. (It should be mentioned that Hinton did not depend entirely upon verbal material for his ratings; he had the patient's interview and ward behavior records as well.)

As might be expected, depression and anxiety were more common in patients who had endured physical distress longer. But there were other findings of special interest. Anxiety proved to be related to particular physical symptoms—not to physical distress in general. Patients suffering from the symptom of dyspnea were the most likely to experience anxiety. This symptom apparently is difficult to relieve. It is not easy for any of us to remain serene when we are having trouble catching a breath of air. It will be recalled that drowning elicited the highest percentage of panic responses among Kalish's subjects. In both instances—dyspnea and drowning—the individual is struggling for his life's breath. Considering that the Kalish and Hinton studies differ so much in methodology, it is interesting to note that similar findings were obtained on such a specific point. And it is also useful to mark this further evidence that anxiety is related to specific variables in the immediate psychosociobiological field. There may be something characteristic about a given individual's orientation toward dying, but the very specific circumstances of his existence, here and now, are of no lesser significance.

Another relevant point is that anxiety and depression did not necessarily go together (although there was a positive relationship between these variables). Anxiety did not seem to have much relationship to the patient's awareness of his foreshortened life expectancy. However, the most depressed patients were those who openly recognized the prospect of death. Why should knowledge or recognition lead to depression and not anxiety? Is it because fear or anxiety involves the concept of futurity, whereas depression is a psychic state that tends to deny futurity?

Most of the dying patients studied by Hinton were facing almost certain death, but within a period of time, the boundaries of which could be specified (at least approximately). Psychologist Kenneth A. Chandler also studied some patients of this type, but directed most of his attention to "patients whose illnesses are such as to lead them to expect to die at any moment, that is, chronic cardiovascular and cerebrovascular patients with histories of many crises." He characterized these people as having "the *presentiment* of death, that is, the recognition that death may occur at any moment yet one might also live for a longer time than might be expected" (59).

Chandler organized a group of elderly cardio- and cerebrovascular patients who were living with the "presentiment" of death. He met regularly with this group, and also with a group of nursing person-

nel who cared for these patients. His observations pertain largely to the disturbed relationships between staff and patients. Most relevant here is his report that the patients had an unspoken fear of death that pervaded all of their interpersonal relationships. Why was the fear unspoken? Chandler brings out certain facets of the patient-staff interaction as well as the staff's own death-related problems. Unable or unwilling to express their death concern directly, the patients developed quite a reputation for hostile acting-out. They resorted frequently to the defenses of withdrawal, negativism, and inappropriate aggressiveness. The group sessions eventually provided a verbal release for their apprehensions, and the acting-out diminished greatly (the same process occurred in the staff group).

This clinical study helps in the delineation of death fear/anxiety as an interpersonal process. Although Chandler did not put it in so many words, it would appear that he found death fear within the patients, within the staff, and *between* patients and staff.

Another of his contributions is intimately related to the methodology employed. If Chandler had limited his research to the description of overt behavior, then it is doubtful that much would have been learned. However, his method was to learn by the process of attempting to bring about *change*. The previously held-in sense of dread came to the surface only after a period of time and after an investment of therapeutic effort. It seems to us that this example of repeated encounters with the subjects, introduction of an "independent variable" (loosely speaking), and attention to the interpersonal milieu might well serve as a paradigm for others. Chandler's study was exploratory. It should be repeated with increased and expanded patient samples, as well as with the methodological refinements that can be expected on the second time around.

One other aspect of Chandler's study

should be highlighted—his experience gives further support to the contention that fear of dying/death is not entirely an invariant. People living with a sense of urgent ambiguity about the timing of their deaths (at the next moment, or not for many years) are in quite a different situation than those of us who are in good health, or those of us who see ourselves moving inexorably toward a terminus that still stands at some distance away.

Psychiatrist Daniel Cappon is another clinical investigator who has taken into account the "differences between those facing certain and uncertain death, at variable speeds of the process; between these and those ill, yet not facing death; and again between these and those ill in mind; and finally between these and those seeking death" (60). He used the bedside interview approach, making a special effort to obtain fantasy material at both sleep and waking levels of awareness. His "experimental" group was comprised of 19 patients who were experiencing the inevitably near approach of death. There were seven "control" groups: patients facing a lingering death, patients facing possible death, physically-but-not-fatally ill people, psychiatrically ill people, suicide attempters, people who died from suicide attempts, and people who died suddenly from medical causes. There was a total of 88 patients in these subgroups, unequally distributed.

One of Cappon's most germane observations is that forebodings of death "bring fear and panic in their wake, which are indistinguishable from thanatophobic outbursts." But he also states that "The stronger forebodings are, the more likely they are to coincide with a positive motivation toward dying. The more primitive and hence intuitive person, say a European peasant, the more hysterical or paranoid the schizophrenic, that is, dissociative and grandiose, the more likely are strong forebodings. Yet if they strike the normal civilized man with magical force,

his conscious defenses tremble at this inner, outwardly-projected assault. Depending much on the equanimity with which the patient regards this event, which in turn is determined culturally no less than individually, meaningful communication may be made" (61).

In other words, it is suggested that what appears to be the same expression of fear on the part of two patients may, in one case, be an accurate foreboding of death, but in another case constitute a phobic symptom. Presumably, the "witchery test" should be applied here: The foreboding patient who does in fact die is vindicated, while the person who fails to die is thus revealed to be a death-neurotic. Nevertheless, Cappon's observations tune our sensitivities to the information value of a patient's utterances. What the patient expresses may be more than a reading of his fears and perturbations—it may also be a reading of internal developments that point to an emergent crisis. It should be added, however, that most of Cappon's patients did not give clear evidence of death-forebodings; in fact, more of the dying patients denied than admitted premonitions.

And how fearful were his dying patients? In his summary description of the emotional status of each patient, Cappon applies the term "fear" in only three of the 19 instances. Furthermore, in each of these cases there were other salient affects and attitudes as well. He found more hostility than fearfulness in this population. "Blind hope" was discerned in two patients while two others conveyed a sense of "hopelessness." Yet there were also two patients who exhibited "normal cheerfulness" and another who was in a state of "elation." Other combinations of affect were also reported. In his characterization of the dying patients' emotional condition Cappon attempts to include the repressed or inner state as well as the manifest (e.g., "apparent serenity, inner fearfulness."). How is one to be certain that he has truly seen beyond the "apparent" into the "inner"? This question cannot be far from our minds when considering many of the psychiatric-type studies.

Cappon was not the first to find some indication that fear can serve as a prognostication of impending death. The most specific previous article on this subject, by psychiatrist Jerome S. Beigler was based upon several of his case studies (62). Beigler offers a brief review of relevant clinical observations that had been scattered throughout the literature—from Aristotle onward. Several of these observations were based on dream material from patients in psychoanalysis, quite in keeping with Freud's emphasis upon the "royal road to the unconscious."

Beigler summarizes seven of his own cases and another that was brought to his attention by a colleague. All but one of these cases revealed that the patient in question had shown a marked change in affect and behavior just prior to death although in most instances imminent death was not expected by physicians and others. "The eyes were deeply sunken, there was a profound expression of terror, and the whole face had a black cast. She looked as though she had been to death's door and would soon return. I tried to resume our friendly relationship, but she immediately rejected me and shook her head with the same hopeless gesture of grim finality as did Patient 3. She, too, died within a few days" (63). In the case of another patient, a woman of 77, "there was a marked change of attitude to one of hopelessness and a direct seeking for help. The internist was impressed by the passivity with which she accepted the hospitalization, complaining of not feeling well and of 'something wrong.' She died suddenly a few days after admission" (64).

The exception is one that proved the rule. A 60-year-old woman with a long and serious medical history "was admitted with a severe cardiac decompensation. Clinically she seemed in extremis; yet she was calm and was able to give herself up to that optimum of passivity which is often essential for somatic recuperation. The lack of anxiety was interpreted as an indication of the relative benignity of her disorder, and the prediction was made that she would live longer than the above cases. She made a rapid recovery from her cardiac decompensation. At the last follow-up she was attending the outpatient clinic, four months later" (65). Beigler states that he had five other cases in which the *lack* of clinical anxiety predicted to recovery despite "markedly abnormal physical and laboratory findings."

The psychiatrist points out that there was a preponderance of uremic and chronic cardiac cases in this series. He believes that chronic diseases such as these are subject to sudden changes in equilibrium which can make themselves quickly known to the patient. The reactions of anxiety (and denial) are obvious enough to be detected by pscyhiatrically-oriented observers. "When such a patient becomes restless and begins to have multiple and insatiable complaints, one becomes alerted to the possibility of an early demise" (66).

Probably of greatest importance here is the indication that emotional changes in people suffering from a chronic disease should be regarded as possible clues to imminent death. It is obvious that there are significant therapeutic implications attached to this knowledge. Similarly, lack of anxiety in a life-or-death crisis might be cause for a cautious optimism. Intensive research on these topics would be quite valuable. From the standpoint of understanding death fear/anxiety, we see that the initial awareness of inner danger is (thought to be) represented by heightened emotional arousal. However, the patient may not remain anxious very long. He may quickly deny his predicament, become depressed, or show other somatic symptomatology (67). We cannot "depend" on manifest anxiety as a prognostication of death—it could be that we have come upon the scene *after* the initial anxiety has been transformed into other symptoms. Although we have been learning something as we traverse these selected studies, we do come back again to the conclusion that anxiety or fear is part of the picture when one is in danger for his life, but cannot be taken as the only significant psychological response. Furthermore, there may be circumstances in which the relationship between anxiety and the prospect for survival runs counter to what has been described above.

In his valuable book, *Psychological Stress: Psychoanalytic and Behavioral Studies of Surgical Patients* (68), Irving L. Janis observed that clinically manifest anxiety is often a favorable sign. The anxious patient is less likely to succumb to surgery or postsurgical complications. Are these two sets of observations mutually contradictory? Not necessarily. There may be a crucial difference between the situation in which presurgical patients find themselves as compared with the patients reported by Beigler and others.

Look at it this way. This individual afflicted with a chronic disease or a sudden emergent condition may be the first to know that something disastrous is taking place. His somatic experience conveys a sense of disintegration, an impending change in his "internal weather." This is a private experience, and one for which he probably lacks appropriate verbal concepts and categories. The vague "something terrible inside" gives rise to anxiety. As has been said before, the anxiety may linger a while, but may also be transformed into other types of symptomatology. For the presurgical patient, however, the phenomenological situation is quite different. The threat to his life is public knowledge, so to speak. Everybody knows he has a condition serious enough to require surgery (we are referring here only to major surgery in the service of saving the patient's life). There is an external locus or placement of the stress: such-and-such a surgical procedure will be carried out on such-and-such an hour of such-and-such a day. The actions of many other people are converged into presurgical preparations. In other words, the patient is confronting a relatively definable and visible challenge.

Under these conditions, an anxiety response may be entirely "natural." It is "normal" for the actor, the soloist, the athlete (and the surgical team itself) to experience a state of emotional arousal before moving into action. The patient does not play an active role in the surgical process (although subsequent research may reveal that his role is more active than what is generally appreciated), but his internal preparation for action in the form of emotional arousal indicates that he is in a sound functional status. He has normal emotional responsivity. Conversely, the presurgical patient who does not exhibit anxiety may be conveying the nonverbal communication that his psychobiological apparatus is not in condition for the challenge ahead. On another dimension, it might be said that the presurgical patient is stirred up by the anticipation of a life/death crisis, while the person whose condition is rapidly deteriorating feels anxious because he is, in fact, dying.

The foregoing is a suggested line of explanation. It should not be taken as a substitute for the additional clinical research that is indicated.

Still another phenomenon has been observed in this area. Psychiatrists Avery D. Weisman and Thomas P. Hackett reviewed five cases of what they judged represented a "predilection" to death (69). These were surgical patients who expressed the conviction that they would die very soon. There was another common characteristic: "Predilection patients may be readily distinguished from preoperative patients with high anticipatory anxiety, depressed patients, suicidal patients, and those rare patients who correctly prognosticate their own deaths and demonstrate no significant lesions at autopsy" (70).

Thus, we have the suggestion that concern with death should not automatically be equated with death fear or anxiety. It is unfortunate that this distinction is not made consistently by other investigators. Weisman and Hackett's discussion of the case histories has made this article one of the classics in its field. Among other contributions, it introduces the concept of the patient's "middle knowledge" of approaching death, and the concept of an "appropriate death." Most germane to our present focus, however, is their emphasis upon the responses to death *other than* fear/anxiety that may be observed in the preterminal patient. Weisman and Hackett also differentiate more carefully than most clinical investigators between fear of dying and fear of death. Studies of preterminal geriatric patients have also suggested that fear of dying is not invariably the dominant affect. Morton A. Lieberman and his colleagues found relatively little preoccupation with death among elders who were soon to die (71). Those who were close to death (as determined retroactively) did show a number of behavioral and phenomenological differences from peers who would survive longer—but heightened fearfulness was *not* detected as one of these trends. Explicit fear of dying was relatively uncommon among the patients studied during an intensive six-year clinical research program at Cushing Hospital (for the aged) in Massachusetts. An attitude of acceptance was found more frequently than apprehension or alarm during the preterminal period (72). Flamboyant expressions of anxiety occurred chiefly among patients who were highly disturbed in general or who showed an advanced degree of organic deterioration.

In a later report from the same project, Weisman and Kastenbaum caution: "Withdrawn and anxious patients often may not be noticed by the staff (while) the process of institutionalization and the duration of disability may serve to conceal depression and anxieties. . . . Subtle changes in affect or attitude are apt to escape notice, and relatively inconspicuous emotions may be neglected in favor of overt behavior and

spoken sentiments" (73). They cite, for example, a woman who ". . . accepted without question the knowledge that an operation to remove an abdominal mass was necessary. The morning after she was told this, she reported dreaming that she had leaped from a 'fright train' [sic] before a nameless calamity occurred. She did not recover consciousness following surgery" (74).

Because this study was a multifaceted and relatively sustained attempt to understand psychological aspects of the preterminal process, it was possible to weigh the relative significance of many factors. Extended institutionalization and disability came to be seen as two of the most important "conditioners" of the geriatric patient's response to both life and death. "In the course of extended institutionalization, emotional extremes become modulated, and affective expression itself is reduced. Periodically there will be outbursts of anger, panic, elation or melancholia, but, for the most part, patients eventually achieve an accommodation to their status. Part of this accommodation includes acceptance of the reality of death, but the prolonged duration of disability itself may also tend to reduce overt emotional responses. In the early stages of serious illness many patients are alarmed and fearful lest they die. However, within a surprisingly short time, anxiety abates and is replaced by bland denial or remote concern" (75).

Obvious death fear or anxiety is not characteristic of most elderly or even most preterminal geriatric patients, from the evidence we now have before us. The detection of less-than-obvious anxiety becomes a sensitive problem. It is fraught with many possibilities of error in either direction: reading too much or too little "between the lines." Furthermore, it is evident that one oversimplifies the inquiry if attention is given only to fear responses when studying the psychological life of the preterminal aged person. (In this section we have been focusing upon the behavior of elderly people whose lives are in jeopardy or who are already in the preterminal phase. Other types of research with elderly subjects will be cited later).

What is known about the other extreme of the life cycle? In the previous chapter attention was given to separation experiences in the development of the child's conception of death. Separation also arouses anxiety. And the fatally ill child is likely to experience physical separation from his home and family at the same time that internal organic changes discomfort and alarm him. It is all too clear that anxiety is an important part of the total situation for both the fatally ill child and his family (the medical and nursing staff can be included here, as well). Consider, for example, the following two studies conducted at the City of Hope Medical Center, Duarte, California. City of Hope is well known as a facility dedicated to the treatment of the seriously ill, as well as a center for advanced medical research. The Center also operates a parent participation program in its pediatrics unit. Parents are encouraged to participate actively in the hospital care of their children, under professional supervision (76). City of Hope thus offers an unusually favorable milieu for the total care of the seriously ill child as well as for research efforts.

Nevertheless, abundant signs of fear or anxiety were observed in a study directed by Joseph M. Natterson and Alfred G. Knudson (77). All 33 children in this study were suffering from cancer, leukemia, or blood disease. All died. The youngest child was less than one year of age, the oldest was almost thirteen. The children and their parents were observed during hospitalization and in the outpatient clinic. This was a multidisciplinary study, involving the participation of physicians, psychiatrists, nurses, the schoolteacher, the occupational therapist, and the social worker.

The investigators report: "In addition to having illnesses which could cause considerable distress, these children were sub-ject to three stresses of environmental origin, namely, separation from mother, traumatic procedures, and deaths of other children" (78). Maternal absence was identified as the most common cause of distress in the child, no matter how advanced his organic condition. Almost all of the children showed some adverse reaction to separation. Such traumatic procedures as venipuncture and bone-marrow aspiration seemed to arouse apprehension in about half of the children, generally the older ones. A few boys struggled actively against these procedures and were not much relieved by the mother's presence.

Anxiety about dying or death was found chiefly among the older children. "However, there were indications that anxiety about death may have been present in more subtle form in younger children, even though overshadowed by fear of separation, or fear of the procedures. Such indications were sometimes found in the drawings and stories of the children" (79). The death of another child in the hospital occasionally was identified as the source of manifest death anxiety.

Natterson and Knudson feel that three fairly distinct types of fear were shown by these children. Furthermore, the fears were closely related to the child's developmental level: "The reactions to separation were most severe in the age group 0-5 years; the reactions to the procedures were most intense in the age group 5-10 years; and the reactions to death were strongest in the age group 10 years and over. It is evident that the reactions . . . consisted largely of anxiety. In fact, they seemed to constitute, in turn, fear of separation, fear of mutilation, and fear of death. The observations suggest that fear of death is related to the other fears in a maturational pattern" (80). Fear of mutilation was regarded as a transitional state between the fears of separation and death. It was not as formidable and pervasive a condition as either of the others.

The investigators do not hesitate to categorize these death fears as *realistic*, in contradistinction to the traditional psychoanalytic emphasis upon the neurotic derivation of thanatophobia. They also noted that fear of death took clear precedence over all other fears in the oldest children, and "seemed to be a function of a highly developed integrative capacity and reality sense" (81).

A subsequent study at the City of Hope was conducted as a doctoral project by James R. Morrissey, a social worker (82). He collected information concerning 50 children who died of leukemia or other forms of cancer during a 27-month period. His data came from medical charts, social service records, interviews with the children, and interviews with the research staff. The assessment of anxiety was based on collective evidence from all sources of data. (This method obviously has much in common with the psychological autopsy procedure utilized with geriatric patients). Not only did Morrissey investigate the degree of anxiety, but also its likely source, the child's awareness of diagnosis and prognosis, the quality of the parents' participation in care, and the patient's overall hospital adjustment.

Almost all of the children were assessed as having some degree of anxiety—severe anxiety in about half of the cases. A child's anxiety usually came from more than one source. But separation anxiety was considered the most prominent type in 60 percent of the children. Death anxiety was prominent in 13 children, most of them ten years of age or older. The older boys tended to "act out" their anxiety, while the older girls were more likely to become depressed. Four children were considered to be experiencing castration anxiety. These observations seem to be consistent with the earlier study of Natterson and Knudson, with "castration anxiety" perhaps being another way of describing what the previous investigators termed "fear of mutilation."

The combination of high anxiety and absence of sensitive parental support was associated with poor general adjustment to the hospital situation. Effective parent participation helped a number of children to adjust fairly well to the hospital even though the young patients retained a high anxiety level. "Conversely, when children were judged to have had low anxiety, all patients [22] were rated to have made a very good or good hospital adjustment. The patient's anxiety level appeared to be the key variable, and qualitative parent participation a primary factor in dealing with the child's anxiety" (83). Additionally, it was observed that some children tended to respond to their anxiety with an "emotional paralysis," while others were able to keep their fears under control. About one-third of the children showed evidence of speculating on the significance of their illness. It was not known whether these speculations arose from death anxiety, led to death anxiety, or had some other relationship.

This pair of studies suggests that anxiety during the course of fatal illness is either more frequent or more obvious in children as compared with adults. The relationship between specific kinds of fear and chronological age is in keeping with what has been learned elsewhere about the child's development of concepts in general, and death concepts in particular. Neither of these investigations utilized a control group of any kind. Therefore we should not conclude that what has been described above is specific to the experiences of fatally ill children. Similar anxieties might be aroused in children who are hospitalized for conditions that have a more favorable prognosis but which also entail separation, painful procedures, and bodily distress. This methodological qualification does not alter our humanistic or therapeutic approach to the fatally ill child. Generalized anxiety and fear of dying/death are central problems, and deserve the most sensitive attention.

Let us take one more research sample, this time from a situation in which the "death sentence" is literally in effect. Psychiatrists Harvey Bluestone and Carl L.

McGahee interviewed 18 men and one woman who were residents of the Sing Sing "death house" (84). Confined to an isolated area of the prison, they had very little contact with other people. It was noted that they had few visitors, even though the authorities imposed no restrictions. "One might expect them to show severe depression and devastating anxiety, yet neither symptom was conspicuous among these 19 doomed persons" (85).

Bluestone and McGahee observed that three types of psychological defense were erected against the overwhelming anxiety or depression that might be expected under the death sentence. *Denial* was said to be the most common defense. They distinguished four types of denial: by isolation of affect, by minimizing the predicament, by delusion formation, and by living only in the present. Isolation of affect seemed to be the most popular response: " 'So, they'll kill me; and that's that'—this said with a shrug of the shoulders suggests that the affect appropriate to the thought has somehow been isolated" (86).

Projection was also in evidence. Usually this took the form of persecutory delusions, "a comforting delusion" that "converts dissolute criminals into martyrs. . . . While it does not deny that death is just around the corner, it tries to lend it dignity and meaning." Apparently, a depression would overcome some of the men who relied upon projection when this mechanism proved inadequate on occasion. *Obsessive rumination* was the other important defense. In effect, the doomed prisoners would think furiously about something else—anything else. "Thus, the depressing thought is elbowed out of consciousness by the crowd of other ideas" (87). Preparing appeals or pleas for clemency served as obsessional preoccupations for some of the prisoners (not to minimize the reality-oriented aspects of this activity). There were also a few condemned men whose ruminations moved into the religious or philosophical spheres.

These investigators came away from their study with this conviction: "Traditional ego defense mechanisms alleviate distress. They also mitigate anxiety and depression which would otherwise overwhelm the prisoner in a death cell" (88). In other words, we are not *that* emotionally vulnerable to the objective threat of death. Our defenses can rise to the occasion. Once again, however, we have an interesting clinical study without a control group (for example, those serving life or indefinite sentences), nor do we seem to have a follow-through to learn how the condemned man's orientation toward death maintains itself if and when he actually is brought to the threshold of execution. Nevertheless, it is important to have inquiries such as this, for illness, after all, is only one type of death threat.

With a few exceptions, most of the relevant studies do not attempt to distinguish precisely between fears of anxieties experienced *during* the dying process and fears *of* dying. One might therefore be inclined to conclude that all psychological insecurity and discomfort centers around either the experience of dying or the prospect of death. The two studies conducted at the City of Hope are among the exceptions. They remind us that fatally ill patients—at least, those who are young children—can be quite anxious because of other distressing circumstances, such as separation from home and family. We consider it likely that there are multiple sources of anxiety or fear for adults as well (including the condemned prisoner as well as the organically ill).

Social workers may be more perceptive in this area than their colleagues in other mental health fields. More than the typical physician, nurse, psychiatrist, or psychologist, the social worker is likely to be concerned with the broad range of practical problems which are encountered by a person who is in distress. Especially relevant here is a study of 60 fatally ill cancer patients conducted by Ronald R. Koenig for the Michigan Cancer Foundation (89). The patients were seen shortly after their admission to a Detroit Hospital, followed throughout their hospital stay, and also during periodic clinic visits between hospitalizations. The researcher attempted to develop close rapport with the patients and their families, and to assist them with problems as they arose. Interview data was collected on a systematic basis. Additionally, the Minnesota Multiphasic Personality Inventory (MMPI) was administered to those who were well enough to respond.

Koenig found that these terminally ill men and women were beset by a variety of practical problems in the social sphere, problems "such as many have never seen before." Stresses arising from these problems often complicated or interfered with medical treatment, "and at times negated the effect of treatment altogether" (90).

Financial problems increased the strain on many patients and their families. About half of the patients were faced with the problem of managing their affairs with a drastically reduced income. Some patients feared that they would be in serious financial straits—and would impose the same upon their family—if the disease "dragged on too long." In effect, then, they were almost in the position of desiring to "bet against themselves," to seek an early death instead of an expensive lingering on. "The financial problems. . . were frequently severe. . . and of a nature not readily ameliorated by the usual tactics of social intervention, since the patients could not qualify for public medical assistance under current income eligibility restrictions. Patients were sometimes asked to borrow in order to pay for their medical care, although they knew they would never live to repay the debt. In this way, life insurance purchased for the protection of their families was consumed by the expense of the disease. Many patients were too well-off to qualify for public assistance, but not sufficiently affluent to meet the financial costs of chronic illness" (91).

The disease process and its treatment also was a source of anxiety to many patients—apart from the prospect of death per se. "There was considerable anxiety among the patients, even in periods when they were free from pain, that it would soon return or increase and could not be relieved. This fear was compounded by what they considered to be inconsistencies in nursing attention" (92). Loss of physical energy, restriction in personal activities, and apprehension about going through unfamiliar medical tests also contributed to anxiety.

For many patients, the progressive nature of the disease had upset their patterns of interaction with other family members. Some patients were concerned chiefly with the prospect or reality of becoming "excessively" dependent upon others; some felt guilty about depriving the spouse of sexual enjoyment, while others experienced a sense of patronization or neglect on the part of their family. It should be emphasized that some families did remain close and affectionate—or even seemed to grow closer together—during the final illness. Nevertheless, anxiety from interpersonal sources was a salient aspect of the cancer patient's experience in many cases.

Koenig also found that many patients were upset by difficulties in their hospital experience. "These complaints were often legitimate and reflected the problems of overcrowding and staffing inadequacies common to most urban private hospitals" (93). It was not rare, for example, for a patient to have to wait up to two hours beyond the scheduled time to receive medication for relief of his pain.

Slightly more than half of the patients reported that they felt more anxious than they had prior to onset of the disease and hospitalization, while depression was also reported by about half of the sample (seven patients expressed an increase in suicidal ideas). About one out of every four patients was considered to be suffering enough psychological distress to be an urgent candidate for psychotherapy—a resource that was almost totally *un*available to them. Nevertheless, Koenig and his colleagues did not find any evidence to suggest that these patients in general comprised a psychiatrically-disturbed population. MMPI scores for 36 of the patients failed to reveal indices of psychotic distortion of reality. "In addition, there was little indication that the current group manifested more emotional disturbance than a group of patients suffering with another debilitating disease (tuberculosis)" (94).

Why have we summarized this study in such detail? Because it is important for both practical and theoretical purposes to see that anxiety "within the shadow of death" can derive from many sources other than the death threat itself. These concerns (which were described earlier in this chapter as "attached fears") often are rooted firmly in "objective reality." We falsify and perform a disservice if we make do with a vague usage of "death anxiety" instead of examining the specific sources of apprehension for a jeopardized individual. We also, in effect, provide ourselves with a rationalization for neglecting efforts that could improve the life situation of the vulnerable or dying person.

Fears of Death

In the preceding section it was not always possible to distinguish between fears of dying and fears of death (as the distinction often was neglected either in data-collection or analysis.) Here we will consider some of the most relevant research into fears of death per se. There is no single operational definition in common among the studies to be cited. They do tend, however, to focus on attitudes toward death as the cessation of life, or as the state which "follows" cessation.

Most studies of death fear have been fairly simple and straightforward. The investigator selects a subject population (or just turns to the type of subjects most easily available to him), and puts a number of death-oriented questions to his respondents. Over the years there has been a gradual (and now accelerating) collection of death-oriented responses from a variety of people at different ages and different life circumstances. Let us begin by trying to determine what has been learned from this approach.

As mentioned earlier, a number of researchers have been interested in the death fears of elderly men and women. Perhaps it has seemed reasonable to assume that there would be something especially characteristic of people whose life expectancy is limited because of their common status, advanced age. The most adequate review of this specialized literature was prepared by a Dutch psychologist, J. M. A. Munnichs, in 1966 (95). He found seven systematic studies into the old person's orientation toward "the end." Munnichs added his own research to this topic, and we have since had several additional studies reported. Those planning to conduct research in this area would do well to consult Munnichs' monograph, although it is now slightly dated.

Do most elderly people have a strong fear of death? Munnichs' own study bears on this point, and is perhaps also the most adequate piece of research from a methodological standpoint. In his sample of 100 Dutch elders (70 years of age and beyond), Munnichs found a variety of orientations toward finitude. But "The most important conclusion is that only a small category of old people [7] were in fear of the end" (96). By far the most frequently observed orientation toward death was one of *acceptance* (40 of the 100). Another common orientation was *acquiescence* [21]. In other words, approximately two-thirds of these elderly people had come to terms with their finitude. Additionally, it was the *psychologically mature* elder who was most likely to acknowledge death in a positive manner. Conversely, negative attitudes tended to be associated with an immature personality, especially when these attitudes seemed to constitute a final point of view. Munnichs believes that finitude (or orientation toward cessation of one's existence) is a central theme in the early phases of the aging process. In fact, he suggests that "we might characterize old age as an *anticipated farewell*" (97).

Do we find these results surprising? If we do, then perhaps one might examine his own assumptions and stereotypes about aging and death. Munnichs' findings with relatively healthy elders in the Netherlands are similar to those obtained by Weisman and Kastenbaum with relatively sick elders in a geriatric hospital in the United States (98). The latter found that *apprehension* (or fear) was less often observed than *acceptance,* and they also noted responses of *apathy* and *anticipation.* As patients entered the preterminal phase of life, fearfulness was not the modal orientation. Two typical patterns were observed. Some patients accepted their fate quietly, and gradually reduced their spheres of functioning. This preterminal disengagement was initiated by the patients themselves and allowed them to bring their affairs to order, and exercise psychological control over a more limited life-space. Other patients also recognized the close prospect of death, but opted to remain involved with daily life activities. It did not seem appropriate to describe them as essentially counterphobic. They were simply continuing to live as they had been living. Death would come, of course, but it would have to tap them on the shoulder and interrupt the business of life.

An earlier study by Wendell Swenson also found a preponderance of forward-looking attitudes to death (99). Only about 10 percent of his relatively healthy elders admitted to fears of death when completing a self-administered checklist. Those who did not express favorable attitudes tended to evade the topic. Fear of death, when found, seemed to be related to solitary residence as compared with

living with relatives or in a facility for the aged. Chronological age and sex differences did not seem to make any difference in death orientation within this sample.

Frances C. Jeffers and her colleagues asked 269 elderly research volunteers from the community, "Are you afraid to die?" (100). Once again, there were not many who admitted to fear of death (10 percent). Many of the subjects invoked a religious frame of reference in replying to this question. As the investigators note, religion is an important part of community life in the region of North Carolina in which this study was conducted. Therefore, it is not surprising that most of the respondents would think of death in religious terminology. From their clinical experiences with this population, Jeffers and her colleagues suggest that "denial is a very important mechanism for dealing with anxiety in old age" (101). In other words, they incline toward the interpretation that denial of death fear represents a defensive response rather than the elderly person's "real" orientation.

Another study of death attitudes among elderly volunteer subjects was conducted in New York City by Samuel D. Shrut (102). His respondents were 60 currently unmarried elderly women, presumably all of Jewish background. They were presented with a self-appraisal health questionnaire, another questionnaire for adjustment in their residence, and still another concerned with claimed participation in activities. A sentence-completion test and the Thematic Apperception Test were also included in this battery. A panel of psychologists rated the projective test responses in terms of attitudes toward death on a 5-point scale ranging from marked dread or preoccupation with death to philosophic acceptance.

In his interpretation of the results, Shrut emphasizes the (rather small) differences obtained in death attitude between subjects residing in apartments and those residing in the central residence of the

Home for Aged and Infirm Hebrews of New York. The women living in an institutional atmosphere showed somewhat more fear or preoccupation with death. This was taken to imply that the apartment dwellers enjoyed better mental health and were "more concerned with planning for continued living. . . " (103). They did, indeed, seem more socially alert, and less suspicious than those living in the institution. Perhaps of more interest, however, is the fact that neither group received a high rating on fear of death. Both samples were rated very close to the midpoint of the scale, a point described as "mild anxiety" (between "evident anxiety" and "attitude of equanimity or indifference").

So far as can be determined from this study, we seem to have another example of the *lack* of pervasive and conspicuous death-related anxiety among the elderly. There are two additional points of interest here. The death anxiety ratings were made from projective techniques rather than from direct questioning, and no attempt seems to have been made to distinguish anxiety attributable to death concern from the subjects' general level of anxiety.

One clinical study does report a high incidence of death concern. Adolph E. Christ interviewed 100 successive geriatric admissions to the psychiatric wards of a San Francisco hospital. He was able to obtain responses in the area of death from 62 of these patients, all of whom were described as acutely disturbed. Christ concludes: "The patients were fearful of death, but on the whole were willing, and in some cases were relieved to discuss it" (104). Unfortunately, the study itself has too many methodological blemishes for the results to be regarded with much confidence. This does not reflect personal discredit upon the investigator, who stepped outside of his usual domain to explore a topic neglected by others. Although not clearly supported by the procedures used, the results of this study might well stand up through further inves-

tigation. It will be recalled that other studies have also found suggestive data to the effect that emotionally disturbed or psychologically immature elders are more disposed to death anxiety than is the case with elders in general.

Overall, the available evidence suggests that fear of death is not especially intensive or pervasive for the elderly. This tentative conclusion derives mostly from straightforward questionnaires and interviews, but also from some intensive clinical follow-throughs and projective test data. One can choose to interpret the lack of salient death fear as *proof* that the elder is very fearful indeed. This is the same interpretation that one would have made if the elder had openly admitted to death fears. With a fixed conclusion in mind, one perhaps should bypass the "middleman," and not study any subjects at all (105). We do not mean to imply that the individual's orientation toward death can be read accurately and comprehensively from "face validity" measures only. But we could all be a little more careful in specifying our criteria and operational definitions. Until appropriate subsequent research demonstrates otherwise, it would appear that we must either accept the low incidence and intensity of death fear in the elderly as a fact, or just ignore the data altogether. We prefer to take the data seriously, although not blinding ourselves to the limitations therein.

Let us now try to gain some idea of how attitudes toward death in the elderly compare with those in the population at large.

Questions about death were included in a public opinion poll of 1,500 adults in the United States under the direction of Jack Riley. Some of the results were recently made available. Unfortunately, data specific to *fear* of death have not been released. There is a summary statement, however, to the effect that among adults of all ages "scarcely four percent gave evidence of fear or emotional anxiety in connection with death" (106). The published data suggest that chronological age may not be a crucial variable per se in determining attitudes toward death. Educational background seems more important, at least in this survey. People with limited educational attainment, whatever their age, were more likely to agree with negative propositions about death.

A point is implied here that, although familiar enough in gerontology, may not be sufficiently evident in the psychology of death. The status of being an elder is comprised of many aspects besides chronological age and the *changes* which *may* accompany advancing age. The elder is also marked by certain characteristics that are special to his *generation*. Most relevantly, elders in the United States today in general have a more limited formal educational background than their juniors. The relationship between educational level and death attitude thus might imply that there is something about growing older that makes one feel more negative about death. However, when Riley controlled for educational level, differences among age groups in the population declined sharply.

Among other results from this survey, it is interesting to see that the great majority of respondents at all age levels agree with the propositions that "death is sometimes a blessing," and "death is not tragic for the person who dies, only for the survivors." It is only the middle-aged groups (41-60) who tend to agree that "death always comes too soon." Younger and older people are about as likely to disagree as to agree with that proposition. Furthermore, the number of those who agree that "to die is to suffer" varies within the limited range of 10 to 18 percent across the various age groups (elders agree somewhat more than others).

The overall trend of Riley's findings is in the direction of showing primarily a positive or accepting attitude toward death in the adult population of the United States. This trend is at odds with the prevailing sentiments of psychologists and psychiatrists who study orientations toward death from an intensive, clinical standpoint, and from the standpoint of many social commentators as well. Perhaps what we have here is a useful study of the "socially acceptable" response that most of us think we should emit on the topic of death. In any event, within the framework of this study itself there is no reason to conclude that elders are very much different from the general population in the attitudes they care to express concerning death.

Perhaps at this point we need to regain our confidence in death as an aversive stimulus. "Fear of death" was added as an item to a standard checklist of fears that was administered, along with other procedures, to several populations of adolescents and elders (107). The younger and older groups were not closely matched, so caution is required in interpreting the results in terms of age differences. Death did prove to be a "popular" fear stimulus in this study—but chiefly for the adolescents. All the subpopulations of adolescents assigned more death fear to themselves than did any of the elderly populations. There was a tendency for incarcerated juvenile offenders to express the strongest death fears. The results take on added interest when we bring into consideration the fact that the elders showed more fear *in general* than did the adolescents. In other words, death fear behaved differently than other fears in the "aversive repertoire" of both young and old. The adolescents expressed fear of death, but not of much else. The elders subscribed to most of the fears available, but not the fear of death.

Another study probed orientations toward death with a projective technique, a specially constructed sentence completion test (108). The subjects were adults in the middle-to-old-age range. As in the above study, evidence suggested that elderly people are less frightened of death than their juniors—at least, elderly people themselves seem to think so. This finding is consistent with another study in which the semantic differential technique was used to provide an indirect estimate of death attitudes in younger and older adults (109). These investigators, Nathan Kogan and Michael Wallach, were more successful than most in matching the groups on at least some of the relevant variables. They found more negative responses to death words among the younger subjects.

One of the few studies to go "beneath the surface" of age differences in death attitudes is the doctoral research of psychologist Stanley H. Rothstein (110). He interviewed 36 men all of whom were married, had children, and were active in an occupation. Verbatim transcripts were prepared from the interviews (respondents were seen from one to four times until sufficient information had been obtained in the individual case.) For purposes of analysis the total sample was divided into two adult age groups: 30-42, and 46-58.

Rothstein was interested in developing a substantive theory for understanding the awareness of aging and what he termed the "personalization of death." In essence, he seemed to be concerned with the individual's experience of growing old as a preparation for the subsequent recognition that he truly is vulnerable to personal death. Although he is not the first researcher to appreciate the mutual implications of aging, time perspective, and death, Rothstein is one of the few to have conducted an in-depth empirical study in this area. We will be able to consider only a few of the most relevant aspects of his investigation here.

It was found that the older respondents personalized death more frequently than did their juniors. The older men also showed a greater tendency to feel that time was passing by quickly in most areas of their lives. Differences in the personalization of death can be illustrated by the following excerpts from Rothstein's material:

One of our men . . . died at 63 . . . some people die at 63 . . . when one of my first real contemporaries dropped dead . . . at 44 or 45 . . . this sort of affected me . . . we are getting a little older . . . and you never know when it might hit you.

I see 670 people were taken on a highway over the Christmas holiday. Planes go down and cars crash . . . I have not thought about death in a personal sense . . . only because I don't think it's going to happen for quite some time (111).

The first excerpt illustrates the awareness of death in its personalized form; this awareness is absent (explicitly denied) in the latter example.

Perhaps the most instructive aspect of this study is its indication that important differences in one's orientation toward death may emerge *during* the middle adult years. Awareness of aging and premonitions of death need not be experienced for the first time when one is in the retirement years. Studies which include only elderly persons might yield the misleading impression that their attitudes toward death are distinctive to their present phase of life. But it might be the case that these orientations had been developing for two or even three decades.

Attention should also be given to the fact that Rothstein has made a contribution to our understanding of the development of death orientations without focusing upon fears per se. His inquiry is concerned with the quality or saliency of thought about death (personalized vs. nonpersonalized). We commend this approach as a useful alternative and supplement to the more conventional emphasis upon death fears. Logically, it makes sense to learn how a person grasps the general topic of death before focusing upon specific feelings and themes.

In his own interpretation of the pattern of findings, Rothstein concludes:

The individual personally learns that he will die through learning that he can become older, and through experiencing the death or debilitation of meaningful others. . . . The personalization of death is similar to awareness of aging in that a person is exposed to differentiated experiences with changes in his positions in social contexts. He responds to these unanticipated experiences with shock. An accommodation is made, expectancies are changed, and previously shocking experiences are accepted as being normal. In our society, as a consequence of usual experiences with death, the individual changes from feeling unconcerned, to feeling shocked, to feeling resigned. It is this process that has been called the personalization of death (112).

While it cannot be said that all of these propositions have been amply documented by this single study, Rothstein's observations appear well worth follow-up investigations.

It may not be entirely out of place here to introduce a finding from another investigation that has nothing directly to do with death attitudes. Bernice Neugarten and her colleagues studied opinions toward the menopause in 267 women of four age groups: 21-30; 31-44; 45-55; and 56-65 (113). They found that the younger women tended to have attitudes that not only were more negative, but also more undifferentiated. The authors muse: "The fact that most younger women have generally more negative views is perhaps because the menopause is not only relatively far removed, and therefore relatively vague; but because, being vague, it becomes blended into the whole process of growing old, a process that is both dim and unpleasant. Perhaps it is only the middle-aged or older woman who can take a differentiated view of the menopause; and who, on the basis of experience, can as one woman said, 'separate the old wives' tales from that which is true of old wives'" (114). We think this study is relevant for the following reasons:

1. Again, we come upon important attitudinal differences within the adult age range (between adolescence and old age). This tends to strengthen the impression yielded from Rothstein's study that much more is going on in these middle years than is generally appreciated by behavioral and social scientists. The possible shift in death orientation may be just one part (although a crucial part) of a more general reorganization of individual values and perspectives.

2. The specific differences noted in this study seem to parallel what has been suggested in a number of investigations into death orientations. Older adults seem to achieve a sharper focus on death, but with less manifest fear than younger adults.

3. There may be an underlying relationship between attitude toward one's reproductive prowess and one's terminus. As will be discussed elsewhere in this book (Chapter 7), there are many reasons for considering birth and death dynamics in relationship to each other.

Continuing our youthward traversal of the life cycle, we find a number of studies that concentrate exclusively upon adolescents. It is difficult to know what to make of the findings from most of these investigations. Short on hypotheses, control groups, and general procedural rigor, the typical study in this group merely serves to whet our curiosity.

Marie Hackl Means asked 1,000 co-eds to respond to a list of 349 fear stimuli (115). Quite a few of these items referred to death explicitly (e.g., Painful Death, Death by Burning, Dying People). Some items appeared innocent of death connotations (e.g., Snails, Dentists, Wild Parties). Still other items conveyed the impression that they either might or might not resonate with the respondent's death concern (Holes in the Ground, High Places, Cancer).

Although the author does not provide a separate analysis of death fear responses, she does offer useful "point value" scores for each item. Inspecting the data, one finds that the explicit death items tended to cluster among the most frequent and intense fear stimuli. No death item, for example, was rated as low as the bottom

30 percent, while the lowest position of any item referring to death of the respondent (Sudden Death) appears slightly below the 50th percentile. Although in the winter of 1929 the co-eds shuddered most vigorously at the thought of snakes, their next most fearsome reactions were to Cancer, Death of Loved Ones, and Death by Burning. Not far behind were Death by Drowning, Murderers, Slow Death, Death by Murder, Death by Suffocation and Painful Death. The number of death-related fears among the most aversive stimuli increases further if we include Cyclones, Reckless Driving, Auto Accidents, Pistols, etc.

In a very general way, Means' study suggests that death-related fears are prominent in the "aversive stimuli repertoire" of educated young women. Another early study by W. C. Middleton involved the use of a questionnaire with both male and female college students (116). Idiosyncracies of the instrument he developed tend to defeat any attempt to derive clear conclusions. However, in looking over the data reported by Middleton, David Lester noticed that the co-eds reported more death thoughts and more death fears than did the males (117). This finding would at least be consistent with Means' responses from her co-eds.

In another questionnaire study on the high-school level, Chalmers Stacey and Marie Reichen obtained responses from both "normal" and "institutional subnormal" adolescent girls (118). The normal adolescents tended to conceptualize their deaths more frequently and vividly. They were more likely to have attended funerals, visited cemeteries, and seen corpses (also more fearful of being buried alive). This group also admitted more frequently to feeling sometimes that they wished they were dead. The subnormal girls appeared to be more "emotional" and overtly fearful toward death. They expected to die from a specific illness, while the brighter girls were more likely to expect death to come in the form of an accident. Thoughts about life after death were more common among the institutionalized adolescents. Most girls in both groups reported that they were not fascinated by death and did not care to read stories about death.

A subsequent study by Adah Maurer tends to support the trends in the Stacey-Reichen data (119). Maurer asked 172 high-school girls to write an essay response to the question: "What comes to your mind when you think of death?" The investigator found the responses difficult to evaluate, but eventually grouped the essays according to the frequency with which "fear words" were used. "Observable differences in the thoughts of adolescence on the subject of death range from very childish to very mature. . . . In general, statements made and vocabulary used in spontaneous essays tend to be associated in degree of maturity with academic achievement. Poor achievement is associated with greater fear, often so pervasive that it can be communicated only indirectly" (120).

It is interesting to have even these less-than-satisfactory data to the effect that manifest death fear is greater among institutionalized or low-achieving high-school students, just as it is greater among immature or emotionally disturbed elders.

In Maurer's study, the low-achieving, death-fearing girls often wrote essays concerned with "separation anxiety, remnants of beliefs in ghosts, spirits, haunts, mention of smells, corpses, accidents, disease, and violence. The greater use of euphemisms and similes, such as 'sleep' and 'journey,' questions as to how the dead 'feel,' and degrees of deadness are stigmata of slow minds" (121).

Research mentioned in the previous chapter has suggested that fear of death is both salient in adolescence and much defended against. Depending upon how one approaches the adolescent subject, one might see either more of the saliency or more of the defensive side. Observations such as these are more likely to emerge

from multi-level and fairly complex studies. One of the best available examples of
refined inquiry into adolescent responses
to death is the multi-level approach of
Irving Alexander and Arthur Adlerstein
(122). With a population of 50 male
college students, these psychologists made
use of the ubiquitous questionnaire approach to assess conscious attitudes
towards death. However, they supple-
mented this measure with Charles Osgood's Semantic Differential Technique
(123). This is a fairly sophisticated instrument that provides an indirect measure of
the meanings individuals assign to various
concepts. Additionally, they interviewed
each subject about their death-related
thoughts and experiences.

Yet there was even more to this study.
Alexander and Adlerstein had each of the
young men respond to a word association
task that included death and non-death
words—while at the same time being attached to a polygraph that recorded the
psychogalvanic skin response (GSR). GSR
was assessed before and after the exposure
to death words, and the subjects also
responded to a manifest anxiety scale
before and after. Certainly the investigators in this study were in an unusually
good position to learn how their subjects
orient themselves to death.

Although this experiment was designed
to explore differences between religious
and nonreligious young Protestant men,
the most relevant findings here concern
the characteristics of the total group
(which was equally divided between the
religious and nonreligious.) The shared
characteristics of these subjects seemed to
prevail over differences attributable to religious orientation. Death words elicited
an increased GSR in almost all of the
men. They also tended to describe death-
related words as both "bad" and "potent"
on the Semantic Differential. During the
interviews, most of the men offered "the
philosophical shrug followed by a justification in terms of God's will and the
afterlife or the natural order of things"

(124) when asked how they felt about the
fact that they must die. Overt expressions
of fear were not common. The possibility
of a painful death was the most repellent
prospect for both the religious and nonreligious. Separation from loved ones, the
thought of being buried in the ground,
and the challenge of facing death "properly" were problems that occurred about
as frequently in both groups.

There were some differences between
the religious and nonreligious subjects, but
we will come to that later. Relevant here
is the observation that "the evidence from
the indirect measures, both physiological
and verbal, points to the fact that death is
a negatively-toned affective concept for
both of our groups. However, as soon as
one begins to deal with the problem directly, on a conscious level, as in our
interview, there is a tendency for subjects
to act as though they are not at all
concerned over the prospect of their own
death. These findings seem to be the same
for both our religious and our nonreligious subjects" (125).

To our knowledge, no research of this
type has been conducted with post-adoles-
cent populations. The studies which reveal
different levels of death response in the
same individual seem to be limited to
children and adolescents, mostly the
latter. We cannot determine, then, whether the discrepancy between a socially put
forth response and a more inward and
alarmed reaction is especially characteristic of being an adolescent, or especially
characteristic of being human (or being a
contemporary American). Nevertheless, we
do have sufficient evidence to suggest that
death stimuli cue off stronger responses
from our adolescents than they generally
recognize or care to admit.

Children think of death fairly often, as
we learned in the preceding chapter. Curiosity seems to be as important as fear in
the child's orientation toward death. It
was even ventured that death poses the
first significant intellectual challenge to
the young child, a prime stimulus for his

subsequent mental growth. Death of the *other* person, resulting in a sense of abandonment and heightened vulnerability, often seems more salient than fear of one's own death. Yet direct fear of death could also be observed in the thought and play of the child. As Paul Schilder has observed, the child finds it easier to understand death through violence than through disease. "The young child, especially the aggressive young child, is constantly destroying things. The ability to destroy gives the child a sense of power, and is accordingly a source of pleasure. . . . [Furthermore] to the child, anything that is unexpected and unusual may kill—ghosts kill and so do the dead" (126). Fear of punishment from adults has a way of becoming translated into fear of death (even though the child may not understand the concept of death in the same way as his parents do).

Developmental level has also been identified as an important influence upon the child's emotional orientation to death. One may feel differently about death when he comes to the realization that it is an inevitable prospect as contrasted with the earlier notion of an unpleasantry one could always manage to avoid were he clever and lucky enough. Personal experiences in the child's life were also seen as contributory to his death orientation, including the presence of fatal illness in the child himself.

Death Fear in Special Populations

With a few exceptions, the studies considered above were concerned with fear of death in "normal" individuals of various ages. More briefly now, we will explore the attitudes found in a few special populations.

Walter Bromberg and Paul Schilder applied a psychoanalytically-oriented clinical technique to the study of death attitudes in a small sample of neurotics and other psychiatric patients (127). Previously they had explored the conscious and unconscious attitudes of relatively normal adults (128). From this pair of studies, Bromberg and Schilder emphasize that "neither neurosis or psychosis produce an attitude towards death which cannot be found also in the so-called normal" (129). This conclusion recalls to mind the similar finding of Sylvia Anthony who studied both normal and disturbed children (130).

Nevertheless, Bromberg and Schilder observed that the psychodynamic meanings of death came more clearly into the foreground in people suffering from neurotic or psychotic disorders. Obsessional neurotics, for example, do not seem to have salient fears of personal death so long as their aggression has an external object. However, when the superego begins to direct aggression inwardly, then the individual is likely to develop an obsessional fear of death. He may attempt to protect himself by investing in symbolic structures, such as metaphysical speculations of an eternal life. These defensive efforts are not invariably successful. The prospect of existence-without-end may come to mean punishment-without-end. For the obsessional neurotic, then, what he may fear most deeply about death is its introduction to an infinite future of sadomasochistic torment.

Different dynamics were observed for neurotics whose syndromes centered around anxiety or hysteria. In these cases death seemed to have the meaning of separation from the loved one. "In the psychopathology of hysteria the notion of space is important. . . . Such types must have people close to them and their anxiety often concerns the fear of not having a libidinous object in close proximity to themselves, as is seen for example in the mechanism of hysterical frigidity. . . . In neurotic anxiety the predominant fear is the dread of sudden death either of oneself or of a person who is close to the patient. Sudden death for this type of neurotic means a separation from objects of libidinous attachment in the environment" (131).

This type of report is difficult to evaluate. One respects the clinical acumen of the investigators, and one finds the case material instructive. The specific interpretations are provocative, e.g., "In this case the anxiety about death is the expression of a repressed wish to be lifeless and passive and to be handled by the father (an undertaker)" (132). Yet in studies such as this one also has to be concerned about:

1. The haste with which generalizations are drawn from a few cases.
2. The plentiful opportunities for inadvertent methodological contamination when it is the same person who obtains and interprets the data in such a wide-open situation.
3. The ambiguity as to whether the case material is being used as a source of *fresh* data, or as a means of *demonstrating* principles already assumed to be true by the investigators.

Certainly, one can gain insights and clues from clinical studies such as the present one by Bromberg and Schilder. But it is not always possible to come away with the conviction that anything has been proven or clearly tested about man's relationship to death. This comment is not intended to imply that the clinical researchers are mistaken in their conclusions, simply that the reader often is not in a position to evaluate the probabilities.

A subsequent study by Herman Feifel did support Bromberg and Schilder's observation that neither neurosis nor psychosis produces attitudes toward death which cannot also be found in normal adults (133). There were differences in frequency, however. Feifel reported a tendency for mentally ill subjects either to deny thoughts of death more often than did normals, or to envisage personal death coming about in a violent mode. Another interesting difference emerged in response to the question, "If you could do only one more thing before dying, what would you choose to do?" While normal subjects emphasized indulgence in personal pleasures, the mentally ill subjects focused more often upon social, religious, or charitable activities ("Know more of God," "Stop war if possible," etc.).

In a later report based upon the same continuing series of interview studies, Feifel and Heller came to the conclusion that mentally ill subjects were more fearful of death than were either healthy or physically ill normal subjects (134). Ideas of failure and punishment were said to occur more frequently among the mentally ill patients with respect to death, while normal adults were concerned more with loneliness and fear of the unknown.

Another study of psychiatric patients' attitudes toward death was conducted in Great Britain by Ijaz Haider (135). All the patients were 50 years of age or older, and were asked a series of direct death questions as part of a routine psychiatric interview. Although only nine of the patients said that they feared death, the investigator included 17 other patients in the death-fearing group because they either said they wanted to have a long life or wanted death to come suddenly. This classification system seems rather arbitrary. As a consequence, we do not know what to make of the other findings that were reported.

A number of observers have been impressed by the significance of death to schizophrenic individuals. One of the most compelling presentations of this viewpoint is to be found in an essay by psychiatrist Harold E. Searles (136). This is not a research paper and makes no pretense of being such. However, Searles draws upon extensive psychotherapeutic experience with schizophrenics. He has gradually come to the conclusion that "the very mundane universal factor of human mortality seemingly constitutes one of the major sources of anxiety against which the patient is defending himself. . . " (137). Searles regards death as a central factor in the schizophrenic pattern: one becomes and remains schizophrenic largely in order to avoid facing the fact that life in finite.

He describes long-term psychotherapy with a young woman who came forth with "a richly detailed, fascinatingly exotic and complex, extremely vigorously-defended delusional system, replete with all manner of horrendous concepts, ranging from brutal savagery to witchcraft, and to the intricate machinations of science-fiction" (138). Despite the exotic and fear-ridden quality of her phenomenological world, this woman showed no awareness of "any of the *innate* tragedy which sane persons find in their world—tragedy having to do with such matters as illness, poverty, aging, and, above all, inescapable death..." (139). As therapy progressed, the patient intensified her denial of death. She would spend much of her time picking up dead leaves and searching for dead birds and animals, attempting to bring them all back to life in one way or another. Finally, she came to the emotional realization that she was mortal, that everybody was mortal, but that this condition was *not her fault*. At the same time she finally became able to accept the fact that both of her parents had been dead for years.

This woman, and other schizophrenic individuals cited by Searles, gave him the impression that they did not really experience themselves as being alive. He suggests that this sense of unaliveness may serve the defensive function of protecting oneself from death—if I already feel dead, what is there to lose through death? Searles also proposes another relationship between the sense of aliveness and denial of mortality. He contends that one cannot bear the anxiety aroused by perception of finitude "unless one has the strengthening knowledge that one is a whole person, and is, with this wholeness, able to participate wholly in living—able to experience one's self as a part of the collective wholeness of mankind, all of whom are

faced with this common fate" (140). Searles' orientation here is remarkably similar to that of John Dorsey who has written eloquently on the desirability of the individual attaining a sense of "allness" (141).

In company with other observers, Searles points out that it is typical to find critical interpersonal losses in the early developmental background of people who grow up to be schizophrenic. He suggests that the early timing of these losses (e.g., death of a parent, or total rejection by a parent) undermines the child's subsequent intrapsychic and interpersonal development. He does not experience the loss as a loss per se—that would require a higher level of psychological development than what has already been attained. Instead, the child is said to experience a basic sense of disintegration within his total self. In desperate reaction to this sense of disintegration, the child clings to *subjective omnipotence*. This state of mind requires the implicit or explicit denial of personal death, and becomes the core of the subsequent schizophrenic pattern.

The propositions offered by Searles strike us as being insightful and promising. Yet they are not easily put to appropriate empirical tests. Somebody could make a valuable contribution here by carrying out an in-depth but well-controlled inquiry based upon Searles' observations.

Let us consider one more special population: people who have nightmares. Marvin J. Feldman and Michel Hersen asked more than 1,300 subjects to classify themselves with respect to frequency of nightmares (142). As one might expect from the large size of their sample, the subjects were, indeed, students in large introductory psychology classes. Besides indicating the frequency with which they experienced nightmares, the students were also asked to indicate if the nightmares had recurrent themes, and if they would be willing to participate in a further study outside of regular class time. The co-eds tended to report more nightmares, and more recurrent themes, and also to volunteer in greater numbers. In general, both the males and the females who had experienced any nightmares at all in recent months seemed quite willing to discuss their fearful dreams. From this total sample, Feldman and Hersen drew a reduced sample of 168 subjects who were then asked to take a Death Scale with each of the 10 items to be answered along a 6-point continuum of death concern. The students were also asked to provide some biographical information pertaining to death and to respond to a battery of personality tests.

A significant relationship was found between nightmare frequency and the subjects' conscious concern about death. This relationship held true for both sexes. Those who reported frequent nightmares were especially likely to think often of their own death, to imagine themselves as dying or dead, to have dreams of dying or death, and to think about being killed in an accident. An attempt was made to investigate the relationship between nightmares, death concern, and personal experiences with death, but this population seemed to have so few death experiences that the analysis came to naught.

Feldman and Hersen, referring to additional unpublished data, also report that concern specific to death is much more strongly related to nightmares than are more general attitudes of anxiety or fear. They believe that "nightmares reflect intense areas of unresolved conflict about which the dreamer feels so helpless that even the fantasy of dreams does not provide solutions that would keep the dreamer asleep. Persons for whom death is a salient concern would seem then to be vulnerable to nightmares" (143).

Have we learned something? Within a few months of the Feldman-Hersen study, David Lester had conducted a study on the same topic that failed to replicate the original results (144). Lester pointed out that the earlier study did not control for the frequency with which people have

dreams, and also used some death concern items that overlapped with nightmare questions. Lester took these factors into account in his own study of 304 co-eds. He found that people who had reported frequent nightmares also tended to report more dreams of all kinds. No association was found between the reported frequency of either dreams or nightmares and the conscious fear of death.

One could criticize Lester's study as well. It was not designed in perfect parallel with the earlier study, and had some intrinsic flaws of its own. Yet Lester has done that rare thing in the still new field of psychological death research: he has attempted to replicate a previous result. Would we know more or less about fear of death if careful replications had been carried out for other studies that are frequently cited in this area?

Death Fear and Other Psychosocial Variables

Occasional studies have attempted to clarify the relationship between fear of death and other psychological or social variables. Several of these inquiries will be reviewed here.

As the reader has had opportunity to observe, many studies have relied upon questionnaires to assess the respondent's attitude toward death. If the reader also sees fit to comment that *too* many studies have been limited to this technique, he will find no disagreement on the part of the present writers. But since attitude measures do have a place in this realm it would be useful to learn more about death attitudes *as* attitudes. Is it not possible, for example, that people may be inclined to offer answers that are socially desirable rather than personally relevant? Barry Crown and his colleagues appear to be the first researchers to explore "attitudes toward attitudes toward death" (145). They prepared a set of 17 statements concerning death attitudes using the Edwards social desirability technique.

The items were selected to differ on two dimensions: "healthy" vs "unhealthy" and "hysterical" vs "obsessive." With 45 male graduate students as subjects it was found that a "healthy sensitivity" to death was considered to be the most socially desirable orientation. This was expressed in such items as "My philosophy of life helps me to deal with death." The *least* socially desirable orientation was that of "unhealthy sensitivity" (e.g., "Death terrifies me.") It was considered more desirable to have a healthy *in*sensitivity than an *un*healthy sensitivity. In other words, it would appear that the socially desirable attitude toward death attitudes is that one should be able to face death with equanimity and perspective—but if one cannot bring this off with a flourish, it is better to avoid the topic altogether. Obsessing about death was the most negatively-regarded orientation of those represented in this study.

It would be premature to generalize these results to other populations. But Crown, *et al* have provided us with the first solid indication that the social desirability influence makes itself known in the realm of death attitudes as well as elsewhere. This relationship has been suspected by some investigators, but not previously made the focus of study. Subsequent attitudinal research might well incorporate the social desirability dimension in order to improve our ability to distinguish between "public" and "private" utterances.

The notion of "social desirability" brings to mind the broader relationship between the individual's position in family and community life and his response to death. Material on this topic will appear in various contexts throughout the book. Let us concentrate for the moment upon a pair of studies which bear directly on this topic. James C. Diggory and Doreen Z. Rothman reasoned that there should be a strong relationship between the goals a person values highly and his social status. Therefore, it was hypothesized that "fear

of various consequences of his own death should vary with ... status or role, whether defined by age, sex, social class, religion, or marital condition" (146).

A list of seven "consequences of one's death" was developed and administered to a catch-as-catch-can population of 563 adults. The "consequences" were set up as paired comparisons and included with a larger questionnaire pertaining to death attitudes. Respondents were asked to indicate which member of each pair they regarded as worse or more distasteful than the other. The items were:

1. I could no longer have any experiences.
2. I am uncertain as to what might happen to me if there is a life after death.
3. I am afraid of what might happen to my body after death.
4. I could no longer care for my dependents.
5. My death would cause grief to my relatives and friends.
6. All my plans and projects would come to an end.
7. The process of dying might be painful (147).

In presenting their results, the authors concentrated upon Item 4 which they believed was most relevant to goal striving and social role. Concern about not being able to care for one's dependents was systematically related to marital status, sex, and age. Married people, for example, were more likely to have this concern than those who were single or engaged. This pattern of findings was taken as supporting the hypothesis that "a person fears death because it eliminates his opportunity to pursue goals important to his self-esteem" (148). And, as has already been mentioned, the goals crucial to self-esteem were thought to be strongly influenced by social role variables.

The Diggory-Rothman study is of interest because it brings together an innovative approach ("consequences of one's death") with a social role theoretical orientation. The total pattern of results is more complex than what has been presented here. The reader who has an abiding interest in the relationship between death attitudes and social role is urged to review the data in detail and form his own conclusions about the extent to which the hypothesis was confirmed.

But we cannot leave this study without commenting upon the data obtained for Item 1, "I could no longer have any experiences." This statement is especially relevant to the fear of extinction, which has been treated in this chapter as the basic death fear. We are impressed—and puzzled—by several points when we inspect the median scale positions assigned to the items by the Diggory-Rothman respondents:

1. For the total subject population [563], the lack of future experiences occupied only the *midpoint* of the scale. Most people did not consider the end of their phenomenological life to be the most disturbing aspect of personal death. Causing grief to others was the most distasteful item. This finding thus goes against the hypothesis that extinction of the self is the most aversive aspect of the death stimulus.

2. Death as a foreclosing of one's *ambition* (Item 6) was rated as a more distasteful prospect than loss of phenomenological life for the respondents as a whole (and at every age level and for both sexes). What does this suggest? Is it possible that the *general* influence of our cultural milieu overrides more specific influences of the individual's social role? Diggory and Rothman concentrated upon role differences, which is certainly a significant research problem, but may have moved too swiftly past the problem of general cultural effects. Perhaps our society's emphasis upon *achievement* has become so deeply entrenched that it has overpowered the appreciation of who-it-is-who-will-be-there-to-experience-the-achieve-

ment. Do we prefer to achieve rather than to experience? Imagine that this preference could be granted a basis in reality: one's inner life blanks out, but the organism still goes through the motions of producing and achieving. We would have a machine-like entity, a zombie, an automaton. (We have permitted ourselves to indulge in this slight digression because, as will be seen in Chapter 6, the image of the automaton does emerge from recent psychological studies.)

We also pause long enough to wonder if the achievement-over-experience orientation may bear a relationship to one of the observations made by Edwin Shneidman and Norman Farberow in their studies of real and simulated suicide notes (149). They found that some people on the brink of suicide engage in a peculiar form of logic. The individual anticipates self-destruction, yet he also projects himself into the future. He writes his final note as though he will be there to see how people react to his death: by implication, the experiencing self lives on although the objectified self has been slain. This eccentric logic may have a parallel in the split/screen consciousness that permits a person to accept his own obliteration with more equanimity than he can muster when his pet projects and plans are threatened. Other interpretations of this pattern in the Diggory-Rothman results are possible, but we think the data should not go unnoticed, whatever one cares to make of them.

3. Religious affiliation was the major social variable that distinguished responses to the experience item. Catholics were markedly less concerned about cessation of personal experience. Jews were more concerned than Protestants, but those subjects who were classified in the "Other-None" group of religious affiliation were decidedly more concerned about loss of phenomenological life than any of the other groups. Diggory and Rothman call attention to this pattern, and suggest that differences in religious beliefs concerning

life after death may account for the findings.

There has been no replication or extension of the study cited above, but it may be useful to set an investigation by Paul Rhudick and Andrew Dibner (150) next to it. These psychologists studied 58 healthy and alert elderly volunteer subjects. Especially germane here is the fact that demographic variables—so important in the Diggory-Rothman study—proved to be *unrelated* to death concern. There are a number of possible explanations for the difference. The most relevant factor, however, could be the differing approaches used by both sets of investigators in defining and assessing death concern. While Diggory and Rothman asked their respondents to make straightforward ratings of presented stimuli (consequences of death), Rhudick and Dibner had their subjects offer stories to TAT (Thematic Apperception Test) cards. Introduction of a death as an integral part of the story constituted a "death concern" response (the specific measure used was a refinement of the foregoing).

It is possible that Rhudick and Dibner obtained a personal or idiosyncratic response from their subjects while Diggory and Rothman elicited responses more heavily weighted with "social desirability." This would be consistent with the positive relationship found with demographic variables in one case but not the other. (It is also consistent with questionnaire data from geriatric hospital personnel reported in Chapter 9.) Neither study is being criticized on these grounds. The point is that relatively straightforward measures of death concern are likely to bear a stronger relationship to external social variables than we will find when more indirect or subtle techniques are employed. A complete picture would require investigation at both levels.

The Rhudick-Dibner study is interesting for more than its negative results concerning demographic variables. They also found that subjects who tended to report many symptoms of either physical or emotional distress had higher death concern scores. This finding is in the same direction as those obtained in several studies described earlier. An attempt was made to relate death concern to the personality variables that are thought to be assessed by the Minnesota Multiphasic Personality Inventory (MMPI). Sixteen scales were used. Hypochondriasis was the only scale on which a significant differentiation was noted at the .01 level, but Hysteria and Dependency and Impulsivity were not far behind. On the whole, one cannot say that much was learned about the relationship between personality structure and death concern here, but the trend is in the by-now expected direction: the more "neurotic" the picture an individual conveys about himself, the more likely he is also to manifest obvious death concern. No significant relationships were found between death concern and any of the scales purported to measure psychotic tendencies. The present writers are impressed by the general lack of relationship between most MMPI scales and death concern in this study.

One other finding in the Rhudick-Dibner study should be mentioned both to recall previously-cited research and to prepare for a discussion that follows: Close examination of their findings led Rhudick and Dibner to conclude that depressive affect, *not* anxiety, was most likely to be aroused by the presence of death concern. Several other studies, using much different methodology, have also wound up yielding the impression that depression may be equally as common if not more common than fear as a response to death stimuli.

Fear of death, of course, has been the basic topic of this chapter. Although many relevant studies have been described, we have not seen much in the way of an experimentally-oriented approach to the determinants of death fear, or its relationship to functional variables. Joyce

Paris and Leonard D. Goodstein have shown that it is possible to conduct well-controlled research of this character (151). They hypothesized a possible relationship between repression-sensitivity as a personality variable and the individual's response to death stimuli when they noted: "Repression-sensitization is conceptualized as a continuum, with the repression extreme involving those behaviors which avoid anxiety-arousing stimuli, while at the sensitizing extreme are those behaviors which involve an attempt to approach or control these same stimuli. Therefore, repressive defenses would tend to involve repression, denial, and rationalization, while the sensitizing defense would involve intellectualizing, obsessions, and ruminative worry" (152).

Paris and Goodstein expected "sensitizers" to express more anxiety to literary material dealing with both sex and death than would "repressors." They didn't. Undergraduate men and women selected as repressors or sensitizers were exposed to erotic, deathly, or "neutral" reading materials and asked to make a set of self-ratings afterward. Most people reported feeling "sexier" after reading the erotic materials. However, there was no tendency for the sensitizers to report more anxiety than the repressors to either the erotic or death-related readings. About the only positive data relevant to the death anxiety hypothesis was a tendency for females to be "less bored" by death than by neutral readings and a bit more "emotionally upset."

Another serendipitous finding, however, is worth mentioning here. The co-eds seemed to find death a little more sexually arousing than did their male classmates. The men reported no sexual arousal after reading death materials, while a few of the women verbalized a slight increase in sexual feelings (the difference was statistically significant). Paris and Goodstein note that this unexpected finding seems pertinent to David McClelland's discussion of a reported tendency for women to sexualize

death (153). It is also relevant to material presented in a later chapter in this book.

Two other experiments have delved into the possible relationships between cognitive and emotional orientations toward death. Irving Alexander and his colleagues asked 31 male undergraduates to provide word associations while their response time and psychogalvanic skin response were being electrically recorded (154). The stimulus words included "funeral," "death," and "burial," along with three other sets of words selected from the standard list developed by Thorndike and Lorge (155). They found that death words elicited responses of greater emotional intensity (as defined by the latency and PGR measures) than did equivalent words drawn from the general language sample. Alexander et al point out that this result is different from that obtained by some other observers when death concern was assessed entirely on the basis of what the respondent said to direct interview or questionnaire items. The discrepancy between overt and covert processes was illustrated in the case of one subject who had shown a strong psychophysiological response to death words, but denied consciously any concern or interest in this topic. A post-experimental interview disclosed that "he was a diabetic . . . whose very existence depended on a dose of insulin administered each morning" (156). This study confirms experimentally what has been said previously about the complexity of our response to death. It also prepared the way for the subsequent experiment of Stephen L. Golding and his colleagues (157).

Taking off from the several studies by Alexander and his associates, the Golding team reasoned that "death-related words have a high emotional content for individuals with a high fear of death" (158). People with high anxiety should exhibit "connotative rigidity" when confronted by death stimuli. "Connotative rigidity" was regarded as a form of resistance in making cognitive associations to death stimuli. Furthermore, an anxious person should also exhibit marked perceptual defense to death stimuli. In other words, he will try to resist the recognition of death stimuli in the first place, and, if such stimuli do sneak by, to control rigidly their place in his consciousness.

Their 30 standard issue subjects (introductory psychology students) were shown death-related and non-death words for tachistoscopic recognition. This was the measure of perceptual defense. A semantic differential form was used to evaluate connotative meanings of death words. Death anxiety was assessed by Sarnoff and Corwin's 5-item scale (159).

Golding, et al were successful in replicating the major findings of earlier investigations: death words did take longer for the subjects to recognize, thus lending support to a perceptual defense interpretation. They also found a fairly substantial pattern of relationships between both forms of resistance to the idea of death: perceptual defense and connotative rigidity. The establishment of an empirical link between these two phenomena should serve as an encouraging outcropping of solid ground in this otherwise rather swampy terrain. However, no relationship was established between the two forms of resistance to death and their measure of death anxiety. This failure must be taken at its face value for the moment: it cannot be said that high-anxiety subjects have been shown to be more guarded when confronted with death stimuli. But the present authors tend to agree with Golding et al in their contention that the results "probably reflect the insufficiency of the instrument (Sarnoff-Corwin fear of death scale) in tapping the deeper aspects of an individual's affective orientation to death. . . . A more sensitive indication . . . might have resulted had word-association or GSR techniques been used (instead)" (160).

It might be useful here to call attention to a recent approach to the assessment of anxiety that could be substituted for the superficial death fear measures that have already been tried in a number of studies without conspicuous success. Louis A. Gottschalk, Carolyn N. Winget and Goldine C. Gleser have devoted an impressive amount of systematic effort to the development of content analysis scales (161). Their Anxiety Scale (and four other independent scales) draws upon verbal communications that can be obtained by a wide variety of techniques. One can use interview data, dream reports, projective test materials, or virtually any other verbal sampling technique imaginable. Detailed instructions are provided in a commendable manual that constitutes one of the two volumes in their new two-volume work.

A death anxiety subscale is included within the larger Anxiety Scale. Many researchers may also be interested in coding verbal material for the other anxiety subscales as well: mutilation, separation, guilt, shame, and diffuse or nonspecific anxiety. It is not difficult to see the relevance of these other content areas for death anxiety per se. Gottschalk et al take the position that the "subtypes of anxiety are of equivalent importance and relevance to the magnitude of overall anxiety of the subject." They also note that "Since the scale is designed to tap 'immediate' anxiety, the scores of an individual may fluctuate considerably from day to day or hour to hour; a single score is not a good indicator of a subject's typical level of anxiety over any extended period of time. The average of five or more such scores suitably spaced, however, does differentiate individuals reliably in this respect" (162).

This content analysis approach thus does not cater to the laggardly researcher. One must first master a detailed and demanding scoring system, and then one must be prepared to take repeated samplings. We have already had more than one occasion to point out that most psychological research on the topic of death, whether concerned with cognitions, affects, or behaviors, has operated within a self-imposed "one-shot" approach. Yet there is no reason to believe that our relationship to death is so static and simple that it can be studied adequately in such a manner. The stringent requirements of the Gottschalk Content Analysis Scale should be welcomed by researchers who really want to learn something.

Death Fear and Religion

Theological and other religious writings are replete with explicit and implicit references to death. Many comments about religion are also to be found in psychosocial essays on death. But the *empirical* relationship between death fear and religiosity is another story. Perhaps the reader will forgive us for not elaborating this story in detail. For all the importance of the religion-death relationship, it has not been served especially well by psychological research. Perhaps one of the difficulties is that religiosity too often has been included as an afterthought instead of an integral part of research design. And perhaps many of us have so many mixed feelings on both subjects that we have not been able to really think through the mutual implications.

In his review of the literature on this subject, Lester surveyed ten studies, some of which have already been described here (but largely for their contributions to other topics). He concluded that the results of the studies conflicted with each other. On the whole, we share that conclusion. One can work at finding explanations for why the apparent contradictions are only apparent, but it remains difficult to arrive at convincing general conclusions. From the available data, however, Lester does suggest that "religious belief does not affect the intensity of the fear of death, but rather channels the fear onto the specific problems that each religion proposes" (163).

What relationship *should* we expect between religiosity and death fear? It seems to us that contradictory predictions might well be advanced on the basis of general experience and opinion. Some historians claim that religion exists universally because mortality is universal—belief in God(s) and supportive ritual has the primary function of reducing apprehension in the face of death. The "more" religious a person, then the more he should be insulated by his faith from the raw encounter with death. But why did he become so religious in the first place? He probably was exceptionally anxious about death. Depending upon when and how we sample his orientation, then, we find the highly religious person to be either much more or much less death-anxious than the less religious person.

Even this approach is much too simple. Religions differ in their approach to death and life after death. Denomination A may offer solid support to the bereaved but little solace to the dying person, the reverse of denomination B. Apprehension about the terrors of the afterlife may haunt partisans of denomination C throughout their lives (an anxiety increment), while those adhering to denomination D may have so little offered to them in the way of postmortem futurity that their orientation differs scarcely at all from the nonreligious on this point. To be devout in one particular denomination or sect may have rather different implications for death anxiety than to be devout in another sect. As a matter of fact, the social geography involved may be almost as important as the variety of church per se. Local social, political, and economic factors can either sharpen or blur the differences among sects, including their orientations toward death. Still further, religious institutions are not static. Just within the span of time encompassed by the earliest and most recent psychological studies of death and religion, changes have occurred (differentially) in various denominations and sects. A relationship that could be more or less taken for granted around the turn of the century may no longer hold true today.

Research has seldom attuned itself to the complexity of one's external relationship to religion, one's internal belief system, and the total spectrum of one's thoughts, feelings, and behaviors with respect to death. More typically, investigators have attempted to discern statistically significant differences between religious and nonreligious subjects, or those belonging to various faiths. There is a place for such studies. We doubt, however, that very much will be learned by exclusive attention to this search-for-different-outcomes approach. Would it not be more informative to inquire into the *processes* through which religiosity and death orientation influence each other? Different types of research design would be required, it is true. And one might have to suspend temporarily the hope of finding statistically significant differences wherever one turns. But we might then be in a better position to develop informed hypotheses for more definitive testing.

OTHER WAYS OF FACING DEATH

The Limits of Fear

Fear has enjoyed the place of honor in this chapter because it is the best advertised response to death. Admittedly, it has been a lengthy exploration. One could devote a thousand pages to this topic, however, and still fail to encompass all the relevant material. Yet there are limits to fear:

1. Much of the empirical research described above has indicated that death responses other than, or in addition to, fear often are observed.

2. Frequently (but not invariably) fear seems to be a self-limiting reaction. One can remain intensely perturbed for only so long. The momentary panic induced by death or any other threatening

stimulus is likely to be replaced by other emotional responses, defensive postures, somatic symptomatology, or coping actions. Thus, even when fear or anxiety is a salient response to a death stimulus it may not continue this dominance over a long period of time, and need not be assumed to constitute the only response.

3. As a psychological concept, fear of death has limited (although as yet indispensable) value. The reader will have noticed that most of the theoretical questions we raised about fear of death and most of the distinctions proposed in the first section of this chapter received relatively little clarification from the available research data covered in the second section. You like the framework we have proposed here, or you do not like it. In either case, we all remain with most of the questions still before us. Taking into account the lack of progress that has been made in empirically contributing to our understanding of death fear per se (in contrast to the real, if limited, progress that has been made in relating death fear to external variables such as age and psychopathology), it seems appropriate to broaden the scope of our inquiry.

This will be a brief and selective discussion. No attempt will be made to examine all the responses that may be called forth by the thought of death. The intention is to show something of the range and flexibility of the human response to death. The details will be left to the reader's motivation and spirit of adventure. We will also try to avoid methodological byways. Many of the technical research problems that we stumbled across earlier will also be found here (plus a few more). We will pretend not to notice them.

163471

Sorrowing

People often feel sad about the death of others or the prospect of their own demise. We do not need fancy research to prove this to ourselves. But it is impressive to see how frequently a sorrowful response has been observed even in clinical studies that seem to focus upon fear or anxiety. "Sad" and "sorrowful" are words that do not appear often in the clinical research literature. We read instead about "depression." There is some reason for this usage. The researcher is attempting to classify individuals into groups on the basis of manifest or covert symptomatology, and thus relies upon standard nomenclature. Additionally, he may be working with people whose psychobiological functioning has reached an extreme that legitimately can be described in psychopathological terms. You and I are feeling sad—but that man over there has such a severe depressive reaction that he makes no effort to keep himself alive. Nevertheless, it may be that clinical terminology has been somewhat overdone in this area. Call a man "depressed" and we have transformed him into a clinical specimen. Without denying the relevance of this approach in some instances, for our purposes here we prefer to speak more simply about sadness or sorrow in the face of death. Fewer assumptions are then involved.

Let us take a few examples from here and there. In the well-designed clinical study by Hinton (164), it was found that a sorrowful orientation was expressed by dying patients even more frequently than anxious agitation. Brown has shown that men stricken with sorrow often have life histories involving paternal death at an early age (165). Freud (166), Lindemann (167), Eliot (168), Jackson (169), and Becker (170) are among the many perceptive observers who have described the varieties of sorrow a person is likely to experience following bereavement (or, in some instances, anticipating bereavement). Although fear of death continues to receive most of the emphasis in psychological writings, it would appear that sadness and sorrow constitute an equally important and deep response.

Some of us may be accustomed to thinking that sadness/grief is the basic response to death of the other, while fear/anxiety is our response to personal death. There may be something to this distinction. However, we have already seen that fear can be a salient response for the child when somebody close to him dies. (It is not necessarily fear of death per se; it can be apprehension about separation and abandonment.) Immature or dependent individuals of any age may also show this type of response to death of the other: fear for one's own fate, or a mixed (poorly differentiated) fear/sorrow response.

It may be less evident that sorrow is a fairly common response to the prospect of our own death. Perhaps we cannot fully appreciate the total loss of self that is death. But we have experienced other losses that prepare us to imagine what is in store. A process of active imagination may not be crucial. It may be enough to have our thoughts and feelings inundated with memories of past losses. We all have learned something of sorrow. The thought of death can be a powerful stimulus for the reactivation of these old sorrows, and the anticipation of sorrows to come.

Extinction ("ceasing to be") has been regarded as the basic death fear. It is also a prime object of sorrow. One might substitute "sorrow" for "fear" and develop a schema parallel to Figure A (p. 45). We sorrow for ourselves or for others—and in the contexts of the dying process, the afterlife (or its negation), and extinction.

Additionally, it might be useful to recognize a condition of *deathly sorrow*. In parallel with deathly fear, this state is not defined by its object. Deathly sorrow itself (as an internal condition of the organism) may be somewhat distinct from other types of sorrow. The reader may recall that one of the forms of deathly fear described above involved an *identification with death*. (To feel that one's life has come to a standstill is perhaps to fear that one's death has begun.) This process was exemplified by an old man sitting in isolation in a geriatric institution. He was said to be experiencing a variety of deathly fear because he was perceiving his own phenomenological life dwindling away, being replaced by a sort of psychological embalming fluid. This sequence can be taken one step further.

There are both theoretical and clinical bases for asserting that anxiety is likely to be the first response in a sequence of psychological disturbance (171). This affect tends to be replaced by other states or behaviors. Suppose that the life situation of our hypothetical (but real) elder does not improve. The intuited and feared condition becomes increasingly evident. Is it not likely that deathly fear will give way to deathly sorrow? He has become that which he feared: a specimen of the "living dead." (See Chapter 5.) A passage from Jules Henry's description of a geriatric facility comes to mind:

So they feel they are not human, and from this comes anguish that expresses itself in clinging. But silence is not the only form of dehumanizing communication to which these people are exposed. Empty walls, rows of beds close together, the dreariness of their fellow inmates, the bedpans, the odors, the routinization, all tell them they have become junk. Capping it all is the hostility of the patients to one another and the arbitrary movement from place to place like empty boxes in a storeroom. At the end is a degraded death (172).

We are familiar with conditions such as these. Anxious agitation still can be aroused in a reflex-like manner by sudden intrusions or the perception of possible threats. But in between these alarms the afflicted elder dwells in a state of sorrow so deep it is almost anesthetic. He is beyond weeping—perhaps because tears have a way of implying washing away the old and giving birth to the new. He is resigned to living in a state resembling death until relieved by the anticlimax (physical death).

One is anxious now and then. But one can sorrow and grieve continuously, almost without limit. And so it may be that—with sensitive research—we are likely to discover that sorrow is a response to death that demands a much greater share of our attention.

We are suggesting that sorrow in the face of death is as "normal" or "typical" a response as any. It may vary from the subtle and barely perceptible to the massive and debilitating. A certain "prenostalgia" toward personal death may develop at a relatively early age in some people—we know very little about the developmental career of sorrow and other responses to loss. The relationship between deathly sorrow, as described here, and other forms of sorrow also remains to be determined. A comprehensive understanding would, of course, make use of concepts and findings from psychopathology, a language we have avoided in this discussion. But we might think twice before equating human sorrow at the thought of death with those "depressive reactions" that happen to somebody else and can be controlled with the flick of an electric switch or the ingestion of a psychotropic chemical.

Overcoming

But why sorrow or fear? Why do we not simply *overcome* death? Religion is one of the highly organized cultural efforts to overcome or transcend death. Procreation at least partially overcomes death, for one "lives on," in a sense, in progeny. That $2,000,000 Chair in Psychosocial Gerontology which you have just been kind enough to endow at your local university also bestows social immortality; your name will be linked forevermore to the professor who holds that enviable title. We have many individual and social strategies for getting past death. We bribe, trick, or bully him aside. These devices for overcoming death may possess a great deal of genuine social value (as a bonus), or they may take foolish and trivial forms. In either case, strivings for personal or social immortality must certainly be construed as responses to the prospect of death.

The interested reader will have no difficulty in finding reading matter on the belief in immortality. Apart from the classic anthropological contributions of Frazer (173), one might also recommend the philosophical works of Hocking (174), Lamont (175), and Ducasse (176). Fascinating as this topic may be, we will not linger here.

We have had opportunity to observe personally two special cases of overcoming. Let us first sample one pattern of response that was found in an experiment conducted by one of the present writers (R.K.).

An experimental interview probed the subject's beliefs and values. What was the best possible life a person could live? The worst possible life? What would he do if he were given an extra year of life? If he had only one year of life remaining to him? If he could have access to a magic time machine, how much time, if any, would he care to add to his life? How would he use this time? Does he believe in God? What kind of God? What happens to a person when his physical existence terminates?

These questions were not rattled off in hasty succession. The subject was given all the time he required to search and express his thoughts and feelings. The interviewer probed until it was felt that he had hit rock bottom. Eventually, both subject and interviewer would reach the conclusion that his beliefs and values had been expressed as fully as possible under these circumstances. This did not terminate the session, rather it provided the occasion for an experimental intervention. (Each session lasted for most of a morning or afternoon.)

At this point in the proceedings, the subject would be asked to accept the "news" that his belief about death and

the afterlife had been mistaken. We now had it on excellent and irrefutable evidence that the actual situation was contrary to his previous beliefs. Thus, the believer in a life after death was asked to accept (temporarily) the proposition that the individual does not survive death in any form. And the nonbeliever was asked to accept the proposition that the individual does survive death in some (unspecified) form. Most subjects were able to accept the counter-assumption, although with varying degrees of protest or ease.

Next, the subjects were asked to judge how they would accommodate themselves to this revision in a basic belief. How much difference would it make to them? In what ways? After a general exploration, we would return to the previous questions to determine if new answers would now be required. This challenge proved to be instructive to both the subjects and the investigator. Following four or five hours of intensive discussion, respondents often remarked that they now knew their own minds on this subject for the first time, or that they had been startled to observe their own reactions and now realized that they had a lot more thinking to do.

The type of reaction that is most germane here was encountered in a full-blown form in three cases, and more subtly in several others. A portion of the interaction with the first person who showed this pattern will be described here. The first half (pre-experimental part) of the interview revealed this young man to be a devout Catholic who had firm opinions on all topics that were raised. In essence, he regarded the good life as commitment to the welfare of others. Even more centrally, it was crucial that, as a human and as a Christian, one faithfully perform his responsibilities to his God and his church. A twisted, ambition-ridden existence would be the worst possible life. It would be spiritual folly to seek personal wealth and power at the expense of others. This young man would have nothing to do with the magic time machine. God had placed everyone here for a purpose, and would claim every individual at the proper time. Consistent with all of the foregoing, he believed in an afterlife. Furthermore, he regarded this belief as basic to the way in which he conducted his life.

He was momentarily stunned by the denial of afterlife. However, he quickly recovered and said there was no harm in entertaining an idea that was so obviously absurd. For the first few minutes he chatted amiably about possible reactions to this "news bulletin." Yes, he supposed that some people would "get shook up" about it. And others, lots of others, would lose whatever scruples they had and deliver themselves over to vices and excesses. He himself would not alter his behavior. It is true that he would *feel* somewhat disappointed. He had been counting on the afterlife, it was something to look forward to. But his moral tendencies and life pattern were so firmly entrenched that they would remain in effect.

However, he began to falter when we returned to the magic time machine situation. "I suppose it wouldn't hurt to have a little extra time, would it? Could I get another ten years of life from that machine of yours?. . . Good. Well, I'd get some more education and get a better paying job . . . live more comfortably."

He brightened perceptibly at this point. "Could you make that 20, 25 years? Then I could get some money together. Start a business and make something of it. Make a lot of money. . . . Say, make that a hundred years! Boy! I could be a rich man. Get into politics. Really have some power. You know. . . ."

With glowing eyes and growing animation he continued his rhapsody. Soon he was demanding 1000, no, make that 10,000 years. He would be President—no, he would rule the universe. And, man, *how* he would rule this universe. He would have absolute power over life and death. Better believe that he would get everything he wanted, and what he wanted was. . . everything.

One could almost hear something breaking when he overcame his last scruple and demanded, "all the time, all the time you've got in the machine. I'm gonna live forever. Everybody's gonna have to come crawling to me."

Then he stopped. There was a sudden awareness. In a faint, sheepish voice he remarked, "Say, I guess that'd make *me* God, wouldn't it?" He slumped back in his chair.

This young man had filled the God-vacuum with himself, inflating his ego boundaries until he reached the proportions of the vanished deity. But the transformation was even more radical than this—he had turned himself into a Devil-God, a being whose mode of existence was the very shadow, the very antithesis of the good person living the good life according to his own previous approach.

In this miniaturized life crisis situation, the subject was confronted with a vision of death that previously had been obscured from his view by faith in an afterlife. At first there was some agitation (anxiety? fear?). A sense of disappointment followed (sorrow?). But his more sustained and elaborated response was a coping effort to overcome the new guise in which death faced him. It did not take very long for this new response to assert itself. He was able to develop this strategy from resources already at hand. Initially the experimenter was impressed most by the radical nature of the transformation— overcoming death by turning his value structure inside out at a moment's notice. In retrospect, we are also impressed by the (at least temporary) effect this experience had upon the subject. He now recognized that he had been only partially aware of his own orientation toward life and death. He departed from the lengthy interview with the thought in mind that his "real" orientation was neither the one he brought with him into the room, nor the surprising Devil-God that made its appearance during the session. His total orientation toward death would involve both facets of his personality in a new integration—providing that he could achieve such an integration.

One experimental case history proves little if anything. But it was instructive to see this small drama unfold before one's eyes. How many other processes, besides the one reported here, are available to the individual who seeks to cope with the prospect of annihilation by somehow overcoming death? Does it make sense to speak of more or less "healthy" or "effective" overcoming techniques? Questions of this nature await the investigator who is bold enough to try to overcome the technical problems in this field.

The other example to be mentioned here concerns group or class behavior. Recently one of the present writers was discussing dying and death with a small group of ministers. Several people were concerned with the problem of attempting to bolster a dying person's faith in the afterlife when the minister is no longer quite so sure himself. Within this context, a black minister declared that "his people" had been changing in this respect, and changing fast. Through years of oppression, black men and women in the United States often had centered their hopes around the hereafter. Life on earth? One thought of misery, humiliation, and scraping by. But *through* death one could overcome the sorrows and tribulations of life. Things would be much better in the next life (they could hardly be much worse). Faith in a joyous life after death thus was an important sustaining force during one's troubled sojourn here.

Today, however, death and the afterlife are less salient as life goals. The black American wants his good life *now*. He is not willing to remain in subjugation during his life on earth in order to pass through the portals of death into eternal bliss. Presumably, death is losing its power to help the black man overcome his disappointments in life. Death gradually may become the stimulus for dread and despair that it seems to be for many Americans who comprise "The Establishment." Heightened expectations for life may thus deprive black men and women of death as a possible "escape hatch." Other strategies will have to be developed if death (instead of life) is to be overcome.

Participating

"If you can't beat 'em—join 'em." This is a familiar strategy in politics and other realms. It also has a place in our relationship to death. Let us first reflect briefly on some of the conditions that may prompt us to overcome (or seek to overcome) death. This may help to clarify the participatory urge.

We suggest that the following general circumstances increase the probability of an *overcoming* response to death:

1. Death is conceptualized as an external contingency.
2. The context of the anticipated death carries overtones of failure, defeat, or humiliation.
3. The individual has a highly developed need for achievement and independence.
4. There is a technological (or magical) prospect for supporting one's objectives.
5. Cultural or group values require an assertion of power against the devastating or malicious forces of the environment.

By contrast, the individual is more probable to seek a *participatory* relationship to death when:

1. Death is conceptualized as possessing an internal locus.
2. The context of the anticipated death carries overtones of honor, reunion, or fulfillment.
3. The individual has a highly devel-

oped sensitivity for cooperative behavior, sharing, affiliation.

4. Techno-magical props against death are not conspicuous; moreover, there are positively-valued social channels available through which the dying person can express himself and distribute meaningful symbols or tokens.

5. The culture feels itself to be in a natural and intimate relationship with its environment (as, for example, in a rural area with low population mobility—grandfather was born here, and my grandchildren will be buried in the same churchyard where their ancestors rest).

These theoretical propositions are stated here for the first time. We hope their implications are sufficiently evident that the omission of a detailed exposition will not be too troublesome. For sake of brevity, we have selected only a few illustrative points.

It has been suggested that both individual and social factors are relevant to the choice of death response. The present cultural milieu in the United States seems to favor overcoming instead of participatory strategies. By and large, we tend to see death as an external menace that is eager to bring us down and strip us of our achievements. Yet there are instances in which it appears that the person has selected a participatory mode. From scattered observations it seems to us that women and elders of both sexes are more likely to enter as a partner in the death process, as compared with men from early to middle adulthood. There is also the impression that people whose life style has remained within a minority group ethnic pattern are somewhat more likely to be participatory than in the homogenized American (with possible exception for "Anglo" patterns).

Women and elders may find it more natural to think of death in terms of reunion with departed loved ones. This sentiment does not necessarily have to be accompanied by an explicit faith in life after death (at least, in our observations). There is just the general feeling that one is moving toward the completion of a circle. Dying is not to be regarded exclusively as an unparalleled event in one's personal biography (as the "overcomers" are likely to feel). Rather, dying is something that many others have done before us. One is treading a well-beaten path "to the peopled grave" (177).

Elderly adults often seem to have fewer illusions about the locus of death. They can intuit the eventual approach of death throughout their bodies—has not death's "advance man," aging, already entrenched himself? We have known geriatric patients who speak of death as a familiar presence, a sort of invisible companion. If one is already an involuntary participant in the death process, then it is not such a big step to acquiesce more openly. Death and the old man may become one. This is not the same quality as a sorrowful identification with death, or a dread of phenomenological death. It is, rather, a partnership. The individual may work toward the achievement of his death by spurning measures that might extend his life. He will gradually reduce his caloric intake, dump the medication, turn down the elective surgery, etc.

In other instances, the individual is not so much rushing his death as he is *treasuring* it. A 93-year-old man beamed affirmatively when one of the writers commented, "I think you *like* talking about your death because. . . well, your death is something you *have*." "It's mine," the elder rejoined. "Don't belong to nobody else." (What is the effect, then, of our usual gambit of evading or denying the reality of impending death for the elderly-and-ill? Does this not reject a vital aspect of the person who has entered into a participatory relationship with his own demise? Love me, love my death.)

Families who cling to ethnic traditions may encourage a participatory orientation toward death by their reliance upon patterns of personal interaction rather than institutionalized procedures. In American life we do not have anything as dramatic as the classic Indian tradition of the widow hurling herself upon her husband's funeral pyre. But we do still come across occasional examples of the dying person taking on a special status within the family. He has his possessions and his blessings to distribute. Furthermore, it may not be going too far to suggest that he has been given the symbolic mantle of representing all those family members who have died before him. He gives and receives not only as himself, but also in his unique role as a sort of liaison man between the world of the living and the world of the dead.

The "wish for death" can be regarded as one form of participation. A simple explanation could be advanced on the basis of pleasure-pain balance. Daily life has come to hold more distress than gratification. The future also looks bleak from this standpoint. If there is no pleasure left in life, then why not embrace death? One is beyond fear, sorrow, or the effort to overcome. Death is the absence of stimulation—a relief. (In its most elementary form, this explanation implies that all persons would long for death when the pleasure-pain balance is upset sufficiently. This may or may not be true factually.)

There is a more complex line of explanation that also should be voiced. Perhaps under some circumstances death is regarded as something more positive than the absence of negative stimulation. Perhaps there is a pleasurable—even erotic—aura hovering around finitude. In psychoanalytic terms, death may be libidinized. Some research evidence is available to the effect that erotic thoughts and feelings can be associated with death (178). Among theoretical essays on this topic we have found Slater's "Prolegomena to a psychoanalytic theory of aging and death" to be of particular value (179). From his sociological perspective, Slater observes:

A death almost always activates collective behav-

ior of some kind or another—a drawing together, a social integration—as well as some sort of loving behavior toward the corpse. In most societies the corpse is in some fashion nurtured like an infant: it is bathed, dressed, decorated, garlanded; sometimes held, rocked in the arms, kissed (180).

In this passage, Slater was referring to social participation in death. But the individual's role is also emphasized. He reminds us that when we bump our knee against a chair there is "an immediate reflexive response" to rub the injured part (he says nothing about the reflexive basis for the verbal commentary with which we may accompany the painful bump). And if we cut our hand there is a natural tendency to put it to our mouth and suck the wound—although in our society the child often is sternly admonished not to engage in this autoerotic self-doctoring.

In a purely physiological sense this is not necessarily functional behavior, and doctors must often interdict such instinctive reactions, particularly with children, lest they exacerbate the injury. It may even increase the pain, as when a man rubs a fracture; or create a new one, as when a tongue is rubbed raw on a broken tooth. What, then is the basis of this response? Why does an animal lick its wounds? (181).

Slater's answer involves the concept of a "primitive caress." We attempt to combat the threat to bodily integrity by rushing libidinal reinforcements to the scene. Affection and sensory gratification help to seduce the injured part back to health, or the whole organism back to life. "As we know from the studies of Spitz, this seduction is vital for human existence: the child must be eroticized in order to live, just as the wound must be eroticized in order to heal" (182).

We cannot pursue Slater's thesis in more detail here, nor begin to do justice to the many psychoanalytic writers, including Freud, who have commented upon possible love-death dynamics. It may be enough to propose that we all have a tendency to participate in our own death through the withdrawal of libido from the external world to the home base, i.e., comforting ourselves with a deep self-interest. Illness, dying, and death may thus be accompanied by a warming current of deep, primitive affect. There is at least a diffuse erotic quality to this affect. In some instances, the eroticism may be more definite and salient. A woman whose own life has been unrewarding sexually may have developed an unconscious predisposition to perceive Death as her mysterious, dark lover (183). Pleasurable anticipations may be part of her total response to the prospect of death—so much a part that she may even reach forward to embrace Death instead of clinging to the sterile life she has known.

At this point it seems appropriate to add one further hypothesis regarding the participatory orientation toward death: *The closer to death one comes, the more likely it is that a participatory response becomes evident, and, ultimately, dominant.* One cannot overlook the total situation—the specific mode of dying, the environmental context, the life circumstances surrounding exitus for the individual. Yet it may be that a new psychobiological orientation takes over at a certain point. The struggle is over. In a sense, one is ready to give birth to death—and even the birth/death pangs can be tolerated because they are part of a meaningful and necessary act.

Other Responses

Fearing, sorrowing, overcoming, and participating have been selected as four of the most important patterns of response by which man attempts to relate himself to death. The list-makers among us should not have much difficulty in adding other responses. We do not see any point in compiling a catalog here. It is probable that a comprehensive catalog would be virtually identical with a description of our species' entire range of attitudes and behaviors. Select any handful of "defense mechanisms" from the traditional catalog—could not all or most of these maneuvers be carried out as a means of relating one's self to death? Discover or invent new psychological strategies for solving, transforming, or avoiding problems and you are also likely to have found a new way of dealing with death.

Let us not emphasize a fixed repertoire of responses that are aimed at death and only at death. It is more realistic for the student of human behavior and experience to learn how to trace the development of death orientations in the individual case, how to read the shifting patterns, and how to discriminate between death as a central or peripheral concern in a particular behavior pattern.

Our response to the stimulus of death has been considered in some detail, although far from exhaustively. Emphasis has been upon the individual's orientation. Only secondary attention has been given to cultural and environmental factors. In later chapters (especially 8 and 9) we reverse this emphasis and give precedence to society's patterns of response to death.

Some tentative conclusions, hypotheses, and suggestions have been offered throughout the course of this chapter and will not be repeated here. Glittering generalizations would be premature. There is just too much that we do not know, at least in that sense of the term "knowledge" that implies strong and clear research evidence. Some of us may "know" a good deal more than what can be demonstrated on the basis of "hard data." However, it remains for more systematic and sophisticated research to help us distinguish between the real and the wax fruits of clinical intuition.

Many of the questions and hypotheses mentioned in the first section of this chapter were scarcely touched upon in our exploration of the available research. How does aversion (and other responses) to death develop? What stages does it pass through? What are the critical factors which influence its scope, particularity, and intensity? How does the development of death responses interweave with other aspects of personality growth? We have picked up a few suggestive findings along the way, but, by and large, we are still dependent upon untested clinical or philosophical formulations. It is doubtful that we are much closer to understanding how much of what kind of death orientation is "normal" or "pathological" within a given situational context. Perhaps this is a topic that will not yield much until we are more willing to examine the implicit value dimensions in what has been formulated, too readily, as an exclusively psychiatric or psychodynamic problem. From what standpoint can we say that one orientation toward death—fearing, sorrowing, overcoming, participating—is "better" than another? Our own assumptions about the meaning of human life must be examined, as well as the death attitudes and attitude-correlates of our subjects.

"Deathly fear" was proposed as a supplementary and alternative approach to the conceptualization of aversive responses toward death. It is understandable in this instance why we do not yet have any relevant research. But it is more difficult to understand why other topics have received so little empirical or theoretical attention. Under what conditions does a strong death fear enhance our chances of survival, and under what conditions does it have the opposite effect? What kinds of people are most adept at "reading" the death orientations of others? How could such a skill be fostered? How amenable is the individual's death orientation to modification—and what procedures are most likely to be effective? What other changes ensue if one's pattern of response toward death is changed? These are just a few of the questions that have come in for little or no research.

Theories? Every approach to human behavior and experience has implications for our relationship to death. For the most part, these implications have not been brought together in the form of concise theoretical statements. In this chapter we introduced a few general and simple elements from learning theory. Dedicated learning theorists could go much farther in offering a broad framework, a set of terms and concepts, and a number of directional hypotheses—if they cared to do so. The richest source of hypotheses at present seems to be within the psychoanalytic realm. A variety of psychoanalytic theories are streaked with death hypotheses. It would still require much effort and acumen to formulate one or more psychoanalytic theories of response to death that could meet with rigorous criteria for theoretical systems. Developmental conceptions of death overlap somewhat with the psychoanalytic, but they also have the potential for providing a distinctive framework. Some developmental considerations have been incorporated in both this chapter and the preceding one. The challenge of formulating an explicit and encompassing developmental theory of death response, however, has not yet been attempted. It seems to us that developmental-field theory would be the most promising approach, as it gives more than the usual amount of emphasis to environmental-situational processes without neglecting the terms of the organism per se (184,185).

Up to this point, we have been concentrating upon death as conceived by and responded to by that notoriously subjective organism—man. Death is "that which we respond to by trembling, sorrowing, etc." Yet we are also accustomed to believing that death is "real" and "objective." This traditional view (for our society) is honored in the following chapter by a brief inquiry into the concept of physical death.

REFERENCES

1. Choron, J. *Modern man and mortality*. New York: Macmillan, 1964.
2. Anthony, S. *The child's discovery of death*. New York: Harcourt, Brace, & World, 1940.
3. Deutsch, F. Euthanasia: A clinical study. *Psychiatric Quarterly*, 1936, *5*, 347-368.
4. Shneidman, E. S. On the deromanticization of death. University of California at Los Angeles, unpublished manuscript.
5. James, W. *Principles of psychology*. Boston: Holt, 1896.
6. Chayefsky, P. *The latent heterosexual*. New York: Bantam Books, 1967. P. 105.
7. *Ibid.*, p. 114.
8. Choron, *op. cit.*, p. 71.
9. *Ibid.*, p. 71.
10. *Ibid.*, pp. 71-72.
11. Kastenbaum, R. On the structure and function of time perspective. *Journal of Psychological Research* (India), 1964, *8*, 1-11.
12. Lifton, R. J. Psychological effects of the atomic bomb in Hiroshima: The theme of death. In R. Fulton (Ed.), *Death and identity*. New York: Wiley, 1965. P. 29.
13. Nagy, M. The child's view of death. In H. Feifel (Ed.), *The meaning of death*. New York: McGraw-Hill, 1959. Pp. 79-98.
14. Feifel, H. Symposium comments, cited by R. Kastenbaum, Death as a research problem in social gerontology: An overview. *Gerontologist*, 1966, *7*, 67-69.
15. Kozol, J. *Death at an early age*. New York: Bantam Books, 1967.
16. Kastenbaum, R. As the clock runs out. *Mental Hygiene*, 1966, *50*, 332-336.
17. May, R. *The meaning of anxiety*. New York: Ronald Press, 1950.
18. *Ibid.*
19. Freud, S. *New introductory lectures on psychoanalysis*. New York: W. W. Norton, (1933) 1964.
20. *Ibid.*, p. 81.
21. May, *op. cit.*, p. 46 ff.
22. Freud, S. *The problem of anxiety*. New York: W. W. Norton, 1936.
23. Freud, 1964, *op. cit.*, p. 87.
24. Freud, S. Thoughts for the times on war and death. In *Collected Papers*. Vol. 4. New York: Basic Books, 1959. Pp. 288-317.
25. Aring, C. D. Intimations of mortality. *Annals of Internal Medicine*, 1968, *69*, 137-151.
26. Weisman, A. D., & Hackett, T. P. Predilection to death. *Psychosomatic Medicine*, 1961, *23*, 232-256.
27. Kastenbaum, R. Premonitions of death and their implications for psychological intervention. *Bull. Division 20* (American Psychological Association), 1969, *16*, 30-32.
28. Riley, J. Data cited in M. W. Riley & A. Foner (Eds.), *Aging and society*. Vol. 1. New York: Russell Sage Foundation. P. 333 ff.
29. Zinker, J. *Rosa Lee*. Plainsville, Ohio: Lake Erie College Studies. Vol. 6, 1966.
30. Shneidman, E. S. Suicide, sleep and death: Some possible interrelations among cessation, interruption, and continuation phenomena. *Journal of Consulting Psychology*, 1964, *28*, 95-106.
31. Weisman, A. D., & Kastenbaum, R. *The psychological autopsy: A study of the terminal phase of life*. New York: Behavioral publications, monograph # 4 of *Community Mental Health Journal*, 1968.
32. Hendin, H. Black suicide. *Archives of General Psychiatry*, 1969, *21*, 407-427.
33. Bluestone, H., & McGahee, C. L. Reaction to extreme stress: Impending death by execution. *American Journal of Psychiatry*, 1962, *119*, 393-396.
34. Ekman, P., Cohen, L., Moos, R., Raine, W., Schlesinger, M., & Stone, G. Divergent reactions to the threat of war. *Science*, 1963, *139*, 88-94.
35. Lester, D. The fear of death of those who have nightmares. *Journal of Psychology*, 1968, *69*, 245-247.
36. Feldman, M. J. & Hersen, M. Attitudes toward death in nightmare subjects. *Journal of Abnormal Psychology*, 1967, *72*, 421-425.
37. Opler, M. E., & Bittle, W. E. The death practices and eschatology of the Kiowa Apache. *Southwestern Journal of Anthropology*, 1961, *17*, 383-394.
38. Lieberman, M. Psychological correlates of impending death: Some preliminary observations. *Journal of Gerontology*, 1965, *20*, 181-190.
39. Kastenbaum, R. The mental life of dying geriatric patients. *Gerontologist*, 1967, *7*, 97-100.
40. Kalish, R. A. An approach to the study of death attitudes. *American Behavioral Science*, 1963, *6*, 68-70.
41. Lester, D. Experimental and correlational studies of the fear of death. *Psychological Bulletin*, 1967, 27-36.
42. Glaser, B. G., & Strauss, A. L. *Awareness of dying*. Chicago: Aldine, 1966.
43. *Ibid.*, p. 10.
44. *Ibid.*, p. 247.
45. Kalish, R. A. Social distance and the dying. *Community Mental Health Journal*, 1966, *2*, 152-155.

46. Kastenbaum, R. Multiple perspectives on a geriatric "Death Valley." *Community Mental Health Journal*, 1967, *3*, 21-29.
47. Hunter, R. C. A. On the experience of nearly dying. *American Journal of Psychiatry*, 1967, *124*, 122-126.
48. *Ibid.*, p. 124.
49. *Ibid.*, p. 126.
50. Pfister, O. Shockdenken und schockphantasien bei hochster todesgefahr. *Zeitschrift fuer Psychoanalytische Padagogik*, 1930, *16*, 430-455.
51. Hunter, *op. cit.*, p. 126.
52. Weisman & Kastenbaum, *op. cit.*
53. Kubler-Ross, E. *On death and dying.* New York: Macmillan, 1969.
54. Kalish, R. A. Experiences of persons reprieved from death. In A. H. Kutscher (Ed.), *Death and bereavement.* Springfield, Ill.: Charles C Thomas, 1969. Pp. 84-98.
55. *Ibid.*, p. 91.
56. *Ibid.*, p. 93.
57. Hinton, J. The physical and mental distress of the dying. *Quarterly Journal of Medicine*, 1963, *32*, 1-21.
58. *Ibid.*, p. 17.
59. Chandler, K. A. Three processes of dying and their behavioral effects. *Journal of Consulting Psychology*, 1965, *29*, 296-301.
60. Cappon, D. The dying. *Psychiatric Quarterly*, 1959, *33*, 466-489.
61. *Ibid.*, p. 480.
62. Beigler, J. S. Anxiety as an aid in the prognostication of impending death. *Archives of Neurology and Psychiatry*, 1957, *77*, 171-177.
63. *Ibid.*, p. 174.
64. *Ibid.*, p. 175.
65. *Ibid.*
66. *Ibid.*, p. 177.
67. Switzer, D. K. *The dynamics of grief.* Nashville, Tenn.: Abingdon, 1970.
68. Janis, I. L. *Psychological stress: Psychoanalytic and behavioral studies of surgical patients.* New York: Wiley, 1958.
69. Weisman & Hackett, *op. cit.*
70. *Ibid.*, p. 254.
71. Lieberman, et al, *op. cit.*
72. Kastenbaum, R. & Weisman, A. D. The psychological autopsy method in gerontology. In D. P. Kent, R. Kastenbaum, & S. Sherwood (Eds.), *Research, planning, and action for the elderly.* New York: Behavioral Publications, in press.
73. Weisman & Kastenbaum, *op. cit.*, p. 24.
74. *Ibid.*
75. *Ibid.*
76. Hamovitch, M. B. *The parent and the fatally ill child.* Los Angeles: Del Mar Pub. Co., 1964.
77. Natterson, J. M., & Knudson, A. G. Observa-
tions concerning fear of death in fatally ill children and their mothers. *Psychosomatic Medicine*, 1960, *22*, 456-466.
78. *Ibid.*, p. 459.
79. *Ibid.*, p. 463.
80. *Ibid.*, p. 465.
81. *Ibid.*
82. Morrissey, J. R. A note on interviews with children facing imminent death. *Social Casework*, 1963, *44*, 343-345.
83. *Ibid.*, p. 345.
84. Bluestone and McGahee, *op. cit.*
85. *Ibid.*, p. 394.
86. *Ibid.*
87. *Ibid.*, p. 395.
88. *Ibid.*
89. Koenig, R. R. Fatal Illness: A summary of social service needs. *Social Work*, 1968, *13*, 85-90.
90. *Ibid.*, p. 88.
91. *Ibid.*, p. 87.
92. *Ibid.*
93. *Ibid.*, p. 89.
94. *Ibid.*
95. Munnichs, J. M. A. *Old age and finitude.* Basel, Switzerland and New York: Karger, 1966.
96. *Ibid.*, p. 124.
97. *Ibid.*, p. 125.
98. Weisman & Kastenbaum, *op. cit.*
99. Swenson, W. Attitudes toward death in an aged population. *Journal of Gerontology*, 1961, *16*, 49-53.
100. Jeffers, F. C., Nichols, C. R., & Eisdorfer, C. Attitudes of older persons toward death: A preliminary study. *Journal of Gerontology*, 1961, *16*, 53-55.
101. *Ibid.*, p. 55.
102. Shrut, S. D. Attitudes toward old age and death. *Mental Hygiene*, 1958, *42*, 259-266.
103. *Ibid.*, p. 265.
104. Christ, A. E. Attitudes toward death among a group of acute geriatric psychiatric patients. *Journal of Gerontology*, 1961, *16*, 56-59.
105. Kastenbaum, R. Death as a research problem in social gerontology: An overview. *Gerontologist*, 1966, *7*, 67-69.
106. Riley, *op. cit.*, p. 332.
107. Cautela, J. R., & Kastenbaum, R. Fears and reinforcers of young and old adults. Presented at annual meeting, Gerontological Society, October, 1967.
108. Kogan, N., & Shelton, F. C. Beliefs about 'old people': A comparative study of older and younger samples. *Journal of Genetic Psychology*, 1962, *100*, 93-111.
109. Kogan, N. & Wallach, M. A. Age changes in values and attitudes. *Journal of Gerontology*, 1961, *16*, 272-280.
110. Rothstein, S. H. *Aging awareness and per-*

sonalization of death in the young and middle adult years. University of Chicago: Ph.D. dissertation, 1967.

111. *Ibid.,* p. 12.

112. *Ibid.,* p. 23.

113. Neugarten, B., Wood, V., Kraines, R. J., & Loomis, B. Women's attitudes toward the menopause. *Vita humana,* 1963, *6,* 140-151.

114. *Ibid.,* p. 150.

115. Means, M. H. Fears of one thousand college women. *Journal of Abnormal and Social Psychology,* 1936, *31,* 291-311.

116. Middleton, W. C. Some reactions towards death among college students. *Journal of Abnormal and Social Psychology,* 1936, *31,* 165-173.

117. Lester, 1967, *op. cit.*

118. Stacey, C., & Reichen, M. Attitudes toward death and future life among normal and subnormal adolescent girls. *Exceptional Children,* 1954, *20,* 259-262.

119. Maurer, A. Adolescent attitudes toward death. *Journal of Genetic Psychology,* 1964, *105,* 79-90.

120. *Ibid.,* p. 89.

121. *Ibid.*

122. Alexander, I., & Adlerstein, A. Death and religion. In H. Feifel (Ed.), *The meaning of death.* New York: McGraw-Hill, 1959. Pp. 271-283.

123. Osgood, C. E., Suci, G. J., & Tannenbaum, P. H. *The measurement of meaning.* Urbana, Ill.: University of Illinois Press, 1957.

124. Alexander and Adlerstein, 1959, *op. cit.,* p. 278.

125. *Ibid.,* p. 280.

126. Schilder, P., & Wechsler, D. The attitudes of children towards death. *Journal of Genetic Psychology,* 1934, *45,* 406-451.

127. Bromberg, W., & Schilder, P. The attitude of psychoneurotics towards death. *Psychoanalytic Review,* 1936, *23,* 1-25.

128. Bromberg, W., & Schilder, P. A comparative study of the attitudes and mental reactions toward death and dying. *Psychoanalytic Review,* 1933, *20,* 173-185.

129. *Ibid.,* p. 25.

130. Anthony, *op. cit.*

131. Bromberg and Schilder, 1936, *op. cit.,* p. 4.

132. *Ibid.,* pp. 6-7.

133. Feifel, H. Attitudes toward death in some normal and mentally ill populations. In H. Feifel (Ed.), *The meaning of death.* New York: McGraw-Hill, 1959. Pp. 114-132.

134. Feifel, H. & Heller, J. Normalcy, illness, and death. *Proceedings of Third World Congress of Psychiatry,* 1961, Vol. 2. Pp. 1252-1256.

135. Haider, I. Attitudes toward death of psychiatric patients. *International Journal of Neuropsychiatry,* 1967, *3,* 10-14.

136. Searles, H. E. Schizophrenia and the inevitability of death. *Psychiatric Quarterly,* 1961, *35,* 632-655.

137. *Ibid.,* pp. 632.

138. *Ibid.,* pp. 636.

139. *Ibid.*

140. *Ibid.,* p. 640.

141. Dorsey, J. *Illness or allness.* Detroit: Wayne State University Press, 1965.

142. Feldman and Hersen, *op. cit.*

143. *Ibid.,* p. 425.

144. Lester, D. The fear of death of those who have nightmares. *op. cit.*

145. Crown, B., O'Donovan, D., & Thompson, T. G. Attitudes toward attitudes toward death. *Psychological Reports,* 1967, *20,* 1181-1182.

146. Diggory, J. C., & Rothman, D. Z. Values destroyed by death. *Journal of Abnormal and Social Psychology,* 1961, *63,* 205-210.

147. *Ibid.*

148. *Ibid.,* p. 210.

149. Shneidman, E. S. & Farberow, N. L. *Clues to suicide.* New York: McGraw-Hill (paperback), 1957. Pp. 3-11; 197-216.

150. Rhudick, P. J., & Dibner, A. S. Age, personality and health correlates of death concerns in normal aged individuals. *Journal of Gerontology,* 1961, *16,* 44-49.

151. Paris, J., & Goodstein L. D. Responses to death and sex stimulus materials as a function of repression-sensitization. *Psychological Reports,* 1966, 1283-1291.

152. *Ibid.,* P. 1284.

153. McClelland, D. C. The harlequin complex. In R. White (Ed.), *The study of lives.* New York: Prentice-Hall, 1963. Pp. 95-119.

154. Alexander, I., Colley, R. S., & Adlerstein, A. M. Is death a matter of indifference? *Journal of Psychology,* 1957, *43,* 277-283.

155. Thorndike, E. C. & Lorge, I. *Teacher's word book of 30,000 words.* New York: Teacher's College, Columbia University, 1944.

156. Alexander, et al, *op. cit.,* p. 281.

157. Golding, S. I., Atwood, G. E., & Goodman, R. A. Anxiety and two cognitive forms of resistance to the idea of death. *Psychological Reports,* 1966, *18,* 359-364.

158. *Ibid.,* p. 363.

159. Sarnoff, I., & Corwin, S. M. Castration anxiety and the fear of death. *Journal of Personality and Social Psychology,* 1959, *27,* 374-385.

160. Golding, et al, *op. cit.,* p. 363.

161. Gottschalk, L. A., Winget, C. N., & Gleser, G. C. *Manual of instructions for using the Gottschalk-Gleser Content Analysis Scales: Anxiety, Hostility, and Social Alienation—Personal Disorganization.* Berkeley & Los

Angeles: University of California Press, 1969. Pp. 30-31.

162. *Ibid.*

163. Lester, *op. cit.*, 1967.

164. Hinton, *op. cit.*

165. Brown, F. Depression and childhood bereavement. *Journal of Mental Science,* 1961, *107,* 754-777.

166. Freud, S. Mourning and melancholia. *Complete psychological works of Sigmund Freud.* London: Hogarth, 1957. Vol. 14, pp. 237-259.

167. Lindemann, E. Symptomatology and management of acute grief. *American Journal of Psychiatry,* 1944, *101,* 141-148.

168. Eliot, T. D. The bereaved family. *Annals of the American Academy of Political and Social Sciences,* 1932, *160,* 184-190.

169. Jackson, E. N. *Understanding grief: Its roots, dynamics, and treatment.* New York: Abingdon-Cokesbury Press, 1957.

170. Becker, H. The sorrow of bereavement. *Journal of Abnormal and Social Psychology,* 1933, *27,* 391-410.

171. May, *op. cit.*

172. Henry, J. *Culture against man.* New York: Vintage Books, 1963. P. 405.

173. Frazer, J. G. *The fear of the dead in primitive religion.* London: Macmillan (3 volumes), 1933.

174. Hocking, W. E. *The meaning of immortality in human experience.* New York: Harper & Bros., 1957.

175. Lamont, C. *The illusion of immortality.* New York: Philosophical Library, 1950.

176. Ducasse, C. J. *The belief in a life after death.* Springfield, Ill.: Charles C Thomas, 1961.

177. Santayana, G. With you a part of me. In Louis Untermeyer (Ed.). *A treasury of great poems.* New York: Simon and Schuster, 1942. P. 1034.

178. Paris and Goodstein, *op. cit.*

179. Slater, P. E. Prolegomena to a psychoanalytic theory of aging and death. In R. Kastenbaum (Ed.), *New thoughts on old age.* New York: Springer, 1964. Pp. 19-40.

180. *Ibid.,* pp. 31-32.

181. *Ibid.,* p. 29.

182. *Ibid.,* p. 30.

183. McClelland, *op. cit.*

184. Kastenbaum, R. Engrossment and perspective in later life. In R. Kastenbaum (Ed.), *Contributions to the psychobiology of aging.* New York: Springer, 1965. Pp. 3-18.

185. Kastenbaum, R., & Kastenbaum, B. K. Hope, survival, and the caring environment. In Edmore Palmore and F. C. Jeffers (Eds.), *Prediction of lifespan.* Lexington, Mass.: Heath, 1971. Pp. 249-272.

4

On the
Logic and Methodologic of Death

A stable reference point would be helpful in understanding our death-related thoughts, feelings, and behaviors. Presumably, such a fixed reference point does exist: death itself. No matter what subjective orientation a person happens to develop, his mortality remains an objective fact. It follows that we should be able to improve our knowledge of the *psychology* of death by relating individual and group behaviors to *physical* reality. Errors, embellishments, and shifting perceptions could be brought into alignment against the simple, immutable criteria of death.

The sophisticated reader, however, will be aware that the task is not as simple as it may appear. The attention given in recent years to organ transplants has renewed interest—and controversy—concerning the precise definition of death. Some readers will also be familiar with efforts aimed at preserving and resuscitating the "dead." Additionally, there are certain lines of research in biology and physics that seem calculated to unsettle fixed beliefs. These developments tend to complicate and perhaps to blur our conceptions of physical death.

One could maintain that essential facts and principles have been altered not at all. Death is what it always has been and will be: the final, inevitable cessation of life. But a more extreme position could be taken. It might be ventured that our conceptions of physical death no longer are viable in their present form. It is not enough to patch things up here and there. A thorough reevaluation is required. This reevaluation might transform our understanding of both life and death or, more accurately, lead to a series of transformations.

One does have the option of ignoring the logical and methodological problems involved in defining death. We prefer to take this topic seriously. At the least, a brief confrontation with "objective death" will provide us with a common framework and with the opportunity to reflect upon personal assumptions that may not have enjoyed an airing recently. Beyond this, it may be that such an exploration will enable us to approach both theoretical and applied problems a little more flexibly.

DEATH AND DURATION

How long does death endure? This is one of the naive questions that will give us an opportunity to consider death from multiple perspectives. From a traditional standpoint one probably would answer by saying: *Death endures endlessly, without limit in time. Death would not be death if it did not last forever.*

Indeed, without the insistence upon the endless duration of death, how would one distinguish this state from other conditions which it may resemble? Death might be merely a disorder.

Death itself has now assumed an aspect and a name less direful and terrific. *Death*, in some of its most alarming forms, has now lost a portion of its terror, and has been hailed by the cheering name of Suspended Animation. We are now assured that the frame may be restored to the full possession of its functions, under the signs of *Death*, as it might be under the signs or symptoms of any other disorder with which the vital energies may be oppressed. This extraordinary fact, so unknown to all former ages, demands a new language to express its operation; and the writer of the present volume has for the first time presented to the attention of the public, researches on the *Disorder* of Death (1).

This assertion does not come from a contemporary enthusiast of artificial hypothermia (cryonic suspension). It was in 1819 that W. Whiter took the position that death may be a *temporary* state. Although he credited himself with being the first proponent of this view, Whiter did make frequent reference to the statements and practices of physicians in ancient times. Oddly, Whiter's work seems to have been totally ignored by the present generation of researchers, advocates, and historians.

It is not essential here to expound and critically evaluate Whiter's dissertation. But it is relevant to distinguish between his conclusions and the material he offers in their support. Whiter describes several instances in which a "dead" person was reanimated either by special attention or by fortunate circumstances. In his opinion, many others could have had their "disorder of death" remedied by appropriate actions. Some of his practical sugges-

tions may sound quaint in our times. Yet one cannot help but be impressed by the range of possible interventions he describes—including the administration of galvanism (electric shock). "Tho' this agent has exhibited the most astonishing effect on Animal Matter ... it has never yet been professedly and scientifically applied to the purpose of Resuscitation in the Human frame" (2).

Whiter challenged his countrymen to persist in resuscitation efforts even, or especially, under those circumstances in which it generally would be assumed that there was nothing more to be done. From a traditional standpoint one might acknowledge Whiter's efforts as a neglected pioneer in the art and science of prolonging life and the snatching of life from the very jaws of death. His basic contention, however, would be dismissed without a hearing. "That man could not have been dead, because he did recover and survive. Were he *really* dead, then dead he would have remained."

But another viewpoint is possible. (We introduce here a logic that is not Whiter's.) Why had the resuscitated drowning victim been considered dead in the first place? He looked dead to somebody, to everybody. According to all observers (including the physician), this man was lifeless at a particular moment in time. Processes regarded as crucial to life had ceased. Isn't this sufficient to rule that he was "really" dead? No? Somebody here insists upon an endurance test? Consider the implications of this requirement.

1. Death criteria become ambiguous. Direct perception, even when it is consensual, is not sufficient. We cannot entirely trust our best judgment. This slips a certain lack of confidence into the definition of death.

2. Absolutely certain determination of death could not be made until it was absolutely certain that there would not be a subsequent observation to the contrary. Anything short of absolute certainty

"robs" death of its peculiar distinction. He looks dead now. He has looked dead for ten minutes. For an hour. All day long. Tomorrow? It is unlikely, but theoretically possible that tomorrow, or the day after, he will give evidence of life. New observations could be made at any time in the foreseeable future.

Under what conditions, then, could we be absolutely certain that no further observations will be made (and, therefore, no likelihood of the present conclusion being overturned?). There will be no further observations if there is nobody left who might be in a position to observe. This condition translates into the disappearance of the entire human race. And that would have to be the *permanent* disappearance of homo sapiens, a condition no easier to verify than the irreversible death of a single individual. Moreover, there is a further complication here, should one care to notice: with the hypothetical disappearance of all possible observers there would be, of course, nobody to observe that the theoretical conditions had been satisfied.

There is another imaginable condition. Death could be certified as permanent (hence, really death) if we had a permanent observer. This might be an observer who survives until "the end of time," or for whom time, as we know it, is irrelevant. Clearly, it is a God-like attribute that is required here. Even this superobserver would have to wait until the last tick of the universal clock before checking in with his final observation (assuming he realizes that time is now up and has, in fact, addressed himself to making this kind of observation). As an alternative, we could imagine an observer who knows "ahead of time" all that will transpire. He knows whether or not this apparent fatality is a "real" death (but will he tell us?).

It should be clear that a big assumption is required if we are to define death as a state that persists throughout time for all time. We need a superobserver, a God to maintain the necessary observational framework. A definition that hinges upon such a speculation or leap of faith cannot be taken very seriously if it is passed off as "tough-minded science" or "inexorable logic." Yet the insistence that death must have a temporal dimension, and the dimension endless, requires the sort of metaphysical assumption that has been described. The assumption of a permanent superobserver may have its merits, but it is difficult to accept as the basis for not-to-be-questioned definitions of life and death.

There is a related implication here. What about the *adequacy* of the observations, whenever they happen to be made? It is tempting to argue that Whiter and his contemporaries were *mistaken* in their judgments. Medical science is more advanced these days. A modern physician is less likely to take the semblance of death for its reality. Empirically, there is something in favor of this argument (although not as much as one might believe—in "the old days" there was sometimes more attention to the hazards of distinguishing between real and apparent death than is the case in today's production-line medical care system). In Chapter 5 we will consider the "dead or alive?" question in more detail from historical and empirical standpoints. Emphasis now is upon logical and methodological aspects.

Two difficulties arise to complicate any second guesses we might care to make. First, there is the implicit invitation to others to second guess our judgments. A more sensitive, more experienced, more knowledgeable observer might challenge both our criteria and our observational skills. Furthermore, a challenge might also come from someone we consider to be less experienced and knowledgeable than ourselves. But he has his own frame of reference, and his own opinion of us. He may see "not-quite-death" where we see death, or vice versa. Most germane, perhaps, is the situation in which one observer has different, additional, more "advanced" methods at his disposal. In this day of rapid medicotechnological advance and hyperspecialization, we are not speaking hypothetically. Adequacy of observation is always subject to dispute. Adequacy of criteria is also subject to dispute, especially these days. It is questionable to insist that we have the perfect or most nearly perfect criteria and, on this basis, to set aside any other observations that might unsettle our beliefs.

The urge to equivocate is the second point. We develop a working definition of death based upon current knowledge and belief. It is the best we can do. This definition is important not only in the individual case, but also as a guideline for systematic theory and research. Logically, we should maintain our definitions and criteria until new evidence prompts us to lay them aside. By remaining committed strongly—but provisionally—to the best available knowledge and procedures, we are able to subject them to constant re-evaluation and, eventually, to whatever modifications are shown to be appropriate. Equivocation betrays us. This person has been declared dead by our usual criteria (except for the untestable assumption of permanence). Later, let us say a short time later, he is found to be living. The steadfast mind would accept both sets of observations: "Dead, then; alive, now." The equivocating mind would scuttle the previous observation, although he probably has nothing better with which to replace it. In fact, through his fickleness, the equivocator undercuts the possibility of improving the existing working definition of death.

Cessation of life/presence of death should be an observable phenomenon at any particular point in time. Human judgment, whether or not assisted by instrumentation, always is exercised at particular points in time. If a decision cannot be made at a specifiable time, then one may doubt whether it truly can be made at all. Perhaps we would befuddle ourselves less if the "alive or dead" decision were based

upon the best available criteria and assessment procedures at a given time. Let there be no half hidden assumptions about the longevity of death.

Question: How long does a creature have to be alive for us to consider it alive? *Answer:* Just long enough for the necessary observations to be made—and that probably means less than a minute. The eventual death of the living creature in no way impugns its former state. How long, then, need a creature be lifeless for us to consider that it is dead? It has to be dead for a moment even if it is going to be dead forever. And if it is dead for a moment, is this not sufficient?

The assumed rigid linkage between death and duration has been called into question here. It was not our intention to develop the argument fully, or to convince the reader. Rather we wished to make explicit some tacit assumptions that often are held about the logic and methodologic of death. Once these assumptions are out in the open, then each of us can decide for himself whether or not they deserve to be maintained indefinitely.

WHO IS DEAD?

In our language it is possible to speak of death without specifying a particular instance, i.e., *sans habeus corpus.* We hear that "death strikes suddenly." It is thus portrayed as a force or agency that is relatively independent of particular individuals who die. And we hear that "death is the ultimate fate of all living creatures." In other words, death is that condition (or non-condition) that begins when life ends—a *common*, not a particularized state.

Liberated from concrete referents, death becomes, in a sense, "bigger than life." ("Life," of course, is another word that is often used in a generalized as well as a specific sense.) This usage invites reification. It becomes tempting to overlook the question: *who* is dead? Perhaps this question never would be raised if we relied entirely upon the word, "death." It seems awkward to inquire, "Who has death?" or, romanticizing, to ask, "Whom does death have?" "Dead" may be the more useful term here. "Death" may roam free, striking now and then, here and there—but somebody has to be dead.

"Who is dead?" is a question that can be asked at more than one level. Consider for a moment organisms other than homo sapiens. Claiborne S. Jones offers the perspective of a zoologist (3). He points out that for many species of life it is difficult to determine how the organism itself is to be defined. If one cannot specify the identity of the organism unambiguously, then how can one be sure who has died? As one of his examples, Jones offers the instance of Plasmodium. This is the protozoan parasite which causes malaria in birds and mammals. The definitional problems encountered here are fairly representative of those found with many other organisms that traverse certain kinds of life cycles.

Plasmodium has a complex life cycle that involves no fewer than eight stages. *"Each of the 'stages' in the life cycle is distinctively different from the others, functionally as well as morphologically, and yet malaria cannot continue to exist without all these separate but interdependent stages"* (4). Jones wonders who or what is dead when Plasmodium is killed at a certain stage in its life cycle. "It seems equally unsatisfactory to conclude that the organism is any one of the stages in its life cycle or that it is the repetitive sequence of all the stages. How can we characterize death in such circumstances, even though we face the undeniable fact of its occurrence?" (5).

We wonder if Plasmodium should be regarded as having eight lives, each of which must be destroyed for "death" to have occurred. Since one cannot kill the "same" Plasmodium eight times—especially at the same time—then, in a sense, perhaps one never slays a Plasmodium no

matter how many infected mosquitoes are swatted or sprayed. At best, one just destroys one-eighth of the organism, nevertheless, this is sufficient to preclude the actualization of its other seven-eighths. Perplexing? No doubt. Absurd? Perhaps. To be dismissed as an idle thought-game? At our own peril. Understanding *who* is dead requires attention to all forms of life, and does not become a simpler problem when we move to the human level.

Let us take another example on the subhuman level, again from Jones. He asks: "Is each honeybee really an individual member of the species, which is to say (very loosely) a population of taxonomically indistinguishable individuals, or is a honeybee a human concept instead of an organism? When a drone—or a worker or a queen—is killed, is it really a honeybee that has died or is it just one dispensable part of the organism (that is, the 'hive' or colony) that has been lost? Despite the beauty of Donne's imagery, if a clod be washed away by the sea, is Europe really the less?" (6).

Here, then, are two forms of challenge to the assumption that it is enough to know that death has occurred. We have been asked to ponder the question of identity-through-time (e.g., the eight-phased Plasmodium), and the question of independent vs group identity (the honeybee). The latter instance should be of special interest to anyone who is imbued with a gestalt psychology approach. There is a fascinating part-whole relationship waiting to be explicated by a good gestalter. We will just muse a little. If each honeybee is a part of the whole, does this mean that it has its own life-identity-destiny, but on a partial basis? Being only a part, perhaps Joe Drone does have his individual death to die, but it should be distinguished from the larger, more complete death that could overtake the whole hive. But then, what actually would constitute death of the larger unit? Assume that some outside force brings about the disruption of the hive as a unit. No single individual component (bee) is destroyed. But the whole has vanished as such. Has a larger death in fact occurred? *Habeus corpus*? Assume again that the hive is intact but that there is a mounting mortality rate among its components. Does the life or death of the hive-organism depend upon the number of surviving components, or upon more abstract structural-functional properties? Perhaps a general systems approach is necessary to analyze such problems. In any event, we see that the mind can turn in many directions when attempting to define the identity of the deceased in certain forms of life—or even when attempting to determine whether "death" has taken place at all. We have also admitted the barest possibility that it might be appropriate to recognize more than one kind of death, depending upon the nature of the organism that has been certified dead.

Up to this point, the discussion has been limited to death within a single species. Is it possible that "who is dead" may require an answer that involves two or more species? Even further out: must we perplex ourselves with the possibility that the "deceased" might turn out to be a complex interdependent network of units whose independence as individuals is more apparent than real? Of course, we still retain the option of backing off from questions of this kind. Ludwig von Bertalanffy, the distinguished scientist and theoretician, is one who has not backed off. Familiarity with general systems theory (7) would greatly facilitate one's appreciation of those observations that are especially pertinent to our topic. We will pick up on just a few of his points here.

Von Bertalnaffy reminds us that symbiosis between two organisms of different species sometimes eventuates in a new organism, e.g., lichens emerging from algae and fungi (8). But the familiar concept of symbiosis merely serves to prepare us for understanding the interdependence of life forms on a much larger scale. Interdependency of life forms, in turn, has impli-

cations for the kind of death that might be said to befall the organisms which are involved.

According to von Bertalnaffy, it is demonstrable that animal-plant communities in certain areas function as total units, not as simple aggregates. The lake or forest region should be regarded as a "population system." Each system has structural properties; the functioning is ruled by definite laws. This position takes us a long way from the usual image of, let us say, a "lone wolf" living and finally dying as a discrete individual. It would be acknowledged, of course, that the wolf exists in an environment, and that the nature of this environment has much to do with the animal's survival. But the wolf nevertheless would be seen as the figure against the background of the environment. For von Bertalnaffy (and now for many others), the wolf would be an inextricable functional unit within a complex system. Every form of life in this environment participates in the common life, or the population system. When the wolf brings down a deer it is unmistakable that a death has occurred. Yet this action has its place in the preservation of the total population system.

Interference by outside forces (e.g., man) could markedly increase or decrease the numbers of a given species. In either case, the balance is upset. It is possible that efforts to *increase* the numbers of a given species might produce disastrous results for the system as a whole. It takes a certain amount of the "right kind" of death for the system to continue. If the system itself falters, then many types of living organism may be doomed to extinction. Conservationists have been trying for years to alert us to many man-induced death threats to specific species or to entire population systems. Areas teeming with life—whether the vast Everglades, or a small local marsh—can lose their life-supporting qualities either by direct or indirect attack. The illegally slaughtered alligator, for example, will burrow no more places for water to accumulate. The other creatures that would have survived on this water reservoir will be real, if indirect casualties of the shot that dispatched the alligator. Draining of wetlands, dumping of refuse, and other such practices have the effect of destroying not only specific living creatures, but the total environment upon which they, and their future generations, depend. (Similar observations have been made about other types of population systems as well as the marshes chosen for illustration here.)

This discussion may appear strangely out of focus to American psychologists. We have a tradition that emphasizes the individual (although there has been considerable movement in the opposite direction in recent years). Therefore, when we think of death it is natural for us to dwell upon individual death. From other standpoints, however, it may be as relevant to consider the death of groups, of species, of life-support systems. An individual can die without endangering the population system. The death may even be regarded as a necessary element within this system. But destruction of the system poses an obvious danger to all the individuals involved. Furthermore, the danger extends beyond the lives of those individual creatures who exist at the moment. The danger encompasses their future generations as well.

We believe that observations such as those of von Bertalaffy imply three different forms of death that might follow as a consequence of disturbed ecological conditions:

1. The "system" itself is dead.
2. Individual organisms within the system are dead.
3. Futurity is dead.

The first proposition requires a few comments. It does not make sense to regard the population system per se as dead unless it can be said to have been alive in the first place. This, in turn, poses

at least two other questions: Can any system be regarded as "alive?" If so, does the population or ecological system qualify? We think a reasonable case can be made for affirmative answers to both questions.

Theoreticians have offered many tightly reasoned arguments for distinguishing among types of systems. These are not necessarily exercises in high-level pedantics. L. Brillouin, for example, is one of those who have wondered: "How is it possible to understand life, when the whole world is ruled by such a law as the second principle of thermodynamics, which points toward death and annihilation?" (9). In his essay on "Life, Thermodyamics, and Cybernetics," Brillouin examines properties of those systems which involve living organisms in comparison with those systems which apply to inert objects. One can agree or disagree with his formulations. The point is that one would be precipitious to dismiss these distinctions simply on temperamental grounds: "I'm not used to thinking of things in this way . . . so they must be mistaken or irrelevant."

But it is one thing to distinguish between life and nonlife systems, and another thing to demonstrate that the former is alive *as a system.* Here comes a "hot grounder" zinging toward the shortstop. He fields the ball cleanly, tosses it to the second baseman whose accurate throw to the first baseman results in a double play. This transaction involved several living components: the fielders and base-runners. The double play thus involved the systematic interaction of organic elements (not to mention the earthly remains of former living elements: the bat, ball, and gloves). But if the double play existed at all it did not exist as exclusive property of any one of the individual components. Skilled behavior on the part of several participants created a superordinate action. Furthermore, the 6-to-4-to-3 doubleplay "retired the side" which is another event on a more-than-individual level, and contributes to determining that superordinate outcome, the final score of "the old ball game." The action is systematic, inseparable from its individual components but not reducible to any of these elements.

Perhaps it does make sense in some circumstances to speak of a system as dead. Even when the individual elements continue to exist, the lack of the requisite contact, balance, and timing may prevent that type of integrated functioning we tend to denote by the term "system." A disrupted and fragmented population system might be classified as "dead" according to objective technical criteria applied by expert observers.

Let us move to a more familiar focus: the individual human. We ignore for a moment the individual's place in superordinate systems. Here he is, a person standing alone with his unique identity. He is his own "superordinate level." His body is literally covered with death, yet both his peers and himself persist in regarding him as alive. Evidently, one's basic identity is not compromised by the layer of dead cells that line the surface of the skin he presents to the world. He may also have a dead tooth in his jaw without himself being certifiable as deceased. If he is in poor health it is possible that laboratory tests might reveal an alarming index of necrotic tissue (dead cells) elsewhere in his body. Once again, however, *he* would be considered alive—fully alive—even though a certain percentage of him must be classified as dead.

Under what conditions, then, is *he* dead? There are two general perspectives from which this question might be examined: a) when he is dead "to himself" and b) when he is perceived as dead by observers other than himself. In either instance we would have to relate the observations to our own conceptions and definitions of individual identity. How challenging and intricate a topic this is goes without saying. Many of the greatest minds in human history have wrestled with the problem of human identity, and

these efforts continue today. The few comments that are being offered here can do little more than remind the reader how complex a problem must be encountered and mastered before we can say with total assurance just who is the "who" who is dead.

Let us begin with the externalistic perspective. Perhaps he is dead when those characteristics which distinguished him from others have been annihilated. We do not recognize him as the particular person he was. What produced this transformation? Perhaps he underwent a lobotomy with resultant brain damage that overreached medical intentions. Perhaps he incurred brain damage spontaneously in a sudden accident. Perhaps he has been reduced by chronic and depressive disease. Or perhaps nobody knows precisely why he is no longer the person he used to be; all we have is the evidence of our direct perception. Somebody is alive, but not the person we knew.

Is this reasonable reasoning? Decide for yourself. The better we know somebody, the more we admire or despise, love or hate him for the particular person he is. He does not exist for us as a standard central nervous system encased in bone and animated by muscle, nor as an interchangeable unit within the social complex. He is a certain person to us, and the dissolution of that personality is perceived as a kind of death.

Death of the person and "physical death" have semi-independent careers, at least in our minds. The personality of a powerful or beloved person may remain "alive to us" long after the funeral. We may not be able to define our terms precisely. But most of us are capable of recognizing clearly that some*body* is dead, while still experiencing the somebody's personality as "with us." Were there such a procedure as a phenomenologic-behavioral analysis, then we would probably be able to discover the cues upon which such experiences depend. Similarly, the person may die *to us* while the body lives.

There is at least another level of person-perception to be mentioned here. We have been considering the disappearance of the particular or distinctive personality previously associated with an individual. But a human can also lose even those characteristics which he shares in common with most other humans. Having lost his particularity (at least, to our perceptions), he may also become reduced to such a low level of functioning that we no longer regard him as a living *person* (Chapters 5, 16). The body remains alive and shows some rudimentary forms of organization or responsiveness. But *he* is not living (and what does that mean, if it does not mean that he is dead?).

Think again of the dead-skin, dead-tooth examples, silly as they may appear. We think it silly to apply the word "dead" seriously when the defunct entity is merely a unit within a larger organic whole. The personality of the individual is superordinate to his moribund molar. When dealing with such extremes (tooth/personality) we are not perplexed. But the other examples given above complicate the situation. How many superordinate systems are there? Just one—total personality? (whatever that is). Or are there several personality systems, perhaps a variable number, depending upon the individual and his developmental level at the time?

When little Betty outgrows babyhood we do not pronounce her baby personality (or her) dead; we are too attentive to the larger, emerging self she is becoming to give that much notice to what is disappearing. And where does the babyness that was Betty go? We don't know and, generally, we don't much care.

But now move forward eight decades. After many years of mature adult functioning, Elizabeth is beginning to slip. She is no longer the "old Elizabeth." The self or personality by which she has been known seems to have come unraveled. "Regressed," we say. In other words, she has peeled back down to some previous self or, more accurately perhaps, to a caricature of a previous self. This time, we are more likely to witness and make salient in our minds the demise of the superordinate structure. The infantile or childish organization that replaces Elizabeth was not quite dead after all. Is there a sort of psychic limbo into which personality organizations disappear, perhaps to return again, perhaps never to return?

The direction of development—toward more complex and so-called mature or desirable selves, or toward simpler and now socially undesirable selves—has something to do with the perception of personality transformations as being either births or deaths. As with almost every other topic we are exploring here, it would be easy to continue to complicate the picture, to show how many frame-of-reference factors influence our perception of death. Let us just select one more topic from the externalistic perspective.

We have been focusing in this section on the disappearance of another person insofar as that other person radiates certain stimulus properties that impress themselves upon us. We see him as dead, or no longer alive. Now let us take a reading from our actions, not our thoughts and words. Elsewhere we have said that "a person is *socially dead* when there is an absence of those behaviors that we would expect to be directed toward a living person and the presence of those behaviors that we would expect when dealing with a deceased or nonexistent person" (10).

Have you ever been "cut dead," been made a persona non grata? Received the "silent treatment?" Been treated as though you were not really there, or just a piece of furniture? Have you ever treated anyone else that way? We expel each other to social deaths over and again in our daily lives. These "little murders" may be more or less complete, and more or less permanent. But few of us have been completely exempt from such experiences, whether on the giving or receiving end.

More specialized illustrations could be cited. Some of these go to an extreme that rival "real" death. Institutionalization may be followed by a response toward the departed as though his departure were not merely from the bosom of the community, but from the face of the earth itself. So-called voodoo deaths, bone-pointing ceremonies, and other ritualistic enactments of social death may, in fact, hasten the outcast's physical death. (The same effect may also be achieved in some instances through institutionalization, lest we be too quick to judge traditional voodoo practitioners.) One might also be unwise enough to engage in behaviors which are *verboten* for one's inner circle or primary reference group. Do something that good Catholics, good Jews, good Ku Klux Klanners, good Black Panthers, good reporters, good soldiers, good athletes don't do, and one risks total ostracism. One becomes dead to the group. Whether or not the group is so moved as to attend to the physical death of the "traitor" is not entirely a matter of indifference, but it is independent of the observation that he became a *social death* first.

Is there a relationship between *thinking* of somebody as though he were dead, and *behaving* toward him in the same manner? Probably so. Thought and behavior are known to be partners in other realms. But the relationship is far from perfect and, in our present limited state of knowledge, may not be very predictable. The relevant methodological point is that we have two fairly distinct ways of registering a person as dead: a) by how we perceive and conceive him; and b) by how we behave with respect to him. The specific relationship between these two modes remains to be determined empirically.

Even more briefly, let us turn to the subjectivistic perspective. Is there a sense in which a person can be "dead to himself?" Once again, we must attempt to find a balance between inflexible thought habits and mere wordplay. Inflexibility in this case would be the hasty assertion that

one could in no sense be dead to himself. If he were dead, then no subjective experiences of any kind would be possible. Obviously, there is something to this argument. We are destined to be ignorant of our own deadness. At best, we are entitled to entertain the bias that we are *not* dead right now.

Yet this argument, for all its hardheaded appeal, contains the same hidden premise that so many other propositions harbor on the topic of death. It assumes that there is an indisputable definition of death that is just out of range of the present discussion. A person cannot really experience himself as dead. But where does the definition of "dead" come from in this instance? It has not been established, merely assumed. That is not quite fair. The argument should be modified to state: by *external* definition, the individual himself cannot be aware of his own demise. This is plausible enough. But the argument now does not overextend itself by declaring what the individual can or cannot experience by *his* criteria.

Objectivity misplaced is no longer objectivity. It is in no wise preferable to an honest subjectivity. In any event, we raise less self-beclouding dust if we respect both the externalistic and the subjectivistic perspective on the definition of who (if anybody) is dead. It would be a mirror-image reversal of the same mislogic if we avered that the individual's experience of himself as dead meant that he "really" was dead. Mere wordplay.

There are at least two ways in which the individual may perceive himself as dead:

1. *He may perceive one or more of his part-selves as wholly dead.* The debilitated athlete, the retired worker, the person whose beloved has died—each of these individuals may participate in the symbolic burial of one of his most fundamental part-selves. The pitcher whose arm troubles halt him in mid-career remains a living person, but not the person he had

been. He may be unable fully to reorganize his life until a certain amount of "mourning work" has been completed for that deceased facet of his total personality. (At the same time he may also become socially dead to the sports public.) True enough, there are instances in which the person who thought he would never play, work, or love again proves to have been mistaken. But if we stay within the immediate phenomenological world of the individual, then we must respect the fact that right now he regards this part-self as dead.

This form of self-perception could be likened to society's perspective on an individual. A particular member of the society is seen as (physically or socially) dead by the group. There is a recognition of loss because survivors remain to experience the loss. In this case, the "experiencing ego" of the individual remains as a survivor to register the loss of one or more of his part-selves. There is, in other words, an objective/subjective distinction within the inner world of the individual himself.

It is conceivable that the experiencing or observing self might continue to function with great clarity while one after another of its part-selves wither away. One eventually may come to regard his experiencing ego as the only living spirit in a sort of psychic graveyard.

2. *He may perceive his total or experiencing self as partially dead.* In the clinical practice of psychology or psychiatry it is not altogether rare to come across patients who feel themselves to be dead. The catatonic form of schizophrenia is a condition in which the "I am dead" sentiment has been noted by many observers. But one does not have to be psychotic in order to experience a *deadening* of his phenomenological life. To feel "less alive" is to feel "more dead," is it not? A sensitive self-observer might chart for himself daily and perhaps even hourly variations in how alive/dead he feels. At this point one anticipates the objection that death is an all-or-nothing affair. We will

explore that question in a little while. But whether or not physical-death-from-an-externalistic-perspective must be considered all-or-nothing has not much to do with how the individual perceives his own condition.

In a previous paper, one of the authors proposed a dimension of *psychological aliveness.* Much of what passes for "normal" human functioning would be located around the midpoint of this dimension. Reference was made to the person whose behavior has become "entirely stereotyped, routinized. He is merely going through the motions." This condition is contrasted with "the person who is vibrantly or violently alive, enjoying a high rate of exchange with his environment, zestful, responsive, and spontaneous" (11). At the opposite extreme (closer to phenomenological death) would be the person who has only a feeble, shallow, or fluctuating self-monitoring system. He feels "out of it." But he retains enough mental functioning to register the difference between his present and former state. He feels that he himself has become deadened. This is different from the condition described earlier in which there is an intact experiencing ego that witnesses the demise of one or more components of the total self.

From the subjective viewpoint, then, one may either experience a general deadening of his inner life, or the death (perhaps total death) of a part-self. In the first instance, when answering the question, "Who is dead?" one would say, "*I am* . . . that is, I am deader than I used to be, and perhaps dead enough to feel completely dead to myself." In the second instance, one might reply, "I am alive, but part of me is dead, the who-I-was who could do certain things or enter into certain relationships."

Phenomenological currents may surge in the opposite direction as well. Fortunate circumstances may help the individual awaken to a fuller sense of inner life than he has ever known before; new part-selves may develop and flourish. He feels "more alive" (and perhaps only in retrospect appreciates the limitations of his previous existence), and there is "more of him" (new part-selves) to be alive.

These distinctions between externalistic and subjectivistic perspectives, and the varieties of each, could be useful in many ways. Under what environmental conditions does an individual appear physically or socially dead to others, or seem physically alive yet phenomenologically dead? Under what environmental conditions does the individual come to regard himself as dead or deadening? How are these conditions interrelated? What are the implications for physical survival of the individual when he is regarded as dead by others? By himself? Can the "death" or "abortion" of a possible future self serve as the cue for despair, disorganization, and physical death? Some adolescents, for example, see their "real" selves as waiting for them in the near future. Their past selves are as outgrown as the clothes that once adorned them, and their present selves are merely points of transition. Any threat to the attainment of the future self may strike as though an actual lethal event had taken place. "The person I was going to be is dead . . . therefore, can I really be alive?"

ALIVENESS AND DEADNESS

Most of us have the bias that death pertains to the ending of life, the absence of life. Clearly, then, death is different from life. It is life's negation.

There are reasons for challenging this bias. We will consider a few of these reasons.

1. *Death has to do with the beginnings of life as well as the ending.* Biologists have known for years that death is to be found in the very early stages of an organism's life cycle, as well as its final stages. Cell death was observed to take place within the embryo itself. Saunders and Fallon inform us that "An earlier generation of biologists emphasized a kind of chance causality for many deaths: death might ensue in cells crowded by pressure from their neighbors during morphogenetic movements; or dying cells might be considered the losers in competition for energy sources and oxygen. An old view also suggested for the phagocyte an assassin's role in the destruction of larval tissues in the metaphosing insect" (12). Now, however, according to Saunders and Fallon (and others), death is recognized as an intrinsic aspect of the developmental programming. Certain cells must die if normal development of the total organism is to proceed. In birds and fowl, for example, the death of specific cells must occur "on schedule" during the embryo stage if the wings are to emerge as functional. In a sense, then, life of the mature organism is dependent upon death of some of its component parts very early in the life cycle.

2. *Death has to do with the maintenance as well as the destruction of life.* The dead cells that line the outer surface of the skin serve to protect our body. The same holds true for our outcroppings of hair. Inside our bodies, bacteria devour other bacteria, and the white blood cells are nothing short of Murder, Incorporated. These scavenging leucocytes gobble up invasion parties and eventually succumb themselves. Jones describes the mass death of leucocytes during infections as a sort of suicide which ". . . serves as a mechanical barrier or dam against more extensive invasion by the foreign agent " (13). The complex system that underlines the maintenance of human personality would quickly fail without a variety of death-making processes at subordinate levels. Some of us dies so that most of us can live.

3. *There are many forms which are intermediate between the "living" and the "nonliving."* All that is alive and all that

is not alive cannot be arrayed neatly on either side of a chasm. The bridges are too numerous and too interesting to be dismissed. Perhaps the best known intermediary is the mosaic tobacco virus. It is crystalline matter in the laboratory, but a living parasite on the tobacco plant. Jones reminds us that spores and seeds can exist in nonmetabolizing (not alive?) states for a long period of time, yet be perfectly capable of burgeoning into life under appropriate environmental conditions.

Depending upon one's definition of life, the line can be drawn here or there along the continuum. Crystals exhibit structural properties somewhat akin to those found in vivo, can increase in size, and can split (reproduce?). But probably there are few of us who would include crystals within the world of the living. Yet what about maverick crystals such as the mosaic tobacco virus? And what about the protein macromolecules that scientists have been able to "create" in recent years? Do these perhaps deserve a place in the world of the living? From Jones again we have the admonition that "it would be foolhardy in our present state of knowledge to attempt (and futile to expect) a simple, precise, adequate definition of death or of life as biological phenomena" (14). We find it easy to concur with this opinion.

4. *The living and the not-so-living may be regarded as comprising an interdependent system.* This proposition is consistent with, but goes beyond what has already been suggested. (It is especially relevant to Bertalnaffy's observations cited above.) Biophysicist Joseph C. Hoffman tells us that "The living process of cells does something to matter. The growth of plants and animals is enhanced by the presence of former living material whether it is in the form of dead tissue or actual manure or other excrement. . . . There are few foods that men eat which have not been at some time or other parts of living things. . . . Even after incineration, living matter serves as an excellent fertilizer. We all know that wood ashes are a superior kind of food for garden plants" (15). He adds that, "Living things spring up from the organic environment that has accumulated over the years. In the mountains there is a gradual piling up among the rocks and gulleys and crevices of humus which accelerates further growth of plants along the rocky slope. The humus is not alive, and yet it is considerably different from the rocks surrounding it. It is a state of matter providing a culture medium for the growth of plants. That there are degrees of deadness of matter can be illustrated by the circulating red blood cell which is no longer capable of dividing and propagating its line of cells. But there is in it an atomic turnover while it circulates in the blood stream" (16).

We cannot resist a further quotation from Hoffman: "The varying degrees of death found in materials that once were living show that these fragments are part of life. The vast amount of organic matter on the earth should be considered to be part of life. The debris and excrement and waste of living things provides nourishment, and fragments of life are not totally dead. This brings up the poetic notion that living things are fully aware that there is organic matter on the face of the earth. . . . The impartial observer might reasonably conclude that living things know more than they can tell. They seem to know that there will be available debris of other living things from which to create new ones. In this sense the thin layer of organic debris over the earth is part of life and not just accidental offal " (17).

All we wish to add to Hoffman's observations is the thought that when intricate and systematic relationships can be observed among a number of phenomena it seems arbitrary to insist that the components must be divided into two mutually exclusive classes (in this case, the living and the nonliving).

5. *"Death" is not synonymous with the cessation of organized processes.* Just as it has been ventured here that there is

death at the beginnings of life, so it may be further ventured that processes resembling life can be found at and "beyond" death. By "death" in this context we mean the expert verdict that an organism (let us say, a human being) is deceased.

In *The Chemistry of Death*, Evans asserts that "Death is not an unaltering state, and far from being an inert mass, the dead body is, under normal circumstances, subject to many complex and, often enough, only partly investigated changes arising from intrinsic as well as extrinsic causes which bring about quite substantial chemical and morphological alterations of the tissues, though attention has tended to be drawn more to the visible structural modifications than to the chemical changes" (18).

A vivid summary of post-terminal processes is offered by Kugelmass in his foreword to Evans' book: "The body remains almost entirely alive after death is definitive. Organs and tissues begin to die, each in their turn. The tripod of life formed by the heart, lungs, and brain may be overturned irreversibly but independently. When the heart stops, the liver continues to make glucose, the muscle still responds to stimulation, the hair reveals growth. Just as there may be local death in a living body, so there may be local life in a dead body. The possibility of life recovery is thus a wholly artificial sign of death. There appears no sharp demarcation between seemingly dead tissue, whose life has flickered to a smouldering ember, fanned back into flame; and the handful of dust, the aggregate of crumbles, with the material returned to the inorganic world for newly formed life" (19).

ON THE PRAGMATICS OF DEATH

Up to this point we have been hassling with the familiar notion that death is an absolute, a monolith, a simple and self-evident fact. We have been attempting to suggest that "death" is a rather complex system of propositions, each of which is subject to examination, challenge, and alternative formulation. Our definitions and determinations would be empty and irrelevant were they not embedded in a complex matrix of observations and ideas. It is artificial, it is misleading to regard "death" and "dead" as terms that are somehow beyond the usual rules that apply to psychological and logical analyses.

Selecting just a few more illustrations from the abundant material available, we will complete this exploration with a discussion of the pragmatics of death. As used here, this term is consistent with the definition of pragmatism as "the doctrine that the whole meaning of a conception expresses itself in practical consequences" (20).

Continued progress in the procedure of organ transplantation adds a new dimension to topics already considered: the duration of death, who is dead, and the basis for distinction between living and dead/nonliving. (Only one without a sense of history, however, would conclude that these issues were created in our own times—they have been with us for centuries.) Even a very brief foray into the topic of organ transplantation will indicate how our definition of death is hinged to the *actions* we propose to take with respect to death.

F. J. Ayd is one of many medical spokesmen who have called for a new *legal* definition of death (21). He also feels that there is an *urgent* need for guidelines to help the physician *decide* when he may terminate *extraordinary measures* to delay *clinical* and *biological* death. Ayd declares that an *updated* definition of death is crucial as organ transplantation becomes ever more common. "Even when it is possible to preserve organs for transplantation, they still must be removed as soon after clinical death as possible; consequently, doctors must be able to determine when death is a fact and when such organs can be legally removed. *Society* must reflect its *moral consensus* about death by *enacting* new legislation which makes the reality of death *compatible* with advances in medical science" (22). [Italics ours.]

This is a most startling and fundamental set of propositions. It may be easy to accept Ayd's position as a sensible, practical utterance. He has good reason to be concerned about the matters he discusses; perhaps we should go along with what he suggests. But it would be unfortunate if we should let such statements pass without recognizing that they imply a worldwide view that is much different from that which comes as first nature to most of us. Ayd and other writers on this subject are, in effect, endorsing the most extreme argument against "establishment" notions of death that anyone might care to advance. Whether or not Ayd and his colleagues themselves are concerned about these theoretical implications, they are something for us to be concerned about here.

Notice the time dimensions involved. The need for redefinition is said to be *urgent*. Are we usually in such haste when considering issues that are philosophic or formalistic? Time pressure is being applied to the definition of a condition which presumably has been constant throughout human history. This is a remarkable instance of a contemporary effort to "hurry up" and control a phenomenon that in other times and places might have been considered fixed, immutable. The definition must be *updated*. We must "do something" about our view of death. It has failed to keep up with the times. Once updated, the new definition of death might itself prove perishable. Although in a sense death may remain as certain as taxes, it may also become as subject to revisions.

Clearly, the pressure for revising the legal definition of death arises from practical concerns. The physician must *decide*. Other people also have decisions to make

that are related to the legal definition of death, and to the physician's judgment. If there was nothing special one could do about death, then this problem would be unlikely to arise. It is because we now have choices (and *expect* to have choices) that the definition of death takes on such significance. Elsewhere in this book (Chapters 8, 9), we discuss the fact that one of the characteristics of our present cultural milieu is that we find ourselves in the position of having to make decisions in circumstances in which most of our forebears would have had to come to terms with the "way things are." And if the pressure to change our definitions of death comes from practical concerns, is it out of place to suggest that the existing definitions also developed within practical contexts? We have become accustomed to thinking of death in a certain way because these thoughts and definitions were compatible with what we believed we could *do* about death. This does not mean that philosophic and religious ideas had no influence. But our intellectual traditions themselves have always been marbled with the veins of social, economic, and technologic circumstances.

Among the decisions that must be made about life and death these days is the one cited by Ayd: when should the physician terminate *extraordinary measures*? But what constitutes an extraordinary measure? This itself is a definition that appears highly unstable. With medical science's talent for discovery and application it does not take long for the extraordinary to become the ordinary. The very notion of an "extraordinary" measure implies a certain context, a certain baseline. How skilled and updated are the physicians? How adequate are their facilities and supplies? How valued are the patients (e.g., is it extraordinary to massage the heart of a stricken nonogenarian but not of a stricken adolescent)? We must have some assumptions—conscious or otherwise—about when it is acceptable for certain kinds of people to die if we are to find the concept of "extraordinary measures" useful.

Ayd also speaks of *society* and its *moral consensus.* But what does this level of discourse have to do with death, with straight-on physical death? Is the definition of death to emerge somehow from the values and spirit of a people as well as from medical research and the findings of the pathologist? Consensus, in fact, implies a sort of context or election to determine the new definition of death. We do not think this approach is too far-fetched (although it should be made clear again that Ayd has not addressed himself to the implications we are spinning out here). Perhaps the most interesting facet is that it is a physician who has opened the doors to the community-at-large. Students of language and culture may be too surprised to take advantage of this opening; they probably anticipated that the walls would have to be battered down.

Let us round off this exegesis of Ayd's position. He emphasizes the close connection between legal and medical systems by calling for the *enactment* of new definitional *legislation.* This could be regarded as the relationship between a ritualistic regulatory system and a direct action system. It is also the relationship between a slow-moving, conservative system and a fast-moving system that replaces its own components with relentless vigor. The definition of death must emerge from and be consonant with both. It is dangerous to permit the two systems to grow further estranged from each other. The definition of death, then, has something to do with the relationships between major systems in our culture. This is a long way from the dictionary definition of death as cessation of vital bodily processes. The dictionary may not be entirely wrong, but it is not precisely correct, either.

Perhaps Ayd's most unsettling (if vague) implications are to be found in the phrase, "Society must reflect its moral consensus about death by enacting new legislation which makes the reality of death compatible with advances in medical science " (23). Does legislation bring "reality" into existence (and then take it away, or modify it?). Is the "reality of death" so easily managed by the legislative processes? And *must* legalistic reality follow with great faithfulness the changing contours of advances in medical science? Why should not "medical reality" take its cue from the legal? Or both "medical" and "legal" realities of death accept guidance from some other source? Which is the real reality of death?

Even less explicit are the implications regarding organ transplants and identity. Who is alive and who is dead when body parts are swapped? One of the first organ transplant poems had its protagonist saying, in part:

> . . . Me, Oldnobodyme
> Shambling Slumofame
> Some of me buried
>   alreaddeadedly
> Some of me patched
> Some of me matched
> Some of me new
> Some of me you
> The New Man, me, hah!
> Heartificial art keep
> A 'smilin' on me:
> First of what is sure to be,
> Your customized refabricatee. . . (24).

Identity transfer might be weighed according to sheer volume (51 percent of the decedent is still alive in the spare parts ward awaiting distribution; therefore, in a sense, the deceased is more alive than dead.) Or attention might be focused instead upon the *centrality* of the transferred organ (the hypothetical brain transplant, for example, should score higher than a grafted kidney or leg). From the other standpoint, how much of the recipient's body can be comprised of imported parts if he is to claim his "own" identity? No, we don't think these questions are worth much pondering at this time; their priority is low. But it is appropriate to remind ourselves that new developments pertaining to the question, "who is dead?" may be expected to emerge as time goes on.

Now back to Ayd for one more point. He referred to the distinction between *clinical* and *biological* death. Two kinds of death? One of the most impressive tomes on this subject is V.A. Negovskii's, *Resuscitation and Artificial Hypothermia* (25). The book contains nearly 900 references (mostly Soviet and American) to research conducted in this frontier area up to 1961. Research has continued since then, of course, but we will find sufficient guidance in Negovskii. Clinical and biological forms of death are to be distinguished in terms of their reversibility. "There is little doubt that 10 minutes or less after the cessation of cardiac activity and respiration, at ordinary temperatures clinical death changes into biological, *i.e.*, irreversible death, although it cannot be stated with accuracy when this change takes place in any given patient" (26).

Negovskii emphasizes "the exceptional mobility and the relative nature of the boundaries between the various phenomena in the terminal stages of life." For example, he states: "If the process causing death is prolonged and exhausting, clinical death may give way to biological death during the first minute after the cardiac activity and respiration cease. In the case of a young and healthy patient or animal, the change takes place later. If inhibition or extreme excitation of the cerebral cortex is present during the terminal process, this will also be reflected in the duration of clinical death. Clinical death changes into biological death in a deeply anesthetized patient at a different time from that in the unanesthetized patient"(27).

Reflecting upon these passages for a moment, we see that we have not really had done with the question of death and duration. We learn that clinical death has a variable duration. It is dependent upon many conditions. Furthermore, it does not reveal itself directly to observation ("It cannot be stated with accuracy when this change takes place in any given patient."). Clinical death, in other words, is a theoretical construct. One infers its presence or absence from observations in a particular instance, but whether or not one chooses to believe in clinical death comes down to a matter of theoretical temperament and the usefulness one finds in invoking this concept. Indeed, clinical death does seem to be a useful concept these days. This is why it is now part of the pragmatics of death. But it does not necessarily mean that clinical death is any more or less real than other conceptions of death one might encounter or develop.

The distinction between clinical and biological death seems to be at least a temporary way out of solving the problem of death's duration and reversibility. We can have it both ways, or so we seem to think: death that might be reversed (clinical), and death that cannot be reversed (biological). But wherein lies the proof? If resuscitation efforts succeed in a particular case, then all hands will agree that the death had reached only the clinical phase. This, of course, is a shuddering tautology and ought not be encouraged. By the same token, if resuscitation efforts fail, then we can make a perhaps gratuitous choice between the alternatives that a) the biological phase of death had already been reached; and b) the clinical phase was still in effect, but the intervention itself inadequate for some reason. In relating clinical and biological death to resuscitation procedures, then, we should exercise some critical judgment. Otherwise we will think we have learned something when actually all we have done is to have recovered some of the assumptions we built into the terminology.

But let us return to Negovskii. He is confident that before very long it will be expected that the physician employ, *as a routine action*, active resuscitation measures on persons dying from certain causes (such as blood loss, collapse under general anesthesia, and neonatal asphyxia). The number and variety of such conditions is expected to increase rapidly in the years ahead. Severe legal penalties may await the future physician who fails to take actions that today may be considered to be optional, exotic, or unnecessary. "To take a more long-term view of this problem, we may prophesy that perhaps at the end of the 20th or beginning of the 21st century active and successful treatment will be given in any case of sudden death" (28). Shades of Whiter!

The more that man can do in crisis situations, the further into the distance the concept of biological death recedes. Every new procedure and device introduces an "operant behavior" between the "participant-observer" (e.g., physician) and the certification of death. What could be more pragmatic?

We should not leave Negovskii without noting the attention he gives to artificial hypothermia, the attempt to preserve life in a state that might loosely be described as suspended or frozen animation. In the United States this approach has been described and advocated by a number of people, among whom Robert C. W. Ettinger has probably attained the greatest eminence. In *The Prospect of Immortality* (29) he describes the state of the art as of 1966 and deals with a number of logical and sociological questions that bear upon the definition of life and death. The questions raised by Ettinger are even more pertinent today. At least 11 humans have now been placed in "cryonic interment" (preserved at low temperatures) following their certification as dead (30).

So where are we now? At the least, perhaps we are at the point of recognizing that there are more relationships and fewer dichotomies than once appeared to be the case. All conceptions of death—whether dressed up as psychological, general systems, biomedical, or whatever—are mediated through the eyes and minds of men. All conceptions of death are intimately related to our total system of language and thought. And how we think and speak about death seems very closely related to what we are prepared to *do* in the encounter with death.

In our own work, we like to cling for security to the Pierce-Bridgman view of knowledge. One of the authors has applied this view in an earlier essay:

We know something only through the specific operations we have employed in entering into contact with it. Thus, a person may or may not be known as dead (in any of the senses of this term) depending upon the specific observational framework involved. The very definition of death becomes limited to specifiable sets of perceptual observations. Another way of saying this is that "death" (and "life") become of decreased scientific value as general concepts. *We have as many degrees of deathness or lifeness as we can support with careful observations and as we find useful to recognize....* No single definition based upon a single observational framework could be selected as *the* death perception.... Our observations about life and death ... depend upon somebody's perception of somebody else. On the strict interpretation we are not entitled to say: "Person A is dead." This statement implicitly locates "death" inside Person A, or makes "death" in some way wholly an attribute of A. What we can conclude is: "Death occurred between Persons A and B." In other words, that pattern of behaviors or "non-behaviors" which we have agreed to define as death was manifested during the time that B, the observer, was in contact with A. An observer who is located outside the A-B interaction will have still another observational framework to contribute. His conclusion might be: "No behavior characteristic of life was witnessed during the period of observation. Hence, a death situation prevailed (behaviorally defined)." If we press him to tell us, "But *who* was dead?" then he would simply report the logical alternatives: "A was dead—perhaps; but it could be that B was dead. Or that both were dead. All that I can properly conclude is that a death *situation* prevailed; the terms lose their moorings to direct observation when I try to attribute an aspect of the total situation to one element within the situation" (31).

In the three chapters which follow, we will continue to follow the trail of death, as we learn more about what death "is" by observing what it "does" in various contexts.

REFERENCES

1. Whiter, W. *A dissertation on the disorder called suspended animation*. Norwich, 1819. P. 14.
2. *Ibid.*, p. 463.
3. Jones, C. S. "In the midst of life. . . " Reflections on some biological aspects of death. In E. A. Grollman (Ed.), *Explaining death to children*. Boston: Beacon Press, 1967. Pp. 127-144.
4. *Ibid.*, p. 129.
5. *Ibid.*
6. *Ibid.*
7. Buckley, W. (Ed.). *Modern systems research for the behavioral scientist*. Chicago: Aldine, 1968.
8. Von Bertalnaffy, L. *Problems of life*. New York: Harper & Row Torchbook, 1960.
9. Brillouin, L. Life, thermodynamics, and cybernetics. In W. Buckley (Ed.), *Modern systems research for the behavioral scientist*. Chicago: Aldine, 1968. Pp. 147-156.
10. Kastenbaum, R. Psychological death. In L. Pearson (Ed.), *Death and dying: Current issues in the treatment of the dying person*. Cleveland, Ohio: Case Western Reserve University Press, 1969. Pp. 1-27 (p. 15 quoted).
11. *Ibid.*, p. 19.
12. Saunders, J. W., Jr., & Fallon, J. F. *In vitro* analysis of the control of morphogenetic cell death in the wing bud of the chick embryo. *American Zoologist*, abstract, 1965, *5*, 213-214.
13. Jones, *op. cit.*, p. 130.
14. *Ibid.*, p. 144.
15. Hoffman, J. G. *The life and death of cells*. New York: Doubleday/Dolphin Books, 1957. P. 311.
16. *Ibid.*, p. 312.
17. *Ibid.*, p. 313.
18. Evans, W. E. D. *The chemistry of death*. Springfield, Ill.: Charles C Thomas, 1963.
19. Kugelmass, I. N. In Evans, *op. cit.*, p. iii.
20. *Oxford Universal Dictionary*. (3rd ed.) London: Oxford University Press, 1955. P. 1561.
21. Ayd, F. J. When is a person dead? *Medical Science*, 1967, *18*, 33-36.
22. *Ibid.*, p. 36.
23. *Ibid.*
24. Kastenbaum, R. Heartificial Art. *Omega*, 1968, *3*, 1 (Newsletter).
25. Negovskii, V. A. *Resuscitation and artificial hypothermia*. (Translated by Basil Haigh.) New York: Consultants Bureau, 1962.
26. *Ibid.*, p. 267.
27. *Ibid.*
28. *Ibid.*, p. 272.
29. Ettinger, R. C. W. *The prospect of immortality*. New York: McFadden-Bartell, 1966.
30. Nelson, R. F. *We froze the first man*. New York: Dell, 1968.
31. Kastenbaum, R., *Omega, op. cit.*, 23.

5

Thanatomimesis

Alive or dead? Sometimes we are mistaken. Imagine a human form that is apparently without life. Place it in a tomb. See it through the eyes of a distraught lover. Who would not repeat Romeo's error? Perhaps under these circumstances even a physician might err in differentiating between a drugged sleep and death.

Every performance of *Romeo and Juliet* climaxes with the "actual" death of the young lovers, following directly upon the misperception of death. As members of the audience, we know that Juliet is alive while Romeo is perceiving her as dead. A moment later we know that Juliet truly is dead (and Romeo as well). But these deaths are "real" only within the framework of the performance—we do not suppose either that the actors who impersonated Romeo and Juliet have died, or that these famous lovers have died to the world of the theater. They will return for the Saturday matinee.

Not all misperceptions of death are followed by "real" death—in fact, sometimes this phenomenon prevents or delays death. And not all misperceptions occur within the peculiar set of multiple frameworks that constitute a theatrical experi-ence. The false impression of death has been emanated by animals as well as humans in a variety of situations. This chapter explores some manifestations of what we will term *thanatomimesis*. This combination of two Greek words—*thanatos*/death and *mimos*/imitation—is intended to provide a neutral coverall for the variety of phenomena that will be under consideration. The phrase, "sham death" has been heard occasionally; but this implies a motivational component that is not necessarily to be found in every instance of misperception. We will regard sham death as one possible subtype. In general, thanatomimetic phenomena are those which are likely to arouse in the perceiver the *false* impression that he is in relationship with a dead rather than a living organism.

This chapter may take us only a step or two toward an appreciation of thanatomimetic phenomena. Observations are scattered in many sources, most of them outside of psychology. This first attempt to develop thanatomimesis as a topic in its own right labors under many limitations. However, we believe that there is some usefulness in at least pointing toward the possibilities that inquiries into thanatomimesis might hold for increasing our understanding of death and deathlike states.

THANATOMIMETIC BEHAVIOR

Thanatomimetic behavior could be classified in various ways. We believe it would be most heuristic to attempt a classification based upon purpose or intentionality. Is it most reasonable to conclude that a certain organism intended to convey the impression of death? Or do the facts suggest that the appearance of death arose despite the organism's intention, or without regard to his intention? With questions such as these in mind, it seems appropriate to make use of a set of categories proposed by Shneidman (1). Although his own use of these categories has been centered on the problem of suicide, Shneidman's nomenclature is equally applicable to the individual's general orientation toward his cessation. With regard to thanatomimesis, then, the organism might be intentioned, subintentioned, unintentioned, or contraintentioned. These terms have been defined by Shneidman in the following way: *intentioned*—"Individual plays direct or conscious role in his alteration;" *subintentioned*—"Indirect, covert, partial, or unconscious role;" *unintentioned*—"Plays no significant role;" *contraintentioned* — "Employs 'semantic blanket' or altered state with conscious intention of avoiding it" (2).

Sham Death

"Playing 'possum" is perhaps the most familiar expression in the entire realm of thanatomimesis. This phrase is used metaphorically to describe a person who we believe is feigning a limitation or impairment. Jake LaMotta, once an eminent pugilist, was famous for his "act" of apparent fatigue and helplessness that sometimes lured unwary opponents to neglect their own defenses. *Didelphis virginiana* himself, the opossum, has long been credited with the ability to deceive the onlooker into believing that he is observing a dead marsupial. Hunters and other observers have vowed that this is a *deliberate* performance, a ruse. The act itself is quite impressive. When attacked by another animal, the opossum immediately will collapse into an inert ball of fur. There is no sound or movement. His head droops down, his mouth hangs open, his eyes are fixed in an empty stare. The attacking animal is likely to leave his would-be prey "for dead." After the danger has passed, the inert ball of fur once again becomes a lively little creature.

No one has questioned the fact that an opossum can behave in the manner described. However, scientists occasionally have disputed the interpretation that the opossum somehow *intends* to deceive. One might reject this interpretation simply because it is mentalistic, i.e., attributes certain cognitive and conative abilities to an animal. (There was a time when many psychologists would not attribute mental life to their fellow humans!) From an empirical standpoint, however, there was a stronger objection. Is it not more likely that the opossum falls into an involuntary state of *tonic immobility*? We should not aspire to a psychological level of explanation when it remains plausible that a physiological explanation will suffice, or so the argument ran.

Recently this question was put to an experimental test. A research team in Los Angeles implanted electrodes into the skulls of 15 opossums. The thanatomimetic state was induced by shaking the animals with an artificial dog jaw. The effect of realism was increased by playing recorded barks and growls through a high fidelity speaker. Electroencephalographic tracings disclosed a *heightened* level of arousal during the episode. This tendency toward a greater than usual alertness persisted for a while afterward. There was no indication that the opossum had fallen into an involuntary state of catalepsy or tonic immobility. The experiment was repeated with a variation designed further to increase the "realism" (live dogs were introduced)—same results. Norton, Beran and Misrahy thus concluded that the opossum really does "play 'possum" (3). That the opossum is alert or phenomenologically alive during the time that it is broadcasting an image of death supports the position that this behavior is *intentioned.*

Verification of the adaptive and perhaps deliberate character of the opossum's thanatomimetic behavior does not end the controversy. Indeed, it stirs the dust of a little-remembered dispute that now becomes more relevant. Charles Darwin was among those who observed that various insects and spiders appear to feign death. Being Darwin, he took an additional step, namely, that of experimentation.

I carefully noted the simulated positions of seventeen different kinds of insects belonging to different genera, both poor and first-rate shammers. Afterwards I procured naturally dead specimens of some of these insects (including a lulus, spider, and Oniscus) belonging to distinct genera, others I killed with camphor by an easy slow death; the result was that in no instance was the attitude exactly the same, and in several instances the attitudes of the feigners and of the really dead were as unlike as they could possibly be (4).

Darwin entertained the possibility that, within their survival repertoire, insects possess a talent for feigning death. Holmes confirmed Darwin's observation that many insects do draw themselves up into a ball or otherwise adopt a deathlike attitude, and that these postures can be maintained for an hour or longer (5). Furthermore, he noted that certain insects, such as the water scorpion, will exhibit thanatomimetic behavior readily on land, but not when they are in water. However, Holmes was

decidedly less impressed with his shammers, whether "poor" or "first-rate." He rejected the notion that there was any conscious or deliberate process at work; rather, he proposed that reflex action was the more likely hypothesis. Holmes did not rule out the possibility that higher animals might well be intentional deceivers.

Writing more than half a century ago, Carrington and Meader seemed to anticipate the recent findings of Norton, Beran and Misrahy. The earlier writers noted that "A fox, when feigning death, will often cautiously open its eyes, raise its head, look around, and finally scamper off, if its pursuers have withdrawn to a safe distance" (6). They suggested that higher animals such as the fox "are perfectly aware of their surroundings, and of the reason for their feigning in this manner." However, Carrington and Meader sided with Holmes in judging that insects and other lower animals probably enter into a state of muscular rigidity resembling catalepsy. This state would be interpreted as a reflex or instinct, not an act of conscious intentionality.

In more recent years the term, *tonic immobility* has been applied to a deathlike state that is marked by total rigidity. Reviewing the information available in 1928, Hoagland (7) pointed out that tonic immobility has been described and induced in a wide variety of animals, including spiders, lizards, birds, guinea pigs, dogs, cats, sheep, and apes. Some birds and mammals can be induced to develop this state by suddenly being turned upon their backs. Abbe Kircher is said to have observed and recorded this phenomenon as long ago as 1562! Some writers have referred to tonic immobility as "animal hypnosis" because of its superficial resemblance to the trance state in human hypnotic subjects. Hoagland (rightly, we think) rejects this term because it tends to bring psychological implications to mind that probably confuse rather than clarify the situation.

A close examination of the tonic immobility state in a variety of organisms might add to our knowledge of life-and-death dynamics, especially on the psychobiological plane. Research on this topic appears to be scant. Nevertheless, Hoagland and the horned toad did collaborate in a careful investigation which is of interest here although it was not intended as a contribution to the psychology of death. The results which are mentioned below are based in part upon Hoagland's work with the lizard, *Anolis carolinensis*, and in part upon that with the horned toad who is, himself, actually a lizard, *Phrynosoma cornutum*.

It is a footnote, a peripheral observation by Hoagland, that first engages our attention:

It was observed in the course of the experiments that certain irregularities in the duration of tonic immobility periods served as an index of the approaching death of the animal. This was true for both *Phrynosoma* and *Anolis*, and it was also true for the isopods with which Crozier worked. It was found possible in several cases to predict the death of an apparently normal animal as much as three days in advance by irregularities in the rhythms. This fact suggests a possible relationship between the durations of immobility and metabolism (8).

This observation obviously raises the possibility that careful assessment of the way in which an organism mimics death can predict the imminence of actual death. Just as obviously, we cannot do much with this line of speculation as long as the data are limited to lizards. Less obvious, perhaps, are the effects of repeated bouts of tonic immobility upon the organism's health. Hoagland induced the immobile state over and again in his lizards. The state appears to involve a formidable set of internal changes, as Hoagland's own work has indicated. Might repeated "shamming" *exhaust* the organism, making it more vulnerable to relatively minor stress, or, alternately, *unbalance* total functioning so that general homeo-stasis cannot be maintained? Might it then be the case that profound thanatomimesis has its own built-in limitation—that overuse of a counterfeiting mechanism may itself induce the real thing? We note in passing that Hoagland's lizards could well have come to his experiments with a variety of "shamming" careers already behind them, thus making them differentially vulnerable to the hypothetically lethal effect of repeated states of tonic immobility. One also bears in mind the possibility that the investigation of rhythmical activities in the body (tonic immobility being just one special case with its own temporal structure) might generally improve the prediction of impending death.

Another peripheral observation by Hoagland raises questions for us. He noted that *Anolis* usually struggled before becoming immobilized. But in the foxes, opossums, spiders et al that were previously mentioned, the thanatomimetic state appeared to be voluntary or spontaneous on the part of the threatened organism. The crafty fox described by Carrington and Meader seems to be playing an intentional role in his sham death, while Darwin's spider might be credited with sub-intentionality (unconscious-instinctive, in this case), or, at the least, unintentionality (it "just happens"). However, Hoagland's lizard seems to *contraintend* (resist) the sham state. Whatever else one might care to make of these observations, it does look as though a convincing exhibition of thanatomimesis cannot be taken per se as proof that the organism is intending or subintending the performance. Perhaps there is a "final common pathway" for the physiological action that underlies sham death. This pathway could be energized either from a psychological ('possum detects an enemy) or a physical (lizard is subjected to laboratory manipulations) inception. Supporting this view to some extent is Hoagland's report that the tonic immobility state is quite the same no matter what stimulus is used to induce it.

We also raise the possibility that some

animals may be capable of behaving either in an intentioned or unintentioned manner with regard to sham death. We would not expect such versatility to be as pronounced among spiders and other "lower animals," on the developmental assumption that versatility of functioning increases with complexity of structure (at least, up to a point). Perhaps the fox and the opossum could be induced into the state of tonic immobility by physical stimuli alone—and against their "will," so to speak. Here we again turn to one of Hoagland's footnotes:

Tonic immobility or a state akin to it has been described in children by Piéron (1913). I have recently been able to produce the condition in adult human beings. The technique was brought to my attention by a student in physiology, Mr. W. I. Gregg, who after hearing a lecture on tonic immobility suggested that a state produced by the following form of manhandling which he had seen exhibited as a sort of trick might be essentially the same thing. If one bends forward from the waist through an angle of 90°, places the hands on the abdomen, and after taking a deep breath is violently thrown backwards through 180° by a man on either side, the skeletal muscles contract vigorously and a state of pronounced immobility lasting for some seconds may result. The condition is striking and of especial interest since this type of manipulation (sudden turning into a dorsal position) is the most common one used for producing tonic immobility in vertebrates (9).

Apparently, then, a state resembling profound tonic immobility can be induced in man by physical means alone; that is, the state need not be intentioned or sub-intentioned. It is possible that incidents sometimes observed in athletic events, such as football games, involve inadvertent induction of tonic immobility. A flanker back reaches forward to receive a pass—instantly he is tackled in such a fashion that his body is flipped backwards quickly and forcefully. He remains flat on his back, immobile, for half a minute or longer. We are afraid that he may have suffered a serious injury, judging by his complete lack of response. But the pass-receiver is soon back on his feet. Chances are that he will return to the game after a rest. The flanker back was not shamming death in the intentional sense, yet his imitation under the condition of tonic immobility could appear to be more authentic than any voluntary counterfeiting performance he might wish to enact.

We are suggesting that tonic immobility in man, and possibly in other higher animals, is likely to occur under different circumstances and involve a different pattern of psychophysiological activity than when the individual is deliberately attempting to convey the impression that he is dead. The latter situation frequently arises when there is the perceived possibility that actual death or serious injury might be in the offing. The soldier, perhaps already wounded, may feign death while his position is being overrun by an overwhelming enemy force. Could he voluntarily induce a profound state of tonic immobility, then his chances for escaping detection (and death) would be increased.

Suspended Animation

We would probably judge the soldier and the opossum—even the spider—successful if their death-feigning performances induced the enemy to pass them by. The horned toad who is on his own time might also engage in thanatomimetic behavior that has the effect of discouraging a possible attack. However, a first-rate performance can also have the opposite effect: it can be fatal. We are not dwelling on the hypothetical effects of repeated tonic immobility in the lizard—the reference now is to strong circumstantial evidence that members of our own species have died prematurely because they have emanated a deathlike appearance. In this section our specific focus is upon thanatomimetic behavior that is related to an altered state of being. "Suspended animation" is a rather loose term but it will suffice as a general indication of our subject matter.

One Thousand Buried Alive By Their Best Friends (10) is an admirably direct title. Fletcher's treatise of 1890 is but one of many reports in which it has been claimed that premature burial of the living does occur, and occurs with alarming frequency. Perhaps the classic in this genre is Hartmann's *Buried Alive* (11) which appeared in 1895. Reports of this nature were especially numerous in the nineteenth century (12). Occasional reports are still to be found in our own time (13), but the heydey of premature burial concern seems to have passed with the nineteenth century. Discussions of premature burial often appeared in medical journals. The authors were usually either physicians or other learned men. During this period of time—particularly the last three decades of the nineteenth century—many articles were devoted to the subject of suspended animation, with or without explicit reference to premature burial.

The basic contention was that individuals who are in suspended animation or some other altered state of being may be taken for dead. The "corpse," so identified, is then denied attentions that might have facilitated recovery. More lamentably yet, the "corpse" is apt to be buried and subsequently regain normal functioning—too late. No doubt many people developed the mental picture of being trapped in a coffin, frantically struggling and straining for release. It is the very stuff of nightmares. Today's reader might find this prospect incredible. However, the vision of premature burial was considered seriously by well-educated adults just a few generations ago. In retrospect, one can now weigh the available evidence and arrive at a more or less dispassionate conclusion either favoring or rejecting the reality of premature burial. But those who were exposed to personal experiences which seemed to involve premature burial, and to freshly-printed tomes by prestigious writers, probably found it more difficult

to remain aloof. Let us consider some of the observations that were being reported approximately one hundred years ago.

Montague Summers, the esteemed biographer of the vampire, has provided one of the most accessible surveys of premature burial reports. The instances mentioned below were reported by a variety of observers and subsequently collated by Summers in *The Vampire, His Kith and Kin* (14). A French physician, Icard, detailed a dozen cases in which a person medically certified as dead had revived. In one instance the revival occurred in the midst of funeral ceremonies and in the presence of several physicians, who independently reported on the phenomenon. Tebb culled from medical sources 219 reported narrow escapes from premature burial, 149 premature interments that actually occurred, ten cases of dissection while life was not extinct, three cases in which dissection of the living was avoided at the last moment, and even two cases in which consciousness returned to the "corpse" during the process of embalmment. Summer also quotes from the work of Hartmann and from several newspaper accounts of premature burial or near-burial. The most recent newspaper dateline was 1908 (many years before publication of Summer's book). From his review of the literature, Summers commented that "There is no greater mistake than to suppose that most cases of premature burial, and of escape from premature burial, happened long ago, and that even then the majority of these took place under exceptional conditions, and for the most part in small towns or remoter villages on the continent. Amazing as it may appear in these days of enlightenment, the number of instances of narrowest escapes from premature burial, and also from this terrible fate itself, has not decreased of recent years, but it has, on the contrary, increased" (15). Summers also cites references to the effect that premature burials had occurred many times prior to the nineteenth century, and occasionally to people of great renown (e.g., the Grand Inquisitor of Spain under Philip II, a Cardinal, is said to have grasped the scalpel of the anatomist with his hand when he recovered consciousness on the embalming table).

A more vivid impression of the premature burial literature can be obtained by looking into a more or less typical article. We have selected a paper by MacKay that made its appearance in *Popular Science Monthly* in 1880 (16). "The difference between death and a state of trance—or, as the Germans put it, *Todt* and *Scheintodt*—has never been quite clearly understood by the generality of mankind," writes MacKay. "Society, which sometimes does its best for the living, does not always do its best for the dead (or those who appear to be dead), and he would be a bold man who, without statistics, should assert that men, women, and children are never, by any chance, buried alive. Are the bodies of the poor always examined with care before burial? Are deaths properly verified in days of epidemic, that is to say in days of social panic" (17)?

MacKay limits his discussion to cases of reported trance or *Scheintodt* in which the semblance of death is maintained for hours and days, not merely for minutes as in the case of fainting spells. The moral of the numerous incidents he reports seems to be: beware of the hasty funeral. Examples are drawn both from ancient times and the current scene. "Petrarch, when a middle-aged man, lay in Ferrara twenty hours in a state of trance, and was to be buried on the completion of the time laid down by law, that is to say in four hours, when a sudden change of temperature caused him to start up in his bed. He complained of the draught and reprimanded his attendants. They had allowed a current of cold air to fall on his couch! Perhaps if the door had been kept shut, the poet, showing no signs of animation, would have been buried that day. Petrarch would have been defrauded of a large portion of his life, and the world would

have lost, in consequence, some of its finest sonnets" (18). Abbé Prevot, author of *Manon Lescaut*, is reported to have been inadvertently killed by a village physician who found his unconscious body in the woods "and commenced what he was pleased to term his *post-mortem* examination. But at the first thrust of the knife the unlucky author awoke, and, with a piercing shriek, gave up the ghost" (19).

Among his more contemporaneous examples, MacKay cites the case of a young woman who was buried on the eve of her marriage to the man she loved.

The doctor was of the opinion that the girl had died from excitement—overjoy, it is said, at the prospect of being married—but the legal name for the catastrophe was disease of the heart, and with this verdict her place in society was declared vacant. When the first shovelful of earth was thrown down on the coffin, strange noises were heard proceeding therefrom, "as of evil spirits disputing over the body of the dead." The gravediggers took to flight, and the mourners began praying; but the bridegroom, less superstitious than the others, insisted on the coffin being unnailed. This was done; but too late: the girl was found in an attitude of horror and pain impossible to describe; her eyes wide open, her teeth clenched, her hands clutching her hair. Life was extinct; but, when laid in her shroud the day before, her eyes were closed, her hands were folded on her breast as if in prayer (20).

Another incident made the point that "the resuscitated victims of apparent death do not always return safe and sound—hale in body and in mind—from the land of shadows." MacKay describes the plight of Luigi Vittori, a carbineer in the Pope's service, who was certified as dead from asthma in a hospital in Rome. "A doctor, glancing at the body, fancied he detected signs of life in it. A lighted taper was applied to the nose of the carbineer—a mirror was applied to his mouth; but all without success. The body was pinched and beaten, the taper was again applied, and so often and so obstinately that the nose was burned, and the patient, quivering in all his frame, drew short, spasmodic breaths—sure proofs, even to a non-professional witness, that the soldier was not altogether dead. The doctor applied other remedies, and in a short time the corpse was declared to be a living man. Luigi Vittori left the hospital to resume his duties as carbineer, but his nose—a scarred and crimson beacon on his face—told till he died (which was soon afterward) the sad story of his cure in the very jaws of the grave" (21). MacKay adds that mental as well as physical infirmities have sometimes accompanied such narrow escapes.

Many other anecdotal reports can be found both in MacKay and elsewhere, sometimes presented as first-person observations, sometimes as more remote gleanings. Not all the accounts are as melodramatic as MacKay's, but the reader may be assured that far more grisly stories have been told than we have seen fit to include on these pages. One can speculate that vivid reports of premature burials aroused strong reactions in opposite directions. Some people probably were convinced that suspended animation deaths posed a genuine risk that they or their loved ones might encounter. Others probably looked askance at these reports, seeking either to discredit the observations per se or to advance less exotic explanations for the phenomena. Let us now consider examples of the critical reaction to the premature burial literature.

William See, a professor of medicine, offered a rejoinder to the article we have just sampled. See took particular issue with MacKay's implicit assertion that the ordinary physician or general practitioner is not capable of reaching a reliable judgement of the signs of death. Along with other critics of the premature burial literature, See did not challenge the basic contention that such events have occurred with some frequency. "That the trance state has been mistaken for death, and that premature burials have taken place, seem to be fully recognized in the system

of morgues or dead-houses in various parts of Europe where bodies are so placed that the slightest movements will be brought to the notice of attendants; and in the laws which in most countries require the lapse of twenty-four hours and longer periods between death and burial" (22). But See argued that morgues or dead-houses are superfluous when ordinary care is taken by the relatives of a deceased person—the onus thus is shifted from the physician to the relative.

See further took note of "the credulity of the public" in accepting all premature burial reports as authentic when, in fact, many are questionable or based upon inadequate information. He also contended that a trance state that resembles death sufficiently to deceive the *trained* observer does not persist beyond a minute or two—certainly not for hours and days. He did not dispute the likelihood that *untrained* observers (such as relatives and morgue attendants) might fail to notice vital signs that would be apparent to the careful physician.

At least some instances of changes in posture after burial can be explained by the general process of rigor mortis, according to See. "With this rigidity is a muscular contraction usually not resulting in any change of position of the body; but the flexor muscles exhibit a greater tendency to contraction than the extensors, and there are instances where this contraction has been quite marked, resulting of course in a change of position. If a body be not properly laid out and placed in a coffin in the cramped position in which rigor mortis has set it, there will necessarily be some change of position when, at the end of the time mentioned, this condition passes off and a relaxation ensues. In one case of death from cholera, half an hour after complete cessation of circulation and respiration, the muscles of the arms underwent spontaneously various motions of contraction and relaxation, continuing for upward of an hour" (23).

See concluded by reiterating his message that "The only motive in preparing this paper has been, not to contradict the fact that premature burials may have taken place and under the most unhappy circumstances, but to place renewed confidence in the ability of the *ordinary* general practitioner of medicine to recognize the distinction between a state of trance and a state of death, and to induce a disregard of the idle stories of ignorant and superstitious persons upon premature burials" (24).

Continued public concern about premature burial prompted another writer, who preferred anonymity, to publish an article that was intended to be reassuring in the *Journal of the Medical Association* (1898). He quickly acknowledged that "There are probably few persons endowed with lively imaginations who have not at some time in their lives had grewsome fancies about being buried alive, that is if the idea has ever been suggested to them" (25). His own opinion was that widespread incidence of premature burials probably was limited to times of social disorganization and panic (e.g., during uncontrolled epidemics), or to any conditions which prompt survivors to rush funeral preparations (e.g., when there is great fear for public safety after a person apparently has died from a highly infectious disease).

He concurs that "The difficulty in some cases of determining whether the condition is actual death or only a suspension of the vital activities with a possibility of their full reinstatement is very great . . . ." Moreover, he notes that "it is claimed by some that it is practically impossible [to make the distinction] under ordinary conditions and with the usually available means" (26). This writer thus appears to be less confident than See regarding the ability of the ordinary physician of the times to arrive at a clear-cut decision in all cases.

What reassurances can be offered to those who have developed "grewsome" fancies? The anonymous author declared that with increasing use of modern methods of preservation of remains, living burial is becoming impossible, "and with reasonable delay and care the possibilities of premature interment are reduced in all cases to almost nothing, if not absolutely destroyed" (27). That the author himself was not entirely swayed by this argument may be gleaned from the fact that he also offered an explanation intended to minimize the terror of premature burials—in effect, an acknowledgement that this phenomenon is still not out of the question. "The horror of finding oneself in a living tomb appeals directly to the imagination of every one; it seems the most terrible of all possible deaths. There is, however, another way to look at it when the physical conditions are considered. The air space in a tight coffin under five feet of earth is limited, not over two or three cubic feet at the utmost outside of the space ordinarily occupied by the body. Unless consciousness returned simultaneously with respiration, asphyxia might possibly precede it and annul it—there might be some evidences of convulsion that might be interpreted as voluntary movement, but they are not necessarily indicative of such. The cases where consciousness exists throughout must be rare, though they have been made much of in fiction, and are popularly believed to be almost the rule. It is no comfort to think that any one can be buried alive, but it is better to believe, as the facts warrant us, that the long lingering death in hopeless horror, and the powerless anticipation of the fate are still less probable events" (28).

But precisely what is the state of trance or suspended animation? In the past, many learned essays, some of them booklength, were devoted to this question. While there was reasonably good agreement descriptively, no truly satisfactory explanation emerged. Even today we are far from understanding all the psychobiological mechanisms that might be involved in altered states of consciousness, although knowledge in this general area has steadily increased. Carrington and Meader observed in 1911 that "When we come to inquire into the cause, the real *essence* of trance and kindred states, we find an amazing lack of knowledge on these subjects—mostly due to the fact, no doubt, that it has always been considered a mark of 'supersitition' to investigate such cases; and so, until the last few years, these peculiar conditions have been left strictly alone by the medical profession. When a condition of catalepsy could be shown to be due to a disordered nervous condition, *then* it was legitimate to study such a case; but when the causes of the trance were psychological or unknown, then it immediately became 'superstition'! Even today this state of affairs is not outgrown. We doubt if more than one physician in a hundred would be willing to recognize the 'medium trance', *e.g.*, as a separate state requiring prolonged psychological investigation. In spite of the fact that Professor William James pointed out the absurdity of this attitude, it is still the one all but universally maintained " (29).

Medical writers in the nineteenth and early twentieth century often attempted to differentiate at least three states that had in common the appearance of insensibility and immobility in a living person. *Catalepsy* was said to be marked by a singular absence of volition; the whole body or parts of the body would remain in any position in which they might be placed. *Ecstasy* was marked by a radiant, visionary expression. The immobility tended to fix itself in statuesque positions. *Trance* most nearly resembled the condition of a hibernating animal, complete mental inertia and insensibility. The trance state was said generally to be maintained longer than ecstasy.

It is interesting to consider that some of the elements of catalepsy remain in the contemporary psychiatric case-book, now generally included in the picture of schizophrenic reaction, catatonic type, while trance also remains very much with us in

hypnosis research and practice. But what has become of ecstasy? This altered state of consciousness was described as often involving a concentration upon some object of admiration or adoration. Were the observations mistaken, or do people no longer enter into profound states of ecstasy, so-called? We will return to this question later.

The relationship between suspended animation and premature burial strongly implies that this form of thanatomimesis is contraintentioned. Had he any choice in the matter, the individual would not have placed his life in such peril. However, we believe there are at least three types of exception to the rule that suspended animation is a contraintentioned form of thanatomimesis:

1. The individual intends or subintends an altered state of consciousness to achieve a psychosocial satisfaction or avoid a psychosocial crisis. A prime example here is the fainting spell that once was rather popular among women as a means of controlling or modifying an interpersonal situation. Apparently some of these spells were so convincing that they conveyed the impression life had fled. No doubt some fainters were barely equal to their task, or found that they could achieve the desired results by merely feigning a faint. Others were more talented, which probably means more adept at subjecting bodily processes to mental control, and could induce a state of "genuine" suspended animation.

2. The individual unintentionally induces a state of suspended animation by the use of drugs or other external means. His intention might be to relieve a distressing physical symptom, combat insomnia, relax, pep himself up, temporarily escape from stress, etc. Inadvertently (or in some instances, subintentionally), he overshoots the mark and induces a greater alteration than he had anticipated.

3. The individual fully intends to induce a state of suspended animation and

this outcome is itself a primary goal (rather than simply the means to fulfill another purpose such as getting one's way in an interpersonal situation). Success is determined largely by the depth and authenticity of the altered state. The person who seeks to induce such a state in himself might have the *cointention* of a) learning how far he can go in controlling his bodily processes, b) achieving a very special phenomenological state that he believes cannot be reached by ordinary means, or even c) pre-experiencing death and/or the state of existence after death. Superior practitioners of yoga have been credited with the ability to induce impressive and long-lasting states of suspended animation. The passage quoted below does not concern a "mysterious man of the Orient," but rather a certain Colonel Townsend whose reputed exploits earn him charter membership in any Hall of Fame that might be established in this field. We have encountered many references to Colonel Townsend in the earlier literature, but each generation freshly refurbishes his fame which rested on his ability to induce in himself a state of suspended animation from which he would make a complete recovery. As recently as 1961, Colonel Townsend was called as a witness in a panel discussion on "The Psychophysiology of Death."

"The ability to willfully influence the cardiac rate is ascribed to a Colonel Townsend who 'possessed the remarkable faculty of throwing himself into a trance at pleasure. The heart ceased apparently to throb at his bidding, respirations seemed at an end, his whole frame assumed the icy chill and rigidity of death, while his face became colourless and shrunk, and his eyes fixed, glazed and ghastly; even his mind ceased to manifest itself, for during the trance it was as utterly devoid of consciousness as his body of animation. In this state he would remain for hours, when these singular phenomena wore away and he returned to his usual condition" (30).

Two physicians and a layman reported the details of the Colonel's death. His pulse was "distinct, though small and thready, and his heart had its usual beating. He composed himself on his back and lay in a still posture for some time. I found his pulse sink gradually, till at last I could not feel any by the most exact and nice touch. Dr. Baynard could not feel the least motion in his breast nor Mr. Skrine see the least soil of breath on the bright mirror he held to his mouth; then each of us by turns examined his arm, heart and breath, but could not by the nicest scrutiny discover the least symptom of life in him" (31). The three examiners waited some time and finally were about to leave, convinced that the Colonel had indeed passed on, "when a slight motion in his body reassured them; upon examination, the pulse and heart were found again in action, and he gradually restored himself. His death-like state lasted half an hour, and recurred at nine in the morning, after which he transacted business with his attorney, and quickly expired at six o'clock in the afternoon; and the body when examined presented, with the exception of the right kidney, no signs of disease" (32).

Between Life and Death

Potential for complete or substantial recovery with little or no specialized intervention is a distinguishing characteristic of those cases which are thought to involve suspended animation. But the signs of death can also be difficult to evaluate in a person who apparently has succumbed to the effects of illness or accident. Is this very sick person now dead, or does a spark of life still flicker? Detection of life in what superficially appears to be a corpse does not necessarily imply that the individual would ever be able to return to the level of functioning he had once enjoyed, or even that life at the barest level could be maintained for much longer. In an earlier chapter (4) we considered some of the conceptual problems in attempting to define death. Here we will be concerned chiefly with the applied question: Is this a living person or a corpse?

This question is relevant in all societies, but perhaps it was of special relevance in the Transylvania of yesteryear. This is the land which, in folklore, abounds in vampires and "their kith and kin." Writers of macabre stories and scripts would have us believe that Transylvanian coffins come equipped with swinging doors, that two way traffic is the rule. This perception of Transylvania does have some support—reports of remarkably well preserved cadavers, "returns to life," etc., have been unusually frequent. Such reports can be transferred automatically to the realm of psychopathology or otherwise dismissed. A more enterprising approach is to examine closely possible naturalistic explanations for some of the phenomena—for example, is there something in the composition of Transylvanian soil that preserves human remains extraordinarily well? We cannot pursue such conjectures here. However, the fact is that one of the earliest detailed medical discussions of the problems encountered in differentiating real from apparent death was published in the *Transylvania Journal of Medicine* for 1835 (33). Dr. Nathanial Shrock apparently was motivated to explore this subject by the near-interment of his uncle. The latter had not been in a true state of suspended animation because he was quite sensible of the funeral preparations. It was a temporary paralysis, an inability to speak or move, that had brought him exceedingly close to the coffin. With his uncle's suffering still in mind, Shrock proposed that his fellow physicians redouble their efforts to avoid erroneous judgments of death.

He proposed that the following signs of death be considered as the most conclusive: "1st. Absence of respiration. 2nd. Coldness of the body. 3rd. Stiffness of the limbs. 4th. State of the circulation. 5th. State of the eyes. 6th. Depression

and flatness of the loins and buttocks. 7th. Lividness of the back. 8th. Relaxation of the sphincters. 9th. Cadaverous countenance. 10th. Insensibility of the body. 11th. Cadaverous odor. 12th. Putrefaction" (34).

In carefully reviewing these signs, in the light of his own experience and current knowledge, Shrock pointed out many instances in which incorrect judgments could be made. He was critical, for example, of the high priority given to respiration as the basic criterion of life.

Formerly, this criterion was esteemed to be of so much value, in determining on the existence of life, or the presence of death, that many methods have been adopted, to ascertain precisely whether life still remain, and the patient still breathe; and each one has been recommended as infallible in all cases. Such as the application of a mirror, or polished metal, to the mouth and nostrils; holding a burning taper before the mouth and nostrils; placing a vessel of water upon the scrobiculus cordis, etc. As to the first of these tests, it was said, if the mirror retained its lustre, the patient was considered as inevitably dead; but if, on the other hand, the surface of the mirror, or polished metal became tarnished from the condensation of the aqueous vapor of the breath, it was received as conclusive evidence, that the vital principle still remained (35).

Shrock denied that any of these procedures offered an error-free way of determining the absence of respiration. For example, "The breathing is often carried on in such a feeble and imperceptible manner, by the gentle actions of the diaphragm, as not sensibly to affect the vessel of water, or give any motion to the fluid, while the fluctuations of the atmosphere may make such an impression on the water, as to beget, in the mind of the friends of the deceased and the physician, a hope that life still remains . . ." (36). Furthermore, the absence of respiration may be only the *suspension* of this activity.

Possible sources of error are pointed out regarding each of the 12 most conclusive signs of death. While coldness of the body is generally taken to be a mark of death, the temperature depends upon many factors, including the mode of death. Sudden death from lightning or an internal injury, for example, may not result in much change of body temperature for several hours, while in some cases a dead body will become cold but then regenerate so much heat in the next day or two that a lifelike temperature returns. On the other side, a severe attack of asthma or some other illness that diminishes respiration may result in a death-like coldness although the person is still alive. Another example: "The loss of the contractile power of the iris has been laid down as a manifestation of the presence of death. . . . " Accordingly, the physician will push the eyelid up with his finger—if the position is maintained, then he concludes that death unquestionably has occurred. "In no disease, let the relaxation and exhaustion be as great as they may, does this occur, but it will cover the ball, and when pushed up, will regain its natural position," or so medical opinion went. But Shrock argued that "the same is observable in deep sleep, apoplexy, asphyxia, drunkenness, injuries of the head, poisoning with the strammonium, etc. It is consequently not a conclusive sign of death" (37).

We need not pursue this critique in all its particulars. However, it is instructive to note that even the most conclusive of all the "conclusive" signs—putrefaction—can also be misinterpreted. "But unhappily for the devoted examiner, it is not always an easy matter to distinguish the putrid smell of a corpse, from the nauseous odor produced by the decomposition of matters in the intestinal tube. The smelling may occur in hysteric cases, counterfeiting death, or it may arise from fermentation during life. Some diseases are attended with spots on the skin, which so much counterfeit these spots, that it is almost impossible to distinguish them from each other" (38). Shrock emphasized that it is

an essential part of medical education to learn and most diligently practice the difficult skill of reading the signs of death, rather than to treat this matter in an overly-assured, perfunctory manner.

Henry W. Ducachet, a New York physician, preceded Shrock by a few years in his examination of the subject (39), and many of his observations were confirmed by the experience of the latter. Ducachet also was concerned with the practice, still somewhat prevalent in his day, for bodies to be interred without obtaining an authentic medical certificate. "But physicians themselves are sometimes so negligent of the duty thus enjoined, that the wise intention of the law is continually defeated" (40).

Occasional articles and chapters on problems in distinguishing between real and apparent death have continued to appear. Barker, writing more than 60 years after Shrock, seemed rather confident about the ability of the physician to ascertain death with great accuracy in most cases, but cautioned his colleagues to be aware of that special instance they might encounter at any time (41). Decomposition or putrefaction, when clearly present, remains the surest sign. "But putrefaction, itself may be long delayed, especially in subjects addicted to the use of certain drugs, as alcohol or arsenic, or in persons poisoned by these or by other antiseptic drugs" (42). Barker's suggestions for determining the presence of life under questionable circumstances include a reference to "the methods of resuscitating the fakirs. . . . Friction and hot water bathing are applied to the body, the eyelids oiled and gently rubbed, the tongue annointed and gently drawn forward and hot, moist compresses applied to the top of the head" (43). In other words, one can attempt experimentally to induce or encourage life rather than restrict the diagnostic efforts to the usual observations. Barker's brief remarks on this point have a very modern sound. He was implying, or on the verge of implying, that death may be a function of the potential physican-patient interaction rather than a fixed, irrevocable fact in its own right. And we have already seen (Chapters 4 and 16) that *diagnosis, treatment and definition of death are now being regarded increasingly as inseparable aspects of the same process of intervention or inquiry.*

The observer, even the physician, sometimes can experience difficulty in determining whether or not life is truly extinct in a person who is thought to be dead. However, the obverse might be more common these days. We are referring to individuals who linger for weeks, months, or even years in a state of severe debilitation and depletion. Officially, these people are alive. But the observer may detect little or no lifelike behavior. Let us observe the observer for a moment. Does he behave as though he is in the presence of a living person? Or does he instead treat the non-responsive person as a sort of object or machine that requires tending, protection, etc., but no distinctly human response? If there is no behavior forthcoming from the body and if those in the environment behave as though the bed were not occupied by a living human being, then the thanatomimetic impression can be overwhelming. We are assured only by the context (the body is in a hospital bed, not on a slab).

Psychology and psychiatry have had relatively little to say about these conditions. Perhaps the prevailing emphasis upon psychodynamics has discouraged attention to these seemingly dynamic-less states. Furthermore, medical-nursing personnel seldom request psychologists and psychiatrists to consult in these circumstances. Whatever the reason, we do not even have a standard nomenclature or set of diagnostic procedures to support us when we find ourselves in the vicinity of "the living dead." Much less do we have any clear theoretical framework to guide our efforts. This is surely one of the areas in which mental health knowledge and skills have remained rudimentary for years.

An Exploratory Study

One of the authors (R.K.) and several of his colleagues conducted an exploratory study of patients who seem to hover between life and death. This study was carried out at Cushing Hospital, a geriatric facility operated by The Commonwealth of Massachusetts. The objectives were limited, but difficult to achieve: a) to develop a reliable procedure for observing and classifying patients whose behavior is at the extreme low end of the spectrum, b) to apply this procedure to the current hospital population, and c) to determine what disparity, if any, exists between the patient's appearance and the behavior that he still remains capable of performing. Additionally, we hoped to interpret the findings within the general framework of the developmental-field theory. This study merely opened the way for subsequent investigations that we hope others as well as ourselves will be interested in pursuing. Here we will report some of the developments and findings that are most relevant to the present topic.

Clincial psychologists and research personnel familiar with geriatric patients made random observations on various wards throughout the hospital. They attempted to condense their observations into "atomic statements," i.e., brief, non-judgmental descriptions of the patients' speech, appearance, behavior, and posture. These observations were culled and studied by the staff. A standard procedure and a preliminary classification system was then devised, and a second round of observations carried out. Next followed a more organized observational effort in which three investigators made twice-daily ratings on 213 patients for three days. Each patient in this study (about one-third of the total hospital population) was seen once in the morning and once in the afternoon. The observers were distributed by patient and by time period in a counterbalanced design. While each of these observations was made by a single staff member, individual bias was distributed evenly throughout the sample, and the three raters had previously conducted a number of joint observations to develop a shared orientation. Later, one of the raters continued his observations on a daily basis on the intensive treatment unit.

Four types of *low-level behavioral syndrome* were distinguished:

Type I

    1. In bed
    2. Supine
    3. Mouth open
    4. Eyes closed or with empty stare
    5. Head tilted back
    6. Arms straight at side
    7. Absence of adjustive movements, fidgeting, speech, verbalizations, etc.
    8. General impression of having been placed or molded into position

Type II

    1. Propped in chair (with pillow and foot support)
    2. Head droops to one side
    3. Eyes closed
    4. Absence of fidgeting and adjustive movements, speech, etc.
    5. Position in chair may be readjusted with no discernible response on part of patient, or with immediate return to original position after brief, slow visual inspection

Type III

    1. If in bed: lying on side, generally with one arm above the head, holding to top railing. This is a stereotyped posture, but more resemblance to normal resting posture than in the case of Type I
    2. May spontaneously shift position, usually with a toppling motion
    3. If sitting: gives impression of supporting self in the chair, at least partially (in contrast to inert bundle appearance of Type II)

    4. Tends to look up when someone approaches, or when receiving direct attention
    5. Responds to simple questions with word or simple phrase
    6. Does not volunteer statements
    7. Absence of emotional expression in speech or demeanor
    8. Often will grasp objects placed in hand

Type IV

    1. Usually found sitting at the bedside or in solarium; does not appear completely inert
    2. May be semi-ambulatory, use walker or wheelchair for short distances
    3. Fidgets, picks at clothes, tries to escape from chair, women often pull dress up, impression of activity-tendencies without clear purpose
    4. Emits sounds—may groan, cry, or speak stereotyped phrases. Verbalizations are made without a shared context for communication. May be bizarre, obscene, or fragments of what sounds like normal discourse, but lacking context and connections
    5. When approached, patient tends to start or increase verbalizations. Mumbling and largely incomprehensible, the patient gives impression of being confused. Often one cannot be sure whether or not the patient is responding to the interviewer

Types I and II might be regarded as syndromes of "the living dead." The major difference seemed to be that Type II patients could be moved from bed to chair and did not exhibit the open, sunken mouth appearance of Type I. Type III patients might be considered as being in a transitional stage between the living dead and the clearly alive. These patients were more likely to be clad in their own clothes. Type IV patients could perhaps be considered as being at the entrance level to what generally is understood as human functioning.

The stereotype prevalent in these four syndromes makes it possible to specify rather definite characteristics with little or no concern for individual differences. But as we move along from one type to the next (particularly after Type II and again after Type IV), the stereotypy begins to diminish and individual differences become of increasing importance. In fact, beyond Type IV, the variety of specific postures and behaviors in our patients was observed to be so great that it was not practical to develop additional categories. Type V patients would have included some who were markedly impaired and reduced in functioning by almost any standard one would care to use, but whose behavior remained so much more complex and variable than the other types that we could not establish reliable categories based upon clearly observable signs. Only the first four categories were considered types of the low-level behavior syndrome.

Each rating was in effect a microcosmic before-and-after study. The contact was divided into two parts: *observation* and *confrontation*. During the observational phase, the rater would approach the patient closely enough to see him well and to give the patient an opportunity to see him and acknowledge his presence in some way. A rating would be made based upon this observation. Then the rater would speak to the patient, introduce himself and attempt to develop at least a rudimentary relationship. Results of this confrontation phase were also rated. Thus, it was possible to learn if some patients were more or less intact or "alive" than they appeared to be on the basis of observation alone. Fluctuations in appearance and response from morning to afternoon and from day to day were also available for analysis.

On the first day of observations three female and two male patients were classified as Type I. These were all "sick ward" patients with the exception of one female. Eleven females and five males were classified as Type II; five of these females and all of the males were located off the "sick ward" or intensive treatment unit. Three of the Type I patients (observation phase) were again classified as Type I after being approached by the rater (confrontation phase). However, one woman responded sufficiently to be given the follow-up classification of Type II and one man was raised to a Type III. Six of the Type II patients remained in this classification during the confrontation phase, but ten exhibited more lifelike behavior. Of the ten whose response belied their appearance, two were reclassified as Type III, and four each as Type IV and Type V (out of the low-level syndrome entirely). None of the Type II patients appeared to decline in their appearance when approached by the raters, but such a decline would in any case be very difficult to observe (and, of course, a Type I patient, being in the lowest category, could decline no further).

The great majority of the patients who were observed turned out to be in classifications beyond "the living dead." It was uncommon for a person in a higher classification on observation to be rated lower on confrontation. During the first contact, for example, only one of the 63 patients rated as Type III was reclassified as Type II on confrontation. Downward shifts were most frequent at the upper end, where 14 of 47 patients initially seen as Type V were rated on confrontation as Type IV. As we examined all six contacts over three days for each patient, we became impressed by the predominance of positive changes during the confrontation phase. Roughly half the time that a Type I or Type II patient was approached, his response to the contact was sufficient to reevaluate him on a higher level. There may well have been a "priming" effect—after several contacts a previously inert patient could have been more ready to respond to subsequent contacts. Possible effects of multiple brief interpersonal contacts with patients manifesting a low-level behavioral syndrome could be evaluated more clearly with an experimental design that adds fresh patients to each round of observations.

There is nothing really surprising, of course, in the finding that people sometimes respond to other people, even in the limited sort of relationship our staff could offer in their research roles. But is is interesting to note that a thanatomimetic state sufficient to discourage ordinary human relationships proved to be relatively easy to modify about half the time. With a more therapeutic and persistent kind of intervention this percentage might have been increased, and the "thaw" become more substantial and permanent. Conversely, if personnel and visitors are overly impressed with the thanatomimetic appearance, then some individuals might remain isolated from significant human contact although they still retain the potential for interaction.

Symbolic Death

Is it possible that a person might subintend a thanatomimetic state in an effort to contraintend actual death? In other words, might a person slay himself symbolically to avoid the real thing? Such a proposition sounds rather Freudian so, appropriately enough, we now turn to Freud.

The life of Dostoevsky in some respects rivals the fascination of his writings. Freud studied both. His attention was drawn to the severe epileptic attacks that Dostoevsky suffered on a number of occasions. Freud concluded that "These attacks had the significance of death: They were heralded by a fear of death and consisted of lethargic, somnolent states" (44). This illness first came over Dostoevsky as a youth in the form of a sudden feeling that he was going to die right on the spot. The seizure, in fact, induced a state markedly similar to real death. Dostoevsky then made it a practice to leave notes about before going to sleep. He was afraid that he would fall into the death-like state and become a victim of premature burial. His notes begged that burial be postponed for five days.

According to Freud, these deathlike attacks signified an identification with a dead person: either with someone who was really dead or with someone who was still alive but whom the subject—Dostoevsky—wished dead. Freud emphasized the implications of the latter alternative. "The attack then has the value of a punishment. One has wished another person dead, and now one *is* the other person and is dead himself . . . . For a boy, this other person is usually his father and the attack (which is termed hysterical) is thus a self-punishment for a death-wish against a hated father" (45). In the specific case of Dostoevsky, Freud bolstered his argument by citing the mock execution and banishment which a father-replacement (the Tsar) was induced to administer. When Dostoevsky could not induce his father or a suitable father-replacement to punish him, then he would have to administer the punishment himself: a mock self-execution, as it were. Freud also observed that, in the aura of the epileptic attack, one moment of supreme bliss is experienced. He proposed that this experience might be a record of the triumph and sense of liberation felt on the symbolic execution of the father, to be followed immediately by the massive punishment of the seizure-death.

A number of questions are left unanswered. Was the feared death itself symbolic, or did Dostoevsky engage in these psychic maneuvers to avert what he sensed to be the prospect of actual murder or annihilation? This question perhaps is a parallel to the better known dispute concerning "the castration complex": how much is realistic, how much is symbolic? Certainly, a death threat within the context of the father-son dynamics described here by Freud suggests a sort of punishment-by-castration that has escalated into the prospect of total castration or death. We are also left wondering to what extent we can generalize from Dostoevsky's plight. Are similar dynamics to be found in all or many persons who suffer from epileptic seizures? Only males? Only those with relatively little organic basis for the seizures? Do the dynamics apply more broadly, with the particular death-equivalent symptom varying from person to person? In other words, although Dostoevsky is said to have experienced his seizures as a substitute for death, might it be the case that others develop different substitutes for death? What might these substitutes be? Oversleeping? Over-medication? Certain "psychosomatic" diseases? Frigidity or impotence? Is it possible that some cases of suspended animation which have been presumed to be unintentioned or contraintentioned might really be subintentioned? And is it out of the question that even some of the 'between-life-and-death' cases might involve symbolic, i.e., subintentional dynamics?

While a person might be "symbolically dead" in several different ways (such as being "cut dead" by his social group), here we have limited our attention to a condition that is clearly thanatomimetic, such as Dostoevsky's seizure-related states. *Perhaps any state* (whether it is sleep, seizure, or whatnot) *that bears a resemblance to death can be used symbolically by the individual as a death-equivalent or substitute.* Thus, whenever we witness a thanatomimetic state we might wonder about the likelihood of subintentionality. Naturally, this would be just one of several hypotheses to be considered, not an automatic conclusion.

Playing Dead

Let us briefly consider one more form of thanatomimesis. Play might be regarded as one of the most serious forms of human activity. Within the rules of the game we can strive for perfection, enact life-and-death dramas, test the limits of our functioning, reaffirm group allegiances, and practice skills that have signi-

ficant applications outside of the game situation. Raw emotions and formidable ideas that would be highly anxiety-rousing in "real life" can be tolerated or even enjoyed in play. The participant who disobeys the rules of the game is quickly notified of the seriousness of his misconduct.

Often the strong feelings and complex ideas associated with death can be accommodated within the framework of spontaneous playfulness or relatively systematized games. Children have been playing dead for centuries. Hide-and-go-seek, in its many variants, has been interpreted as a death game, along with the thinly-symbolic game of medieval origin, ring-around-the-rosie (46). Maurer asserts that even the infant plays at death or nonexistence in his universally popular peek-a-boo antics (47). And we have all seen youngsters "die" melodramatically as they enact cowboy-and-Indian or spaceman-and-creature games inspired by what they have witnessed on the screen or television.

The child who playfully intends the thanatomimetic state is learning how to accommodate the meaning of death into his general outlook on life. How better to become acquainted with the implications of death than by trying it on for size, and under varying circumstances? Mere verbal discussion of death is not likely to resolve the curiosity and uncertainty that the child is beginning to experience. Acting it out is more satisfactory—and also has the advantage of linking one's own feelings to group behavior. We might increase our respect for children's death impersonations if we kept in mind the strong likelihood that this play is a significant part of a developmental-learning process that will have implications for their total life view and adjustment (see chapter 2).

CONCLUDING REMARKS

This chapter has introduced thanatomimesis as a subject deserving study in its own right. It has been proposed that categories already in use in one area (suicide) also are applicable here. These are the concepts of intentional, subintentional, unintentional, and contraintentional participation in one's deathlike state. Cointentionality has been proposed as an additional category. A considerable range of thanatomimetic behavior has been cited, with several applied and theoretical points discussed in passing. We conclude by highlighting a few questions that deserve futher exploration:

1. What can we learn from thanatomimesis that will improve our understanding of *actual death that is induced by subtle and complex mechanisms?* We are thinking in particular of incidents that tend to be classified as "psychosomatic deaths," or "voodoo" or "hex" deaths.

2. What can we learn from thanatomimesis that will improve our understanding of the *reversibility* of what appears to be the terminal process?

3. What can we learn from thanatomimesis that will contribute to our understanding of the *changing relationship between cultural patterns and psychobiological states?* For example, it has been noted that ecstasy, once a relatively prevalent form of suspended animation, is seldom, if ever, reported these days. Now let us add the observation that conversion reactions and multiple personalities, phenomena that seem to have a good deal in common with ecstasy, also have become clinical rarities. All these phenomena were topics of considerable interest to leading clinicians as recently as the first decade of the present century (48, 49). Yet today there are many clinicians who have never encountered or, at any rate, identified these syndromes, who perhaps never heard of ecstasy and disbelieve that such a state as multiple personality ever existed. Without launching into a full discussion here, it can be suggested that culturally sanctioned or facilitated modes of psychobiological expression might change from

generation to generation. We speculate that in parts of the world that enjoy a lag in psychological sophistication, one might still find many examples of ecstasy, conversion reaction, and multiple personality (especially the first two). There is increasing acceptance of the proposition that patterns of "conventional" illness may be related to cultural and subcultural factors (Chapter 5). Perhaps thanatomimetic states—their form, frequency, and intentionality—also vary with cultural factors, and may thus provide a new pathway for the investigation of cultural differences.

4. What can we learn from thanatomimesis that will improve our understanding of *how people perceive and react to an altered state of functioning in others?* No doubt people differ with respect to their implicit criteria for judging that a person is dead. Some nurses, for example, continue to speak and minister to comatose patients, giving them the benefit of the doubt. Other nurses adopt a nonhuman form of relationship even while the patient appears to be alive. Motivational as well as perceptual-cognitive factors probably are involved. For example, a person motivated by anxiety for the health of a loved one might fearfully interpret a deep sleep as death, or persist in demanding a response from what in fact is a corpse. We would like to know something about possible differences in how people behave when they are in the presence of an indisputable corpse as compared with a person known to be alive but functioning in a profound thanatomimetic state.

5. What can we learn from thanatomimesis that will *improve our care of people who are in a state resembling death?* The authors have heard many accounts of people who recovered from a thanatomimetic state with decidely negative aftereffects based upon what was said about them within range of their hearing. A recent example is typical: An experienced and senior nurse reported that her brother was brought into the emergency

room of a general hospital after he and his two companions had been in a severe automobile accident. The man in question was bloodied and unresponsive. He could easily have been taken for dead or near-dead. As a matter of fact, however, he was conscious and able to hear all that was said. In his presence the hospital personnel a) spoke casually about the death of one of his companions, which was news to him, and b) spoke disparagingly about his own chances of survival. "He's a goner—don't bother with him now." This man could have died with these words ringing in his ears. He tried desperately to offer some behavior that would demonstrate he was still alive and capable of life. This story had a happy ending, otherwise we would not have known it. It could be that the thoughtless comments made in his presence actually challenged him to rally his resources, an interpretation that the patient later made himself. But these remarks might also have finished him off. He remains rather haunted by this experience.

Considering that we know so little about thanatomimesis, it would seem that special care would be given to people who are observed to be in this condition. Who knows precisely what short-range and long-range effects might be induced in a person who is in such a drastically altered state of being? It is possible that suggestibility might be greatly heightened, resulting in something akin to a posthypnotic suggestion or (inadvertently) conditioned response.

This chapter will have accomplished its purpose if the reader now considers certain extremes of human behavior—specifically thanatomimesis—to be "in bounds" for scientific research and enlightened professional practice.

REFERENCES

1. Shneidman, E. S. Orientations toward death: A vital aspect of the study of lives. In R. White (Ed.), *The study of lives*. New York: Atherton Press, 1963. Pp. 200-227.
2. *Ibid.*, p. 206.
3. Norton, A. C., Beran, A. V. & Misrahy, G. A. Experiment summarized in *Scientific American*, 1964, *211*, 64.
4. Charles Darwin. Quoted by Carrington, H. & Meader, J. R. *Death: Its causes and phenomena*. London: Rider, 1911. P. 55.
5. S. J. Holmes, cited by Carrington & Meader, *op. cit.*, p. 56.
6. Carrington H. & Meader, J. R. *Death: Its causes and phenomena*. London: Rider, 1911. P. 51.
7. Hoagland, Hudson. On the mechanism of tonic immobility in vertebrates. *Journal of General Physiology*, 1928. Pp. 715-741.
8. *Ibid.*, p. 731.
9. *Ibid.*, p. 716.
10. Fletcher, M. R. *One thousand buried alive by their best friends*. Boston, 1890.
11. Hartmann, F. *Buried alive*. Boston, 1895.
12. Haberstein, R. W. & Lamers, W. M. *The history of American funeral direction*. Milwaukee, Wisc.: Bulfin, 1955.
13. Blythe, R. *Akenfield. Portrait of an English village*. New York: Dell, 1969. Pp. 313-314.
14. Summers, M. *The vampire, his kith and kin*. New York: University Books, 1960.
15. *Ibid.*, p. 45.
16. MacKay, G. E. Premature burials. *Popular Science Monthly*, 1880, *16*, 389-397.
17. *Ibid.*, p. 389.
18. *Ibid.*, p. 391.
19. *Ibid.*
20. *Ibid.*, p. 390.
21. *Ibid.*, p. 392.
22. See, W. The extreme rarity of premature burials. *Popular Science Monthly*, 1880, *17*, 527.
23. *Ibid.*, p. 529.
24. *Ibid.*, p. 530.
25. Anon. Premature burial. *Journal of the American Medical Association*, 1898. P. 273.
26. *Ibid.*, p. 273.
27. *Ibid.*, p. 274.
28. *Ibid.*, pp. 273-274.
29. Carrington & Meader, *op. cit.*, p. 44.
30. Herbert C. C. Life-influencing interactions. In A. Simon, C. C. Herbert & R. Strauss (Eds.), *The physiology of emotion*. Springfield, Ill.: Charles C Thomas, 1961. P. 190.

31. *Ibid.*, p. 190.
32. *Ibid.*, p. 191.
33. Shrock, N. M. On the signs that distinguish real from apparent death. *Transylvanian Journal of Medicine*, 1835, *13*, 210-220.
34. *Ibid.*, p. 211.
35. *Ibid.*, p. 212.
36. *Ibid.*, p. 213.
37. *Ibid.*, p. 217.
38. *Ibid.*, p. 220.
39. Ducachet, H. W. On the signs of death, and the manner of distinguishing real from apparent death. *American Medical Record*, 1822. Pp. 39-53.
40. *Ibid.*, p. 52.
41. Barker, C. F. On real and apparent death. *Clin. Chic. Med.*, 1897, *18*, 232-238.

42. *Ibid.*, p. 235.
43. *Ibid.*, p. 238.
44. Freud, S. Dostoevsky and parricide. *Collected psychological papers of Sigmund Freud.* London: Hogarth, 1961. Vol. 21, p. 183.
45. *Ibid.*, p. 183.
46. Weber, F. P. *Aspects of death and correlated aspects of life in art, epigram and poetry.* London: H. K. Lewis and Co., Ltd., 1922.
47. Maurer, A. The child's knowledge of non-existence. *Journal of Existential Psychology*, 1961, *2*, 193-212.
48. Prince, M. *The dissociation of a personality.* New York: Longmans, Green, 1905.
49. Binet, A. *Alterations of personality.* (Translated by J. M. Baldwin.) New York: Appleton, 1896.

6

The Personification
of Death

TWO VIEWS OF DEATH

Death is "the final cessation of the vital functions of an animal or plant" (1).

Death is "a very old woman with horribly wrinkled skin and long, grey hair. She is a very ugly person with a long, thin nose and thin lips. She is tall and very thin, dressed always in black. Her hands are the most noticeable things about her— being in the shape of claws with long green fingernails. Death's personality is a very morbid one, yet she is continuously laughing. She rarely speaks, but that horrible laugh can be heard whenever she is near. She doesn't like most people because she resents life itself."

The first of these two strikingly different views of death is a formal and rather typical definition such as may be found in dictionaries. Although the phraseology may differ somewhat from one definition to another, the general message is clear enough: Death is an impersonal fact to be formulated in an intellectual manner, shorn of any obvious feelings or attitudes. The formal definition provides "the truth and nothing but the truth" about death.

By contrast, the second view seems to abandon objectivity. Death is cast in a human form and described in emotional language. There is the impression that this view of death has personal meaning to the individual who offered this description. In quasi-spatial terms, the second view seems "close" to the individual, while the first view is "distant." Correspondingly, the second view is particularized and perhaps idiosyncratic, while the first view is available and acceptable to any reasonable person.

The formal, objective view of death is the one that appears to make the most sense. The idiosyncratic, subjective personification of death appears to have little in its favor: factually, it is absurd, and psychologically it is burdened with the particular fears and fancies of its inventor.

These considerations, however, are rather superficial, and of value chiefly in how they enable us to formulate a set of problems worthy of psychological investigation. Perhaps the first step might be to examine more carefully the similarities as well as the differences between these two views. We suggest here that these contrasting views are similar in that each is a special case of a more general cognitive mode. The formal, intellectualized view of death seems to represent the cognitive mode that Heinz Werner has characterized as *geometric-technical*, while the personification of death seems to represent the functioning of what Werner has termed the *physiognomic* mode of cognition (2). According to Werner, these two modes of cognition are quite basic in human functioning, and quite distinct from each other. The g-technical mode is employed in scientific and mathematical thought; objects are seen in what is taken to be their "matter-of-fact," or "realistic" aspect. The physiognomic mode is particularly evident in artistic activities, the emphasis being placed upon the "expressive" or "aesthetic" qualities perceived in the world. Support for this line of reasoning has been provided by several controlled studies. Particularly clear-cut is Comalli's investigation of perceptual differences between scientists (chemists) and artists (3). Artists were found to be more greatly affected by physiognomic qualities than were the scientists.

Werner and Comalli conceive these two cognitive modes as being intimately involved with our habitual view of the world in general, a notion that is consistent with the findings cited above. It appears in keeping with this rationale to hypothesize that preference for a "realistic" or personifying view of death would be related to one's general bias in the direction of either the g-technical or physiognomic mode. These considerations imply that perhaps we should not be too hasty in dismissing personifications of death as fantasies, quirks, or distortions of "what death really is." If personification is closely linked to the physiognomic mode of cognition, as suggested, and if the physiognomic mode is as basic an aspect of human functioning as Werner has suggested, then we might attend more seriously to how our minds register and act upon the qualities of death that are excluded by objective definitions. Even the dictionary acknowledges the existence

of this alternate mode of viewing death, e.g., the words that immediately follow the quoted definition ("the final cessation of the vital functions of an animal or plant") are: "often personified."

There is a further implication. If the g-technical and physiognomic modes are equally basic to human functioning, then the former mode may no longer go unchallenged as the only "correct" orientation to death. Might it not be the case that each mode offers a combination of insight and attitude, but that neither mode by itself is sufficient to define completely man's view of death?

The formal view is not merely factual— it also expresses an attitude. The attitude is one of detachment; death is regarded as impersonal. To define death without including a personal or social meaning surely conveys an attitude toward the subject, and an attitude toward the *relationship* between the definer and the defined. Even though the definition may contain "the truth and nothing but the truth," it is doubtful that it contains "the whole truth." Correspondingly, the personification of death is not merely a thrown-together patchwork of feelings and attitudes—it also conveys information. Is death personified as a young woman? As an old man? As an appealing or a frightening person? Are some individuals unable to personify death, and others unable to regard death in the g-technical mode? Does the personification change as the individual approaches the prospect of his own death? Do personifications of death tell us something about a culture's "death system" and its relationship to an entire way of life? Do personifications of death tell us something about the individual's conception of his place in the universe and the meaning of his own life?

PLAN OF THIS CHAPTER

The authors have obtained personifications of death from a variety of people:

liberal arts college students, student nurses, graduate nurses, funeral directors, students in a morticians' training program, and staff members of a geriatric hospital. Further information about these samples is given in Table 1. An open-end procedure was administered to 240 subjects; 421 subjects responded to a multiple choice procedure.

The open-end version: "If death were a person, what sort of a person would Death be? Think of this question until an image of death-as-a-human-being forms in your mind. Then describe Death physically, what Death would *look* like. . . . Now, what would Death *be* like? What kind of personality would Death have?" If the subject did not spontaneously indicate the age and sex of Death, he was then requested to add these specifications. Additionally, he was asked to indicate from what sources he had derived his image of Death and how difficult or easy the task had been for him.

The multiple choice version most frequently used:

1. "In stories, plays and movies, death is sometimes treated as though a human being. If you were writing a story in which one character would represent Death, would you represent Death as a) a young man b) an old man c) a young woman d) an old woman? If other, please specify.

2. "Would Death be a) a cold, remote sort of person b) a gentle, well-meaning sort of person c) a grim, terrifying sort of person?"

From responses to the open-end question, we have been able to establish several relatively clear types of personification. These images are described and briefly discussed in the following section of this chapter. Next, consideration is given to a simple analysis of quantitative findings regarding characteristics of death personifications and their relationship to the personifiers. The concluding section offers an exploration of possible meanings of death personifications with some attention to philosophical and cultural as well as personality factors.

CONTEMPORARY PERSONIFICATIONS OF DEATH: QUALITATIVE ASPECTS

What human shape represents death in our minds today? There is not one all-pervasive image that is shared by everybody in our society; rather, a variety of images can be found even within the limitations of the present samples. An even greater variety might be found if one inquired into the personifications of, let us say, Southern sharecroppers, survivors of concentration camps, professional artists, etc. The present data, however, are sufficiently rich to provide a starting point for classifying and understanding contemporary modes of personifying death.

As mentioned earlier, this section offers a classification of the verbal portraits of death that were given in response to the open-end form of our inquiry.

ⅹ *The Macabre* ⅹ

The vivid, horror-laden, disfigured personification of death that was so prevalent in fourteenth and fifteenth century Europe is still with us today, although it is no longer without competition.

One image of the macabre was given in the introduction to this chapter: "A very old woman with horribly wrinkled skin . . . very ugly person with a long thin nose and thin lips. . . ." This image, offered by a female undergraduate in a liberal arts college, emphasizes repulsive physical characteristics associated with advanced age. She has auditory as well as visual aspects ("a horrible laugh"), and is, one might say, "dead-set" against life.

A male undergraduate offers a similar image, except that he imagines death to be a man and is even more explicit in describing repugnant physical characteristics:

Physically, Death is a walking death. He is a male, about eighty-nine years old, and is very bent over. His hair is scraggly, his face is wrinkled, almost not recognizable as human flesh. His eyes are sunken, his teeth are rotting (the ones left). As noted above, he is bent, if not a hunchback, and can hardly move. His hands and other appendages are also in terrible shape. Personality-wise, he's grouchy, cranky, sullen, sarcastic, cynical, mean, evil, disgusting, obnoxious, and nauseating—most of the time—only, very, very seldom does his good side show through. But even here, one must be quite sharp to catch it, for it only appears very infrequently, and is gone again an instant after it appears.

The idea of deterioration, sometimes associated with the image of a skeleton, is another medieval representation of the macabre. Here is one contemporary personification offered by another male undergraduate:

The only thing that comes to mind immediately is the classical illustration of a skeleton with a white sheet over his skull and part or all of his body, with hollow black eye sockets and nasal openings. This I imagine only because I have seen it represented this way in illustrations such as ghost stories, National Safety Council signs, etc. The personality is a coldness, hollowness, absolute nothingness. I imagine death as being a ceasing of existence, and you can't really put a personality into a void or nothingness.

Still another male undergraduate imagines:

An extremely thin, and emaciated form, scarred, burned, contorted, about twelve feet tall. There is something indefinable about this person. When I look at this person—don't think it isn't possible—a shivering and nausea overwhelms me. Its face is blank, a mere flat surface, blank eyes, nose, and mouth, an unsensing thing. Claws on both hands and feet. This form is completely nude, very hairy and useless.

Another female undergraduate would picture death as a "gigantic being of super-human strength. A body to which one would relinquish all hopes of resistance. He would be cold and dark, in such a way that one glance would reveal his mission. He would be always dressed in black and would wear a hat which he wore tightly over his head . . . self-confident, with an over-abundance of ego. He would naturally be callous and would enjoy his occupation. He would get a greater thrill when the person whom he was claiming was enjoying life to a great degree."

Additional illustrations could be given, but those presented above represent the most salient and typical characteristics encountered in contemporary versions of the macabre personification. Physically, death is either repulsive or overpowering. The vision may be of an emaciated or decaying human, or of a monster with only faint resemblance to human form. Often implied and sometimes explicit is the image of a death-like death, i.e., the form is that of a being which is consumed or in process of being consumed by death (e.g., "Death is a walking death"). This theme was also central to those medieval representations of death which emerged at the high tide of the macabre sentiment. Frequently there is the suggestion that mass media of the present day serve to perpetuate the medieval image (e.g., "National Safety Council signs"). Perhaps it is simply that the death-engrossed artist of the Middle Ages discovered modes of expression that are difficult to improve upon for clarity and impact of communication. It is worth noting that an apparently more sophisticated, g-technical attitude may co-exist along with the physiognomic macabre personification, as in the "skeleton with a white sheet over his skull." On a verbal level, the young man who presented this image *conceived* of death as a "ceasing of existence"; but this abstract conception did not inhibit him from *imaging* death in a concrete way.

Macabre personifications also tend to be "close" to the emotional life of their creators. A clear example is that of the young man who reported that "a shivering and nausea overwhelms me" when he contemplates the image he has produced.

Advanced age frequently is attributed to the macabre personification. This attribute is also found in some other types of death personification. But here we are given pictures not merely of advanced age, but of grossly infirm, even hideous old people. One is reminded of those infinitely miserable Struldbrugs encountered by Captain Gulliver in the Land of the Luggnaggians, beings fated not to death but to endless aging (4).

In summary then, the type of personification we have termed macabre is one which emphasizes disfiguration and decay, often in the form of a very old person. Death the macabre is seen as a horrible being who is the sworn enemy of life. The characterizations frequently are vivid, detailed, and emotionally close to their creators.

The Gentle Comforter

The macabre vision of death presents a raw encounter with the decadent and demonic. In vain does one search for comfort and reassurance. However, there is another type of personification which seems to possess at its very core a theme of soothing welcome. Here are three examples, the first given by a co-ed at a liberal arts college, the others by young nurses.

Physically, Death would be male. He would be very strong, very powerful. He would be quiet; he would speak very softly and gently. He would be light-haired and have darker skin, that is, not a fair, whitish complexion. The physical attributes are very, very difficult to imagine in any detail. Death, if a person, would not be so easy to see as an image of any man, but he would be very strong, powerful, with a quiet gentleness and tenderness.

Psychologically, Death would be very comfortable and comforting. He would bring the meaning of life, the quiet whisper would allow one to know what life is about. The entire reason each

one is living will become clear when Death comes. He will be kind, tender, and gentle. He will come to envelope and take me with a quietness.

Death would be about middle-aged or even younger.

This young woman found the task "relatively easy to do—I have grappled with the problem and come to this conclusion. It may change with age. The idea came to me in my sophomore year when I was wavering over a fellow I am now pinned to and we have intentions of being married. My idea about this was formulated at this time, at least the psychological part. I had not pictured Death as a physical person."

The Gentle Comforter may also be seen as an old person, as illustrated in this personification from a registered nurse:

A fairly old man with long white hair and a long beard. A man who would resemble a biblical figure with a long robe which is clean but shabby. He would have very strong features and despite his age would appear to have strength. His eyes would be very penetrating and his hands would be large."

Death would be calm, soothing, and comforting. His voice would be of an alluring nature and, although kind, would hold the tone of the mysterious. Therefore, in general, he would be kind and understanding and yet be very firm and sure of his action and attitudes.

This young woman believed that she had developed her picture of death from the traditional image of Father Time.

The comforting theme occasionally is embodied in a person whose sex is not entirely determinate, as illustrated by this response from another registered nurse.

Physicially, Death would be a large, tall person but I am unable to say whether it is male or female. Death has fair skin and strong but artistic hands—one would say they are beautiful, another handsome. The face of Death is stern but not ugly. It is almost a gentle face. It seems strange that a face could be stern and gentle at the same time, but that is how I see Death. It is an understanding face. The more I think about it, the more Death is masculine but not a male. Not a female either. But more masculine than feminine.

Mentally, Death is *aware* enough to be *sympathetic*. Death is also understanding but unable to often times do other than what must be done though Death would like to change its "plans."

Death was thought of as being somewhere between 30 and 50, although actually "it never grows older." This woman's final word about its sex: "Death is neither male nor female and could be both. Although Death is more masculine than feminine." This young woman experienced the task as being a difficult one, and had a hunch that "the ideas I had about it were from my experience: the death of my father."

The Gentle Comforter may be an adult of any age. When he is in the form of a very old person there is none of the decay and repugnance with which advanced age is caricatured in the macabre personification. Rather, he is portrayed as a wise and noble person whose character is enhanced rather than impaired by age.

While the Gentle Comforter usually is seen as a male, there are also a number of images in which the sexual differentiation is either ambiguous or regarded as unimportant. Female personifications occur, but not often in our samples.

The idea of a powerful force quietly employed in a kindly way is perhaps at the core of the Gentle Comforter personification. Death thus embodies a favorable integration of qualities that are valued when they occur in actual human beings. In this personification, death is sometimes felt as being close and intimate to its creator; never is its presence treated as a casual encounter. The parent-child relationship is the one which appears most analogical to the qualities discerned in the typical Gentle Comforter personification. However, it is also this form of personification which appears most similar to the sexualized dynamics studied by Greenberger (5, 6) and described by McClelland

as constituting the "Harlequin complex" (7). This interpretation will be discussed later.

The Automaton

In a class by itself is the image of death as an objective, unfeeling instrument in human guise:

Death, physically: Lean, pale, clothed in the color of nothing; sexless; not senile but older-looking, about 60 years of age. Death, mentally: Unthinking and automatic, inured to and bored by suffering, having no moral values or need of them.

The physical and mental characteristics cited by this male liberal arts undergraduate are fairly typical of those we have classified as the Automaton. Another male undergraduate portrays Death as:

Tall and skinny, probably wearing black. His face would bear a serious expression. He would be a habitually taciturn person. He would never speak. He would be void of all emotions. He would exist under a superhuman type of energy. He would move slowly as if remorsefully, but he would not be so in the slightest. He would never tire, nor would he ever become energetic. He would just go about his business in a matter-of-fact way.

A student in a training institute for funeral directors saw death this way:

He is a sort of blank in human form. I don't know what he looks like, I don't know if he's short or tall. Probably he is not very short or very tall or very good-looking or very ugly. He is just somebody you would never notice because he just goes his own way. He looks angry or sullen, but he really doesn't feel anything. I guess he is more like a machine than anything else. You would probably never have anything in common with a guy like that.

Another student at this institute thought that:

Death would look like any normal physical being, only mentally he wouldn't be there at all. I don't mean he would be stupid. I mean he wouldn't care what he was doing. Death would go around in a trance. He wouldn't really have any personality, though, and you couldn't make him happy or get him mad. This may sound odd, but that's what I thought of.

Women tend to describe the Automaton's physical appearance in more detail than do men, as in this image from a co-ed:

Death, we will not call him Mr., is not the frightening person one would imagine, but he is not a jolly sort of person either. Physically he is above average height with dark hair and clear dark brown eyes. He is of medium build with no trace of obesity. He is not over-imposing, but his appearance is what you might call "sharp," dressed in a dark suit with a conservative tie. His walk is almost military, as if he were a man who is formal in most of his dealings. Death would be around 35, retaining a good physical appearance, but having reached complete mental maturity. This man, Death, is definitely masculine in gender.

Psychologically he has no feeling of emotion about his job—either positive or negative. He simply does his job. He doesn't think about what he is doing, and there is no way to reason with him. There is no way to stop him or change his mind. When you look into his eyes you do not see a person. You see only death.

The Automaton, then, appears in human guise but lacks human qualities. Unlike other personifications, he does not establish a human relationship of any kind. He advances with neither diabolical pleasure nor gentle compassion, but as an automatic—should we say, soulless?—apparatus. From a mere apparatus one can expect no emotionally meaningful response, no matter how humanoid its superficial appearance. If one cannot discern any human thought or feeling in The Automaton, then what is one to do with his *own* thoughts and feelings? The macabre personification might terrify, but terror is at least a human condition: one can respond to the terrifying with terror. Peculiar as it may seem, even such grotesque personages as the vampire and the were-

wolf were regarded as capable of establishing some kind of relationship with their victims. The scream of terror was an interpersonal response of sorts. By contrast, one can express nothing to a "blank in human form."

It strikes the authors that there is something absurd about personifying death as a nonperson. The absurdity does not reside in the characterization of death as an instrument indifferent to its own actions, but in the establishment of such an instrument in human guise. At least since Capek's introduction of the robot (8), the image of a nonhuman force in human form has haunted much contemporary literature and philosophy. Leites (9), Camus (10), and Giraudoux (11) are among those contemporary writers who have described or created a type of "real life" person who appears quite similar to the personifications we have obtained of death as The Automaton. Consider, for example, this passage from Giraudoux's play, *The Madwoman of Chaillot*. It is Act 1, and The Ragpicker is trying to bring The Countess up-to-date on conditions in the world.

RAGPICKER: Countess, there was a time when you could walk around Paris, and all the people you met were just like yourself. A little cleaner, maybe, or dirtier, perhaps, or angry, or smiling—but you knew them. They were you. Well, Countess, twenty years ago, one day, on the street, I saw a face in the crowd. A face, you might say, without a face. Not a human face. It saw me staring, and when it looked back at me with its gelatine eyes, I shuddered. Because I knew that to make room for this one, one of us must have left the earth. A while after, I saw another. And another. And since then, I've seen hundreds come in—yes—thousands.

COUNTESS: Describe them to me.

RAGPICKER: You've seen them yourself, Countess. Their clothes don't wrinkle. Their hats don't come off. When they talk, they don't look at you. They don't perspire.

COUNTESS: Have they wives? Have they children?

RAGPICKER: They buy the models out of shop windows, fur and all. They animate them by a secret process. Then they marry them. Naturally, they don't have children. . . (12).

Perhaps this "automatic" humanoid who "goes about his business in a matter-of-fact way," and is "void of all emotions," "in a trance," and in whose eyes "you do not see a person" is an emanation arising from our science and technology. Perhaps The Automaton is a creature of our own times, while Mr. Macabre and the Gentle Comforter linger as inheritances from earlier relationships to death. Perhaps The Automaton is one part of a broader image, an image of the universe as a vast chamber whose design, if any, is indifferent to the feelings and purposes of man. By implication, there is no purpose to inquiring about purpose. Automatized death does not punish, welcome, glorify or explain. Death is a machined termination. What meaning, then, might be attributed to the life that has been terminated?

The Gay Deceiver

Death is either a man and/or a woman. This death person is young to middle-aged and very good looking. The man is about 35 or 40 with dark hair, graying at the sides. The woman is tall, beautiful with dark hair and about 30. Neither is repulsive in any way. Both have very subtle and interesting personalities. They're suave, charming, but deceitful, cruel, and cold. While death may be cruel, however, it's a pleasant cruelty at times. It can't be generalized too much (the personality) since it's dynamic, capable of change, and a sort of selective behavior. Death is flexible, but never strikes a mediocre, mundane position.

Both are dressed formally, she in a black gown and he in a formal suit, i.e., dinner jacket (black), etc., with a diamond tie tack. The atmosphere I see them in is a gambling casino. Another atmosphere is a black scene I can't define. Both are really sharp. You like them and they lead you on.

Some personifications, such as the above example written by an undergradu-

ate male, describe an attractive or even elegant individual who has many worldly graces. Death is represented as a poised, sophisticated person. This form of death does not repulse the viewer, as does Mr. Macabre, nor does it welcome and support him as does the Gentle Comforter. Still less does it present the aspect of an impersonal tool as does The Automaton. Rather, one tends to be enticed, led on by this lively-appearing personality.

Another undergraduate male imagines:

Were death a person he would be a man of medium stature and medium build. He would be slightly below middle age, say in his thirties, have soft features such as small nose, thin eyebrows, shallow eyes, narrow lips, and medium complexioned, unwrinkled skin. His dark brown hair would be neatly combed back and it would be distinctly parted on the left. It would be shiny and moist but not greasy. Death would speak in a slow, modulated tone of voice. Death would be wearing clothes of conservative colors, probably gray or blue. These clothes are clean and neatly pressed. All in all, death would give the appearance of somebody one could trust.

Psychologically, however, one could not trust him. He would be elusive in his manners, hypocritical, a liar, persuasive. Death would first gain your confidence. Then you would learn who he really is, and it would be too late.

A young man in training to become a funeral director viewed death as:

A pretty sharp looking guy. He always looks like he's ready to go out and have a helluva time. You say to yourself, "Hey, I'd like to go with him!" He looks like he knows his way around. But, brother, it's all a front. He's as nasty as they come. (The young man estimates age of Death as "about 25 or 30.")

A student nurse writes:

It's very hard for me to think of Death as a human being. But if he was, somehow I think he'd be young, tho not very young, and on the good-looking side tho not necessarily very handsome. It is easier to think about him as I go along. Death is a likeable person. His conversation is sparkling and his promises are tempting.

He doesn't seem at all like the Grim Reaper. He is mysterious and everyone wants to know him a little better although when his identity is uncovered he turns cold and forbidding. (Age?) He is about 35 or 40 years old.

The Gay Deceiver seems to embody many characteristics that are associated with the "high life." He is often pictured as a companion that one would seek out for amusement, adventure, or excitement. Frequently, although not invariably, it is explicitly stated that he tempts, lures us on, and "Then you would learn who he really is, and it would be too late." That "Who he really is" might be a modern dress version of the devil is a possibility. There are occasional direct references to the devil, as in the following protocol from a male undergraduate:

I picture Death as being fairly tall, having clearly cut features. His nose is straight and his eyes sparkle. He is a little on the slim side though looks fairly powerful. He has a very dark goatee coming to a point, black hair which is in need of a haircut. He is wearing a dark suit. He also has a light complexion. I see death right now almost in the same way as the devil.

Death is a quiet person and kind of scary. He does not say much but is very sharp and it is almost impossible to outsmart him. Although you would like to stay away from him, there's something about him that kind of draws you to him. You like him and fear him at the same time. I picture Death as being millions of years old but only looking about 40.

The Gay Deceiver seems to embody characteristics of both an ego ideal and a con man. He or she is still young, but a few years older than most of the respondents. And he has the poise, sophistication, good looks, and capacity for pleasure that many people might incorporate in their own ego ideal. Yet, behind the "show," there is the intent to deceive. Perhaps on one level, the Gay Deceiver is a character who has stepped out of a morality play. Like the serpent in the Garden of Eden, or Sportin' Life in Porgy and Bess, he seeks to divert one with promises and smooth words. Death is the penalty for going his way. Perhaps on another level, the Gay Deceiver represents the respondent's own efforts to divert himself from the prospect of death. In effect, one declares: "By immersing myself in all the pleasures that life has to offer, I will have neither the time nor the inclination to admit dark thoughts. The very fact that I revel in sophisticated enjoyments suggests that death cannot really be formidable. . . . Am I kidding myself? Of course! But that is the solution I prefer."

A Few Other Images

The personifications described above were the clearest and most frequently given types by people who responded to the open-end question. A few other types will be more briefly noted.

Death is occasionally personified as taking the form of a deceased person who was known to the respondent. The specific characteristics of this personification depend upon the characteristics of a deceased person. One undergraduate male described death as:

Emanciated, lanky, loose-jointed, slack lips, hollow eye sockets, brittle "nicotined-stained" hair, red eyes, hot breath, loose clothes, most likely in a stooped or hunch-backed position with face down in grief, up in anguish, or directed over the shoulder in tragic, helpless resentment. His personality is constricted, detached, hostile, rigid, relatively unresponsive, self-oriented, withdrawn, enclosed." The respondent had his grandfather in mind: "My grandfather is dead—I attended his funeral and hated it violently. My grandfather and his behavior came to mind in answering this question."

A nurse reported:

My father comes to me in my dreams two or three times a year. He looks very tired and sad. He looks like he has something he wants to say, but can't say it or maybe he doesn't want to. That's the only way I can think of Death, as a person.

Some people were not able to visualize death as a person, but did conjure up a rather vague image.

"Death would be a darkness related to complete silence," replied one undergraduate male. "Coldness also would be implicated in death. The coldness would be of a wet or slimy type. I can't really see a person. I just get the feeling of darkness and cold and everything being wet or slimy. I also get a sense of helplessness and a loss of hope could also be thought of. Most important, however, is defeat. Death is a defeat as far as I'm concerned." Although this young man did not directly personify death he answered with hesitation that it was "old" and "female." He added, "I really can't think of a reason for this, but that's what came right into my mind when you asked."

Occasionally, a respondent gives two rather contrasting images and cannot choose between them. A female undergraduate first described a woman "in long, flowing clothes of chiffon. She's attractive, long black hair, beautiful hands, graceful, soft-spoken. . . the motherly type who would lead someone by the hand." But she then added, "Death could also be a man—old, scrawny, revengeful sort of laugh. He would be sinister."

No doubt, the range of images would increase with increased sampling of subject populations. We will return for a general interpretation of death personifications after considering findings from the multiple-choice form and a few quantitative aspects of both forms.

CONTEMPORARY PERSONIFICATIONS OF DEATH: QUANTITATIVE ASPECTS

A few questions about the personification of death can be answered in a clear-cut manner from responses to the multiple-choice form. It should be kept in mind that our samples (421 subjects) consist entirely of college students and of people who work in nursing and other paramedical fields.

TABLE 1. DEATH PERSONIFICATION SUBJECTS

A. Open-end procedure

Sample		Male	Female	Total	Age Range	Median Age
College students*		61	77	138	18-27	20
Nurses		0	31	31	20-59	31
Student nurses		0	34	34	18-24	19
Mortician students		34	3	37	18-37	19
	N	111	129	240		

B. Multiple-choice procedure

Sample		Male	Female	Total	Age Range	Median Age
College Students **		56	61	117	18-30	20
Nurses***		0	46	46	24-52	26
Student nurses***		0	51	51	18-23	19
Geriatric nurses & aides		23	152	175	18-57	43
Funeral directors		31	1	32	23-64	46
	N	110	311	421		

*Clark University and Brandeis University.
**Clark University only.
***These samples were retested at ten- and six-week intervals, respectively.

The Sex of Death

Death was most frequently perceived as a male in all of the research samples. Percentages are given in Table 2. The preference for a masculine personification was always decisive, sometimes overwhelming. The geriatric hospital personnel offered the largest "minority vote" for a female personification (39 percent). Although this sample was predominantly female and middle-aged, other predominantly female samples gave much smaller percentages of female personifications, and male personifications were given almost exclusively by the middle-aged funeral directors. It is possible, of course, that being *both* female and middle-aged, rather than just one or the other has some bearing on the sex of the death personification. Whatever might be the explanation for differences among the samples, it seems clear enough that the masculine personification is most prevalent.

The Age of Death

Death was more frequently pictured as an old rather than a young person by all subjects (Table 2). Again, the preference was clear-cut. Since the multiple-choice form limited the respondent to a young vs. old decision, it is useful to examine the ages attributed to Death by respondents to the open-end form. The funeral directors, who were given a variant of the multiple-choice form, also had the opportunity to attribute an age to Death rather than make a dichotomous judgment. In all instances there was a marked tendency to regard Death as a person who is in the later years of his life. The funeral directors, for example, attributed a median age of 59.5 years to Death, and only one respondent in this sample gave an age under 40 years. No subjects in any of the samples portrayed Death as a child. While the tendency to see Death as middle-aged or elderly seems well established, there are more exceptions to this generalization than was the case with sex. Personifications of Death as a young adult were given by many college students, although these responses were still in the minority. For the college samples, median age of Death was 50 years. A number of respondents to the open-end version cited ages that project beyond the usual human life-span, e.g., 120 or 150 years.

Personal Characteristics of Death

Respondents were given three alternative characterizations of death from which

TABLE 2. SEX AND AGE OF DEATH PERSONIFICATIONS
(IN PERCENTAGES)

	Sex				Age	
Sample	M	F	Other*	Young	Old	Other*
College students	90.6	6.1	3.3	26.6	67.4	6.0
Nurses	74.5	15.7	9.8	11.8	74.5	13.7
Student nurses	68.6	27.5	3.9	17.7	78.4	3.9
Geriatric personnel	61.0	39.0	0	21.7	78.3	0
Funeral directors	85.4	3.1	15.6	Median age:	59.5**	

*Subjects were given the option of writing in their own responses if they did not consider the stated alternatives appropriate. Sexless and bisexual, indefinite and ageless categories were introduced by some subjects.
**This sample was asked to attribute age, not choose between "young-old." The 81.3% who specified sex also specified age, with the same percentage in the "other" category for both age and sex.

to choose. The same relative popularity was observed in every sample, although the distances among the alternatives varied somewhat. All samples most frequently viewed Death as "A gentle, well-meaning sort of person." The second most popular image was that of "A cold, remote sort of person," followed by "A grim, terrifying sort of person." Percentages are given in Table 3. The geriatric personnel and the student nurses were strongest in their preferences for "gentle" Death, but the margin was decisive in all groups.

TABLE 3. PERSONAL CHARACTERISTICS OF DEATH (IN PERCENTAGES)

Sample	Gentle	Cold	Grim
College students	46.2	31.6	22.2
Nurses	50.9	31.4	17.7
Student nurses	80.4	11.7	7.9
Geriatric personnel	67.4	22.9	9.7
Funeral directors	71.8	18.8	9.4

Difficulty of the Task

Apart from the content of the response, we were interested in learning something about the difficulties posed by the task itself. Is the personification of death an easy task for most people, or a difficult one? Obviously, this line of inquiry is related to the previous discussion of physiognomic vs g-technical modes of perception. Information available on this point comes from two sources: the percentage of omissions (no personification given) and subjects' rating of task difficulty on a 5-point scale from "very easy" to "very difficult." Omission data are available for all samples, but the subjective ratings were obtained only from subjects who took the open-end form, and the nurses and funeral directors who took the multiple-choice form.

The numbers (N) given in Table 1 and the percentages in Tables 2 and 3 represent only those subjects who actually gave responses to death personification questions. The number and percentage of those who were asked to respond but did not give a personification may be found in Table 4. As the death personification item was embedded in a battery of diverse questions and tasks, it was possible to differentiate lack of death personification from a more general "anti-response" set. It was our observation that an appreciable minority of subjects failed to come up with a personification although they were able to respond to other inquires.

TABLE 4. SUBJECTS WHO DID NOT PERSONIFY DEATH

Sample	Total N	No Personification f	No Personification %
Open-end			
College students	146	8	5.5
Nurses	34	3	8.8
Student nurses	40	6	15.0
Mortician students	52	15	28.8
Multiple choice			
College students	124	7	5.7
Nurses	47	1	2.1
Student nurses	56	5	9.1
Geriatric personnel	197	22	11.2
Funeral directors	48	16	33.0

The self-ratings on difficulty of the task support the impression we gained from the omission data that it is fairly common to experience some difficulty in personifying death (Table 5). Eventually, we should explore the relationship between personification of death and the ability to conjure up images in general. Lacking information on this point, we cannot say how much of the difficulty some of our subjects experienced was related to the specific subject matter, and how much to individual variations in physiognomic and, particularly, visual perception.

There are hints that individuals who favor a biological approach experience more difficulty than most other people in attempting to personify death. One of these hints is in the data from student morticians. Other hints come from personal observations and from attempts to

TABLE 5. SELF-RATINGS OF TASK DIFFICULTY*

Sample	Very Difficult		Moderately Difficult		Not Difficult		N
	f	%	f	%	f	%	
Open-end							
College students	40	28.9	51	36.9	47	34.2	138
Nurses	7	22.6	19	61.3	5	16.1	31
Student nurses	12	35.3	16	47.1	6	17.6	34
Mortician students	23	62.2	7	18.6	7	18.6	37
Multiple choice							
Nurses	8	17.4	33	71.8	5	10.8	46
Funeral directors	11	34.4	16	50.0	5	15.6	32

*5-point scale collapsed to 3-point scale by combining all non-extreme ratings.

study the relationship between personification and the student's major field of study and occupational goal. It might be correct to say that young people who are biologically minded do not approve of death personifications, and encounter much inner resistance when they try to set themselves to the task. At present, however, we know very little about the personality correlates of death personification. We should not miss the obvious point, however, that most people who were asked to personify death did manage to come up with a response, and that some people found this to be an easy task.

Changes Over Time

Two of the multiple-choice samples (nurses and student nurses) were retested for death personifications. The nurses were retested after an interval of ten weeks, the student nurses after an interval of six weeks. From these small follow-up studies we learn that death personifications are stable with respect to sex and personality characteristics, at least within the time period studied. However, there was an increasing tendency to regard death as an old person the second time around. Only 5.9 percent of the nurses saw death as a young person on retest, as compared with 11.8 on test; similarly, only 9.8 percent of the student nurses

saw death as a young person on retest, while 17.7 percent had seen him as a young person the first time they were asked this question. There was a slight tendency in both groups for masculine personifications to increase their margin over feminine personifications on retest. There was also a slight tendency for the number of "grim" personifications to decrease. In general, then, retest changes were in the direction of emphasizing those preferences which had already been established by the first inquiry. Most subjects in both groups made the same choices on both occasions.

Other Analyses

A number of possible relationships within the data have been explored, but mostly these do not yield any conclusions that are worth reporting here. However, there is the strong suggestion that feminine personifications are less likely to be regarded as "cold," but more likely to be regarded as "grim," in comparison with masculine personifications. Geriatric personnel, the largest of the subpopulations who responded to the multiple-choice version, characterized 13 percent of their feminine personifications as "grim, terrifying," as compared with 6.6 percent of their masculine personifications. But 26.4 percent of the masculine personifications were "cold, remote," as compared with

17.4 percent of the feminine. Findings were comparable in the other samples.

DISCUSSION AND SUMMARY

Recapitulation

It has been suggested here that it is normal—and useful—to personify death. As an alternative or counterblance to the biological approach, personification enables one to express something of his own emotional and symbolic orientation toward death. Personification might be considered to be one manifestation of the more general mode of perception which Werner has termed *physiognomic* (13), while matter-of-fact definitions of death emerge from a *geo-technical* orientation.

Several types of personification were distinguished, based upon inspection of 240 brief essays. *The macabre personification* is a portrayal of repulsive physical decay animated by a personality that is viciously opposed to life. This image usually is presented in a vivid, detailed style with a sense of being emotionally close to the person who is visualizing it. Macabre personifications have striking similarities with medieval representations of death. *The Gentle Comforter* has a wise and reassuring appearance. He is quiet and powerful, sympathetic and understanding. *The Automaton* has the appearance of a human being, but lacks "soul." He performs his deadly assignment without registering any emotions of his own—he is a humanoid blank. It was suggested that this image is a relatively new one on the cultural scene. *The Gay Deceiver* is a physically attractive and sophisticated person who tempts his victims with veiled promises of pleasure—then delivers them unto death. A few other images were more briefly described.

Next, we considered the responses that 421 subjects gave to a multiple-choice version of the personification inquiry. It was found that death was most frequently perceived as a male, as a late middle-aged or elderly person, and as one who is "gentle, well-meaning." This does not mean, of course, that all respondents pictured death as an elderly, gentle man (which would be a close approximation to The Gentle Comforter). Gentle old women, cold young men, etc., were also selected as images. Some people had considerable difficulty with the personification task. We got the impression that this difficulty was particularly common for those subjects who deal with death in their daily business (e.g., funeral directors and mortician students), and students who are priming themselves for a career in medicine or the biological sciences. Repeated testing on two groups of subjects indicated that personifications are relatively stable over time; the largest change was in the direction of an even greater prevalence of "old" as contrasted with "young" images. Although masculine and feminine personifications were about equally pictured as "gentle," relatively more feminine personifications were seen as "grim, terrifying", and relatively more masculine personifications as "cold, remote."

With the present findings in mind, let us turn to observations and hypotheses that others have made on the topic of death personification. This brief and incomplete survey is intended to highlight some problems that invite further research.

DEATH PERSONIFICATIONS AND SOCIETY

Slater (14) points out that the tendency to personify death is quite ancient. "As soon as the gods cease to be beasts, and through conquest or diffusion begin to be mingled together in a pantheon of some sort, specialization begins to occur. And in this division of labor among the previously all-round gods, one of the first functions to be differentiated out is that of god of the dead, who ultimately comes to represent Death itself.''

But what determines or influences the particular image of death that a society creates? Slater suggests that death is more likely to be portrayed as a woman in societies which have matriarchal leanings. More specifically, whichever sex seems the more powerful in a given society will appear as the death image. Death will be male or female, young or old, etc., according to the power generally attached to these categories. He notes that one can find many examples of both feminine and masculine personifications—in fact, the word ''death'' itself is feminine in some languages (e.g., the romance languages), and masculine in others (e.g., German). Slater gives particular attention to the possibility ''that death will be seen as masculine or feminine according to whether it typically occurs in a phallic-penetrating or vaginal-enveloping form. Thus in a hunting society, or a martial one, death is most likely to occur in the form of some kind of wounding or tearing, whether by the goring, clawing, or trampling of beasts, or by the weapons of man. Such events will tend to be associated with masculinity, and with paternal strength and power.''

By contrast, Slater observes that ''In an agricultural or peasant society . . . death is more apt to come from starvation and disease and hence to be experienced as an envelopment and associated with maternal deprivation. It is no coincidence that human sacrifice to blood-thirsty goddesses is typically found in highly developed and stable agricultural societies with considerable specialization and interdependence, such that crop failures cannot be compensated for by branching out into other modes of subsistence, but simply cause mass starvation.''

Neumann gives particular emphasis to the feminine death image, likening the tomb to the womb. ''Thus the womb of the earth becomes the deadly devouring woman of the underworld, and beside the fecun-dated womb and the protecting cave of earth and mountain gapes the abyss of hell, the dark hole of the depths, the devouring womb of the grave and of death, of darkness without light, of nothingness. For this woman who generates life and all living things on earth is the same who takes them back into herself, who pursues her victims and captures them with snare and net . . . . This terrible mother is the hungry earth, which devours its own children and fattens on their corpses; it is . . . the flesh-eating sarcophagus voraciously licking up the blood seed of men and beasts and, once fecundated and sated, casting it out again in new birth, hurling it to death, and over and over again to death'' (15).

This vivid description seems consistent with Slater's idea of feminine-style death as taking a ''vaginal-enveloping form.'' However, it should be added that both Roman and Greek personifications included the image of a violent, conflictive sudden death which is inflicted by a woman or female creature with dreadful fangs and claws. These personifications are feminine, yet the death they bring seems more similar to the ''phallic-penetrating'' than the ''vaginal-enveloping'' form.

Regarding the age that is attributed to death, Slater proposes two alternative hypotheses: that societies in which the old are revered will view death as old; that societies in which individuals usually perish at an advanced age will view death as older than societies in which death usually comes early. Reviewing a number of societies, he notes that ''one typically associates veneration of the elderly with China, and such personifications of death as we find there do suggest great age. An equally positive evaluation of the aged is found in the pastoral cultures of the Middle East, however, which in their attitude contrast rather strongly with the classical Greek view. Whereas the Greeks said, 'whom the gods love die young' and regard old age as an unmitigated misfortune, the Middle Eastern groups to this day adhere to the biblical adage that it is the wicked who die young, and that such early death is the worst catastrophe that a man can undergo. Yet Hades is middle-aged like his brothers, while Middle Eastern culture gives us no personification at all" (16). In primitive tribes personifications seem to be relatively uncommon, but those that have been gathered tend to represent death as an aged person.

In a society as complex as ours one would expect many images of death, with various combinations of age, sex, and personality or temperament. And this is what we have found. The prevalence of masculine personifications might imply that we are more like a hunting or martial than an agricultural society, and that matriarchal influences upon us are not particularly strong. But this line of interpretation is too simple. It does not reckon with the marked differences among images in which masculinity predominates (e.g., The Automaton and The Gentle Comforter are quite dissimilar, although both are most often seen as masculine). And it does not provide a satisfactory explanation for the equal prevalence of "gentle, well-meaning" images of death for both feminine and masculine personifications, nor does it account for the emergence of new personifications such as we may have in The Automaton.

We may have some indirect support for the observations of Neumann and Slater with respect to feminine interpretations of death. Neumann speaks of "the terrible mother," and Slater of "blood-thirsty goddesses." In our multiple-choice data, the "grim, terrifying" personification, least popular of the three alternatives, was more frequently associated with femininity than with masculinity. There were also some vivid examples of feminine macabre personifications in the open-end data—but none of the cold, emotionless automatons were described as female.

With respect to age, perhaps our data can be interpreted more adequately by the second of Slater's two hypotheses:

that societies in which individuals usually perish at an advanced age will view death as older than societies in which death usually comes early. If death personifications were collected on a systematic, long-term basis we might find a steady increase in the age attributed to death as a society overcomes health problems which cause high mortality rates in the early years of life. We should also consider, however, a third hypothesis: death is so often perceived as an elderly person because we wish to keep death at a distance from ourselves.

ILLNESS, PERSONALITY, AND DEATH PERSONIFICATION

What is the relationship between the personifier and the personified? How does serious illness or the prospect of imminent death influence the personification? We do not have much information in this area, but several reports are worth considering.

The noted psychoanalyst, Felix Deutsch, suggested from his case experiences that "normal" or "peaceful" dying seldom occurs. There is usually some kind of psychological threat which mobilizes the dying person's resources and keeps him agitated (17).

Heightened fear of death may lead to a (spontaneous) personification. "The illness may be personified as an actual enemy and persecutor; so that either paranoia may ensue or profound depression, even melancholia, which reevalutates the menace of the illness as a menace proceeding from the super-ego" (18).

A man whom Deutsch was treating referred to the intense pain of angina attacks in the following way: "Now the devil is loose once more in my chest; he has me again in his clutches." Exploration revealed that the devil was his mother. Working through his infantile relationship with his mother relieved this patient both from his angina attacks and his great fear of death—and, as a consequence, no more personifications.

Many observers over the years have remarked upon the tendency of dying people to behave as though they were being visited by a loved one "from the other side." If we choose to believe that deceased persons actually appear to the senses of those who are close to death, then, of course, we are dealing not with personification but with "the real thing." However, if deathbed visions are to be understood in psychological terms, then it might be useful to consider them as a form of personification. The realm of death sends as its representative the image of a person who was known to the patient and particularly significant to him. As reported earlier, there were a few personifications in our data which depicted death in the form of a person actually known to the personifier.

Possibly, deathbed personifications offer a source of comfort, an intimation that one will be welcomed when he has passed through the transition of death. It would be tempting to say that the dying person's wishes and hopes are converted into an image that is projected outward and then perceived as though it were an external reality. But such an explanation at this time would be glib and premature—we need more facts. As circumstantial evidence supporting this hypothesis, we might expect to find that spontaneous personifications in the form of visitations from the grave would occur more frequently among seriously ill people than among people in general, and that the personifications would most generally behave in a reassuring, anxiety-alleviating manner.

One recent investigation has approached this subject. Osis (19) seems to be the first researcher to use IBM procedures in studying postmortem behavior. He obtained deathbed observations from 640 physicians and nurses by questionnaires and follow-up contacts. In all, he counted 1,370 hallucinatory persons. Osis concluded that "the terminal patients predominantly hallucinate phantoms representing dead persons, who often claim to aid the patient's transition into postmortem existence" (20). He adds: "In most cases the patient's perception of and response to the actual environment was intact during the experiencing of the hallucinatory visitor . . . . The large majority of our cases came from patients whose mentality was not disturbed by sedatives, other medication or high body-temperature. Only a small proportion had a diagnosed illness which might be hallucinogenic. Most patients were fully conscious . . . ."

Osis' study tends to support the comfort-giving hypothesis of deathbed visions. The "phantoms" or personifications seemed to be on missions of welcome. And there is some indirect evidence, cited by Osis, to suggest that death personifications are given more frequently by those who are close to death than those who are in good health. Evidently, the tendency to witness—and perhaps interact with—personifications and representatives of death is an aspect of the dying process that deserves further attention.

Interesting speculations about the psychodynamics of death personification have been advanced by McClelland (21) and investigated by Greenberger (22). McClelland begins with the observation that some people—especially women—appear to be looking forward to death with a sense of excitement. "The possibility both thrills and attracts her, at the same time that it frightens her. Yet often the thrill seems as strong as the fear, in much the same way that it is for a person who is about to make a ski jump or a high dive" (23). He then develops the theme of death as a dark, mysterious lover. There is ample historical precedent for this death personification theme in art and literature, as both Greenberger and McClelland note.

The term, "Harlequin complex" is proposed by McClelland as an appropriate designation for this theme. He believes that the burlesque, *commedia del-l'arte* Harlequin character serves as a double agent: for love and death. Seduction, death, and demonic power are said to be under the surface of Harlequin's slapstick antics. In fact, McClelland traces the clown, Harlequin, to the medieval French devil, Herlequin. We cannot digress here into the interesting case that McClelland makes for the pedigree of Harlequin as a demon lover. But we should note that he finds many modern representations of Harlequin, including the hypnotist, Svengali, and "the dark, mysterious foreign psychoanalyst." He mentions two particulars in which psychoanalysts have enacted the Harlequin role. "They (Freud and other early psychoanalysts) carried out their treatments with their patients, in the beginning usually women, stretched out on a couch as if ready for sexual intercourse and also as if dead on a bier; and the treatment involved a specifically sexual relationship between the woman and her 'hidden' male analyst (transference). While the death and seduction aspects of psychoanalytic treatment were muted and treated only symbolically, much of the force of the popular image of psychoanalysts as dark foreign 'devils', and perhaps even of the treatment itself, may have come from its re-creation of the eternal Harlequin theme of a woman being sexually seduced by death" (24).

At this point, we leave the general discussion of death personified as a mysterious lover and turn to a pair of careful psychological studies by Greenberger (25). She reasoned that "If death is perceived as a lover, with certain unsavory characteristics either mentioned or repressed, women confronting death may produce fantasies of illicit sexuality. This category would consist of theses of rape, abduction, seduction, and infidelity" (26). In the first of her studies, Greenberger presented selected TAT cards to 25 women who were hospitalized for known or suspected cancer. Another 25 women who were hospitalized for relatively minor dis-

orders that did not present a threat to life were used as the control group. The second study included another 25 experimental subjects, this time, women with a variety of severe illnesses, and another control group. Six of the TAT cards administered in the first study were used again; additionally, Greenberger employed seven new pictures developed especially for this study. The new pictures: 1) girl running through large construction pipes; 2) girl looking down stairwell; 3) dark man with woman's shadow on stairs below him; 6) old woman looking out of hearse window; and 7) boy carrying large blank clock-face. Five scoring categories were developed: 1) denial themes; 2) punishment themes; 3) separation themes; 4) reunion themes; and 5) illicit sex themes.

Since it is the last category with which we are most concerned here, it may be useful to add Greenberger's specifications for "illicit sex themes." These were defined as "mention of illicit sexuality, i.e., seduction, intercourse out of wedlock, pregnancy, rape or abduction, a woman's betrayal of her husband or boyfriend." Several brief examples are given from actual protocols: "He seduced a girl that wasn't altogether unwilling." "That man is there to take her away on his horse and she doesn't want to go. That's her mother. She don't want her to go." "Her husband could have come home on a drunk, beat her, threw her on the bed . . . she had a boy friend . . . her husband didn't care to see that . . . he told her to be a good wife . . . I didn't want to make it like the other one, being sick and all that."

Greenberger was able to conclude from results of both studies that death does seem to have sexual overtones for many women. In particular, the death encounter is most frequently associated with a sexual rendezvous in the minds of terminally ill women who were unmarried. She observes that these fantasies cause anxiety in some women, but seem to be a source of comfort to others. "These may be the women in whom oedipal fantasies are on a low ebb, for whom Death is not a forbidden and, hence, forbidding partner." Greenberger then suggests that, "Here the therapist might subtly strengthen the connection between the sexual experience and the experience of dying."

Greenberger's final remarks support our general impression that greater knowledge of death personifications can help us to understand the dying person's orientation toward his demise: "It is sometimes said that women die with less anguish than men. A familiar type of explanation invokes female passivity. But may it not also be due to the woman's greater tendency to libidinize death? . . . At the very least, this tendency would produce ambivalence, rather than outright dread of dying. At most, it would produce a positive and sexually toned desire for death" (27).

How do the various observations on this topic relate to each other? Methodological differences are too great to permit close comparison. McClelland analyzed death themes in literature and other art forms. Greenberger asked ill women to invent stories based upon projective test materials, and then interpreted the responses in terms of death theme categories. We asked directly for death personifications from men and women in good health (but a large number of these subjects were drawn from the health professions).

Nevertheless, certain comments might be offered. First, it should be said that quite a few of the personifications we elicited were sexy. In this respect, our findings merely support the general observation that sex is ubiquitous, and likely to be a component of almost any relationship, actual or personified. Secondly, however, we do not find it easy to set the sex-death or love-death personification into any single stereotype. Where is Harlequin in our data? The love offered by The Gentle Comforter is tender and parental, although not lacking in sexual overtones. Has Harlequin grown up, matured? He is

alluring and mysterious, in the words of some respondents, but not dark or exciting. Our impression is that the personifier is prepared to surrender to The Gentle Comforter as a tired, trusting child might surrender to his parent. Enveloping protection and acceptance is primary; the sexual tone is diffuse.

Dangerous, palpitating sex-death can be read in the features of Mr. Macabre, "A body to which one would relinquish all hopes of resistance." Perhaps this is Harlequin. But, again, The Gay Deceiver, the accomplished, sophisticated seducer may also be Harlequin. Without belaboring the point, we are attempting to suggest that the "Harlequin complex" is not without a certain kind of validity—but, in practice, it takes on a number of individual forms, each of which involve different combinations of tenderness, passion, danger, etc. We need not ignore the sexual overtones of death personifications, but other aspects—such as the parental or even the existential (cf. particularly, The Automaton) should also be kept in mind.

FOR THE FUTURE

So little research has been conducted on this topic, that new contributions of many kinds would be welcome. In particular, it would be helpful to obtain both direct and indirect personifications from the same individual (e.g., by combining Greenberger's method and ours); to incorporate the personification inquiry into longitudinal designs so that we can understand the role of personification at various stages of life, in health and illness; to examine more carefully the male counterpart of the "Harlequin complex"; and to relate personification not only to sex, age, and personality, but also to ethnicity.

We have already suggested that personification is a natural, functional response to the prospect of death, even beyond that period in middle childhood in which personifications flourish (28). Perhaps it will be possible to devise and conduct investigations to extend our knowledge of precisely how imagery contributes to our total comprehension of death. Imagination may in part be responsible for the terror and despair some people feel when death is in the air—but imagination may also be part of the remedy as well!

One further comment. It is risky to read culture from individuals, or individuals from culture. But it is possible that individual images of death, in the many forms that they might be studied, offer an unusually good opportunity to explore our culture's changing stance toward both life and death. Does grandmother personify a Gentle Comforter, while mother images The Gay Deceiver, and daughter, The Automaton? Do we *think* of death in one way, and *image* it in another? If so, which modality leans toward futurity, toward our next orientation to death? We await further contributions to this topic by philosophers, artists, and writers, as well as psychiatrists, experimental and clinical psychologists, and other social scientists. (See also Chapter 16.)

REFERENCES

1. Oxford Universal Dictionary. (3rd ed.) London: Oxford University Press, 1955. Pp. 459-460.
2. Werner, H. *Comparative psychology of mental development*. New York: International University Press, 1957.
3. Comalli, P. Studies in physiognomic perception: VI. Differential effect of directional dynamics of pictured objects on real and apparent motion in artists and chemists. *Journal of Psychology*, 1960, *49*, 99-109.
4. Swift, J. *Gulliver's travels*. Boston: Beacon Press, 1957. Pp. 216-223 especially.
5. Greenberger, E. Fantasies of women confronting death. *Journal of Consulting Psychology*, 1965, *29*, 252-260.
6. Greenberger, E. 'Flirting' with death: Fantasies of a critically ill woman. *Journal of Projective Technology and Personality Assessment, 30:* 197-204.
7. McClelland, D. The Harlequin complex. In Robert White (Ed.), *The study of lives*. New York: Atherton Press, 1963. Pp. 94-119.
8. Capek, K. R.U.R. In R. W. Corrigan, *Masterpieces of modern central European theatre: Five plays*. New York: Collier Books, 1967.
9. Leites, N. The stranger. In William Phillips (Ed.), *Art and psychoanalysis*. New York: Criterion Books, 1956. Pp. 247-270.
10. Camus, A. *The stranger*. (Translated by Stuart Gilbert) New York: Knopf, 1946.
11. Giraudoux, J. The madwoman of Chaillot. In *Jean Giraudoux. Three plays* Vol. 1. (Translated by Phyllis La Farge and Peter H. Judd) New York: Hill & Wang, 1964.
12. *Ibid.*, pp. 256-257.
13. Werner, *op. cit.*
14. Slater, P. E. The face of death. Unpublished manuscript. Framingham, Mass.: Cushing Hospital, 1963.
15. Neumann, O. Quoted by P. E. Slater, *ibid.*
16. Slater, *op. cit.*
17. Deutsch, F. Euthanasia, a clinical study. *Psychoanalytic Quarterly*, 1936, *5*, 347-368.
18. *Ibid.*, p. 353.
19. Osis, K. *Deathbed observations by physicians and nurses*. New York: Parapsychology Foundation, 1961.
20. *Ibid.*, p. 104.
21. McClelland, *op. cit.*
22. Greenberger, 1965, *op. cit.*
23. McClelland, *op. cit.*, p. 95.
24. *Ibid.*, p. 106.
25. Greenberger, 1965, *op. cit.*, p. 255.
26. *Ibid.*, p. 257.
27. *Ibid.*, p. 259.
28. Nagy, M. The child's view of death. In H. Feifel (Ed.), *The meaning of death*. New York: McGraw-Hill, 1959. Pp. 79-98.

7

Birth and Death:

Some Mutual Implications

The puppy grew into full spanielhood and then into a doddering old age under the affectionate auspices of a childless couple. Finally, "the union was blessed," as the saying goes. A daughter was born and, on that very day, the old dog drew his last breath. The parents did not seriously entertain the proposition that there really was a connection between the two events. Nevertheless, they could not escape the sentiment that a kind of exchange had taken place, a "new life for the old."

The death of one character closely followed by the birth of another is a frequent theme in literature. It is also encountered occasionally in daily life, as exemplified above. And people in some societies have deemed it important to convey the breath of a dying person directly to the mouth of the new-born infant (1). Symbolic relationships between birth and death come readily to mind. As Henderson and Oakes have proposed, the question, "What will it be like to go to sleep and never wake up?" irresistibly suggests the corollary: "Where and who was I before my father and mother conceived me?" (2) Thoughts of death or birth give rise to each other in many contexts. In this chapter we examine some of the ways in which birth and death have come to be linked, and explore a variety of beliefs about the nature of this relationship.

ON THE DEVELOPMENT OF BIRTH-DEATH IDEAS

What Kalish designates as the level of "biological life" begins at conception or shortly thereafter; it does not wait for the act of parturition (3). Furthermore, we are not likely to forget that many societies have accepted or at least considered the proposition that a form of life persists after death. However, birth and death often impress us as strong opposites, the beginning and end of life as we know it. The fact that one opposite brings to mind thoughts of the other is not altogether unexpected. Experience with classic word association tests has demonstrated that many stimulus words regularly elicit responses of opposite meaning (4). Psychoanalysts also assure us that giving-and-receiving, and many other pairs of apparent opposites, are equivalent in the unconscious.

Personal experiences also teach us that birth and death are related. Even today, giving birth entails some risk to mother and infant; and, too, in becoming a neonate, the fetus passes through a time of stress and danger when death is in close prospect. Laymen are well aware of both of these facts. In *A Tree Grows in Brooklyn*, Mary Rommely says with regard to her daughter's approaching accouchement: "When a woman gives birth, death holds her hand for a little while. Sometimes he doesn't let go" (5). One of our common expressions derives from and reminds us of the frequency of death-at-birth. We apply the phrase, "died a'borning" to almost any unsuccessful new venture. Nevertheless, many of the reasons for the complex interrelationships between birth and death obviously lie at deeper layers of the psyche than those involved only in one's personal experiences with childbirth and bereavement. Nor does an hypothesized unconscious translation of words into their opposites constitute sufficient explanation. Let us now turn to approaches which have often provided clues to the understanding of our mental life: developmental psychology, psychopathology, mythology, and the study of (so-called) primitive peoples.

Adah Maurer proposes that we take seriously the familiar peek-a-boo game. The infant may be attempting to master the contrasting states of isolation and togetherness, of being and nonbeing. "By the time he is three months old, the healthy baby is secure enough in his self feelings to be ready to experiment with these contrasting states. In the game of peek-a-boo, he replays in safe circumstances the alternate terror and delight, confirming his sense of self by risking and regaining complete consciousness. A light cloth spread over his face and body will elicit an immediate and forceful reaction. Short, sharp intakes of breath, vigorous thrashing of arms and legs removes the erstwhile shroud to reveal widely staring eyes that scan the scene with frantic alertness until they lock glances with the smiling mother, whereupon he will wriggle and laugh with joy. . . . It is obvious that he enjoyed the temporary dimming of the light, the blotting out of the reassuring face and the suggestion of a lack of air which his own efforts enabled him to restore, his aliveness additionally confirmed by the glad greeting implicit in the eye to eye oneness with another human" (6). In a sense, then, the infant may be alternating between births and deaths.

After interviewing and testing children on the subject of death, Sylvia Anthony suggested that birth and death become linked primarily as a result of "three meanings given death in the child's earlier explorative phase. These are 1) separation, departure, disappearance; 2) sleep; and 3) going into a grave, coffin, earth and water" (7). The notions of separation and going into a dark place appear similar to the dynamics suggested by Maurer for the infant. When he has words at his command, the child expresses even more clearly the relationship in his mind between death and separation. The most obvious effect of death is that the deceased person has disappeared or gone away. Informed that a relative has died, children will often inquire where he has gone—for the departure of death seems, at first, much like any other. For example, despite explanations, the daughter of one of the authors (R.A.) has several times inquired when a dead uncle would "come back." Previous departures had always been followed by reappearances; why not this one? Reappearance after an absence probably parallels to some extent the idea of rebirth, just as the absence itself carries some of the impact of death.

Nagy concurs with the finding that for young children death is simply "a departure" (8). (Adults give evidence of trying to maintain this pain-easing fiction in the euphemism, "She is *gone*." A popular sympathy card offers not condolences but denial: "He is just away.") Nagy also agrees that children may consider death to be a "diminished life exclusively restricted to sleep," adding that in psychoanalytic thinking "sleep and death are considered as synonymous in the unconscious" (9). She also reports that West Africans have no special word for sleep. "The verb for sleep is written, 'to be half-dead.' " It is interesting to note that in English we use this same phrase to mean "tired." In fact, in our speech we often connect death with sleep or fatigue which is closely related to sleep, for example, "dead to the world," "dead tired," "dead on my feet," etc.

Shneidman has taken the similarities between sleep and death seriously enough to obtain Sleep Form diaries on the possibility that these might be predictive of suicidal behavior (10). He reports that just before her self-inflicted death, a 67-year-old widow began to think of sleep as an escape from the world, a reunion with loved ones, and a temporary death. Shneidman's discussion makes it clear that relationships between sleep and death are important in the minds and lives of adults as well as children.

Anthony finds that when the concept of death is linked with the concept of birth, "there results a belief that the actual pattern of life in time will be symmetrical with the symmetry suggested by the common aspects of birth and death as union with and separation from the mother. . . " (11).

The hypothesized connection of birth and death with each other, and of both with the relationship with the mother, gains further significance in the light of certain psychopathological phenomena. Psychotic patients sometimes voice the delusion that they are now dead or have been dead, or that the world has died. Indeed, such ideas are fairly common in the early stages of schizophrenia. And it is well known that the onset of psychosis, especially schizophrenia, often follows upon the death of, or separation from, a person with whom the patient had previously shared an important relationship

(12). It will also be remembered that the life histories of schizophrenics reveal a disproportionately high incidence of maternal death (13). When we add to this the likelihood that schizophrenic adults are largely recruited from children who clung to their mothers' apron strings (14) the following statement appears reasonable: *In some cases the primitive equation: "separation from mother (or other significant person)=death" is one of the factors at work in producing such delusions as, "I am dead." "The world is coming to an end."*

Clinical experience with geriatric patients has led to a parallel observation by the authors. A number of institutionalized elderly men and women exist in an apathetic, passive, virtually anesthetic or "dead" state. Often a past bereavement serves as a sharp dividing line between the elder's former life and his present afterlife. Separation from a spouse upon whom the individual had been almost entirely dependent seems to be the most frequent example, although death of the most significant or last remaining parent is also found to have been the turning-off point in some cases. Discussion of the bereavement sometimes has resulted in a breakthrough. Narrow, stereotyped functioning gives way to a more personal relationship in which the elder has a sense of recovering from a semi-death, thinking and feeling in ways that had seemed to be permanently lost to him. Thus, an octogenarian who has been "psychologically dead" for 30 years may "come alive" temporarily in discussing the last real event in his life—the death of a person who had "meant everything" to him. The case of a grossly confused aged woman who temporarily snapped back into life after exploration of previous bereavements has been reported (15). Thus, the hypothesis mentioned above might be extended to include some aged, not necessarily schizophrenic individuals. Further discussion of "psychological death" and related concepts will be found elsewhere in this book (Chapters 5 and 16).

Anthony's observations are quite consistent with certain of Freud's hypotheses. According to Freud, delusions of world destruction result from "the inner perception of the loss of object relationships" (16). In later stages of this process there often occur fantasies of world reconstruction, or feelings that salvation or rebirth are imminent (17). Harry Stack Sullivan treated what he termed the "world disaster psychosis" somewhat differently (18). The rebirth or reconstruction phase was not mentioned. Occasionally this becomes a stage during which the individual actually begins to recover, develop an improved sense of reality, and work out new strategies for coping with his problems. Most often, unfortunately, recovery does not follow. Nevertheless, the idea that the death of one's whole world or way of life is a prerequisite to the achievement of a new mode of functioning is not so atypical as it may at first appear. It is certainly not confined to the realm of psychopathology. Who has not wished that he could undo—destroy, if necessary—the existing situation, in order to begin anew?

Initiation ceremonies often involve "the belief that a state cannot be changed without first being annihilated. . . ." In his investigation of birth and rebirth meanings in primitive societies, Eliade has found that "images and symbols of ritual death are inextricably connected with germination, with embryology. They already indicate a new life in course of preparation" (19).

Especially relevant here is Eliade's account of ceremonies in which the initiates are separated from their mothers. In some Australian tribes the mothers are told that their sons "will be killed and eaten by a hostile and mysterious divinity" (20). They are then assured that the novices will be resuscitated as grown men-initiates. "The novices die to childhood." Among some tribes, "mothers mourn over the initiands as the dead are mourned." The initiates are also informed that they will be killed by a deity. "The very act of separation from their mothers fills them with forebodings of death" (21).

Belief in the linkage of birth and death is expressed openly by some primitive and some psychotic people. By contrast, such notions occur but fleetingly to the typical modern Western man and are seldom voiced plainly. Even in the scientific community there have been precious few who have devoted a major portion of their efforts to considering, let along unraveling, the theoretical problems of birth and death. One such pioneer, a psychoanalyst, has made birth and its psychological effects the cornerstone of his theory and of his therapeutic principles.

Otto Rank saw birth as a traumatic experience for the individual—one which affected the entire course of his life. For Rank, the birth trauma initiated two sets of strivings: "an impulse to return to the womb in order to restore prenatal conditions of security and . . . an impulse for *rebirth* or separation from a maternal object" (22). These contradictory impulses were thought to lead in two directions: to strivings to relate to others in a dependent fashion, and to an effort to achieve individuality.

Throughout life, each new separation is thought to revive the anxiety which accompanied the birth trauma. This point is interesting in view of the fact that Anthony, Freud, et al imply that separation arouses what is usually called death-anxiety, not birth-anxiety. To Rank, of course, the latter is the prototype of the former; the problem is theoretical, rather than merely semantic. Freud denied that death-anxiety could be traced to the trauma of birth (23). He argued, as others have since, that the mental apparatus of the neonate is far too undeveloped to appreciate the prospect of death. Rheingold replies that Freud's criticism is beside the point. "Of course the fetus has no knowledge of death—it requires almost all of childhood to arrive at a naturalistic understanding of its meaning. But even the fetus *fears* death, in the same way that an animal fears death without knowledge of death. Perception of threat is an innate given, a biological mechanism serving survival. . . . The fetus and infant act *as if* they knew death. I regard it as an acceptable assumption that the process of birth contributes a universal factor to the fear of death, even in persons born by section, and that variations in the natural process help to explain individual differences in sensitivity to danger situations" (24).

Certainly the *feeling* that each separation is something of a death is widespread. It is apparently an emotional if not a literal truth, if such a distinction be allowed. A popular song of a few years past proclaims, "Every time we say 'Goodbye', I die a little," a sentiment that was also expressed three centuries ago by John Donne: "When last I died, and dear, I die/as often as from thee I go/. . . . "

There is at least one other psychoanalytic foray into birth-death relations that demands our attention. In his imaginative little book, *Thalassa: A Theory of Genitality* (25), Sandor Ferenczi offered an interpretation that rivals even the bold views of Rank in its daring and scope. As the title implies, Ferenczi's book is concerned chiefly with explicating the meanings of genitality or sex. The details of his theory are not especially relevant here. But it is pertinent to note that Ferenczi presents a case for the possibility that higher forms of life—including man—exhibit what he terms a "thalassal regressive trend." Sexual behavior is one of the most significant ways in which we manifest our "striving towards the aquatic mode of existence abandoned in primeval times. . . " (26). The act of sexual intercourse may be regarded as fulfilling a striving to return to the moist and nourishing womb. Coitus, then, expresses our desire to regress to a more primitive state of unity.

What about death? Although Ferenczi does not dwell long upon this topic, he is alert to possible parallels between sex and death as strategies for returning to the prenatal situation. "It would indeed seem as though there were discoverable in the symptoms of the death struggle regressive trends which might fashion dying in the image of birth and so render it less agonizing. Immediately before the individual breathes his last, often indeed somewhat sooner, complete resignation supervenes, nay, expressions of satisfaction which proclaim the final attainment of a state of perfect rest, somewhat as in orgasm after the sexual struggle which has preceded it. Death exhibits uteroregressive trends similar to those of sleep and coitus" (27). In support of this proposition, Ferenczi, like Rank before him, points out that "many primitive peoples inter their dead in a squatting or foetal position, and the fact that in dreams and myths we find the same symbols for both death and birth cannot be a mere coincidence" (28).

Rank, then, emphasizes the pivotal experience of *separation* with its bi-directional implications (go back? go forward?). Birth is crucial because it is the first separation, preparing the way for one's response to all other separations, including death. Ferenczi does not emphasize the process of birth so much as the striving to return to the aquatic state that prevailed before birth in the individual's biography, and in earlier stages of evolution in the biography of the species. Coitus and the death-struggle are somewhat equivalent in the sense that both are ways of propelling oneself "home," against the stream of development and complexity. Both of these concepts differ from the proposition that birth and death are primarily to be regarded as opposites.

Furthermore, one could offer other alternatives involving different combinations of the same variables. Perhaps coitus itself is a sort of death-struggle, motivated in part by the desire for self-destruction in a symbolic reunion. For a variation on this theme, it could be proposed that coitus aims simultaneously at birth and death through the general route of a "uteroregressive trend." Still again, one might argue that lethal behavior (such as a suicidal attempt) is the symbolic substitute for that perfect sexual act which might induce the desired reunion and rebirth.

All of the foregoing raises many problems regarding the possible birth-death relationship. Under what conditions is it appropriate to regard birth and death as opposites? As equivalents? Rank's postulation of a primal anxiety that flows from birth trauma may seem less bizarre when viewed as just one of the many possible factors in Everyman's death-anxiety. But is there in fact always a psychological birth trauma? Are birth and death always related symbolically as "union with or separation from the mother?" Ferenczi's equation of coitus and dying as strategies for returning to the womb is not patently absurd. But how can such an hypothesis be subjected to clear-cut empirical investigation? As is so often the case in this area of inquiry, the questioner is hard put to discover information substantial enough to resolve the problem one way or the other.

We are in no position to spurn the fragmentary evidence that sometimes is encountered during clinical and research contacts. It has been found by the authors and several of their former colleagues at a geriatric hospital that elderly people who are presumed to be close to death may be preoccupied not with their immediate affairs, but with their earliest relationships. For example, patients' responses to sentence completion tests were more often concerned with parents, long since deceased, than with spouses and children, many of whom were still living. The "home" mentioned in responses often proved, upon further investigation, to be that of the patient's early childhood (29). These observations may provide indirect support for Deutsch's views on "peaceful dying" (30) which are considered elsewhere in this book (Chapter 6). It may be that these elderly and ailing people were contemplating a "going home" journey

whose psychological destination was both the womb and the tomb. Whether those who spoke of "going home" were fantasying a return to a Heavenly Father, a reunion with deceased natural parents, both or neither is open to conjecture—or, better yet, research. Other explanations of the focus upon early relationships can also be advanced (31).

It has already been noted that the concept of life and death as part of a symmetrical pattern is commonplace in childhood. Similar conceptions are encountered in the mythology of the ancients and the beliefs of contemporary primitives.

Henderson and Oakes have examined mythology in a depth and detail to which we cannot do justice here (32). They report: "the unthinkable after-death appears to be the same as the unthinkable before-birth, so that if I once came out of nothing, the odds are that I can come again and again. Nothing seems to create something by implication, just as low implies high. This is why the cycle of birth, death and rebirth is about the most basic theme in mythology and religion." Moreover, the theme of death, whether it is found in recurrent myths or contemporary dreams, "is never seen to stand alone as a final act of annihilation. Apart from extreme forms of pathology...death is universally found to be part of a cycle of death and rebirth, or to be the condition necessary to imagine transcendance of life in an experience of resurrection" (33).

In some cultures, the difference between birth and rebirth is not clearly defined. Consider the natives of central Australia. These tribesmen believe that after death the spirit of the deceased remains near its former home. Here it awaits the opportunity to enter a woman so that it can be reborn again as a baby. Thus, the spirit survives death and is reborn on this earth in a new body—to live again precisely the kind of life already known to the tribesman. Nevertheless, these people are not altogether comfortable with the idea that spirits of the dead may be hovering nearby; pregnant women try to avoid straying near lonely areas of the village where spirits may enter them (34).

Remnants of this birth-death conception may still be with us although not consciously recognized in current belief systems. When, for example, a newborn is seen to bear a striking resemblance to a recently deceased relative, the similarity is often greeted with mixed emotions. There may be the uneasy feeling that uncanny forces are in operation. Attitudes toward the deceased may exert an influence on attitudes toward the infant, or even on one's conceptions about death itself. Perhaps the words, "the Lord gave and the Lord hath taken away," frequently uttered at funeral services, contribute to the notion that a new birth is in some mysterious way a payment for the old life that was recently taken. This may be one reason why the literary theme, "a new life for an old" is so common. In the psychic economy this seems only just and proper.

THE PERSISTENCE OF "PRIMITIVE" IDEAS

Up to this point discussion has centered on the apparent linkage between the concepts of birth and death in childhood, in pathological conditions, in mythology, and in the beliefs and practices of primitive peoples. It has been hinted that much of what has already been said may also apply to the unacknowledged convictions of modern, normal adults as well. Now it is appropriate to consider more closely those clues which suggest that primitive conceptions of birth, death and rebirth continue to exist alongside and sometimes in opposition to the usual Judeo-Christian tenets.

The major Western religions do not support belief in reincarnation—physical rebirth into this world—nor in the continued life on earth of discarnate spirits. In fact, such beliefs have at times been openly and vigorously combatted (35). Nevertheless, there appears to be widespread, if largely unverbalized, sympathy for at least the latter of these two notions and possibly for the former as well. In some of the more elaborate memorial parks (i.e., cemeteries) on the West Coast of the United States, some families have arranged to have music piped into burial vaults. The practice of burying toys or prized possessions with the deceased is also popular (36). Promoters sell burial lots described as "Companion Spaces" for occupancy by husband and wife. "Garden crypts" ("part of the trend toward outdoor *living*") are also available. Such practices and the great emphasis on embalming to preserve physical remains are reminiscent of the customs prevalent in ancient Egypt where the professed beliefs were markedly different from our own. One can argue that the funeral industry is guided by motives that are monetary rather than religious or philosophical. However, the fact remains that people do purchase the services and trappings mentioned. This appeal can hardly be explained solely on the basis of the purchaser's ignorance of alternatives or desire for prestige, although undoubtedly these factors often play a part. We must also consider the likelihood that there survives in the minds of many contemporaries the consciously disavowed notion of continued postmortem life on earth (or under it).

That spirits of the deceased can return to their former homes is another of the beliefs which, while little discussed, is not entirely foreign to modern thought. The employment of spirits as characters in works of fiction has long been accepted. This practice persits even in literature which is noteworthy for its realism. We see an example of this in James Agee's touching novel, *A Death in the Family* (37). Jay, a central character, has been killed in an automobile accident. His wife, Mary, knows of his death and is home with the family.

It began to seem to Mary, as to Hanna, that there was someone in the house other than themselves. . . . She felt in it a terrible forcefulness, and concern, and restiveness. . . . ''

The elderly, deaf grandmother inquires: ''Has somebody come into the house? Why how very stupid of me, I *thought* I *heard* footsteps.''

''It was Jay, Andrew,'' [Mary says later].

''It was *something*. I haven't any doubt of that, but—good God, Mary.''

''It was Jay, all right, I know! Who else would be coming here tonight, so terribly worried, so terribly concerned for us, and restless! Besides, Andrew, it—it simply *felt* like Jay.''

''I just mean it felt like his *presence*'' (38).

And again,

''His presence became faint, and in a moment of terrible dread she cried out 'Jay!' and hurried to her daughter's crib. 'Stay with me one minute,' she whispered, 'just one minute, my dearest;' and in some force he did return. . . '' (39).

It is not uncommon to have recently deceased friends or relatives appear in one's dreams. We continue to be surprised, however, by the number of instances in which the dreamer assumes that the spirit of the deceased actually had paid a call. A recent example is typical:

INFORMANT (a registered nurse): She had something on her mind. I could tell she was worried. Oh, she really scolded me, but in a nice way. . . . She reminded me that I hadn't done what I said I'd do, what I'd promised her, to burn some envelopes she kept in her bedroom.

INTERVIEWER (R.K.): Were you surprised to see her in your dream?

INFORMANT: No, not at all. It was my fault. I'd really forgotten to do what I promised, so she just came to remind me.

INTERVIEWER: Do you think this dream was a way of reminding yourself to carry out this mission? I mean, did you have an image of Helen in your dreams, or did Helen herself call upon you?

INFORMANT: It was like I said. She came to remind me. She had every right to.

INTERVIEWER: Then you mean it was Helen herself who visited you, your dead friend, not a trick of your dreaming mind?

INFORMANT: That's right.

INTERVIEWER: And this didn't surprise you at all?

INFORMANT: (matter-of-factly) Like I said. She had to make sure I burned those envelopes.

This woman, an educated person with professional responsibilities, was not flustered or even particularly curious about the experience of having been visited by a dead friend. Her interest centered upon the content of the visit, rather than the event itself. Instances such as this make it difficult for us to believe that the ghost of the ghost-idea has been truly laid to rest.

Of course there have always been those who believed that discarnate spirits return to their former dwellings. Many of us can recall being warned at least once during childhood about a ''haunted'' house. Interest in poltergeists traditionally has been more popular and reputable in England than in the United States. A recent hour-long network television program was devoted to ''The Stately Ghosts of England'' (40), thus focusing the attention of millions of viewers on alleged phenomena usually the province of the atypical few. England has also been relatively tolerant of efforts to subject such phenomena to systematic investigation. In the United States, those who attempt to study spirits, mediums, reincarnation, and the entire realm of extrasensory perception (ESP) or parapsychology are frequently met with hostility and ridicule by the scientific establishment. Even at this date, it is unusual to find a behavioral scientist who will examine and discuss research in parapsychology with a mind both rigorous and open. This prejudice is unfortunate for it inhibits one possible method for direct investigation of the relationships between birth and death as well as many other unexplored areas.

Those who are interested in the *psychology* of death would be placing an unnecessary limitation upon themselves if they neglected the observation and analysis of ESP and related experiences. What people believe they have experienced and how they respond to the experiences is subject matter that is well within the reach of conventional psychological investigation. Perhaps researchers have been frightened off from studying many phenomena that are amenable to empirical operations because even to express an interest in the topic seems (mistakenly) to commit oneself to a metaphysical position, and an unfashionable one at that.

The field of science fiction, because it is so labeled, permits the writer great latitude in formulating hypotheses and offering predictions. Fantasies otherwise too weird to be tolerated are given free reign; solutions which violate physical laws can be applied to problems that have yet to arise. Since the science fictionist can treat birth and death in any way he chooses, it may be instructive to examine at least one example.

J. T. McIntosh's *Immortality—for Some* (41) envisions a rebirth which precedes physical death of the body, although it necessitates death of the original personality. It can be seen at once that this is a reversal of the conventional religious conception in which the body dies but is survived by the essence of the personality, or the spirit. The immortality to which McIntosh refers is limited to the individual's hereditary characteristics and capacities. All of the reborn person's life experience, including learned behavior and speech, is wiped out, and his body is regressed (through unspecified processes) to that of a 14-year-old. Thus, the reborn must be schooled for about four years to bring them up to the general level of knowledge and experience of the rest of the population. Only citizens considered to be of value to the community are eligible for rebirth. In fact, the valuable citizen has no choice: his worth is too great to be lost forever through death. He must be reborn.

The hero of this tale, an eminently valuable citizen, does not desire rebirth:

I wanted to live my life to the full and die when it was over. When a man goes for Rebirth, does he survive? No. He remembers nothing of his previous life, of his own personal history. He becomes another person. . . . At 80 I was subject to increasing pressure to accept Rebirth. I didn't want it. I wanted the 20 years I've had since then, the 20 or 30 more I could have. . . . I wanted to go on being myself (42).

The author in this case uses his freedom to envision a time when a) a life expectancy of 120 years will be quite usual, and b) technological advance will enable a physical rebirth. Mankind will then be torn by a new conflict: the desire to live out life maintaining one's sense of personal integrity and identity, and the desire for immortality. Two points are worth noting:

1. The kind of immortality depicted in this story has features in common with one of the few types of quasi-immortality already available: the survival of the genes. Hereditary traits and capacities do continue after the individual's death, if he is survived by children. In the story the reborn have no recollection of a previous life; they do not know that they have lived before. Thus, in effect, the hero is asked to renounce what is left of his own personal life simply so that he will not experience death, and so that society might possibly again make use of his abilities. Also, this form of immortality is not granted automatically to all individuals, but must be earned in some way—just as the creation of offspring to carry one's genetic structure onward is not vouchsafed to all humans. Other conceptions of a "conditional immortality" have been proposed by philosophers, notably William Earnest Hocking (43).

2. Except for the facts that the regression process returns one only to

adolescence and that the rebirth occurs before physical death, the basic idea in this example from contemporary science fiction obviously is related to a very ancient one—reincarnation, or the transmigration of souls. Rejected by most Western theologians, this doctrine now presents itself in a new guise in which it can tantalize the reader with the implicit prediction that technological development will bring ancient myth into future reality.

Scientists as well as science-fictionists and philosophers have occasionally offered conceptions of birth and death that deviate markedly from our usual notions. A particularly interesting example is that provided by Gustav Theodor Fechner. Students of psychology learn early of Fechner's fundamental contributions to experimental method. He is generally credited with being the pioneer of the field of psychophysics. Yet Fechner was guided by a world view much broader than the field of psychology. In *Buchlein vom Leben Nach dem Tode* (44) he proposed what might be construed as a developmental model of the birth process that extends throughout the entire life-span— and beyond!

The usual dichotomy between life and afterlife is rejected. It is more appropriate to think in terms of a *development into life* that begins long before birth and continues long after death. "The consciousness with which the child awakes at birth is only a part of the eternal, preexisting, universal, divine consciousness which has concentrated itself in the new soul" (45). This most elementary and undifferentiated seed of life becomes slightly more particularized in the womb, but even the postnatal years fail to bring a complete individualization. The new soul becomes a sort of part-person, i.e., an ordinary human on earth. The part-person alternates between sleeping and waking in a spiritual as well as a literal sense. His self-knowledge is severely limited; a flash of understanding illuminates; an intuition

suggests; then the part-person once again is drowned in his own limitations. The part-person requires time and effort to comprehend his expanded new possibilities after death. Just as the new soul is confused, disoriented, and bewildered by its entry into life, so the evolving soul finds itself temporarily at a loss upon its entry into the afterlife. Birth and death are merely way stations in the continuing development of the part-person into full spiritual personality. Furthermore, birth and death are semipermeable boundaries through which souls may interpenetrate for mutual influence. A "dead" man is still a citizen in the universal human community, his spirit contributing to the progress of mankind.

The idea that birth and death are not ultimate, but merely way stations in the infinitely gradual development of the individual spirit or soul is somewhat reminiscent of the reincarnation doctrine which has been so influential in Oriental thought. The Buddhist seeks release from the repetitious cycle of birth-death-rebirth in various earthbound forms. The state of nirvana is attained when he no longer must seek for an understanding of the world or himself. "*Nirvana* is the way of life which ensues when clutching at life has come to an end.... [The self is freed] from 'the Round of incantations.' " (46). Fechner's variation on this theme, emphasizing the *continuation* of development rather than the final state, may reflect a distinctive characteristic of technologically-tinged Western thought.

Although he contributed significantly to several fields of science, Fechner obviously developed his vision of birth-death relationships upon other grounds than the empirical and operational. More recently it has become possible to advance rather unusual ideas that have some basis in scientific and technological developments. Consider *The Prospect of Immortality*. Its author, Robert C. W. Ettinger, proposes that people be frozen immediately after death to prevent their physical deterioration. Then, whenever future technological developments permit, the deceased could be defrosted, repaired, and revived. "No matter what kills us, whether old age or disease, and even if freezing techniques are still crude when we die, *sooner or later* our friends of the future should be equal to the task of reviving and curing us" (47).

What influence the introduction of such practices would have on man's attitudes toward birth and death, or his entire philosophy of life, can only be guessed at (Ettinger himself has discussed some of the more practical problems). However, every work is to some extent a product of its time. The fact that *The Prospect of Immortality* has appeared in our day and has met with serious discussion rather than outright censure and rejection is another manifestation of the growing interest in death-related topics. Perhaps the technological trappings which support the "freeze-wait-reanimate" approach (48) make the topic more acceptable than the parapsychological approach which is more dependent upon mental (i.e., "invisible") phenomena. There is a characteristically American accent to the cryonic movement that has followed in the wake of Ettinger's book; the reliance on technological advances for the solution of life's problems. For whatever reasons, whether in fiction or the scientific laboratory, the second half of the twentieth century finds Western man more willing to grapple with matters of life and death than he has been for a long time.

A 'PERMANENT ENCOUNTER WITH DEATH'?

In pursuit of evidence that modern man retains age-old ideas about the linkage of birth and death, we move from the sublime to the ridiculous. No doubt one could argue that the freezing of dead bodies is something less than sublime; but most would agree, perhaps, that the re-cent outbreak of monster television programs, masks, dolls, stories, games, cookies, etc., is, on the surface at least, ridiculous. Because of the wealth of material they present, the television monster programs are of special interest.

Two recent series, "The Munsters" and "The Addams Family," relied heavily for their humor on the conversion of almost everything into its opposite. Characters regard as good or beautiful that which is usually considered bad or ugly and vice versa. Lions, man-eating plants, octopi and venomous spiders are household pets. Beings of bizarre and frightening visage are described as beautiful and sexy. Unusually attractive people are reviled as ugly or horrible; the image of The Macabre (Chapter 6) is radically transformed. Earlier reference to word association tests and psychoanalytic theory emphasized that opposites are often equivalent in the unconscious. Hence, to the psychologically sophisticated, the interchange of opposites is comprehensible and not unexpected. To the layman, however, such substitutions have surprise value. He laughs at the unexpected element. This laughter may serve to relieve the anxiety that has been aroused by the perception of something horrible and frightening (and perhaps also by the unacceptable feelings of attraction they may hold for him). He reassures himself: "Of course, that's not really beautiful; it's hideous. I think so, too. Calling it pretty is actually funny, an off-beat joke."

A second interesting facet of at least one of the programs is the cavalier fashion in which birth and death are treated. It is hinted that the father who works at "the parlor," presumably a funeral parlor, was not born but assembled, either from inanimate objects or parts collected from various corpses. His wife and her father are hundreds of years old. "Grandpa" has apparently died several times previously. In one episode he is transformed into a wolf and back again into human form. Such ingredients would hardly be thought to constitute wholesome family fare, much less a prescription for comedy. It is probable that in previous decades they would have met with less success, if not with outright rejection. Why is it that monster programs were so recently initiated and welcomed into the living room?

It is a truism that behavior is over-determined. The motivation for television viewing preferences is certainly no exception. Undoubtedly many factors, including some highly idiosyncratic ones, underlie the appeal of the monster programs. However, it would appear that monster programs and the products they advertise have been tailored largely for young people. And it is the younger generation that has been raised entirely within the shadow of imminent thermonuclear destruction. The following proposition suggests itself: *The "atomic age" and its accouterments are partially responsible for the attitude change which is fundamental to, or facilitates the acceptance of, the monster craze.*

In discussing the ramifications of the Hiroshima disaster, Robert Jay Lifton details what he terms the "permanent encounter with death," a psychological state common among those who were exposed to the first thermonuclear explosion. Lifton describes a "sense of total contamination"; a "bomb disease"; the fear of an enduring taint which leads the sufferer to see every symptom as related to radiation exposure; and, not of least importance, the *identification* with death and dying (49).

All informed people today are, to some extent, involved in a permanent encounter with death. However engrossed we may be in our daily activities there lurks somewhere within us, ready for arousal, a complex of attitudes and anxieties based on the realization that any hour of any day could be doomsday. A single international incident might precipitate nuclear war. Nor are we discomforted only by what-might-be. What already-has-been is brought to our attention with

every new report of the fallout in our food supply. Among the very young, the unstable, and those who for other reasons lack perspective, the total orientation to life can fluctuate with the daily news. One cannot help but wonder if our society's pressure on the young to act "grown up" at ever earlier ages, callousness toward death, and unwillingness to get involved with others—all characteristics that have been imputed to our era—relate not only to our burgeoning population and its increased mobility, but also to a pervasive sense of impending disaster. Of course, there have always been some people whose philosophy was to "live fast, die young and leave a goodlooking corpse." But there is something distinct in the widespread readiness to see the Frankenstein monster, the vampire, the bizarre creature from another age or world as a part of a lovable, if not 100 percent, red-blooded American family.

There is now, perhaps, an *identification* with the monsters, the dead, and the inhuman. Perhaps this psychic arrangement reassures the viewer that death is not so bad after all or, at least, that it might not be final. Best of all, even while he derives these benefits from the monster program, the viewer can laugh at it as an impossible comedy and deny that it has any deeper meaning.

An additional factor may be involved in our readiness to embrace the monster: *the desire to humanize so that we can contend more comfortably with the proliferating, still unfamiliar, thinking machines and other space-age "hardware."* We try to warm up to the robot-like computers, neither living nor dead, who may soon be our colleagues. This desire to humanize the monster may be related to attitudes that underlie some contemporary personifications of death as well as medieval depictions and enactments. (See Chapter 16.)

Finally, the advent of space exploration may have increased the credibility of phenomena once considered bizarre. The problem of whether or not there is life on other planets is no longer a completely remote or idle inquiry. We may soon be in a position to investigate this question directly, and the moon has already started to reveal its mysteries. The wildest of Jules Verne's dreams, the most fantastic of Flash Gordon episodes, might prove tame when compared with what future explorations could reveal. At the very least, it now seems appropriate to accommodate ourselves to the possibility that the universe—as probed by science, not simply as conjured by imagination—may have many more surprises in store for us.

It is not mere chance, therefore, that programs about space exploration have been one of the major successors to the monster series. There are several reasons why this should be so: 1) They are topical. Plans for future space travel are now part of our daily news. 2) They provide new pastureland for the jaded. "Space" is one of the last external virgin territories that remains to be explored. 3) They present basic problems of life and death in a new context. Writers can capitalize even more freely on some of the underlying fantasies and motivations which made the monster fad successful—in a setting which, by its very uniqueness renders the bizarre plausible. 4) Anything goes. Since space, and the planets to which one can travel through it, are unknown quantities, only the writer's imagination limits the plots and characterizations. 5) They may serve a preparatory function. The psyche of the earthbound must eventually come to accept other planets and perhaps other forms of sentient life as well. Space exploration programs allow us to try out new roles, encounter new kinds of problems and, perhaps, to release in fantasy some of the anxieties associated with both of these. Note some of the characteristics of two of the most successful space programs. In both *Star Trek* and *Lost in Space* human earthlings and near-human creatures have superhuman capacities and proceed through time and space (if it is

still useful to separate them) in defiance of traditional physical laws. *Lost in Space* frequently employs monsters and completely programmed robots as major characters. Some are "good" and some are "bad." As in the monster series, the "ugly" is sometimes "good." Villains are not ordinarily vanquished by conventional means. They are made to disappear by mysterious techniques or are banished or escape to other planets. How these creatures originated is not explained and death, as we know it, is almost never seen. It is common for the space creatures to appear "out of nothing" and to assume such a variety of forms that one cannot speak easily of their birth or death. "Can this really happen?" the child asks his parents. The young mind is opened even further to the prospect that so-called fantasy and so-called reality are not easily distinguishable.

What has all this to do with our ideas about the relationship of birth and death? Possibly, a great deal. The young child receiving religious instruction hears that when people die they go "up" to Heaven. From other sources he learns that there may be living creatures on other planets to which astronauts expect to travel. The child takes in television programs about monsters, assembled from debris rather than born, who have apparently lived before and can turn themselves into beasts. He discovers that man can travel beyond the earth and return. For the adult, too, our present era opens vistas that can be both exciting and unsettling. Ideas that one had been taught to regard as fantastic are now being implemented or at least explored. This cannot help but raise the suspicion that other seemingly unbelievable notions may also be true. In both child and adult, fantasy and fact join hands to form a circle. Primitive ideas about birth and death supply a rich source of raw material for monster stories. *The facts of our nuclear-space age, which provide a fertile soil wherein monster and interplanetary fantasies may flourish, fur-*

*ther awaken, stimulate, and lend credence
to man's primitive ideas about birth and
death.*

BIRTH, DEATH, AND PERCEPTUAL
ORGANIZATION

There are still other possible explanations for the persistence of ideas about birth and death that would superficially appear to be out of tune with contemporary knowledge. Viktor Frankl submits that one need seek no complex motive for the idea that part of man is immortal. It keeps cropping up as does the observation that 2+2=4 simply because it is so (50). Emerson voiced a related idea: "The blazing evidence of immortality is our dissatisfaction with any other solution" (51). Lifton reiterates the familiar observation that man has "an innate need for a sense of immortality" (52). Are there other reasons why many people do not think of birth and death as merely defining the ends of a continuum but, rather, as having been preceded by or to be succeeded by some other stage?

Ducasse offers two reasons why belief in life after death is "easy and widespread" (53):

1. *Because of "psychological inertia,"* which he defines as "a tendency to assume that what we're accustomed to find present will continue to be so."

This reason becomes more convincing when one notes the great difficulty that young people frequently encounter in attempting to project themselves intellectually and emotionally into advanced age. Being young (and never having been old) they find it difficult to image the situation will ever change; similarly, their grandparents or even parents, being "old" now, could never really have been young (54). The "emotional distance" from life to death would seem to be greater than that from youth to old age (although the latter should not be underestimated);

thus, the force of what Ducasse terms "psychological inertia" must be tremendous in this regard.

2. *Because we wish there to be a life after death.* It may well be true that most people wish for a life after death. Perhaps it is also true, since expectations are rooted in past experience, that "psychological inertia" plays a part in the credibility given to immortality. However, many other hypotheses are plausible. Let us consider one simple alternative which, if less obvious, is nonetheless within the realm of the plausible and is also reasonably parsimonious. This hypothesis is related to the basic principles of gestalt psychology, specifically, the laws of form.

Gestalt psychology teaches that the human organism's perceptual field tends to become organized in accord with certain principles. Since these are fairly numerous, however, only those germane to the hypothesis will be reviewed (55):

1. A perceptual field tends to become structured in terms of a *figure* and the *ground* upon which it appears to be superimposed.

2. "Good" forms are generally well articulated and closed.

3. Good forms tend to persist and recur.

4. There is a tendency for a figure to be perceived as having as "good" a form as possible. Thus, if a circle that is interrupted by a small gap is viewed from a distance there will be a tendency for it to be seen as complete (law of closure).

5. Forms tend toward *symmetry*.

6. Form persists despite transposition. "Organization, form and therefore object character usually depend on the *relations* between parts and not on the particular characteristics of the parts. It follows that, if the parts change and the relations remain the same, the form or object remains the same, as in the transposed melody" (56).

In addition to the foregoing, it can be demonstrated experimentally that habitual and/or instructional sets influence what we perceive (57). For example, subjects presented with identical stimulus figures (0-0) but different instructions reproduced the stimulus in accord with the instructions received instead of the objective characteristics of the stimulus. Stimulus: 0-0. Eyeglasses: o⌒o. Dumbbell: o——o (58).

a) Some of the basic principles said to govern perception have been reviewed. b) In the ideas of children and primitive peoples (and, we suspect, in our own as well) there is a tendency to conceive of life and death as part of a symmetrical pattern. c) There is much evidence that needs and ideas as well as set influence our perceptions.

It seems reasonable now to raise the possibility that the reverse is also true: what we *perceive* may help determine what we *conceive*. Of greater interest still, perhaps the laws which determine the way we perceive are actually identical with the laws which determine how we conceptualize. For example, in addition to a) and b) above, it is known that the circle and the sphere (two and three dimensional, respectively) are considered the most perfectly symmetrical figures. Hence, if there is a tendency to conceptualize as well as to perceive in such a manner that the "product" (percept or concept) is as "good" or perfect as possible, it would be reasonable to hypothesize that we would think of birth and death as part of a symmetrical, circular pattern.

This hypothetical circular pattern, to be complete, would have to include something between death and birth as well as the reverse: Birth   Death. This could be one factor which underlies some people's belief in rebirth and reincarnation: the perceptual apparatus favors the organization of experience and ideas into symmetrical, "good" concepts.

It is possible that this tendency may be rooted in early experiences of temporality that persist through the adult years although somewhat masked by 'higher level' thought. For example, for both the infant and child, time seems to be apprehended primarily as a symmetry in motion, a cycle of events-and-feeling-states that repeats itself over and again (59). This nondirectional sense of time may develop from the interplay between psychobiological rhythms and the environmental context in which they occur (e.g., patterns of hunger and feedings). A complicated developmental sequence must occur before abstract and linear notions of time are achieved (60), and such concepts do not seem to develop very far in some primitive societies (61).

Although the earlier sense of time as a cycle or set of cycles gradually becomes subordinate to the developing individual's more abstract frameworks for organizing his experience, it does not vanish. On many subsequent occasions, the sense of time as a symmetrical cycle may become dominant, or may continue to operate influentially on its own level with some independence from the more conceptual frameworks that the individual may believe he is using to regulate his life (62).

Death constitutes a formidable challenge to human cognitive operations at their highest levels of functioning, and even when directed with prolonged concentration upon this subject. Few individuals appear to have either the intellectual training or the inclination to meditate productively and at length upon the nature of death. Thus, the more primitive sense of cyclical, symmetrical time is likely to be applied to the question of death that has not been answered satisfactorily by articulated thought operations. Waking and sleeping, and waking again; living and dying, and living again—this reliable primitive logic easily works out its own conclusions. It will be suggested below that familiar principles in experimental psychology tend to confirm this interpretation of the birth-death relationship as a natural construction of a symmetry-seeking bias that is basic to human functioning.

Let us explicate what has been implied in the foregoing discussion:

Death seemingly is an unique event that terminates the individual's lifeline, and thus implies a unidirectional flow of time. But the child, the primitive man, the myth-maker, and all three of these within ourselves interpret death within a cyclical time structure that recognizes beginnings and ends but not one absolute beginning and one unique and final end. Ideas of death do not exist independently from ideas of time—a relationship that is considered further at other points in this book—in Chapter 2, for example.

Does the application of gestalt perceptual laws to birth-death relationships seem at once too farfetched and too simplified? We should remind ourselves that:

1. Geometric figures and curves frequently are employed as models in discussions of life and death. Pelikan has relied upon geometric figures to describe the "shape of death" disclosed by Christian theologians (63). Jung likened the "curve of life" to "the parabola of a projectile which, disturbed from its initial state of rest, rises and then returns to a state of repose" (64).

2. Discovery of general laws of behavior is one of the goals of psychology (the only goal, say some). Hence, principles which appear valid in one realm (e.g., the perceptual) should be tested in other realms to determine the extreme limits of their applicability. Psychological problems, whether those of birth and death, perception and cognition, brain function, etc., are, after all, interdependent.

Undoubtedly, many other hypotheses could be advanced to help explain the development of ideas about birth and death. Perhaps the time has come at last to subject some of these ideas to experimental investigation.

A parting word about the general relevance of this chapter is in order. It is obvious that the question of the linkage between concepts of birth and death is in part theoretical or philosophical. This does not make it an empty, impractical inquiry. How can man avoid grappling with the meanings of birth and death if he proposes to discover or create "meanings" for the life that flows between these two phenomena? What is one to make of his personal time that moves so incessantly from birth toward death? While waiting for Godot, Pozzo turns suddenly furious: "Have you not done tormenting me with your accursed time! It's abominable! When! When! One day, is that not enough for you, one day he went dumb, one day I went blind, one day we'll go deaf, one day we were born, one day we shall die, the same day, the same second, is that not enough for you?" (Calmer.) "They give birth astride of a grave, the light gleams an instant, then it's night once more. . . " (65). The question is psychological, but not in the narrow sense of the word.

Continued scientific advances make it increasingly clear that if one pursues any subject far enough he is confronted eventually by the data and unsolved problems of many, if not all, others. In every field one encounters the question: "How did it begin?" The microbiologist, the philosopher, the chemist attempt not only to identify and define the tenuous line that divides plant from animal, but also to distinguish the animate from the inanimate. The astronomer seeks to discover, among other things, the very origin of the universe. When Abner Dean's lonely, naked cartoon character inquires at the information booth: "What am I doing here? What does it all mean in the vast infinite scheme of things?" (66) the laugh is on us. What answer each person, as an individual and as a minute constituent of the universe, develops to meet such basic questions, how he regards birth and death and his place in the sun, can influence all of history. There may be no indisputable single answer to "What is the relationship between birth and death?", but it certainly remains a most relevant question.

REFERENCES

1. Henderson, J., & Oakes, M. *The wisdom of the serpent.* New York: Braziller, 1963.
2. *Ibid.*, p. xi.
3. Kalish, R. Life and death: Dividing the indivisible. *Social Science and Medicine*, 1968, *2*, 249-259.
4. Postman, L., & Egan, J. *Experimental psychology: An introduction.* New York: Harper & Bros., 1949. Pp. 262-264.
5. Smith, B. *A tree grows in Brooklyn.* New York: Everybody's Vacation Publishing Co., 1943. P. 283.
6. Maurer, A. Maturation of concepts of death. *British Journal of Medicine and Psychology*, 1966, *39*, 35-41.
7. Anthony, S. *The child's discovery of death.* New York: Harcourt, Brace, 1940.
8. Nagy, M. The child's view of death. In H. Feifel (Ed.), *The meaning of death.* New York: McGraw-Hill, 1959. P. 83.
9. *Ibid.*, p. 84.
10. Shneidman, E. Suicide, sleep, and death: Some possible interrelations among cessation, interruption, and continuation phenomena. *Journal of Consulting Psychology*, 1964, *28*, 95-106.
11. Anthony, *op. cit.*, p. 167.
12. Barry, H. H. Orphanhood as a factor in psychoses. *Journal of Abnormal and Social Psychology.* 1936, *30*, 431-438.
13. Edelson, S. R., & Warren, P. H. Catatonic schizophrenia as a mourning process. *Diseases of the Nervous System*, 1963, *24*, 2-8.
14. Hinsie, L. E. Cited by Robert White: *The abnormal personality.* New York: Ronald Press, 1948. P. 531.
15. Kastenbaum, R. Multiple personality in later life—a developmental interpretation. *Gerontologist*, 1964, *4*, 16-20.
16. Fenichel, O. *The psychoanalytic theory of neurosis.* Washington, D.C.: W. W. Norton, 1945. P. 417.
17. *Ibid.*, pp. 424-425.
18. Sullivan, H. S. *Conceptions of modern psychiatry.* Washington, D.C.: W. W. Norton, 1947. Pp. 83-84.
19. Eliade, M. *Birth and rebirth: The religious meanings of initiation in human culture.* (Translated by Willard R. Trask) New York: Harper, 1958.
20. *Ibid.*, p. xiv.
21. *Ibid.*, p. 8.
22. Rank, O. *The trauma of birth.* New York: Brunner, 1952.
23. Wolberg, L. *The technique of psychotherapy.* New York: Grune & Stratton, 1954. P. 69.
24. Rheingold, J. *The mother, anxiety and death: The catastrophic death complex.* Boston: Little, Brown, 1967. P. 78.
25. Ferenczi, S. *Thalassa: A theory of genitality.* (Translated by Henry Alden Bunker) New York: Psychoanalytic Quarterly, Inc., 1938.
26. *Ibid.*, p. 52.
27. *Ibid.*, p. 95.
28. *Ibid.*, p. 95.
29. Aisenberg, R., & Kastenbaum, R., et al. Unpublished data, NIMH project MHO-4818. Framingham, Mass.: Cushing Hospital, 1963.
30. Deutsch, F. Euthanasia: A clinical study. *Psychoanalytic Quarterly.* 1936, *5*, 347-368.
31. Kastenbaum, R. On the meaning of time in later life. *Journal of Genetic Psychology*, 1966, *109*, 9-25.
32. Henderson & Oakes, *op. cit.*
33. *Ibid.*, p. 4.
34. Lueba, J. H. *The belief in God and immortality.* Boston: Sherman, French, 1916. P. 17.
35. Ducasse, C. J. *The belief in life after death.* Springfield, Ill.: Charles C Thomas, 1961. P. 290.
36. Harmer, R. M. *The high cost of dying.* New York: Colliers, 1963, *51*, 55-56.
37. Agee, J. *A death in the family.* New York: Avon, 1963. P. 141.
38. *Ibid.*, p. 142.
39. *Ibid.*, p. 145.
40. "The Stately Ghosts of England." NBC television production, January 25, 1965.
41. McIntosh, J. T. Immortality...for some. In Groff Conklin (Ed.), *Twelve great classics of science fiction.* Greenwich, Conn.: Gold Medal, 1963. Pp. 157-192.
42. *Ibid.*, pp. 189-190.
43. Hocking, W. E. *The meaning of immortality in human experience.* New York: Harpers, 1957.
44. Fechner, G. T. *The little book of life after death.* (Translated by Mary C. Wadsworth) Boston: Little, Brown, 1904.
45. *Ibid.*, p. 91.
46. Watts, A. W. *The way of Zen.* New York: Pantheon, 1957. P. 59.

47. Ettinger, R. C. W. *The prospect of immortality.* New York: McFadden-Bartell, 1964. P. 15.

48. A catch-phrase that appears regularly in *Cryonic Reports*, newsletter of the Cryonics Society of New York.

49. Lifton, R. J. On death and death symbolism: The Hiroshima disaster. *Psychiatry*, 1964, *27*, 191-210.

50. Frankl, V. *From death camp to existentialism.* Boston: Beacon Press, 1959.

51. Curtis, C. P. & Greenslet, F. (Eds.), *The practical cogitator.* Boston: Houghton Mifflin, 1945. P. 510.

52. Lifton, *op. cit.* p. 209.

53. Ducasse, C. J. *Nature, mind and death.* Springfield, Ill.: Charles C Thomas, 1951. P. 444.

54. Kastenbaum, R. The crisis of explanation. In R. Kastenbaum (Ed.), *New thoughts on old age.* New York: Springer, 1964. Pp. 316-323.

55. Boring, E. G. *A history of experimental psychology.* New York: Appleton-Century-Crofts, 1950. Pp. 611-612.

56. Munn, N. L. *Psychology.* Boston: 1966.

57. *Ibid.,* p. 327.

58. Sargent, S. S. *Social psychology,* New York: Harper & Bros., 1950. Pp. 261-262.

59. Schecter, D. E., Symonds, M., & Bernstein, I. Development of the concept of time in children. *Journal of Nervous and Mental Disease,* 1955, *21,* 301-310.

60. Kastenbaum, R. On the meaning of time in later life, *op. cit.*

61. Werner, H. *Comparative psychology of mental development.* New York: International University Press, 1957.

62. Schecter, et al., *op. cit.*

63. Pelikan, J. *The shape of death, life and immortality in the early fathers.* New York: Abingdon Press, 1961.

64. Jung, C. The soul and death. In H. Feifel (Ed.), *The meaning of death.* New York: McGraw-Hill, 1959. Pp. 3-15.

65. Beckett, S. *Waiting for Godot.* New York: Grove Press, 1954.

66. Dean, A. *What am I doing here?* New York: Simon & Schuster, 1947.

8

The Cultural Milieu of Death

1: *Yesterday*

We are told that it is futile to contemplate death. "Ignore death" is the advice, for to dwell upon this subject sickens heart and mind, and to no good purpose. And we are told that the only proper way to conduct one's life is through the daily, if not hourly, contemplation of that inevitable moment toward which all flesh moves.

We are told that death is a biological fact that is no more important than the punctuation at the end of a sentence. And we are told that death is the supreme fact of our existence, a fact that shapes the meaning of everything else in our lives.

We are told that death negates or destroys all the values we develop in the course of our lives. And we are told that death transfigures our values, raising them to a higher level of being.

We are told that fear of death is instinctive, deeply rooted in human nature. And we are told that in the depths of our psyche none of us can truly accept or even understand the proposition that we are mortal.

Healthy people who contemplate death do so with nervous laughter, or with composure, or with denial, resignation, intensity, indifference, doubt, certainty. Critically ill people and others who face imminent death maintain a silence. Sometimes this is an agitated silence—at other times, it is stoical, tranquil, or enigmatic. Or, they face death with desperate maneuvers, eager anticipation, dread, apathy, or rather mixed sentiments.

These are among the interpretations that have been put upon the prospect or fact of death within our cultural milieu. Most if not all of these interpretations come to us as part of our heritage from previous generations, earlier cultures. Yet our own *zeitgeist*—make that *zeitgeisten*— are very much in evidence. We are more likely to accept some alternatives than others, and our cultural milieu may be generating significant new variations on ancient themes, perhaps new themes as well.

In this chapter we explore some of the cultural factors that contribute to the individual's orientation toward death. By "orientation toward death" we intend the total range of thought, feeling, and behavior that is directly or indirectly related to death. This includes conceptions of death, attitudes toward dying persons, funerary practices, and behaviors that have the effect of shortening or lengthening the individual's life-span. Several of these topics are discussed in more detail elsewhere in this book. Here we are chiefly interested in developing a general perspective on the relationship between cultural milieu and death orientation.

DEATH AND ITS BACKGROUND OF LIFE

Let us begin by considering a few characteristics of the cultural milieu that seem particularly important in shaping our interpretations of death. The prevalent situation in the United States today will be compared and contrasted with conditions that have obtained elsewhere or at other times. This presentation is necessarily brief and selective.

One is impressed by the great differences that can be observed as various societies come into view. Yet certain basic conditions of life have prevailed in most societies from ancient times to at least the fringes of our present age. We propose that the four conditions cited below have contributed significantly to the general background of life against which interpretations of death have emerged.

Perhaps the most obvious condition was the rather limited life expectancy that confronted man throughout most of his history. Relatively few people survived beyond the years of early maturity. So high were the death rates among infants and children that census takers often did not bother to include them in their tallies. Deaths associated with childbearing included not only the women who died while giving birth or soon after, but also those whose health was undermined by multiple births, of which a high proportion might be stillborn. Associated with the foreshortened life-span that characterized most societies prior to our own was the relative unimportance of both adolescence and old age. There was not much

time to dawdle in the transition from childhood to adult responsibility, given the prospect that the adult years would be so limited in number (1). Relatively few people died of old age, although one who survived into advanced years while retaining mental and physical prowess might wield considerable social influence (2).

A second and related condition was exposure to death—that is, to the sight of dying and dead persons, and animals as well. The average person had relatively little insulation from standing as witness to death.

A third condition was the sense of possessing relatively little control over the forces of nature. The world was an untrustworthy abode, comfortable and dependable at times but, at other times, crushing, devastating, uprooting its inhabitants. And for what purpose or reason? The ways of the world were mysterious, difficult to comprehend. If ancient man felt relatively powerless in the world because of what we might now describe as his lack of substantial scientific knowledge, then he could not have been much reassured by his technology. Without minimizing some of the technological feats that the ancients performed, we can appreciate that, for many centuries, man had rather limited resources for altering the unfavorable circumstances in which he frequently found himself.

In earlier cultures, then, man's hold on life was quite precarious, with death most frequently occurring within what we now would regard as the first half of the life-span. Furthermore, dying and death were everywhere visible, and one generally did not expect to exercise control over his environment (although the desire to do so was present and contributed to the development of magical practices and mythologies). To these environmental conditions we should now add at least one psychosocial element: the status of the individual.

Philosophers and social historians have

expressed the opinion that the concept of individualism was relatively little developed in the ancient world (3,4). The person was primarily a social component, a unit that fulfilled its role expectancies within the dictates of custom. One's lineage and his station in life were the important things. The extended family and the clan, tribe, or city provided the needed strength and continuity. Most persons in most societies were not expected to make individual decisions about basic issues or ultimate matters, nor was the emotional satisfaction or fate of the individual as an individual considered to be of primary significance. The well-being of the individual was important chiefly as it related to his performance of obligations to the group.

Not all the conditions that have been mentioned here were of equal salience in a given society at a particular moment in its history. But these factors do seem to have provided an important part of the context for earlier interpretations of death. We would be mistaken to consider myths and other conceptualizations of death apart from these background conditions of life.

THE DEATH SYSTEM

We suggest that *words and actions concerning death may be considered as jointly constituting a system.* All societies have developed one or more death systems through which they have tried to come to terms with death in both its personal and social aspects. Let us sample a few of the death systems that developed against the background of life conditions that has just been sketched.

The Egyptians of antiquity developed a death system that was quite explicit and detailed. Their *Book of the Dead* (5), like the Tibetan counterpart with the same title (6), provided the outlines of a comprehensive death system although cast largely in the form of prescriptions for funerary practice. This system transmitted—or at least was intended to transmit—a relatively integrated approach that would enable individual members to think, feel, and behave with respect to death in ways that they might consider to be effective and appropriate. The Egyptian system offered an explicit world view which was sponsored by the governing authorities, shared by the community, and linked to individual behavior in specific terms. Within this system, the individual's belief was the community's belief. He was not alone. And he had important actions to perform in the total death situation, ranging from the dying process through the care of the dead.

These actions were important from two standpoints. From the standpoint of the individual, his actions were important because, through sacrifices and rituals, he was actually producing an effect in the whole sequence of events that transpire between the process of dying and full status in the community of shades. From the standpoint of a psychologically-oriented observer, the actions were important not because they had any actual effect upon the fate of the deceased or future relations between deceased and survivor, but because they performed functions vital to the individual and his society. Perhaps the most important function was the behavioral prescription that gave the person something to do in situations that otherwise might have exposed him to a sense of utter helplessness. Belief in magical control over the powerful forces of death and the afterlife further encouraged the Egyptian to think of death as an event that was well within his province of action.

Whether or not the Egyptian death system actually functioned as smoothly as advertised is open to question. How effective is even the most elaborate death system in helping the individual to cope with his personal distress? It is also possible to argue that the very existence of an elaborate, formalized death system demonstrates an unusually strong sense of discomfort in the presence of death, a discomfort that perhaps was only masked by ritual. And we may not be entirely justified in portraying the ancient Egyptians as a people who were dedicated to the subject of death. Anthropological findings suggest that preservation of death-related artifacts may have been unusually great because of favorable conditions in the soil; thus, it would be possible to overestimate their relative preoccupation with death (7). Nevertheless, it appears reasonable to regard the authors and practitioners of *The Book of the Dead* as exemplars of a most determined effort to place death within the scope of cultural sanctions.

The Egyptian death system emerged within a society that had achieved a relatively high level of intellectual and technological development. But much can be learned from the death systems in the numerous less advanced societies that have existed both before and after the ancient Egyptians. Anthropological observations are abundant (8,9,10). We will focus upon one example, the Malayan tribesmen described by Robert Hertz (11).

The Malayan death system resembles many others that have been reported for preliterate or "primitive" societies. Death was *not* a final and immediate event—that is to say, the cessation of what we would call life or vital functions in a human being constituted only one phase of a gradual process. This was a process of transition analogous to such other transitional events as birth, weaning, coming of age, and marriage. The death process began in advance of the physical demise in the minds and actions of the community (assuming the death was not sudden and unexpected). Physical cessation introduced the intermediary phase during which time the body was given a provisional burial. The soul remained near its previous habitat while the survivors performed the necessary work of mourning. Bereavement rituals continued until the physical re-

mains had reached such a state of purified decay that it was obvious the soul had completely abandoned its body and had gained entrance to the spiritual world. At this time a final burial would be enacted and the rites completed.

There are several points here that we consider to be particularly important:

1. As with the Egyptians, the Malayan death system was centered around funerary practices.

2. The funerary practices were decidedly communal; individual reactions were secondary.

3. The distinction between life and death was softened rather than sharpened. This was accomplished by a) conceiving of death as a process instead of an instantaneous event, b) regarding this process as just one more transition within a social framework, and c) providing the survivors with a sense of participation or interaction with the deceased.

4. The total pattern of funerary rites served the function not only of relieving the anxiety or misery of individuals, but also of affirming the strength and viability of the community. The death system was society's way of reconstituting its integrity after the loss of one of its parts.

This latter point deserves amplification. Hertz writes:

Death does not just end the visible bodily life of the individual; it also destroys the social being grafted upon the physical individual, and to whom the group attributed great dignity and importance. His destruction is tantamount to sacrilege, implying intervention of powers of the same magnitude as the community's but of negative nature. Thus, when a man dies, society loses in him much more than a unit; it is stricken in the very principle of its life, in the faith it has in itself (12).

From this reasoning, one might expect that the group's response to death would be proportional to the significance it attached to the particular individual and to the manner of death. The descriptions reported by Hertz support both of these hypotheses. The faith of the group in its life-magic appeared to be most threatened when a young, vigorous person was taken by sudden death. Rituals were intensified under such circumstances. The group attempted to overcome the death-magic of alien forces. And, sooner or later, the power of the group would triumph over death.

Hertz suggests that death is both a critical test of a group's integrity and an occasion for strengthening this integrity (if the death system, as we would call it, is in good repair). There is the further implication that each society may develop a characteristic idea of what death *is*, based upon its particular combination of background circumstances (e.g., mortality rate, level of technology, etc.) and its response to these circumstances (the death system). Therefore, we should not be surprised to find that our familiar definitions and feelings with respect to death lack universality.

In our own society the generally accepted opinion is that death occurs in one instant. The only purpose of the two or three days' delay between the demise and the burial is to allow material preparations to be made and to summon relatives and friends. No interval separates the life ahead from the one that has just ceased: no sooner has the last breath been exhaled than the soul appears before its judge and prepares to reap the reward for its good deeds or to expiate its sins. After this sudden catastrophe a more or less prolonged period of mourning begins. On certain dates, especially at the "end of the year," commemorative ceremonies are held in honour of the deceased. This conception of death, and this particular pattern of events which constitute death and which follow it, are so familiar to us that we can hardly imagine that they are not necessary. But the facts from many societies less advanced than our own do not fit into this framework . . . . This difference in custom is not . . . a mere accident; it brings to light the fact that death has not always been represented and felt as it is in our society (13).

THE BLACK DEATH AND ITS TIMES

The experience and representation of death is not always contained within existing social frameworks. A society can buckle when it is assulted by intense and pervasive encounters with death—especially when it is a society that is already afflicted with severe economic, social, and psychological disorders. Under massive and prolonged stress it is possible that the death system itself can contribute to chaos, perhaps analogous to the way that an organism can be menaced by its own mechanisms for adapting to stress (14). The late Middle Ages provide us with a vivid example of a society that was tormented not only by uncontrollable and repulsive death, but also by its own runaway death system. The fourteenth century may be taken as the crest of this period and deserves our careful attention.

The conditions of short life expectancy, exposure to scenes of dying and death, and helplessness in the midst of catastrophe were never in greater evidence. Gowen, for example, writes:

In the fourteenth century. . . were crowded more pestilences and peculiar epidemics than have ever been known at any other time. Not to mention the famine which, in the second decade of the century, strewed the roads with the dead, and caused imprisoned thieves to devour one another, nor the severe scourges of some of the more common diseases, such as measles and smallpox, there were probably twenty visits of the plague in various parts of Europe; besides, the witch mania still held sway, and the craze of the Flagellants was almost universal; the dancing mania in some form or other overran a number of European countries—St. John's and St. Vitus's dance in central and northern Europe, and tarantism in Italy; and that most terrible (though not the most widespread) of all disease, St. Anthony's fire,* raged particularly in France and England. Truly, this was a century of putrid malignant affections (16).

---

* This condition, thought to be of historical interest only, made a sudden reappearance in the French village of

And this horde of "putrid malignant affections" was ravaging a society that had expended generations of children and young adults on a succession of crusades— ventures that, among other effects, may have served to reintroduce the bubonic plague. Furthermore, this was also a century of warfare in which brutalities were commonplace. War and plague sometimes struck at the same time, as when the Tartars died by the thousands—of disease —each day while laying seige to Theodosia. Diseased corpses were hurled into the city, spreading the pestilence to the defenders who then transported it throughout Europe in their desperate (and useless) flight (17). The weakened populace could offer little resistance to fires, earthquakes, and other disasters. Moreover, it was during these very years of heightened vulnerability and suffering that the Inquisition began to use torture and death as official instruments of administrative policy (18).

Even within this nightmarish configuration there was a special terror associated with the bubonic plague. Although the topic is unpleasant to an extreme, we cannot entirely bypass the specific phenomena of the plague if we hope to appreciate the circumstances that confronted the fourteenth century European. From a safe perspective today, one can describe the plague in its etiological, clinical, and statistical aspects:

· A rod-shaped microorganism, *Pastuerella pestis*, moving through a rat-flea-man cycle; highly contagious.

· Headache, dizziness, and fever, followed by nosebleed or spitting of blood, swelling of the glands in the armpit, groin, or neck, severe inflammation of lungs and throat, intense thirst, violent chest pains, delirium, and dark spots on the skin which gave the disease its familiar name, The Black Death.

· Probably was fatal to at least 90 percent of those who were infected; probably destroyed at least one-fourth of the earth's population, including entire communities (19).

This recitation of facts merely hints at the actual situation of the individual. He could all but see Death stalking through the land. Medicine, religion, and magic had little if any effect, although all were thrown into the combat. Children as well as adults were clearly aware that death might be in close prospect for them— those who were not yet afflicted with the plague were already suffering from the food shortage and general social turmoil that accompanied mass annihilation. The mind of the individual had to absorb the sight and prospect of death in a particularly disturbing form—death that was premature, death that seized one as though by an invisible hand, death that inflicted unbearable torment and turned one into an object repulsive both to himself and others until the final delirium. Let the reader imagine the most appalling situations in hospitals, ships, and prisons, the crudest sort of funerary practices, the most desperate combinations of disease, famine, and ignorance and he will probably be close to the mark. Perhaps we need not pursue the details further.

Bubonic plague and its associated terrors made a severe impact on the entire social structure. Things were never quite the same again. It would be a significant and fascinating venture to explore the total impact of death in the late Middle Ages upon succeeding generations—including our own. Such an endeavor is beyond the scope of this book and the compe-

---

Point-Saint-Esprit in 1951. In his report of the outbreak, John G. Fuller describes bizarre physical and psychological symptoms that closely resemble those noted at the height of the fourteenth century afflictions (15). Fuller develops a careful circumstantial case for the possibility that "St. Anthony's fire" is an extreme form of what today might be called "a bad trip." The explanation proposed is that a fungus with LSD-like properties had infiltrated a small quantity of flour and subsequently affected those who purchased the bread. Fuller's account also raises questions about the role of sociocultural and attitudinal factors in causing premature death. (See also Chapters 15 and 16, this book).

tence of its authors. What we are chiefly concerned with at this point is the psychological and social response to a form of death that overwhelmed the cultural milieu.

The medieval death system was unable to offer an effective *technological* defense. Most medical and quasi-medical procedures were completely useless; the necessary sanitation methods were not comprehended. *Social* controls and adjustments did not ease much of the burden from the individual. Authorities were exceedingly hardpressed even to direct the mass collection and disposal of corpses, let alone offer much solace to the living. We therefore must conclude that it was the individual—ready or not—who had to bear the psychological onslaught of The Black Death, bear it with whatever intellectual and emotional resources he could muster. We turn now to the *psychological* component of the medieval death system. How did the man of the fourteenth century attempt to alleviate his anxiety? How well did he succeed? And what are the lessons for us?

Many interpretations of death had emerged long before the late Middle Ages. A study of Greek and Latin epitaphs, for example, makes it clear that death aroused a wide variety of emotions and attitudes, although it was most generally regarded as a misfortune, an evil (20). An observer two thousand years before The Black Death episode might have concluded with high plausibility that all possible themes had been explored. But this hypothetical observer would have been mistaken.

The fourteenth century European saw death not only through his own eyes, but also through the eyes of theological doctrine that had continued to ferment and change over the centuries. Choron points out that the Old Testament offered no escape from death, no promise of a glorious immortality. How, then, was one to overcome anxiety and depression? "It was faith in the unique and all-powerful Creator that brought solace in the face of death. We cannot even begin to fathom the intensity of this faith and the complete reliance on the will of God and the complete surrender to Him" (21). Unlimited trust was the answer.

This answer did not serve all people. The Pharisees held firmly to a belief in resurrection of the dead, and the Romans occupied themselves with rituals for assuring immortality (some thought they had a pill for it). According to Choron, the time was ripe for a new and more affirmative answer. "The New Testament proclaims the victory over death.... The last and greatest enemy . . . is already conquered" (22). St. Paul's message, with the resurrection of Christ as evidence, had enormous appeal. The beginnings of a Christian theology offered the prospect of resurrection in the flesh as well as the spirit, a bold promise. Those who developed their death systems around this central belief had cause to be joyful.

By the fourteenth century, however, little joy remained. Victory over death had become less certain, while visions of eternal torture were increasingly paramount:

The hereafter has become, through the efforts of the Church, a source of terror and not consolation. Instead of reward, most people could expect only retribution. In order to secure a blissful existence in the other world, and not to be condemned eternally to unimaginable torture so vividly depicted by Hieronymus Bosch and others, it was necessary to lead such a life in this world as was beyond the endurance of most people, except for a few over-zealous ascetics. At the same time, as a result of the activity of priests and of monastic orders, an acute death consciousness became widespread. It is best expressed in the words, *Media in vita in morte sumus* (in the midst of life we are in death) (23).

Postmortem unpleasantries were only part of the darkening picture. The fact of death—the very moment of death—assumed a new and forbidding significance. Death was now considered to be God's punishment of man. It is not dismal enough to know that one dies. The more complete story is that dying demonstrates one's guilt and unworthiness, even as it transports him through a dreadful crisis to endless mortification and torment. This seems to have developed as a truly original theme. "To despise human life, to contemplate death and to think of the other world were not, of course, doctrines that have been invented by the Middle Ages," Spencer reminds us. He continues:

The philosophy of Plato, which taught that true reality lay outside the shadowy world of the senses, the metaphysical hierarchy of the neo-Platonists, which virtually identified evil with matter, the teaching of the Stoics, who were compelled to face the worldly ills they did their best to deny, the visions of the Near-Eastern ascetics, who elaborated with increasing fervency of detail the tortures or delights of the next world—all these things made men look forward to death, and had prepared the way for a scorn of man's natural abilities and an emphasis on the next world which should be the only satisfactory attitude for serious minds to maintain. But Christianity added one remarkable doctrine which pagan disillusionment and transcendental philosophy had never mentioned. *It taught that death was a punishment for man's sin* (24).

The moment of death became the most dread moment of life. The agonies of dying were widely advertised throughout the fourteenth century. Physical pain is merely the prelude. One is helpless before the devils and demons that prance menacingly around him as he draws his last breath.

They will make horrid noises and faces like mad lions, they will try to bring the dying man into despair by threatenings and fear of the hopelessness of his sins. They will surely come, for they came to St. Martin when he died, and to St. Bernard. It is impossible to imagine how horrible they are; no living man could bear the sight of them, hence they come only at death. . . (25).

Furthermore, one has the pain of recollecting his past life—listening while the devils recite all his evil deeds with great

relish. And, if one still retains the capacity to imagine further sorrows, the moment of death also separates the sinful or unprepared spirit from the realm of God. One is totally abandoned. "O death, where is thy sting? O grave, where is thy victory? Thanks be to God which giveth us the victory through our Lord Jesus Christ" (26). The triumph proclaimed by St. Paul seemed far less certain than it had in past generations.

In retrospect we can hardly be surprised to learn that the collision of The Black Death with medieval theology led to the development of a bizarre and intense psychological reaction. It is unfortunate that some of the most useful descriptions of this psychological reaction have omitted consideration of the total context. We are shown the response, but not the stimulus. Hopefully, enough of the physical and intellectual context has been sketched here to permit us to regard the psychological reaction to death during the fourteenth century as more than a curious phase of social psychopathology.

There is general agreement on the propositions that the subject of death was central, pervasive, vivid, intense—in short, *the* concern of fourteenth century man. Spencer concludes that:

More than any other period in history, the late Middle Ages were preoccupied with the thought of death. In Northern Europe for two hundred years—from the middle of the fourteenth century to the middle of the sixteenth—death was the favorite topic of preachers and moralistic writers, it was one of the most common subjects for popular art, and if a man of the period followed the prevailing doctrine, there was no object so frequently or so vividly before his mind's eye as the skeleton he would one day become (27).

The increasing preoccupation with death as both a physical and theological terror found its expression in what one might term the "pop art" of the fourteenth century. Certainly, death had become as familiar an object of perception and thought as the cans of soup and other objects that have captivated some artists in recent years. Depictions of death were also popular in the sense of being very nearly ubiquitous—statues, jewelry, paintings, woodcuts, poems, all the media for communicating an artistic vision of the world were devoted to themes of death (28). Death became the coin of interpersonal communication; in fact, memento mori showed up on coins, tokens, medals, clothing and all sorts of items of human commerce.

What psychological orientation toward death was expressed through these diverse media? Huizinga states:

At the close of the Middle Ages the whole vision of death may be summed up in the word macabre, in its modern meaning. Of course, this meaning is the outcome of a long process. But the sentiment it embodies, of something gruesome and dismal, is precisely the conception of death which arose during the last centuries of the Middle Ages. This bizarre word appeared in French in the fourteenth century.... Towards 1400 the conception of death in art and literature took a spectral and fantastic shape. A new and vivid shudder was added to the great primitive horror of death. The macabre vision arose from deep psychological strata of fear; religious thought at once reduced it to a means of moral exhortation. As such it was a great cultural idea, till in its turn it went out of fashion, lingering on in epitaphs and symbols in village cemeteries (29).

Art, as an expression of the death system, seemed in this case to represent and perhaps heighten the sense of anxiety, rather than to offer much consolation. It is difficult to see much that is reassuring in the grim and fantastical examples of medieval art and literature concerned with death (30,31,32). These are the decades during which the Dance of Death, the Triumph of Death, The Art of Dying *(Ars Moriende)* and the Encounter of the Three Living with the Three Dead flourished in all art forms. The Dance of Death may have originated from the custom of public dancing on the village green transfigured by The Black Death into a grisly

whirl wherein Death himself becomes a participant. Indeed, nothing was more common in artistic productions than the depiction of Death as a person. The Dance of Death was also enacted as a theater piece in a direct form, as well as thinly disguised in burlesque, whose comedy was a fusion of sex and death.

The Triumph of Death theme, according to art historian Gottlieb, "shows death no longer as a delegate of God, but as His substitute. Revolt at the injustice of fate, dread of the unknown, the abdication of God in favor of Death—these are the moving ideas of the fourteenth- and fifteenth-century themes" (33). The *Ars Moriendi* theme, in both literature and art, centered around the very moment of death with all its attendant pains and risks. One was urged to live with the thought of death uppermost in his mind, especially death interpreted as an event, an act:

And when it was so important, there was one thing particularly to be avoided, a sudden death; to die suddenly was to be deprived of all the rites of the Church. Without the religious viaticum, those black devils which hovered about every deathbed would have it all their own way, and the miserable soul would be hurried off to hell; hence fear of sudden death was commonplace (34).

Perhaps the first of these death themes to become prominent was the Encounter of the Three Living with the Three Dead. Huizinga has found a thirteenth century example in which "three young noblemen suddenly meet three hideous dead men, who tell them of their past grandeur and warn them of their own near end. Art soon took hold of this suggestive theme..." (35). Weber notes that the artists "delighted in contrasting death and the emblems of death with the strenuous ambitions, careless indulgences, vices and follies of everyday life ... in representing the universal power of death, how it carries off rich and poor alike, kings and peasants, wise men and fools, good and bad, old and young, beautiful and ugly" (36).

It would be difficult to exaggerate the intensity and vividness with which these themes were portrayed. Sepulchral monuments, for example, now began to take the form of partially decomposed representations of the deceased. Half of the statue might be fashioned as the stalwart person the deceased once had been, while the other half was shown in various stages of decay, e.g., rotting flesh being consumed by worms, or skeletal remains.

The psychological reaction to death was not limited to artistic media. Childrens' games, some of which have survived to the present day, often were ritualistic enactments of the events they saw about them. "Ashes, ashes, all fall down" had meanings to the fourteenth century child that it probably does not have for children today. Hide-and-go-seek apparently was played in quite an elaborate way with chanting and other quasi-liturgical accompaniments that suggest the children knew precisely what they were hiding from (37). Magical thinking flourished among adults as well as children. No proposed prophylactic or cure for The Black Death was too arcane, repulsive, or foolish to find a ready market. The mysterious triangle reproduced below has left its residue in our language and thought, although one doubts its reputed efficacy as a prophylactic measure for the plague (38):

```
A B R A C A D A B R A
A B R A C A D A B R
A B R A C A D A B
A B R A C A D A
A B R A C A D
A B R A C A
A B R A C
A B R A
A B R
A B
A
```

Behavioral reactions were among the most bizarre ever developed by our species—which is saying something! Flagellation and the persecution of the Flagellants, plague-spreading and the persecution of the plague-spreaders, dancing manias, death-sex mixtures of the most extreme form, and the renewed influence of witches, werewolves, and vampires were among the behaviors that seem to be related to the overtaxed death system (39). It is even possible that lingering superstitions regarding the malicious properties of cats derive from the vampire tradition that was one of the offshoots of the medieval reaction to death, although it had not been completely unknown before that time.

Even this brief sketch of the psychological reaction to overwhelming death would not be complete without adding that some individuals and social institutions turned these phenomena to profit. One of the most flagrant examples was the persecution of the Jews for monetary gain on the basis of hearsay that they were responsible for the plague. "The massacres of the Jews in the fourteenth century are so deeply revolting, because the ruling classes, as well as the clergy and the educated classes of the time, were perfectly conscious of the lack of foundation in the accusations brought by the people against the Jews; but from fear of the rabble and still more for the sake of material profit, not only held their peace, but in the most cruel manner participated in the slaughter of the innocent victims. . . " (40).

One reads not only that Jews were falsely accused of plotting against society, but also that "Germany seems to have been the scene of the most diabolical treatment of these people. . . " (41). In several cities all the Jews were herded together—without even the pretense of a trial—and burned alive; elsewhere Jewish communities committed mass suicide by burning rather than deliver themselves over to the multitudes. It takes a moment to remind oneself that these events occurred six hundred years ago.

EVALUATION OF THE MEDIEVAL DEATH SYSTEM

How effective was the death system that developed during the fourteenth century, particularly in its psychological aspects? The following analysis—quite speculative, of course—might provide useful background for later interpretations of our own cultural milieu.

By now it is no secret that the medieval death system had its negative elements. Should a death system alleviate fears associated with death? If so, then the medieval system was a conspicuous failure. Realistic apprehensions of a vulnerable populace were heightened by lurid theological interpretations of the deathbed scene and its aftermath. Should a death system accommodate its subject matter with sufficient ease that people may pursue their other interests relatively free from death preoccupations? If so, the medieval system failed again—had, in fact, the opposite effect. And should the death system perhaps contribute to the actual reduction of premature, gruesome, or unnecessary death? Failure again—and, again, the circumstantial evidence indicates that the psychological reaction intensified rather than minimized the affliction. Gowen, for example, quotes a number of authorities to the effect that fear, panic, and feverish imaginings increased the lethality of The Black Death and other pestilences of the time (42).

One might also propose the criterion that a valuable death system is one which contributes to the psychological growth of the society. This psychological growth could take a number of forms; development of a broader and more sophisticated perspective on life, improvement of formal and informal systems for safeguarding the welfare of the individual, encouragement of knowledge-gaining and humanistic activities, and enhanced appreciation for the value of life in all its forms. Once again, the evidence suggests that the death system which crystallized in the four-teenth century operated in the negative direction.

"Negative," of course, is a value judgment made from our own perspective. In a sense it is unfair to apply a set of criteria that occur to psychologists who were not part of the cultural milieu under consideration. Knowledge-gaining activities, for example, are more salient and positive values for us than for the man of the fourteenth century. But we cannot pretend to be culture-free; instead we simply hope to make our bias reasonably explicit so that it can be taken into account. The medieval death system probably was not judged so harshly in its own time, but it is difficult to escape the conclusion that many people truly suffered from its excesses and distortions.

Now it is time to explore the positive aspects of the medieval death system. We have already granted that the psychological reaction was dismal, macabre, and stress-inducing. But we find it difficult to believe that the interpretation of death had no adaptive value whatsoever. Perhaps, in fact, there were some rather subtle psychological strategies involved. Let us entertain the following hypotheses.

1. The overwhelming emotional impact of The Black Death and its associated terrors had to be met on its own terms, with a counterattack of intense emotionality.

2. An emotional counterattack requires its object. One cannot easily do battle with an abstraction or a technicality. The raw fact of death was relatively useless as an enemy. But Death could be fashioned into a more palpable form, converted into an object worthy of emotional response. And what object would lie closer at hand or be more appropriate than the human body itself? Medieval man, then, personified death. Now his thoughts and feelings no longer had to be diffuse—there was Death, a most formidable opponent indeed, but at least an opponent one could picture in his mind,

could interact with. This represented a "savings" in the psychological economy, providing a focal point. Furthermore, it helped to free the individual from being choked with his own pervasive and inexpressible anxieties. As we point out elsewhere in this book (Chapters 6 and 16), the encounter with a vicious, depraved Death is not necessarily the worst alternative. One might encounter an automatized Death whose presence makes all emotional reactions strangely irrelevant. Terrible meanings may be preferable to meaninglessness.

3. Personification may have achieved a sort of "one-upmanship" over Death. The mighty conquerer was depicted as a most hideous, miserable-looking specimen. "You are the revolting death you bring," the artist seemed to be saying. "You are as wretched as you make us feel. We deny you beauty and glory. We grant you symbolic life, but merely as a caricature, a macabre." Thus, Death was belittled and mocked at the very moment of his triumph. "You are no better than what you do to us!"

4. Those with a counterphobic defensive strategy could cloak themselves with the personification of Death. Identification with Death the Aggressor could be achieved by enacting his role in popular entertainments or by wearing his emblems on one's own person. At least one religious order adapted the skull and crossbones as its official insignia, and death's-head rings were on the fingers of many prostitutes. In field-theory terms, these actions could be interpreted as attempts to diminish the impact of death by dedifferentiating the boundaries between Death and the individual.

5. The very fact that representations of death were widely produced and disseminated suggests that a certain kind of control had been established. Death could not be controlled by the technological system, nor by rational thought. But the artist, poet and actor were willing and able to act upon death. Almost everything that made death so frightening as a physical event or spiritual crisis also made death an admirable subject for art. One was assured of a fascinated audience. Death that owed its shape, its features, its speaking lines to a sculptor, a painter, an author or actor was a Death that did not completely run its own show. The medieval artist was quite successful in transforming death into a material for creative manipulation. Much of our present imagery of death derives from this heritage.

6. The Black Death was exploited by some people for their own gain, as indicated earlier. But it also had the effect of providing the common man with one of his first glimmers into the possibility of equality with the noble and privileged. We are referring particularly to the theme, Encounter of the Three Living with the Three Dead, and some of its variations. One can sense the grim sort of satisfaction that must have been aroused in ordinary folk when they saw vivid depictions of lordly people reduced to a common and miserable grave. Death was portrayed as "the great leveler" of social and economic differences, well before significant political power and access came to the populace at large.

7. Apparently one can gaze intently at the same object for just so long—then a satiation effect is registered. And satiation may turn to a search for variation, even playfulness. As the years went by, representations of death in all media began to lose some of their impact. Now the death-transformed-into-art itself began to be taken as the subject matter. Representations became more clever and subtle, humor and perspective began to intrude upon the original macabre vision. Psychological satiation, then, may have been one of the consequences of the initial, intensive reaction to the forms of death in the fourteenth century. Having exposed themselves to seeing and imaging the worst, the survivors could move with some confidence toward greater flexibility and ease.

8. The   individual's   intense   pre-

occupation with death did not isolate him from society. Preoccupation with death was spread through all sectors of society; it was the norm. Although the death system may not have functioned as adequately in this respect as in some other societies (e.g., the Egyptians and Malayans cited earlier), nevertheless there was a clear sense that "we are all in this together." If death had been made a socially taboo topic, then the weight upon the individual probably would have been crushing. As it was, the psychological strain must have been enormous, but the individual could look around and appreciate that everybody else was just as concerned, and had approximately the same interpretation of the situation.

9. Finally, the dramatization of the deathbed scene and its real or supposed horrors should not be classified as a total psychological disaster. At the least, the dying process was regarded as important, the nature of the *person* remained a crucial concern up to the very last breath, and determined efforts were made to specify and actualize what we might call a "dying role."

There is much room for disagreement in what we have said about the cultural milieu of death in bygone times. The survey has been highly selective and infused with our own prejudices and speculations. However, perhaps the ways of thinking that have been illustrated here may be of value to others in considering not only historical but also contemporary relationships between the cultural milieu and the individual's relationship to death. In the following chapter we turn to the contemporary scene.

REFERENCES

1. Guillerme, J. *Longevity.* (Translated by Mark Holloway). New York: Walker, 1963.
2. Simmons, L. *The role of the aged in primitive society.* New Haven: Yale University Press, 1948.
3. Brandon, S. G. *History, time, and deity: A historical and comparative study of the conception of time in religious thought and practice.* New York: Barnes & Noble, 1965.
4. Choron, J. *Death and western thought.* New York: Collier Books, 1963.
5. *The book of the dead.* (Translated by H. M. Tirard). London: 1910.
6. *The Tibetan book of the dead.* (Translated by W. Y. Evans-Wentz). New York: Oxford University Press, 1960.
7. Cottrell, L. *The anvil of civilization.* New York: Mentor Books, 1962.
8. Frazer, J. *The belief in immortality.* London: Macmillan, 1913.
9. Lueba, J. *The belief in God and immortality.* Boston: Sherman, French, & Co., 1916.
10. Devereux, G. Primitive psychiatry, funeral suicide, and the Mohave social structure. *Bulletin of the History of Medicine,* 1942, *11*, 522-542.
11. Hertz, Robert. *Death and the right hand.* (Translated by Rodney and Claudia Needham) New York: The Free Press, 1960.
12. *Ibid.,* p. 77.
13. *Ibid.,* p. 28.
14. Selye, Hans. *The stress of life.* New York: McGraw-Hill, 1956.
15. Fuller, J. G. *The day of St. Anthony's fire.* New York: Signet Books, 1969.
16. Gowen, B. S. Some aspects of pestilences and other epidemics. *American Journal of Psychology,* 1907, *18,* 1-60 (quoted, p. 2).
17. *Ibid.*
18. Lea, H. C. *A history of the inquisition of Spain.* New York: Macmillan, 1906.
19. Nohl, J. *The Black Death.* New York: Ballantine Books, 1961.
20. Lattimer, R. *Themes in Latin and Greek epitaphs.* Urbana, Ill.: University of Illinois Press, 1962.
21. Choron, *op. cit.,* p. 83.
22. *Ibid.,* p. 84.
23. *Ibid.,* p. 91.
24. Spencer, T. *Death and Elizabethan tragedy.* New York: Pageant Books, 1960. Pp. 4-5.
25. *Ibid.,* p. 11.
26. I Corinthians 15:51-57.
27. Spencer, *op. cit.,* p. 3.
28. Weber, F. P. *Aspects of death and correlated aspects of life in art, epigram, and poetry.* London: H. K. Lewis & Co., Ltd., 1922.

29. Huizinga, J. *The waning of the middle ages.* Garden City, N. Y.: Doubleday Anchor Books, 1963. P. 144.
30. *Ibid.*
31. Weber, *op. cit.*
32. Spencer, *op. cit.*
33. Gottlieb, C. Modern art and death. In H. Feifel (Ed.), *The meaning of death.* New York: McGraw-Hill, 1959. Pp. 157-188 (quoted, p. 172).
34. Spencer, *op. cit.*, p. 23.
35. Huizinga, *op. cit.*, pp. 144-145.
36. Weber, *op. cit.*, p. 66.
37. *Ibid.*
38. Nohl, *op. cit.*
39. Gowen, *op. cit.*
40. *Ibid.*, p. 17.
41. *Ibid.*, p. 18.
42. *Ibid.*

9

The Cultural Milieu of Death

2: Today

The ancient Egyptians, the Malayan tribesmen, and the fourteenth century Europeans oriented much of their thinking and behavior around the fact of death. In the preceding chapter we attempted to learn something from them and, in general, from members of all cultures that preceded our own. We attempted to identify some of the major conditions of life that influenced the form of the death encounter. And we attempted to identify some of the major components and dynamics of the death systems which the individual and his culture developed in response to these conditions.

Now it is time to explore our own relationships with death. To gain perspective on ourselves it will be useful to make a few comparisons with yesterday's cultural milieu of death.

TRANSPOSED, INSULATED, TECHNOLOGIZED, DECONTEXTUALIZED

America's orientation toward death has struck a number of observers as being quite peculiar. We will consider their opinions later. At the moment we are concerned with a few broad factors that are too often neglected when judgment is passed upon our culture's death system. It is not simply our response to death that sets us apart from most previous cultures. It is also the nature of the background conditions that have fostered our style of response. We differ markedly from most earlier cultures with respect to all four conditions that were identified in the preceding chapter as exceedingly influential in shaping death interpretations.

By present standards, the individual's life expectancy in olden times was astonishingly limited. Death was a constant menace at the beginning of life, a menace to the mother and to her newborn infant. Survival continued to be in serious jeopardy throughout childhood. Even in the prime of life one faced mortality risks of great magnitude. In all probability, both the community and the individual had a keen appreciation for the uncertainty of survival. One could not count upon a complete traversal of the life cycle for himself, nor a safe coming-of-age for his children.

Our own situation contrasts so vividly with the above that it is hardly necessary to labor the point. Life expectancy in the United States today is more than twice as great as it was for most of our ancestors on this planet. In making this statement we should not lose sight of the fact that there is considerable variability within our own society. People who are classified as living at the lower socioeconomic levels within our population seem to be much more vulnerable to premature death than are more affluent members of the community. It has been clearly documented, for example, that mortality rates for influenza and pneumonia are higher for those in the lower socioeconomic levels (1). As will be seen repeatedly in later chapters of this book, this finding is by no means an isolated one.

Nevertheless, it is still appropriate to remind ourselves that we carry a relatively light burden of premature mortality risk, as compared with mankind's traditional burden. This condition probably contributes much to our general interpretation of death. We are less likely to regard death as a knife at our throat or a scourge at our child's bedside. Death stands at a more reassuring or "proper" distance from the young and middle-aged adult. Who dies? Old people (not us). The increasing statistical association between mortality and advanced age thus encourages us to transpose death from an immediate and perpetual menace to a distant, remote prospect.

This line of reasoning is, of course, highly biased. It is biased in the direction of youth. How an old person himself regards death is a topic that will receive separate attention later. Relevant here is the frequently made observation that we are a youth-oriented society. The power and the glory belong to the young. Increasingly, then, death is becoming detached and transposed from the valued core of society, the young. We could say, in a sense, that death is becoming obsolete. It is an event that befalls only those

people who have already become obsolete, therefore Death himself has been mustered out of his employment. He is retired from his full-time pursuit, now awarded only the secondary job of gathering those souls who have persisted in surviving beyond their day in the sun.

One point should be underlined here. We have been considering primarily what passes for "natural" death. It is no longer natural to die young. "Unnatural" deaths continue to be associated with the young, a topic that is explored in several contexts throughout this book.

We are insulated from the perception of death. The insulation is not perfect; death has its way of intruding upon the most carefully patrolled environments. Yet we are protected from the sights of dying and death to an extent that could hardly have been imagined in most previous cultures. The average citizen in yesterday's world (and many who live in struggling nations today) was exposed repeatedly to the visual impact of death. He saw his children and elders die around him. All the details of the dying process, whether sudden or prolonged, impinged upon his eyes and ears. It is probable that many of these deaths were made more painful to behold because of the relative lack of medical comforts and the terrifying symptomatology which accompanied major causes of death in those days. Furthermore, death periodically would sweep through his experience on a rampage. Many lives would fall before the onslaught of epidemics, famines, and disasters such as fire. These precipitants of mass death often were intensified by the almost continuous warfare that also produced its direct fatalities. The presence of death, then, was felt as an authentic part of daily life.

By contrast, the dying-death sequence in our own culture is increasingly shunted to teams of specialists. The medical people and the burying people are licensed experts. They perform their functions in special settings, inviting us to participate only at certain approved stages of the process. Our participation is peripheral. We can, in fact, opt out of the dying-death sequence completely if we lack the stomach for it.

Illness-and-death, just as illness-and-recovery, is a sequence that is becoming removed from household management. We pull through or we die on the crisp white sheets of an institutional bed. We actually have the choice as to how we will inform or fail to inform children of deaths. Not so many years ago we seldom had this choice—the children saw what was happening as directly as we did.

Even within hospital walls there are implicit rules and choices. The hospitalized patient is not supposed to die in just any place at any time. It is deemed important that he not expose the survivors (other patients, staff, visitors) to the phenomenon of death except under carefully specified circumstances. The obliging terminal patient will first provide clear evidence, either through clinical symptoms or laboratory findings, to the effect that his condition is worsening. This enables the medico-administrative process to add his name to the DL (danger list). He will then show clear signs of further deterioration or jeopardy which require either that special treatments begin on his present ward, or preferably, that he be transferred to an intensive treatment unit. Here he eventually will provide indices of impending death. Now he may be removed to a private side-room. Death is expected. The approved sequence is winding to its finale. The chaplain and other nonmedical constituents of the system can enact their roles in the customary manner.

There is a sense of discomfort, sometimes an actual outburst of rage, when a patient dies in the wrong place at the wrong time. We have become very fond, it would seem, of the insulation our culture offers us from the perceptual impact of death. Even the death specialists whom we have delegated to carry out responsibilities that formerly were our own, even these specialists demand a certain insulation.

The symbolic aspects of death also have relatively little place in our daily life. Our eyes are seldom greeted by the memento mori which flourished in the past; our ears are seldom exercised by old-time fire and brimstone sermons. Visions of the afterlife, whether beatific or terrifying, seem to have but a small foothold in the media of mass communication. Granting that there are some interesting exceptions here and there, our culture does not hold up the prospects of dying and death for our steady attention.

Both physical death and its symbolic portrayal and elaboration are almost out of sight to us. . . . Out of mind as well?

The conditions already mentioned imply that we may be as extreme in our relationship to death as was the fourteenth century European. If death consituted the overwhelming fact of life to the man of the late Middle Ages, then to many of us, death may seem all but irrelevant. Perhaps more than any other society the world has known, we have succeeded in relegating death to a small, peripheral corner of our conscious mental life. Death befalls the aged, who are semi-invisible on our phenomenological screen anyhow; and death is the business of specialists whose work is largely unseen by our eyes.

This general situation is also related to our attitude toward the physical environment. The growth in scientific knowledge and its visible technological applications has greatly increased our powers for reshaping the world. But it has done more than that—it has also led us to *expect* ourselves to be capable of control, of mastery. "Science" potentially can solve any problem in which we care to invest sufficient time and resources. Money changes the world.

Similarly, the physician and his colleagues in the life sciences are expected to continue their breakthroughs against disease. Medical science has won so many skirmishes with death in recent decades that it must just be a matter of time and tax-free deductions until death is completely defeated (or, at least, relegated to a gerontophagic role). We are overstating the case for sake of emphasis. But it is clear that our cultural milieu does continue to encourage expectations and fantasies about the virtually unlimited control of the world that is within the range of our know-how. Indeed, it is not easy to draw the line between realistic expectation and bootless fantasy. The work of Claude Beck (2) in the United States and V. A. Negovskii (3) in the Soviet Union (popularized in this country by Robert Ettinger) (34) has demonstrated that animals who would ordinarily be considered totally defunct can be reanimated on occasion by careful laboratory procedures.

The most relevant point, however, is not how far we can go in sweeping death back from our daily lives. Rather, it is the culturally-sanctioned expectation that *technological* answers can be found for all problems, the expectation that man can remove or remake whatever stands in the path of his desires—death not excluded.

Finally, we no longer participate in a society that is dominated by tradition, lineage, or accepted dogma. The older systems of social control within our culture have lost much of their ability to shape our behavior and support us in times of crisis. It would be difficult to maintain that these systems have been adequately replaced.

We experience this situation as freedom, as responsibility, as anxiety. The *individual* is the primary unit now. He is free to pursue his own self-actualization. But he also faces more doubt and anxiety than did his ancestor who grew up in a milieu which had firmly entrenched ideas and practices regarding life-and-death mat-

ters. Increasingly, the individual is held responsible for his own ideas and actions. Decisions that once were almost automatic must be made anew.

These decisions are particularly evident in the realm of death. The orientation of the healthy person toward the prospect of his own death, the orientation of the dying person, the orientation toward funerary practices—these are among the situations which now require decisions by the individual. Death, in this sense, has become *decontextualized*. There is not the reliable, heavily-reinforced social fabric that enabled the ancient Egyptian, for example, to know that he was doing the right thing in the right way. The necessity for making individual decisions is multiplied for those who have repeated encounters with death in their professional roles. It also weighs upon people in various walks of life who occasionally find themselves in life-and-death situations. Decisions and responsibilities, then, are salient characteristics of our relationship with death in the present cultural milieu—which is not to say that everybody *accepts* the responsibility for making and abiding by his own decisions.

PROFESSIONALS IN OUR DEATH SYSTEMS

It has already been implied that we do not possess an integrated, consensually validated death system. Participants in the death situation, whatever their role, often are not provided with effective answers and emotional support. Instead, we have been elaborating a cultural system for depersonalizing, neutralizing, specializing, and fragmenting the topic. Some of the background conditions that encourage this approach have been explored.

How is the death situation managed within this context? We will begin with a consideration of the professionals among us—those to whom we are likely to look for expertise. The funeral director is one kind of "death expert." The physician is another. The nurse has a vital role here and deserves consideration on her own terms. The mental health professional is also a candidate for consideration as a death expert. Perhaps the most traditional expert is the minister. Let us attempt to portray these experts and their modes of functioning within our own times. We will make use of empirical findings wherever possible, but other sources of observation also must be utilized to round off the picture.

The Funeral Director

It was not long ago that the funeral director was made conspicuous in a manner that could not have been very pleasing to him. Jessica Mitford's book, *The American Way of Death* (5), and Ruth Mulvey Harmer's, *The High Cost of Dying* (6), both made their appearance in 1963. These publications were severely critical of the funeral director's style of practice. The American public's responsiveness to this topic was demonstrated by the high sales volume both books enjoyed, and by a wave of formal and informal discussions.

Mitford and Harmer challenged the funeral director on two basic counts: Do funerals really have to be so expensive? Is the funeral director behaving in a callous and unprincipled manner? The facts and opinions mustered by these books, which are still readily available, need not be repeated here. The economic issue is important on its own terms, and does have some psychological implications. However, we will focus upon the contention that funeral directors somehow are violating the public trust that is invested in them. Instead of contributing to an authentic and relevant experience, the funeral director is said to impose an artificial, hollow ceremonial. Harmer, for example, concedes that:

... "a funeral can be of value; it does provide during a period of crisis a set of customs and rituals that minimize the traumatic effect of the

experience and offer other members of the group an opportunity for spiritual and secular communion. ... . Funerals can help to alleviate the pain of individuals affected by offering a series of actions that must be performed and by offering the solace that grief is shared by others" (7).

It is evident that Harmer is arguing here for the kind of support that funeral customs have provided in many societies prior to our own (as illustrated in the preceding chapter). But, she adds:

Unfortunately, current funeral practices do not serve those ends, but negate them. They encourage irrational responses by enhancing the feeling of unreality survivors often experience when death occurs. By forcing bereaved persons to play publicly their parts as chief mourners during the first terrible wave of grief, funerals intensify their emotional shock and dislocation. The social value has also been minimized because the undertaker, the entrepreneurs, have appropriated the members' traditional roles and usurped their functions. Even though a number of mourners may show up somberly clad for the ceremony, they have surrendered to the florist the expression of their thoughts and feelings and to the mortician the expression of their ritualistic gestures. The occasion, therefore, merely isolates and alienates them from other members of the group (8).

To the extent that Harmer's impression is representative, it means that current funerary practices expose the technologization and decontextualization of our death system just as vividly as older funerary practices displayed the strength of a culture's death system. We are inclined to concur with Harmer's observations, although several of her remarks seem to go beyond the present stage of our empirical knowledge. For example, we do not have any substantial research to document the proposition that current funeral practices enhance "the feeling of unreality survivors often experience when death occurs." It would be informative to test this out, and a challenging research task as well.

Mitford does admit that funeral directors:

...are always telling each other about the importance of ethics (not just any old ethics but usually "the *highest* ethics").... They exhort each other to be sincere, friendly, dignified, prompt, courteous, ... and, it goes without saying, so to conduct themselves that they will be above scandal or slander. In short, they long to be worthy of high regard, to be liked and understood, a most human longing. Yet, just as one is beginning to think what dears they really are—one's eye is caught by this sort of thing in *Mortuary Management:* "You must start treating a child's funeral, from the time of death to the time of burial, as a 'golden opportunity' for building good will and preserving sentiment, without which we wouldn't have any industry at all." Or this in the *National Funeral Service Journal:* "Buying habits are influenced largely by envy and environment. Don't ever overlook the importance of these two factors in estimating the purchasing possibilities or potential of any family.... It is the idea of keep up with the Joneses.... Sometimes it is only necessary to say, "Here is a casket similar to the one the Joneses selected" to insure a selection in a substantially profitable bracket" (9).

Sharp merchandising practices would, of course, increase the cost of funerary services that Mitford and others find so objectionable. But what Mitford finds even more objectionable here is the funeral director's *attitude*. He may strike the posture of a dedicated professional, or even fancy himself to be a "grief therapist"—but his motives are those of the cash register. To the extent that these accusations are well-founded, then the customer is in danger of becoming harshly disillusioned. The semi-physician, semi-priest who mediates between death and himself is not really devoted to performing his solemn office, after all. The specialist's expertise is in merchandising, not in death. One may then feel even further alienated from society in time of bereavement, having been let down by a major functionary of the death system.

Even the innocuous-sounding remark that the funeral director longs "to be liked and understood, a most human longing" takes on a critical tinge when it is included in the barrage that Mitford and others have aimed at him. One thinks back to a once-popular character in the "Life of Riley" radio comedy. Digby O'Dell, the "Friendly Undertaker," could always be counted upon for a few laughs. Most of the humor revolved around double entendre remarks such as, "Well, I must be ... shoveling off." Behind the "funny lines," however, there was an atmosphere of incongruity. Imagine that—an undertaker actually thinks he can behave the way anybody else does, just stopping by for a visit. The listener was uneasy to begin with at this "abnormal" juxtaposition of a death expert into a family's daily affairs, an uneasiness that was ready to discharge itself through the release of humor. We will return to the funeral director *as a person* in a moment.

It is worth persisting a little longer in our focus upon the funeral director as one constituent of our cultural death system. Let us consider the views of a professional sociologist who has made *The American Funeral* (10) a subject of intensive study. Although LeRoy Bowman's book on this topic was published several years before the works by Mitford and Harmer it did not reach the public in so dramatic a fashion. Bowman could be credited with prior identification of many of the points that subsequently have been disseminated by others.

While Bowman is no less critical than the lay authors regarding alleged deficiencies in funerary practices, he has a broader perspective at his disposal. It is not quite fair to blame the funeral director for everything that has gone wrong: "The trouble lies basically in the failure of the culture to hold up clear and authoritative norms or ideals. The need of individuals for them is the same as in former generations, and probably will be much the same in the future" (11).

He agrees with the authors of the present book in observing that "This is an era of hectic effort to understand the continuing wonders of science and technology. Accompanying this effort is a casual reliance on an automatic preservation of the deeper values. It is an era of transitional and confused beliefs and half acknowledged doubts. There is no unifying center to the culture, and hence no place or occasion on which convincing and unquestioned answers to cultural needs can be enunciated. . . " (12).

In other words, the funeral director, in our terms, has not created a faulty death system, but is merely one of the inheritors. From this standpoint, we would be rash to heap accusations upon those among us who have accepted funerary responsibilities. *We* do not know what to make of our lives in general—how can we expect the funeral director to conjure up guaranteed and convincing symbols for death? Here we have leaned the other way a little too much. The funeral director is not a passive agent. He contributes to the present situation and has his special share of responsibility. Nevertheless, we wish to emphasize Bowman's point that the inadequacies arise from broad problems in our culture, not simply from the maneuvers of a particular professional group.

Bowman proposes a set of ideal conditions toward which he believes funerary practices should move. He suggests that we persuade or force morticians to share funeral planning with other elements in the community. It should no longer be under the virtual domination of one group, and a commercially-oriented group at that. Technical and materialistic features of the funeral should be subordinated to the public's psychological, social, and spiritual needs. Less emphasis should be placed upon adorning and displaying the body, and more sensible methods employed for disposing of the physical remains. Funeral cost should be reduced substantially. The family should receive some form of support from institutional and collective action when it comes to negotiating with the funeral establishment.

He also urges that the procedures which follow a death be "geared into the operations of the functioning community and

brought back from the shadowy, tangential status they now occupy" (13). Let us, in other words, de-specialize the death situation. Furthermore, "Funeral practices should become an integral part of all institutional efforts to develop maturity and self-control in every individual" (14). Finally, "When a death occurs the focus of thought and feeling of everyone concerned should be on the enhancement of life's values for the living" (15).

Although Bowman is not overly optimistic about the successful introduction of such changes, he reminds us that these are not wild innovations in any sense. All have been put into practice in various times and places—and all are needed in full measure for our own time and place.

A questionnaire study by Geoffrey Gorer suggests strongly that most of the observations made above would apply as well to Great Britian (16). The cost of funerals did not seem to matter very much to Gorer's respondents, probably because of common law tradition regarding churchyard burial and National Insurance provisions. However, he was impressed by the number of respondents who seemed to require more assistance than was offered to them during and after the funeral. The rituals and the broader cultural system that stands behind the rituals could not be counted upon to help the mourner reorganize himself and return to his own life in an integrated manner.

What about the funeral director himself? In contrast with the reasonably thorough attention that has been given to the mortician from economic, sociological, and anthropological vantages, almost no attention has been given to his psychology. There is one available study. It is certainly neither extensive nor intensive enough to permit vast generalizations, but we cannot afford to be too choosy at this time.

Kastenbaum and Goldsmith took advantage of the opportunity to study 47 funeral directors who were attending a regional conference, and 150 students enrolled in a college of mortuary sciences. Procedures employed included a sentence completion test, questionnare, hypothetical situations, and brief essays. Additionally, in the case of the students, background demographic and intellectual performance data were available. Some of the results were published in *The American Funeral Director (17)*.

It was found that many of the people who plan a career in this field (to the extent that the population sampled was a representative one) have a fairly low level of intellectual interest and output. There was little indication that intellectual challenges were welcome. The typical student expected to absorb certain necessary facts or know-how from his course work, but showed no zest for further knowledge or inquiry. He neither regarded himself as a thinker, nor supposed that successful performance of the funeral director's role would require an informed and disciplined mind. This does not necessarily mean that the typical student in a mortuary science program is absolutely incapable of productive thinking—it just does not come naturally to him, or seem important enough to cultivate.

Such a disinclination to open one's mind must surely limit the student's comprehension of the complex issues that will soon swirl around him, including the ethical, philosophical, social, and psychological meanings of death and burial. The problems associated with death cannot always be presented in a form so simple that one can comprehend them without putting forth a substantial intellectual effort.

The intellectual passivity was closely related to passivity in the motivational and emotional sense of the term. Life goals of most students were few and stereotyped. They expected that the desirables of life would drop into their lap by-and-by without requiring much effort or risk-taking behavior. Essays and sentence-completion responses suggested an overall style of skating on the surfaces of

emotional life with occasional outbursts of displeasure when significant demands are placed upon them.

It is conceivable that people who are not distinguished with respect to either intellectual zeal or emotional maturity might nevertheless have developed secure attitudes toward death. This possibility, however, was not supported by the available data. The typical student in this sample had a pained and brittle attitude toward death. Discomfort became evident as soon as the first death question was raised in the classroom. Instantly the room was filled with cigarettes that looked like so many emergency flares burning for help; the young men and women began to twitch as though their chairs had just been electrified, and there was a scattering of giggles and obscene remarks. This was by far the strongest reaction either of the researchers had ever encountered when introducing the topic of death in a classroom situation—and the students were tomorrow's funeral directors!

The completed tests and questionnaires confirmed the anxiety that had been evident in the group behavior. Responses were often constricted and stereotyped and included many more outright refusals and incompletions that we usually anticipate. The discomfort with death was limited to human or psychosocial aspects. Death as an impersonal biological phenomenon did not ruffle them.

There were also many expressions of insecurity regarding their future roles as death experts. The students were well aware that other people would be looking to them as a model of how a person should behave at a funeral. They worried about their ability to "make the right impression."

In general, there was no evidence to indicate that the career choice had been based upon a particular commitment to the problems of bereavement, or an exploration and resolution of the meaning of death in their own lives.

The exploration of death attitudes and

thoughts of established funeral directors failed to brighten the picture. There was no evidence to support the hope that experienced funeral directors, as a group, possess a perspective on death that might be characterized as unusually deep or mature. With both students and senior groups, it was typical to find stereotyped expressions which, under slight probing, gave way to self-contradictions or stymied responses.

It is likely that our own expectations of the funeral director increase his difficulties. We may be expecting him to provide a kind of expertise and quasi-sacred mystique that is not within his scope. And we may also, as Robert Fulton suggests, expect him to meet conflicting demands: "On the one hand, he is encouraged to mitigate the reality of death for the survivors who may no longer receive the emotional support once provided by theology to deal with it; on the other hand, he is impelled to call attention to the special services he is rendering. If he is to justify his role as an important functionary in death he must focus attention on the body. In so doing, however, he invites the anger and hostility of a society that is experiencing a growing need to repress death" (18).

Fulton, a sociologist, recently conducted a study of the attitudes which the American public holds toward death, funerals, and funeral directors. His particular interest was to determine whether or not "criticisms of the American funeral program reflected the opinions of an active and articulate minority or whether they did in fact reflect a common concern or a basic attitudinal shift among the majority of the American public toward contemporary funeral procedures and mourning rites" (19). He obtained questionnaire data from 1248 respondents who had been selected randomly from telephone listings in major urban centers, and 458 members drawn from 11 memorial societies. Additionally, Fulton and his staff conducted 315 personal interviews. They found that members of memorial societies (dedicated to the funeral reform movement) were more likely than the general public to consider that death marks the final cessation of individual identity. Expressions of religious conviction in salvation, eternal life, and so forth were approximately three times more frequent among the general respondents than among the memorial societies' members. The two groups had fairly similar views of the major functions a funeral should serve; however, those involved with the reform movement were more critical of the actual effectiveness of funerals in fulfilling these functions. Common criticisms were that the funeral today is "too formal," "too impersonal," "too long," and "too emotional."

The two groups also differed somewhat in their evaluation of the funeral director. The memorial society members tended to see the funeral director primarily as a businessman who should attend to the specifically physical and administrative aspects of the funeral. The general public group also emphasized the funeral director's physical-administrative function, but they felt that, in addition, he should be a source of emotional comfort to the bereaved. Fulton's findings also indicated that many of the respondents who had negative attitudes toward the funeral or the funeral director actually had rather little direct information about funeral practices, including economics.

In Fulton's opinion, some of the hostility aimed at the funeral director may have less to do with the man himself and his specific practices than with the role he plays. "The guilt generated by desire on the part of the bereaved to rid themselves quickly of the body and by the death itself, the possible confusion and anxiety in the selection of the 'right' casket, and the attitude of the funeral director as the constant reminder and associate of death, prompt the public to lash out at him" (20).

We believe this position deserves to be

taken seriously. The funeral director may be held responsible for death, just as the meteorologist is half-jokingly blamed for bad weather. Sophisticated adults are not likely to speak openly of the funeral director as the man who brings death—but he certainly is one of the men who brings death to mind. The distinction between a mental and a physical relationship is sometimes blurred over in our thinking, especially on a topic that seldom is brought to the light of day. Children may be more direct in postulating a relationship between the funeral director and death. A secretary who was typing the Kastenbaum-Goldsmith article mentioned earlier, suddenly recalled an incident in her own childhood. As a five-year-old girl she developed a fear of the funeral director because there he was—taking away a person who had always been alive, so obviously he was the man who brought death!

In summary, it seems reasonably accurate to state that our culture's death system has neither been created by the funeral director nor passively received by him. The system operates *through* him. He is called upon to perform a significant function that is open to both rational and emotionally-inspired criticism. But he cannot draw upon an effective cultural tradition or upon special personal characteristics to fulfill his responsibilities. There is pressure—and it probably is an increasing pressure—for the funeral director to alter his practices. It would be in the general interest for all of us to remember that the problems are not his alone. We take flight from our own responsibilities and deny our own involvements in death if we seek to blame the funeral director for everything that has been going awry.

Perhaps we should also be reminded that one of the historic functions of the funeral director now is carried out so effectively that we are likely to forget past disasters. Improper burial procedures can produce serious hazards to public health, as well as offend our sensitivities.

In earlier generations there were frequent reports of debilitating and sometimes fatal diseases spreading from burial grounds. Gravediggers and their families were in special jeopardy. We will refrain from quoting these reports: they are vivid. However, publications such as G.A. Walker's attack upon burial practices in London (1830), *Gatherings from Graveyards* (21), did much to stimulate a burial reform movement from which we benefit today.

The Physician

The mortality rate in life is 100 percent. Barring sudden death, each one of us will go through the process of dying as an experience of life and notwithstanding the writing on the wall we shall seek its denial with whatever means at our disposal; dismissal of symptoms, preoccupation with trivialities, trust in our doctor, faith in God, metamorphosis, or belief in life after death. Naked and horizontal we shall expect more than platitudes from our physicians or surgeons (22).

In the practice of our art it often matters little what medicine is given, but matters much that we give ourselves with our pills. Until the doctor has had the sad experience of standing by to the very last those nearest and dearest to him, he can only imagine the heartache of his dying patient's family and their sore need of sympathy, nor until he himself has been nigh unto death can he more than imagine the comfort that even the firm clasp of a friendly hand can give to one in such extremity (23).

Both of these statements were made by physicians. Michael S. Rose and Alfred Worcester are among those medical practitioners who have attempted to persuade their colleagues to comfort their dying patients psychologically as well as physically. Should the physician feel obliged to accept this responsibility? Is he, in fact, equipped to do so? Should he also be expected to alleviate the distress of the dying person's family? Is it not sufficient that the physician dedicate himself to preserving life, so long as there is a prospect that the battle can be won? Should he ever relax his efforts to preserve life even when it appears certain that his patient cannot recover?

These are among the many significant decisions that are within the physician's realm of life-and-death responsibilities. As we might well expect from what has already been said about our culture's death system, the physician often is "on the spot." There are conflicting expectations about almost every aspect of his functioning. He should be objective and scientific. He should be warm and personal. He must exert himself with equal vigor to save all lives. He is free to be selective, favor the "more valuable" lives over the "less valuable." He is responsible only to himself and his professional code of ethics. He is responsible to the community. He is responsible to the patient. He is a sage and all-around authority on life. He is a technician, a repairman.

As the pivotal figure in our culture's death system, the physician exerts much influence over the general climate of thought and feeling, and also over the specific functioning of others in the system—including the patient and his family. The physician himself is an even more salient target than the funeral director for all the thoughts and feelings about death that we wish to externalize. Because the physician enjoys an especially honored place in our society, he is less often attacked openly and directly. Nevertheless, most physicians probably are well aware that their patients are beaming strong emotional signals to them. These feelings range from the worshipful to the enraged to the desperate—and these feelings may succeed each other rapidly or even coexist. We are just trying to make it clear that the physician is not free to engage in his vocation as an insulated expert (although some physicians may fancy themselves in this role). Rather, the doctor is influenced markedly by the death system that he serves.

It has been suggested on occasion that many physicians were motivated to choose their occupation because death is an unusually salient personal problem for them. The front line of our death system thus would be manned by volunteers who are more intimidated by the enemy than are many of the civilians behind the lines. In other words, counterphobic action has been proposed as an explanation for entrance into the medical profession. Perhaps the unspoken sentiment is, "I am protecting others from death, therefore, I myself must be invulnerable."

Herman Feifel and his colleagues recently explored this possibility in an empirical study (24). Experienced clinical psychologists and psychiatrists conducted depth interviews with 81 physicians. The physicians were drawn from three specialties: internal medicine, surgery, and psychiatry. To have a basis for comparison, the investigators also studied three other groups of people: 38 medical students, 92 seriously or terminally ill patients, and 95 apparently healthy normal individuals.

The subjects were asked open-end questions such as, "What does death mean to you personally?" "What do you think will happen after you die?" They were also given questions to rate along various scales, e.g., "How often would you say you think about death? Never, rarely, occasionally, frequently, all the time?" Responses were classified independently by two members of the research team, with a high interjudge agreement.

Feifel interpreted his results as supporting the contention that physicians (and medical students) tend to have an above-average fear of death. He found "the implication that a number of physicians utilize the medical profession, through which the individual secures prominent mastery over disease, to help control personal concerns about death" (25).

Specifically, Feifel and his colleagues found that more of the physicians than other subjects tended to respond in an introversive way to the death of another person. While most other subjects would "feel bad" when learning of a death, the physicians were inclined to "reflect on my own mortality." They were also more afraid of death and more apprehensive about the dying process than either the physically sick or healthy normal groups. It is interesting to note that the physicians displayed more negative verbal death imagery and blocked more frequently on death questions, relative to the other subjects. This finding is consistent with research on the personification of death described in Chapter 6.

But how well does the medical profession protect its practitioners against their own discomfort with thoughts of death? Almost two-thirds of the physicians stated that they now feared death less than they had in the past. This self-report could be taken to support the contention that being a physician does shield one against personal problems in this area. However, better controls would be necessary to make this conclusion fully acceptable. And we should not forget that the expressed death fears of physicans remained relatively high, despite their diminishment over the years. Feifel believes that the physician remains quite vulnerable to twinges of death fear, even to the extent that his behavior toward his patients may be altered. "In those instances where the physician's professional narcissism comes under attack—particularly in encounters with the fatally ill—his reawakened anxieties about death may lead him to unwittingly disinherit his patient psychologically at the very time he enhances attention to his physiological needs" (26).

An independent exploration of the physician's orientation toward death was carried out by Peter B. Livingston and Carl N. Zimet, physician and psychologist, respectively (27). These investigators studied future surgeons, internists, pediatricians, and psychiatrists (total of 116 men drawn from the same school of medicine). The students responded to a 44-item questionnaire dealing with authoritarianism and death-anxiety. (We should keep in mind

that one investigator's "death fear" may be another's "death-anxiety." These terms have not yet received a consensual meaning.)

Livingston and Zimet hypothesized that there is an inverse relationship between authoritarianism and death-anxiety, i.e., students high in authoritarianism will be low in death-anxiety, and those low in authoritarianism will be high in death-anxiety. They also expected that surgeons would prove to be high in authoritarianism and low in death-anxiety, with the reverse pattern for the future psychiatrists. Furthermore, all students were expected to show increased death-anxiety as they continued through medical school and came into more direct contact with death and dying.

Indeed, it was found that those students who received high scores for authoritarianism also tended to express relatively little death-anxiety, and that death-anxiety (but not authoritarianism) increases as students move from academic to clinical training. The future psychiatrists proved to be less authoritarian and more death-anxious than the other medical students. The future surgeons were less anxious about death than any of the other students, although not much more authoritarian than the future internists and pediatricians.

Commenting upon their findings, Livingston and Zimet suggest that "high degrees of authoritarianism and non-authoritarianism, low death-anxiety and high death-anxiety, are potentially crippling for the physician's sense of reality and render him incapable of a beneficial relationship with his patients, too little makes the physician liable to doubts, extreme introspectiveness, and a pathologic insensitivity that makes him unable to retain the detachment necessary for useful service to a suffering human being" (28). They also suggest that a physician's underlying values and attitudes are well entrenched before he enters medical school, and that they play a significant role in his selection of a specialty, not only his choice of medicine in general.

One aspect of this study is especially pertinent to our understanding of death in our present cultural milieu. It has been suggested earlier in this chapter that our prevailing tendency is to remove death from our lives by means of insulation, "technologization," and decontextualization. The surgeon is a man who is in an almost perfect position to fulfill these culturally-sanctioned missions. It is considered very proper for him to adopt a bloodless, "objective" attitude toward his craft. While he is doing culture's bidding ("Defeat death, or at least make it seem like a technical matter.") he is also able to control his own personal anxieties.

Livingston and Zimet perhaps share this view when they observe:

Surgery is certainly the specialty most characterized by protocol, privilege, and hierarchy, from the long, carefully graded progression of its training to the intricate ritual of the operating room. Thus, it is the medical specialty most clearly organized along the lines of authoritarianism (29).

It would seem that the physician, especially the surgeon, is particularly fortunate in being able to shield himself from personal anguish on the topic of death by the very mechanisms that bring him favorable notice from a death-avoiding populace. But some observers are outspokenly critical about the results of this orientation. August M. Kasper, a psychiatrist, proposes that "The doctor should know more about dying and death than any other man. The greater part of his life is spent with people who consider death, or its herald, pain, pressing enough to seek the doctor's help." How much does the doctor actually know of death? Kasper declares:

I am not impressed with either the volume or profundity of medical thought concerning death or dying people. It is as if this one certainty of life were to be avoided not only by vigorous positive thought and action, but also by giving it, as an event, no more attention than one gives to a period at the end of a moving, impressive novel (30).

Kasper believes that medical training frequently encourages an attitude of counterphobic bravado, a desensitization toward death. The emphasis upon "scientific objectivity" is not all to the good. "There are some very useful similarities between science and medicine, but whereas a scientist is interested in death, a doctor is against it" (31). He argues forcefully for the physician to come to terms with death in its full emotional and social meaning. Failure to do so can only have unfortunate consequences for the relationship between the physician and his terminally ill patient.

At present there is no accurate way to assess the general quality of the physician's management of the dying-death sequence. It is a multidimensional problem, with considerable disagreement regarding what should be expected from the physician, as well as his success in meeting these expectations. But it should be obvious that the prevailing conditions warrant close and systematic inquiry. One agency of the Federal government held a small, intensive conference on this topic but, so far as can be determined, none of the recommendations have been implemented. Recent books by Barney Glaser and Anselm Strauss (32, 33), David Sudnow (34), and Adrian Verwoerdt (35) have contributed to our knowledge of what transpires in and around the death situation. All of these authors suggest that there is much room for improvement on the physician's part, although he is by no means the only person in the situation who should reexamine his role.

We shall not delve fully into the physician's orientation toward death and dying patients. But we should like to offer here just a few additional illustrations of the problems that have come to the attention of some physicians, psychiatrists, and social scientists.

Feifel (36) and Gorer (37) are among those who point out that physicians tend to regard patients as being quite different from themselves with respect to terminal illness. The physician often insists upon knowing the truth: he seldom feels that it is appropriate to tell the truth to his own terminal patients. Even such a man as Sigmund Freud, surely a persistent explorer of "reality" in its most threatening forms, had cause to worry that his own physician might not provide accurate information to him. Charles D. Aring, a physician, teacher, and administrator of extensive experience, finds the disparity between physician's orientations toward death and those of nonphysicians to be a "fascinating statistic, and, if true, it is likely to reflect the doctor's perturbation and confusion in a situation reputed to be natural. Does the necessity to administer to the dying involve the doctor in ways of which he is unaware?" (38).

Answering his own question in a summary, Aring believes that "To be graceful among the dying requires the physician to become aware of his feelings about death. With energies neurotically encumbered, graceful use of the self is not likely. Death can be natural if we will make it so; it is not a taboo surrounded by disapproval or shame" (39). Aring urges "everyone to reexamine his position continually."

Four independent reactions to a case history in terminal care were offered recently by a physician, a psychiatrist, a minister, and a social psychologist. There was general agreement that in the dying situation today:

1. We tend to impose emotional isolation upon the dying person.
2. We tend to treat him in a routinized manner.
3. We tend to treat him as though he were an irresponsible child, unable to cope with his situation on an adult level.
4. Among the people who are intimately involved with the patient's well-

being, the patterns of communication are inadequate and unreliable. This ranges from what the doctor says to the patient and how he says it, to all the little ways by which everybody withholds or misinterprets significant information.

5. There is a failure on the part of all persons involved to recognize and fulfill their share of the total responsibility (40).

It is clear that the physician has a particularly large share of the total responsibility. It is reasonably clear that the way in which he manages (or manages to avoid) his responsibilities cannot be separated from the kind of person he is—especially the kind of arrangement he has made with his own intimations of mortality. And it is reasonably clear that his functioning is much affected by the expectations, ideologies, resources, and blind spots that characterize our culture in general. Aring puts it this way: "A realistic, positive, and courageous approach to dying seems to have been lost in the noises this century makes" (41). Perhaps this view is unnecessarily pessimistic. This century has also developed many resources that have strengthened the front line of the death system. Perhaps what we have yet to learn is how to utilize these developments in the best interests of the total person and those around him as he moves from the jeopardy to the certainty of death.

Furthermore, in these times we cannot easily lose sight of the extensive changes that are taking place in all aspects of medical practice. Yesterday's "heroic procedures" that would be attempted in rare and selected cases now are routine in enlightened medical practice. (Remember when the intravenous needle was a "far-out" device?) Organ transplants are moving rapidly from the category of the extraordinary to the expected—if not yet quite ordinary. The peculiar and disturbing notion of a "spare parts ward"—bodies kept alive for their yield of intact, transplantable organs—is also moving into the realm of the actual. The physician must come to terms not only with the technical aspects of such developments, but also with their challenges to his professional ethics and his personal psychology.

And yet it may be that the physician is confronting an even more perplexing series of changes from another source. The economics and style of medical practice, two closely related factors, have changed a great deal in recent years and continue to change. We should not be surprised to find corresponding changes in the physician's sense of who he is and what his fundamental responsibilities are. Especially, we should not be surprised if we occasionally find him to be as confused as we are by new developments whose final configuration is anybody's guess.

The physician's place in our culture's death system is much more complex than the funeral director's, and it would not be useful to stretch the analogies between the two. Nevertheless we seem to be observing two sets of "death professionals" who have significant inner struggles to wage on the subject of death, while simultaneously attempting to cope with a variety of powerful cultural pressures. However, neither the funeral director nor the physician become trapped in the death situation in quite the way that many nurses do.

The Nurse

One of the authors recalls a series of brief visits with nurses stationed on a particular ward in a geriatric hospital. He had been requested by a staff physician to assist in the total management of a recently admitted patient. At 67 years of age, this woman was "young" relative to the average patient in this hospital (mean age: 83 years). But she would be outlived by most of the other patients, for Miss F. had cancer; it was terminal; the course would be rapid.

The staff physician had been unusually direct. "See here, Kastenbaum, I don't want to talk to this woman. It makes me terribly uncomfortable. Just the case for you, I should think!" He explained that, so far as he knew, no one had told the patient of her prognosis. Furthermore, her former physician in the community had expressed the opinion that she should *not* be told. The staff physician did not care for any of his options. He did not like to tell people they were going to die soon. Particularly, he did not like to give them such information when a colleague specifically had requested otherwise. He did not like to lie and deny the facts. He did not like to continue seeing a person with whom he felt honest communication was impossible. And he did not like to abandon a patient because of a psychological "hang-up." The only remarkable part of this preliminary discussion was the physician's candor in expressing his thoughts and feelings. At this moment, for this particular patient, he did not feel capable of doing the whole job. He was secure enough to admit his feelings and ask someone else to share the load.

It was agreed that the consultant would "do what seemed best to do" once he was in the situation. One of his goals was to form an opinion of what the patient should be told, if anything, and, if it seemed appropriate, to break the news. Another goal was to provide some degree of comfort to a patient whom the staff was finding inaccessible. Still another (although tacit) goal was to make it possible for the staff to behave toward this patient in a more natural and effective manner.

Where did the nurses fit into this situation? The two registered nurses on this ward were competent professionals and warm human beings. But they had been semi-paralyzed by the conflicting and ambiguous demands placed upon them. The nurses were taut, apprehensive, and defensive when the consultant first indicated that he was interested in Miss F. There was the strong sentiment that Miss

F. needed them more than most of their patients did, but that they could not really approach her. The problem was not so much Miss F. herself, although she seemed to be a reserved, inward-looking person. It was that the nurses were trapped in an apparent—what shall we call it?—"responsibility vacuum." They did not know what, if anything, the patient had been told. They did not know what the patient knew or suspected. They did not know what they themselves should say and should avoid saying. "I find it hard to go near her. What if she asks something? I don't want to say the wrong thing." By "wrong thing" the nurse was referring both to a comment that might affect the patient adversely, or to a comment that might be *out of line* for her, regardless of its effect.

This quandry is not an unusual one for the nurse. In many situations the nurse is the person whose hands most often touch the dying person. She is more likely to have the hour-by-hour responsibility, the physical proximity. It is more difficult for her simply to avoid a difficult situation by disappearing "for urgent business elsewhere" (although this tactic is not entirely unknown in the nursing profession). Yet there are substantial restrictions upon her behavior in the dying-death sequence. As we have already suggested, one important source of restriction derives from her subordinate role in the professional status system. The physician is the person who is enfranchised to make the crucial decisions. The nurse is obligated to enforce and implement these decisions, regardless of her own opinions and preferences. At times, she may feel that she knows the patient better than the physician does. At other times, she may be concerned not so much by what the physician has written in his orders, but by what has been left unsaid. When a responsibility vacuum exists in the dying situation, the nurse is apt to feel, "damned if I do—damned if I don't."

In the particular situation described above, it proved very easy to reduce the level of anxiety that had inhibited the nurses' natural behavior toward Miss F. The consultant simply indicated that (with the physician's permission) he would take responsibility for the question of "telling or not telling." He did not have any preconception about the best course of action, but would attempt to form whatever kind of relationship the patient desired and would permit. He suggested that all who were involved (nurses, physician, consultant) could talk things over whenever any of them felt the urge. The nurses relaxed perceptibly. From that point on, they and their supporting staff of licensed practical nurses and aides, circulated around Miss F.'s bedside in a freer, more natural manner. Of course, the patient noticed the difference. She felt a little more at home in the hospital environment, a little more secure. Being somewhat less anxious about Miss F. seemed to make the nursing personnel more open and spontaneous in their transactions with other patients as well.

Miss F. died more or less "on schedule." The nursing staff accepted her death with a certain ease. They felt, justifiably, that they had done all they could for her. Furthermore, she was "lucky to be out of all that misery." In other situations we have observed tension, defensiveness, and recriminations in the wake of a "bad death." This might have been another one of those instances if the staff had been left with the uneasy feeling that they had failed the patient while she was alive.

It may also be of interest to mention that Miss F. never had to be told her prognosis, nor was it necessary to deny or blur the issue. She proved to have a sensitive use of what Dr. Avery D. Weisman has called "middle knowledge." Weisman has observed:

Most dying patients are aware that they will not recover, but they vacillate between knowing and not knowing. We call this condition of uncertain certainty "middle knowledge." It is defined as that portion of the total available meaning of being sick which the patient is able to acknowledge. The range of middle knowledge is sometimes quite narrow, but at other times it seems to be almost equivalent to full acceptance of death (42).

During the second interview, Miss F. commented spontaneously, "Sometimes I doubt that I ever will get better. Even the doctors don't seem to know what's wrong." Two weeks later (fifth interview) there was a long silence while the patient and the psychologist looked through the window at the first yellow-green buds on a small tree. "If they told me that I was going to die soon, I'd just fall apart." This statement by Miss F. had no verbal context, but it appeared entirely appropriate and understandable. It also confirmed the impression of the community physician who had urged that she not be informed that her condition was terminal. She could accept the prospect of death, but on her own terms, gradually increasing her range of "middle knowledge." This woman, who had always been a lonely, inward sort of person, died a lonely death, but a death that remained within her emotional control.

Partially released from "the trap" in this particular instance, the nurses performed their tasks efficiently and humanely. But could a nurse have gone beyond the expected? Could she have offered the kind of relationship Miss F. seemed to need? Could nurses in general offer much of the interpersonal support that a terminal patient requires, regardless of his or her age? We believe that affirmative answers might be given to these questions. The nurse who happens to be a mature person should also have the makings for being a truly comforting person to her dying patient. Being an important functionary in our culture's death system and one of the few people who remain within the vicinity of the dying person, the nurse would seem to be in a good position to offer comfort.

Yet there are observations to suggest that the nurse frequently is trapped by more than the responsibility vacuum. She is trapped by "her own people" and by herself. Consider first some observations regarding the verbal and nonverbal behavior of nurses when death is salient in the situation.

Lawrence LeShan, a psychologist who has himself worked intensively with many dying patients, found a direct yet unobtrusive way to study the response of nurses to their terminal patients (43). He simply stop-watched the interval between the sounding of a bedside call and the nurse's response. Nurses took more time to respond to calls from patients with terminal prognoses than from patients less seriously ill. The nurses had not been aware that their responses varied according to the patient's condition. (Some of the nurses consequently attempted to respond more rapidly to calls from terminal patients, but this effort faded away over a period of time) (44).

There are many things that this little study does not tell us. But it does demonstrate actual behavioral differences in response to terminal and nonterminal patients—as well as the lack of awareness that one was behaving in an "undemocratic" manner. We are reminded of earlier comments regarding the physician's possible lack of awareness regarding his own behaviors in the dying-death situation.

Verbal behavior also reflects a discomfort with the topics of dying and death. What do nursing personnel say to a patient when he brings up the subject of his own death, e.g., "I think I'm going to die soon" or "I wish I could just end it all"? Kastenbaum asked approximately two hundred attendants and licensed practical nurses at a geriatric hospital to describe their usual reactions to this type of statement and to elucidate the basis for their reactions (45). Five general categories of response were evident:

Reassurance. "You're doing so well now. You don't have to feel this way." "You're going to be feeling better soon, then you won't be thinking this way.

You'll be feeling more like your old self again."

Denial. "You don't really mean that." "You are not going to die. Oh, you're going to live to be a hundred."

Changing the subject. "Let's think of something more cheerful." "You shouldn't say things like that; there are better things to talk about."

Fatalism. "We are all going to die sometime, and it's a good thing we don't know when." "When God wants you, He will take you. It's a sin to say that you want to die."

Discussion. "What makes you feel that way today? Is it something that happened, something somebody said?" Could you tell me why? I'd like to know."

Fatalism, denial, and changing the subject were the most popular responses. Only 18 percent of the total group indicated they would enter into a discussion of the patient's thoughts and feelings (the licensed practical nurses were more likely to favor discussion than were the attendants). In other words, the odds were stacked against a patient happening to find a member of the ward staff who would attempt to learn *why* he had death on his mind. No inclination was shown to pass the message to "higher-ups" in the nursing or medical hierarchy. The clear tendency was to "turn off" the patient as quickly and deftly as possible.

Those who were inclined to "turn off" the patient often explained that they did not like to see their charges looking so glum. Mention of death was equated with a state of fear or surrender—states of mind that were unacceptable to the nursing personnel. Patients should want to live and should expect to live. Therefore, it is appropriate to try to get the patient's mind off death. Some of the respondents were direct enough to say that "Death talk bugs me." In general, silencing a patient who speaks about death seemed to derive from both a humanistic (I like to

see them happy) and a self-protective (it shakes me up to talk about death) viewpoint. When the facts in the situation were too obvious to permit an easy denial, then the fatalistic response was deemed appropriate. This response came naturally to many of the attending personnel "Because I believed it myself."

Those who tended to follow up the patient's death remarks with an open discussion seemed to have a problem-solving orientation. "They are exhibiting emotion and asking for psychological assistance. I want to see if maybe an answer can be found to their problem—or help of some kind." This sort of response is almost "too good," suggesting perhaps a desire to say what one believes psychologists like to hear. But there definitely was a minority group that was interested in finding out what the patient really had in mind so that some constructive action could be taken.

A more extensive sampling of experiences with and attitudes toward death was carried out in the same geriatric hospital three years before the study cited above (46). Several of the items included in this 60-item questionnaire are of interest here. The respondents were 221 staff members, representing most of the hospital's services. This sample included 28 registered nurses, 37 licensed practical nurses, and 119 attendants.

As might have been expected, most of the nursing personnel had had repeated experiences with death. How did they *feel* about these deaths, and what did they *do* in response to their own feelings? One multiple choice item required: "The first time I was with a dying patient I (had no particular feelings) (had feelings and tried not to let my feelings show) (had feelings and let them show)." Fully 90 percent of the respondents indicated that they did have feelings but tried not to let them show. For a related item: "When I am with a dying patient I usually" (same three alternatives as above), the response was even closer to unanimity: 94 percent indicated the "tried not to let my feelings show" alternative.

Another item is relevant here: "When a patient starts to go downhill my feelings about him usually (become weaker) (stay the same) (become stronger)." It was rare for nurses to report a weakening of affect (3 percent). The most frequent reaction was to feel even stronger (57 percent), while it was also common to retain feelings at the same level as previously held (40 percent).

These self-reports seem to support our observations made while working alongside nurses in the chronic hospital setting. The nurse is likely to be a person with at least average, often above average, compassion for the ill and suffering. While some nurses, as some physicians, manage to insulate themselves from the emotional implications of their work, it is more typical for the nurse to *care* about what her patients are going through. Yet it is also typical for the nurse to believe that she should not "give in" to her feelings, even to the extent of "letting them show" to others. It might be said that she is trapped by her own role image. Other nurses would not think well of her and, accordingly, she would not think well of herself if she gave natural vent to her feelings.

Most nurses like to believe they are practicing "benign equalitarianism from a distance" (47). Those who observe the nurse's actual behavior (including LeShan's stop-watch) may be dubious about her success in carrying out a flawless policy of nondiscrimination. Successful or not, the nurse seems to enact her role in the dying-death situation with the intention of emulating the "new-look" physician—objective, scientific. It is entirely possible that she may even outdo the physician in this respect, proving that she can be as efficient and objective as the most refined product of our medical schools.

The medical model of efficient but essentially impersonal care exerts its influence not only over the physician, but also over the nurse and, increasingly, over the patient himself. What we are most directly concerned with here, however, is the nurse's quandry. She begins with strong feelings toward her dying patient; she continues to have strong feelings toward him; as the downhill process accelerates, her feelings grow even stronger—yet she remains impelled to "keep a stiff upper lip, all over."

It is worth considering specific responses to this questionnaire within the context of the nurse's general orientations toward life and death. A definite consensus (ranging from 81 to 93 percent) was found on a cluster of items. The typical nurse in this study considered herself to be a devout person with a strong belief in some form of life after death. This included the conviction that one would be personally accountable to God after death. Very few nurses agreed that "A person's life is his own to do with as he likes, so long as he does not hurt anyone; if he feels he wants to end his life, that's his own business." Few reported that they had ever wished someone else would die; few were in favor of "mercy killing" under any circumstances. Interestingly (for people who are attempting to save lives), most of the nurses agreed that "The length of a person's life is pretty much decided when he is born. No matter what you do, when it's your time to go, you go."

This cluster of attitudes and beliefs (which have not been exhaustively reported here) is discernibly different from those of staff members of the same hospital who had different educational and occupational backgrounds. It seems fair to suggest that the ethnic, religious, and socioeconomic background that a woman brings with her affect the way she thinks and behaves even when she has donned the nurse's uniform. How much of the nurse's role in the death situation is influenced by her general background and how much by her occupational training and role expectations cannot be ascertained at present. It is probable that personal background and occupational style come together at certain junctions to emphasize a particular behavior. For example, the nurse may have had a fatalistic outlook on death as part of her ethnic heritage. This is likely to be reinforced by the tacit occupational rule, "Cool it. Don't show emotion on the job." As we have seen, it may be easier to control the outward expression of feeling than it is to live with the feelings that continue to percolate inside.

The nurse's difficulties in coping with the emotional needs of terminal patients is compounded by lack of adequate training. She must fall back upon whatever guidelines are available from other sources: the life-and-death orientations that she learned within her particular ethnic and socioeconomic background; the pressure of colleagues to conform to their definition of what constitutes a good nurse; her own personal experiences and quirks. Presumably all these influences would be less potent if the nurse had received the advantages of knowledgeable training and supervision in this area.

A leading advocate of improved training for terminal care is Jeanne C. Quint, herself both a nurse and a social scientist. In her recent book (48) and in numerous other presentations, she has called attention to the heavy burden of care which falls upon the nurse's shoulders:

Educational programs in nursing have not generally provided environments through which nursing students develop the capacity to function effectively in situations which are either personally or professionally threatening. Neither have nursing instructors always recognized the emotional impact carried by certain types of patient assignments. This educational heritage is not surprising when one considers that nursing in the United States is by tradition somewhat authoritarian, with a premium attached to self-control and dedication (49, 50).

Quint finds that terminal care is one of the most demanding and stressful situations encountered by many nurses. "Keeping the patient clean, fed, and comfortable until he dies is not always easy or pleasant, nor is working with families living under the stress of impending death." Added to these difficulties is the responsibility for making decisions that could have a life-or-death effect.

According to Quint, the nurse's preparation for working with terminal patients is one-sided. She is made to feel very concerned about committing errors. Consequently, the apprentice nurse defends herself by investing in routines and rituals that tend to alienate her from the specific patients she is serving. Moral, ethical, and legal considerations—including the patient's right to be informed of his condition—are much neglected. Furthermore, the enormous attention given to techniques of life-prolongation and to the most tenuous hopes of recovery has no counterpart in attention to providing comforts to those who will die. It is difficult to strive to keep the patient alive at all costs and simultaneously to help him die in a dignified and comforted manner. And both of these conflicting goals are made more difficult to attain by "the relative unimportance attached to conversation as a significant component of professional nursing practice. Educational programs in nursing generally provide explicit instruction in the technical aspects of nursing care but little specialized direction in the use of conversation in the best interest of patients. In part, this state of affairs can be traced to nursing's historical associations with medicine and to the 'handmaiden' role which was subordinate to the doctor's position of authority. It also reflects the present elementary state of knowledge in behavioral science content as it has relevance for nursing practice" (52). Quint offers a set of recommendations for improving the nurse's preparation to cope with the dying situation, recommendations that are well worth serious attention by those in the position to implement them.

It is evident that Quint's observations are consistent with the experiences and findings we have reported above. We arrive at a general view of the nurse as a person who must cope with the daily challenges and demands of the death situation—yet lacking the authoritative leverage of the physician, lacking relevant training from her own profession, and lacking an on-the-job atmosphere that would support her in times of personal distress or in her more adventuresome and involved efforts. It is no wonder that she may lean heavily upon unexamined cultural values and attitudes. Nor should we be hasty in asking her to abandon the self-protective rituals that enable her to function within the vicinity of the terminal patient. As with the funeral director and physician, we send the nurse forward with conflicting orders ringing in her ears. We are not sure precisely what we want her to do with death except, somehow, to keep it out of sight.

The Clergyman

Death and religion. These two concepts have been together a long time. It is a familiar contention that the roots of all religions are to be found in man's encounter with death, his need to adorn and interpret the bare fact of mortality. However one cares to regard this contention, it is difficult to deny the strong mutual influences between our orientations toward death and deity. The minister, then, represents perhaps our most ancient and traditional resource in the death system. Presumably, his role should be less affected by the passage of time than the other "death professionals" we have already considered. The others must attempt to keep pace with rapid technological innovations and shifting cultural demands. The minister can hold fast to faith and dogma that have been honored by time—or can he?

There is reason to believe that the minister increasingly is being cut adrift to manage as best he can in the swirl of current developments. He is a man of his times. He may have his doubts about

certain religious traditions. He is likely to be concerned about his general role in society and his specific role in the death system. And he is not necessarily immune to stereotyped notions and personal anxieties about death that flourish in our society at large. Religious establishments are in turmoil over a number of issues that are relevant to the ministry of death, including birth control and euthanasia. There are fewer and fewer places of refuge left for the person who wishes to draw his life orientation entirely from religion. Even the nunnery has begun to accomodate itself to the times.

It is one thing for a man to face up to the doubts in his own mind and the changes that are occurring around him. It is quite another thing to expect this man to front the world as though he were perfectly confident in his views—especially if we are asking him to demonstrate his total and reassuring command in situations that tend to bring out feelings of anguish and impotence in most of us. The minister, in short, may be expected to say and do precisely the right thing in a death situation because he is really "in the know." A number of clergymen have told us how burdensome this task can be. In a recent book, Rev. Carl G. Carlozzi has acknowledged the pastor's "paradoxically complicated situation in which he represents God to man, and as such must speak with an authoritative confidence; but yet, as a man, he is in no way in a privileged position with the God whom he serves. . . " (52).

Caught between his public role and his private doubts, the minister may develop a defensive style of functioning. Margaretta K. Bowers, M. D., and three colleagues representing psychological and pastoral viewpoints have observed five "masks" that frequently are donned by the clergyman as he enters the death situation (53):

1. *Set-apartness.* "The act of ordination marks a man as a custodian of the sacred mysteries, as if he knows more of

the truth than others, and is granted powers that are reserved for those of special goodness."

2. *Ritualized action.* "The use of formalized prayers and traditional procedures makes it possible to enter into a human relationship protected against the full encounter with the person, because the communication is general rather than specific. . . ."

3. *Special language.* "Phrases like 'saving grace' and 'redemptive power' may have a familiar ring associated with acts of public worship, but they may mean little and say nothing to the patient, for the deeper substance of the words has never been fully employed. They may mean something to the pastor, or they may be comfortable phrases that can be said with assurance that their deeper meaning will not be called in question."

4. *Special attire.* The clergyman's special clothing tells the patient that " 'I am different from you' at the moment when it is important to say 'In this moment I share with you the thoughts and feelings that penetrate your aloneness.' "

5. *Business.* Some pastors carefully cultivate the idea that they are "terribly busy about a number of important tasks and that they break in upon these many duties to pay the dying patient a quick favor by their short visit. . . ."

Both Bowers et al and Cardozzi have called attention to these defensive maneuverings in an attempt to permit ministers to gain insight into their own behavior and, hopefully, to deal more openly with the dying person. The reader will easily recognize that others who contact the dying person in official capacities can develop their own variations on the "masks" mentioned above.

Reverend Robert E. Buxbaum, an experienced hospital chaplain, has contrasted two types of ministerial approach that fail to meet the patient's needs. One approach is exemplified by "the minister who enter-

ed my wife's hospital room while she was recovering from major surgery. He smilingly asked her how she was feeling. Before she could begin to reply, he was commenting on the weather. He announced that he was compiling a list of people who wanted to receive Holy Communion the following morning. As she began to form the reply on her dry lips, he had already commented on the flowers at the foot of the bed and disappeared through the door in order to inflict himself upon as many sufferers as possible." The other extreme is represented by "the clergyman who walks into the sick room with a Bible or prayer book clenched tightly in his hand. He has already decided what passage he will read, what prayer he will say, what questions he will ask, and what areas of concern he will avoid. Like the Boy Scout, he is prepared! But his anxiety level, which made it necessary for him to prepare himself in this way, is so high that he must concentrate on the devices he has chosen and misses the human being that lies before him. The ritual which protects him from his anxiety too often shuts off the possibility of a helpful and dynamic relationship that is attuned to the patient's real human needs" (54).

In recent years, those clergymen who have made their views public seem to agree that to be useful in the death situation one must function as a mature and sensitive *person* as well as a living symbol of God and church. However, other questions remain. What does the minister actually do when he is with a dying person or a mourner? What should he do? Is there a place for a nonmedical, nontechnological, noninstrumental presence in our current milieu? Perhaps the minister no longer can "show the way." Perhaps he is even *in* the way.

It seems to us that the minister retains a significant role in the death system precisely because he does not have medical or technological functions to perform. We tend to agree with Reverend Buxbaum when he observes:

On the most significant level, the (adequate) minister doesn't *do* anything in the sick room. He has not come to *see* the patient. He has not come to *treat* the patient. He has not come to perform any magical rites. He has come to *be with* the patient. Simply that. And yet, this is not very simple! The busy hospital routine is such that many people go in and out of the room during the patient's waking day. They have come to feel, to feed, to provide, to take away, to treat, to inspect, to advise, and on and on *ad infinitum*. It is the task of the pastor, and that which makes him so valuable a resource to the busy hospital personnel, to be there for no other reason than simply to *be with* the patient! (55).

We would add the following considerations:

1. In our mobile and achievement-oriented culture we tend to disapprove or be suspicious and uneasy with a person who is "doing nothing." Even leisure time is regarded by many people as a demand upon them to work hard at recreation. We like to see palpable evidence that people are doing something. The nurse is almost always doing something. The physician often must exercise his ingenuity to convince the patient that he is "doing something for him," in situations in which there is nothing the physician can or should be doing except to monitor the course of events, and to prevent the patient from inadvertently exacerbating his own condition. As a product of this culture, the American clergyman may feel that others expect him to do domething visible and, preferably, "special." It may require a high degree of self-confidence and inner tranquility for the minister simply to be with the patient.

2. There is ambiguity in Buxbaum's characterization of the pastor as a valuable resource to the "busy hospital personnel." It is possible to infer that any of the really busy people on the hospital staff could offer the same comfort to the patient as the clergyman does—except that the former have more important things to do. However, we have no assurance that

most hospital personnel are psychologically capable of *being with* the terminal patient and his family. In fact, it is possible to regard some of the "busyness" as staff maneuvers to avoid deep interpersonal contact with the patients and their intimates. Furthermore, the emphasis upon the personal qualities that are required of the clergyman should not allow us to underestimate his particular significance as a representative of the religious establishment. A nurse clinician, a social worker, a psychologist, a psychiatrist are other sorts of people who might be helpful in the death situation. But the minister can be helpful in a *distinctive* way that these others cannot.

3. More than most other people in our society, the clergyman represents a tradition that has attempted over the centuries to provide an integrative framework for man's total life experience. Not every person is inclined to think long and hard about the relationship between his own very personal life at the moment, and all that has gone before him and all that is to come. The minister need not offer an extended lecture series in theology to the person he is attempting to comfort. He can find his own way to communicate and reinforce the sense of the individual's relationship to enduring values.

4. The "busy hospital personnel" also are in need of a counterbalancing orientation. If chaplains evade their responsibilities in any of the ways that have already been mentioned, then the technical specialists in the death system are likely to feel more isolated themselves, and under even greater pressure. The professionals are perhaps more likely to be distressed when there is nothing palpable left for them to *do*. The positive presence of clergymen can reduce the staff's insecurity and guilt. Somebody else is around to accept a share of the responsibility. The minister who is able to communicate meaningfully with the patient and his family may bring about a favorable medical effect, albeit indirectly. The staff may

be less inclined to subject the patient to the harassment of "treatment" procedures that are quite unlikely to improve his condition. And, of course, the minister's contact with the dying patient can improve the latter's interpersonal life by: a) demonstrating to staff and visitors that *somebody* still considers the patient to be a person who is deserving of full attention, and b) enabling the patient to come to better terms with his own situation and, thereby, making him more "appealing" to the hospital staff.

Most of what has been said here about the minister's relationship to death has been drawn from experiences with or observations made by Protestant clergy. It has been our impression that the "death ministry" is being subjected to more re-evaluation and discussion by Protestant clergy than by those of other faiths. In any event, since our exploration here must be a limited one, we decided to concentrate upon the Protestant approach. Yet it is important to remind ourselves that important differences continue to exist among the various faiths, despite the fact that all religious establishments have been feeling the winds of change.

Let us consider, for example, the differences between Protestant and Catholic views of the funeral. Sociologist Robert L. Fulton sent questionnaires to approximately 1,800 clergymen throughout the nation. Slightly more than a third of the questionnaires were completed and returned. Although Fulton had hoped to obtain adequate numbers of returns from Jewish and black Protestant clergy, there were too few to justify statistical analysis. This is what he found concerning the views of white Protestant and Catholic clergy toward the funeral (56):

1. Priests regard the funeral as a vehicle for prayer and the salvation of the soul. Emphasis is upon honoring both the memory and the body of the *deceased.*
2. Protestant clergy see value in the funeral for what it does to bring peace and understanding to the *survivors.* The funeral exists primarily to comfort those who are bereaved. It also reinforces the hope of a future life.

3. The great majority of priests in this sample regard the present-day funeral as adequate for its purposes. While a majority of the Protestant clergy sampled shared this view, there was also a large minority report (35 percent). Those ministers who were critical of today's funeral decried ostentatious displays, the open casket, emphasis upon social aspects of the funeral, and the excessive control they thought was being exercised by funeral directors.

4. Not too surprisingly, in view of the above, almost all Catholic priests thought that there was no urgent need to alter funerary practices—but the majority of Protestant ministers felt that changes should be made.

Both the priests and the ministers regarded the funeral ceremony as one of their most significant rituals. Both had concern for the survivors as well as the deceased. In general, however, the priests placed greater emphasis upon conducting a proper service for the dead, while the ministers emphasized their role as counselor-comforter-friend of the bereaved. Protestant and Catholic clergy also expressed different viewpoints regarding the disposition of the corpse at the funeral. According to Fulton, the priests "stressed the importance of the body as the temple of the Holy Spirit and indicated that the body, as a result, deserved the same respect and consideration in death as in life. This viewpoint may help account for the Catholic clergy's lack of concern for the attention shown the body at the time of death, and their noticeable lack of interest in what the Protestant clergy condemn as the wasteful trappings of death" (57).

Let us pursue for a moment the friction that often seems to exist between ministers (but not priests) and funeral directors. We take this as an example of the influence of social and psychological factors upon the professional's functioning in the death system, including his difficulties in relating to other professionals. Fulton suggests that *threatened loss of status* is one of the most powerful conditions that influence the minister to feel antagonistic toward funeral directors and the modern-day funeral. He refers to "the relative shift in status that clergymen, and particularly the Protestant clergymen, have experienced over the last few decades. Less than a century ago the local parson or priest enjoyed comparable or greater prestige in the American community than his professional colleagues, i.e., the doctor, lawyer, or dentist. He had sole authority in regard to the funeral. When requested, the cabinet maker or church sexton undertook to lay out the dead.

Today clergymen see the new-found prestige enjoyed by doctors, lawyers, and other professional men in the community and are aware, as well, of the material rewards that these professions offer. Relative to these professions many clergymen sense a loss of status, for in a manner of speaking, these other professions have moved ahead more rapidly than the clergy. But in addition, clergymen discover that the cabinet maker who assisted him yesterday in the conduct of a funeral, today not only offers to take complete charge of the funeral, but also is prepared to hold the service in his own 'chapel.' To many clergymen this is not only galling personally, but is also contrary to the tenets of their faith (58).

Fulton believes that the threatened loss of status is not as severe for the priest. The Catholic church has insisted upon keeping the funeral service within the church and, in general, provides the priest with the opportunity to exercise a greater degree of control over his parishioners. The minister is the one who often must conduct services in a funeral director's "chapel." He is also apt to feel embarrassed and chagrined about his honorarium, which tends to compare quite unfavorably with the funeral director's fee.

It is not that the minister is eager to profit from a funeral (many follow the practice of refusing honorariums from their church members). But he cannot help but notice that the *value* of his services (as expressed in the language of money) is regarded as much inferior to that of his commercial colleague, the funeral director.

Throughout this book we encounter illustrations of the ways in which social and psychological factors influence the death system—including who is launched upon what particular pathway to death at what time. What we have just reported is one line of reasoning that pertains to the role of the professionals in the death system. (And we would expect that ministers would be interested in replying to Fulton's analysis with their own views of the sociopsychological constellation that operates upon both funeral directors and themselves.) Factors that change or threaten our status are relevant to death as well as to life. This is no less true for ministers, physicians, nurses, and funeral directors than it is for "amateurs" in the death system. Whether the expert's mandate is to cure or comfort, he should not be expected to function as a pure craftsman. His training, attitudes, interpersonal relations, and behavior with respect to death all develop within a complex and dynamic milieu.

At least one more trend should be noted. We have already touched upon the impact of science and technology upon our culture's death system. Specific attention has been given to the role of the minister. He seems to be flanked on one side by medical technology and on the other by the funeral marketplace. It has been ventured here that the minister's role in the death system *as a minister* (not, for example, a paramedical semi-volunteer) is a distinctive one that should be maintained and strengthened. However, it is also possible for clergymen to improve their situation by applying concepts and techniques from related disciplines. There is now a growing body. of knowledge regarding the behavior and attitudes of ministers that has been acquired by ministers who have taken the trouble to learn the necessary research skills. In a recent doctoral study, for example, Reverend Rutherford E. Everest conducted an intensive inquiry into the bereavement ministry of Protestant clergymen (59). His work stands as a contribution both to the minister's understanding of his own behavior, and to the general social psychology of death. He found, for example, that the nature of the minister's emphasis before, during, and after the funeral was related to his age, experience, and training—but not to his particular denomination. Additionally, those clergymen who favored a "meaning-integrative" approach (helping the bereaved to integrate the death event into a cognitively meaningful structure) had a significantly greater exposure to death when they were young than was the case with clergymen in general. These are just a few of Reverend Everest's findings. Obviously, it is possible for ministers to select and apply useful techniques from our culture's scientific resources without any concomitant need to surrender their own values and purposes.

The Mental Health Specialist

"Conspicuous by his absence" is a fairly accurate appraisal of the role of the mental health expert in our culture's death system. At least, this statement would have been close to the mark up to a few years ago. Freud and other major figures in psychiatry had a few things to say about the psychodynamics of death. But one could not report that the mental health movement in general had any explicit involvement in dying, death, bereavement, or the promotion of longevity. There was a mere smattering of speculation and anecdotal clinical reports, and only an occasional isolated study. The pioneering research on bereavement by

sociologist Thomas D. Eliot proved to be much ahead of its time (60). Professor Eliot's colleagues could not understand why he would waste his efforts on such a morbid topic. The much-admired physician, William Osler, had made some famous observations on care of the dying patient (61) that might well have been taken up by psychiatrists and psychologists—but were not. The lucid, humane little book by another physician, Alfred Worcester, also contained much that could have interested and guided mental health specialists (62). But again—no takers.

Even the appearance of a genuine "classic" did not guarantee that anybody would move vigorously toward mental health action. Emil Durkheim's work on suicide (63) was original and provocative. Yet it was a long time before intensive and systematic efforts were made to investigate and *prevent* suicide. Brilliant journalistic muckrakers (an honorable term) repeatedly showed how self-serving and callous practices endangered human lives, and several novels written in this tradition achieved great popularity (e.g., Upton Sinclair's, *The Jungle*) (64). Some people did become aroused by these revelations and reforms eventually followed. But academic psychology, and psychiatric practitioners apparently saw no correlation between culturally-generated hazards to life and the pursuit of their own professional and scientific interests.

The rapid growth of the mental health movement in the United States was not accompanied by a parallel increase in attention to death and related topics. Even today, the dimension of "death" is scarcely touched upon in the academic classroom from whence tomorrow's researchers and clinicians will emerge. A year-long course on developmental psychology—nay, a four-year graduate program—may include almost nothing on the intimate relationship between growth and death. The future clinical psychologist is expected to master a rather startling array of material; but the psychodynamics of death is seldom included. He is not expected to understand how motives, cognitions, defenses, and all the rest of the psychic and social apparatus can lead to premature death. If he has any exposure at all to the problem of suicide, it is slight. But neither the budding clinical psychologist nor his colleague in psychiatry are likely to go forth with a) adequate knowledge, or b) a sense of involvement in death-related questions—it has never been presented to them as a "job specification."

The situation is changing. Progress appears fairly substantial when seen against the previous base line of inactivity. But there is still so little in the way of research and practice on death-related topics that colleagues remain inclined to raise their eyebrows when they come across a "death man" every now and again (65).

Several questions come to mind:

· Why have "mental healthers" been so inconspicuous in the death system until very recently?
· What is responsible for the "mental healther's" recent growth of interest in this topic?
· What pattern of participation is beginning to emerge for the "mental healther," and what are likely to be his contributions and tribulations?

These questions could be approached from several standpoints. It is most appropriate here to examine them (briefly) within their context in the cultural milieu of death, as the latter has been interpreted in this book. The answers offered below are neither exhaustive nor beyond dispute, but should yield some impression of the relationship between psychologists and other mental health specialists and our culture's death system.

· Why Have Mental Health Specialists Been so Inconspicuous in the Death System?

1. Because they *could* avoid the confrontation with death. The funeral director, physician, nurse, and clergyman have chosen occupations in which their professional activities expose them to dying, death, and bereavement. Once in the situation, they cannot avoid or minimize deep involvement by a variety of psychological and social defenses (e.g., the minister's "masks" described earlier). But the psychologist and psychiatrist does not have to jeopardize his feelings in the first place. Neither his profession nor any one else defines him as a responsible agent in death situations.

2. Because academia *was* academic. Psychology had not strayed far from the classroom and the experimental laboratory. Universities did not see themselves as a resource for meeting (or meddling into) community needs. University psychologists were occupied with fashioning their field into a respectable science of behavior. Although there was strong concern for basic processes (e.g., perception, feeling, and thought), this concern worked itself out chiefly in terms of laboratory-sized hypotheses and investigations. The life and death of real people wherever they happened to be, and ruminations on the nature of life and death, were rarely considered to be within the province of the new scientific psychology—after all, wasn't much of our effort devoted to shedding the philosophic tradition that seemed to bog down fresh empirical inquiry? No, psychology would study what it could study under controlled conditions in the academic sanctuary.

3. Because clinicians were "neurotic" or "organic." The new cadre of psychoanalytic psychiatrists made a great impact in the field. Those who were outside of the movement had much to learn and evaluate. Gradually, the influence of psychoanalytic theory pervaded much of psychiatry and drew recruits from psychology, social work, and related fields. Most relevant to our present topic is the characteristic psychoanalytic view that *intrapsychic* dynamics hold the key for understanding and modifying behavior. This was

especially true in the earlier days of psychoanalysis. So-called "reality" problems were of less interest. Exciting discoveries and insights were being achieved mostly within the intrapsychic realm. Psychoanalytic theorists and clinicians seemed confident that virtually all human problems could be understood by depth analysis of the individual. Where did this leave death? *Out.* In a pale and indirect way, death could be translated into a purely intrapsychic matter. Preoccupation with or fear of death might be interpreted as part of a neurotic constellation. Death as an "objective" or "reality" factor, however, was largely beyond the ken of psychoanalytic psychiatry in its vigorous early days.

Meanwhile, those clinicians who were not persuaded to join the psychoanalytic ranks tended to favor organic explanations for disturbances of thought and behavior. Emphasis upon the demonstrated or suspected organic components in behavior disorder was accompanied by a distinct lack of emphasis upon the psychosocial components. One would not be likely to give serious attention, for example, to socioeconomic influences on suicide, or parental attitudes and emotional stability as determinants of the child's probability of survival. It also should be recalled that the organically-toned psychiatry of which we are speaking was concerned mostly with grossly disturbed persons. The typical psychiatrist did not have much opportunity within his professional role to explore the multiple and subtle relationships that a "normal" person develops with respect to his own death.

4. Because our nation had been relatively free of mass death by war, starvation, and epidemic. Violent death, malnutrition, and rampaging diseases had, indeed, been conspicuous in the United States for many years. Gangland slayings, dust-bowl victims, diphtheria—these are a few of the names by which such lethal conditions have been known to us. However, considering the general extent of human vulnerability and suffering that has been so great over the centuries and that persists even into our own time, our nation has been very well favored in comparison with most other lands. Since our bloody Civil War, there have been no full-scale battles fought on our mainland. We have not learned to *expect* millions of citizens to perish each year of famine and its secondary complications. Similarly, we are not prepared to be ravaged periodically by truly virulent diseases that would carry tens of thousands of us to the grave. Yet in many other parts of the world, those same years of relative exemption for us were years of mass death. The American youth who would some day be a psychiatrist or psychologist was not likely to be conditioned from birth by the alarms and symbols of death. Born in Mexico, India, or any of a number of other places, he might well have organized his personality around the reality and prospect of death.

5. Because material progress and social optimism still abounded. We had become an achievement-oriented culture that was, in fact, achieving. If land frontiers were gradually diminishing, there was, nevertheless, a remarkable succession of new technological frontiers waiting to be identified and exploited. In comparison with most times and places the world has known, it was relatively easy for a person to convince himself that the "good life" was near at hand (if only one had a lot of ingenuity and perseverance and a bit of luck). It was not a mental and emotional climate in which one cared to be reminded of death. Morbid sentiments were out of keeping with the new spirit.

6. Death was unproductive, and indicative of failure. From the increasingly prevalent materialistic-technological standpoint, there was not much point in associating with those who were soon to die. The dying person was not likely to be productive in any economic sense. And there was "not much in it" for the professional who comes to his side. All he could

anticipate is chagrin in his ultimate failure and discomfort until then, for "in terms of the market place it is really not good business to invest in such a transient and doomed enterprise. 'This man will be dead, you know, and all your science and craft will have been wasted'" (66). Once the opinion has been formed that a person is soon to die, then it no longer makes good business to "invest time" in him.

One clinician has wondered: "What quantitative indices ought one establish to guide the psychotherapist? Should he treat a person who can expect to live twenty years, but not one who can expect to live only ten years? Or, perhaps, we should make that ten years? Yes! Five years, no! Or, perhaps, a more refined measure could be developed: so many hours of psychotherapeutic time conducted at such-and-such a quantitative level of effort will be provided for persons whose life expectancy has been estimated at such-and-such a figure. The more seriously we take the quantitative transformation of human life, the more absurd we feel. All human beings have a limited life-span. How can a therapist accept one patient in treatment and then ever again deny treatment on the implicit or explicit basis of "not enough time to make it worthwhile?" (67)

Another clinician reported that his colleagues reacted to the idea of intensive psychotherapy with dying patients as 'obscene' and 'disgusting' (68). He also observed that the psychotherapist cannot protect himself by the defense maneuver that necessity sometimes dictates to the purely medical specialist whose patients often die—a brusque, armoured, uninvolved manner, and a way of viewing the patient's disease as of primary interest and concentrating on its technical details to the exclusion of as much else of the person as possible. This may save the physician a great deal of heartache, but it is a defense that one who is in a psychotherapeutic role cannot possibly assume.

In other words, the "mental healther" exposes himself to personal distress and wastes his valuable time if he moves into the front line of the death system—or so it has seemed to many practitioners.

7. Because unimportant people die. It has already been pointed out that death now comes later in the life-span for more people than has usually been the case throughout history. There is a stronger tendency to view old age and death as being intimately related. There is also a strong tendency to devalue aged men and women. ("What have you done for me lately?"). The upshot of this combination is that a dysvalued event (death) befalls a dysvalued person (aged). To the extent that "mental healthers" have avoided contact with aged people—to that extent they have also further insulated themselves from contact with the death system.

Still other factors could be mentioned. True, "mental healthers" were free to avoid death situations. But *why* were they so free? In other words, why did physicians and ministers make no demands on them? Did the "death pro's" perhaps even bolt the door to the newcomers in psychology, psychiatry and social work? On another dimension: did our nation's independent-isolationist orientation insulate us from feeling-knowledge of lethal scourges elsewhere in the world? Were some internal factors operating in our culture that permitted us to erect and maintain a psychological wall? Reference is made to the wall that stands between ourselves and those among us who have been extraordinarily vulnerable to degradation and death. American Indians may be mentioned as just one example of people whose vulnerability has been arranged and perpetuated with very little expression of public concern. Or, on still another dimension: How did the American clergy lose its hold on the emotions and imaginations of its parishioners?

Something must have happened (and other things failed to have happened) for us to have moved so far away from the traditional religious focus upon death.

The early "mental healthers," then, may have grown up within a social climate that no longer was served by stern, influential men on the deathwatch (the clergy). Furthermore, this same climate was lacking in adequate compensatory development of the social justice sentiment. The admonishment that "All men are brothers" had not been sufficient to create a milieu in which we felt that our brother's life and death intimately concerned us.

·*Why Is There Now a Surge of Interest in Death?*

1. Because *we face the prospect of mass death.* Perhaps many of us would have absorbed the immense impact of World War II somewhat as an earlier generation attempted to go on as though World War I had never occurred. But then there was (and is)—THE BOMB. Massive annihilation *here* as well as *there* became a nerve-twitching possibility. Furthermore, the multilateral development of "overkill" capabilities has confronted us with a prospect that has few if any historical precedents: the prospect that in one swift cataclysm we will lose not only our own lives, but all posterity. (This time, Noah and his Ark are not in sight, and there are many who take the "God is dead" rumor more concretely than the rumormongers had intended.)

For many thoughtful people, this prospect has done more than to serve as just another threat to their lives. It has led them to question anew the meaning of life. What is this stuff of life that it can be burned from the earth in a twinkling? What is this stuff of man that he has brought himself so close to total conflagration? A new visage of Death has been turned toward us. It is the visage of a death to end all deaths, because it ends all life (as we know life).

This new form of death awareness has begun to reveal itself to psychologists and psychiatrists, whose work brings them close to the thoughts and feelings of others. They also are likely to find evidences of this awareness within themselves. One cannot overlook the mushroom-cloud-of-the-mind in post World War II society any more than an earlier generation of clinicians could overlook chained and distorted sexuality.

2. Because *we are less isolated from violent death.* Earlier in this chapter we touched upon the American penchant for insulating ourselves from death. We are adept in shielding ourselves from exposure to so-called "natural" dying and death. Violent or unexpected death is something else. It is more difficult to insulate ourselves from exposure to unscheduled deaths. And this difficulty has increased sharply with the heightened influence of mass media. Consider television. That little window inside our living room opens into a world of commercial make-believe much of the time. But there are more and more occasions when a turn of the knob brings us into a world both nightmarish and real. Suffering and death in a physically remote part of the earth instantly is part of our household environment. "They shouldn't show that sort of thing," some viewers have complained about television coverage of the war in Vietnam. Others are so troubled and aroused that they give over much of their lives to social and political activism. Each of us may have his own idiosyncratic way of reacting to this exposure. But we all are much more likely to feel the impact of violent death. Automobile accidents, fires, assassinations—think of any form of violent death and we will be considering something that has been put on display in our own living room.

3. Because *we now have more "mental healthers" who have been through the mill.* The mental health professions have been established long enough by now to have developed large senior echelons. In

other words, there are more psychologists and psychiatrists growing old now than previously. They have experienced the death of loved ones, and their own mortality stands forth as a prospect that is difficult to interpret according to the psychodynamic formulae they learned decades ago. And there are more "mental healthers" who have themselves been through the most harrowing experiences of our century, including battle, military imprisonment, and concentration camps. The mark of Nazi inhumanities is to be found deep within the spirits of many people who are active in the field of mental health, either by direct personal experience or by the loss of family, friends, and colleagues. Let us remind ourselves: psychoanalysis made its first wave of remarkable contributions before World War I, and while its proponents were mostly young or in early middle age. Rivers of blood have been spilled since then. Psychoanalysis has become an Establishment instead of a Revolution—and this Establishment is manned in part by elderly psychiatrists who have seen too much brutal and unnecessary death in the past, and have their own deaths in prospect.

4. Because *simple faith in material progress is on the ebb.* We have become aware that technology does not necessarily solve social or human problems. In fact, every technological boon (e.g., improved agricultural techniques, automation, progress in space exploration) seems to bring about its equal and opposite reaction (we already grow too much food, people may be thrown out of work, funds badly needed for upgrading our cities are diverted elsewhere, etc.). Even the development and application of life-prolonging techniques is often assailed as undesirable or wasteful. The beatnik-hippie-yippie axis has been trying to alert us to the possiblity that our society may have already moved too far into commercialism and technology, at the sacrifice of the individual self. Black Power advocates

have found their ways of reminding us that the Gross National Product is no suitable measure of our society's success in making available to all its citizens the opportunity for a livable life. In short, there are fewer of us today who are willing to trust in the automatic benefits to be reaped from material progress. Unacceptable types and levels of suffering, and unnecessarily premature deaths have not vanished, and show little inclination to do so.

5. Because *we suspect that our very way of life has lethal components.* Who pollutes the air we breathe? Who pollutes the water? Who upsets ecology to such an extent that species after species of animal life is brought to the edge of extinction? Who slaughters us on the highway? Who pours alcohol and drugs into our bodies? Who points that gun at us? Who writes that suicide note for us? Who batters our children? And who makes war for us?

There are perfectly adequate *objective* reasons for these questions to concern us (as is documented in Chapters 10-16 which deal with longevity). It has just taken a while for us to develop enough general social sensitivity to forge these questions into open public concerns. But it is possible that there are important *subjective* reasons as well. We may feel ourselves to be responsible for the deaths of others in a distinctly unpopular war. There are memories of our nuclear attacks on Japan. We may even be starting to feel some responsibility for the wretched living conditions (conducive to death) of some of our fellow citizens. Some of us also have come to develop misgivings about the threats our land development and technology pose to animal life. In other words: *guilt.*

Some of the factors that have been mentioned here are clearly within the realm of mental health (e.g., suicide); others are on the borderline (e.g., accidents); and still others seem remote from conventional definitions of mental health concern (e.g., water pollution). But the *sense* of intrinsic involvement with lethal circumstances obviously is well within the bounds of psychology and psychiatry. To the extent that we are beginning to suspect that the way we think, feel, and behave may be relevant to when and how we (and others) die, to that extent we are inviting a mental health approach to dying and death.

Again, we could cite additional factors that probably have contributed to the recent surge of interest in death on the part of "mental healthers." But perhaps enough has been said already to allow us to move on to the next question:

• *What are Mental Health Specialists Doing with Respect to Death?*

1. *Attempting to prevent suicide.* Self-destruction is a recognizable mental health problem (more accurately, it is a recognizable problem some of whose aspects fall within the province of mental health). The topic of suicide is treated at length in Chapter 11. Here we simply wish to point out that suicide prevention has become the most visible mental health activity within the general realm of death. Suicide prevention centers are functioning in many of our cities. Educational and training efforts are being made to improve our identification of potential suicide victims and develop effective countermeasures. On the federal level there exists a Center for Studies of Suicide Prevention (CSSP). The CSSP is an administrative unit within the National Institute of Mental Health, charged with the responsibility for encouraging and evaluating mental health efforts pertaining directly or indirectly to suicide prevention. Apart from the specific contributions with which the CSSP has been associated, it stands as an important symbol. The government of the United States, through the CSSP, acknowledges the existence of a life-and-death problem which requires the efforts of mental health specialists. And

the government stands prepared to provide financial support for at least some of the research, training, and demonstration proposals regarding suicide prevention that are brought to its attention.

2. *Attempting to identify psychosocial components in other types of death.* Psychiatrists Avery D. Weisman and Thomas P. Hackett, for example, have observed that certain attitudes or predispositions on the part of the patient seem to be associated with failure to recover from surgery (69). Sociologist Irving K. Zola has contributed to our knowledge of the relationship between socioeconomic class membership and a person's tendency to seek or delay treatment for illness (70). Psychologists Frank Kirkner and Joseph Gingerelli have presented material suggesting that personality factors may be related to the body's defense against cancer (71). Sociologist August B. Hollingshead and pediatrician Raymond S. Duff have illuminated the relationship between human factors on both the patient's and physician's side and the quality of hospital care that is rendered (72). These are just a few of many possible illustrations. There is now a growing body of knowledge on the role of psychosocial factors in the various pathways to death: illness, accidents, and murder, as well as suicide. Some of these studies have implications for prevention and intervention.

3. *Attempting to improve the care of the terminal patient.* In the last few years some mental health specialists have been focusing attention upon the dying person—how is he being treated *as* a person? How should he be treated? Many people thought it passing strange when psychiatrist Kurt Eissler devoted a book to *The Psychiatrist and the Dying Patient* (73) not so very long ago. Now a variety of books and articles are appearing on the scene regularly. Some are written by professional "mental healthers," others by nurses, clergy, and physicians who have taken a psychosocial viewpoint. As an example of the new abundance of mater-

ial, consider a specialized survey of the literature conducted recently by sociologist-social worker Ronald R. Koenig (74). He selected just one of the many questions that have been raised in the field: Should a cancer patient be told of his diagnosis? Apart from carrying out his own empirical research, Koenig found no fewer than 51 articles in the professional literature which deal explicitly with this question. Not all questions have received this much observation and comment, but it is clear that psychosocial aspects of dying has emerged as an identifiable area of inquiry within the broader field of death research.

4. *Attempting to decontaminate the topic of death.* More than a decade ago, psycholgist Herman Feifel argued that death was being treated as though a taboo topic in our society (75). Feifel's own vigorous work, gradually joined by others, is beginning to have its impact. He recognized that there could be no really useful psychology of death until people (including his own colleagues) were willing to accept this topic as relevant and legitimate. Feifel encountered much resistance to his interest in death. The *attitude* of resistance thus became an obvious and immediate research topic itself. There has since developed the tradition of investigating death attitudes in order to confront the public with its own biases and resistances.

5. *Attempting to integrate the dimension of death into educational and training programs.* Future psychologists, psychiatrists, sociologists, and social workers should, we think, be given an opportunity to consider death as it is relevant to their prospective life's work. (In practical terms, this also requires some attention to the personal meanings death holds for them.) The same might be said of future nurses, physicians, clergymen, police officers, and some others. Not a great deal has been accomplished yet in this direction. There have been a few university course offerings on psychosocial as-

pects of death. Symposia and lecture series are no longer oddities. But, there is still little awareness in psychology that death could be usefully interwoven with course materials on a variety of subjects—personality, learning, cognition, developmental, community mental health, to name a few.

One very recent development might prefigure more extensive future efforts. A Center for Psychological Studies of Dying, Death, and Lethal Behavior has been established at Wayne State University in Detroit. With a multidisciplinary staff and its university base, this center has at least a foothold in potential educational and training programs. Already it is offering courses to undergraduate and graduate students, as well as to adults in the community. A versatile training program is being developed that is intended to reach selected people in the community and graduate and postdoctoral students from a variety of fields. Trainees will have active involvement in field situations, basic research, prevention-intervention programs, and public information services. One of the aims is to create a corps of specialists in the psychosociology of death (possessing both research and intervention skills). But another, equally important, aim is to provide enough learning experiences for *non*-specialists to enable them to introduce the death dimension into their subsequent activities, whatever these might be.

We have surveyed some of the activities which psycholgists and other "mental healthers" have started to carry out in this area. It should be emphasized that, although on the increase, the number of professionals thus involved remains small. And it is also important to bear in mind that not all of these endeavors prove to be effective. We have yet to learn how to devise appropriate research strategies for many of the most vital questions. Indeed, we are still having trouble formulating the questions. Furthermore, pathways for collaborative activities between "mental healthers" and others in the death system have just begun to be explored. Wasted effort, confusion, and unnecessary conflict will probably be encountered on occasion. In terms of prevention and intervention, we still have almost everything to learn. And we have scarcely touched upon the possibilities for making large-scale contributions at the levels of mass media, legislation, governmental programming, etc. Within the mental health community itself, there are those who oppose some or all of what we have been discussing (and there are more who just do not care to become involved).

But, for better or worse, the "mental healthers" are beginning to make places for themselves in the death system. Chances are that neither the mental health movement nor the death system will be quite the same again.

HOW EXPERT OBSERVERS VIEW OUR DEATH SYSTEM

We have been examining the ways in which various professionals function within our death system. But there are also some expert observers among us who attempt to stand back and put the entire system into perspective. To minimize repetition, we will concentrate upon those viewpoints which add new facets to what has already been discussed in this and the preceding chapter.

What Has Our Death System Done with the Dead?

The dead have been expelled. They are no longer important to the social structure in general or to the "death system" in particular (Chapter 8). This observation has been made by sociologist Robert Blauner (76). He agrees with the present authors' belief that today there is a "diminished visibility of death." However, he goes further and suggests that the relative invisibility of death in our technological society has made the dead seem less real and less powerful to us.

Blauner reminds us that the dead continue to circulate as influential spirits in most preindustrial societies:

Their spheres of influence . . . are many: Spirits watch over and guide economic activities and may determine the fate of trading exchanges, hunting and fishing expeditions, and harvests. Their most important realm of authority is probably that of social control: They are concerned with the general morality of society and the specific actions of individuals (usually kin or clansmen) under their jurisdiction. . . . The dead have the power to bring about both economic and personal misfortunes (including illness and death) to serve their own interests, to express their general capriciousness, or to specifically punish the sins and errors of the living. . . (77).

But this hardly serves as an accurate description of our contemporary relationships with the dead. "Our concept of the inner life of spirits is most shadowy. In primitive societies a full range of attitudes and feelings is imputed to them, whereas a scientific culture has emptied out specific mental and emotional contents from its vague image of spirit life." Generally speaking, we do not feel that the dead exert influence over us as we go about our daily lives. Perhaps the most significant point here is that we no longer need the dead. But what does this mean? How can it be that our ancestors "needed" the dead, but that we find them dispensable?

The answer to this question has already been offered in this book, but in another context. In comparing background conditions for developing death systems, we pointed out that one of the most important differences between past and present circumstances is the age at which one is most likely to die. It was suggested that death has become less important to our society because we associate death with advanced age—and we regard our elders as relatively unimportant and disconnected people. In attempting to account for the unimportance of the dead, Blauner refers to these same factors. He also refers to our relative lack of affinity for tradition and authority—and tradition and authority are, of course, frequently associated with the elderly. Blauner holds that "the dead and their concerns are simply not relevant to the living in a society that feels liberated from the authority of the past and orients its energies toward immediate preoccupations and future possibilities" (78).

These observations lead to a pair of further implications:

1. *Our social distance from the dead is increasing.* Blauner refers to the widening "social distance" between the dead and the living in our own society. This is a fascinating extension of the familiar social distance concept. (Psychologist Richard Kalish has independently studied our social distance from the *dying*, but that is a less extreme application of the concept (79).) Blauner's discussion implies that social distance between the living and the dead can be employed as a variable in both cross-culture and subculture research. It should be possible, for example, to test his own hypothesis that, with increasing industrial and scientific development, a society widens the gap between living and dead. Subgroups within the same culture could also be classified with respect to their social distance from the dead. As Fulton's previously cited research has shown, in our own society Catholic clergy seem to maintain a relatively closer relationship with the dead than is the case with their Protestatnt compatriots (80). Furthermore, we would think that this variable could also be applied to individual differences within the psychological realm. The individual's sense of being related to the dead may vary with his developmental level, his social learning experiences, and his personality organization.

Let us linger for a moment on the relationship between developmental level and social distance from the dead. Elsewhere in this book (Chapter 2) we have explored death as a *concept*. It has been shown that the concept of death has a developmental history within the individual, and that this history is intimately related to the emergence of other basic concepts such as time perspective and self-conservation. The concept of death has also been approached from logical and biological standpoints. The social distance variable has implications for all these perspectives on death. It is one of our reminders that death is not a static concept. We oversimplify and distort our relationship to death if we suppose this concept to be independent of developmental level, socioeconomic context, and so forth. For example, death does not mean the same thing to a child who feels that he still moves within a dead person's orbit that it does to an adult who is convinced that there is no possible contact between himself and the departed.

2. *Our attitudes toward the dead as indices of social structure and change are changing.* In this chapter we have been concerned chiefly with what we can learn about the cultural milieu that can enable us to improve our understanding of our relationship to death. However, it is also possible to move in the other direction: how can our understanding of the psychosociology of death illuminate the structure of our society? Blauner's observations (which have not been reported here in their entirety) provide a basis for moving in this reverse direction. How rapidly is the structure of a particular society changing? How are certain age groups regarded in this society? What is the prevailing orientation toward authority and tradition? Questions such as these can be approached in part from specific inquiries into the culture's death system.

Where Is Death?

Not here!

We have already pointed out that the act of dying has been placed in isolated compartments within our society. We are shielded from direct perceptual encounter with the mortality of our species. Death strikes some place else (and his victim, of course, is somebody else). Although this phenomenon has been touched upon in several different ways, there is more to say about it. Let us discover what can be added to our understanding by an observer who is steeped in mortality statistics. Murray Projector, an actuary for an insurance firm, has integrated his personal observations of our death system with the mass of statistical data that is available to him.

Projector argues that we Americans are literally *obsessed* with the occurrence of *accidental* deaths (81). In developing his case he uses the following points:

1. Accidental deaths (especially from auto, airplane or fire) are given feature coverage in our mass media. Attention is focused upon vivid details of the *particular* case, rather than the general picture or underlying causes.

2. We have become accustomed to believe that accident fatalities comprise a large proportion of the total mortality rate. In other words, death is "out there," waiting for us on the highway or in other hazardous and chancy situations.

3. But: "the significant statistic . . . is that only five percent of all deaths in the United States are caused by accident. Put negatively or positively, ninety-five percent of all deaths are from natural causes" (82). (He does point out that the fatality rate from accidents varies according to the age of the victim, with young adults being especially vulnerable. We will have more to say about the relationship between age and accidents in Chapter 14.)

4. We have also become accustomed to believing that accidental death is a much more frequent occurrence today than in earlier and simpler times. Again, the drift of this belief is to strengthen our feeling that sudden and external death is Public Enemy Number One. Projector denies the validity of this assumption:

"The horse and carriage years were years of horse and carriage accidents, of railroad accidents, of steamboat sinkings, of conflagrations, of falling buildings. The railroad passengers then were greater daredevils than aircraft passengers today. The railroad empire included poor maintenance, unconcern with safety, and low employee morale, so that railroad fatalities were unexpectedly high. The Casey Jones folk song is set against the background of a then commonplace type of railroad accident.

"Steamboat travel was not safer. The commercial concern was for speed and capacity, not safety. Boiler explosions and fires, and sometimes both, were great risks on inland waters. The steamboat Sultana exploded on the Mississippi River in 1865 killing over 1500. The steamboat General Slocum burned in the New York City Harbor in 1904, causing the death of over 1000.

"Fire was always a menace. Firefighting equipment was more primitive, materials more combustible. . . . The runaway horse hazard was not spectacular in terms of fatalities per accident, but did reach respectable totals. *When we think of annual total fatalities from runaway horses, railroad accidents, steamboat explosions, fires, falling buildings, industrial accidents, drownings, and so forth, we then conclude that pre-automobile America was truly the land of sudden death* (83). [Italics ours.]

5. Why is there such a prevalent "overbelief" in fatal accidents? Projector draws his answer from one of the most fundamental propositions in either folk or technical psychology: We believe what we want to believe. But he goes a step further, and this is where his viewpoint is particularly interesting with respect to the cultural milieu of death.

"Why should we be so enamored of accidental death? . . . Excessive concern with accidental death must be equivalent to insufficient concern with natural death. . . . It is the inevitability of death that is at the root of our behavior. Man wishes not to notice, not to think about, not recognize that his own death is inevitable. What simpler way to repress the consciousness of his own mortality than by concentrating on those who die in 'unlucky' accidents in avoidable situations?"

Projector has other provocative comments to offer as well, but we will consider only his main line of argument. Overemphasis upon accidental fatalities is, indeed, a convenient device for diverting our attention from so-called "natural" death. It is a way of reinforcing our belief that death is some place else. Most particularly, *death is not within ourselves.* It is an external act that may befall us. We wish to add the following considerations:

1. The notion that death is accidental can be interpreted as an inclination to remain within the child's universe of causality. We have already seen (Chapter 2) that children tend to see death threats as being closely related to concrete circumstances. Avoid those circumstances and one avoids death. It is only later in the developmental sequence that one achieves the concept of *inevitable* death (a concept that now may be further complicated by current developments in life-prolongation techniques).

2. There is a second sense in which we deny that death is within us. We are speaking here of the many ways in which longevity (of ourselves and others) is influenced by our attitudes and behaviors. As you may have noticed from the table of contents, much of the material which follows in this book is concerned with the influences of psychological and social factors on longevity. In the minds of many people, to classify a death as "accidental" is equivalent to saying that one could not really have prevented its occurrence. This attitude itself is a rather lethal influence, and will be challenged in subsequent chapters. For the moment, it may be sufficient to recall that Projector has pinpointed a number of avoidable causes of accidental death ("unconcern with safety, poor employee morale," etc.). If people were concerned about "accidents" in pre-automobile America, why did they permit hazardous conditions to develop and flourish? If we are concerned about "accidents" today, why do we still permit ourselves to become accomplices? Perhaps this puzzler deserves the same kind of answer that Projector has already provided: Perhaps we secretly have a stake in continued "accidental" fatalities in order to bolster this phenomenon as a diversion from concern with inevitable death that has roots within ourselves.

3. Our cultural milieu of death now begins to resemble those of preindustrial societies in at least one respect: We also shrink from confronting "natural" or inevitable death. Anthropologists and other cross-cultural observers have sometimes "excused" primitive societies for their alleged difficulty in managing abstract concepts. But we deal in abstractions all the time. It may have been customary in primitive societies for an unexpected death to be interpreted as a hostile act on the part of some human or supernatural power. This is an understandable kind of logic to apply when one does not subscribe to a scientific world view. But what are we to make of ourselves when we overly anticipate accidental death, and neglect the much greater odds of a natural demise? Among the possibilities that come to mind: a) In our hearts, we believe that it is really a sort of "accident" to be stricken by illness or age (84); b) we do not really subscribe to a scientific world view, despite its ready availability; c) we cancel our subscription to the scientific outlook when personal matters are at stake; d) we have a magnificent capacity for shifting between sophisticated and primitive-regressive levels of thought. It is possible, of course, that more than one of these factors is involved.

Why Do We Die?

Because we deserve to die.

Because there is no good reason why we should not die.

This question and the answers we have supplied for it are intended to be interpreted within the context of the increasing secularization of our society. In the preceding chapter we commented upon the salient role of religion in social death systems of the past. In this chapter we have mentioned the decline of religious influence as one of the contributing factors in the fragmentation of our own death system. Sociologist Robert Fulton adds another point: "Death . . . in such a secularly-oriented society as ours is no longer the wages of sin; the medical insinuation is that it is the wages of loose living. The fear of death no longer is the fear of judgment but, psychiatrically, the expression of a neurotic personality. Modern America with its emphasis upon youth, health, sports cars, long vacations, and longevity has come to view death as an infringement upon the right to life and upon the pursuit of happiness" (85).

We have the following comments to add:

1. This view of death cannot be separated from a certain view of life—namely, that we are here to have the "good life" on earth. Furthermore, we are under considerable pressure to achieve whatever it is we take to be the "good life." There is not much point in learning to adapt ourselves to suffering, deprivation, and frustration. These experiences are not "worthy" in themselves, nor do they win points for us on the celestial scoreboard.

2. The implication is that we waste our lives unless we give ourselves over to the pursuit of happiness. Yet the *achievement* of certain forms of "happiness," paradoxically enough, can be interpreted as "loose living." Take some obvious examples. A person who is untroubled by traditional strictures on sexual morality pursues sensual happiness to the hilt. Achievement also happens to be accompanied by venereal disease. Another person finds his brand of happiness in the bottle. Liver disease and other ailments follow, as well as a general deterioration in his occupational and social life. These people obviously had the "right idea"—pursuing happiness. But they were "unlucky" enough to be "caught." Take a slightly less obvious example. I have the "right" to smoke, and as much as I "feel like." Puffing on a cigarette either brings me positive satisfaction or masks the frustrations and disappointments I have been encountering in my own pursuit of happiness. And if it "happens" that *my* lungs are ruined, why, then, I suppose I deserve to die. I took my chances with one variant of the pleasure-seeking quest. The "loose living" I enjoyed proved to be my undoing, that's all. It is not that I have been wicked. It is not that my life has been evaluated and found wanting. It is just that I was foolish or unlucky enough to be caught.

3. The same basic logic may prevail even when one takes a different *attitude* toward life-prolongation. Let us persist with the cigarette example. You disapprove of premature or avoidable death. Perhaps you are with the Internal Revenue Service and do not wish to lose a taxpayer before his time. Or perhaps you are just an inveterate busybody who feels compelled to meddle into the lives that other people seem to be throwing away. In any event, you take a moral position with respect to my smoking habits. Filling my lungs with tars, resins, and gases is *wrong*. (Ditto for my failure to use seat belts, and for other death-tempting behaviors). Your attitude certainly contrasts with mine. However, you agree with me on a basic point: it is "loose living" that causes death. I am willing to take the chance; you think I am morally misshapen for doing so. When both of us learn that some one has died, we tend to respond

with the same mental reflexes: We assume that he was "done in" by loose living.

At this point it should be emphasized that we have added an entire structure of speculation that should not be charged to Fulton's account, just as we have roamed beyond the basic observations of Blauner and Projector. We have also been employing the broad strokes of generalization in order to chart some pathways for your own exploration and evaluation. Corner us some place and we are likely to qualify and equivocate a bit.

But there was a second answer to our question: We die because there is no good reason why we should not die. Individuals have come to this conclusion before. What we are concerned about here is the possibility that there may now be *socially normative* dispositions toward accepting death as a "makes-no-difference" alternative to life. We are not suggesting that this is the most prevalent orientation today, but that it *is* a recognizable orientation that must be considered on social as well as individual terms.

One orientation has already received the implicit approval of our society. We are thinking of the elderly person who has come to feel that his present life (and future prospects) are so dim that there does not appear to be much difference between this form of existence and the state of nonexistence. One might go on. Or one might just as well quit. One way or the other, it doesn't seem to make much difference. (As we will see, suicide and other self-destructive behaviors occur with high frequency among our elders, an indirect but potent testimony to the reality of this orientation.) In fact, an influential theory of aging holds that it is *normal* for people to disengage themselves from the network of social relationships and obligations that formerly provided them with identity and satisfactions (86). Elaine Cumming and William Henry, co-authors of *Disengagement Theory*, caution that if adequate compensations or substitutions are not developed for what has been lost, then the elder may suffer a devastating blow to his morale. Feeling useless and disconnected he may prefer death to life—or, as we have seen in our clinical experiences, he may not have a consistent preference at all.

There is another orientation which is less specifically related to a particular age group. It does seem to require a fair amount of experience with life, but this experience can be intensive as well as extensive. The attitude to which we are now referring has a number of variants. The common theme is that life itself does not possess such a deep and intrinsic meaning that one ought to prefer it to death. Philosopher Jacques Choron declares that "someone who has known and reflected upon the fate of the flower of European and American manhood and the military and civilian casualties of the two World Wars cannot close his eyes to the absurd aspect of such deaths, and in good conscience suppress the question of the meaning of life which ends prematurely and horribly" (87).

Absurd. That's the word we need here. There are many people among us today who have had painful encounters with the waste and destruction of human lives. Some of them feel, as Choron has indicated, that life is an absurd phenomenon if it can be brought to such absurd contortions and conclusions. Others, perhaps even more introspectively, feel it is absurd to be a member of a species that has shown such a genius for brutality and senseless destruction. Still others—the young—take a threshold perspective. They have not *experienced* the absurdities that others have directly encountered. But they can *sense* the distortions of the system into which they are expected to enter as full-fledged participants. The college student passes through a slum area on his way to class, and thinks: "Brotherly love: I spit in your face. How can a human come out of this place?" (88) The now familiar bumper sticker advises us to "Make Love—Not War!" Perhaps the basic sentiment here is that we are functioning within a system that makes human life absurd. Hypocrisy, exploitation, and indifference to the sufferings of others gives the lie to our nationally advertised virtues. The young person who experiences his society in this light may also feel that death cannot be any more absurd than life—in fact, may be preferable to "selling out." Is it coincidental that suicide and death-risking behaviors rise sharply in the adolescent years as well as in old age?

The notion that death *and* life might be absurd poses an extreme challenge to our culture. The viewpoint itself is challenging, and so is the fact that its adherents include some of the people from whom important social contributions ordinarily would be anticipated. We do not know how many people hold this outlook. The number may still be quite small in proportion to the total population. But for every person who *experiences* life and death as absurdities, there must be a larger circle who feel that "I know what he means, even though I don't usually feel that way myself." It seems to have become, in short, a recognizable orientation, and one which a troubled society cannot easily dismiss with a negative sanction.

LONGEVITY AND THE CULTURAL MILIEU

Many potential lines of inquiry lie before us at this point. But one problem takes precedence: how does our way of life—as individuals and as a society—affect the length of our lives? How do we move the hour of our death closer or further away by our individual actions and social customs? This exceedingly practical question also involves a variety of theoretical problems that merit our attention.

Accordingly, the pages that follow will be concerned largely with the effect of psychological and social variables upon the timing and manner of our death. Further explorations of the cultural milieu will be made along the way, and use will also be made of other materials that have been introduced in the preceding pages.

Our death system is in flux. We have attempted to sketch some of the major trends which distinguish our present death system from those which preceded it. What will be the future shape of death in our society? We are not ignoring this question, but we are holding it off until we have had the opportunity to examine in detail some of the ways in which our milieu arranges our rendezvous with death.

REFERENCES

1. Anonymous. Variations in mortality from influenza and pneumonia by socioeconomic level. *Statistical Bulletin* (Metropolitan Life Insurance). January, 1968, *49*, 5-7.
2. Beck, C. S., & Mautz, F. R. The control of the heart death by the surgeon, with special reference to ventricular fibrillation occuring during operation. *Annals of Surgery*, 1937, *106*, 525-537.
3. Negovskii, V. A. *Resuscitation and artificial hypothermia.* (Translated by Basil Haigh). New York: Consultants Bureau, 1962.
4. Ettinger, R. C. W. *The prospect of immortality.* New York: McFadden-Bartell, 1966.

5. Mitford, J. *The American way of death.* New York: Simon & Schuster, 1963.
6. Harmer, R. M. *The high cost of dying.* New York: Collier Books, 1963.
7. *Ibid.*, p. 225.
8. *Ibid.*, pp. 225-226.
9. Mitford, *op. cit.*, p. 228.
10. Bowman, L. *The American funeral.* Washington, D.C.: Public Affairs Press, 1959.
11. *Ibid.*, p. 145.
12. *Ibid.*
13. *Ibid.*, p. 147
14. *Ibid.*,
15. *Ibid.*,

16. Gorer, G. *Death, grief, and mourning in contemporary Britian.* London: Cresset Press, 1965.

17. Kastenbaum, R., & Goldsmith, C. E. The funeral director and the meaning of death. *The American Funeral Director*, April, May, & June, 1963.

18. Fulton, R. The sacred and the secular: Attitudes of the American public toward death, funerals, and funeral directors. In R. Fulton (Ed.), *Death and identity*. New York: Wiley, 1965. P. 101.

19. *Ibid.*, p. 89.

20. *Ibid.*, p. 104.

21. Walker, G. E. *Gatherings from graveyards.* London: 1830.

22. Rose, M. S. Motivation in medicine. *Lancet*, September, 10, 1966, p. 583.

23. Worcester, A. *The care of the aged, the dying, and the dead.* Springfield, Ill.: Charles C Thomas, 1961 (first printing, 1935). P. 48.

24. Feifel, H., Hanson, S., Jones, R. & Edwards, L. Physicians consider death. *Proceedings, 75th Annual Convention*, American Psychological Association. Washington, D.C.: American Psychological Association, 1967.

25. *Ibid.*, p. 202.

26. *Ibid.*

27. Livingston, P. B., & Zimet, C. N. Death anxiety, authoritarianism, and choice of specialty in medical students. *Journal of Nervous and Mental Diseases*, 1965, *140*, 222-230.

28. *Ibid.*, p. 229.

29. *Ibid.*, p. 230.

30. Kasper, A. M. The doctor and death. In H. Feifel (Ed.), *The meaning of death*. New York: McGraw-Hill, 1965. P. 261.

31. *Ibid.*, p. 262.

32. Glaser, B. G., & Strauss, A. *Awareness of dying.* Chicago: Aldine, 1966.

33. Glaser, B. G., & Strauss, A. *Time for dying.* Chicago: Aldine, 1968.

34. Sudnow, D. *Passing on.* New York: Prentice-Hall, 1967.

35. Verwoerdt, A. *Communication with the fatally ill.* Springfield, Ill.: Charles C Thomas, 1966.

36. Feifel, H. The functions of attitudes toward death. Group for the Advancement of Psychiatry: *Death and dying: Attitudes of patient and doctor*. GAP Symposium *L* 11, Vol. *5*, October, 1965. Pp. 632-641.

37. Gorer, G. *Death, grief, and mourning.* New York: Doubleday (Anchor), 1956.

38. Aring, C. D. Intimations of mortality. *Annals of Internal Medicine*, 1968, *69*, 137-151.

39. *Ibid.*, p. 150.

40. Kastenbaum, R. Death and responsibility: A critical summary. *Psychiatric Opinion*, 1966, *2*, 35-41.

41. Aring, *op. cit.*, p. 151.

42. Weisman, A. D. Crisis, conflict, and disease. In: *The clergymen's relationship to action for mental health in the community.* Windsor, Conn.: Connecticut Association for Mental Health, 1963. Pp. 10-19 (quoted, p. 19).

43. Bowers, M., Jackson, E., Knight, J., & LeShan, L. *Counseling the dying.* New York: Thomas Nelson & Sons, 1964.

44. Lawrence LeShan. Personal communication.

45. Kastenbaum, R. Multiple perspectives on a geriatric "Death Valley." *Community Mental Health Journal*, 1967, *3*, 21-29.

46. "Training for work with the aged and dying." NIMH project *L* MHO-4818. Framingham, Mass.: Cushing Hospital, 1963-1968.

47. Kastenbaum, 1967, *op. cit.*, p. 27.

48. Quint, J. C. *The nurse and the dying patient.* New York: Macmillan, 1967.

49. Quint, J. C. The social context of dying. Presentation at the conference, "Terminal illness and impending death among the aged." Washington, D.C., May 10, 1966.

50. *Ibid.*

51. *Ibid.*

52. Carlozzi, C. G. *Death and contemporary man: The crisis of terminal illness.* Grand Rapids, Mich.: Eerdmans, 1968.

53. Bowers, et al, *op. cit.*, pp. 67-68.

54. Buxbaum, R. F. What does a minister do in a sick room? Presentation to Bexar County (Texas) Medical Society Committee on Medicine and Religion, March 19, 1963.

55. *Ibid.*

56. Fulton, R. L. The clergyman and the funeral director: A study in role conflict. *Social forces*, 1961, *39*, 317-323.

57. *Ibid.*, p. 322.

58. *Ibid.*, p. 323.

59. Everest, R. E. *Protestant ministers and the church's ministry to the bereaved: A study of patterns of emphasis.* Doctoral study, Boston University, 1965.

60. Eliot, T. D. Bereavement as a problem for family research and technique. *Family*, 1930, *2*, 114-115.

61. Osler, W. *Counsels and ideals.* Boston: Houghton, Mifflin, 1905.

62. Worcester, A. *Care of the aged, the dying, and the dead.* Springfield, Ill.: Charles C Thomas, 1935.

63. Durkheim, E. *Suicide: A sociological study.* (Translated by J. A. Spaulding and G. Simpson.) New York: Free Press, 1951.

64. Sinclair, U. *The jungle.* New York: Vanguard Press, 1926.

65. Weisman, A. D. The birth of the "death-people." *Omega* (Newsletter), 1966.

66. Kastenbaum, R. The reluctant therapist. *Geriatrics*, 1963, *18*, 296-301 (quoted, p. 300).

67. *Ibid.* P. 298.

68. LeShan, L., & LeShan, E. Psychotherapy and the patient with a limited life span. *Psychiatry*, 1961, *24*, 318-323 (quoted, p. 322).

69. Weisman, A. D., & Hackett, T. F. Predilection to death. *Psychosomatic Medicine*, 1961, *23*, 232-256.

70. Kosa, J., Antonovsky, A., & Zola, I. K. (Eds.), *Poverty and health: A sociological analysis.* Cambridge, Mass.: Harvard University Press, 1969.

71. Gengerelli, J. A. & Kirkner, F. J. (Eds.), *Psychological variables in human cancer.* Berkeley: University of California Press, 1954.

72. Duff, R. S., & Hollingshead, A. B. *Sickness and society.* New York: Harper & Row, 1968.

73. Eissler, K. *The psychiatrist and the dying patient.* New York: International University Press, 1955.

74. Koenig, R. R. Anticipating death from cancer —physician and patient attitudes. *Michigan Medicine*, Vol. *68*, No. 17, September 1969, 899-905.

75. Feifel, H. In H. Feifel (Ed.), *The meaning of death.* New York: McGraw-Hill, 1959, xiii-xviii.

76. Blauner, R. Death and social structure. *Psychiatry*, 1966, *29*, 378-394.

77. *Ibid.*, p. 390.

78. *Ibid.*, p. 391.

79. Kalish, R. A. Social distance and the dying. *Community Mental Health Journal*, 1966, *2*, 152-155.

80. Fulton, *op. cit.*

81. Projector, M. The American way of looking at accidental death. *Omega* (Newsletter), 1968, *3*, 43-47.

82. *Ibid.*, p. 44.

83. *Ibid.*, p. 45.

84. Kastenbaum, R. The crisis of explanation. In R. Kastenbaum (Ed.), *New thoughts on old age.* New York: Springer, 1964. Pp. 316-323.

85. Fulton, R. L. *The sacred and the secular. Attitudes of the American public toward death.* Milwaukee: Bulfin Press, 1963. P. 8.

86. Cumming E., & Henry, W. *Growing old.* New York: Basic Books, 1961.

87. Choron, J. *Death and western thought.* New York: Collier Books, 1963. P. 273.

88. Hnider, W. From: A house on Compton street. *Milestone.* Los Angeles, Calif.: East Los Angeles College, 1951. P. 9.

10

Psychological Factors

in Death and Longevity:

An Introduction

Murder is a leading cause of death in childhood; the victims are usually killed by their parents.

At one point in history, composers of classical music tended to outlive most of their contemporaries—but at a later point in history, the longevity of composers was markedly reduced.

Many insurance companies offer lower rates to schoolteachers because they have so few accidents.

More single than married men commit suicide.

Physical ills and psychoses apparently alternate in some people.

The prognosis for coronary patients is more favorable for those of high socio-economic status.

More white people than Negroes kill themselves, but Negro suicides are increasing.

In most age groups males have a higher death rate than females.

The incidence of coronary disease is unusually high among physicians.

Young servicemen traveling too fast or too slowly in old cars are among the most dangerous drivers on the road at night.

Adult males were once the usual victims of peptic and duodenal ulcers. Now both women and men are increasingly affected.

Why?

1. It is possible that observations such as those listed above represent only the operation of random processes. Survival is really a matter of "luck," unpredictable circumstance, "hit-or-miss." Should we choose to accept this explanation, then there would be very little point to studying psychological factors in longevity. Occasionally the phenomena may seem to fall into a coherent pattern, but this apparent coherence would be regarded as a "chance" occurrence, not to be taken seriously. We would be deceiving ourselves to believe that differential longevity is explicable on the basis of psychological or other systematic, orderly processes.

2. Again, it is possible that longevity is "fated." Many people have expressed the opinion that there is an underlying principle, but a principle which is beyond the reach of ordinary human understand-

ing. If one's day of death is a pre-established fact, then no amount of research is likely to produce further explication; the significant variable or variables exist in a special realm far beyond the scope of science. Furthermore, no matter how one might tinker with his own behavior or with his environment, he is quite unlikely to influence longevity by as much as a millisecond.

3. Genetic determinism is still another possible explanation. Wholehearted acceptance of this viewpoint would involve the assumption that there is a strong component of "lawfulness" or systematic processes which contribute to the length of life. In contrast to the fatalistic position, this view generally does not insist that survival is entirely a matter of predetermined conditions. Rather, so the argument would go, whatever is systematic and inherently predictable about longevity can be attributed to factors in the realm of genetics. As an important corollary, we note that this realm is amenable to research and understanding, and might also be amenable to modification or control. The genetic position further differs from the other views in that it can draw support from an impressive and rapidly growing body of scientific research.

4. The remaining possibility also seems to be the most complex. In recent years there has been an increasing tendency on the part of behavioral scientists and psychiatrists to regard the human person as a truly psychobiological or holistic entity. Both the individual's momentary state of behavior and experience, and his characteristic lifestyle, are interpreted as emergents from a multiplicity of interacting factors at all levels of organization. An adequate description—let alone an explanation—of the individual would require attention to his biological condition, environmental circumstances, basic psychological processes, and phenomenological world. Perhaps, then, *length* of life should be conceptualized in the same manner as we attempt to conceptualize *quality* of

life. The quest for understanding, predictability, and, perhaps, modification of longevity, would require a) investigation at each level taken separately, and b) careful efforts toward integrating the results to develop the whole picture.

The psychobiological viewpoint does not require a guarantee that longevity be 100 percent predictable, even in theory. In making this statement we are aware that some behavioral scientists believe that one must assume perfect determinism as a conceptual cornerstone for the research endeavor. This assumption we find quaint, irrelevant, and trouble-begging. Our reasons for rejecting the extreme deterministic assumption are too varied to describe here. It will suffice to adopt the simpler assumption: Our present knowledge of factors associated with longevity can be improved to some unknown extent by appropriate research into the individual's total life situation. The extent to which "purely psychological" variables will contribute to increased knowledge is also unknown, but these variables are deemed to be an essential part of the total configuration.

Which line of explanation should we accept? All these viewpoints can muster some observations in their support. None are totally lacking in plausibility. The "chance" and "fate" arguments usually are formulated in such a loose manner that it is exceedingly difficult to devise a crucial test. Furthermore, these positions tend to protect themselves by ignoring and discrediting research endeavors which might yield discordant results. However, it does not seem appropriate simply to dismiss these viewpoints. To prove that chance or fate do *not* govern the universe in general, or human longevity in particular, is a philosophico-logical problem more than it is a scientific task if, indeed, these assumptions can be overthrown at all. Perhaps we should welcome the continued presence of these not-quite-testable explanations as both goad and balance, lest we too readily convince ourselves that all the mysteries are within the reach of technologically-oriented inquiry.

To deny that longevity is related to genetic factors would be ridiculous. It is not ridiculous, however, to wonder whether or not the genetic approach is sufficient unto itself. One of the main thrusts of current research and theory in genetics is toward interpenetration of what formerly had been regarded as the radically different realms of "nature" and "nurture" (1, 2). The emerging field of behavioral genetics exemplifies this new approach. Indeed, it is often the far-sighted biological scientist who has prodded his colleagues in the behavioral sciences to contribute their share to problems of mutual interest. To clarify the nature and limits of genetic and other biological mechanisms it is necessary to observe their behavioral effects in a sensitive and appropriate manner. Disagreements regarding the relative contribution of genetic and non-genetic factors in longevity probably will continue. But we are likely to find that fewer and fewer investigators will insist that the story is all in the chromosomes. The story seems to be in the interaction between the chromosomes and—dare we say it—the entire psychological and cultural context within which the chromosomes develop. Perhaps not many investigators are ready to deal with the whole range of phenomena from cultural pattern to biological mechanism, but the day is coming, and advance signs already can be discerned.

In opting for the remaining approach—the psychobiologic or holistic—we are not losing any of the advantages that can be derived from the genetic. It is a matter of starting with a frame of reference that is broad enough to encompass contributions from the biological sciences and facilitate their integration with psychological, social, and other environmental data. Even a rather silly example might be used here. Suppose that, in the strictest sense, human longevity were completely dependent upon genetic endowment. Would this factor obviate the significance of environmental factors? Not likely.

Genetic transmission still requires that intervening variable known as mating. Selection of a mate, age at time of mating, number of children produced and other such factors are strongly shaped by personality, cultural, and physical forces in the environment. *Who* is conceived by *whom* is affected by a plethora of non-genetic variables, e.g., prejudice against mixed marriages, ghetto vs diffused residential patterns, peace-time vs war-time social climate, expectations regarding the proper age for marriage, the proper age differential between husband and wife, etc. Parental age at time of conception may differ markedly from Alabama to County Cork and produce significant differences in the transmitted genetic endowment. Yet, the differences between Alabama and County Cork seem to be geographic, psychologic, political, and economic, rather more than genetic. Behavior, interpersonal behavior, is required for initiation of genetic processes. Furthermore, the biological program for longevity that is implicit in the embryo will have no chance to unfurl if personality or cultural patterns happen to dictate abortion or infanticide. These, perhaps, are the simplest kinds of possible genetic/non-genetic interactions, but sufficient to suggest that complete separation of the two realms would be artificial and burdensome.

How variables of many kinds converge and interact to influence death will be discussed in the chapter that summarizes this section. First, however, it will be necessary to consider some of the variables and problems separately. We have not hesitated to introduce material from a variety of fields other than psychology, hoping to cut across artificial boundaries that handicap us in making use of each other's work.

Let us begin by categorizing what are usually considered to be the causes of death: suicide, murder, warfare, accidents, illness and "natural causes." We are already in difficulty, for obviously these categories are not mutually exclusive. Apparent accidents or illnesses may represent suicidal efforts. The discovery that one has a terminal illness may prompt him to suicide. While committing suicide, one may deliberately or inadvertently "murder" or produce an "accident" that takes the lives of other people. Mental illness may lie at the root of both suicide and murder; and both physical and mental disease can set up accidents. Warfare undoubtedly contributes to all of the other categories: it can serve as the reason or excuse for suicide and murder, produce unusual numbers and types of accidents, and increase the incidence of diseases, especially contagious diseases. Death from "natural causes" is even more of a problem. What causes are "natural?" Is it "natural" for a man of 90 to die in his sleep of the effects of cerebral arteriosclerosis? How about a man of 35? Is it natural for the heart of a 19-year-old

basketball player simply to stop beating one day during intermission? And how many times have we read that a death first thought due to "natural causes" was later found to be the result of an overdose of drugs or a coronary thrombosis?

For purposes of clarity we will discuss these categories as if they were "solid" and discrete. The amount and kinds of overlap will be easily enough discerned. We will move from a consideration of those kinds of death in which the role of psychological factors seems to be paramount and most obvious to those in which it is less apparent, poorly understood, or controversial. Each of the following chapters is titled with a "cause of death" as it might appear on a death certificate or in a newspaper account. But what we seek to explore here is, in that overworked but still relevant phrase, "the story behind the story." What are the hidden causes of death? What subtle factors combine to do man in? And how "guilty" is he of complicity?

REFERENCES

1. Fuller, J. L., & Thompson, W. R. *Behavior genetics.* New York: Wiley, 1960.
2. Vandenberg, S. G. Contributions of twin research to psychology. *Psychological Bulletin,* 1966, *66,* 327-352.

Suicide

I know a hundred ways to die.
I've often thought I'd try one:
Lie down beneath a motor truck
Some day when standing by one.

Or throw myself from off a bridge—
Except such things must be
So hard upon the scavengers
And men that clean the sea.

I know some poison I could drink.
I've often thought I'd taste it.
But mother bought it for the sink,
And drinking it would waste it.

       Edna St. Vincent Millay (1)

Would you like to escape from all your responsibilities and problems? Do you want to make certain people feel guilty for the way they have treated you? There is a way to ensure this. You have only to trade for these imagined pleasures the sum of your present and future rewards and experiences—in short, life itself. To most people this would hardly seem an attractive bargain. Yet at least 24,000 Americans are willing parties to it yearly (2). Suicide has been known to occur in al-most every conceivable type of society; and the American rate is not the highest (3). Probably at some time in their lives many adults have thought, albeit fleetingly, of "ending it all." Yet only a minority of them actually make the attempt. A desire to escape the less pleasant aspects of life is certainly understandable; but what explains the willingness to forfeit all chance for a better future? In short, why does *anyone* commit suicide?

Because he is psychotic and doesn't know what he is doing.
Because he acts on impulse and doesn't think about the future.
Because his discomfort is so acute that he cares about nothing but escape.
Because he believes he is already dying and has no earthly future.
Because he believes that the future will be no better, or even worse.
Because he feels that what he can gain symbolically through death is more important than anything continued life can offer.

Or, most generally, because "life has no meaning."

Most people who have contemplated suicide have at least one of these "reasons." Yet any seemingly hopeless situation or tragic event that prompts a person to consider suicide has been successfully weathered by countless others. Indeed, it is likely that most middle-aged adults have already faced and overcome one or more problems that have supposedly compelled others to commit self-murder. Therefore, we might reasonably inquire: Why doesn't *everyone* commit suicide?

There are those who would contend that, at some level, all of us do kill ourselves—that eventually we actively seek out or passively submit to death when continued life is still possible. The universal applicability of this proposition may be questioned; but it is doubtless true that everyone does, in some way, help to determine his time and mode of death. This is one of the themes with which we will be concerned in the chapters ahead. First, however, there are at least two reasons for attempting to uncover the roots of suicide per se:

1. What we discover might aid us in finding ways to prevent this type of death.
2. The factors basic to suicide may be found to underlie other, more subtle, forms of self-destructive behavior as well.

Is it really true that all of us are basically suicidal? If we are not, then what determines who is and who is not oriented toward self-destruction?

A large number of complexly interrelated variables are correlated with suicide rates. We will begin this exploration by examining a summary of the data on which most statisticians would agree: *The incidence of suicide is highest among the elderly, males, Caucasians and Orientals, the divorced and widowed, people at both extremes of the socioeconomic ladder, and immigrants from certain nations.* Ob-

viously, most of these categories are not mutually exclusive. What is not apparent is the nature of their relationship to each other and the degree to which any are of true causal significance in suicide. Is one factor or set of factors common and/or basic to all of them? In quest for an answer we will first attend to the variables known to be correlated with suicide.

THE MAJOR VARIABLES ASSOCIATED WITH SUICIDE

The variables associated with suicide (age, sex, race, subcultural group membership, marital status, socioeconomic level, mental illness, suicide preventatives) differ in complexity. This is a statement of the obvious. Yet, one might expect the relationship between suicide and at least some of the variables to be simple, direct, and easily understood. If so, he is doomed to disappointment. Let us consider first the variable which may prove to be most deceiving.

Age

Whoever said "Growing old is not so bad when you consider the alternative" was certainly not looking at the suicide statistics, for suicide rates and advancing age go hand in hand. Although suicide is rare in childhood (but see below), the rate rises gradually during adolescence and rather sharply in early adulthood. The upward trend continues to parallel the advance in age until it reaches the maximum rate of 27.9 suicides per 100,000 for people in the 75- to 84-year-old bracket; thereafter, it declines slightly (4). The relationship between suicide and age is deceptively simple; in fact, at first glance the data appear to be unequivocal: up to age 85, suicide is almost directly proportional to age, and relatively few people live beyond that age. If one focuses on the very elderly alone, this finding hardly seems surprising. The later years of life are usually characterized by decreasing physical powers, if not actual incapacity; and illness and discomfort are often the constant companions of older people. Many of our aged have outlived their relatives and most intimate friends and are in a poor position to acquire new ones. Jobs are not generally available to the elderly either, even to those who are still capable and who want to work. Fifty-six percent of the jobless in the United States are 45 years of age or older (5). This is reflected in the suicide rates which are higher for the retired than for the employed of the same age (6). And the rate of unemployment among our elders has steadily increased from decade to decade. Even recreational activities require the investment of more money and energy than many older people have at their disposal. Furthermore, throughout life each new decision eliminates other possible choices: therefore, there is a tendency for alternatives to become progressively fewer as one grows older; and one may become disillusioned with those already selected.

Are these, then, the major causes for the high suicide rate among the elderly? We think not. All of these objective problems of later life are understandable reasons for concern and dissatisfaction; yet, suicide in later life is quite obviously not "caused" by old age per se, nor solely by any of the problems which accompany it. What other explanations are available? Batchelor contends that in old age "the great majority of suicidal people are suffering from psychosis—and fall into two clinical groups: the depressive states and the organic dementias" (7). On the basis of two independent investigations of suicide attempters, he concludes that, after the age of 60: a) the majority of attempters are in the depressive stage of manic depressive psychosis; b) the minority suffer from organic psychoses typical of old age; and c) a small number are in states of transient confusion which he believes are most often organically determined. This investigator notes that in a

few cases such confusion appears to be psychogenic, for example, a "sudden panic reaction in a setting of despair and bewilderment. . . " (8).

In the absence of more detailed information about studies that have been conducted, it is difficult to know to what extent one can use the findings as a basis for generalizations. Is it really only the psychotic older person who is likely to commit suicide? Batchelor noted a family history of suicidal acts in 17 percent of a series of 40 cases, and found a history of "psychotic abnormality in the majority." He concludes, therefore, that "an apparent familial manic-depressive trait is commonly important" (9). The extent to which it is possible to attribute this "familial trait" to psychological and environmental influences rather than to purely hereditary and organic ones is a point that is neither discussed nor raised. What is important to us here is the fact that even Batchelor, who sees suicide primarily from an organic standpoint, nevertheless concedes that "mental illness in itself is not often a sufficient explanation of suicide. . . . One should scrutinize the individual's situation to discover the causes of unhappiness" (10). He mentions loneliness, social isolation, loss of a loved one, unemployment, and financial worries as some possible causes for suicide attempts. All of these causes direct attention to the area of social and self attitudes.

One cannot subjectively experience old age until it is upon him. In the absence of previous personal experience of this state, from what sources do the elderly derive the negative self attitudes that suicide usually implies? The process of developing attitudes toward the self originally involves internalizing the attitudes of others (11). In early life, the significant others are usually the parents. There is no reason to assume that in later life the process is basically any different except that, for the elderly, the whole contemporary society constitutes "significant others." Generally speaking, the elderly are condemned because they are guilty on several counts: They impede progress (i.e., change) by adhering to old, familiar ways and products. They get in the way of younger people who can think and move faster. They take up space which the young feel could be used more profitably by themselves. What is even more important, but not usually acknowledged, is that the elderly remind us of the inevitable (12). The association of death with old age and its physical characteristics is a common one (13). The fact is that many people do not like the elderly (14, 15); and apparently the elderly often do not like themselves either. The situation appears to be much the same throughout the Western world, and so is the relationship between age and suicide (16).

In France, the negative view of aging, in which anyone nearing 40 is considered "old," has begun to have serious economic repercussions. Highly competent people in their late 30's are finding themselves unemployed and unemployable. The French government is trying, somewhat belatedly, to reverse this attitudinal trend. It may be instructive and perhaps discouraging to see what effect, if any, this will have on the French suicide statistics (17). Of course it is not likely that any society will ever surpass ours in efficiently disseminating negative attitudes toward the aged. Occasionally, one still hears that "you are as young as you feel," and that what is important is "to be young at heart," but, for the most part, the impression conveyed by our mass media is that it is important to be young—period (18). Naturally, the ultimate effect of this is to increase the sense of anxiety and impotence among the elderly. Small wonder that suicide is sometimes preferred to an ignominious old age. But we cannot contend that social attitudes toward old age are the basic cause of suicide among the elderly, for if they were, then would not most, or even all, of the elderly commit suicide? Quite obviously, however, social attitude toward change is a contributing

or, sometimes, a precipitating factor in suicide and thus is worthy of emphasis since it is possible to alter social climate in a favorable direction. Some of the other factors with which we are concerned in this chapter are less amenable to manipulation.

What, then, are the basic reasons for suicide in old age? How do they differ, if at all, from the causes of suicide in younger people? Farberow's and Shneidman's provocative paper, "Suicide and Age," sheds light on this question while raising others (19). Using suicide notes as their raw data, the authors classified the motives revealed in each on the basis of the three factors which Menninger has theorized "are present in varying degrees" in all suicides: the wish to kill, the wish to be killed, and the wish to die (20). Farberow and Shneidman found that, especially in males, the wish to kill and the wish to be killed decreased with age, while the third factor, the wish to die, increased with age. At first, these findings may seem to contribute but little to our discussion since they appear to say merely that old people, especially men, commit suicide because they wish to die. Their implications, however, are far deeper and broader. Farberow and Shneidman agree with Menninger that the three elements that he enumerates are present in all suicides, but "the pattern or the constellation of the various dynamics motivating the suicidal person tends to show marked shifts depending on his age" (21). We could not agree more strongly, and shall enlarge on this theme not only as it applies to suicide, but in our discussions of other forms of death as well. It is quite obvious that it would be difficult to uncover the basic etiological factor in suicide in old age without considering the problem of suicide in all other age groups. Only then can we formulate, compare, and contrast hypotheses.

Despite the fact that the incidence of suicide is highest among the aged, many young people do kill themselves, and without apparent "benefit" of social prodding. What role, if any, does chronological age per se play in these deaths? At the beginning of life chronological age plays a decisive part. Obviously, one must have lived for a certain length of time in order to have achieved some physical and mental mastery of his environment. In infancy, the organism's rudimentary state of development precludes the occurrence of suicide as it is ordinarily defined. The infant is incapable of deliberately executing simple motor activities, much less of understanding its situation or planning ahead. Should it tumble from a crib or a window, or swallow a poisonous substance, the outcome is considered an accident, or, more rarely, murder, but never suicide.

It would be difficult to ascertain at what age one should begin to label self-destruction as suicide. Psychoanalytic theory provides, by implication, a partial explanation for those cases of suicide assumed to be caused by depression related to object loss. Schmale has proposed "a developmental concept of the manifestations of depression based on theoretical object relationship models." He postulates that "psychobiological depression can occur at any time after there is a beginning psychic representation of the mother-child symbiosis" (22). There may be an age below which such "beginning psychic representation" cannot exist, but apart from that, there is certainly plenty of room for individual variation. Furthermore, we do not know precisely to what extent suicide in childhood can be attributed to depression at all. Several years ago a newspaper carried an account of the death of a two-year-old boy who fractured his skull by deliberately running into a wall after being denied a piece of candy. This death was undoubtedly more the accidental outcome of a temper tantrum than a true suicide. The death was classified an accident because the victim's immaturity was taken into consideration. Yet, many an adult death which follows a "temper tantrum" is called suicide because it is assumed that adults can foresee the consequences of their acts and have greater self-control. In many cases the validity of such an assumption is highly questionable. Physical and psychological development do not always proceed apace. After age two, this presents serious classificatory problems.

Very young children do, certainly, have some ideas about death. Suicide threats are not at all uncommon in childhood, even in the early years. Naturally, the death to which little children refer is unlike that which adults usually envision. But the fact remains that children are concerned about death, and some do commit suicide. Currently, in fact, the number of childhood and adolescent suicides appears to be increasing (23). We may gain some insight into why anyone commits suicide by trying to understand what lies behind changes in the suicide rates among children.

Why should childhood suicide be on the rise? The ready answer is that, although basically children may have changed very little from generation to generation, the childhood they are expected to live through has changed a great deal (24). It is hardly necessary to remind anyone today that children are pressured to grow up at ever earlier ages. The child is goaded to conform, to achieve academic excellence, to be productive, to be popular, to be a joiner, to be a leader. More important still is the fact that parental acceptance and love, which should be the child's birthright, are often made contingent upon his social and academic success (25). The plight of the adolescent may be even worse than that of the younger child. Northwestern University's Professor L. Carrol King feels that the total of 17 hours of work required of high-school students daily is "a crime against a generation" (26). Later at college "he is faced with four more years of seventeen-hour days. It's too much; he just quits. The tired, beaten, defeated Mr. Good Student asks for academic death." Or real death? Certainly many children today are allowed but little time for quiet contemplation or for digesting their experiences. All of this is frequently and piously deplored, but little has been done to remedy the situation. Someone has said "If Booth Tarkington were to write *Seventeen* today, he'd have to call it *Twelve.*" This may well be true, but it is not very funny. The infant born today has the same basic equipment as infants of earlier eras. He still has his own built-in timetable which can be accelerated only so much. It may be true that people tend to enter adolescence about a year earlier than formerly (whether due to better nutrition, as usually suggested, has yet to be determined), but a year is only a year and dressing like an adult does not make a boy a man. It certainly seems likely that the rising rate of childhood suicide is partly attributable to all of these increasing educational and social demands which some children feel they cannot meet. Quite probably, the parental and social responses to such failure are even more crucial.

Two other factors may play a significant role in childhood suicide rates. One of these is closely related to the father image in the modern family. Adults, too, are subjected to increasing pressures, many of which have their roots in family economics at a time of technological change. Only the lowest paid, least secure jobs are now available to the untrained individual. As machines replace men, and synthetics supplant older materials, frequent job changes are becoming the rule. The father no longer has the security of a lifetime job and its long-term interpersonal relationships, and the child no longer has the security of a stable father image. For the highly-trained individual the situation is somewhat better, although hardly ideal. Scientific developments and technological advances rapidly render the skills of even the recent graduate obsolete. The age at which one becomes "old" and, therefore, prey to all the ills of the el-

derly, is forever being revised in a downward direction (27). Continued study to keep up with his field as well as refresher courses to remind him of the basics, take up whatever slack there may once have been in the professional man's schedule. In addition, to ensure upward professional mobility, one must often resort to geographic mobility, a factor already known to be correlated with suicide (28). The uprooted child, deprived of friends and familiar surroundings, is more than ever dependent upon his parents for emotional support and recognition of personal worth. But the parents themselves are pressured and preoccupied. They are ambitious for their children's social and educational success but, paradoxically, they have little time for their children. It is not difficult to understand how—buffeted by conflicting pressures, and apparently rejected by preoccupied parents whose standards they cannot meet—children's elemental defenses may be overwhelmed and suicide used as an escape.

A second set of factors in the increasing rate of childhood suicide includes certain facets of modern Western culture that undermine the development and exercise of emotional control. In a mobile society, people often find themselves in places where they know or are known to no one, and their expressive behavior is likely to be freer than in a stable, smaller community where they are known. Because children pick up underlying, unspoken attitudes quickly, those in mobile families may not develop patterns of thought and behavior that are basic to self-control. Too, travel brings people into contact with others whose standards are different. For the adult or older child this can be a broadening, enlightening experience, but for the young child it may prove confusing and disruptive. With his own controls not really "jelled," he is suddenly confronted with people who act freely in ways he has just begun to label "wrong." If the reasons for such behavior are not adequately explained by the parents, the child may develop a cynical outlook: any-thing is all right so long as you can get away with it, and why should you control yourself, anyway, if nobody else does? Impulse control and postponement of per-sonal gratification may also be subtly un-dermined by the attitudes implicit in the "fly now, pay later" approach to property acquisition and personal debt. *Thus, our present society may exert great pressure on the young, tend to deprive children of the contact with parents whom they need as a source of emotional support and as figures for identification, and at the same time undermine the development of an adequate control system and the ability to sublimate.* All of these factors are proba-bly relevant to suicidal behavior in general but they are especially relevant to that in young children whose incomplete develop-ment renders them especially vulnerable.

Thus far in our discussion of the rela-tionship between age and the suicide rate we have focused attention on the ex-tremes of the chronological continuum. What, if anything, can be said about the suicides of people in the intervening years? Is it at all useful to regard suicide as a function of age?

A familiar biblical quotation tells us "To everything there is a season, and a time to every purpose under the Heaven." Shakespeare speaks of the seven ages of man. Yet, once physical maturity is reached, these times or ages certainly can-not be considered objective. In fact, chronological age itself does not mean the same thing to all people. Therein lies an important limit to any purely chronologi-cal approach to suicide. For example, knowledge of one's objective age does not tell us anything about his ideas of age-appropriate behavior, how rigid they are, or what their significance is in his total life perspective (29). It does not reveal what time schedule, if any, governs his decisions, and what deadlines he must meet to be successful in his own eyes (30). Each individual whose life style in-cludes planning ahead has his own pecu-

liar goals and deadlines. His behavior is not really comprehensible without an understanding of his personal time schedule.

One of the authors is acquainted with a man who had always hoped to go to college, but lacked sufficient funds. Upon his return from military service, however, the money was available. But at the age of 24, the man felt he was much too old to be a college freshman. Since a degree was not essential to this man's self-concept, he was able to proceed with an alternate life plan. Suppose, however, that he had considered a college education essential because life could have no ac-ceptable meaning to him unless he could enter a particular profession and to do so he had to have a degree. The conflict between the need for a degree and his idea of age-appropriate behavior would well have been his undoing. Similarly, a person who derives all of his satisfactions and feelings of worth from activities tradi-tionally restricted to the very young might become suicidal in middle age if he is unable either to find another basis for his self-esteem or to challenge the existing conventions.

Despite the cultural stereotypes, atti-tudes toward aging may be highly idiosyn-cratic. They may be primarily a function of what proportion of one's life he be-lieves he has already lived. People with long-lived relatives may think 60 is not very old, for they anticipate another 20 or 30 years of active life (31). Conversely, the individual whose parents died before 50, may approach age 40 with anxious foreboding. An unusual attitude toward age may also result from an especially unfortunate family history. A young man who had lost all his brothers to sickness or accident before they were 20 might be so convinced of his own impending de-mise that he "robs" death by committing suicide the night before his twentieth birthday. Consider this striking example reported by Dublin. "Until the age of 53, I had good health; I had no troubles, my temperament was quite cheerful. Then, three years ago, I began to have gloomy thoughts—for the past three months they have persecuted me constantly and I am tempted to kill myself at every moment. I will not conceal that my brother committed suicide at the age of 60; I had never thought seriously of it, but on reaching my fifty-sixth year the memory recurred to me more vividly and now it never leaves me" (32). These are all examples of unusual attitudes toward age which can influence suicide among those who are not yet aged.

Of course, many people live primarily in the present and are little given to rumination. Such people may not consciously recognize age as a factor relevant to suicide at all. However, for most individuals, time and age do pervade life. For example, it has recently come to light that the biological activities of every known type of plant and animal are characterized by pulsations or circadian rhythms that are independent of external events (33). Stated anthropomorphically, each organism, even each cell, "tells time" and alters its functions rhythmically as the day goes on. Flies and rodents have been found to be more susceptible to poisons in the afternoon than in the morning. Heart muscle kept alive after removal from the body continues to recognize time by beating faster during the day than at night. Crabs that change color at night continue to do so even when placed in dark enclosures during the day and in illuminated ones at night. In health, human body temperature typically drops at night, reaches its lowest point in the early morning and its highest point in the late afternoon (34). Professor Lawrence Scheving, who discovered a 78 percent mortality rate among rodents injected with amphetamine at certain hours of the day, but only a 6 percent mortality rate among controls injected at other hours, is unable to specify why the time variable is crucial (35). In light of the available data, however, it is reasonable to hypothesize that mental and emotional vulnerability also vary rhythmically with time of day. Might vulnerability not vary with biological age and thus with chronological age as well? Do the daily periods of increased physical and/or emotional vulnerability to noxious stimuli increase in duration, frequency, or intensity with increasing age? Is this one of the reasons why suicide increases with age? Biologically speaking, is this why the elderly "run out of time," i.e., enjoy fewer and fewer "good hours" per day? We shall have more to say of this later, but must first turn our attention to other variables that cast a different light on the whole problem of suicide and biological time.

Earlier in this chapter we characterized the relationship between age and suicide as "deceptively simple." The reasons for this note of caution will become clear as we discuss the other variables.

Sex

One authority on the subject has described suicide as "a masculine type of behavior" (36). The ratio of male to female suicides is between three and four to one at earlier ages, and about ten to one after age 85. Furthermore, in almost all European countries the suicide rate has been found to be two or three males for every female, except in Norway and Finland where the disparity in rates is even greater. This difference crosses racial as well as national boundaries: The suicide rate among nonwhite persons in the United States is higher for males than females and increases correspondingly to the increase in age. The data are clear: the reasons behind them are not. Do males have an intrinsically lower frustration tolerance and/or heightened responsiveness to thwarting situations? Are they better able to foresee future difficulties and predict catastrophic outcomes, or are they simply less capable of carrying on in the face of adversity? Is suicide one of the chief ways for males to escape from problems that females solve by utilizing other techniques? It would be important to know whether factors basic to the high male rate of completed suicides are related ultimately to biologically sex-linked characteristics, or whether they are derived primarily from roles, traits, and expectations which result from social indoctrination. Some statistics and scientific information may be helpful here. There is some evidence that biological factors may be related to the differential vulnerabilities of males and females.

1. Despite comparable environments, the male fetus is apparently more vulnerable than the female—"three out of five abortions are of male embryos" (37).

2. During both childhood and adolescence the male death rate exceeds that of females by significant amounts.

3. Many more men than women die of coronaries, tuberculosis, and accidents.

Some biologists believe that the cellular attributes fundamental to masculinity are partially responsible for this. Every cell in a woman's body contains 23 pairs of matched chromosomes. Every cell in a man's body also contains 23 pairs of chromosomes, but only 22 are matched. In the twenty-third pair, one is an X chromosome and the other is a smaller Y chromosome which contains fewer genes. The theory, somewhat oversimplified, is that there are insufficient genes in the Y chromosome to compensate for any defective gene which the X chromosome may contain. Thus, males may have certain diseases like hemophilia which females usually only carry, without themselves being afflicted (38). If mental and physical functions are as intimately linked as most scientists believe, then perhaps this vulnerability extends to what we have come to call the psychological realm.

Another biological explanation stresses the relationship between male sex hormones and longevity. Several investigators have attacked this problem, but one example will suffice. James Hamilton explored the relationship of castration and sex to survival and longevity in domestic cats. His findings are illuminating. The death rate of intact males was particularly high in the years immediately following sexual maturation. If the cats survived these years they had a good chance for a long life. "When the deleterious effects of testicular functions were eliminated by castration the percentage of long-life cats was as large in the males as in the females." Furthermore, "mortality rates tended to be lower in castrated than in intact males throughout life" (39). This would imply that the death rate from all causes, including accidents which are not usually considered to be biologically determined, were lower among castrated than intact male cats. Of course, the findings would have to be explored more thoroughly, but they are certainly suggestive. For example, we know that among humans, as well as cats, the rate of accidental deaths among males immediately following sexual maturation is unusually high. Perhaps it would be well to pursue this from a biological as well as from a social and psychological standpoint.

It is certainly reasonable to assume that variations in the amount of sex hormones in the human organism can produce changes in affective tone ("mood"), energy level, and tension, thus altering one's perception of the world. Is it not also reasonable to assume that such perceptual alterations may render one more prone to depression, and/or suicide; or make suicide appear temporarily to be a desirable alternative—or the only one? There is one further statistic which may be of interest in this connection. It has been reported that the suicide rate among pregnant women is only one-sixth that of the nonpregnant (40). When one considers the difficult situations in which some pregnant women find themselves, this statistic is all the more noteworthy. Do the amount and kind of hormones secreted in pregnancy so alter the psychological state that difficult situations appear less so? Or is the knowledge and the fact of pregnancy itself—that one has someone to live for or a special role in life—primarily responsible?

There are, of course, a number of equally plausible alternatives to the purely biological explanations. In the first place, there is no evidence that suicidal behavior, with sex held constant, is "inherited." Kallman's studies of identical twins indicate that twins are not concordant for suicide (41). "Familial suicide" is apparently not the result of hereditary, but of environmental influences. Secondly, one cannot ignore the obvious and crucial impact of social attitudes and sexual stereotyping. The adventurous risk-taking behavior generally thought to epitomize occidental masculinity can have dire consequences. One of these is the involvement in situations that are likely to prove lethal. The "all-boy" boy who plays *Tarzan* and fractures his ankle in a fall from a tree might just as easily have fractured his skull. Whatever it is that prompts a young man to leap into the water to save a drowning girl may prove his undoing when he is caught in the same undertow that has trapped her. The bravado an ailing man musters to carry on despite annoying symptoms may postpone what could have been a lifesaving visit to his physician.

The female, by contrast, tends to display less physical bravery. This is reflected in accident statistics which reveal that the home is one of the few places in which the accident level for girls exceeds that for boys (42). In adulthood, too, the female spends more time at home and is less likely to expose herself to automobile, industrial, and hunting accidents. When she is ill, a woman generally consults a physician sooner and dutifully follows the therapeutic regimen he prescribes. Moreover, she very rarely engages in direct physical combat, even with those of her own sex and weight. Finally, while she attempts suicide with much greater

frequency than does the male (43), she usually manages to ensure that the outcome will not be fatal. But why? Are the culture and its customs—in short, primarily "external" factors—responsible for the higher male suicide and overall death rate? We do not have a definite answer. What we do have is another example of the chicken-egg controversy. For, after all, what can we blame for society's stereotyping of masculine characteristics if not masculine behavior itself?

Men today seem to be killing themselves at a faster rate than do women (Chapters 14 and 15). If both biological and cultural factors play important roles (which certainly seems likely), we can attribute the higher male suicide rate at least partly to so-called "masculine" traits regardless of their origin. Since males apparently are more aggressive, they must also have more hostility available to introject and, since they are also supposed to be more impulsive and/or more decisive, and possessed of greater physical bravery, men may be more willing and able to make a decision that is irrevocable, and to follow it through despite pain and mutilation. In support of the foregoing, it should be noted that female suicide attempters are more likely to employ such techniques as sleeping pills or relatively ineffectual poisons—techniques that bespeak ambivalence and require but little bravery (44). Men are likely to use a gun or an explosive, a technique that is not only more effective but may also possess unconscious masculine or specifically phallic significance as well. The fact is that the patterns of both the suicide rate and what constitutes masculine as opposed to feminine suicide behavior seem to cross national and racial boundaries. This could be construed, rather loosely, as a kind of support for a biological hypothesis. However, there are other data that may undermine this hypothesis.

According to Hutchin (45), "while today the number of men who die in middle age is double the number of women, a hundred years ago the figures were roughly equal." Furthermore, in this country, male suicides have not always exceeded female suicides at every age. In 1910, for example, white girls between 15 and 19 years of age had a suicide rate significantly higher than that for boys of the same age (46). Thereafter, the rate for girls declined, crossed that for boys in 1920, and decreased until by 1960 it was less than one-third that of young men. The boys' rate has remained essentially unchanged. One might assume that basic human nature, especially that of the female, has altered radically over the past half century. But it may be better simply to recognize that significant changes have occurred in living conditions, expectations, opportunities for self-expression, and a host of other psychological and social aspects of life. In fact, one might say that as the social, individual, and economic opportunities for American women increased, their suicide rate decreased.

Another kind of evidence that may seem to support the role of cultural rather than biological factors as determinants of masculine, and hence, *perhaps*, of suicidal behavior, is the data accumulated by cultural anthropologists. Early in her career, Margaret Mead studied several primitive societies in which the patterns of masculine and feminine behavior were very different from our own (47). In some, the men and the women "reversed" traditional roles; and in others the men and the women tended, to a great extent, to share each other's roles. These variations may cast doubt on the view that sex typing is primarily biologically based. However, let us look again at the suicide statistics for the period 1910 to 1960. We have already noted that the suicide rate for women changed drastically during that period of social change and that the rate for males 15-19 remained constant. Yet, there were social changes for the men too. The constancy of the male suicide rate in that half century might possibly be construed to lend some support to a biological hypothesis. We must come around to the conclusion that sex per se may have somewhat greater relevance in determining suicide than was previously believed, although we cannot specify precisely how this role is played. For whatever reason, there seems to be a greater development in males of those personality characteristics that predispose to self-destruction, or a lesser development of these characteristics in women.

Another question might be raised: are the differences in the male and female suicide rates ultimately and subtly related to sexual differences in the "biological clock?" It is in women that life has usually been thought to be governed by a biological clock. Cycles of physical and psychological change associated with the menstrual cycle and its termination have been recognized for centuries. The geometric figure most consistent with the female adult life would probably be the circle that is forever self-renewing. Could this cyclical pattern in some way be reflected in women's view of the world? Or perhaps the feminine time clock and suicide are related in another way. Some women do commit suicide; and the female suicide rate also rises with age. Since the rate is highest after the menopause when the "circle is broken," one might also inquire what relationship, if any, there is between the phase of menstrual cycle and its termination and the time of suicide or suicide attempts.

What of the masculine biological time clock? Does it in some way determine that male psychological resistance shall run down sooner or more completely than female? Are males so constituted that they have more vulnerable periods each day or each year? If there are differences in the biological clocks of males and females, are these necessarily biologically determined? Even if they are, can they not be altered? Or are all such notions too far-fetched? The biologist and comparative psychologist studying life patterns of lower organisms may yet have the last word about sex and death.

By now it should be quite apparent that there is more to the suicide statistics than first meets the eye. Even in the realm of sex, where we deal with two more or less discrete groups, it is almost impossible to discover the relative relationships among biological, environmental, and individual psychological factors. When we look for causes that are not directly observable, it is generally useful to find out what changes precede and/or accompany changes in the phenomena under investigation. We utilized this technique to some extent in discussing the increase of suicide in childhood, which we discovered was positively correlated with disturbed parent-child relationships, decreased family cohesiveness, intense stress, and geographic mobility. We will find this method to be of even greater value in the following paragraphs.

Race

We cannot clearly define the relationship between suicide and race when we consider race as a purely biological entity. Membership in a particular race tends to select and shape the individual's participation in many categories of experience. Be that as it may, the statistical fact is that suicide rates do differ from race to race and, moreover, these rates are changing.

Let us first consider some group differences that remained fairly stable for a long time. Formerly, the suicide rate of non-white Americans was significantly lower than that of white Americans. In 1959, for example, Dublin found that the suicide rate for whites of all ages was 11.2 per 100,000. At the same time, it was only 4.5 for the non-white population (48). He observed further that the rates for non-whites were even lower in the rural south and central United States than in the urban area of the north. In 1960, the rates for white and non-white males were similar in 25- to 34-year-old men,

but after age 34 "rates for the whites are from two to five times as high as those for the non-whites" (49). Dublin pointed out that it is the Negro rate that is (or was) low, while that for other non-whites was actually rather high.

Some of the reasons for this become clearer when one examines the fragmentary evidence now becoming available. For example, suicides among Negroes in Washington, D.C., have jumped 16 percent over the past six years but, during the same period, the Negro population has increased only 17 percent (50). In a recent article in *Ebony Magazine*, John Woodford discussed the problem of why Negro suicides are increasing. Woodford observes that since 1946 "the suicide rate of Negro men has almost doubled," and that of these suicides "almost two-thirds take place in the financially secure, even wealthy group" (51). Woodford notes that this belies the contention that "suicide is monopolized by the sensitive, the rich, the intelligent—meaning the white man," an hypothesis sometimes advanced to explain the fact that white Americans previously had a suicide rate three times that of Negroes. He calls American suicide "a kind of luxury—because it is committed by those whose physical needs are satisfied enough to free them to mull over personal internal problems" (52). Woodford also believes that segregation may have "preserved the sanity of many Negroes, for when the mind is occupied by daily external problems it cannot feed upon itself. . . . During World War II, for instance, the suicide rate for Negroes dropped twenty percent but the postwar economic boom has brought a suicide boom too" (53). (This last, incidentally is true for the population as a whole, not just for Negroes. It has been demonstrated repeatedly that suicide rates decrease in times of war. See Chapter 12.)

Woodford's comments are particularly enlightening because they show how the increased suicide rate among Negroes can be directly related to increased vertical mobility, psychological stress, shifting roles, social instability, and a host of other factors that are part of the Negro revolution.

We have been discussing and comparing primarily white and Negro suicide rates because they provide insight into the kinds of factors that can lead to suicide. However, the suicide rates for Oriental Americans can also be understood as illustrations, albeit less dramatic ones, of some of the same points. Historically, Oriental Americans, although at first subjected to prejudice, have had a much more favorable position in American society than have Negroes. Having emigrated voluntarily from their homelands, rather than being forced to come as slave laborers, Orientals could maintain an intact family, and were paid for their work. With less discrimination to impede them, and an opportunity to secure better education, the Orientals as a group have always belonged to a higher socioeconomic class than have the Negroes. They have also had suicide rates that have been at least comparable to—often higher—than those of white Americans (54). They have not only been in a position to "enjoy" the dubious luxury of suicide, of which Woodford speaks, but they also have had a traditional acceptance of suicide which places few psychological barriers between the potential suicide and his act.

How can we reconcile the high suicide rate of a more highly privileged minority group with the increasing suicide rate of one of the most suppressed minorities? For a clue, let us return for a moment to the statistics on suicide of young American girls living early in the present century. We have already mentioned that their suicide rate decreased as their social, individual, and economic opportunities increased. At first glance, the statistics on the Negro American seem to be the reverse. As their opportunities are increasing, so also is their suicide rate. But what does this phenomenon mean? In 1910, the young American woman was begin-

ning to question the traditions which bound her to hearth, home, and silent servitude. She eventually took up arms, so to speak, in defiance of social custom (and often of her husband as well) and campaigned openly for the real and symbolic vote. It was during this era that the suicide rate of young women—unsettled by present changes and unsure of their place in the future—was at its height. This situation appears similar to that in which the Negro in America, especially the male, finds himself today. People in a society of rising expectations are more vulnerable, psychologically, to increasing frustrations. To live in marginal economic circumstances in a society that is poverty-stricken in general is less difficult to bear than the perceived contrast between one's own plight and the "high life" being enjoyed by others. This contrast becomes truly painful when the underprivileged person recognizes that he does have some opportunity to better his circumstances. He is likely to develop a state of disequilibrium in which he can neither continue to accommodate himself to a relatively deprived way of life nor develop much confidence in the prospect of achieving the more desirable way of life that now tantalizes him. Living with this kind of discomfort, the individual may be tempted to resolve the ambiguity and uncertainty by extreme behavior such as violence directed either inwardly or outwardly.

One might venture, then, that when an American Negro is relatively unaffected by this sort of "suicidogenic" situation, he: a) has not yet taken seriously the prospect of breaking out of his disadvantaged circumstances; b) has exceptional talents or good fortune, and thus is able to fulfill his rising expectations without going through a long period of uncertainty and frustration; or c) has an unusual ability to tolerate uncertainty and frustration. It would naturally follow that suicidal risks would be found most frequently among those Negroes who a) are oriented toward improving their life situation, but b) encounter serious obstacles that result in a prolonged phase of uncertainty and frustration, while c) their personal capacities for tolerating inner tension and ambiguity are not exceptional. And, of course, it is entirely possible that the frustrations can be so intense and pervasive that even a person with exceptional abilities to tolerate inner tension is finally forced to a breaking point.

Attainment of a more favorable way of life does not necessarily remove the possibility of suicidal risk. Vertical mobility may have the correlates of weakening the bonds between the "emerging" Negro and those who have yet to "make it" while, at the same time, locating him in a new social context, predominantly white, that does not grant him full emotional acceptance. The first few waves of "successful" Negroes thus may experience continuing insecurity and uncertainty related to their very recent transition.

Psychological and social factors such as those we have been considering often appear to have more utility in understanding self-destructive behavior than does the bare fact of membership in a particular racial or quasi-racial group. Furthermore, it is now distinctly unpopular even to raise the question as to whether or not certain behaviors or psychological characteristics can be attributed to one's membership in a particular race. The brutal misuse of hypotheses about racial characteristics—and the extremely dubious nature of many of the hypotheses themselves—has led many behavioral scientists and others to discredit the subject entirely. It is painful to recall the misery that people have inflicted upon each other in the name of so-called "racial superiority"; one would not wish to add any materials that might lead to further distortions. However, this consideration of possible racial factors in suicide would not be complete without discussion of the hypothesis that there is a relatively direct relationship between self-destructive behavior and race.

William McDougall argued that certain personality predispositions as well as physical characteristics are inherent in people in accord with the mixture of racial "bloods" in their endowment (55). While strongly denouncing the proponents of an alleged super-race, McDougall proposed that temperament varies widely among different racial strains. Based upon his interpretation of the then-current state of knowledge in physical anthropology (circa 1919-1925), he distinguished among three great racial strains that have contributed to the population of Europe: Alpine, Mediterranean, and Nordic. We will consider here only his comparisons of the "Mediterranean" and "Nordic" strains, which happen to be most relevant to the topic of suicide.

The Nordic individual, tall, fair-haired and fair-skinned, is said to be "constitutionally introvert" while the Mediterranean, shorter and darker, is "constitutionally extrovert" (56). McDougall follows Jung (57) in his specification of the introvert-extrovert contrast. In McDougall's words, "The well-marked extroverts are those whose emotions flow out easily into bodily expression and action. They are the vivid, vivacious, active persons who charm us by their ease and freedom of expression, their frankness, their quick sympathetic responses. They are little given to introspective brooding; they remain relatively ignorant of themselves; for they are essentially objective, they are interested directly and primarily in the outer world about them. When and if they break down under strain, their trouble takes on the hysteric type, the form of dissociations, paralyses, anesthesias, amnesias; in spite of which they may remain cheerful, active, and interested in the world." By contrast, the introvert ". . . is slow and reserved in the expression of his emotions. He has difficulty in adequately expressing himself. His nervous and mental energies, instead of flowing out freely to meet and play upon the outer world, seem apt to turn inward, determining him to brooding, reflection, deliberation before action. And, when he is subject to strain, his energies are absorbed in internal conflicts; he becomes dead to the outer world, languid, absorbed, self-centered, and full of vague distress" (58).

McDougall insists that this difference between constitutional types cannot be explained adequately on the basis of differential environment or training. Hereditary factors, he says, are the most important. What is especially relevant here is McDougall's effort to demonstrate: a) that people of Nordic and Mediterranean racial strains differ markedly in their suicide rates; and b) that this specific difference is but one example of general and basic differences that are expressed in such characteristics as type of religious experience preferred, the nature of the art that is created and appreciated, tendencies toward homicide, and leadership capabilities.

Examining the frequency of suicide by geographical regions, especially in England and France, McDougall offers the conclusion that high rates prevail in those locales that are populated chiefly by people with Nordic ancestry and characteristics. He acknowledges that Nordics generally occupy the regions of greatest industrial activity and prosperity, "but *that* they occupy these regions is a fact which in turn requires explanation" (59). Obviously, McDougall is proposing that constitutional differences strongly influence the kind of environment that a given people select or develop.

In further support of his position, McDougall suggests that "Suicide is a form of violence, of homicide; we might, then, on superficial consideration, expect to find suicide most frequent where other forms of violence and of homicide abound. But the facts are just converse of this expectation. It is in Southern Italy, Corsica, and Sardinia, where the population is mostly Mediterranean, that crimes of violence, especially homicide, are most

frequent; while suicide is very infrequent" (60). Finally, McDougall finds that "these peculiar features of the distribution of suicide and homicide are in perfect harmony with the conclusions we have drawn from the comparison of the arts of Northern and Southern Europe; they are just what we should expect, if the three European races differ in mental constitution in the ways assumed by our hypothesis" (61).

According to McDougall, then, the Nordic tends to be an introvert, a rather unsociable person who will brood over his discontents and develop strong internal conflicts. The Mediterranean, by contrast, is not likely to brood—he attacks the problem directly, which, in some cases, means physical assault upon those who have offended him.

Today it seems more difficult to make out a persuasive case for the validity or even the usefulness of the assumed Nordic-Mediterranean-Alpine racial triad. Undoubtedly, however, the last word on this topic has yet to be spoken, and such distinctions might again come into good repute. The extrovert-introvert distinction, apart from its possible link with racially-determined constitutional endowments, continues to attract scientific and clinical attention (62). Whatever one cares to make of the racial hypothesis put forth by McDougall, there may be value in further explorations of the possibility that very early in life individuals exhibit temperamental predispositions that either favor or inhibit the development of suicidal tendencies. The significance of environmental factors (economic, social, etc.) in shaping one's orientation toward self-destruction need not deter us from investigating the possibility of predispositions that may be linked directly to genetic endowment.

If race, biological endowment, age, and sex are held constant, what then determines which people will be prone to suicide?

Thus far we have emphasized the role of social and biological factors in suicide, with periodic reminders that it is not usually the objective situation but one's attitudes toward the situation and himself that are crucial. For every individual who sees economic reverses, a chronic illness, or the loss of a loved one as a sufficient reason to end it all there are countless others who have met and mastered situations that are objectively similar. Even the Nordic who is "full of vague distress" may not destroy himself. Obviously the key word here is "objective," for situations which externally may seem identical can be vastly different in their subjective, symbolic significance and intensity for those who actually experience them. Yet, we cannot usefully consider suicide the result solely of *individual* psychological factors. If we did, then how could we explain the significant differences in the suicide rates of different national and religious *groups?* Before we can focus on the individual psychological bases of suicide, we must first find some way to bridge the gap, or at least to define the relationship, between culture and personality. Only then can we hope to understand both the social and individual roots of suicide. Let us examine first the nature of these group differences: What explanations are plausible as well as consistent with the facts we have already discussed?

Subcultural Group Membership: National Origin and Religion

Dear God,

I am the only one in my class who is Chinese. They all say that you are American but, I am too, so you could be Chinese, right?

Your friend,

Kim (63)

Man is said to have created God in his own image. Children are more direct about this than adults. The son of one of the authors recently informed her: "God

has brown hair and wears blue sneakers." It doesn't take much imagination to figure out the hair and shoe color of this juvenile seer. In a mixed society it is doubtless hard for people to feel secure in their own beliefs and customs. They can attempt to perpetuate their particular views of life and death and to follow family and group traditions, but they are constantly being challenged by the external, larger, superimposed culture that is the "American way of life." Does subcultural group membership affect suicidal *potential?* To what extent and why?

In the early years of twentieth-century America, separate little subcultures based on national origin and/or religion were commonplace and easily discerned. Almost every large city had its Germantown, Little Italy, and neighborhoods that were predominately Irish, Polish, Greek, Jewish, etc. Generally, each of these subgroups had its own special marital, dietary, and child-rearing customs. People from the same country often shared the same religion and tended to agree in their attitudes toward death, bereavement, and burial customs. It was possible to be born, grow up, live, and die in one's own little neighborhood and scarcely ever have contact with anyone living in another ghetto of the same city. In fact, when young people of one area ventured into the territory of another, open warfare often ensued. It was not uncommon for people to be beaten, or even killed. Although the melting pot philosophy and the consequent increasing assimilation have appreciably altered this situation, there still remains some tendency for people of the same national origin or religion to congregate in one area and attempt to perpetuate some of their forebears' customs and institutions. In light of this, it is scarcely surprising to discover that the suicide rates of the various national groups in the United States (and, presumably, in other mixed societies) differ both from each other and from that of the native born population. Dublin found that "the differences which exist among foreign born populations are like those found in their respective homelands, although they tend to be greater here than there" (64).

Let us examine, for future reference, the specifics of the suicide rates for certain groups in the United States. The Germans, Scandinavians, and Austrians have consistently had high suicide rates. The English and Norwegian rates are somewhat lower, although still fairly high. Further, and by contrast, almost all studies that include them show that the Irish and Italians have rather low suicide rates (65). How can these findings be explained? We cannot attribute these group differences in suicide rates to intrinsic biological characteristics or to the effects of racial prejudice, for the national groups considered do not constitute separate races, unless one supports McDougall's thesis that "Nordics" and "Mediterraneans" truly represent racial types. If we are to understand the data, we must turn our attention to the area of cultural differences. Since it is the individual and not the entire culture which commits suicide, it is legitimate to ask:

1. How does the culture contribute to personality development?
2. Why do some cultures produce more suicidal individuals than others?

Several theories that attempt to explain the role of culture in personality development are available but it is not within the scope, or consistent with the goals, of this book to review all of them here. However, if we are to develop tenable hypotheses concerning the effects of group differences on suicide rates, it is necessary to present at least one of the theories that can bridge the gap between culture and personality. The theory we have chosen for this purpose is that of Abraham Kardiner (66). Apparently, there is something in this theory which makes it appear uniquely applicable to suicide, for Herbert Hendin selected it to use in his cross-cultural study of suicide in Scandinavia (see p. 268).

Kardiner's fundamental concept is "basic personality," which is defined as "that personality configuration shared by the bulk of society's members because of the early experiences they have in common." Reduced to its barest essentials, the theory holds simply that the child-rearing practices of any culture tend to be institutionalized. Thus, these practices provide a common core of experiences to which most of the children are exposed. Frustrations in childhood are responsible for the modifications of personality that, in adult life, will constitute unconscious character patterns. These, in turn, are the wellsprings of projective systems that are characterized by symbolic extension or the application to situations vastly different from those on which they were based. Since the projective systems arise under the influence of the Freudian pleasure principle, their purpose is adaptation in the form of tension reduction. Often this adaptation takes the form of long-range anticipation of tension reduction. The widespread belief in a personalistic deity who will reward the earthly sufferings of the virtuous after death has frequently been explained in this way. In fact, Kardiner considers religion and folklore to be the purest manifestations of the prevalent systems which constitute the culture's basic personality. What the child is not permitted to do is replaced by compensatory behavior and comes to be defended by rationalizations. The rationalizations—later ideologies—form the basis of the institutions that govern the training of future children and, hence, perpetuate the basic personality. Kardiner's theory originally had reference to so-called "primitive" societies.

The societies of industrialized countries, but most particularly those of the United States, are more complex. Yet, even these highly complicated societies are made up of a multitude of sometimes overlapping, sometimes quite discrete subcultures, each with its own more or less unique customs and institutions. Each of these self-perpetuating subgroups undoubtedly does exemplify to some extent the processes described by Kardiner. Each, therefore, lays the foundation for a somewhat different "basic personality." However, in the United States, the integration of different groups, the exposure of groups to each other and to the leveling influence of the mass media tend to dilute subcultural differences, or at least to render them less obvious. Nevertheless, more or less distinguishable basic personality configurations for different subcultures do persist and, we hypothesize, are responsible for the different suicide rates in the various subcultures.

What kinds of child-rearing practices and early experiences set the stage for suicide? Hendin's study of suicide in Denmark, Sweden, and Norway provides an example of one type of research into this problem as well as important data and provocative leads (67). In each country, he tried to discover the underlying dynamics and link them to the child-rearing practices which, in turn, he related to the suicide rate. Hendin found that Danish mothers tended to encourage their children to be dependent, to inhibit open expression of aggression, and to use the arousal of guilt (for causing others to suffer) as "the principal form of discipline" (68). The suicide rate in Denmark is very high; the homicide rate very low. Hendin believes that the marked dependency concern of Danes explains their vulnerability to depression and suicide following the termination of relationships (69). Suicidal patients' fantasies of "reunion after death with a lost loved one" are so "common as to be almost the rule" (70).

The suicide rate in Sweden is also very high, but Hendin found the child-rearing patterns and problems of suicidal patients to be very different from those in Denmark. He noted that Swedish mothers strongly encourage children to be inde-

pendent and self-sufficient. Mothers are described, by a child psychiatrist whom Hendin quotes, as "not experiencing . . . pleasure from their children whether playing with them or caring for them" (71). Hendin believes that Swedish children's early separation from their mothers is responsible for much anxiety and resentment. Although both boys and girls are separated from their mothers early in life, boys are outside of the house and are left alone more than are girls between five and ten years of age. Because girls are expected to help with the housekeeping, they are in the house more and in closer contact with their mothers than are the boys. Hendin suggests that this proximity may work to the girls' psychological advantage (72).

This may be an important idea. Girls in most modern societies, even in our own relatively emancipated society, are home with mother more than boys are. Thus, they have a double advantage: a) more and closer contact with mother; and b) the availability, for identification purposes, of the parent of the same sex. Perhaps this partially explains why women have a lower suicide rate than men. Hendin believes that Swedish women who are suicidal have been influenced by experiences associated with relatively early separation from their mothers. Thus, in one suicidal group "repeated male infidelity or total abandonment" were found to be precipitating factors (73). We noted earlier that, even in Scandinavia, the female suicide rate is far exceeded by the male rate. In addition to greater contact with the mother, females are allowed, from childhood on, greater latitude in expressing feelings. Little girls may even be allowed an undirected temper tantrum (74). Boys, by contrast, are expected to be quiet, calm, and unemotional even when under great stress. Furthermore, the Swedish male not only experiences early separation from his mother; he is also subjected to great pressure to do well at school. This is apparently of much importance, for Hendin found that, when he is suicidal, the Swedish male is likely to suffer intense anxiety and frustration about his lack of success.

In Norway, where the suicide rate is low, Hendin discovered still a third set of child-rearing patterns. Although Norwegian mothers want their children to be independent, they are likely to make them the center of their own emotional life. Despite this, they allow children much physical freedom and are happy about their accomplishments. The mothers do not make affection conditional upon success. Children may win affection by being good and behaving well, something most of them can learn to do. Norwegians are also found to be much freer in expressing aggression verbally. Young boys are encouraged to fight back if attacked. Since suicide is considered by many to be the result of directing against the self the murderous hostility one feels toward another, it follows that extrapunitive behavior may be a kind of protection against suicide.

Much of the above discussion could be considered over-simplification. Our purpose here has been merely to point out the contrasts which Hendin noted in the child rearing practices of three Scandinavian countries and their possible relationship to the differential suicide rates. But, obviously, if Kardiner's theory, on which Hendin's study was based, is correct, it should also be applicable to the subcultures in the United States. Since German-Americans and Italian-Americans have widely different suicide rates—the former high, the latter low—we should expect the child-rearing practices and family constellations of these two subcultures to differ significantly in some consistent ways. Although this possibility remains to be determined, we do have some information about the "basic personality" of Italians. Luigi Barzini has commented extensively on Italian national character (75). Some of his ideas may help to explain the relatively low Italian suicide

rate. He claims that there has never been a "race" (sic) so desolate as the Italians, whose pessimism he attributes to the sad, often dangerous lives they lead in Italy. He claims that Italians have been able to escape suicide and madness by adopting the view that life is a show. Italian men feign exaggerated interest in women and food, and live in what Barzini describes as a "baroque" style in which they derive their pleasures by playing to an audience (a point on which McDougall would agree). He stresses that there is a side to Italian character that requires bolstering by formalities and that rates external appearances as very important. Barzini considers that, for most Italians, family life is true "patriarchism": Italian families tend to be fairly large, and when two people marry, their families, in a sense, marry also. Defense of the family and loyalty to it are paramount. How might a child reared in such an atmosphere be protected from suicide? For one thing, he would always have someone to turn to, a group to whom he is important, and a sense of belonging. Secondly, woes and joys could, in a way, be distributed among family members, who present a united front to the outside, and to common "enemies." Since Italians are much given to expressive behavior, one could also argue that aggression is thereby released and not available for introjective self-punishment.

On the basis of the foregoing, it would seem that differences in the suicide rates of various national groups are at least partially attributable to different child-rearing practices and family styles. The same kinds of explanations, somewhat modified and refocused, can be applied to differences in the suicidal behavior of the major religious groups in the United States. Generally speaking, Catholics and orthodox Jews have lower suicide rates than do Protestants (76). It should be noted, however, that there is considerable overlapping of national and religious groups. For example, most Italians are Catholics; most Swedes and Danes are

Protestants. The English (with intermediate suicide rates) tend to be Protestant also; and many American Jews came originally from Slavic countries where the suicide rates were formerly intermediate or rather low (77).

Child-rearing practices and social structure are no less pertinent to the understanding of suicide in Oriental nations. Reviewing his own studies and those of other investigators, Iga has recently proposed that there is a modal personality type among those who attempt suicide in contemporary urban Japan (78). A triad of personality factors begins to emerge early in the life of the potential suicide: dependency, self-assertion, and insecurity. The child is encouraged to become very dependent on his mother, whose needs for self-assertion and achievement can be fulfilled only through her son. Furthermore, the "child is the only object for unrestrained expression of the mother's affection in a formalistic authoritarian society . . ." (79).

The child lives in something akin to a pressure cooker. He *must* succeed if he is to satisfy his own achievement needs and those of his mother. However, the roads to success are relatively few and the obstacles are many. Incessant competition in school must be survived if the youngster is to gain admittance to a "good" university—and only by graduating from such a university is he likely to receive a desirable job offer from a large firm. Employment by a large firm is considered desirable because it provides a measure of financial security in a society where "unemployment is a constant threat . . . where the superior's whim and rumor can ruin the individual's security. Once unemployed, a person seldom obtains a respectable job. Even if fortunate enough to find a new job, he will have to start again at the bottom, with a low salary and with little hope of rapid promotion" (80).

Strong dependency and an intense desire for success are characteristics that seem likely to produce a continuing sense of insecurity. Frustrating encounters with a social structure that does not provide ready fulfillments for the needs it has fostered could well escalate insecurity into a crisis of despair. Yet we should bear in mind that in Japan, as elsewhere, the combination of potentially suicidal dynamics and a frustrating external situation does not invariably lead to an attempt at self-destruction. It is possible, for example, that many people continue to live with a feeling of despair, reducing their expectations for gratification and generally showing a resigned attitude. A partial death of the self might be the alternative to outright and complete self-murder. Why does one Japanese youth commit suicide while another who appears to be in identical life circumstances takes an alternate pathway? Obviously, we have much to learn about the relationship between the individual's inner personality dynamics and his relationship to the social structure.

In addition to the unique institutionalized practices of the different countries and those implicit in the teachings of various religions there is another factor that may be of significance in determining the individual's susceptibility to suicide: the attitude of his religion toward death in general and suicide in particular. The Japanese suicide rate, for example, has always been high. It seems likely that this high rate has been related to the traditional attitude which held suicide to be an especially honorable death. Thus, cultural differences in suicide can themselves be seen as an "over-determined" function of many variables.

Marital Status and Socioeconomic Level

The statistical relationship between marital status and suicide can be summarized briefly: among males, the suicide rate is lowest for the married, higher for the unmarried, still higher for the widowed, and highest for the divorced. Among females, the suicide rate is lower overall. However, the rates do differ depending on marital status and, while these differences are less pronounced, they follow a pattern similar to that for males. One further factor should be noted. The suicide rate is lower among those who have children, especially among women (81). It goes without saying that one can hardly attribute suicide to marital status per se. Physical health, the sex ratio in various locales, socioeconomic status, religion, and a host of other factors affect those who can and will marry. Since institutionalized people and those with severe physical and mental handicaps are likely to be excluded from marriage as well as from participation in a host of other social institutions, we would expect their suicide rate to be higher than that of married people. This in fact is borne out. Since suicide frequently follows upon object loss, the high suicide rate for the widowed appears understandable. For the divorced, the determinants must be more complex. The "object loss" in this case is often arranged by the victim. This fact raises many questions. What kind of individual gets divorced and why? What life situations and/or family constellations are related to divorce? Are these same social and family situations positively correlated with the suicide rate in the absence of divorce? In other words, is marital status ever really a determinant of suicide or do some of those factors that result in divorce, of themselves, predispose to suicide?

The relationship between suicide and socioeconomic status is not altogether clear. In Britain, data show that the suicide rate during the working years is higher in the upper and lower classes than in the middle class. From the age of 65 on—the so-called retirement years—the highest suicide rates are found among lower-class unskilled males (82). These findings differ from those in the United States in that there is little variation in the suicide rates of all the upper classes. The rate among non-farm laborers is the highest, although that for farm workers is also high (83). In general, however, although varying in particular from country to country, suicide rates in the Western world tend to be highest at both extremes of the socioeconomic ladder. There is also some evidence that members of certain professions are particularly suicide prone, e.g., physicians, dentists, lawyers. On the basis of limited data, the suicide rates of teachers and of clergymen of some denominations are quite low (84).

Are these findings primarily a function of the personality traits possessed by people who enter these professions or do they result from the kind of life that the occupations require one to lead? We all know, for example, that physicians, dentists, and some lawyers are likely to be under a good deal of pressure much of the time. They must often put other people's needs before their own, make important decisions rapidly, and follow an irregular schedule. In addition, it has often been pointed out that physicians and dentists have ready access to materials that can be employed in suicide attempts and they know how to use them. On the other hand, people are rarely forced into entering these occupations. Physicians, dentists, and lawyers choose their professions freely and usually know in advance about some of the difficulties they are likely to encounter. Furthermore, the vast majority of people in these professions are male and, until recently, have tended to be mostly Caucasian Protestants as well. Teachers, by contrast, are more likely to be female and to live more predictable lives. It also appears that a significant proportion come from the middle or lower-middle classes. Clergymen, of course, would be likely to have strong negative attitudes toward suicide and to lead fairly well regulated lives. The socioeconomic groups from which they come vary greatly. It would be interesting to determine the relationship between the suicide rates of clergymen and their socio-economic levels as well as their denominations.

Despite all the complicating factors of sex, occupation, etc., it is possible to see relationships between a society's overall economic state and its suicide rate. It has been found that, roughly, suicide rates fluctuate in accord with business cycles. When the employment level is high and the country prosperous, the male suicide rate is usually low and the female rate remains unchanged. During periods of economic depression it is the suicide rate of "higher level" men that is most affected (85). Is this because men at higher socio-economic levels tend to fall into categories that generally have a higher level of suicides? Perhaps. We noted earlier that older males have the highest suicide rate, and that, before one achieves economic success, he has usually entered middle age. Then, too, in the past only whites and Orientals were allowed access to the "gateways" (education and entry occupations) to economic success; and most of them came from, or descended from, people who came from western Europe or the Orient, both of which have high suicide rates. Which of these interrelated factors came first and set the whole pattern in motion?

Let us reconsider the foregoing data for a moment and summarize what we have discovered thus far. This should enable us to establish the suicidal potential of broad categories of individuals, provided that past trends persist. For example, divorced white, elderly, upper middle-class, Protestant, Swedish-born American males will be among the most likely to commit suicide. We have already discussed some of the possible reasons for this. However, it is obvious that all that has been said is of little or no value in predicting, and hence, ultimately preventing the suicide of any *one* particular individual. If all of the interacting variables discussed are basic to suicide, then why do not all of those in the high suicide risk group kill themselves? And what explains the occasional suicide of the young married, middle-class Irish or Italian born Catholic girl? Many laymen think they know the answer: mental illness.

Mental Illness

It is often said: "You have to be crazy to kill yourself." If by "crazy" one means only being emotionally upset or possessed of personality problems, this contention can scarcely be disputed. If, however, what is meant by "crazy" is mental illness per se, or psychosis in particular, then we cannot agree. The incidence of recognizable mental illness among suicidal victims has been variously reported ("one-third," "more than half," "twenty percent") (86) as has the incidence of suicide among those previously diagnosed as being psychotic (30 to 40 annually per 90,000 patients at a New York State Hospital, 34 annually per 100,000 New York State residents between April, 1957, and March, 1959) (87). In no instance does the reported incidence of psychosis among suicide victims or suicide among psychotics even remotely approach 100 percent. Obviously: a) one does not have to be crazy to commit suicide; and b) most people who are psychotic do not kill themselves.

Not surprisingly, however, suicide rates are high among patients who suffer from involutional melancholia or manic depressive psychosis (88). There also appears to be a marked suicidal hazard among some, but by no means all, schizophrenics (89).

Schizophrenia itself could be considered a sort of suicide equivalent or "psychic death." Perhaps it is the individual not yet deep in his psychosis or just emerging therefrom, and hence symbolically not completely dead, who is most likely to be suicidal. This could be: a) because he has not completely satisfied his wish for death in psychosis; or b) because he is not totally out of contact and hence realizes his situation. This latter reason has sometimes been invoked to explain the suicide of psychotics who are emerging from psychosis but are still depressed. When they begin to understand the gravity of their situation they may attempt suicide. Both authors have seen this occur, and such "data" are much more compelling in real life than in theory.

Despite all of this, it is of little use to say that so-and-so committed suicide because of a particular mental illness unless the diagnostic label employed is a shorthand term for constellations of symptoms or underlying dynamics that inevitably lead to suicide. For, if one attributes suicide to schizophrenia, we can legitimately inquire, "Why does one become schizophrenic, or what is it about this disease which often results in suicide?" Farberow, Shneidman and Leonard studied 60 schizophrenic patients, equally divided between those who committed suicide and those who did not (90). They noted that certain characteristics seemed to distinguish the suicidal from the control patients. The hospitalized schizophrenics who were suicidal seemed to feel under stress and were "tense, restless, and impulsive" (91). This kind of behavior can by no means be considered characteristic of suicidal schizophrenics alone. It is undoubtedly also common to many nonpsychotics who commit suicide as well as to many people who, under stress, decide to "do something" about their tension other than committing suicide. This something may frequently be of an adaptive or creative nature. In the majority of cases, one would, of course, have no information. However, the fact that it may sometimes be possible to distinguish potentially suicidal schizophrenics could of course be of great practical value.

It is also interesting to note that the differences between suicidal psychotics and nonpsychotics may not be primarily a qualitative one at all. It is quite possible that the basic causes of suicide among psychotics are often much the same as those for suicide among nonpsychotics and have their roots in the childhood experiences and present life situations of the victim, as does the illness itself, perhaps. It is interesting, for example, that the rates of nonpsychotic suicides and of psychosis among people bereaved in early childhood are both unusually high (Chapter 7).

Bettelheim has spoken of the "delayed action mines" of childhood, and it may be useful to think in terms of such "mines" when we attempt to understand the adult suicide victim. Apparently, the potentially suicidal individual: a) has severe underlying problems for which the usual kinds of adult psychological defenses are inadequate when challenged by additional stress; or b) has, because of his basic problems, been fixated at an early developmental stage and has never developed adequate adult defenses—consequently, ordinary life problems seem overwhelming; or c) has a combination of these two defense problems.

The credibility of these propositions is supported by the fragmentary data concerning the motives for suicide. Tabachnick, who studied a group of suicide attempters, found that a feeling of rejection seemed important, and that the suicide attempt was made sometime after criticism by a "mothering figure." He believes that an early disturbance of the child's relationship with the mother or the mother surrogate is a major dynamic factor in attempted suicide (92). Batchelor found that the breaking up of their homes during childhood seemed to play a significant part in causing the suicide attempts of young psychopathic individuals (93). Family disorganization was implicated as a major factor in suicide in a series of studies by Tuckman, et al (94, 95, 96). Tuckman suggests that a wide variety of maladaptive behaviors may be attempted before the victim of a broken or disorganized home resorts to suicide. "Mentally ill" behaviors may or may not be among the pre-suicidal alternatives for a given individual. Wahl holds that the major problem which suicide tries to solve is an identification conflict. If the individual is abandoned by his parents or if he believes that his parents hold negative attitudes toward him, his self-concept may be that of a "debased and inadequate person" (97). Such a person may well become preoccupied with suicidal fantasies, but what determines whether he will act on them?

SUICIDE PREVENTATIVES

What kinds of objects, situations, or events interfere with the initiation or completion of suicidal acts? Of course, we seldom know of the seemingly insignificant events that break a train of thought or interrupt a plan of action that would have culminated in suicide. (The accidental discovery of a dying suicide victim who has almost gained his end does not really enlighten us about the psychodynamic and social factors basic to the act unless we can demonstrate that his "accidental" discovery was, in fact, planned.) However, some information concerning suicide prevention is provided by two groups of suicidal individuals:

1. The first, and perhaps largest group, consists of *those who do not actually attempt suicide* but who appeal directly to others for help because of their suicidal thoughts. We would include in this category people who voluntarily contact suicide prevention centers, patients who commit themselves to mental hospitals, and those who inform psychotherapists, physicians, social agencies, or teachers of their suicidal promptings and appeal for aid. The amount and type of information available from such resources is uneven, incomplete and not always in a form which makes possible its organization and comparison. We have no way of determining how many people who ask for assistance are not taken seriously and later turn up in the suicide statistics. However, "in a recent New Hampshire

study nearly fifty percent of patients had consulted a physician shortly before suicide for a range of illnesses that were actually a mask for underlying depression or anxiety" (98). According to Dr. Mathew Ross, the most practical alerting clue for the physician to note is the presence of emotional disorder. He estimates that "about half of this illness is associated with depression and more than one-fourth with alcoholism (99). In these cases, Ross sees prevention as the responsibility of the physician who must recognize the danger signals and arrange hospitalization.

2. The second group, the suicide attempters, receive considerable attention. The following quote concerns some of those attempters referred to the Los Angeles Suicide Prevention Center: "It became immediately apparent that the individual's interpersonal relationships were very important in precipitating the suicide attempts and that the nature of these continuing relationships was significant in determining the prognosis. Thus a number of cases involving marital and parental relationships could be seen as family neuroses . . . " (100). The significance of this observation in the light of Kardiner's theory which we have already discussed and psychoanalytic theory per se, to be considered later, is compelling.

Wolberg has succinctly summarized the salient characteristics of a common type of suicide attempt: "Suicidal attempts in hysterical personalities are common and consist of histrionic gestures calculated to impress, frighten or force persons with whom the patient is in contact to yield attention and favors" (101). In these cases, an indirect request for help is made via the suicidal gesture itself. The danger is that the attempt may be too realistic and enthusiastic, and thus inadvertently become an accomplished suicide. The chief factor which often prevents the hysteric's suicide attempt from resulting in death is the matter of advance planning.

He must arrange to be found before it is too late. Unfortunately, an individual who is sufficiently disturbed and immature to resort to this kind of behavior may not be the world's best planner. It may even be that such apparent failures in foresight actually represent the unconscious intent of the victim. Perhaps by reassuring himself that it is only a gesture he is then able to accomplish his own death in what Shneidman has termed a 'subintentional' manner (102). These dynamics may not operate in every case. But the safest course is to regard every suicidal gesture, however superficial, as a genuine attempt. It may be relevant to remind ourselves at this point that *more suicides are attempted but not completed by females*. Are females more likely to be ambivalent and thus more likely to appeal for help? Or are the recipients of the pleas more willing, perhaps, to help females than males because of some reason that is presently obscure? Again, might it be that the methods utilized to assist female attempters are more appropriate to their basic problems than the methods utilized to assist male attempters? It is conceivable that the offer of a new and constructive interpersonal relationship operates as a more potent lifeline for women than for men.

In both of these groups of suicidal individuals, the only factor known to prevent suicide is the intervention of others. What does this tell us? The message could be that the individual abdicates responsibility for his own behavior. As a corollary, he delegates that responsibility to an outside agent who may or may not accept it. The suicidal person places himself in a position not unlike that of the small child. His life is in the hands of stronger outside agents. If they do not shoulder this heavy responsibility, then he will die—but, in that case, there may be nothing to live for anyway. Yet it could also be argued that, in some instances, the movement toward self-destruction actually begins with an enhanced sense of responsi-

bility. The person who sees his life as drifting out of control, heading from bad times to worse, possibly burdening others with his problems, might conclude that only one responsible action remains in his repertoire: suicide. One could protest that his action is in fact irresponsible. Yet the most relevant consideration might be that the individual himself has become convinced that this is the only responsible option that is left to him.

Attempters who fall into still another group, small but well publicized, may be able to teach us something about suicide prevention. These are the people who dramatize their attempts by climbing to the top of a tall building or by teetering on a high window ledge while a tense crowd watches. MacKenzie, reporting one such case, stated that people frequently can be induced to come down by reminding them of their family responsibilities, especially to their children (103). ("Think of how your children will feel," etc.) Why might this verbal intervention be effective? Perhaps reminders of this kind temporarily stabilize the vascillating self-image and bring the adult self into focus. The relatively mature and socialized aspects of the personality are reinforced at a critical moment of psychic instability.

Precisely what is it that hospitals, social agencies, or individual counselors provide that sometimes prevents suicide? They probably offer various mixtures of the following components: support for failing psychological defenses, external substitutes for internal controls, the feeling of personal worth (others are interested in saving his life, so it must be of value), affiliation with other human beings (he is not all alone in the world), a chance to release tension verbally ("to lay his burden on the Lord"), and an external object toward which to direct those impulses for which he previously had no real object other than self.

It would seem to follow logically that the potential suicide victim is often immature, psychologically alone, and possessed of low self-esteem and inadequate or rigid defenses—for such are the conditions which the interventions seem designed to mitigate. But it is one thing to draw up a list of characteristics that may be common among suicidal individuals, and another thing to construct a cohesive theory that integrates all the relevant variables. Is there an adequate theory of suicide? Let us examine what might be regarded as the two "classic" suicide theories, which are, to some extent, prototypes for all of the others.

THEORIES OF SUICIDE

Emile Durkheim's theory of suicide is primarily sociological, although it does take into account certain psychological factors. He proposes four categories of suicide but attention is usually limited to the first three: a) *egoistic* suicide, which results from the individual's lack of integration into society or into family life; b) *obligatory altruistic* suicide, which occurs when the individual sacrifices his life because "it is my duty" (e.g., on the basis of religious beliefs, commands received from a superior officer, etc.); and c) *anomic* suicide "results from man's activities lacking regulation, and his consequent sufferings" (104). In other words, there is a disruption in the system of sanctions and regulatory devices which govern the individual's needs and the manner in which they may be satisfied. The fourth category, d) *fatalistic* suicide, is associated with over-regulation, with lack of opportunity for the individual. It may be regarded as the opposite of the anomic suicide. This type was considered too uncommon to be worth much inquiry by Durkheim himself, and most subsequent researchers have also neglected it. However, there are indications that fatalistic suicide is beginning to come in for more serious consideration.

Durkheim's work encompassed such factors as culture, sex differences, religion,

imitation, and contagion. This very brief summary does not begin to do justice to the vast amount of research and thought that went into his formulations. However, a quick glance is sufficient to identify the kinds of questions which a primarily sociologic theory tends to leave unanswered. In the first place, this theory does not answer the basic question of why many people do restrain themselves from suicide although they are being assailed by problems peculiar to the suicide typology. Some people simply remain unintegrated with society, find an alternative to equating the performance of duty with the sacrifice of their lives, or accept anomic sufferings indefinitely. Second, it does not explain to what extent people are responsible for exposing themselves to the influences of those factors which, in Durkheim's judgment, cause suicide. Almost any sociologic theory is, by definition, likely to share these flaws since psychological factors are considered only secondarily, if at all. This is not to say that sociologic theories of suicide are not 'right' as far as they go, but rather that they do not go far enough.

The second major conceptual approach to suicide is psychoanalytic theory, two aspects of which have special relevance to suicide—the interpretation of depression, and the postulation of a death instinct.

When a depressive patient commits suicide he is, in effect, turning the sadism of his own superego upon himself. This is one of the psychoanalytic contentions that has been offered by Fenichel. The depressive suicide is said to prove the thesis "that nobody kills himself who had not intended to kill somebody else.... From the standpoint of the ego, suicide is an ... expression of the fact that the terrible tension, the pressure that the superego induces, has become unbearable. Frequently the passive thought of giving up an active fighting seems to express itself; the loss of self-esteem is so complete that any hopes of repairing it is abandoned." The ego sees itself deserted by its superego and lets itself die. "To have a desire to live," Fenichel believes, means to feel a certain self-esteem—"to feel supported by the protective forces of a superego. When this feeling vanishes, the original annihilation of the deserted, hungry baby reappears" (105).

What brings about depression in the first place? Fenichel's observations merit close attention. He suggests that certain conditions lead to a predisposition for subsequent depressions: "The decisive, narcissistic injuries must have taken the form of severe disappointments in the parents at a time when the child's self-esteem was regulated by 'participation in the parents' omnipotence' because . . . at this time a dethroning of the parents necessarily means a dethroning of the child's own ego." Fenichel believes that "after disappointments of this type the child asks for subsequent compensatory, external, narcissistic supplies throughout his life, thus disturbing the development of his superego; he also tries to compensate for his parents' insufficiencies by the development of a specially 'omnipotent,' that is, strict and rigid superego and subsequently needs external, narcissistic supplies in order to outweigh the unbearable demands of this qualitative and different superego" (106).

This theoretical approach does not share the inadequacies of Durkheim's. It does seek to explain why some people are predisposed by early experience to depression and, hence, suicide, and why others are not so predisposed. It also explains why some individuals unconsciously might seek to place themselves in situations where suicide is "required" and why some others might make such unreasonable demands on their environment that they become frustrated and, ultimately, suicidal. This psychoanalytic approach, however, does not explain why males are more prone to successful suicide than females, or why external, impersonal factors should influence the suicide rate at all. Furthermore, as Hendin has quite rea-

sonably pointed out, not all who commit suicide are depressed, and certainly all depressive people do not commit suicide (107).

The psychoanalytic school provides yet another approach to the understanding of suicide, namely, Freud's formulation of the death instinct. He proposed "a kind of mythology and, in the present case, not even an agreeable one." This psychomythology posits the existence in human nature of two basic qualities that we might regard as super-instincts. One of these is the death instinct which "is at work in every living creature and is striving to bring it to ruin and to reduce life to its original inanimate matter . . . . The death instinct turns into the destructive instinct when, with the help of special organs, it is directed outwards, onto objects. The organism preserves its own life, so to say, by destroying an extraneous one. Some portion of the death instinct, however, remains operative *within* the organism, and we have sought to trace quite a number of normal and pathological phenomena to this internalization of the destructive instinct" (108). The death instinct is to be contrasted with *Eros*, which represents the effort to live. *Eros* includes the instinct for preservation of the species as well as the self (109). It aims toward the establishment of higher and more complex unities, while the death instinct aims toward reduction and destruction. These two primal or super-instincts mingle together in various combinations. Seldom is a thought or behavior comprised of just one of the elements; usually there is a dialectic or contest between the two oppositional forces.

Suicide, then, could be regarded as a triumph of the death instinct over *Eros*. Beyond this statement, however, it is questionable that the very broad theory of primal and competitive instincts can contribute much to our understanding and prediction of suicide in the specific case. The death instinct theory, to be considered in more detail later (Chapter 16), might serve to sharpen the observational powers of some investigators or suggest directions of research. Yet in itself, the death instinct formulation does not seem to offer a practical framework for interpreting suicidal behaviors.

It is true that Menninger, who agrees strongly with Freud's death instinct formulation, has discussed the three sources of suicide cited previously—the wish to kill, the wish to be killed, and the wish to die. He has also contributed importantly to an understanding of the role of psychological factors in death. However, Menninger's contributions (110, 111) can be seen as quite independent from the concept of a death instinct. Whether or not the death instinct adds anything to his more specific observations is problematical.

Numerous other writings on suicide could be regarded as theories, albeit incomplete ones. Most of these contributions are related either to Durkheim's conceptualization or to that of psychoanalysis. Farberow and Jackson have both provided summaries of a variety of theories (including those mentioned above), and these summaries can be read with profit by any student of suicide.

Jackson found that suicide theories often emphasize early influences (112). He states that arrested psychosexual development based upon the physical or psychological absence of parents has been indicted as a fundamental cause of suicide. Jackson also found that spite, object loss, heredity, aggression, loss of goals, failure of adaptation, onanistia, incest, inversion motives, aggressive reaction patterns to "insecurity provoking situations," disappointment and frustration of narcissistic personalities, compensatory behavior for homicidal impulses, breakdown in adaptive processes, weather conditions, and fluctuations in economic cycles are some the many other factors that have been proposed as causative in suicide. Additionally, Jackson refers to Zilboorg's idea (113) that suicide enables a person both to thwart external sources that make life impossible and to gain a sort of "immortality." Jackson himself proposes that suicide theories can be classified on the basis of the varying emphases given to underlying motives: "self-directed aggression," "rebirth and restitution," and "despair, loss of self-esteem, or the real or imagined loss of the love object" (114).

In Farberow and Shneidman's book, *The Cry for Help*, a case of attempted suicide is independently analyzed and discussed by eight theorists of more or less different orientations (115). Farberow has rendered a valuable service by extracting and discussing the dynamics which seem "to appear both frequently and consistently" in the theorists' discussions (116). It is clear when we face the atypical individual case that general, primarily sociological theories are inadequate to explain suicidal behavior. It is equally clear that focusing only on individual psychodynamics and idiosyncratic past experiences is of little help in understanding group differences in suicide rates. What is the logical alternative to these two broad approaches? Quite obviously, the solution is to integrate them. A preliminary step to integration would be the identification of factors that are common to a variety of theoretical orientations, such as those represented in the Farberow-Shneidman book. The factors discovered by Farberow in his summary of various theorists' approach to the single case of attempted suicide are: a) *dependency* "noted frequently in the constellation of motives important for suicide or significant in the general make-up of the general personality in which suicide can appear;" b) *aggression* and *hostility;* c) *guilt*; and d) *anxiety* (117).

Farberow's summary of common factors suggests that different theoretical orientations do have much in common, and points up implicitly that the time has come for an attempt to integrate the various theories and experimental findings concerning suicide into a unified approach. Although we shall not attempt such a feat here, we should like to suggest an approach which hopefully might stimulate others to formulate a unified theory of suicide.

SOME PROPOSALS

Let us begin with a rather broad proposal: to understand suicide it is not sufficient to study suicide. Overt suicide has too frequently been regarded as a special topic, quite removed from death in general and from behavior in general. (The work of Shneidman and his colleagues is one of the constructive exceptions.) The conceptualization of suicide as a unitary phenomenon runs counter to what has been learned about the general dynamics of human behavior. It would be convenient to assume that the occurrence of behavior A can be associated invariably with motivation X, and conversely, that the presence of motivation X leads invariably to behavior A. This simple principle of commutability seldom can be supported in any facet of human behavior, let alone so complex a facet as life-and death dynamics. Suicidal intent can lead to outcomes other than suicide. Furthermore, outcomes that might be classified as suicide can flow from combinations of motives and circumstances that did not bear the mark of deliberate intent toward self-destruction. Suicidal behavior, like behavior in general, cannot be assumed to spring invariably from the same fixed, universal psychological constellation. Even within the experience of the same individual, two suicidal attempts may be based upon two rather different life situations.

We suggest, then, that the topic of suicide be incorporated fully into the general study of human behavior and experience, not sealed off as a separate domain in which fundamental laws of human functioning are suspended. Naturally, we would anticipate an especially intimate relationship between phenomena pertaining to suicide and other phenomena pertaining to death. A number of psychiatrists, psychologists, and sociologists have observed that accidents and certain kinds of illness may serve to convey or actualize a suicidal intent. In Shneidman's nomenclature, deaths that come about in this manner would be regarded as "subintentioned." That is, the individual has not directly taken his own life but has achieved the same effect by playing an "indirect, covert, partial, or unconscious role" (118). Most writers of a psychoanalytic persuasion seem to support this view. However, only Freud's death instinct, elaborated and illustrated by Karl Menninger, has been advanced as a unifying concept or explanation of the psychological aspects of death in general. This interpretation, evaluated in Chapter 16, is found to have serious inadequacies.

We do not have an adequate alternative to propose. However, we shall offer here a series of proposals which might be of some value in stimulating new conceptual approaches to suicide and other modes of death. Some of these proposals simply concentrate ideas that have been scattered in the literature. Others attempt to organize diverse findings and concepts that seem relevant to suicide although originally presented in other contexts by a variety of writers. And a few convey ideas of our own.

1. Suicide can be regarded as only one subtype within the general category of self-murder. This notion may prove helpful later in the identification of potentially suicidal individuals.

2. It might prove useful to divide the so-called "causes" of suicide into three categories. The *fundamental* causes are to be sought within the psychobiological makeup of the individual himself. External factors (situations and events) can serve as *contributing* causes for individuals with suicidal tendencies, and can also serve as *precipitating* causes in triggering the overt self-destructive act. A particular

situation or event might either contribute to or precipitate a suicidal attempt, but the same objective circumstances will neither contribute to nor precipitate an attempt in a person who lacks a fundamental orientation toward suicide.

This admittedly rough categorization may bring some order out of the proliferating articles on suicide which often focus on only one facet of the problem or on only one kind of "cause." It is difficult to believe that people kill themselves purely in reaction to objective situations such as failing a subject in school, or being hit by an economic recession, asked to retire, or subjected to dysphoric weather conditions. Any of these factors, however, can be plausibly regarded as possible contributing or precipitating causes. External (contributing and precipitating) factors can be identified in every suicide attempt, at least that is what we are assuming here. However, with the exception of what will be described later as "objective suicide," these factors are *necessary but not sufficient* causes of self-destructive acts.

3. Since it is the individual who commits suicide and not the whole society or subculture, it seems reasonable to regard personality variables as playing the major role in suicide. Biological factors, which are also intrinsic to the individual, can function as fundamental causes through their effects on the personality system.

Some readers might balk at this view. It might appear that social factors (about which more below) are not being emphasized strongly enough. It has frequently been proposed that under sufficient external pressure anyone might commit suicide. We cannot agree. This is much like arguing that "every man has his price," or "every man has his breaking point," neither of which has been substantiated. In fact, information about "brainwashing" and other extreme methods employed in prisoner-of-war and concentration camps indicates the opposite. Not all give in. Every man has his *physical* breaking point— when maltreated to an extreme, he may lose consciousness or die—but many are never *psychologically* broken (119).

4. If the suicide rate in any given society is high, then we should expect, as Hendin has demonstrated, that the institutionalized child-rearing practices and patterns of family life will embody elements that tend to predispose toward suicide.

5. Drawing heavily on psychoanalytic theory, we would like to raise the possibility that there is another kind of "basic personality" somewhat analogous to that which Kardiner describes. This might be called a "Basic Suicidal Personality" (BSP). All individuals possessed of this kind of basic personality would have in common certain pathological attributes or potentially lethal "flaws." Naturally this statement should not be taken to imply that all people who commit suicide have identical personalities, nor that certain kinds of personality traits inevitably lead to suicide.

6. What is responsible for the pathological attributes or lethal "flaws" in the BSP? Undoubtedly, inherited temperamental attributes and biological factors are of some relevance. However, the experiences of early childhood probably should be considered as of prime importance. These would include:

a. Any institutionalized child-rearing practices that result in the separation of mother and child in early life.

b. Individual idiosyncratic experiences of early deprivation and rejection, or unusual kinds of separation such as those often encountered in the histories of schizophrenics and psychopaths (120, 121).

c. The "psychological absence" of parents or adequate parental substitutes (i.e., adults were physically present, but were psychologically inaccessible to the child).

7. Other factors that are frequently mentioned as being of etiological significance in suicide could then be seen in one of four ways:

a. As *contributing* to the cultural or home environment that led to the development of a BSP.

b. As *contributing* stress that overburdens precarious defenses and undermines sources of satisfaction.

c. As *precipitating* events which, by their symbolic nature, reawaken earlier, more fundamental problems (e.g., object loss).

d. As *precipitating* events in the sense of "the last straw" that crushes the individual's system of psychobiological defenses, a system that has already been weakened by illness, failure, etc.

8. How might the flaws in the BSP actually predispose to suicide?

a. By sensitizing one to object loss. Very early in life, object loss can lead to the actual death of the individual and so, symbolically, may signify death to the person when he is older.

b. By sensitizing one to failure and rejection. Since he suffers from a fundamental insecurity and low self-esteem because of his early abandonment or rejection, the individual with a BSP may unconsciously look for failure and rejection and/or overrespond to any that he meets.

c. By preventing one from developing defenses adequate in scope and flexibility to the amount and kinds of stress one ordinarily encounters in adult life. (The early experiences summarized under point 6, above, would undermine the process of identification which is essential to normal progress through subsequent developmental stages, i.e., they would encourage "fixation" at an early stage of psychological growth).

d. By burdening the individual with hostility that is derived from his early frustrations.

e. By burdening him additionally with anxiety and perhaps guilt concerning this hostility.

f. By increasing the likelihood of failure. A person with all of the problems enumerated above not only *feels* less adequate than others—in a certain sense, he *is* less adequate. His later difficulties are superimposed upon and serve further to aggravate his basic anxiety. Hampered by a negative self-concept ("If I had any worth, then I would not have been deserted") he may court defeat more or less deliberately. So it is that frustration of normal dependency needs in infancy and early childhood can contribute to an eventual suicide by leading the individual to a repugnant, devalued sense of who he is and what he is capable of accomplishing.

9. There may be a fairly specific developmental "flaw" in many individuals who commit suicide. Earlier in this chapter, a number of references were made to "loss of control," "impulsivity," and the lack of "regulatory devices" by which to guide individual conduct. Terms such as these have been used in a variety of contexts, including both psychoanalytic and sociologic. Furthermore, there is a sort of 'face validity' to the general proposition that one person puts on the brakes, inhibits his impulse to perform a self-destructive act while another person completes the action because of a defective "braking system." A clear explanation (which would include the integration of this phenomenon within the general body of psychological knowledge) has not yet been offered. We propose that an explanation be sought along the following lines. The conceptual framework from which this tentative explanation derives is that of a phenomenologically-oriented developmental-field theory (122).

a. In normal psychobiological development there is an increasing ability to conceptualize the future and the past (123).

b. Correspondingly, the maturing child is less "stimulus bound," and can, in effect, use his appreciation of pastness and futurity as a buffer against the present.

c. A general consequence of this maturational process is the ability to attach both intellectual and emotional significance to *what is not here-and-now*. An event that will occur here, but not now and an event that is occurring now but not here are both regarded as "real." Thus, tomorrow's birthday party psychologically preexists for the child and will influence his behavior today, and the beleaguered graduate student can almost taste the degree he expects to earn in several years' time.

d. It is probable that at every level of development there is a sort of stop-go behavioral dialectic: the organism has good reasons both for facilitating and for inhibiting a prospective action. This concept appears in many forms in the psychological literature. The eye falls on psychoanalytic notions of ambivalence, but also on Pavlovian discussions of inhibition (124) and very up-to-date neo-Pavlovian therapies (125). Psychological maturation (which includes progression to "higher levels" of organization) results in the construction of systems or frameworks within which this dialectic can be regulated "from central office," as it were. The stop-or-go decision is based only in part upon the immediate situation; it is also mediated by the entire personality system which includes past-scanning and future-scanning functions. One can entertain a thought of action and yet restrain from performing the action, or modulate the action in many subtle ways.

e. Crucial indeed is the extent to which the individual develops an adequate framework within which priorities and values can be selected and modified. Many of the etiological factors already mentioned in connection with suicide (e.g., object loss in early life) can exert their potentially lethal influence by retarding the development of an integrative psychological framework. The individual who cannot attach emotional and intellectual salience to the not-here-and-now is at the mercy of the immediate situation. The environment can almost literally pull him in. The coming together of a mood of especially low self-esteem or high anxiety and the presence in the environment of opportunities for action might be sufficient to induce suicidal behavior. There is the gun, the bridge, the poison. The thought of "ending it all" flashes on the mental screen. Considerations that would encourage another person to inhibit his action (i.e., somebody needs him or loves him even though this person is absent at the moment) have no impact, and so there is a direct translation of the thought into the deed.

The conceptual approach that has just been sketched would have the effect of focusing more attention than usual on the question of why many people do *not* commit suicide. The general answer has already been proposed: As part of normal maturation we learn to regard people and events that are not-here-and-now as psychologically "real" factors. From the standpoint of application, we should be able to improve the identification of suicidal risks by examining the individual's capacities for taking "remote" consequences and events into account. It is important to add that biological factors, including fatigue and drug-induced states, may produce a temporary developmental regression (126). The distinction between thought and action becomes fuzzy, as does the entire symbolic system. In this transient state of vulnerability the individual might lose himself for the moment—and for all time.

Individuals with basic personalities flawed in the ways described above could be conceived of as members of a "suicide pool." Membership in the pool would not of itself guarantee that any given individual eventually would commit, or try to commit suicide. It would mean simply that such individuals are especially vulnerable to the various factors—social, climatic, etc.—which are often labeled "causes," but which result in the suicide of only a small number of the people who are subjected to them. The pool would not necessarily include all individuals who commit *objective* suicide. By this term we mean self-murder in such a situation as a concentration camp in order to avoid a slower, degrading, inevitable death by torture. And the pool would not necessarily include all suicidal individuals who are suffering from severe organic psychoses.

At this point, some readers may have the impression that they have just been seduced into visiting Wonderland. Upon what grounds have all these propositions been based? Many readers might have reservations about psychoanalytic theory, and it is possible that developmental theory has more or less escaped their notice. Is there any actual evidence to support even the fundamental assumption that separation from parental figures in early life can alter development in an *objectively measurable* way? There certainly is some evidence, and one doesn't have to step behind the looking glass to find it.

Recently, Dr. Boris Senior, an endocrinologist, has discovered that emotional deprivation in early childhood can result in severly stunted physical growth (127). Of several patients examined he said: "These children were deprived of the emotional support and human contact that appear to be vital for normal development. Placement in a foster home or other situation where intensive mothering is available produced sharp and rapid increase in growth rates." One of the youngsters described stood only 34 inches

tall at the age of four, when he should have been at least seven inches taller. Placed in a foster home, he grew over five inches during the first year. (At what age such stunting becomes irreversible was not indicated; but it seems likely that there must be some point after which the damage is permanent.) According to Senior, "At any big hospital, among children seen for failure to grow at the normal rate, the biggest single cause is emotional deprivation.... *These children also exhibit retarded mental development and personality disorders.*" [Italics ours.]

As is well known, René Spitz found long ago that children deprived of their mothers suffer "anaclitic depression." Spitz observed that "This state is manifest clinically by increased demandingness and weepiness, the loss of weight, and the arrest of developmental progress, with the child by the third month refusing contact with people and assuming a prone position in the crib with averted face" (128). According to Spitz, the provision of an adequate mother substitute within three to five months can result in rapid improvement. Spitz also described the effects of total maternal deprivation on 91 children in foundling homes. These children were separated from their mothers after the first three or four months of life. "The developmental progress was progressively delayed, with the children becoming completely passive and supine, with an empty face, defective eye coordination and an imbecilic expression. The children might not be sitting, standing, walking or talking even by the age of four. Thirty-seven percent of such children died from malnutrition and infection at the end of two years" (129). (For a detailed case history of a boy whose physical and mental defects were directly traceable to the absence of his mother in early life, the reader is referred to an interesting paper by Gelinier-Ortigues and Aubry) (130).

Examples such as those above are commonplace in psychological, psychiatric, and pediatric literature. They are cited to illustrate for the doubter the fact that hypotheses about the great import of the early years are neither unrealistic nor overdrawn, but well supported by clinical experience. If severe early deprivation can have the catastrophic results described, then it is reasonable that deprivation that is less severe will have less devastating, but still negative, effects on the individual. Some of these effects may not be apparent at all in the physical realm, but may exert a lasting influence on the personality.

One might grant these contentions and still question the usefulness—in a field already rife with special labels, loosely-defined concepts and incomplete theories—of the new concept of a basically suicidal personality belonging to a suicide pool. Does this add anything to our understanding? If most suicides occur primarily or ultimately because of the personalities of the victims, then why should the incidence of suicide increase with age, vary with economic conditions, war, changing expectations, and the host of other factors we have reviewed?

The answer may be close at hand, in the mediating concept of *stress*. Let us define stress in its broadest sense merely as any "pressure" or "strain" on the individual. Obviously, any important change in status, physique, or health is likely to be accompanied by stress. Major changes in life situation require not only modifications in overt behavior, but psychological adjustments to an altered self-concept as well. Certainly, the BSP individual, possessed of inadequate defenses and developmental abilities, will be prone to disorganize or actually break down under stress. (What kind and amount of stress will be sufficient to induce disorganization for a particular person will be a function of the severity of his early deprivations, inborn temperamental attributes,

later experiences with success and failure, and the amount and strength of available external supports.) This could explain why suicide increases with social disorganization and economic recessions. Furthermore, the amount of pressure exerted on certain segments of the population is greater during certain periods of history than during others. Thus, we can begin to understand why blacks, children, and adolescents have a higher suicide rate than formerly without altering our original propositions. *In periods of unusual stress no extra people are added to the suicide pool, but a larger than usual number of those already in the pool are "withdrawn"; i.e., they kill themselves.*

One point should be emphasized. "Psychological factors" do not exist in a disembodied state. Even in those suicides which appear quite clearly to have been precipitated by specific external events, it is likely that biological factors have also played a significant part. Perhaps external precipitating events are crucial only if they happen when internal biochemical and physiological resources are in flux or at low ebb, as occurs, for example, when there is more or less of the usual amount of certain hormones, or an excessively large accumulation of toxic substances within the body, or an inadequate supply of oxygen to the brain and other tissues. Some of these conditions may be more likely to obtain at certain stages of development or periods in life (e.g., old age, adolescence) than others, just as certain psychological problems and kinds of death are more common at some stages of development. There may be, in short, a lethal intersection between psychological and biological variables.

In the following two chapters we devote further attention to the relationships among age, developmental level, psychological state, and the mode and time of death.

REFERENCES

1. Millay, E. St.V. From a very young Sphinx (excerpt). In *Edna St. Vincent Millay: Collected lyrics*. New York: Harper Torchbook P 3092, 1969. P. 188.
2. Solomon, P. The burden of responsibility in suicide and homicide. *Journal of the American Medical Association*, 1967, *199*, p. 231.
3. Dublin, L. L. *Suicide: A sociological and statistical study*. New York: Ronald Press, 1963. P. 211.
4. *Ibid.*, p. 22.
5. Lepso, A. Topic. . . "The Unemployed." *Boston Globe*, Feb. 9, 1967.
6. Batchelor, I. R. C. Suicide in old age. In E. S. Shneidman & N. L. Farberow (Eds.), *Clues to suicide*. New York: McGraw-Hill, 1957. P. 144.
7. *Ibid.*, p. 145.
8. *Ibid.*
9. *Ibid.*, p. 144.
10. *Ibid.*
11. Newcombe, T. *Social psychology*. New York: Dryden Press, 1950. Pp. 316-318; 400-401.
12. Aisenberg, R. B., & Kastenbaum, R. Value problems in geriatric psychopharmacology. *Gerontologist*, 1964, *4*, 75-77.
13. Feifel, H. Attitudes toward death in some normal and mentally ill populations. In H. Feifel (Ed.), *The meaning of death*. New York: McGraw-Hill, 1959. P. 122.
14. Kastenbaum, R., & Durkee, N. Young people view old age. In R. Kastenbaum (Ed.), *New thoughts on old age*. New York: Springer, 1964. Pp. 237-249.
15. Kastenbaum, R., & Durkee, N. Elderly people view old age. In R. Kastenbaum (Ed.), *New thoughts on old age*. New York: Springer, 1964. Pp. 250-264.
16. Dublin, *op. cit.*, pp. 214-215.
17. *Boston Globe*, Nov. 24, 1966. P. 63.
18. Rosenfelt, R. H. The elderly mystique. *Journal of Social Issues*, 1965, *21*, 37-43.
19. Farberow, N. L., & Shneidman, E. S. Suicide and age. In Shneidman & Farberow (Eds.), *Clues to suicide*. New York: McGraw-Hill, 1957. Pp. 41-49.
20. *Ibid.*, p. 42.
21. *Ibid.*, p. 47.
22. Schmale, A. H., Jr. Relationship of separation and depression to disease. *Psychosomatic Medicine*, 1958, *20*, p. 270.
23. Terry Ferrer in *Boston Sunday Globe*, Feb. 28, 1965.
24. Lee, D. *Freedom and culture*. Englewood Cliffs, N.J.: Prentice-Hall, 1959.
25. Schildkrout, M. S., in report to National Education Association—American Medical Association Joint Committee on Health Problems and Education. Reported in *Boston Record American*, Sept. 29, 1965. P. 21.
26. King, L. C. Quoted in *Time*, Feb. 17, 1967.
27. Loomba, R. Layoffs in defense industries. *International Science & Technology*, March, 1967. Pp. 14-26.
28. Cavan, R. S. *Suicide*. Chicago: University of Chicago Press, 1928. Pp. 80-81.
29. Kastenbaum & Durkee, *op. cit.*, pp. 237-264.
30. Fraisse, P. *The psychology of time*. New York: Harper & Row, 1963.
31. Aisenberg, R. Unpublished data from survey of older psychologists: Natick, Mass. For data on this topic already published: Aisenberg, What happens to old psychologists? In R. Kastenbaum (Ed.), *New thoughts on old age*. New York: Springer, 1964.
32. Dublin, *op. cit.*
33. Sollberger, A. Biological measurements in time, with particular reference to synchronization mechanisms. In Roland Fisher (Ed.), Interdisciplinary perspectives on time. *Annals of the New York Academy of Sciences*, 1967, *138*, Art. 2, pp. 561-599.
34. Harmer, B., & Henderson, V. *Textbook of the principles and practices of nursing*. New York: Macmillan, 1960. P. 272.
35. Quoted in *Boston Globe*, Dec. 29, 1966.
36. Dublin, *op. cit.*, p. 23.
37. Guttmacher, A. F. *Having a baby*. New York: The New American Library, 1955. P. 79.
38. Patten, B. M. *Human embryology*. (2nd ed.) New York: McGraw-Hill Blakiston Division, 1953. Pp. 56-57.
39. Hamilton, J. B. Relationship of castration, spaying and sex to survival and duration of life in domestic cats. *Journal of Gerontology*, 1965, *20*, p. 103.
40. O'Connell, W., M.D. Interview on "Contact" television program, Channel 4, Boston, June 22, 1967.
41. Kallman, F. J., Deporte, J., Deporte, E., & Feingold, L. Suicide in twins and only children. *American Journal of Human Genetics*, 1949, *1*, 113-126.
42. Schulzinger, M. S. *The accident syndrome*. Springfield, Ill.: Charles C Thomas, 1956. P. 176.
43. Dublin, *op. cit.*, p. 11.
44. *Ibid.*, pp. 40-41.
45. Hutchin, K. C. *How not to kill your husband*. New York: Hawthorne Books, 1965. P. 24.
46. Dublin, *op. cit.*, p. 23.
47. Mead, M. *Sex and temperament in three primitive societies*. New York: Morrow, 1963.
48. Dublin, *op. cit.*, p. 33.
49. *Ibid.*, p. 34.

50. *Boston Globe*, Dec. 13, 1966.
51. Woodford, J. N. Why Negro suicides are increasing. *Pageant*, Oct. 1965. P. 13.
52. *Ibid.*
53. *Ibid.* p. 14.
54. Dublin, *op. cit.*, p. 35.
55. McDougall, W. *Is America safe for democracy?* New York: Scribner's, 1929.
56. *Ibid.*, p. 87.
57. Jung, C. *Analytic psychology.* New York: Pantheon Books, 1968.
58. McDougall, *op. cit.*, pp. 85-86.
59. *Ibid.*, p. 93.
60. *Ibid.*, p. 97.
61. *Ibid.*
62. Eysenck, H. J. *The structure of personality.* London: Methuen & Co., 1953.
63. Marshall, E., & Hample, S. Children's letters to God. *Saturday Evening Post*, Nov. 19, 1966. P. 31.
64. Dublin, *op. cit.*, p. 35.
65. *Ibid.*, pp. 30-33.
66. Kardiner, A., & Ovesey, L. *The mark of oppression.* New York: Morton, 1951.
67. Hendin, H. *Suicide and Scandinavia.* New York: Grune & Stratton, 1964.
68. *Ibid.*, p. 33.
69. *Ibid.*, p. 39.
70. *Ibid.*, p. 41.
71. *Ibid.*, p. 60.
72. *Ibid.*, p. 61.
73. *Ibid.*, p. 67.
74. *Ibid.*, p. 80.
75. Luigi Barzini narration of CBS news special program on his book, *The Italians.* Aired January 17, 1967.
76. Dublin, *op. cit.*, pp. 78-79.
77. *Ibid.*, p. 32.
78. Iga, M. Relation of suicide attempt and social structure in Kamakura, Japan. *International Journal of Social Psychiatry*, 1966, *12*, 221-232.
79. *Ibid.*, p. 228.
80. *Ibid.*, p. 229.
81. Dublin, *op. cit.*, p. 27.
82. *Ibid.*, p. 63.
83. *Ibid.*
84. *Ibid.*
85. *Ibid.*
86. Henry, A. F., & Short, J. F. *Suicide and homicide.* New York: The Free Press, 1954.
87. Dublin, *op. cit.*, pp. 170-171.
88. *Ibid.*, p. 172.
89. *Ibid.*
90. Farberow, N., Shneidman E., & Leonard, C. V. Suicide among schizophrenic hospital patients. In N. L. Farberow & E. S. Shneidman (Eds.), *The cry for help.* New York: McGraw-Hill, 1965. Pp. 78-97.
91. *Ibid.*, p. 81.
92. Tabachnick, N. Observations on attempted suicide. In E. S. Shneidman & N. L. Farberow (Eds.), *Clues to suicide.* New York: McGraw-Hill, 1957. P. 166.
93. Batchelor, *op. cit.*, pp. 144-145.
94. Tuckman, J., & Youngman, W. F. Attempted suicide and family disorganization. *Journal of Genetic Psychology*, 1964, *105*, 187-193.
95. Tuckman, J., Youngman, W. F., & Feifer, B. Suicide and family disorganization. *International Journal of Social Psychiatry*, 1966, *12*, 291-295.
96. Tuckman, J., & Youngman, W. F. Identifying suicide risk groups among attempted suicides. *Public Health Reports*, 1963, *78*, 763-766.
97. Wahl, C. W. Suicide as a magical act. In E. S. Shneidman & N. L. Farberow (Eds.), *Clues to suicide.* New York: McGraw-Hill, 1957. P. 24.
98. *Medical News*, Jan. 2, 1967. Pp. 1 & 20.
99. *Ibid.*
100. Shneidman, E. S., Farberow, N. L., & Litman, R. E. The suicide prevention center. In N. L. Farberow & E. S. Shneidman, (Eds.), *The cry for help.* New York: McGraw-Hill, 1965. P. 10.
101. Wolberg, L. R. *The technique of psychotherapy.* New York: Grune & Stratton, 1954. P. 584.
102. Shneidman, E. S. Orientations toward death: A vital aspect of the study of lives. In Robert White (Ed.), *The study of lives.* New York: Atherton, 1963.
103. MacKenzie, J. (former assistant superintendent, Boston State Hospital). Presentation to staff of Veterans Administration Hospital, Brockton, Mass., 1957.
104. Durkheim, E. *Suicide,* (Translated by J. A. Spaulding & G. Simpson.) New York: The Free Press, 1951.
105. Fenichel, O. *The psychoanalytic theory of neurosis.* New York: Norton, 1945. P. 400.
106. *Ibid.*, p. 405.
107. *Ibid.*
108. Hendin, H. Suicide: Psychoanalytic point of view. In N. L. Farberow & E. S. Shneidman (Eds.), *The cry for help.* New York: McGraw-Hill, 1965. P. 185.
109. Freud, S. *Beyond the pleasure principle.* In: *Complete psychological works of Sigmund Freud.* London: Hogarth, 1955, vol. XVIII.
110. Menninger, K. *Man against himself.* New York: Harcourt Brace, 1938.
111. Menninger, K. Psychoanalytic aspects of suicide. *International Journal of Psychoanalysis*, 1933, *14*, 376-390.
112. Jackson, D. Theories of suicide. In E. S. Shneidman & N. L. Farberow (Eds.), *Clues to suicide.* New York: Mc Graw-Hill, 1957.

113. Zilboorg, G. The sense of immortality. *Psychoanalytic Quarterly*, 1938, 7, 171-199.

114. Jackson, *op. cit.*, pp. 12-13.

115. Farberow, N. L., & Shneidman, E. S. (Eds.), *The cry for help.* New York: McGraw-Hill, 1965. Pp. 153-290.

116. *Ibid.*, p. 298.

117. *Ibid.*, p. 299-302.

118. Shneidman, 1963, *op. cit.*

119. Ewalt, J. R., Strecher, E. A., & Ebaugh, F. G. *Practical clinical psychiatry.* (8th ed.). New York: McGraw-Hill, 1957.

120. Barry, H. Orphanhood as a factor in psychoses. *Journal of Abnormal Social Psychology*, 1936, *30*, 431-438.

121. Goldfarb, W. Emotional and intellectual consequences of psychological deprivation in infancy: A reevaluation. In Paul Hoch & Joseph Zubin (Eds.), *Psychopathology of childhood.* New York: Grune & Stratton, 1955.

122. Kastenbaum, R. Engrossment and perspective in later life: A developmental-field approach. In R. Kastenbaum (Ed.), *Contributions to the psychobiology of aging.* New York: Springer, 1965. Pp. 3-18.

123. Pressey, S. L., & Kuhlen, R. G. *Psychological development through the life span.* New York: Harper, 1957.

124. Pavlov, I. P. *Lectures on conditioned reflexes.* London: Lawrence and Wishart, 1928-1941.

125. Cautela, J. R. Manipulation of the psychosocial environment of the geriatric patient. In D. P. Kent, R. Kastenbaum, & S. Sherwood (Eds.), *Research, planning and action for the elderly.* New York: Behavioral Publications, in press.

126. Krus, D. M., & Wapner, S. Effect of lysergic acid diethylamide (LSD-25) on perception of part-whole relationships. *Journal of Psychology*, 1958, *48*, 87-95.

127. Boris Senior cited by Carl Cobb *The Boston Globe*, Dec. 1, 1966. P. 13.

128. R. Spitz cited by J. R. Ewalt, E. A. Strecher, & F. G. Ebaugh. *Practical clinical psychiatry.* (8th ed.) New York: McGraw-Hill, 1957.

129. *Ibid.*

130. Gelinier-Ortigues, M-C. & Aubry, J. Maternal deprivation, psychogenic deafness and pseudo-retardation. In Gerald Caplan (Ed.), *Emotional Problems of Early Childhood.* New York: Basic Books, 1955. Pp. 231-247.

12

Murder

Our lives are in jeopardy at every moment. The unseen virus or the automobile with "our number" on it may be overtaking us while our minds are filled with everything but intimations of immortality. And it is all too obvious that, throughout life, we negotiate a gauntlet of threats only to terminate in a dead end. The reasonable man reflects: Life is fragile. Life is short. Humankind should draw together, enhance, and preserve life against the menaces and fate common to all.

How little resemblance there is between this reasonable view of human affairs and the events we see and hear about us! In fact, we are fortunate if experiences of human-generated violence reach us only through the morning news report. It is anomalous, from a rational viewpoint, that humans should slaughter each other. Why offer this assistance to Death? It is disturbing, from any viewpoint, that murder* has become so well established a part of our problem-solving repertoire. And it is probably not much consolation to learn that murder (if not charity) begins at home.

OF THE "BATTERED CHILD" AND MURDERING PARENTS

Love, nurturance, and protection are terms we tend to associate with the parent-child relationship. Yet this relationship has become a lethal one often enough to arouse our concern. Pediatrician Vincent Fontana maintains that if complete statistics were available, we would probably learn that parental abuse and neglect is the most common cause of death in childhood (1). Fontana applies the term "maltreatment syndrome" to a wide spectrum of behavior ranging from poor or inadequate care to outright physical attack. This latter type of behavior may be the first to come to mind when one thinks about child abuse. However, it is not the only kind of maltreatment nor is it the

---

Murder: "to kill (a human being) unlawfully and with premeditated malice or wilfully, deliberately and unlaw-

fully;" also, "to slaughter in a brutal manner . . . to put an end to, destroy. . . ." *(Webster's Third International Dictionary,* unabridged. Springfield, Mass.: G. & C. Merriam, 1966.) *Homicide* means the killing of one human being by another. Strictly speaking, murder is a legalistic term, qualifying the act by an assessment of intention. From a psychological standpoint it is often difficult to determine whether an action is "willful," while the "lawfulness" of the act may depend upon many complex factors including the skilfullness of the attorney and the social status of his client. In addition, popular usage sanctions interchangeable use of these terms—we shall use these terms interchangeably as well.

only kind that may lead to the death of a young child. Lack of appropriate behavior—"sins of omission" if you will—accomplish the same result. Let us cite just one example from the current literature.

"He was found dead in his crib by a family friend who had stopped in at the home. A bottle of sour milk was in his crib and maggots were crawling around in his soiled diaper. The mother had gone to visit an aunt, leaving the child alone . . . " (2). The reasons for the neglect in this case are not explained. We know nothing of the mother's motives, and there is no indication that she carried out a direct assault on the victim. The child, however, is no less dead than if he had been the object of a violent physical attack.

The direct physical abuse of children has often given rise to spectacular headlines, but only recently has it become the object of the systematic research it deserves. C. Henry Kempe and his colleagues were the first to formalize child abuse as a diagnostic entity when they coined the term, "battered child syndrome" (3). Their nationwide survey revealed that subdural hemotoma and fracture of the femur were the most frequent physical findings. The extent of the problem is revealed by such statements as: "Seventy-one hospitals reported 302 cases within a single year; thirty-three of the children died and eighty-five suffered permanent brain injuries" (4).

This finding is by no means an isolated one. Another study obtained reports from 77 district attorneys. Collectively, it was found that 447 cases had reached their attention in one year, "including forty-five deaths and twenty-nine brain injuries. In New York City alone one such fatality is reported each week!" (5) Mothers were the parents most frequently involved in the cases that have been studied, but it is not uncommon for fathers to administer severe or lethal beatings (6). One should also bear in mind that the infliction of permanent brain damage also operates, in

general, as a factor that decreases the individual's survival potential. Thus, we suggest that the number of fatalities that might be attributed to the battered child syndrome ought to include the life-shortening effect of significant injuries as well as immediate deaths.

Some of the victims have been very young babies and toddlers (7). It is all too obvious that babies are extremely vulnerable and frequently succumb:

"James Leonard Forman of Forth Worth, Texas, was only 19 months old, and had lived with foster parents until this past August, when a court order directed that he be returned to his real parents. This weekend the foster parents, who wish to remain anonymous, went out to buy a suit for little James, so he could wear it in his coffin. The foster parents also chose a blue, three-foot casket. The real parents may not be at the funeral. They are in jail, charged with beating little James to death. Mrs. Forman, 39, signed a statement saying she kicked James before he died. She said she "flew into a rage" at his toilet habits (8).

Such cases are particularly distressing because of the helplessness of the victim, the brutality of the attacks, and the fact that the perpetrators often had enjoyed the reputation of being good citizens. Yet criminal acts of this kind are not as rare as we should like to suppose.

Why Do They Do It?

How is it possible for parents to batter and kill their own children? Are they really bent on murder, or do they fail to understand the likely effects of their assaults? Do murdering parents have much in common with those who commit other kinds of homicide? To what extent are personality defects responsible for the acts of destruction? To what extent does the role of parenthood itself or environmental factors serve to instigate or "release" this lethal behavior?

The fragmentary bits of evidence are suggestive but not altogether consistent.

Bromberg states that mothers who have murdered their children often are found to be psychotic. Murdering fathers, by contrast, are said to be characterized by extreme immaturity and "psychopathic emotionality" (9). Fontana became acquainted with 50 parents of battered children. He concluded that these parents, as a group, were immature, compulsive, and often plagued by problems in managing alcohol or money. Furthermore, they were operating under a great deal of stress at the time of the beatings. It was Fontana's impression that these young people could not adjust to the demands of the parental role. The child became the focus of frustration although the parents' own problems were more generalized (10).

Kempe conducted a five-year psychiatric study of parents who had assaulted their children. He concluded that such parents behave as they do because:

1. They think the child does not love them.
2. They expect the child to behave at a more mature level than is possible for him at the time.
3. They feel compelled to punish the child when he does not meet their expectations (11).

According to Kempe, the unrealistic expectations are ". . . rooted deeply in the parent's own feelings of insecurity and unlovedness fostered by the manner in which he was raised." The parents, especially the mother, felt valued in childhood only when they pleased their own parents. In adult life "they unconsciously repeat their own experience—they make demands on their infants and punish them when they don't meet these demands" (12).

Kempe's observations seem to support a contention that has been offered by many experts on child-rearing practices—parents tend to treat their children as they themselves had been treated (or maltreated). This pattern may emerge even when the parent makes a deliberate effort to avoid repeating his own upbringing. The battered child thus becomes the battering parent. It would be useful to follow up the careers of children who are battered (but not slain) by their parents to learn if they will later enact the aggressor's role. Yet it is questionable that the repetition dynamics constitutes a completely adequate explanation for the murder of children by their parents. We note that:

1. Children who are the most severely battered (i.e., those who die) obviously will not live to become parents and have their own turns as aggressors.
2. The repetition pattern does not really *explain* child abuse. Rather, it projects the critical context backward in time. Theoretically, we would have an infinite regress—generations of child-beaters. It is not especially helpful to limit the understanding of parental violence to a kind of "original sin" doctrine, with every succeeding generation merely replaying the first event in the series (which itself, of course, needs to be explained).
3. A theory of child-battering that adheres strictly to the repetition dynamics would not seem likely to lead to useful innovations in preventing or ameliorating the phenomenon. One cannot do much about the past per se. It is entirely possible, however, that appreciation of the repetition dynamics would be helpful in developing interventions when integrated with other information and concepts.

It is possible that Fontana's observations, already mentioned, might fill in some of the gaps in the repetition dynamics hypothesis. If Fontana's sample is representative in that abusive parents tend to be young and operating under great stress, then we might give particular attention to such variables as impulse control and perspective. These personality characteristics tend to develop slowly as the individual matures. In general, one would expect young parents to have less impulse control and perspective than older parents. Situations that require patience, self-discipline, and seeing beyond the immediate moment are more likely to be stressful to the young parent. Even the routine demands of raising a child may prove to be quite frustrating to the parent with limited impulse control and perspective. And one of the most familiar propositions in psychology is that frustration can lead to aggression (13).

This line of reasoning fails to account for the fact that most young parents do *not* batter their children. But it would be worth exploring the possibility that the parent who was himself the victim of abuse as a child (as Kempe has observed) has a psychological scar to show for his misfortune: defective impulse control and perspective. Not only does he have the relatively limited level of impulse control and perspective that is sometimes associated with the young, but he suffers a more severe defect in these abilities because of his adverse earlier experiences. Impulse control and perspective are more likely to flourish when the individual has grown up in a dependable, trust-inducing environment (14). Furthermore, defective impulse control and limited perspective tend to increase one's general level of life stress. Defective impulse control that is a consequence of one's own tribulations in childhood could tip the balance toward aggression in parents who are already finding it a struggle to manage their personal affairs and raise a family because of their limited experience.

Frustration, however, does not *always* lead to aggression—nor does aggression always take the form of physical assault. The frequency of parental attacks upon children would be even greater if physical aggression toward the young were the invariable response to parental frustration. A more complete explanation would have to take into account those environmental conditions which encourage or discourage physical violence in the home. We would also need to consider those personality factors which seem to make the difference as to whether a person takes his frustrations and aggressions out on himself, or directs his attacks toward others. Even in those situations involving a frustrated, outward-acting parent in an environment conducive to physical violence we would still want to know why a child is selected as the object in one instance but not in another.

Perhaps the specific pattern of child-abuse that is most consistent with the preceding considerations would be as follows: A young parent has had relatively little previous experience in managing family affairs and consequently often does the wrong thing or fails to do the right thing. When a difficulty arises the parent feels threatened and does not have the inner strength to tolerate a build-up of anxiety. An immediate—often impulsive and poorly-advised—solution is attempted. In all probability, this solution does not meet the demands of the situation, and pressure continues to build. Meanwhile, a similar pattern is developing in other spheres of the young parent's life. The infant or child's behavior is likely to become more abnormal as it attempts to accommodate to its abnormal environment. Inadvertently, the child may show more and more of precisely that kind of behavior which enrages the parent. And the parent—deliberately or unwittingly—may seek to provoke "bad" behavior so that he will have a justifiable object to attack. At the moment that it occurs, a violent attack upon the child may seem to the parent to be a natural and appropriate reaction to the child's alleged misdeeds. Seen from a psychological perspective, however, *the child has been made the victim of the inadequate parent's urgent impulse to obliterate the complex problems that surround him in adult life.*

Such hypotheses are worth considering, but, again, they do not constitute the whole story. For example, it is fairly common for parents to select one of their several children for neglect and abuse while continuing to treat the others well. Here is an illustrative case reported in the press of April, 1967 (15):

For four years, police said, Debbie C., 11, lived much like a little animal in her own home. She subsisted on a daily bowl of dry cereal and she was forced to stay out in the cold while her brothers and sisters got more loving care. . . . Police, acting on a tip, entered the suburban . . . home of Donald C. . . . and found the frail girl tied to her bed. "Nobody's been treated like that little girl since the dark ages," said Westland Municipal Judge Douglas W. Craig. "It's unbelievable, just unbelievable!" The judge said that police had to cut the bindings and the ropes from the child's body. They couldn't even be untied, they were so tight. Debbie told police that she was forced to use the backyard as a lavatory, walk alone three miles to school in the same tattered dress, stay out until 11 o'clock at night in the cold and was strapped to her bed the rest of the time. Her five brothers and sisters, aged 2 to 9, meanwhile ate and dressed well and rode to school, police said. . . .

Why is a particular child selected for abuse or murder? No one, as yet, can answer this question with certainty. There are several possibilities, however:

1. In the case cited above, the abuse may have been directed against Debbie because she was the oldest child. The birth of a first child generally causes a greater dislocation in the husband-wife relationship and the family routine than does the birth of subsequent children. If this is one of the bases for "selecting" which child to abuse, then a disproportionate number of abused or neglected children should be the firstborn. Whether or not the facts support this hypothesis, we do not know. (And it is worth keeping in mind that the firstborn child is often considered to enjoy certain advantages, including the prospect of a longer life! (16) It is not easy to reconcile these two lines of reasoning.)

2. The child selected for abuse may be the one who most closely resembles, either physically or temperamentally, the parent primarily responsible for the maltreatment. The parent who was himself abused in childhood might be recreating the situation he had previously experienced, but this time he would be in charge—the beater, not the battered. This could be seen as an attempt to gain mastery of a situation in which previously he had been helpless. There is also another possibility. The child who most closely resembles the parent may be maltreated because he serves as a reminder of the parent's own shortcomings. The parent's "bad" characteristics may be less acceptable in a child than other "bad" traits which he is not himself trying to suppress or for which he feels no sense of responsibility. Again, the child may have the misfortune to resemble a despised or hated person who is known to the parents. There is yet another variation which may be observed at times: one parent strikes back at the other parent by assaulting the child who resembles not oneself, but the spouse.

3. It may be the child's misfortune to resemble a parent or remind a parent of some of his unacceptable characteristics—but the *lack* of resemblance to other members of the family also may serve to set the child apart as "not really one of us," or "the black sheep." The parents might not know what to do or what to make of a child whose appearance and behavior departs markedly from their own, or their other children. The child is expendable, unwanted.

4. The abused child might be the one who (unwittingly) best fits the role of a maltreated victim. He may be the weakest or least assertive child, the one who is unable to fight back or least likely to report his maltreatment. If he does have some masochistic tendencies these may be (unconsciously) perceived, cultivated, and exploited by his parents.

5. The maltreated child may be the one whose birth intruded on a previously stable domestic scene. This was the unplanned and unexpected "extra" baby,

perhaps, or the "disappointment" (the "wrong" sex, or defective in some way). Some parents have very specific ideas about the characteristics they want their child to have. He may be punished when he fails to conform to these expectations.

The alternative explanations suggested above may be of some utility in trying to determine which particular child is most likely to be made the victim of parental abuse. However, we lack substantial evidence regarding the *function* of this selective process. It appears to be the case that long-term abuse of one child in the family—including a homicidal climax—often is associated with relatively adequate treatment of other children. Would parental abuse have been directed to a different child if the actual victim had not been available? This alternative suggests that certain types of inadequate parents require an object for the release of feelings of frustration and hostility, and will find an object one way or another. The other alternative is that the child-abuse was incited by factors that are specific to the given child, such as the factors mentioned above. Perhaps future research will provide an answer to this question.

It has already been pointed out that many battered children do succumb. Yet it remains difficult to accept the fact that some parents commit deadly assault upon their own children. Often we are willing to find excuses for the perpetrators' behavior: "It must have been an accident. . . . They didn't mean to do it." Some of the reasons behind our readiness to deny the reality of child murder will be discussed later. For the present, we will focus upon psychological factors that are thought to be operative in the *murder* of infants and children, as distinguished from general abuse and assault.

The noted psychiatrist, Walter Bromberg, views the "paradox of maternal aggression toward infants as related to a concept ancient in the human race: those

who create may destroy that which they have created" (17). Bromberg's interpretation recalls to mind other views which emphasize the close relationship between creation and destruction, or birth and death. Bromberg also quotes Marston Bates' conclusion that aboriginal women "killed their offspring without too much compunction." Bates holds that infanticide was quite generally practiced and accepted by prehistoric peoples" (18). However, we believe it is important to distinguish between infanticide that has become an accepted behavior in a particular culture and infanticide that occurs in a culture that is shocked and dismayed by such an action. Culturally-sanctioned infanticide has not been limited to aboriginal and prehistoric peoples. Female infants have been considered expendable by a number of cultures that could not fairly be classified as "primitive." Usually there seems to have been a strong circumstantial factor involved—people whose survival potential is marginal because of inadequate food supply sometimes have "thinned their ranks" to maximize the survival rate of the core community. This process often enough includes both ends of the age spectrum—those who are seen to be liabilities because of advanced age (19) as well as those who are too young to contribute directly to group survival. Lamentable as these practices may be, it is clear that they have been carried out under conditions of severe deprivation and threat to the total community. This is a far cry from the murder that occurs in an affluent society which seems to place so much positive value upon the lives of its children.

One possible contributing factor to the outright murder of young children is the assumption that a very young human being is not possessed of any rights. It is, rather, an object, a possession of which the parents can dispose in any way they please. The immature parent may see himself as merely "playing house," rather than establishing an authentic family.

Children would then be treasured as diverting playthings. Everything is all right so long as the children are interesting, amusing, and gratifying to the parent's needs, without making any unusual or excessive demands themselves. But the insistent assertion of the child's own developing needs, his own individuality, or a family crisis which punctures the "houseparty game"—these occurrences are likely to puzzle, enrage, and frustrate the parents. Striking out with the fury of an angry child, such a parent may turn on his "dolls" and destroy them. Emotionally, this type of killer-parent may never have accepted the responsibilities of his biosocial role. The parent himself has been functioning at an immature level of emotional development, still embroiled in a child's relationship to his own parents.

One is tempted to suggest that immature couples be given their own set of dolls to play with and destroy as necessary, rather than vent their helpless rage upon real children. Or perhaps the boiling point could be avoided if the parents multilated child dolls in the living room, while the children did likewise with Mommy and Daddy dolls in their rooms. Such would be a "family of the absurd" indeed—but one alternative to the intramural murder family.

What other factors might be contributory to infanticide? Bromberg is of the opinion that murdering mothers often are psychotic. He suggests that, "in the mentally ill mother, motherhood itself is unconsciously negated as too great a price to pay for distortion of her body image, an assault on her narcissistic integrity and a drain on her impoverished emotional life. The psychosis itself represents a denial of the child's birth. The aggressive components in these patients are warded away from the ego; hence, the homicide occurs under a cloud of confusion, as in a depression" (20).

Is this psychodynamic formulation widely applicable? What other explanations of infanticide have been proposed?

Let us review a few clinical studies and see what interpretations have grown out of them.

Tuteur and Glotzer studied five patients who had committed infanticide (21). All five had the following characteristics in common: They were female. They appeared to have been schizophrenic at the time of the murder. All "appeared regretful" and claimed that they would never do it again! All had "experienced a definite coolness either from one or both parents during their childhood years when the concept of motherliness begins to develop in the female" (22). All had serious problems with their husbands. Four of the five attempted suicide following the filicide.

Several differences existed among these women. Chief among these were the methods utilized in the murders (two shootings, one strangulation, one poisoning, one drowning), and a number of differences in their general backgrounds and life histories.

Tuteur and Glotzer's interpretation of their patients' behavior is not inconsistent with Bromberg's but it has a totally different focus. They feel that "suicide-murder may be interpreted as an attempt to remove the 'total-all', the actual and the *extended* self, so that nothing of the self remains" (23). This subjective view of the parent-child relationship is only a little different than the one hypothesized for parents of battered children. With regard to the latter, we suggested that the parents may tend to see their children as possessions—objects, not independent selves. Tuteur and Glotzer apparently are convinced that the patients they studied *still* see the children as part of themselves. If anything, this view attributes an even more primitive quality to the pyschosocial developmental level of the murdering parent. The child has never been perceived as differentiated and separate from the parent. Nevertheless, the two misperceptions described here do share an important characteristic. In neither view is the child seen as an individual human being with rights of its own. As we shall see later, this *dehumanization of the victim is a common prelude to all kinds of murder.*

Tuteur and Glotzer's interpretation, if correct, could explain much about the frequent combination of filicide and suicide. The fact that four of the five patients discussed above attempted suicide supports Lauretta Bender's position which was cited by Tuteur and Glotzer, and differs only slightly from their own: Bender found that the depressed mothers she studied used their children psychologically as "hypochondriacal organs." "These mentally ill mothers identify with their children to a point where murder becomes a symbolic suicidal act" (24). Bender holds that what originally began as a *suicidal* urge becomes altered to a homicidal urge directed toward the child as well as the self. However, this double-edged sword ultimately eventuates in the killing of the child alone. She hypothesizes that filicide may represent an "attempt to escape life's turmoil and stresses . . . and the child victim becomes part of the escaping personality" (25). A confused mother might even rationalize that since the child is just part of herself, she is not really committing murder!

What has already been discussed might lead one to conclude that the two types of infanticide cannot be understood in the same theoretical terms. We need a different approach for comprehending the filicide committed by psychotic mothers and those deaths which result from maltreatment at the hands of nonpsychotic parents. But these differences are not as great as they may seem. All kinds of homicide, as we shall see, have much in common. Particularly, they have in common the dehumanization of the victim—and sometimes the dehumanization of the murderer as well.

Helene Deutsch's remarks concerning mothers and mothering undoubtedly apply to psychotics and nonpsychotics alike. Deutsch, like Fontana, Kempe and a host of others, agrees that women who were not adequately mothered do not themselves become motherly. (A position that seems to be consistent with subsequent laboratory experiments that have manipulated the mothering received by infant rats.) Deutsch explains: "The well-integrated mother expands her ego through her child; the maladjusted feels restricted and impoverished through him. Unbearable pressure of reality in the conflict between self-preservation and motherhood leads to complete rejection" (26).

Furthermore, child murders in general may share many characteristics that are usually thought to typify only filicide. Steven Myers has reported a 25-year survey (1940-1965) of felonious homicides of preadolescent children in Detroit (27). From a total of 134 cases, verdicts of guilty were rendered for 71 defendants. These defendants were held accountable for the felonious homicides of 83 victims. Myers found no important discrepancy in the number of male and female victims, and "no racial preponderance." The victims included 23 percent who were under one year of age and another 25 percent between the ages of one and three. Myers points out that these figures are almost exactly the same as those obtained by Adelson in a study of 46 child homicides committed over a 17-year period in another state. Hence, this sample appears representative.

Except for those killed during the first year of life, the largest number of victims were two years of age. (This small point is of interest. It will be discussed more fully later in this chapter in connection with the role the victim plays in his own demise.) Most of the homicides (60 percent) were committed by a parent of the victim—42 percent of the total group by the mother. Victim and slayer were acquainted in almost every case. Most of the mothers adjudged psychotic murdered their children by asphyxiation. Most of the fathers or other males left in charge of the children employed manual assault:

"These assaults were frequently in response to a sudden, intense, uncontrollable rage, experienced by the assailant after the child had defecated on the floor or could not be quieted from crying. The slayer frequently confessed readily and exhibited great remorse, tearfully stating that he simply could not stop beating the child until it was motionless." This behavior was characteristic of some fathers and some males who were unrelated to the child. Myers noted that in those cases in which the battered child syndrome eventuated in death, "the outstanding element was the sadistic nature of the assault. In these cases the assailant frequently attempted to falsify the circumstances surrounding the child's death . . ." (28). Myer's paper confirms much of what we have already learned:

· Children are more likely to be killed by their parents than by anyone else.
· More mothers than fathers commit filicide.
· A large proportion of the women who kill their children are psychotic.
· Paternal filicide (and male filicide in general) usually follows upon some external event which evokes a rage the man cannot control.

We have already remarked upon the relative immaturity and impulsiveness of some abusive parents. We now add two other pieces of information and one personal opinion. First, given similar provocation, some fathers and some males who are not fathers to the particular children involved will respond with lethal physical assault. This suggests that personality traits and the external stimulus situation may be much more relevant and powerful variables than fatherhood per se. Fatherhood may be relevant only in that it ensures in the intact home a greater amount of contact between a potential killer and the child, thus the likelihood that it will be the father rather than some

other male who destroys the child is maximized.

Second, there may be some consistent differences, psychodynamically speaking, between those who kill a child impulsively following a "provocative act," and those who maltreat a child over a long period prior to the actual death. The latter, it will be recalled, were found to be more sadistic and less honest with their report of the lethal assault. Additional investigation may or may not substantiate these differences. In either event, the children remain dead.

Finally, Myers is of the opinion that the *reported* cases of child homicide tell only part of the story. He believes, for example, that many infants are killed without their births even being recorded. Those concerned with the death of an unwanted infant sometimes agree to "look the other way"! (29). This possibility brings us face to face with a question that most of us would probably prefer to ignore.

How Do They Get Away With It?

Child abuse and murder cannot be understood solely in terms of individual characteristics, either of the attacker or the victim. The environmental context is inextricably involved. Such "external" factors as social attitudes can tacitly permit or actively encourage lethal behavior. For the present, let us focus on the problem of tacit permission.

No crime can be considered apart from the society in which it occurs. We are all part of a society in which child murder is increasingly common. Therefore, we can hardly allow ourselves to condemn the parents of maltreated children as though their crimes are irrelevant to our own lives. This is in no way meant to suggest that abusive parents are not guilty—that only "society" is to blame. Of course, such parents are guilty, but they are not alone. It is highly probable that many of us have "aided and abetted" a crime or "harbored a known criminal." Criminal acts of child neglect and maltreatment often are not taken very seriously. Many people—perhaps most people—prefer to consider such unpleasantness to be "none of my business." We can only guess at how many outright filicides or deaths attributable to neglect and abuse could have been prevented by the intercession of "innocent" observers. The number would be large, we believe.

Why is it that many "good citizens" do not intervene? Return for a moment to the case of Debbie, the 11-year-old who was both abused and neglected by her parents. In this instance, four years—four years!—elapsed between the beginning of the abuse and its discovery. Actually, many people must have been aware for a long time that something was wrong. It was, in fact, admitted that "the neighbors knew it and kept silent. Relatives said they didn't want to cause trouble in the family." Yet there was obviously plenty of "trouble in the family" already. More likely, the trouble they wished to avoid was to themselves. And what about Debbie's teachers? The principal? The school nurse? Couldn't they see that the child was frail and under-nourished, that she always wore the "same tattered dress"? Yet it was four long years until someone voiced an anonymous complaint. Had Debbie died, could the neighbors, relatives, and school personnel really have been considered innocent?

There are many examples of the guilt of the innocents. It is frequently noted that the battered child who succumbs has a long, well-documented history of physical trauma. X-ray examinations may reveal multiple, old, healed fractures. Hospital records often show several previous admissions for peculiar "accidental injuries." Why, then, do social agencies, individual physicians, nurses, and others seldom step forcibly into the situation to prevent further injury and possible death? Fontana feels that physicians often are loath to report such cases, on the chance that they might be in error. He points out that it is hard to believe—even when the evidence is there—that the victim's own parents really would do such a thing. Fontana also observes that physicians, as well as many other people, may *not want to get involved*—an attitude that a number of writers fear is assuming epidemic proportions in our society. In any event, Fontana proposes that maltreated children be taken to a hospital rather than to an individual, thus making it possible for institutional authority to take the responsibility for reporting the abuse (30).

Kempe proposes a slightly different explanation for the frequent failure to report cases of the battered child syndrome. He suggests that it is psychologically easier for the physician "to deny the possibility of such an attack than to have to deal with the excessive anger which surges up in him...when he faces the truth" (31). If this reaction does occur, it is possible to sympathize with the physician's situation—yet it is questionable that one person's feelings should be protected at the possible expense of another's life.

The "excessive anger" explanation centers on the proposition that one's own impulses may inhibit effective response to another's potentially lethal behavior. We think it likely that there is also a variation on this general theme: namely, the observer experiences vicariously something of his own latent "murderous impulses." The excessive anger may, in fact, include a partially disguised destructive component. In other words, the physician or other responsible citizen may feel both that "If I acknowledged the reality of this child abuse, I would get so angry that I could clobber the parent myself," *and* "I have sometimes felt angry enough to beat a child myself—these parents have done it for me."

Let us now take just one example of a social agency's, rather than an individual's, failure to function quickly and efficiently when a child's life may be at stake.

"A charge of neglect of minor children

had been made and the Aid to Dependent Children Agency was supposed to have placed the children in foster homes eleven days prior to No. 2's death. This had not been done because of an administrative oversight in the agency" (32). Is not "neglect of minor children" a serious charge? Should it not be treated as an emergency? The failure of agencies and clinics to execute follow-up services must tell us something about social concern for children's lives, whether the "cause" is to be located within the agency itself or within the larger sociopolitical context that ties the agency's hands or limits its treatment resources. As Adelson remarks: "Merely requesting that the mother bring the child to a clinic or hospital is obviously not adequate in some instances" (33). Yet, agency and hospital personnel are not murdering monsters. They often feel acutely frustrated by the red tape and other restrictions that stand in the way of their optimal functioning. They are simply people, like everyone else. Their shortcomings and attitudes, their defenses and rationalizations reflect those of the society which they try to serve. If society—all of us—genuinely placed a high value on human life, then this is what they would reflect.

Our discussion has now come full circle. We must conclude that child abuse, neglect, and infanticide would be far less frequent if most of us were not guilty of indifference or collusion. We will find that much of what we have learned about factors that motivate or contribute to child murder applies with equal force to other types of homicide. This is especially true in regard to the "innocent bystander" role.

There may be substantial emotional resistance to accepting the available evidence. It is more comforting to bask in the (false) security generated by the notion that murder is a rare deed, worlds removed from our normal behavior, and committed only by individuals who are "crazy," brain-damaged, or both. Admit-

tedly, it is easier to accept this hoary explanation than to try to understand the complexities of human aggressive behavior. No one wishes to be implicated, however indirectly, in the crime of homicide, or to feel that there is anything he could have done to prevent it. We prefer to maintain as much psychological distance as possible between ourselves and anyone who commits murder.

MURDER, HEREDITY, BRAIN DAMAGE, AND PSYCHOSIS

Our denial of any possible resemblance between murderers and ourselves is made more absolute by labeling killers as "crazy" or "funny in the head." (We also saw this to be the case with victims of suicide.) How much validity is there in this allegation? We have already learned that many of the mothers who kill or abuse their children are, indeed, mentally ill. Nevertheless, there is a great difference between demonstrating that some murders are committed by people afflicted with psychosis and maintaining that all, or almost all murders can be attributed to this factor.

Time was when criminality in general and the propensity to murder in particular were considered heritable pathological traits. People spoke of "bad blood," or "bad seed" or atavism (34). The father's sins were thought to be visited upon the son who was inevitably wicked and forever beyond redemption. To a large extent, this was the attitude toward mental illness as well (35).

Today we are, or purport to be, much more sophisticated. For example, most of us would readily acknowledge the crucial influence of home and family on personality development and mental health. Few would care to deny that both of these influences must be considered if we wish to understand the total causation and meaning of a criminal act. Nevertheless, our minds still retain vestiges of mankind's earliest ideas about murder. These cognitive remnants are usually made presentable for conscious dialogue in the form of two hypotheses, the clinical evidence for which is then over-generalized to fill the void by now-discredited hereditarianism. One of these hypotheses is that all crime (and therefore, murder) is caused by the organic characteristics of the criminal. The other is, quite simply, that criminals are "out of their minds." Of course, these contentions need not be mutually exclusive, but it will be more useful to examine them separately.

The Organic Approach to Murder

Some of the basic laws of heredity have been known for at least a century (36). Moreover, our understanding of the processes basic to transmission of hereditary characteristics is becoming increasingly sophisticated all the time (37). As Patten points out, since we are all "mosaics" in inheritance, one occasionally encounters an individual who is vastly different from his ancestors. Patten emphasizes, however, that, genetically speaking, "by and large, 'like begets like' " (38). It was undoubtedly the layman's recognition of just this tendency that was partially responsible for the widespread acceptance of the hereditary view of crime in earlier times. It also has the virtue of being (on the face of it) a simple explanation. What evidence is there today that heritable organic factors may play a role in criminal behavior?

Few would dispute that, given good health and nutrition, physique is largely a function of heredity. This general proposition, however, does not by itself improve our understanding of criminal behavior. A possible connection between physique and behavior became of scientific interest when William Sheldon identified three major components of physique: a) endomorphy—the softly rounded body type; b) mesomorphy—the vigorous, well-muscled, athletic variety; and c) ectomorphy—the

tall, thin, poorly-muscled type (39). Sheldon's research demonstrated a degree of correlation between each of these physical types and a constellation of temperamental traits. The traits were designated viscerotonia, somatotonia and cerebrotonia, respectively.

For reasons that will soon become clear, we are most interested in the mesomorph. The mesomorph's traits are said to include assertiveness, desire and aptitude for vigorous physical activity, and a tendency to dominate others. This constellation is coupled with the relative absence of sensitivity to one's own inner feelings (40). This is relevant to our discussion because Sheldon and Eleanor Glueck found in a rather famous study that juvenile delinquents as a group tend to be mesomorphs (41). It was reported that "the delinquents are more harmoniously organized for direct physical activity, probably making easier the conversion of impulse into action" (42). The Gluecks noted also that there was a characteristic developmental pattern for many of the delinquents they studied. Their growth was regarded as having been somewhat retarded until the thirteenth to fourteenth year. At that point they experienced a growth spurt that permitted them to catch up with or even surpass the physical development of non-delinquents (43).

We have no substantial information concerning the proportion of adult offenders who are mesomorphs. Neither do we know to what extent, if any, the more aggressive behavior of the mesomorph represents either an attempt to compensate for his small stature early in life, or a response to other people's expectations of what he "should" be like. Still, the Gluecks' data do tend to support the reasonable hypothesis that inherited physique may imply behavioral traits that predispose one toward particular patterns of solving problems or discharging impulses. It may be recalled that constitutional influences on suicidal and homicidal behavior had been emphasized previously

(Chapter 11) by the distinguished physician and psychologist, William McDougall.

Nevertheless, the value of the Gluecks' data for our purposes is somewhat limited by the fact that there is disagreement concerning the likelihood of juvenile delinquents to "graduate" to adult crime. The National Crime Commission finds that "the earlier a child is arrested for some offense, the more likely it is that he will become an adult offender. . ." (44). By contrast, the Gluecks report that follow-up studies show a steady *de*crease in the number of youths who continue to be offenders: by age 29, fully 40 percent of the former delinquents included in their studies had terminated their illegal behaviors. The Gluecks concluded: "The physical and mental changes that comprise the natural process of maturation offer the chief explanation of this improvement in conduct over the years" (45). Thus, the developmental sequence through which the human organism must progress on its way to maturity may be of importance in determining criminal behavior. There will be more to say of this later.

The crime-through-inherited-tendencies hypothesis and the evidence adduced in its behalf require more extensive and critical attention than can be provided here. We would like to suggest, however, that the possible role of inherited factors is likely to be modified, perhaps even overpowered by social and technological changes. Perhaps we still picture a brutish mesomorph clobbering his helpless victim at short range. This situation would indeed involve the direct expression of (misoriented) bodily vigor. Yet in today's world it is remarkably easy to commit the most destructive and lethal crimes with a minimum of direct physical action. One can murder from both a physical and a psychological distance. Also, it does not require brawn or a physicalistic orientation in order to fire a high-powered rifle from a window, tower, or bridge, or to hurl a fire bomb through a window of a house while the occupants are asleep.

Perhaps some readers would not accept the concept of *administrative murder*. We refer to the lethal consequences of administrative decisions. By signing or not signing an enabling act, by promoting or impeding a program that has vital implications for human welfare, the administrator often exerts a massive influence on the survival odds of an individual or group. Negligence, ignorance, indifference, or actual malice on the part of people in administrative positions is seldom if ever interpreted as "murder" in the legal sense of the term. But the *effect* of their administrative behavior may be quite lethal. This notion is introduced here as a reminder that it is possible to have considerable responsibility for bringing about the death of other people without engaging in direct physical assault. It is doubtful that "administrative murders" (or whatever you choose to call such happenings) can be attributed to mesomorphic characteristics. In fact, there are so many ways to unleash murderous forces that every person, regardless of his constitutional tendencies, could find a physique-syntonic mode of becoming a killer. The mesomorph may, in effect, be losing his "advantage" in this area.

Evaluation of the inherited factors hypothesis of murder and other crimes requires an accurate record of the offenses. The same, of course, holds true for other hypotheses in this area. But it is generally recognized that one's likelihood of being arrested, charged with a major crime, and found guilty of same depends to some extent upon one's ethnic and socioeconomic background. This selective factor in law-enforcement and legal systems makes it difficult to determine the true crime rate. And, of particular relevance here, it becomes difficult to determine the specific contribution of constitutional factors. Suppose we are informed that murder rates are relatively high in a particular socioeconomic range or a particular ethnic group. We usually have no way of knowing whether this statistical fact means: a) the high-murder population has an unusually high proportion of constitutional types who are predisposed to physical aggression; b) the number of reported crimes has been inflated relative to other population groups because of selective factors in law enforcement and/or judiciary processes; or c) environmental—not constitutional—determinants specific to this population group have provoked an unusual amount of criminal behavior (e.g., overcrowding, poor housing, chronic unemployment, and so on).

Organic Disorders and
Murder

Up to now we have been discussing the role of inherited constitutional factors in murder and other crimes. But the individual's organic condition bears the mark of his experiences as well as his genes. Furthermore, in practice it can be exceedingly difficult, even impossible, to determine whether certain traits or lesions were inherited, congenital, or acquired. Let us sample some of the investigations that have been undertaken to clarify the possible relationship between organic attributes and disorders and antisocial behavior.

Many electroencephalographic studies have been conducted of criminals. In reviewing some of this material, Bromberg concluded that "evidence of a direct relationship between cerebral dysrhythmia (organic brain disorder) and violent crime is ambiguous" (46). While there are indications that "the epileptic complex" is related to violent crime, Bromberg cautions that "numerically this relationship is not impressive" (47).

One of the problems involved in trying to link abnormal EEG readings with criminal behavior is illustrated by the findings in one study of psychopaths: "In seventy-five criminal psychopaths . . . the great majority were found to have either an abnormal EEG, or an unsatisfactory early home life, or both" (48). It is almost impossible to sort out the organic

and environmental influences in such cases. We do not know what role cerebral dysrhythmia played in the psychopaths' behavior. It is even possible that environmental factors (e.g., faulty nutrition or physical trauma) were originally responsible for initiating pathological changes in the brain.

Joyce Small conducted a more thorough study of 100 felons who had been referred for psychiatric evaluation (49). Each of the criminals received a full battery of physical, psychologic, and electroencephalographic diagnostic procedures. The attempt was to construct a comprehensive picture of factors which might have contributed toward these criminals' commitment of serious crimes. She found that:

1. "Age, sex, race and psychiatric diagnosis were not significantly correlated with the nature of the alleged crime" (50).

2. According to the criteria employed, 33 percent of the felons studied showed strong evidence of brain damage (51).

3. Of this 33 percent, both those whose brain damage had an early onset and "those with equivocal indications of brain dysfunction were significantly more often accused of theft than any other kind of offense" (52).

4. "In contrast, persons with brain damage beginning in adult life and individuals without indications of central nervous system disorders were mostly charged with assault, murder, or sex crimes" (53).

5. "Habitual physical violence was characteristic of one-half of the subjects in the early onset classification, of two-thirds of the late onset and negative groups and in three-fourths of the equivocal category" (54).

6. All of the subjects were considered to be mentally ill.

In considering these findings it is important to keep in mind that the subjects of this study had all been referred for psychiatric examination in the first place. Hence, they are not a representative sample of felons. This makes it all the more striking that most of those charged with murder and assault (the latter, of course, sometimes leading to the former) either showed no sign of central nervous system disorder or gave evidence of late onset of brain damage. It is of interest, too, that habitual physical violence was more characteristic of felons without brain damage, or with equivocal damage, than of those with clear evidence of brain damage since early life. This pattern of findings certainly tends to undermine the thesis that homicidal behavior is primarily a function of central nervous system pathology.

Berman offers a variation on the organic theme. He regards criminal behavior as primarily a function of disordered endocrinology: "Crime is due, in a Gestalt sense, to a perversion of the instinctive drives dependent upon a deficiency and imblance of the endocrine glands." Additionally, "Certain types of crime are associated with certain types of endocrine malfunctioning" (55). Berman attributed murder to an imbalance involving relative overactivity of the thymus and thyroid and relative underactivity of the parathyroid and adrenals.

Flanders Dunbar, who conducted an unusually thorough analysis of the literature on this and related topics, felt that Berman's formulation was "most extreme" (56). And we know of no other endocrinologist who would support or substantiate Berman's thesis.

There would be little point in quoting authorities or citing references and statistics ad infinitum. Even the very limited sample we have presented should illustrate the fact that the role of organic factors in crime is by no means a consistent or predictable one. This is not to deny that these factors undoubtedly do play a role in many murders and other violent crimes.

But we cannot be sure that the organic factors are necessary, let alone sufficient for criminal behavior. Certainly it would be possible for a person to have brain damage or an illness that has nothing in particular to do with the crime he commits. Furthermore, we know very little about the opposite situation—the case of the person who has an organic disorder but never engages in any sort of criminal behavior. What inhibits or insulates certain victims of brain damage from becoming involved in criminal actions? What releases or facilitates criminal behavior in others? It is likely that the answers to these questions, if they were known, would have psychosocial as well as biological overtones.

The XYY Factor. The questions we have raised about organic factors in crime remain with us even when significant new discoveries come to light. It has been reported in recent years that some criminals possess genetic abnormalities. The specific abnormality is an extra Y chromosome in the male (making him an XYY rather than an XY model). It has been roughly estimated that one in every 300 men may have the XYY makeup (57). Advocates of the latest "bad seed" theory believe that this genetic quirk is related to a variety of undesirable personality characteristics (as well as acne). Aggressive and violent behavior by such men is thought to be especially frequent and extreme. Richard Speck, convicted slayer of eight nurses, is a conspicuous, perhaps "textbook" example of an XYY man.

Although the existence of XYY genetic structure seems to be well documented, its implications for personality and behavior are unclear at present. There is only flimsy data on which to base the contention that XYY is related to violent behavior in any systematic manner. The preliminary findings now available may fail to hold up as more rigorous investigation is pursued. But let us suppose that eventually a statistical relationship could be established between XYY heritage and acts of violence. Would this settle the "cause of homicide" question for once and all?

We doubt that *the* answer to homicidal behavior will be found in the extra Y chromosome. It has already been pointed out that many people suffer from organic disorders—including disorders that might be expected to affect judgment and impulse control—but never engage in antisocial behavior, let alone conspicuous acts of violence. Possession of the XYY genetic structure might increase the probabilities of violent behavior when large populations are considered. But many XYY men refrain from criminality. That still leaves us with the familiar question: Why does one person kill while another person, similar in some crucial respects to the killer, never take a human life?

Furthermore, even if the contention that an extra Y chromosome contributes to criminality in some men were proven, we would not have increased our understanding of women who commit murder. Are we to imagine that men kill because of organic factors, but women slay because of psychosocial factors? This is one of the seldom-aired implications of the current "bad seed" theory. It is a debatable assumption, to say the least.

Among other shortcomings of the XYY hypothesis we briefly note: a) the logical and methodological pitfalls that are usually encountered when one attempts to generate imputations of causality from correlational data; and b) failure to answer the question of behavior specificity—why was this particular victim selected, at this particular time, and slain by this particular mode? XYY can be an important aspect of the total pattern which eventuates in homicide—in some individuals—but is unlikely to provide a general and convincing explanation of homicide in general.

In the absence of firm and substantial evidence, why do so many people persist in the notion that organic attributes or pathological states are the prime causes of murder? Perhaps it is because these hypotheses serve a number of useful purposes—purposes that should be made explicit if we are to understand why it is so difficult to reduce murder and other crimes of violence.

The "Out of His Mind" Approach to Murder

Hypotheses of organic etiology are rather comforting, are they not? They seem to provide both a specific "cause" and, at least in some cases, the basis for specific treatment as well. Beyond this, the organic approach supports the common feeling that murderers are monsters who, from the very outset, are different from normal people such as ourselves. We are thus absolved of any guilt for having contributed to the development of a homicidal trend in these individuals and for its ultimate expression in lethal crimes. The person who accepts these hypotheses probably feels relieved of the need to do anything about preventing the crimes himself. In fact, his biological orientation convinces him that he lacks the requisite skills to take any action. He is just an ordinary person. Only professional specialists have the capacity and responsibility to manage the offenders and to try to prevent others from following in their footsteps. These specialists and their charges can then be hidden away conveniently in institutions where they cannot disturb the rest of us. (Note the similarity to attitudes sometimes expressed toward people whose only crime is that of growing old; again, the assumption is often made that the condition is 99 percent biological and those afflicted with it should be shut away from society under the care of specialized custodians.) (58, 59.)

In short, the organic approach to the etiology of murder provides most of the same advantages that are intrinsic in the notion that all killers (or all suicide victims—see preceding chapter) are "crazy." But perhaps it is unfair to anticipate. There is, after all, much to be said for the role of mental illness in homicide. Therefore, let us proceed with the second of the two hypotheses mentioned earlier—that murder is primarily a function of mental illness.

Certain kinds of murder are often cited to substantiate the hypothesis that it is only or primarily the psychotic person who becomes a killer. What is the nature of the crimes which one must be "crazy" to commit? Mostly, they tend to be one or the other of two general types: a) those that lack an obvious motive—the so-called "senseless killings"; and b) those for which the motive is the satisfaction of a perverse sexual impulse. Crimes of the latter type evoke intense feelings of horror and revulsion. They also boost the circulation of the newspapers and magazines in which they are reported. These two interrelated factors result in a tendency to over-report sex crimes. The impression created thereby is that homicidal "sex fiends" commit a sizeable proportion of all murders. Actually, this impression runs counter to the facts: "sex murders" are of only minor statistical significance (although we have already acknowledged their psychosocial significance).

Let us consider briefly the causes of two major types of "crazy" killings, lust and necrophilia.

Lust Murder. The term "lust murder" often is used rather loosely in reference to a homicide that is associated in any way with sexual behavior. Thus, if a rape victim is murdered so that she will not be available to testify against the rapist, newspaper headlines are likely to proclaim that a lust murder has been committed. In true lust murder, however, it is *the actual killing* of the victim (and sometimes the mutilation of the body, as well) that provides sexual gratification to the slayer. There is some theoretical controversy regarding the source of the killer's satisfac-

tion. According to Sandor Lorand (60), the lust murderer so fears rejection by a live woman that he kills in order to have sexual relations with a corpse. However, Krafft-Ebings' conception of lust murder holds that it is the killing per se which affords the gratification. Coitus is not involved (61).

Surely this type of crime supports the thesis that the murderer must be out of his mind. It may seem totally inconceivable that anybody could engage in such an abnormal and savage form of behavior. But is it? Psychoanalytic theorists think not. Otto Fenichel, discussing sadistic behavior in general, reasons:

If a person is about to do to others what he fears may be done to him, he no longer has to be afraid. Thus, anything that tends to increase the subject's power or prestige can be used as a reassurance against anxieties. What might happen to the subject passively is done actively by him, in anticipation of attack, to others (62).

About sex murder in particular, Fenichel theorizes:

The sadistic act not only means "I kill to avoid being killed" but also "I punish to avoid being punished"—or, rather, "I enforce forgiveness by violence." Persons who are in need of narcissistic supplies tend, when frustrated, toward intensive sadistic reactions: Under certain conditions such a tendency may grow until it culminates in an action that is a denial of the fear, "If I do something sexual, I have to be punished," by means of the other one, "I torture you until I force you, by the intensity of your suffering to forgive me, to release me from the guilt feeling that blocks my pleasure, and thus, through and in your forgiveness, to give me sexual satisfaction." The sadist who pretends to be independent thus betrays his deep dependence on his victim. By force, he tries to make his victim love him, the love he seeks is a primitive one, having the significance of a "narcissistic supply" (63).

To some readers these hypotheses may seem almost as bizarre and distasteful as the crimes they purport to explain. Certainly, their validity has yet to be demonstrated. Fenichel himself admits that up to the time his book was written not one sex murderer had been psychoanalyzed (64). Nevertheless, the psychoanalytic approach to lust murders serves several constructive purposes: It demonstrates the possibility of deriving a logical explanation of even the most irrational-seeming actions. By providing a logical explanation, it divests such acts of some of their literally nameless horror. Consequently, it brings preventive programs and management of offenders within the realm of possibility. These influences are all to the good. Not one iota is thereby subtracted from the proposition that this particular type of murder is likely a function of mental aberration. Nevertheless, Fenichel's reasoning does have the effect of returning some of the responsibility for "crazy killings" to the man on the street. And it is appropriate to add that the difficulty one might have in trying to *prove* Fenichel's thesis does not necessarily mean that he is mistaken or fanciful. The behavioral sciences still show quite a gap between the sensitive observations and subtle reflections of a Fenichel and the research strategies that would permit one to subject the ideas to rigorous investigation.

Necrophilia. It would be difficult to ascertain whether lust murder or necrophilia is usually considered more abhorrent. People seem to be no more eager to discuss or understand the necrophiliac than the lust murderer. What is necrophilia? Unlike lust murder, necrophilia is generally agreed to include sexual activity with a corpse. However, the term is sometimes used rather loosely (as in the case described below) to mean primarily a preoccupation with dead bodies. Necrophilia and lust murder overlap in cases where a person commits murder in order to obtain a corpse.

Necrophilia ordinarily is considered to be an adult perversion. However, a few years ago Joseph Bierman reported a case of necrophilia in a 13-year-old boy (65). This seems to be the first published report of necrophilia in a child or early adolescent. Bierman attempted to discover the reason for his patient's obsessive interest in death and corpses and his preoccupation with becoming an undertaker. He found that the symptoms followed the death of the boy's 22-year-old sister whom he had helped to nurse during her terminal illness. The boy's preoccupation with becoming an undertaker was interpreted as an "attempt to turn his traumatic passive experience of sister's illness, death and funeral into an experience he can actively control."

Bierman also feels that necrophilic preoedipal determinants may be present in the successful adult choice of professions which involve the human body. Thus, the original impulses or fantasies basic to necrophilia may not be so weird—or, at least, not so uncommon—as we would like to believe. In any event, there is nothing about necrophilia and necrophiliacs that forces us to abandon the principle that all human behavior is amenable to psychological analysis. The potential necrophiliac or lust-murderer required certain patterns of experience in order to develop this predisposition, and probably requires other experiences in order to become an actual killer. It should be possible to identify the crucial experiential and behavioral factors and alter them before a violent crime has in fact occurred. But the possibility of successful intervention is seriously weakened if we choose to regard these behaviors as completely "crazy" and, thus, unpredictable and inevitable.

What of the hypothesis that psychosis causes one to become a murderer? There can be no serious doubt that both lust murderers and necrophiliacs are mentally aberrant, or that their aberrations are directly responsible for some slayings. There is also no doubt, however, that the proportion of such murders is extremely small, so this hypothesis can hardly be used to justify the conclusion that all killers are "sex" maniacs, or any other kind. Nevertheless, because of reasons stated earlier, sex murders continue to exert a disproportionate influence on our conception of murder in general. Taken together with the "senseless" crimes described below, sex murders do much to perpetuate the notion that murder is caused by psychosis, or its legal counterpart, "insanity."

Murders for which there are no obvious motives or, seemingly, no motives whatever, are often assumed to be caused by mental illness. There is no question that "senseless crimes" have been committed by psychotics. But if a psychotic person commits murder, does this automatically prove that the murder was *caused* by the psychosis? Let us explore two types of "motiveless" homicides.

Murders without Motives

The Individual Homicide as "Episodic Dyscontrol." Menninger, Mayman, and Pruyser have described and discussed several crimes that appeared to be senseless and unnecessarily violent (66). One of these will be recounted for illustrative purposes:

A 24-year-old corporal looking for a prostitute near a French town was approached by a 13-year-old boy who persistently asked him to change Army scrip into French currency; when refused, the boy seemed to mock or make fun of him, whereupon he struck the boy. The corporal insisted he had no intention of killing the victim and did not recall the actual killing. When he "found out" what he was doing, the victim's body had been severely mutilated" (67).

According to the authors:

Such instances of episodic dyscontrol . . . represent an effort to forestall something worse. But what . . . is worse than murder? The ego in distress often "thinks" in primitive language, in primary-process terms. According to this, the ego would rather kill than be killed, or, what amounts to the same thing, suffer a completely

disruptive disintegration. Thus, murder is frequently committed, according to our theory, to preserve sanity (as well as in other instances to preserve life). Some colleagues have proposed that murder and suicide may both serve as defenses against "psychosis." Certainly this would sometimes seem to be the ego's "intention." And it usually works. Such temporary "insanities" rarely become long term "insanities," and indeed, it is just this fact that so perplexes juries in attempting to fix a degree of blame on an offender whose "insanity" seems to them to have been too brief to have been real (68).

Menninger and his colleagues acknowledge that "From the standpoint of society, the explosion of murder is disastrous, but from the standpoint of the individual himself it may be the way to survival, the only solution which, at the moment of decision, the crippled ego could find" (69). The authors also point out that murder is not the only possible result of episodic dyscontrol—and, in fact, it is not a very frequent one.

Here, then, we have a somewhat different kind of hypothesis: murder (during a temporary psychosis) can serve as a defense against a more permanent state of psychosis or disintegration. But we also have the authors' observation that murder as a function of temporary psychosis is a relatively unusual phenomenon; there is no suggestion that most murders are of this type. The theory as a whole does not really answer many questions about even this exceptional "cause" of murder. What factors determine when an episode of dyscontrol will occur? Why does episodic dyscontrol sometimes result in murder and at other times not? Under what environmental circumstances is what type of person likely to experience an episodic dyscontrol that culminates in murder? Is the person who commits murder in an episode of dyscontrol likely to have eventually killed anyway? Is the psychosis really "necessary" to the murder? Let us keep these problems in mind as we consider the second category of senseless homicide.

Mass Murder. The term, "mass murder" is open to a number of interpretations. It can be used to designate a series of individual murders all committed by the same person. It can mean the wholesale killing of a rival gang or a group of individuals for understandable if scarcely laudatory motives—to obtain revenge, for example, or to take over some one else's turf, to silence witnesses, to eliminate dissident elements, to "purify the race." Our concern here is with none of these. We refer instead to the sporadic murder, at the same time, of several people who are often unknown to the assailant, murders that are committed for motives that are not readily apparent or which seem totally inadequate.

During a period of just a few months in 1966, the United States experienced three incidents of mass murder. Quite naturally, there was widespread speculation as to the causes—what could explain these extremely regrettable and threatening events? Most readers will recall these murders, for they became the subject of nationwide news and commentary media. The first in this series took place on July 14th when eight nurses were slain in their Chicago apartment. A sometime merchant seaman was convicted of the crime. It is almost impossible for one who is not privy to all of the sworn testimony to gain a clear idea of what transpired on the day of the crime. Press and magazine reports were sometimes contradictory and confusing. For example, the slayer was reported to have raped as well as strangled one of the victims (70); he was also reported to have raped no one (71). Suffice it to say that eight extremely sadistic murders were committed and the crime reported in great detail in the press. The following month a young college student by the name of Charles Whitman first killed his wife and mother, then made his way to the tower of the University of Texas. Equipped with a veritable arsenal of weapons, he blasted away at the people who moved about the campus 27 stories beneath him. Before Whitman was himself finally felled, he had killed 16 persons and wounded 30 others (72). In November of the same year, an adolescent boy shot five people through the head in a beauty parlor. He told a police officer that "I wanted to make a name for myself" (73).

The seemingly motiveless, unfeeling quality of these crimes is impressive. This aspect, taken together with the sheer number of victims involved in each crime, might be considered as ipso facto evidence for the mental illness of the perpetrators. Certainly this was a prevalent opinion among laymen. Individuals who were informally polled by the writers were of one mind in this respect: "They're all nuts." "You'd have to be out of your mind to do a thing like that." "They lost their sense of personal balance." "That's the work of a maniac—it has to be!"

What evidence is there to support this hypothesis in the specific cases described? We know only that the convicted killer of eight nurses had a history of drinking, may have taken drugs, had had an unsuccessful marriage, was frequently unemployed, had a prison record, seemed to be depressed and/or confused after the crime, admitted to having a bad temper, and claimed amnesia for the actual slayings (74). He could hardly be considered to have been a well-adjusted person prior to the murders, and might be characterized as a sociopath. However, it is obvious that the jury was not convinced that he was insane in the legal sense and so far as the public knows, no clear evidence of psychosis was presented. What of other mass killers?

There is even more ambiguity regarding the case of Charles Whitman, due in part, perhaps, to the fact that his lethal outburst was concluded by his death from a bullet fired by a police officer. Raised by a father who had beaten his own wife and was unusually strict with his children, Whitman learned at an early age to handle guns (75). He gained more experience with firearms on hunting expeditions and in the Marine Corps. Fighting, wife-beating and passing bad checks had all figured in his life (76)—but there was no documented episode of blatant psychosis. Whitman did consult a psychiatrist before committing his crime. In fact, he informed the psychiatrist that he had been thinking of shooting people from the University of Texas Tower. However, as the psychiatrist later indicated, this is not really an unusual *idea*. In his experience, people who voiced antisocial ideas to him almost never engaged in the actual behavior they threatened.

At autopsy it was discovered that Whitman had a brain tumor. It was generally discounted that this organic disorder may have played any role in causing him to commit mass murder. However, there are still some who maintain that the tumor was responsible, at least to some extent. In light of the information available, it is impossible to be certain whether or not Whitman was actually psychotic at the time he killed 16 people. It is not out of the question that he was psychotic by the time he reached the tower, but not psychotic while murdering his wife and mother. Violence and gun usage had been enough a part of his background that one could hardly maintain the premise that his murderous episode was entirely discontinuous with his previous life pattern. Yet the circumstances do suggest that he may have been psychotic at the time—we will never know for sure.

Hamill unearthed some relevant fragments about the adolescent killer of five. He found that the boy was an admirer of Jesse James and Napoleon, had once advocated germ warfare "to wipe out the people of Southeast Asia—they're all animals and they're not important;" and was reported to have first begun acting strangely after the birth of his five-year-old sister (77). The accused entered a plea of innocent by reason of insanity. One of the items admitted into evidence was a note, purportedly written by the accused, in which the writer indicated that he had lied when apprehended because he was trying to get into a hospital (presumably a mental hospital so that he would not be convicted of murder). The question of whether a person is mentally ill often is a most difficult one to determine in a court of law. The jury in this case, as in the case of the convicted murderer of the eight Chicago nurses, did *not* believe that the youth's behavior satisfied the criteria of insanity. He was also convicted.

Thus, in none of these three incidents of mass murder can we be quite sure that the perpetrator was "out of his mind." In one case, psychosis seems probable, but not certain. In two cases, the legal semi-equivalent of psychosis, insanity, could not be demonstrated to a jury's satisfaction (78). So it is that even the relatively unusual "senseless" mass crime is of but limited value in supporting the notions that killers usually are out of their minds. Even if we could demonstrate conclusively that the mass killers were all grossly psychotic, would this *explain* any or all murders—including the ones they had committed? Not really. We would not know for certain that the "psychosis itself" (to reify a mental condition) had "caused" the crime. We would not know *how* a psychotic condition operates to produce a lethal crime, assuming that it does operate in that direction. We would be no closer to understanding the possible effects of psychosis in *reducing* the likelihood that a person might engage in violent crime. And we would not know why mass rather than individual murder is sometimes committed, how the time and place of the crime are decided, how the victims are selected, etc. In short, to regard either type of murder solely from a standpoint of the perpetrator's "mental health," in the usual understanding of this term, is of limited explanatory or predictive value. There is a very good reason for this.

Murder is a Social Act, Psychosis Notwithstanding

Is any psychotic person 100 percent out of contact 100 percent of the time? Most probably not. Mental illness does not entirely insulate the individual from the character of his environmental context. He may experience the environment differently than a "normal" person does, but he is far from oblivious to what goes on about him. In fact, many clinical psychologists and psychiatrists have observed an extraordinary sensitivity to certain aspects of interpersonal behavior on the part of individuals who are suffering from a major mental disorder. And it is also worth keeping in mind that the highly influential "milieu approach" to managing the total environment of mental patients is predicted upon the belief that society can be used as a treatment modality.

All murders are socially relevant. And it is likely that all murders are, to some extent, socially engendered. This proposition is a strong one whether we are considering a murder that has been committed by a psychotic or a nonpsychotic person. Homicide, after all, is not committed within the dark recesses of the sick mind nor even (very commonly) within the closed ward of the mental hospital. It erupts in the real, external society, a society which in some ways permits or even encourages its occurrence. Here are two illustrations of the fact that the psychotic person is influenced by what goes on outside of himself, whether it be in the international world or the immediate sphere of his own hospital ward.

It is common knowledge that some deluded mental patients believe themselves to be famous personages. Almost everyone has seen those tiresome cartoons in which a "loony" is depicted with his hand inside his jacket, apparently trying to emulate Napoleon's famous stance. The patient who enacts a Napoleonic role may be trying to fulfill deeply personal needs.

However, social factors are undoubtedly also germane. A psychiatrist known to one of the authors pointed out that there are "fads" or "styles" in delusional systems. True enough, there was a time when "Napoleons" were frequently encountered. But during and after World War II it became more common to find "Hitlers." Thus, the *content* of delusional systems, which includes both verbal and nonverbal behaviors, are often drawn from the external world, the current scene.

Obviously, then, the nature of the material which the external world has available for selection will help to determine which symptoms the patients incorporate into their self-presentation. It is also likely to influence those aspects of the patients' behavior which are based on elaborations of the delusional system. A ward "Hitler" may, for example, attack others on the ward whom he perceives as "racially inferior." And it could scarcely be denied that part of the etiology of "Napoleon's" or "Hitler's" disorder must be sought in the social context of his development.

Here is a second simple illustration that even the psychotic person responds to his social milieu. Psychiatrist P. Stefan Kraus observed many patients who were transferred from wards filled with very deteriorated, regressed people to wards where there were higher standards of behavior and personal hygiene. Substantial improvement on the part of the transferees was noted in many cases (79). The patients were able to respond to changed expectations about their behavior. Similarly, patients who were transferred from "good" to "bad" wards tended to alter their behavior accordingly. Such observations have been made by many other mental health workers.

Apparently, the more we *expect* patients to be out of control, the more we will be so obliged. It is conceivable that our expectation confers a sort of permission for the asocial or antisocial behavior to occur. This proposition does not deny the significance of other factors which also influence aggressive behavior on the part of a psychotic. Nor does it obviate the fact that some murders are directly related to psychotic symptomatology—for example, the person who kills because he has been directed to do so by hallucinated voices. What we do wish to emphasize is that psychosis per se often fails to explain homicidal behavior. A change in the environmental context might have prevented the killing. Psychosis does not remove the killer or potential killer from the influence and, therefore, the responsibility of society in fostering murder.

A violent or murderous society might give rise to more psychoses than a society which handles its tensions in other ways, or which has fewer tensions. Perhaps it is more likely that a violent society will encourage the development of more violent *forms* of psychotic behavior even if the absolute number of psychotic reactions is not unusually high. One could be "crazy" in the benign and even joyous manner of a Johnny Appleseed, as contrasted with the lethality of a mass murderer. These considerations go far beyond the available evidence, although anthropologists and other students of culture have reported much that is consistent with at least the latter proposition.

It appears entirely appropriate at this point to broaden our discussion to include the nature of the society in which we are now living. Does our society expect or encourage its members, psychotic or nonpsychotic, to behave violently?

OUR HOMICIDOGENIC SOCIETY

Is Murder "Contagious" in Contemporary Society?

Many laymen and professional people feel that the occurrence of several incidents of mass murder within the span of just a few months in 1966 was no coincidence—that, in some way, one crime "suggested" or "triggered" the next one. This outlook is part of the more general view that American society condones and spreads violence. Fredrick Wertham, one of the leading proponents of this view, has declared: "I would state it as a law that if any act of violence is not properly resolved it will be repeated" (80). He explains his proposition as follows:

When you talk about murder, or other crimes, the proper resolution is for society to make clear what it wants. Society must say, *No, this we will not tolerate.* . . . Justice must be done, it must be seen in an open courtroom. This is not revenge, or retribution, of course. Punishment is a language. It says that society will hold people accountable for their acts (81).

Wertham's approach seems to be at odds with that of the school of thought which holds that mental illness is responsible for murder and, therefore, the perpetrators should be treated, not punished. About crime and mental illness, Wertham is very explicit:

If a man is really so mentally ill that he couldn't help himself, I'm the first to defend him. . . . But most people who commit crimes are not mentally sick. They are the result of society's failure and its acceptance of violence as an inevitable part of human life (82).

He is critical of those who take a soft approach.

Unfortunately, many people today who think they are humanitarian feel that society mustn't punish criminals and delinquents . . . we must understand them and turn them over to the psychiatrist. Well, psychiatrists are not trained for this. There's not much about controlling crime in the textbooks we've studied. Crime is society's problem. If you start off by saying "let's call the psychiatrist, the poor man must be insane" . . . you're not telling the world that they can't get away with violence (83).

Are violence and murder really contagious? If so, what are the specific ways in which our society encourages violence?

What are the conditions that make a particular individual especially vulnerable to this "contagion"? Evidence bearing upon these questions is disappointingly scant. This limitation must be kept in mind if we are to avoid jumping to conclusions prematurely. However, it may be possible to find some clues in three sources of information—statistics, case records, and controlled experimental research. Thorough understanding of the psychosociology of murder will probably require integration of observations made within each of these approaches (once there is enough evidence to be worth integrating).

Let us first consider the statistical approach. One possible medium of "contagion" is the press. Jerome Motto examined the possible role of newspaper coverage in "suggesting" suicidal behavior. Similar research could be conducted on the topic of murder. Motto compared the suicide rates in seven cities during periods when newspapers were not being published (because of strikes) with the rates for the same months in the same cities for the previous five years. None of the cities showed significant differences in the suicide rate during the news blackout period. The suicide rate did decline slightly during the newspaper strike in five of the cities, a finding that was in the expected or hypothesized direction. But two cities (Detroit and Honolulu) showed increases. The study in general offered no proof that newspaper reports increase the incidence of suicide *by suggestion*. Motto, however, remained of the opinion that "the value system inherent in the manner news is usually reported has a deleterious influence on the emotional growth of immature readers, which in turn can later be conducive to increased suicide potential" (84).

Perhaps we see in this study one of the limitations of an approach that is limited to descriptive statistics, even if on a large scale. Motto's hypothesis involves the possible influence of manner of news presentation on the emotional growth of immature readers, but would it not be more to the point to study this process directly? Better yet, would it not be more useful to focus upon the suspected *process* by which suicide or murder potential is heightened, and then find appropriate statistical data to determine whether or not the *effect* (actual suicide or murder) occurs? Interaction of the two approaches should enhance the possibility of obtaining statistical data that are most relevant to the suspected processes.

Returning to Motto's study, it is a little surprising that he found even weak evidence for the effect of news blackout on suicide. While it is reasonable to consider amount and manner of news coverage to be a factor in "suggesting" extreme behaviors, there is no firm basis for considering this to be a dominant factor. It should be obvious by now that both suicide and murder are affected by multitudinous factors. And we would not want to forget that radio and television coverage in these cities prevented the newspaper blackout from resulting in a total restriction of mass communications.

The hypothesis that mass media may trigger lethal behavior is still viable. Some of the data uncovered by Motto in his survey of the suicide literature are worth keeping in mind. The following observations link statistical data on lethal behavior with case material.

1. In 1913 "a wave of suicides by ingestion of bichloride of mercury was noted to subside after newspaper accounts deleted mention of the drug" (85).

2. There was a 40 percent increase in suicides in Los Angeles during the month of the suicide of Marilyn Monroe in August, 1962, although this did not significantly alter the suicide rate for the whole year. The increase noted was primarily among males, which Motto feels represents "a reaction to loss" (86).

3. There was a 42 percent increase in female suicides the year following

Marilyn Monroe's death which, according to Motto, "raises the issue of identification with the person whose suicide is publicized" (87).

If it is likely that newspaper and other reports play a role in suggesting suicide to some people, may they not also suggest murder? With respect to "unresolved" crimes, of which Wertham speaks above, would not such an effect be even more likely? During part of the time this chapter was being prepared, two of the three incidents of mass murder mentioned earlier could have been considered "unresolved." In one case, the death sentence was being appealed. In another, the trial was in progress. (Information about the conviction of the adolescent killer of five was incorporated into the chapter after it had been completed.) The third mass killer was himself slain at the scene of the crime. Has anything happened to indicate that these cases, these unresolved crimes, have suggested or otherwise influenced similar behavior in susceptible individuals? Consider the following item, reprinted in its entirety, from a newspaper dated September 20, 1967 (88).

John M. Whitman is the 19-year-old brother of Charles Whitman, the slain University of Texas sniper who killed 16 people in Austin, Texas, on August 1, 1966. Two months before the massacre John was found guilty of possession of alcoholic beverages while a minor. On Tuesday he had his fourth arrest since that time. John was charged with breaking and entering with intent to commit rape in Lake Worth, Fla. The youth fought with his father on the steps of the courthouse before being freed on $2,000 bond. Neighbors said John had left his father when he was 17. Police said the youth told them: "You've heard of my brother . . . well, you haven't seen any reputation yet."

The above example could be considered "contaminated" from many standpoints. The mixture of various factors in a given case is typical, and complicates the quest for a single or "basic" explanation. In the case of John Whitman it would seem that news coverage and other mass media notice of his brother's crime did exert an influence over him ("You've heard of my brother . . . ."). Yet the influence of the media is difficult to assess because of circumstances such as the following: a) The young man in question certainly was not dependent upon news or other indirect accounts of the mass killings. One of the slayers was his own brother. b) Factors in Charles Whitman's upbringing that were germane to his crime may also have been operative in the early life of John. Similarity in early experiences may have led to antisocial behaviors by both brothers, rather than their later exposure to reports of mass killings. c) A poor relationship with the father, highly probable in this case, has often been cited as an etiologic factor in juvenile delinquency and adult crime. This could be considered of causal significance. On the other hand, does the poor relationship with the father explain why cases of mass murder tend to occur in clusters? We doubt it.

Given that characteristics of the individual may determine susceptibility or predisposition, we are still left primarily with social factors as the likely trigger mechanisms. If the social triggering mechanism were absent or if powerful inhibiting forces were at work in society, would not many crimes be prevented? John Whitman himself referred to the behavior of his brother when he was arrested. Apparently, his knowledge of his brother's behavior and its "fame" had exerted a strong influence on his own attitudes and activities. (We might also note in passing that one hypothesis about the etiology of Charles Whitmans' actions—that they were cued off somehow by his brain tumor—tends to be undermined somewhat by indications of antisocial tendencies in his brother. In fact, working from the social line of explanation, one might "postdict" that had John Whitman been the first to commit a violent crime, then his brother Charles might have been influenced to "do him one better.")

Did any other crimes subsequent to the mass killings bear the stamp of their influence? A possible second example was not long in presenting itself:

On October 23, 1967, "a 'quiet, peaceful' gun fancier staged a mass slaying . . . killing 6 persons and wounding 6 others in a 90-minute reign of terror that ended when he was critically injured by police during a gun battle in the backyard of his home in nearby Loganton" (89). The report further stated that Leo Held, the killer, was the father of four, had been active in the Boy Scouts, and knew his victims (five co-workers and a neighbor). As we have already indicated, there is no intention to imply here that the behavior of either of these individuals can be attributed solely to the influence of the previous mass killings. If this were the case, then why would not most Americans who can read newspapers also commit homicide?

The factor of "susceptibility" or "resistance" unquestionably is of prime import. Society's problem, then, appears to be threefold: how to determine who is especially susceptible to homicidal suggestions; how to reduce the number and virulence of the homicidogenic cues they receive and/or to prevent them from acting in response to these cues; and how to keep others (such as children) from developing similar susceptibilities. There is a strong temptation at this point to switch the focus from society to the individual— to delve into psychodynamics, to examine personality traits. This inclination is understandable and, up to a certain point, the information gained by such techniques may be quite valuable. We can emphasize the fact already touched upon that all of the mass slayers mentioned (with the possible exception of Leo Held about whom we lack the relevant information) had poor relationships with their fathers. There is also the knowledge that both of the Whitmans and Held were keenly interested in guns (which may be viewed as subjective phallic symbols as well as objective weapons).

However, we have seen (in Chapter 11) that child-rearing practices are crucial to personality development; and that when certain practices are institutionalized by a given society they produce certain common traits in both children and adults. In light of the fact that the United States has an unusually high rate of violent crime (see below) and, up to now, a virtual monopoly on mass murder, it would seem more important in attempting to understand homicide to direct our attention to the society in which the crimes occur. Moreover, if we choose to focus only on the individual roots of crime we are left with the nagging "coincidence" of many murders occurring closely together in time. Would all of the "bad genes," brain tumors, and aberrant personality traits just happen to manifest themselves one right after the other?

Finally, let us consider what controlled experimental research might be able to teach us about the ways in which social processes trigger lethal behavior. We are using the term "experimental" here in contradistinction to "empirical-only" or "descriptive." Experimental research involves the planned manipulation of conditions to test hypotheses, rather than the observation of events as they happen to occur. Although there has not been much experimental investigation of the phenomena in which we are interested here, the research that has been done is ingenious and valuable.

Leonard Berkowitz and his colleagues at the University of Wisconsin have examined the possibility that our society may encourage violent and murderous behavior by "even so small a matter as the casual sight of a gun" as well as "the sight of violence" (90). In one experiment, the Wisconsin psychologists involved 100 undergraduates in a two-part experience. During the first part of the study the students were administered either a relatively low or a relatively high number of mild electric shocks by an unseen "partner" in another room (the shocks were tripped off by a telegraph key). Supposedly, the number of shocks served to inform the subject as to how his partner evaluated the subject's performance on an idea-generating task. In actuality, however, 50 of the subjects were selected to receive the high number of shocks in an effort to arouse in them feelings of humiliation and anger. This technique did indeed seem to create 50 angry young men.

During the second, and critical part of the study, all of the subjects were called upon to evaluate the work of their (still unseen) partners. The subjects were seated at a table upon which was resting the telegraph key that would (they thought) inflict electric shocks upon their partners. Here is where the critical variable was introduced: Some subjects worked at a table that was completely empty, except for the telegraph key. Other subjects worked at a table that "happened" to have badminton racquets and shuttlecocks lying about ("left over from the last experiment"). But some subjects worked at a table upon which reposed a 12-gauge shotgun and a snub-nosed .38 caliber revolver (also said to have been absentmindedly left there from a previous study). "Our *most significant finding was that the angry men who saw the guns gave more shocks than any other group*" (91).

On its own terms, this experiment is a clear demonstration that an environmental condition (sight of weapon) can influence a person to inflict an unnecessarily great amount of pain upon another, in this case to riddle him with electric shocks. Perhaps the most obvious action-implication is to work for a decreased exposure to the sight of guns and the elimination of easy access to these weapons. But the experiment also demonstrates that the effect is greatest when the individual already is predisposed because of his own affective state (anger, following upon humiliation). Does this not suggest something further—

that social conditions that engender humiliation, anger, and frustration may be critical factors in unleashing lethal behavior? It would seem that our society encourages violence with guns by both pathways: systematically humiliating and frustrating certain people, and making available extreme outlets for the anger that results.

Berkowitz agrees that "our society offers its citizens a wide array of anger-producing frustrations." He continues:

Aggression is more likely to result from unrealized hopes than from deprivation alone. The deprived person who has no hope cannot really be said to be frustrated, because he does not really have a goal he is trying to move toward. A person works harder to get something—whether it is food, a sexual object, or a new car—if he thinks he has a chance. Similarly, his frustration is most severe when he is blocked from a satisfaction he thinks should and could be his. In social terms, this concept of frustration reveals itself in "revolutions of rising expectations." Poverty-stricken groups are not frustrated merely because they have suffered severe deprivations; they are frustrated when they begin to hope. Privation is far less likely to cause violence than is the dashing of hopes (92).

The causes of homicide, then, might be sought in the social disequilibrium that finds some people tempted by exposure to the "good life" that is around them, while at the same time being handicapped by many circumstances in their striving to acquire a share of these desirables for themselves. One thinks immediately of the rising expectations for social equality that has accompanied the enactment of civil rights and anti-poverty legislation. The rise in level of expectation (renewed hope) seems to have led to new levels of frustration for many individuals. As Berkowitz has suggested, violence may be a more frequent consequence of "the dashing of hopes" than of deprivation per se. Perhaps some deprived people began to hope for "too much, too fast." Perhaps society has backed up its promises "too little, too slow." In either case, we have the gap between expectation and fulfillment.

This viewpoint might lead to the formulation and testing of hypotheses regarding *the social function of homicide*. One possibility, for example, is that violence and murder are just the unfortunate by-products of important *transitions*. Regarded in this manner, the rising homicide rate (see below) represents casualties from an undeclared war. We are at war with ourselves on a broad front of social issues. The final outcome (to the extent that any outcome is final) may be a favorable one: the revised system works more equitably for more people. But in the meantime, there is upheaval and frustration—and, hence, more violence shooting off in all directions.

One of the authors recalls a conversation with a dynamic, action-oriented psychiatrist who was in the throes of introducing radical changes in the treatment program of a mental hospital. The innovations were designed to produce a new social climate, changing the expectations of both patients and staff. Results had been encouraging, and the full potential had not yet been actualized. But there was a casualty rate to consider. The psychiatrist recognized the strong prospect that the suicide rate would be elevated for a period of time, at least until the change-over had been completely effected. One may or may not agree with this psychiatrist's judgment that the value of the program overrides the risk of increased lethal behavior. However, perhaps we see in this example a microcosm of increased lethality in a society that is temporarily disorganized while (presumably) en route to a beneficial reorganization.

We also suggest a second hypothesis: that homicide and other forms of lethal behavior may be *crucial* to the purposes of a society, not merely a fallout we do not know how to prevent. Admittedly, this is an appalling idea. But we cannot pretend it is entirely implausible. Has political purpose ever dictated the systematic massacre of certain groups of people? Or

the selective "elimination" of those individuals fancied to be a threat to the regime? Have midnight arrests and public executions ever been used to create fear and weaken resistance in a population?

We are not implying that our society is ruled by premeditated murder or the threat of same. What we are doing is simply raising the possibility that homicide (in at least some of its forms) may have become entrenched as an expected and patterned phenomenon. In other words, homicide may be something that can be "depended on"—and what can be depended on can be *used*. We cannot pursue this hypothesis further here. Let us just recommend that qualified observers begin to ponder the possibility that certain motives and purposes in our society may be well served by the high frequency of lethal behaviors, both self- and other-directed.

Our speculations have run far ahead of Berkowitz's experiment. Additional controlled studies could be undertaken to test and elucidate the hypotheses offered above. We need further analysis and research at all levels: from naturalistic case study through controlled experiments through statistical and intellectual examination of large-scale social trends.

Homicide in Our Society

Perhaps it appears that too much is being made of a few examples. Are we actually experiencing an epidemic of violent crime? It is appropriate to turn now to some of the available statistics.

A few mass killings may dominate the headlines, but it is the accumulation of individual crimes in the back pages that really tell the story. The homicide rate across the United States has been skyrocketing. In the first half of 1967 alone, the homicide rate in a dozen American cities soared alarmingly:

TABLE 6. INCREASE IN HOMICIDE RATE:
JANUARY—JUNE 1967
COMPARED WITH THE SAME PERIOD, 1966

City	Increase
Boston	153%
Chicago	43%
Cleveland	45%
Dallas	26%
Dayton	162%
Houston	28%
Kansas City, Mo.	23%
Memphis	200%
New York	25%
Philadelphia	30%
St. Louis	80%
Washington	22%

Jack Star, who reported these statistics in a national magazine (93), pointed out that the number of murders would have been even greater were it not for improved lifesaving techniques developed since World War II. He cites as illustration the fact that in Chicago only 12 to 13 percent of gunshot victims perish. Thus in the absence of adequate medical care, we might have had a much larger number of homicides in that city. The situation may be similar in other locales. According to Martin Lipset, professor of government and social relations at Harvard University, "the United States has the highest homicide rate, and the greatest propensity for violence among the major western industrialized nations" (94). The homicide rate has continued to climb, with no limits yet in sight. *The Uniform Crime Report: 1970* issued by the Federal Bureau of Investigation reveals a steady increase from 12,090 murders in 1967 to 15,810 in 1970. During the same time span, murders in the Detroit area soared from 220 in 1967 to 550 in 1970. Not only did the annual murder rate more than double within a four year span, but in 1971 the alarming record set only twelve months previously was exceeded by the new total of 690 (*The Detroit News*, January 2, 1972).

A brief look at the relationship between certain key variables and the homicide rate may help us later to determine: a) why the homicide rate is rising so rapidly, and b) why an emphasis on individual psychodynamics and treatment is not adequate to explain or modify antisocial phenomena.

Age. A comparison of crime statistics for 1966 with those for 1960 reveals the following with respect to age. Among persons under the age of 18, arrests for homicide increased 33.3 percent; arrests for aggravated assault (which can lead to homicide) increased 114.9 percent (95). Among individuals 18 years of age and older, homicide increased 19.9 percent and aggravated assault 46.9 percent (96). Of all persons arrested for murder, 9 percent are under 18 years of age, 37 percent are under 25 (97). The overall crime rate among those 21 years of age and under rose 50 percent between 1962 and 1967 (98). More serious crimes are committed by 15-year-olds than by any other age group; 16-year-olds are not far behind (99). FBI figures for 1966 indicate that *children under the age of 15* were accused of committing 144 homicides, 425 forcible rapes, 5338 robberies, 5938 aggravated assaults (100). Crimes in the last three categories are included here since they tend to be repeated and can result in death—some day the young perpetrator may hit his victim too hard or once too often, or perhaps he may begin to use a gun. (Aggravated assaults involving the use of a gun have also been increasing. They jumped 23 percent in the first 9 months of 1966) (101).

Sex. The ratio of males to females is 5:1 among murderers and 3:1 among victims. Of the 15-year-olds committing crimes (see above), ten times as many were male as female (102). (Crime is also increasing among females. However, their crimes usually do not involve violence. The most common one is shoplifting) (103).

Race. A disproportionate number of murders now involve Negroes in some way. Negroes comprise 11 percent of the population, but 54 percent of the murder victims and 57 percent of those charged with homicide (104).

Locale. More murders are commited in the South than in any other region of the United States; nearly half of all American homicides occur in this area. It should be noted also that one region of the South, the hill country around Tennessee and Kentucky, has what amounts to a monopoly on one bizarre technique—murder by mail. The killer eliminates his victim by sending him bombs, poisoned food, etc. The geographic area in which this occurs is one in which family feuds and vendettas are common (105).

Cross-Cultural Data such as the following:

1. Columbia's homicide rate is seven times that of the United States.
2. In 1966 there were 204 murders in Tokyo, Japan, which has a population of just over 11 million. There were 738 murders in greater New York which has a population of 11.5 million (106).
3. In a recent decade (1957-1967) Tokyo's crime rate dropped by one-third while its population *increased* by 50 percent (107). In the past six years alone in our capital city, Washington, D.C., homicides and housebreakings doubled and robberies and auto thefts almost tripled (108).
4. Whether a particular kind of murder is a crime at all, or how serious a crime it is considered to be varies from nation to nation. For example:

Giuseppe Bellusci, a resident of Cosenza, Italy, killed his wife's lover in 1937 and received a three-year sentence. Now a Cosenza court has sentenced him to 27 years in prison for killing his wife in 1963. The court said Bellusci did it because of his love for another woman. The earlier sentence was light, the court said at the time, because Bellusci had acted to defend his honor as a husband (109).

In some cultures, apparently, a husband's honor is important enough to all but justify murder. Several unique "justifications" for homicidal attacks are being offered with some frequency by citizens of post-war Germany. Consider these excerpts from an account of the recent rash of assaults taking place on German highways (110).

Passing another car on a high-speed road is chancy anywhere in the world, but in Germany there is an additional hazard. The man you overhaul almost certainly will consider the action an affront—and may attack you at the next red light.

A group of men in Nuernberg passed a car from Mainz. The Mainz driver made an obscene gesture. The Nuernbergers stopped and one of them spit in the Mainzer's face. A nearby construction site provided both sides with weapons and the fight was pretty much a well-bloodied draw until one of the Nuernberg men produced a pistol and shot the Mainz man dead. . . .

In Cologne, a pedestrian complained to a driver that his lights were too bright and blinding to walkers along the road. The driver leaped from his car, knocked down the pedestrian so forcefully he died, and [the driver] fled.

A Frankfurt man recently shot his neighbor when the neighbor scratched the bumper of his car.

All these cases have occurred within the last 20 months and are only representative of many more.

Various explanations of these violent behaviors have been offered: It "results from the general feeling of insecurity following two lost wars"; or German drivers are aggressive "because most of them are new drivers who haven't yet learned to consider their cars simply as a means of transportation" (111).

In this connection, we would like to

raise again the possibility of the suggestion and contagion of crime. Once this type of crime occurred and was widely reported, susceptible individuals may have come to define highway discourtesy as personally provocative acts. Perhaps the predisposed individual is unconsciously seeking an excuse to act out his aggressive impulses. Highway incidents, once utilized in this fashion, could provide such an excuse for others.

Evidence has been presented here that murder is not simply a function of individual pathology, that even the *psychological* determinants have roots in the social environment, that one cannot fully understand a particular crime without reference to the milieu in which it took place. Even within a particular city, for example, there are locales that are especially hazardous. A black man who lives in one of three high-violence precincts in Detroit runs 10 times as great a risk of being murdered as does a white man residing in another area of the same city (*The Detroit News*, January 3, 1972). We have also specified the relationship between certain variables and the homicide rate. Despite this, one may still lack a clear conception of what characterizes the typical crime of violence in the United States today. One may, in fact, be surprised to learn that most of our stereotypes about murders and murderers have no foundation in fact.

1. *Most murderers are not mysterious strangers.* In at least two-thirds of the cases of willful homicide and violent assault, the perpetrator and victim are at least acquainted (112). In fact, fully 29 percent of the homicides recorded in 1966 were committed by relatives of the victim (113).

2. *Family members or acquaintances behave more violently toward their victims than do total strangers* (114).

3. *"Senseless" assaults by complete strangers are rare* (115).

4. *It is likely that more policemen are killed while investigating domestic disturbances than in any other type of duty* (116).

5. *"The odds in favor of being the victim of a violent crime decline very quickly with increases in neighborhood income"* (117).

6. *"Robbery is the principle source of violence from strangers"* (118).

7. *In most crimes of violence the perpetrator and the victim are of the same race* (119).

Here, then, are the facts of the "ordinary" homicide or aggravated assault. Stripped of allusions to homicidal maniacs, mysterious strangers, and racial bigotry, the events surrounding homicides are in some ways all the more disturbing because they are so commonplace. (The same could be said for many of the other psychosocial pathways to premature death.) Friends and relatives slay each other in the privacy of their homes. Thieves wantonly murder for the sake of what the victim's wallet may contain. Policemen summoned to quell a domestic disturbance are set upon and murdered. Increasingly, homicide is our ready answer to a wide variety of problems. But why? Let us return again to the basic data of contemporary crime cited above. Two alarming features emerge clearly from the statistics: the youth of the perpetrators and the increasing frequency of violent crimes. It is difficult to escape the conclusion that "homicidogenic" influences in American society must be increasing in number, intensity, or both. What are these homicidogenic influences? Can they really be related to antisocial behavior, or is this all pure conjecture?

The Mass Media and Violent Entertainment

The finger of accusation has been pointed at the mass media with increasing frequency. Real and self-appointed experts maintain that television, newspapers, magazines, radio, and motion pictures are all promoting crime. We have already touched upon the problem of whether or not newspaper accounts of suicides have the effect of increasing the suicide rate. Although this is both a matter of theoretical and general significance, few thinking people in a free society are likely to advocate the suppression of unbiased reports of events that have already taken place. Our contention here is that when observers indict the mass media for inciting to homicide, the material to which they refer is usually billed not as news but as "entertainment."

We are bombarded daily with a remarkable amount and variety of violent "amusement." Much of its content is far removed from the "fair and square fight" we purport to favor. It could more accurately be described as downright sadistic and perverse. Frequently it is presented in both "living" color and excruciating detail. Fredric Wertham collected, organized, and discussed varied examples of such material in his challenging book, *A Sign for Cain* (120) which was published in 1962. For evidence that our chief topic of entertainment has changed not at all since then, one has only to turn on the television set, peruse the movie advertisements, or glance at the paperback book rack at the local drugstore.

One of the authors noted the contents of popular television programs over a period of several months. Two of the principle ingredients were violence and death—death at the hands of a crazed axe wielder, death in a Western shootout, death by a "disintegrator gun," death by hanging, death in the jaws of a devouring sea monster, death in a torture cell where spiked walls gradually closed in on the victim, death by bombing, death by man-eating ants in the desert, death by being thrown from a rooftop, death from being pushed off a water tower, death by forcible drowning in a bathtub, death by throwing a man in a wheelchair down an elevator shaft, death by machine gun, and

innumerable war deaths on the battlefield and in submarines. All of these edifying events were witnessed *not* at one o'clock in the morning, but in prime viewing time. It would seem that the gentle interlude once known as "the children's hour" has been replaced by a vicarious bloodbath.

Psychiatrist Karl Menninger has been quoted as saying:

A third or a fourth of our television programs for the amusement of children are exhibitions of how you can slug them, how you can knock them out, how you can kick them, how you can kill them at long distance and short distance. Don't think that violence is condoned, my dear friends, it's enjoyed. . . (121).

Menninger might also have pointed out that in addition to the children's programs, youngsters are also exposed to some of the even coarser fare intended for their more jaded elders. What relationship, if any, has all of this to the increasingly violent behavior of the young?

It is no secret that little children are splendid imitators. They copy and reenact what goes on around them. (What parent has not been witness to and cringed before a public performance by his children of remarks and gestures that were supposed to be "private"?) The potential influence of television is especially great. Movies are also capable of influencing the child's behavior. It can hardly be a matter of indifference that movies seem to be becoming more blatantly violent all the time. Films such as *Bonnie and Clyde* and *The Dirty Dozen* are but two examples. The following advertisement, headlined simply "Horror-Grave," illustrates another and rather specialized type:

"Bloody Pit of Horror" and *"Terror Creatures from the Grave,"* two new shockers, are combined on the thrill bill opening Wednesday at the Orpheum and nearby drive-ins. The films are said to show many of the tortures actually used in Medieval times (122).

Despite the violent and gory content, movies may be less harmful than television. To attend a movie the child must leave his home and usual surroundings, pay admission, and sit in a special building with the lights dimmed. Although the darkness and the rapt, if nervous, attention of his fellow viewers may intensify his experience of what is transpiring on the screen, there are two elements which may reduce the deleterious effects. The most important of these is that the movie is set apart from everyday life. The viewer emerges from darkness, as from sleep, rubs his eyes, and reenters the familiar offscreen world. This decontamination process serves to remind him that what he has left behind is fantasy; it has not altered the circumstances of his daily life. This is not to deny that films may awaken aggressive impulses in the viewer, or contribute to crime by demonstrating techniques. But, at least, the mode of presentation can help the reasonably well-integrated youngster to separate the violence on screen from his own life. Secondly, the admission price and minimum age required for unsupervised attendance at the cinema have heretofore made the movie an infrequent, special event for the very young child.

There are no such built-in restrictions to keep children from viewing the violence depicted on television. In some homes the tube is glowing almost continuously from early morning until late at night—the programs are, after all, touted as "family entertainment." Parents who would not consider taking young children to see a realistic war movie think nothing of allowing them to watch whatever kind of death and destruction happens to be featured on television during their waking hours. In fact, children often are encouraged to watch television to keep them quiet and out of the parents' way. This brings up a more subtle and, we believe, a more ominous aspect of television violence: the parents' tacit approval or, at least, acceptance of whatever television

presents. The home is the mainstay of the young child's existence. Television programs viewed in the broad light of day are an objective part of that home. There is no leaving the theater to return to the "real world" of light when the show is over. Television happenings are part of the surroundings. Mother and perhaps father, too, are there. They continue eating or talking while the mayhem proceeds on the tube. This cannot help but create the impression that what is happening on the tube is "all right" and just a normal part of everyday life. And we would not be suprised if this emotional split between "everything is normal" and bloody violence encourages the susceptible child to develop a dangerous warp in his affective life. One can observe others killing and being killed while daily life flows around the scene as though it were nothing out of the ordinary. Do experiences of this nature—repeated daily—encourage a child to grow into an involved adult who becomes appropriately concerned when the realistic prospect of violence arises? Or does it instead train him to be the callous perpetrator or the callous on-looker?

Some readers might protest that children *must* know that what they see on television does not happen off-screen every day. This is not really so. Babies and toddlers cannot know much of what takes place outside of their own homes. Moreover, young children characteristically have difficulty separating fantasy from reality from television, even without the effects of television (123). The preschool child is likely to be exposed to the longest periods of television viewing. But he is at a stage of life at which he is also least able to distinguish between the real and the "pretend." It should be mentioned at this point that the reasons we have cited for believing that movies may exert a less harmful influence than television are rapidly being negated by two recent developments. The first is the increasing tendency for the entire family to accompany parents to the drive-in theater. The rationalization offered to counteract any objections to this practice is an optimistic assertation that the younger children will "sleep right through it." One of the authors has tried this on several occasions with more than one child, only to find that the asserted soporific effect fails to develop. The second factor is the increasing use on daytime television of old movies that were intended originally for adult audiences. This injects into the toddler's home life depictions of a wide variety of behavior that he is capable of imitating—without understanding their motivations or action-consequences.

We believe that all of the features of the mass media discussed above when added to any constitutional and/or idiosyncratic personality factors can predispose the young viewer to violent behavior. Faced later with a problem or stressful situation, the predisposed individual's aggressive impulses may overwhelm his defenses and be expressed directly in the kind of antisocial behavior he has witnessed scores of times on the screen or tube. But this viewpoint is by no means the only—or even the most popular—opinion held by professional people. Many who are highly experienced see violence in the mass media from a different perspective. One of the foremost of these is the noted psychologist Bruno Bettelheim.

Bettelheim's basic premise is that violence is "an ineradicable part of human nature" (124). He feels that in trying to deny violence a place in our society we force the individual to suppress his tendencies in that direction. These tendencies are then said to accumulate to such an intensity that "he can no longer deny or control them." They can erupt suddenly in the isolated act of explosive violence—whether against eight Chicago nurses or against the president of the United States. Bettelheim thinks it is the conspicuousness of such outbursts that has led us to conclude, erroneously, that ours is an age of violence. He reminds us that we no longer burn witches or hold public hangings. These are taken to support his thesis that we do not live in particularly violent times.

Bettelheim also disagrees that playing with guns or other toys of destruction is bad for children. "At their age such play provides the safety valve that drains off small amounts of violence, leaving a balance that can be managed" (125). He is also convinced that television, comic books, and the mass media in general do *not* "seduce the innocents" (Wertham's term). "It is high time that the myth of original innocence be dissipated to the land of the unconscious along with its opposite, the myth of original sin. Violence exists all right, and each of us is born with the potential for it. We are also born with opposite tendencies and these must be carefully nurtured if they are to offset the violence" (126).

What is the explanation for observed violence by young people today? Bettelheim offers a partial explanation, about as follows: Our society today is an affluent one. We no longer have child labor and sweatshop conditions. The modern child is economically dependent upon his parents for a long time. He has been asked to obey customs that run counter to his biological needs and which have only recently been created. He questions these customs and his parents' right to impose them upon him. "Many youngsters submit and grind out a boring existence, or drop out of society and become beats. But others explode and resort to violence." For them "violence seems a shortcut toward gaining an objective. And by their very revolt they show that they do not know what they are doing. . . they have not been taught what violence is: It is so primitive that it is not suitable for obtaining the subtle satisfactions desired" (127). Finally, Bettelheim deplores a) that channels for the safe discharge of aggression are fewer today, and b) that children's school readers do not include aggression. "Maybe there was some wisdom to the old-fashioned readers where the child was told what cruel fate befalls the evil-doer" (128).

Undoubtedly there are many who would agree with Bettelheim; but we are not among them. Feelings of aggression are appropriate responses to some circumstances, and a certain amount of hostility and aggression may be aroused in times of stress and frustration. However, we do not find it necessary to believe that *violence* is an "ineradicable part of human nature." Neither do we believe that Americans are "trying to deny violence a place in our society." Violence is ubiquitous in this culture; we *should* be trying to curtail it. This does not mean that varied outlets for aggressive, competitive, and assertive impulses should be eliminated. But we cannot agree that the hostile, antisocial, murderous behavior which the word "violence" implies is inevitable and, therefore, acceptable.

We must also take issue with another of Bettelheim's propositions. One may contend on theoretical grounds (especially psychoanalytic formulations) that playing with toy weapons or witnessing homicidal behavior on television safely releases aggression. Nevertheless, as Wertham points out, there is "no shred of clinical evidence" to support it (129). Furthermore, when we consult our own experiences it is likely that we will discover many instances of just the opposite effect. We become involved in a motion picture or television drama. The "bad guy" is so bad that we would like to take a crack at him ourselves. Our pulses race. We are really upset, angry. The aroused sympathetic nervous system and the stream of retaliative and aggressive impulses do not turn off automatically at the end of the production. Often there is an overflow. We were not filled up before watching the drama; it did not assuage preexisting feelings—the story itself precipitated a rise in aggressive sentiments. Chances are that we will survive this little experience without "doing anything rash," but we have been given at least a temporary nudge in the direction of violent behavior. (Much can be learned from exploring the relationship between the structure and content of a dramatic production and its effect upon our emotions—beginning with the observations of Aristotle and Plato. The kind of theatrical experience that we find ourselves describing as "noble," "great," or "humanizing" appears to exercise a more complex and positive effect upon our state of mind than does the usual fare of violent "entertainment" to which we are exposed.)

The available experimental evidence also runs counter to Bettelheim's views on this point. Berkowitz has summarized several experiments conducted by his own and other research teams. The common finding among these studies is that vicarious exposure to violent episodes (e.g., a prize-fighting sequence from *Champion*, a Kirk Douglas movie) is followed by indications of *increased* aggressiveness on the part of the viewers. Additionally, some of these studies suggest that overflow aggression is most likely to be expressed when the individual believes he has observed a scene of *justified* violence. "Rather than feeling purged of their hostility, the students seemed to feel freer to express it. It was as if the justified aggression on the screen justified as well their own aggression against their tormenters" (130).

Berkowitz reports that the effect is halted and even reversed when the viewer comes to perceive the violence as much too severe for the circumstances. When the aggressive actions become too vivid or too excessive, the spectator is likely to experience a sense of horror. This experience in turn leads to a *reduction* in the tendency to behave aggressively toward others.

However, the line between violence that is justified and unjustified, fictional and real, uninhibiting and inhibiting, is anything but clear. . . . At some point on the continuum, viewed violence *stops* horrifying and *starts* exciting. Once this point has been reached, vicarious experience with aggressiveness begins to lower restraints against the real thing (131).

There is reason to believe that the effects we have been considering may be particularly strong upon children and adolescents. The child tries various identities on for size, and many of the available mass-promulgated characters are specialists in violence, whether nominally presented as "good guys" or "bad guys." The adolescent, although more sophisticated than the child, also has more formidable *outlets* for aggressive behavior. He can go further in modeling himself upon celebrities. If, for example, most of the "heroes" to which an adolescent boy is exposed prove their "masculinity" by assaultive actions, is it so surprising that some of their admirers try on this behavior? Can we overlook the possible relationship among these three variables: a) the adolescent's need to find models for his own behavior, b) the ready availability of high-violence models in our mass media, and c) the soaring crime rate in this age group?

By now, some readers may feel that we have belabored our points (again!) and over-generalized. It might be objected that, statistics notwithstanding, most young people who have been exposed to the mass media all their lives do not identify with the shabby heroes, nor commit mayhem on the streets. That is a perfectly valid objection, but we cannot help but feel that the climate in which crimes occur is shaped in part by the influences that have been described above, as well as in various other places throughout this book.

In addition, the hero's role is not the only important one in a saga of violence. There is also the victim. Who would care to identify with the victim of violence or murder? There are a few prime candidates. The potentially suicidal individual is one. The masochist is another. He may not be death-seeking, but he finds the victim's role appealing for its harvest of self-pity and sympathy-recruiting. Stories can suggest subtle ways to arrange a crime so that one can become an "innocent victim." How is that? Victims don't cause crimes. Or do they? John MacDonald, who has explored the role of the victim, believes that often he is not as "innocent" as pictured (132). Better still, he provides concrete examples:

1. When one man threatened his wife with a loaded shotgun, she retorted: "Go ahead, you might just as well kill me." "Whenever the husband announced his intention of selling the shotgun, his wife would insist on his keeping it" (133).
2. "A daughter, overhearing father beating mother, came between her parents. Her mother said, 'Never mind, honey, let him kill me.' After she left the home to seek help, her father obtained his revolver from another room and killed his wife" (134).

MacDonald reports that wives "often responded to production of firearms during an argument with provocative comments, such as, 'What are you going to do, big man, kill me?' and 'You haven't got the guts to kill me.'" These statements strike us as combining elements of seduction and lethality. The victim seems to be asking for it—although neither victim nor murderer may be certain what "it" really is. There is also the obvious implication in these quoted statements that the ability to kill is a trait both masculine and desirable. The Big Man is the one who pulls the trigger.

Some people are "homicide prone" just as others are "accident prone," according to MacDonald (135). He cites the work of Wolfgang, whose study of 588 criminal homicides showed that, in 26 percent of these cases, it was the victim who first resorted to physical violence.

There are cases, of course, in which the "complicity" of the victim is entirely unwitting. Steven Myers, speaking of the large number of two-year-olds slain by parents and parent surrogates, says that this statistic lends validity to the appellation the "terrible two's" (136). The two-year-old's behavior can, indeed, be discomforting to the parents, and his very defenselessness may serve as provocation to those with strong sadistic tendencies. However, it is extremely doubtful that the child of this age has any real conception of the danger in which he places himself.

Nevertheless, it does seem that many people who end up as murder victims have the world's worst judgment. We read about the discovery of the body of a woman who, it later turns out, had walked alone through a dimly-lit neighborhood, entered a shabby bar, accepted drinks and the attentions of half-intoxicated men, and agreed to accompany them in their car. There is also the less deliberate, subtly provocative behavior of those who do not say, "Stop!" or attempt to leave the scene when verbally or physically assaulted. Silence, coupled with failure to leave the scene, gives tacit approval to continued attack—just as the silence of society and its failure to counteract antisocial behavior encourages its continuance.

On the television screen, of course, victims are not always silent. They may writhe around, grimace, groan. Children who are just beginning to develop their ideas about life and death can be quite taken with this behavior. Look in on your children at play. "Bang, bang, you're dead!" is closely followed by a falling child, happily gasping.

Bettelheim has decried the lack of violence in school readers where children might learn about the fate of the perpetrators. Perhaps he is right. Perhaps violence and retribution should be given at least equal time in school-books. But this does not appear to be possible in television. For the child, the major and most attractive portion of many programs is the action, the mayhem. After witnessing these scenes, children are often so stimulated that they race around the room and fight with each other. They may pay

scarce attention to the quieter scenes which follow. Besides, advertisers customarily interrupt the action to insert their messages just before the final scene in which "justice is done." Prolonged dialogue, courtroom scenes and quiet conversations simply cannot compare, for most small children, with the attractions of motor activity—their own, or the action on the tube. The small viewer may drift off to other pursuits or not attend well to the final scene in which the "bad guy" is sent to prison and thus, the crime they have witnessed goes essentially unpunished.

Bettelheim says that ours is not a time of increased violence. Unfortunately, statistics run counter to his assertion. There doesn't just *seem* to be more violence today. There *is*.

We have discussed at some length the preponderance of hostile, aggressive material in the mass media, and have attempted to demonstrate how this can be related to the increasing crime rate among the young. Let us look now at some of the other homicidogenic factors in American society.

The Tradition of Violence in Our Early History

Violence has deep roots in early American history. Harvard Professor Martin Lipset raises the possibility that present-day violence in our nation "stems from our frontier traditions" (137). Perhaps so. Carving a settlement out of the wilderness, often on land forcibly taken from the Indians, hunting and fishing for food, defending the homestead against wild animals and Indian raids—all this required not only physical courage but also involved a great deal of outright killing. Those who lingered to consider the feelings of others, or to weigh decisions too heavily, were less likely to survive. The lynch mob and vigilante justice actually did characterize one period of our history. "Shooting first and asking questions later" was justifiable self-defense. During the first six years of the Gold Rush, 4,200 murders were committed in California, 1,200 in San Francisco alone. Yet there was only one official conviction for murder during the entire period (138).

Although the phrase "the only good Indian is a dead Indian," which now epitomizes provincial bigotry, dates from an earlier era, both the phrase and its underlying attitudes remain with us. However dubious such an assertion may have been in its own time, it has far outlived the self survival function it once served. In our fiction, we glorify the killers of yesteryear as heroes, and offer them up as role models to our children who will grow up in an entirely different kind of world. No wonder that we often still deprive the Indian of his land and do not accord him the full privileges of citizenship. Malnutrition and tuberculosis are far from uncommon on the reservations at a time when the average white American is healthier and wealthier than ever before. In short, we are still killing the Indians. Perhaps the reader will recall an hypothesis offered earlier in this chapter: Homicide and other forms of lethal behavior may be *crucial* to the purposes of a society. We have destroyed the Indian nations, and are still destroying the Indians. Do you suppose this means anything?

The American Indian is but one case in point. The most striking example of how an entire people can be exploited, degraded, and decimated is provided by the tragic history of the Negro in the United States. Violently uprooted from his homeland, transported under subhuman conditions, deprived of family ties, and condemned to permanent, involuntary servitude—such was his early history in this land. Efforts to escape this fate met with severe reprisals during the days of the slave trade. We are only beginning to learn how many of the captives sought the most painful forms of self-destruction in an attempt to avoid a lifetime of servitude (139). We scarcely need to point out the relevance of this oppressive tradi-

tion to current crime statistics, or to remind the reader of the violence it has continued to spawn, the brutalization it has permitted to flourish: a) We have not even done away with outright lynch murder. As recently as 1964, three civil rights workers, one Negro and two Jews (all "inferiors") were murdered in brutal fashion by a large group of white men in Meridian, Miss. (140). b) It has already been noted that the Negro is over-represented in the homicide statistics, *both as slayer and slain.* c) In addition, ghetto disturbances, increasing over the past few years, have resulted in many "accidental murders." Various theories have been advanced to explain the Negro's recent propensity to violence. We need not look far for an answer. The Negro's history of maltreatment, the perpetuation of many of the sources of frustration and rage, the unavailability of socially constructive outlets, the factors which raise expectations while limiting actual progress—these must surely play a significant role. Nor should we overlook the abundant opportunity that the black man has had to learn the methods and values of violence from— well, who would that be? We have learned that the child who is beaten is likely to become the battering adult.

Other useful explanations have been advanced. White people are deserting the core city for the suburbs; southern Negroes are moving in. Some observers feel that the increase in urban violence is partly due to the fact that newly-arrived Negroes have come from areas which have a firmly entrenched tradition of violence (141). You will recall our earlier statement that the South perennially has had a higher homicide rate than the North.

The family pattern forced upon the Negro by his previous white owners has also been indicted. Psychiatrist Lawrence Friedman states: "The passions leading to a Negro's murder of his girl friend are the passions related to the humiliations of fatherlessness or being a male in a culture where the adult female is the male"

(142). However, sociologist Charles V. Willie doubts that "efforts to strengthen family ties and increase family stability in the non-white population will be successful ... until financial upgrading opportunities are provided." Willie's study of the court records of 6,269 juveniles in Washington, D.C., revealed that delinquency rates increased as the socioeconomic status of the families decreased. (Of course, it is likely that the intact family has a higher socioeconomic level.) He theorizes that "the solution of some social problems appear in 'serial patterns': White and non-white populations are in different stages of the series. Most whites have passed beyond the stages of economic insecurity" (143).

Political scientist Norton Long makes another point: "Areas without effective community organization are particularly prone to violence; and urban political machines, which at one time reached into every precinct, are in decay and no longer provide an effective social linkage ..." (144).

Thus, economic and political factors interact with all of the other social and personal variables to over-determine the response of violent acting out among some urban Negroes. Another frequently ignored but potent force behind ghetto "rioting" (145) and individual homicide is our society's unwritten assumption that violence in general and murder in particular are adequate solutions to a broad range of problems.

Legal Homicide

Execution. (Conversation of two college graduates overheard in a department store):

"Did you hear? They got that guy who killed the nurses."

"Yeah, they oughta take him out and shoot him."

"Don't you think he should have a trial?"

"Yeah, sure. Give him a trial, and take him out and shoot him."

Whenever the alleged perpetrator of a brutal murder is apprehended, there is an impulse on the part of the populace to slaughter him. The possibility that he might turn out to be innocent has little impact at this point. And in times of stress, our society is usually prepared to "do"—whether or not its acts can be undone.

Arguments for and against the death penalty are rehashed perennially as one state or another struggles with the decision to abolish or retain it. A thorough discussion of the legal problems involved does not lie within the scope of this book or the competence of its authors. However, for purposes of future discussion, we would like to review the major arguments of retentionists and abolitionists.

Typical retentionist arguments can be summarized as follows:

1. "Life is sacred and he who violates it must pay the supreme penalty." "The law of capital punishment must stand as a silent but powerful witness to the sacredness of God-given life" (146).

2. "The prospect of the death penalty deters the hardened criminal from killing" (147).

3. The death penalty protects the public. "What kind of a zoo-keeper would he be if he opened the cage doors and released the voracious beasts to prey upon the public?" (148).

4. Imprisonment is really no more irrevocable than the death penalty. "If the dignity of the individual has any meaning ... the wrongly imprisoned men who are released ... broken, friendless, useless, 'compensated ... would have been better off dead." "I shall believe the abolitionist's present views only after he has emerged from twelve months in a convict cell" (149).

5. "Capital punishment is more economical" (150).

6. "Capital punishment is necessary to prevent the public from lynching criminals" (151).

7. "Capital punishment is the only certain penalty. People sentenced to life imprisonment are often pardoned" (152).

The first two arguments have often been rebutted by the abolitionists, whose views are summarized below. Comments about the others, however, are in order here. The third argument is based on the assumption that the only alternative to the death penalty is the release of "beasts" who would prey upon the public. This is simply not the case. Indeterminate sentences which would sometimes be tantamount to life imprisonment and other times not, as the individual case warranted, could be meted out. Furthermore, although it is now true that the term "life imprisonment" is a misnomer, the fact is that imprisonment often seems to have worked quite well: studies indicate that the paroled and pardoned, and those whose death sentences have been commuted, are the least likely of all types of criminals to repeat their crime (153). In fact, several penologists have found that, within the prison, murderers are often the best and safest "citizens" (154). And we cannot resist adding the point that the retentionist's analogy could be regarded as slanderous to the animals imprisoned in the zoo. Most beasts are not "voracious." The meat-eaters most typically kill for their own survival, and do not wantonly destroy life.

Barzun's unusual argument (point 4 above) is predicated on the false assumption that the only alternative to the death penalty is imprisonment under debasing, inhumane conditions. It is true that conditions in many prisons are unsanitary, degrading, and dehumanizing. However, it would seem more reasonable to attempt to improve such conditions, rather than to execute prisoners because they'd be better off dead. If Barzun's argument were to prevail, then it could also be used as a rationalization for killing everyone sent to prison regardless of the offense.

Whether or not capital punishment is really more economical (point 5) is open to question as a statement of fact, and we shall discuss this at greater length later in this chapter.

The argument that the death penalty is necessary to "prevent lynchings" borders on the absurd. It brings to mind the saying, "If you can't beat 'em, join 'em." It also undermines the impartial rule of law by expressing doubt in man's ability to enforce it.

The final retentionist argument is certainly valid and this, too, needs to be discussed further. At this point, let us just remark that the desire for a penalty that permanently rids society of the offender (a) presupposes that people are never mistakenly convicted, and (b) assumes that people cannot change. If this last assumption is correct, then our efforts in education, rehabilitation, and counseling must all be for naught—something we know to be untrue.

Consider now the major arguments of the abolitionists (155):

1. *Protestantism, Judaism, and Catholicism all formally recommend abolition of the death penalty.* This is a fact that should be made better known. A member of the Catholic clergy has gone on record as stating that although his church has taken no formal stand on the issue, it is inclined "by history, doctrine, spirit and example to favor abolition . . . ." Reasons for this position include some or all of the following: "Belief in God's unceasing mercy, forgiveness and redemptive power"; "faith in rehabilitative efforts"; the death penalty "brutalizes the human spirit . . ."; legal justice is fallible; the death penalty is not an effective deterrent to crime.

2. *Capital punishment is criminologically unsound.* It undermines rehabilitation and the non-punitive philosophy of twentieth century penology. It is consid-

ered necessary and useful only by those who take an hereditary or organic approach to crime—those who wish to use it for "disposing of society's jetsam."

3. *Capital punishment is morally and ethically unacceptable.* Killing in self-defense is permitted both in private life and during a war; but "the individual citizen has no right in law or morals to slay as punishment for an act, no matter how vile, already committed."

4. *Individuals in groups or societies are subject to the same moral and ethical codes that govern their conduct as individuals.* The Geneva Convention holds that "killing of one's enemy . . . after he has laid down his arms, surrendered or been taken prisoner . . . will not be countenanced." This should also apply to the individual prisoner.

5. *Capital punishment in the United States is applied inconsistently with regard to race, age, sex, and socio-economic level.* A significantly large proportion of those executed belong to minority groups and/or have no money. The wealthy or professional killers are almost never executed.

6. *Many innocent people have been executed.* Some who have been convicted of murder were later found to be innocent and released. However, when the innocent have already been executed, there is nothing that can be done to compensate for the miscarriage of justice. MacNamara mentions that 65 such cases were cited by Prof. Edwin Borchard, and another 36 by Judge Jerome Frank. There are other known cases as well.

7. *Other alternative penalties are available.* Information from areas where there is no death penalty shows that prison sentences, whether specified or indeterminate, are of at least as much protection to society as capital punishment (156). Where the death penalty, although retained, is used very little, the capital crimes rate is lower than in areas where the death penalty is used frequently. In areas where the death penalty was abol-

ished and then restored, "we find a consistently downward trend in capital crimes unaffected by either abolition or restoration" (157). This tends to refute the notion that the death penalty deters.

8. *Studies have shown police and prison officers to be at least as safe, if not safer, in states without the death penalty than in those which retain it* (158).

9. *Capital punishment actually costs more (in dollars and cents) than its alternatives* (159).

10. *What capital punishment deters is penal reform.*

11. *If the penalty for murder is death and one has already committed murder, then there is nothing to deter him from killing repeatedly until he is apprehended.* This is not true if the penalty is imprisonment; the sentence could be increased for additional crimes.

These, in summary, are the major arguments against the death penalty. We agree with them. But another side of the argument should be discussed. MacNamara, who has spoken to many of the ideas listed above, has said that history makes it clear that "punishment, no matter how severe or sadistic, has had little effect on crime rates" (160). Here we must disagree. The death penalty, when exacted, does have an inexorable effect upon the frequency of death-by-violence: it serves to increase it. How can this be? First, there is the logical inconsistency in a society attempting to prevent murder by itself resorting to killing. Execution adds one more assaultive death to the total. Furthermore, capital punishment fosters and exemplifies the notion that killing solves problems. It also tends to provide an excuse for taking the easy way out and resorting to violence: if execution is the best answer the state can offer after years of deliberation, what can we expect of the less contemplative individual who is spurred by momentary stress or passion? More important still, what can he expect of himself?

Execution contributes to the atmosphere of violence simply by being one more example of a life destroyed. After seeing evidence, day in and day out, of an increasing number of killings, beatings, and maimings, one becomes hardened and disinterested. We no longer are shocked, sometimes not even impressed by this mayhem. Individual life may have become devalued in our minds. The very existence of the state-supported occupation of executioner helps to legitimize killing and to dehumanize both executioner and victim: killing is just another job; the dead product becomes an object, not a person with feelings like our own. All of these effects are only intensified by the publicity attendant upon executions, and what Wertham has described as the circus-like atmosphere in which they sometimes take place (161). (It should be added, however, that in recent years, there has been a marked reduction in the frequency of public executions. In many societies other than our own the public execution has often, indeed, been a grand spectacle intended to impress and entertain the masses).

Much of this material could be reconceptualized in traditional psychological terms. Most students of human learning and practitioners of behavior therapy have come to emphasize the power of positive reinforcement in altering the probability of occurrence of certain behaviors. The effects of punishment (negative reinforcement) are less predictable, less controllable. There is little evidence to suggest that imposing massive punishment on one individual will "improve" the behavior of others. There is, in fact, the possibility that what is massive punishment (obliteration) for one person serves as positive reinforcement for others—e.g., increases the frequency of hostile, murderous fantasies, or the fascination with modes of lethality-dealing. Social learning theorists who have been elaborating the concept of learning-through-modeling should also have something to contribute to our un-

derstanding of what is really communicated to the public by exacting capital punishment.

If all of the negative effects described in the preceding section can obtain with executions, how can we even begin to assess the influence of war? We will try.

• *Warfare.* "War is merely an extension of capital punishment on a grand scale."

In these days, nobody needs to be reminded that death by human violence is the one certain outcome of war. It should also be obvious by now that psychological factors are potent in determining whether or not an unstable situation erupts into open warfare (as well as in determining the initial instability of the situation). We are encouraged by a number of psychologists and other students of human behavior who have started to turn their attention to this matter. Any insights that improve our understanding of warfare, or enable us to minimize the probabilities of further international violence, deserve an honored place in the psychology of death. The fact that we cannot include many of these considerations in the present book does not mean that we consider the topic to be irrelevant or insignificant. The reader is invited to consult the considerable range of material that has become available on this subject. One might begin, for example, with Immanuel Kant's forward-looking essay on *Perpetual Peace* in which the great philosopher addressed himself to the need for international controls to avoid mass killing (162). Then, one might quickly come up to date with Ralph K. White's lucid exploration of *Misperception and the Vietnam War* (163). White's contribution is particularly effective in its emphasis upon distortions in national perceptions and communications *that occur over and over again*, with very little learned from past mistakes.

Here we are concerned principally with the indirect or overflow lethality that war is likely to produce. Both war and capital punishment utilize killing as a (purported) problem-solving technique. But war elevates killing into national policy. A large proportion of the nation's resources is mobilized for the related purposes of self-defense and other-destruction. The build-up in weaponry and supportive systems provides financial rewards to some people. Financial gain often leads to increase in social and political power. It is not easy to withdraw from a situation which offers both money and power. The system thus generates pressure for its own perpetuation and expansion, independently to some extent, of the objective need for military strength. Weapons continue to be produced, and what use can be given to implements of destruction? They can serve the economy by growing obsolescent without direct use, thereby requiring expensive replacement. Or they can be put to their intended use: destruction.

Kenneth Boulding has examined the role of the war industry in international conflict. He indicates that it is part of the economic folklore in the United States that "it is only the defense industry which saves us from depression" (164). This belief remains in circulation despite the fact that many communities have demonstrated the ability to survive, equal, or even surpass their previous levels of prosperity after defense industries were dismantled. Boulding emphasizes:

It is not the reality but the image which dominates behavior, and as long as there is a prevailing folk image of the war industry as a source of prosperity, this is an important factor operating to resist a reduction in military budgets. Furthermore, in order to justify military budgets, we almost have to be reactive, and we have to interpret the messages which come from abroad as hostile (165).

The relationship between economic and military power is Boulding's primary concern. But his argument also reveals one of the ways in which war can gradually foster the attitude that killing is an effective and advantageous approach to international problems. Even the skeptic must

admit that, at the very least, the time, money, and effort expended in preparation for killing are subtracted from the amount available for more constructive purposes. Who is to say how many have died for want of the care and material goods that could have been provided if the resources had not been put into the service of warfare? Much of the current wave of protest in the United States centers around the relationship between international war and the basic rights of the individual. "Stop the war!" and "Freedom now!" are two cries of protest that are being voiced conjointly. Perhaps it is a way of asking, "How can we love and kill at the same time? How can we be expected to solve our individual problems without violence when violence is an approved method for solving national problems—especially when the military budget maintains priority over mobilization for improvement of domestic problems?" Each of us may have his own way of reacting to these protests, but it is difficult to deny the relevance of war to the social climate at home. And it is perhaps even more difficult to deny the relevance of social climate to the lethality of its citizens.

Let us turn our attention now to some of the more obvious ways in which war (apart from actual combat) can foster homicide or the atmosphere in which it takes place. The discussion will be divided into two sections: the war zone and the "home front."

• *Killed, But Not in Action:* Habit is important in everyday life, but probably more so to the soldier than the civilian. The decisive person is more likely to succeed (i.e., survive) as a combatant. His gun at the ready, he learns to fire quickly and accurately at what he believes to be the enemy. If the soldier is to survive psychologically as well as physically, and continue to be an efficient killer, he must learn to respond automatically. It is distracting and dangerous to think that he is destroying a person much like himself. This knowledge must be encapsulated away from his current thoughts and attitudes. It is important to keep this in mind when reading accounts of soldiers mistakenly killing civilians or their own comrades in the war zone. After being engaged in the close-range exchange of fire, one's readiness to shoot can easily acquire dominance over the "look first" orientation. The soldier may fire in what he believes is self-defense before determining the identity of his target:

I shot a little girl, Mom. I didn't want to, but I couldn't see her clear, and I knew it wasn't a Marine, so I had to (Excerpt from a letter) (166).

A former bombardier (now a behavioral scientist specializing in perception) recalls instances of having bombed moving targets that "could have been ours or theirs." He explained that the response (bombing) had become so dominant that momentary indecisions usually were decided promptly in favor of "bombs away!" There is a target. Dropping bombs is the assignment, also the purpose of one's present existence. The bombs are dropped. This ex-bombardier reported that such behavior was far from unusual (167).

Of course, combatants realize that their predicament will be taken into account. It is conceivable that the plea of accidental life-taking could be used as a defense in cases of cold-blooded murder. It is easier to kill (and engage in other ordinarily disapproved actions) in an environment that the person experiences as new and temporary. The familiar supports for conventional morality are lacking; there may be no one to observe and report the criminal actions. An extra body on the battlefield may seem of little moment when it is almost impossible to determine whose bullet did what. The battlefield can also be used as an accessory to self-murder. The suicidal individual can fail to

take proper precautions and seem to die an heroic death. This would make it unnecessary for him to admit his self-destructive motivations to himself. The outcome would bring honor, rather than shame, to his family. Decisions to enlist now, rather than wait to be drafted, to volunteer for hazardous assignment, to resist capture by heroic means, to attempt a daring escape that is all but destined to failure—these decisions *sometimes* may derive more from suicidal impulses than from patriotism.

The effect of the prolonged and realistic need to kill-or-be-killed may carry over to off-duty periods, exerting a lethal influence in the form of brawls and "accidents." Too, the knowledge that new buddies may soon be killed and the survivor left to mourn their loss can militate against the formation of close personal relationships. It is easier to witness the destruction of a person with whom one has no ties; it may be easier to help cause his destruction as well.

Whatever the number of "incidental" murders in the war zone, they are overshadowed by the casualties that fall to the silent enemy who appears after any battle. In every war disease kills more soldiers than combat wounds (168). For example, until February, 1967 (in the Vietnamese war), it was estimated that three-fourths of the troops requiring hospitalization were sick rather than wounded. Factors basic to this include the lack of natural resistance to diseases indigenous to the foreign battleground, lowered resistance because of psychological stress, poor and unfamiliar living conditions, and contact with diseased prostitutes. At one point, approximately 59 percent of the American casualties in Vietnam were estimated to be due to venereal disease.

During prolonged wars, poor nutrition and lack of sanitary facilities may cause disease to run rampant in the civilian population, thus embittering the fruits of any victory. Turning again for illustrative purposes to the most recent war in which the United States has been involved, we find that just between January 1st and August 5th of 1966, there were 2,002 cases classified as plague in South Vietnam. This total included the bubonic disease that once decimated much of Europe, as well as pneumonia and septicemia. Fatalities were 116. This figure represents only the diagnosed cases of one general type of disease in one part of the country (169). The number of civilian casualties in this relatively small war has been estimated to be between 100,000 and 150,000 per year. Some reasons for high death rates among civilian sick and wounded in any war are found in excerpts from one summary of testimony about one particular war (170):

"Hundreds . . . are . . . lying in sheds and hospital corridors and other temporary quarters awaiting surgical work. . . . There are an inadequate number of surgeons available."

"Many civilian casualties are not reaching hospitals because of lack of transportation."

"Tuberculosis, plague, cholera and typhoid problems are growing, but there is no clear-cut high priority program of preventive medicine in existence."

"Drugs and supplies are short because of theft and other unauthorized diversion."

"Nurses, medical workers and laboratory technicians scheduled to fill urgent needs . . . are being kept waiting in this country for months and in some cases over a year because they were not given housing priority."

One might add that whatever encourages the spread of contagious disease in one part of the world also increases the vulnerability of the rest of the world. We could have learned that lesson from the "black death" (bubonic plague) that swept through much of the civilized world

with incredible lethality in the wake of warfare (see Chapter 8), or from hundreds of other experiences of this type. Despite greatly increased medical knowledge and health standards, it is still possible for virulent diseases to reach the home front from distant battlefields. The war zone thus has the local civilian population within its grasp and may even embrace those who would seem to be at a perfectly safe distance.

There is no reason to believe that the problems mentioned above are unique or more severe in the Vietnamese war than in any other. In fact, the relatively smaller scope of the war, and recent medical and technological advances, probably make this conflict somewhat less lethal than others. The suffering of civilians in Vietnam may be less than in some previous wars. During World War II, as most of us know, it became national policy in Germany to eradicate whole categories of people. Thirty thousand of these people, although infirm or mentally defective, posed no threat to the government, and held no anti-government sentiment. Others were defined as "inferior," "undesirable" (6,000,000 Jews), or "anti-government" (thousands of Christians and Gypsies, for example). The government considered these people worth more dead than alive. "Products" from one concentration camp included 25 freight cars of women's hair and 319,000 pounds of wedding rings, for example (171). Repeat: 25 freight cars of women's hair and 319,000 pounds of wedding rings.

Another group upon which war has a disastrous impact is made up of refugees. It is hardly necessary to belabor the details of their plight, whichever war we happen to be considering. Poor living conditions greatly increase the probability that the refugee will die before his time. In addition, the despair generated by individual and community disorganization is likely to have two different types of deleterious effect: a) Some refugees are likely to become hardened and cynical, turning to crime and violence for a livelihood and b) others may find their will to live slipping away. They become easy prey to every form of stress and illness. Thus, violence and death beget even more violence and death.

In time of war people die from many proximate causes but chief among these are direct violence, illness, and malnutrition. However, it is difficult to avoid recognizing that, during wartime, a more general cause of death finds multiple pathways to achieve its objective: *People die in time of war because human life becomes a low priority item in the prevailing value system.* The life of a civilian may count for even less than that of a combatant. How often would nations wage war if the preservation of human life were truly a strong and secure fixture in the individual and group value system?

• *Murder in the United States as a Function of Foreign War:* Although the mainland of the United States has not been assaulted physically in recent wars, our psychology of life and death may have been deeply affected by wars we have engaged in. The soldier returns from combat duty to his homeland with a new set of experiences. He may feel alienated from or hostile toward his fellow citizens. They do not know what he went through. This feeling of being set apart from the people around him was one of the factors that made it possible for him to be an agent of destruction during his active service—a feeling that was so carefully nurtured and which became so useful is not easy to turn off.

The creation of a sizable pool of people who have been trained in the techniques of death and encouraged to cultivate a sense of human alienation in the use of these techniques, can be a dangerous step for any society. The additional factors of weaponry training and alienation can produce a lethal combination in the occasional veteran who has been predisposed to violence by his early upbringing or the

tacit approval of his subculture. It may be no coincidence that two of the mass killers mentioned above were skilled in the use of firearms. If people are trained to use weapons and we allow them easy access thereto, it stands to reason that some will turn to violence in times of stress. Moreover, when a large number of citizens have been taught that the way to deal with an adversary is to shoot him, then society may select leaders and representatives who endorse this approach.

In addition to the fact that returning servicemen create a sort of lethal reservoir in the civilian population, the diseases they may bring with them may not become known immediately. For example, inadequately treated venereal disease can be transmitted to others at some stages, or can slowly spread through the central nervous system of the unsuspecting victim and destroy his mind and personality in later years. More exotic ills can catch both physician and soldier or veteran unawares. In the Vietnamese war, a disease called *melioidosis* cropped up. It is a bacterially-induced, but noncontagious, affliction which can be fatal. The disease "has the unpleasant ability to lie dormant in a victim for as long as six years. When it flares up, death occasionally follows within a few days or weeks" (172). This cannot be contemplated tranquilly. However, neither an atmosphere of violence nor the increased death rate attributable to war result simply from isolated individual cases. They are related primarily to war's influence on social attitudes. Therefore, we will shift our focus now from the individual to the larger society.

The mobilization of sentiment for a war and against an enemy usually involves the mobilization of bigotry as well. When an entire nation is defined as "bad" or as "the enemy," the people who comprise that nation are deprived of their individual characteristics, leveled, and dehumanized. Any latent feelings of distrust, fear, or prejudice are given license to free expression under the guise of patriotism.

During World War II, for example, many loyal, law-abiding Americans of Japanese ancestry were deprived of their homes and property. They were herded into segregated camps far removed from their own communities. In retrospect, it has become obvious that this treatment was a result of hysterical overreaction (and, to some extent, ruthless persecution of people who were disliked because they were thriving too well) (173). The relocation program had little justification in terms of national self-defense. But it was done—in a democracy, an open society. It should not be difficult for us to imagine how more drastic actions have taken place under totalitarian regimes.

With society's blessing, the bigot can act out against the chosen victim with little fear of disapproval or punishment. Even the government may sometimes be willing to close its eyes or stretch the law to accommodate social "customs." In Mississippi, for example, up to the 1967 conviction of seven men for the slaying of three civil rights workers, no white man had ever before been convicted of killing a Negro. In the West Virginia mountains, the famed Hatfield-McCoy feud involving multiple homicides was not investigated by the authorities until years after the killings began. Mountain subculture simply did not consider this to be a "crime." The police were unwilling to "interfere" until the feud threatened to embroil two states in hostilities tantamount to civil war (174).

War can exert a homicidogenic influence on the population in at least one other way: by its tendency to disorganize both the individual family and the social mores. The literature on juvenile delinquency and mental illness has demonstrated a relationship between family disorganization and antisocial behavior. Glueck and Glueck found, in their comparison of juvenile delinquents with non-delinquents, that the delinquents' homes were characterized by poorer management, poorer supervision of children,

looser family ties, and a greater incidence of broken homes and prolonged absence of one parent. They suggest that warm ties between father and son, and affectional relationships between both parents and children, are of paramount significance in preventing delinquency (175).

Obviously, the number of fatherless homes increases during wartime. Moreover, and partially on this account, the quality and quantity of family life are likely to deteriorate. In society as a whole, the goals and standards of behavior are subject to frequent change. The mobile service family frequently is forced to give up its former values in favor of those current in a new community or nation. The changing requirements of the war effort dictate corresponding shifts in attitudes and priorities at home. Attention is focused on death-dealing weapons and casualty figures. We are expected to applaud enemy losses and deplore our own. A sense of impending doom or catastrophe may be present to exert a powerful psychological impact. The philosophy of "live and love today, for there may be no tomorrow" introduces a note of urgency into personal life. Impulsive actions are more likely to occur, some of which will contribute to further disorganization ("quickie marriages," illegitimate births, etc.). Adverse effects also are felt in society's entire range of life-supporting programs. As already noted, the expenditures for destruction leave correspondingly less money available for constructive programs, especially those which require long-term planning and application.

The United States has been existing, more or less continuously, in a war or post-war state for at least the past half-century. Hence, varying combinations of some or all of the conditions we have detailed have become abiding elements in our society. Earlier in this chapter, we considered the reflection, concentration, and perversion of these conditions in the homicidogenic material presented as entertainment in the mass media. Now, let us look briefly at some of the homicidogenic attributes of the mass society itself.

• *The Mass Society: Its Exploding Population and Values:* America is increasingly an urban society, and a relatively overcrowded one at that. Although our population's rate of growth is nowhere near that of some of the underdeveloped nations, it has been considerable until very recently. This simultaneous increase in urbanization and population has had some unfavorable consequences. In agrarian society, additional mouths to feed also mean additional hands to help provide the food. But in our urban society, especially the larger metropolitan centers, additional mouths to feed are just that. Children can scarcely be expected to contribute to the family financially in most urban settings where even an unskilled adult has a hard time finding work. A new child today consumes a disproportionate amount of material goods, time, energy, and space in a family in which these may already be in short supply. There is no question that the consequent psychological, as well as the physical "overcrowding" is often a factor in homicide. We have noted earlier that murderers are often relatives of the victims. We should note also that domestic quarrels are also often responsible for homicide. Officer Charles Feeley believes that dealing with angry married couples is one of the toughest jobs a policeman must face. He says, "More police have been killed trying to settle family troubles than by the bullets of bank robbers . . ." (176).

Population growth and overcrowding present problems to the larger community as well as to individual families. Hordes of people crowd together in subways, in stores, on the highways. Frustration mounts as people compete for parking space, theatre seats, admission to college, professional opportunities, desirable jobs. The ensuing anxieties and hostilities may prove particularly dangerous in a highly mobile society where people are not well acquainted. We are no longer kept in line by the watchful eyes of long-time neighbors, or deterred from antisocial behavior by social ostracism. The insecure person may become overwhelmed by the sheer force of numbers pressing against him in a thronging city where everyone else seems to be "in the know" while he is alone. Lack of communication between individuals who nevertheless must literally brush against each other daily may be a potent influence in fostering violence.

What has been said above might apply, in greater or lesser degree, to the highly populated areas of any industrialized nation. However, it would seem to go doubly for American cities, for the value system of our mass society is a rather distinctive one. We seem to be first and foremost a society of consumers. It is important—no, vital—to acquire and consume. We work to obtain more money to buy *things*. We enter contests of every imaginable kind to win things. The merchandiser and the consumer can hardly wait until a product becomes obsolescent so that its shiny new replacement can be introduced. Many observers have noted in various ways that products mean much more to us than the specific functions they are supposed to serve. One of the authors is acquainted with the proprietor of a small radio and television shop who could not even *give away* a number of used television sets that were still functioning within normal limits. We will not attempt to make a deep analysis of a topic that has engaged the minds of many perceptive social observers. We simply submit that there is something peculiar about a society that encourages the scrapping or destruction of serviceable products, while continuing to turn out more of the same. Each reader probably has his own favorite examples of our strange obsession with products.

What is wrong with the acquisition of possessions by legal means? Perhaps nothing. But what is to be said about the tendency to acquire possessions—even "legally"—over someone else's dead body? It is our sense of priorities that is homicidogenic. Our luxuries sometimes come before other's necessities. While some people in our own country are "starving in the sense that acute malnutrition shortens their life span, dying young from an accumulation of hunger-induced diseases that go untreated for years," most of us shop in super-stocked supermarkets where we buy, among other things, low-calorie foods to lessen the more obvious effects of our chronic overeating. The couple who thinks nothing of spending $30 for a "night on the town" may feel it cannot afford half that amount to feed a starving child overseas for a month. We spend approximately $5,000 to kill one enemy soldier, but allot only $3.50 a year for each poverty-stricken person in the United States (177). This is by no means the total picture of the American attitude toward life, but it is a salient part of the picture. We do not have to say anything about our values. Our children observe; they get the message. They learn early what is important; and it is certainly not human life.

Counteraction for Homicidogenicity —Make Violence Less Easy

"When the citizen gives his consent to acts of violence on his behalf he never really believes that they will be used against his own person." (178).

Our attitude toward violence has much in common with our general orientation toward death. As suggested earlier in this book (Chapters 2 and 3) one important trend in our thinking is to regard death primarily as an external contingency. The Adversary is "out there," not in us. We have a fighting chance to outsmart or bribe him. Specific pathways of lethality are also regarded as external. The sentiment that "accidents always happen to the other fellow" and have no intrinsic connection with our own thoughts and motives has been exposed by many observers. The same sentiment seems to prevail with respect to homicide and suicide. But we are less often confronted with the alternative view—that there are personal quirks by which we increase the probabilities of violent death for our neighbors and ourselves. We did not commit that murder. But the event did not simply occur "out there." Something about our own thoughts, feelings, and actions may have served to increase the probability of violence. The disposition of which we have been speaking—to see violence as external and unrelated to ourselves—may, in fact, be one of the most influential factors in facilitating lethal behaviors. We apply the technique of psychological isolation to protect ourselves from a full comprehension of our implicit relationship to the murderer and his victim. Let us now summarize the psychic maneuvers which have been found to facilitate murder. These maneuvers prepare us to tolerate or condone violent behavior in others even if we do not ourselves become direct agents of lethality.

1. *Anything that physically or psychologically separates the potential killer from his victim.* The weapon itself can serve to separate the potential slayer from his prey. One concentrates upon the means rather than the end. "I'm not really killing a person; I'm just squeezing the little trigger on this gun." The potential assailant who balks at attacking his victim physically might find it easy to plant a bomb in his car or poison his food. Focus upon the physical means, then, can shield the killer from the impact of his action; but this is not the only way to by-pass the direct experience of murder.

The eventual killing may be prepared for long ahead of time with the assistance of verbal mythologies. The potential murderer begins by defining his victim or victims as vastly "different" from himself or his people. This form of self-deception has been widely used throughout the world to establish the necessary psychological distance between slayer and slain. The "different" person often is perceived as less human than us ("different" usually being a thinly-veiled euphemism for "inferior"). It is a persistent myth, for example, that "primitive" people do not suffer as much in illness, famine, or exposure to the elements as we sensitive souls would suffer under similar conditions. "Life is cheap" to some of these "different" people; they are thought not to mourn as deeply the death of a child or other intimate. The Us/Them distinction may permit us to remain detached, unperturbed, and inactive in contemplating their calamities. How "They" suffer in famine, war, and pestilence is regrettable in an abstract sort of way. But it doesn't really count for much in our scale of personally relevant values (there are too many people in the world anyway, right?). Yet our blood would boil instantly if anyone else displayed so cavalier an attitude toward our life-and-death problems.

Not everyone cultivates the type of insulation we have been describing. It would be enlightening to conduct intensive studies into the differences between people who characteristically insulate themselves from the agents and victims of lethality, and those who truly regard another person's misfortune as part of their own life. Specialists in child development and parent-child relationships should have much to contribute on this topic. Nevertheless, it is a haunting thought that many of us can purchase relative peace of mind only at the expense of attenuating our relationship with mankind in general. It is as though we felt it necessary to defy John Donne's message in order to survive ourselves: "I *am* an island. I am *not* diminished by what happens to others. I do not *care* to ask, " 'For whom the bells toll.' "

2. *Anything that permits the killer to define murder as something else.* We are not committing homicide. We are just doing this as an example to the rest of them, saving the state the expense of executing him, protecting society from those blasphemous rabblerousers, making sure that this crime won't happen again, or testing this new weapon (which ultimately will make the world a safer place). Additional psychological distance can be achieved if the fact of death itself is overlaid with jargon. We accomplish a "final solution": this sounds more like the completion of an intellectual task than the massacre of millions of men, women, and children. Or we note the "extermination" of "terrorists" who have "infested" certain territories. What comes to mind is the image of repugnant vermin being destroyed, not the killing of humans who may differ from us on ideological or other grounds, but who hardly belong to a different species.

Definitions of murder are highly variable, to say the least. Under some legal jurisdictions, a person may be subject to severe penalties for assisting an individual in ending his own life. The individual in question may have been suffering greatly in the advanced stages of a fatal illness, and have beseeched his intimate friend or relation to help him terminate a life he no longer wanted. We are not judging the merits of such a case here. But it is instructive to compare the stern view taken of this act of murder or quasi-murder with the facile definitions that are sometimes employed on a large scale basis. In Nazi Germany gassing 70,000 people to death was not murder, but "euthanasia" (179). Hitler's definition of the act of killing was accepted by enough of his countrymen to accomplish this mass slaughter. Thousands of "useless eaters" (Hitler-ese for chronically ill people) were also killed deliberately but, again, this was not to be regarded as murder.

3. *Anything that fosters seeing people as objects and animals.* Our habit of referring to people as "cases," "subjects,"

"examples," or by number makes it easier to escape from a relationship without emotional trauma when something happens to them. In this way, it is a subcase of the first point above. However, maneuvers in this category include other kinds of phenomena also. The utilization of planes in warfare, for example, not only ensures distance between slayer and slain, but also helps the attacker literally to see the victims as objects. Those infinitesimal things down there are not real people like us. They look more like microscopic organisms that race about on a laboratory slide. The miniature buildings are toys that flame and explode in ways that are interesting to observe. On the high seas, a *ship* is torpedoed (it is incidental that there are people inside who die). The enemy we kill are "krauts," "gooks," alien objects with funny-sounding names.

In reviewing accounts of concentration camp experiences, Shere and Kastenbaum were struck by the frequency with which oppressors and killers addressed their captives as animals (180). Perhaps it is emotionally easier to maltreat another person by convincing oneself that it is really a subhuman creature one has in his power. The "sheep" were herded and beaten. The "dogs" were kicked and starved. One did not feel compelled to develop a human relationship with his captives. The resulting deaths had nothing to do with "murder." On the contemporary American scene, some people have come to speak of police officers as "pigs." This appellation makes it easier to attack officers verbally and physically. It is probable that some officers have employed the same technique to free-up their own aggressive propensities, i.e., referring to low status and minority group individuals in demeaning, dehumanizing imagery.

4. *Anything that permits one to escape responsibility for killing by blaming someone else.* Among the most familiar examples of murderers who use this maneuver are professional killers in the un-

derworld and the Nazi war criminals. The slayer was merely carrying out orders, functioning as a loyal employee. To the extent that the killer actually believes this rationalization, he is telling us that he himself is something less than a complete person. He is just an instrument of destruction. Judgment and purpose are invested entirely in the individual or system that passed the assignment on to him.

5. *Anything that encourages seeing one's self as debased, worthless, an object, less than human.* This is the reciprocal of the earlier proposition that murder is facilitated by regarding the victim as infrahuman. The person who *accepts* a reduced and negative self-image himself becomes a potential agent of violence. The beaten, abused child often becomes the beater. He was regarded merely as a possession that could be knocked around. Now it is his turn. The victim of racial or other prejudice may grow up with the underlying conviction that he really is worthless, inadequate, to be exploited and humiliated. This self-view is potentially explosive for a number of reasons. Being worthless, what does he have to lose? Being less than a human, how can others expect to receive considerate human treatment from him? Being an (unwilling) student of brutality, what other skill can he exercise so proficiently? The negative self-image may develop from a wide variety of circumstances apart from those mentioned here. The point is that self-hatred, regardless of its origins, heightens the probability that one will treat others in a hateful way—even to the point of lethality.

6. *Anything that reduces self-control or is reputed to do so.* Alcohol and, increasingly of late, "psyche-expanding" drugs (such as LSD and methedrine) often are associated with crime. Since these substances can have the effect of distorting judgment, they can be considered dehumanizing agents. Furthermore, the psychological effect of *knowing* that one is taking alcohol or drugs can be conducive to crime, even if the actual dosage is so

small as to preclude most physical effects. "Operating under the influence" of alcohol or a drug can be a convenient responsibility-shedding excuse for behavior that ordinarily would bring severe retribution. The list of possible alibis is extensive, of course. One need only to accept the general proposition that "responsibility" can be turned on and off as suits our purposes at the time. Whatever leads people to believe that they cannot control their own actions, and whatever actually diminishes opportunities for self-control must be considered as part of the lethal sequence. This would include extreme emotional appeals to arouse mass antagonisms, and the withholding or distorting of information that is vital to decision-making.

7. *Anything that forces or encourages a hasty decision, or which permits no time for a "cooling off" period.* The soldier mentioned above, who shot a little girl because he dared not wait to determine her identity is a case in point. The fatal shooting that follows a demand for an immediate showdown, and which provides the combatants with no opportunity to reconsider, is another. Deciding to shoot or not to shoot on the basis of an arbitrary deadline is a third. The ready availability of weapons also has a place in this category. The gun in our hands seems to have a mind of its own. It is easier to obey the gun's implicit command than to prevail upon ourselves to think things over.

8. *Anything that makes one feel "above" or "outside" the law.* Political rank, wealth, and prestige tend to confer power—sometimes the real power—to operate outside the law and escape retribution. Occasionally one only *feels* that he has such power. This heady sensation may be enough to encourage him to commit crimes—only to be surprised later when he discovers that he must suffer the consequences, like anyone else. Any group which a society calls "privileged" may come to feel that it can "get away with murder" literally as well as figuratively.

All of the above conditions enable people to isolate themselves from others, and thereby contribute to the atmosphere in which murder can take place.

SOME IMPLICATIONS FOR THE PREVENTION OF MURDER

There is not much in this chapter to support the assumption that most homicides have a single primary cause that can be abolished by a few rigorous measures. We see instead that murder is as complex as our society itself and the individual dynamics of all who constitute the society. This situation should not surprise us, nor should it lead to deep pessimism. By and large, the "homicidogenic variables" are familiar variables in psychology and related fields. It is well within the competence of the social sciences to improve our understanding of the specific ways in which homicide emerges as an outcome of individual and cultural pressures—and to exert appropriate influences to modify the variables.

In the next few paragraphs, we will simply make explicit some of the general directions that are likely to reduce the frequency of murder and other forms of violence in our society. Others are better equipped to provide more detailed recommendations. A "how-to-do-it" manual for the prevention of murder probably would be premature at this time, but a few years of intensive basic and applied research might well yield such a source book. For now, let us just remind ourselves of some of the principles that are implicit in the material we have been considering.

1. *Avoid the use of prejudicial, dehumanizing, or derogatory labels—whether applied to others, or to one's self.* Our behavior becomes more impersonal, uncaring, and potentially brutal when we perpetuate such labels as "cases," "preemies," "vegetables," "spicks," "kikes," etc. Violence is invited when we accept, or

select, such labels for our own identity. "Black Panthers," for example, have adopted the name of a more powerful and attractive animal than the "pigs" they despise. Nevertheless, this still means that some men have seen fit to cloak their human identity with that of an animal. Would it be surprising if both "pigs" and "panthers" were to become more hardened in their dispositions toward mutual violence as a result of this image-making?

2. *Avoid the establishment or perpetuation of conditions that underlie dehumanizing perceptions of self or others.* Poverty, discriminatory practices, and excessive emphasis upon the acquisition of material goods are among the conditions in our society that foster dehumanizing perceptions. When we work toward remedying these conditions (usually with other and broader purposes in mind) we are also working toward a reduction in the homicide rate.

3. *Promote communication and contact with enemies, personal and national, emphasizing our similarities and common goals rather than our differences.* This statement can become something more than platitudinous if communications are bolstered by a sophisticated knowledge of those conditions under which contacts are most likely to result in favorable change. Social psychologists have learned that, even when their intentions are the best, efforts to try to increase communication between antagonists sometimes have an adverse effect. We would be well advised to consider their experiences when we try to reduce psychological distance between "warring parties" on the domestic as well as the international scene.

4. *Refrain from using physical punishment as a prime disciplinary technique.*

5. *Glorify the "good guys" for a change, and always give them equal time.*

6. *Teach children that violence is not "fun," "cute," or "smart," and that they will be held responsible for their behavior.*

7. *Identify and foster those human*

resources which provide alternatives to violence. These resources can be found in individuals and in larger units of society. The normal infant is quick to display behaviors that should become part of a non-lethal personality—for example, sharing of food. It is all too easy to ignore or unwittingly punish this behavior. But encouraging the baby to offer a bit of his food to us (even if he gives it to us in something less than A-1 condition) could be one small way of fostering personality traits of openness and involvement. Throughout the course of our children's development, there are many opportunities for us to recognize and reinforce peace-enhancing behaviors. Certainly, the ability to think before acting is one of the critical points in avoiding possibly violent behavior. While delaying capacity tends to develop "naturally" as the child grows up (181), not all youngsters acquire this knack. Whatever we do to identify and foster the child's emerging capacities to control his impulses toward immediate, thoughtless action will be in the service of reduced violence later. (This is not at all the same thing as inhibiting spontaneity.) On a different level, we can give our support to those groups of citizens who are addressing themselves in various ways to the reduction of violence and killing, including unnecessary destruction of wildlife. We can attempt to introduce broader and more effective humanistic emphases in education, both at school and at home. We can support laws and law enforcement, while at the same time attempting to develop wiser laws and more equitable enforcement.

8. *Reduce the attractiveness of violence in the mass media* by making it known to sponsors that we are opposed to the unnecessarily aggressive, life-cheapening content of their programs, by staying away from films that base appeal largely upon gun play and destruction, by finding other toys for our children in the place of guns, etc. Such displays of resistance or disinterest to violence-purveying

can be quite effective. There are already some reports that toy guns have lost much of their popularity, possibly in the wake of public concern after the recent assassinations (182).

A six-year-old we know once observed: "That boy is great big and fat and funny-looking; but *inside he's just like me*" (183). Now there is an idea that is worth packaging and marketing!

REFERENCES

1. Fontana, V. J. *The maltreated child.* Springfield, Ill.: Charles C Thomas, 1964.
2. Adelson, L. Homicide by starvation. *Journal of the American Medical Association,* 1963, *186,* 458.
3. Kempe, C. H., et al. The battered child syndrome. *Journal of the American Medical Association,* 1962, *181,* 17-24.
4. Bromberg, W. *Crime and the mind.* New York: Macmillan, 1965. P. 170.
5. Wyden, P. *The hired killers.* New York: Morrow, 1963. P. 220.
6. *Ibid.,* p. 221.
7. *Boston Globe,* October 5, 1966.
8. *Boston Globe,* November 5, 1967.
9. Bromberg, *op. cit.,* p. 170.
10. Vincent J. Fontana, M. D., interviewed on "Contact," a television program. Boston, March 6, 1967.
11. Helfer, R. E., and Kempe, C. H. (Eds.), *The battered child.* Chicago: University of Chicago Press, 1969.
12. C. H. Kempe, M.D., quoted in *Boston Globe,* October 5, 1966.
13. Dollard, J., Doob, L., Miller, N. E., Mowrer, O. H., & Sears, R. *Integrational possibilities of the frustration-aggression hypothesis for the social sciences.* New Haven: Yale University Press, 1939.
14. Hartmann, H. *Ego psychology and the problem of adaptation.* (Translated by David Rapaport.) New York: International University Press, 1958.
15. *Boston Globe,* April 16, 1967.
16. Bromberg, *op. cit.*
17. *Ibid.,* p. 170.
18. *Ibid.*
19. Simmons, L. *The role of the aged in primitive society.* New Haven: Yale University Press, 1945.
20. Bromberg, *op. cit.,* p. 171.
21. Tuteur, W., & Glotzer, J. Murdering mothers. *American Journal of Psychiatry,* 1959, *116,* 447-452.
22. *Ibid.,* p. 450.
23. *Ibid.,* p. 452.
24. Bender, L. *Aggression, hostility, and anxiety in children.* Springfield, Ill.: Charles C Thomas, 1953.
25. *Ibid.,* p. 67.
26. Deutsch, H. *The psychology of women.* Vol. 2. *Motherhood.* New York: Grune & Stratton, 1945. P. 38.
27. Myers, S. The child slayer. *Archives of General Psychiatry,* 1967, *17,* 211-213.
28. *Ibid.,* p. 211.
29. *Ibid.,* p. 213.
30. Fontana, television interview, *op. cit.*
31. Helfer & Kempe, *op. cit.,* p. 51.
32. Wyden, *op. cit.,* p. 221.
33. Adelson, *op. cit.,* p. 105.
34. Alexander, F., & Selesnick, S. *The history of psychiatry.* New York: Harper & Row, 1966. Chapter 10, especially p. 162.
35. *Ibid.*
36. Holman, R., & Robbins, W. *A textbook of general botany.* (4th ed.) New York: Wiley, 1939. P. 598.
37. Smith, E. B., Blamer, P. R., Vellios, F., & Schulz, D. M. *Principles of human pathology.* New York: Oxford University Press, 1959. Pp. 6-7; 637-638.
38. Patten, B. M. *Human embryology.* (2nd ed.) New York: McGraw-Hill, 1953. P. 12.
39. Sheldon, W. H., & Stevens, S. S. *The varieties of temperament.* New York: Harper & Bros., 1942.
40. *Ibid.*
41. Glueck, S., & Glueck, E. *Delinquency in the making—paths to prevention.* New York: Harper & Row, 1952. P. 97.
42. Sheldon & Stevens, *op. cit.,* p. 100.
43. *Ibid.,* p. 97.
44. *U. S. News & World Report,* Oct. 9, 1967. P. 74.
45. Glueck & Glueck, *op. cit.,* p. 136.
46. Bromberg, *op. cit.,* pp. 133-134.
47. *Ibid.,* p. 225.
48. Henderson, D., & Gillespie, R. D. *A textbook of psychiatry.* (8th ed.) New York: Oxford University Press, 1956. P. 389.
49. Small, J. The organic dimension of crime. *Archives of General Psychiatry,* 1966, *15,* 82-89.
50. *Ibid.,* p. 84.
51. *Ibid.,* p. 86.
52. *Ibid.,* p. 87.
53. *Ibid.*

54. *Ibid.*
55. Berman, L., quoted in Flanders Dunbar: *Emotions and bodily changes.* (4th ed.) New York: Columbia University Press, 1954. Pp. 236-237.
56. *Ibid.,* p. 237.
57. Stock, R. W. The XYY and the criminal. *New York Times* magazine, Oct. 20, 1968. Pp. 30-31; 90-104.
58. Markson, E. The geriatric house of death: Hiding the dying elder in a mental hospital. *Aging and Human Development,* 1970, *1,* 37-50.
59. Bockoven, J. S. Aspects of geriatric care and treatment: Moral, amoral, and immoral. In R. Kastenbaum (Ed.), *New thoughts on old age.* New York: Springer, 1964. Pp. 213-228.
60. Lorand, S. *Clinical studies in psychoanalysis.* New York: International University Press, 1950.
61., Krafft-Ebing, R. *Aberrations of sexual life after the psychopathia sexualis.* (Translated by Arthur Vivian Burbury.) Springfield, Ill.: Charles C Thomas, 1959.
62. Fenichel, O. *The psychoanalytic theory of neurosis.* New York: W. W. Norton, 1945. P. 356.
63. *Ibid.*
64. *Ibid.*
65. Bierman, J. S. Necrophilia in a thirteen-year-old boy. *Psychoanalytic Quarterly,* 1962, *31,* 329-340.
66. Menninger, K., Mayman, M., & Pruyser, P. *The vital balance.* New York: Viking Press, 1963. P. 238.
67. *Ibid.,* pp. 238-239.
68. *Ibid.,* p. 240.
69. *Ibid.*
70. *Boston Globe,* April 16, 1967. P. 1.
71. Hamill, P. The mass murderers. *Good Housekeeping,* Spring, 1967. Pp. 162-163.
72. *Ibid.,* p. 161.
73. *Ibid.*
74. *Boston Globe,* July 27, 1966. P. 1.
75. Hamill, *op. cit.*
76. MacDonald, J. M. Homicidal threats. *American Journal of Psychiatry,* 1967, *124,* 61.
77. Hamill, *op. cit.*
78. Szasz, T. *Law, liberty and psychiatry.* New York: Macmillan, 1963.
79. Kraus, P. S. Admission conferences notes, Acute Intensive Treatment Service, Veterans Administration Hospital, Bedford, Mass., 1954.
80. Wertham, F. An end to violence. *SKF Psychiatric Reporter,* 1967, No. 30 (Jan.-Feb.). P. 5.
81. *Ibid.*
82. *Ibid.*
83. *Ibid.*
84. Motto, J. A. Suicide and suggestibility. *American Journal of Psychiatry,* 1967, *124,* 156-160.
85. *Ibid.,* p. 160.
86. *Ibid.,* p. 157.
87. *Ibid.,* p. 159.
88. *Boston Globe,* Sept. 20, 1967.
89. *Boston Globe,* Oct. 23, 1967.
90. Berkowitz, L. Impulse, aggression and the gun. *Psychology Today,* 1968, *2,* 18-22.
91. *Ibid.,* p. 19.
92. *Ibid.,* p. 20.
93. Star, J. Shocking rise of murder. *Look,* Sept. 19, 1967. Pp. 28-34.
94. *Ibid.*
95. *U. S. News & World Report,* October 9, 1967. P. 74.
96. *Ibid.*
97. Star, *op. cit.*
98. *Boston Globe,* Feb. 12, 1967.
99. *Time,* Feb. 17, 1967. P. 19.
100. *U. S. News & World Report, op. cit.*
101. *U. S. News & World Report,* March 27, 1967. P. 55.
102. Star, *op. cit.*
103. *Boston Globe,* March 8, 1967.
104. Star, *op cit.*
105. Rivers, C. Murder by mail. *Boston Sunday Globe,* May 21, 1967.
106. Star, *op. cit.*
107. *U. S. News & World Report,* Oct. 9, 1967. P. 75.
108. *Boston Globe,* March 12, 1967.
109. *Boston Globe,* October 1, 1967.
110. *Boston Globe,* March 12, 1967.
111. *Ibid.*
112. Pillsbury, F. Uniform crime reports of the FBI. *Boston Sunday Globe,* March 19, 1967.
113. *Boston Globe,* Sept. 4, 1967.
114. Pillsbury, *op. cit.*
115. *Ibid.*
116. *Ibid.*
117. *Ibid.*
118. *Ibid.*
119. *Boston Sunday Globe,* May 21, 1967.
120. Wertham, F. *A sign for Cain.* New York: Macmillan, 1962.
121. *Boston Globe,* March 19, 1967.
122. *Boston Globe,* Nov. 5, 1967.
123. Spock, B. *Baby and child care.* New York: Pocket Books, 1958, p. 395.
124. Bettelheim, B. Children should learn about violence. *The Saturday Evening Post,* March 11, 1967. P. 10.
125. *Ibid.*
126. *Ibid.*
127. *Ibid.*
128. *Ibid.*
129. Wertham, *Cain, op. cit.,* pp. 219-220.
130. Berkowitz, *op. cit.,* p. 20.
131. *Ibid.,* p. 22.

132. MacDonald, *op. cit.*
133. *Ibid.*, p. 67.
134. *Ibid.*
135. *Ibid.*
136. Myers, *op. cit.*, p. 211.
137. *Boston Globe*, Sept. 14, 1967.
138. Jackson, J. H. (Ed.), *San Francisco murders.* New York: Duell, Sloan, & Pearce, 1947.
139. Spears, J. *The American slave trade.* New York: Ballantine Books, 1960.
140. *Boston Globe*, Oct. 21, 1967.
141. Star, *op. cit.*
142. Quoted in *Boston Globe*, Sept. 19, 1967.
143. *Boston Globe*, April 9, 1967.
144. Quoted in *Boston Globe*, March 19, 1967.
145. Vellenga, J. Christianity and the death penalty. In Hugo Adam Bedau (Ed.), *The death penalty in America.* New York: Doubleday Anchor Books, 1964. Pp. 124; 129.
146. Hoover, J. E. Statement in favor of the death penalty. In Bedau, *ibid.*, p. 134.
147. Allen, E. J. Capital punishment: your protection and mine. In Bedau, *ibid.*, pp. 136-137.
148. Barzun, J. In favor of capital punishment. In Bedau, *ibid.*, pp. 162-163.
149. Sutherland, E. H. & Cressey, D. R. *Principles of criminology.* (6th ed.) New York: Lippincott, 1960. P. 292.
150. *Ibid.*
151. *Ibid.*
152. *Ibid.*
153. MacNamara, D. E. J. Statement against capital punishment. In Bedau, *op. cit.*, p. 192.
154. *Ibid.*
155. Various authors in Bedau, *op. cit.*, pp. 169-191.
156. Wertham, *op. cit.*
157. Bishop, G. *Executions—The legal ways of death.* Los Angeles, Calif.: Sherbourne Press, 1965.
158. MacNamara, *op. cit.*
159. *Ibid.*
160. *Ibid.*, p. 192.
161. Wertham, *op. cit.*
162. Kant, I. *Perpetual peace.* (Translated by L. W. Beck.) New York: Bobbs, 1954.
163. White, R. K. *Misperception and the Vietnam War Journal of Social Issues,* 1966, Whole No. 3.
164. Boulding, K. The role of the war industry in international conflict. *Journal of Social Issues,* 1967, *23*, 55.
165. *Ibid.*, p. 56.
166. *Boston Globe*, March 12, 1967.
167. Personal Communication.
168. *Time*, Feb. 10, 1967. P. 84.
169. *Ibid.*
170. *U. S. News & World Report*, Oct. 16, 1967. P. 37.
171. Wertham, *Cain, op. cit.*, p. 158 ff.
172. *Time*, Feb. 10, 1967. P. 84.
173. Myer, D. *Uprooted Americans: The Japanese Americans and the war relocation authority.* Tucson, Ariz.: University of Arizona Press, 1970.
174. Jones, V. C. *Hatfields and the McCoys.* Durham, N. C.: University of North Carolina Press, 1948.
175. Glueck & Glueck, *op. cit.*, p. 62.
176. *Boston Globe*, Sept. 30, 1967.
177. *Boston Globe*, March 19, 1967.
178. Bishop, *op. cit.*, p. 191.
179. Wertham, *Cain, op. cit.*, pp. 153-191.
180. Shere, E. S., & Kastenbaum, R. *Crisis and transformation.* Unpublished manuscript. Tel Aviv: University of Bar Ilan, 1963.
181. Singer, J. L. Delayed gratification and ego development: Implications for clinical experimental research. *Journal of Consulting Psychology,* 1955, *19*, 259-266.
182. Radio news feature, December 23, 1969, WWJ, Detroit, Michigan.
183. Mark Aisenberg, 1967.

13

Suicide and Murder:

Some Possible Relationships

Suicide and murder are often discussed together and it is not difficult to understand why this is so. These two actions seem to have much in common. Both destroy life. Both are thought by many observers to arise from hostile impulses. Both imply a distortion, suspension, or flouting of conventional Western mores. Both involve the expression of ideas or impulses which ordinarily are suppressed or repressed. Both acts are generally either antisocial or asocial; yet neither can be understood apart from its social context. By attempting either suicide or murder, one typically sets himself apart from the rest of society.

We have hypothesized that the conditions that predispose to suicide are established early in life, and that only certain kinds of stress are required to precipitate the self-destructive act. We proposed, in fact, that without such early preparation, only the most extreme or special external events could induce one to attempt self-murder. (Self-immolation as a desperate act of political protest would be one of the important exceptions to this generalization—perhaps.) To what extent do such statements apply to homicide? What is the nature of the relationship between suicide and murder?

There is much circumstantial evidence to suggest a relationship, or several sets of relationships, between the two acts of destruction. Murder and suicide often occur together and, under some conditions, the nature of their relationship can be specified. Suicide rates generally decrease during war time, when the destruction of other humans (enemies) is encouraged. One might expect, then, that cultures with a militaristic orientation would tend to have a relatively low suicide rate. One of the leading students of suicide, Dublin, has supported this position. He declares that "The followers of Islam have always been a warlike race and tend to look upon each individual as potential fighting material. Though it is not openly admitted, the military point of view has always been a potent factor in discouraging suicide" (1).

Presumably the suicide rate is inhibited by the availability of culturally-sanctioned targets for external aggression. This conjecture could appeal to us for several reasons: a) it sounds simple; b) it is general enough to accommodate a large range of observations, and c) it assimilates well into familiar psychodynamic frameworks. One should be cautioned, however, that the plausibility of this explanation rests heavily upon a broad assumption that itself is extremely difficult to evaluate. When we accept the statement that "more" external aggression results in "less" self-directed aggression, we are being asked to accept a closed systems model. There is a certain amount of aggression in any individual or in any society. This aggression will express itself in one kind of aggressive action or another, and we just have to expect this. The basic differences between individuals or societies consist of differences in their outward-to-inward aggressions, and perhaps in the severity or lethality of the consequences. Not every reader will be enthusiastic about accepting the closed systems model that underpins this assumption of suicide-homicide relationships. Indeed, this model is not an especially optimistic one upon which to base either suicide or homicide prevention efforts.

Dublin himself makes two more points that suggest alternatives to the simple more-of-one-and-less-of-the-other-hypothesis: a) during wartime one is more likely to feel needed and thus have less time for dwelling on personal insecurities; and b) the lower suicide rate may be more apparent than real. (We have already seen that suicide can masquerade as an accident of battlefield death during wartime.)

Margaret Mead emphasizes that it is sometimes difficult to draw the line between suicide and murder, since "some forms of homicide are essentially ways of forcing others to carry out an execution" (2). Mead describes *amok*, a form of insanity traditional among the Malays, in this way:

Characteristically a man goes into a deep depression. Then, suddenly and without warning, he starts to kill people until he himself is killed. During the Western colonial period among Malay people it proved possible to control the syndrome of running amok by insisting that the man should not be killed, but should be brought in alive" (3).

This observation illustrates not only a particular kind of relationship between homicide and suicide, but two other points as well. First, it strengthens the case for believing the psychosis takes forms that are determined by the particular culture in which the individual lives, and perhaps becomes more or less frequent as cultural practices change. Secondly, it demonstrates that homicidal behavior, even when it is related to psychosis, can be prevented by appropriate techniques. Knowing something about the *purpose* of the behavior is not necessarily idle information.

Many theoretical propositions about the relationship between murder and self-destruction are simply modifications or extensions of psychoanalytic theory. You will recall the psychoanalytic contention, reported earlier, that no one kills himself who had not first intended to kill someone else. Suicide is a sort of egotropic movement of the lethal impulses originally aimed at another person. Fenichel, for example, proposed that suicidal deeds have a very "active character.... They assert themselves as desperate attempts to enforce, at any cost, the cessation of the pressure on the superego. They are the most extreme acts of ingratiatory responses to punishment and to the superego's cruelty; simultaneously, they are also the most extreme acts of rebellion, that is, murder—murder of the original objects whose incorporation created the superego" (4). In other words, one kills the parents or a significant other by the act of self-destruction. Bergler has offered an interesting variation on this theme (5). He believes that creative writers and other artists who have "blocks" in pursuing their work may engage in a sort of partial murder-suicide (he does not use this expression). Writers in particular are prone to become alcoholics. Why? This "solution" has the symbolic effect of poisoning, slowly destroying the internalized mother whom the writer feels is responsible for his dilemma. In a moment we will consider Rheingold's more recent formulation of a similar theme.

Hypotheses such as Fenichel's are supported by the clinical experiences of many psychoanalytically-oriented therapists. It reflects no discredit on these practitioners to remind ourselves that they are not disinterested observers who can evaluate the material objectively. One can generate and refine hypotheses while practicing psychotherapy, but in most circumstances it is exceedingly difficult to test these propositions rigorously at the same time. Nevertheless, the large proportion of murders that are perpetrated by relatives of the victim does suggest that at least one important aspect of the psychoanalytic hypothesis may be valid: homicidal impulses toward family members are common. Moreover, the propensity to suicide is probably largely determined in early life by child-rearing practices and the quality of early interpersonal relationships (6). To conclude, however, that suicide and homicide are *always* closely related in the individual, or that the murder victim always substitutes for the hated parent figure is—well, fanciful. The unplanned homicide committed incidentally in the course of a robbery, for example, does not fit into this theory very well.

Rheingold has elaborated on the foregoing psychoanalytic hypotheses in a recent book (7). In reviewing some of the literature on homicide, suicide, and maternal destructiveness, he found special relevance in a clinical study by Smith (8), a psychiatrist who attempted to analyze the dynamics of eight young murderers. He found that their backgrounds included disintegrated family structures, emotional deprivation, or primitive violence between the parents.

A common denominator in these cases is a sense of abandonment, with a consequent embittered distrust of relationships and hyperalertness to the possibility of the recurrence of the experience of loss. The earliest expressions of the child's rage are displaced to an object that clearly carries symbolic import as a substitute for the hated parent, and in every instance the parent or a parent symbol becomes the murder victim. *In the act of violence there is a reversion to a precognitive symbiosis in which the self and the other are no longer distinctly separated and the panicky destruction is related to the fear of being destroyed (9).* [Italics ours.]

This last-mentioned hypothesis might be especially relevant to some of the murders that stem from heated family quarrels.

Rheingold also gives particular attention to Schrut's study of children and adolescents who either threatened or attempted suicide (10). Schrut found that "in the majority of the cases a basic feeling of being a burden was unconsciously conveyed to the child by his mother." The feeling of "being 'something wrong,' of being unworthy and a source of displeasure to the mother was accompanied by helpless rage at his rejection" (11). Schrut felt that the mother of the depressed, suicidal child is intensely rejecting. The child of a rejecting mother who feels guilty may react by using self-destructive behavior. This is thought to be effective because it "punishes" the mother, making her feel more anxious and guilty.

MATERNAL FILICIDE

The hypothesis advanced by Rheingold himself brings us full circle to a reconsideration of maternal filicide. He believes that "the mechanism can be seen more clearly if one assumes that these mothers are not merely rejective but suicidal. The filicidal wish means not only the wish to kill but also the wish that the child kill himself" (12). Here we have a somewhat novel twist to the general hypothesis of a relationship between suicide and murder. In such cases as those considered above, Rheingold holds that suicide is more than the murder of the introjected other—the lethal act derives from homicidal impulses in that other (mother). He further suggests that three aspects of maternal destructiveness have not received the attention they merit (13):

1. Maternal destructiveness is universal. One should not think in terms of "good mothers" and "bad mothers." *All* mothers exert some salutary influences, but more that are harmful. Accordingly, he hypothesizes that *all mothers have filicidal impulses.*

2. The crucial variables are in the realm of the unconscious. Murderous impulses have a harmful effect "even in the presence of a conscious benign disposition toward the child."

3. There is probably "an underappraisal of the pathogenic consequences of maternal destructiveness. . . . If we should make all mothers nurturant (or just eliminate the unconscious aggressive impulses) and observe the results after a generation or two, not much mental (and social) disorganization would remain."

This viewpoint warrants further comment. Here Rheingold is proposing that maternal destructiveness ultimately is responsible for much of the homicidal and suicidal behavior in the world. What is to be said about this contention? His emphasis is upon the deleterious effects that all mothers are presumed to exert upon their children, but he also allows that the mothers have some happier influences as well. This general proposition is neither novel nor controversial. From an empirical standpoint it is possible to identify "good" and "bad" influences in *any* interpersonal relationship. From a theoretical standpoint it has long been suggested that we have mixed feelings toward all the people in our lives (whether this observation has been couched in the language of "unconscious ambivalence" or behavioral "approach-avoidance gradients").

Let us grant that the relationship with the mother or mother-surrogate exerts a more important influence on the child than any other early relationship. Let us also grant that this influence includes "unconscious" factors. It still seems rather sterile, if not downright inaccurate, to ascribe the destructive aspects of the mother-child relationship to the state of motherhood per se. This is what Rheingold seems to be saying when he alleges universality. The view might be more plausible if it were broadened to encompass *prolonged dependency relationships* rather than focusing on motherhood. When one person is dependent and demanding upon another person for a prolonged period of time, it may indeed be natural for the depended-upon to feel angry and irritable on occasion. These negative feelings might develop occasionally into crests of murderous intensity. The depended-upon wants to be liberated from his or her situation and there may be moments when destruction seems to be the answer. These dynamics do not require a mother-child relationship. They can be found at times in the relationship between chronically ill people and their caretakers, and in a number of other interpersonal situations.

Environmental factors are likely to influence the intensity and frequency of "hostile impulses" toward the dependent member of the dyad, and also to reduce or increase the probability of lethal behavior. It is reasonable to expect, for example, that the potential lethality of the relationship is reduced when there is rich contact with the outside world, when there are sources of emotional support available for both partners independent of their relationship, and when there are safe outlets available to discharge destructive impulses.

One could then reformulate Rheingold's thesis in something like the following manner: The young mother may be "house-bound," cut off from the larger world much of the time. She may not be receiving the kind of understanding emotional support needed to maintain her equilibrium. She may not have outlets available to express her personal feelings in general, including, but not limited to, her negative affects. And she may well be under stress from other sources (e.g., economic, sexual). But all this time she is called upon to meet the strong dependency needs of another person (her child). To add to the difficulties, she may not possess the particular skills, traits, or knowledge that can reduce the wear and tear of child-rearing (e.g., it *is* possible that she never related to a small child before, and that nobody gifted her with a "Spock"). Such a combination of circumstances is not infrequent in young mothers. It is not difficult to imagine how violent behavior could arise when personal resources wear thin under prolonged usage. And, of course, the probability of destructive behavior would be further increased if the woman in question had certain personality defects or idiosyncrasies.

While we suggest that this revised formulation is more plausible and in better accord with available knowledge, it must be admitted that it lacks the allure of Rheingold's own thesis in which homicide and suicide are predicated largely on the basis of a single variable—maternal destructiveness. The revision we have sketched is prosaic and encumbered.

But let us suppose, for the sake of argument, that Rheingold is correct in implying that filicidal impulses harbored within the mother's breast are much more important than environmental factors, and are qualitatively different from homicidal impulses that are engendered in other interpersonal relationships. We have already seen that some theorists think that mothers feel they have a right to destroy that which they have created (14). (What a variety of motives are read into the maternal mind by theoreticians—most of whom are of the opposite gender!) The create-and-destroy sentiment may or may not be universal, but it is doubtful that this sentiment can contribute much to explaining an individual case of filicide. Similarly, if merely being a mother means the inevitable presence of filicidal impulses, then we are at a loss to understand why some children are spared literal or figurative destruction. Why did this mother kill or warp this particular child? Why did this mother's son commit suicide at this time in this particular way? The general explanation we have been offered by Rheingold does not seem to help much in elucidating these all too familiar problems.

Furthermore, there may be some pragmatic dangers inherent in this approach, which sees maternal destructiveness as universal and accepts it as "entering causatively into a greater range of disorders than any other factor...." (15). This statement is not only limited in the predictive and explanatory value it offers but it may also provide a convenient rationalization for those who find themselves moving toward actions destructive of self or others. In short, this is the kind of explanation that may "permit" its behavior to occur. The individual mother may feel liberated from personal responsibility for her destructive behavior: if *all* mothers are filicidal, how could one, in particular, be blamed for exhibiting these "normal" impulses? While the popularization of such a theory would not necessarily grant women legal license for expressing unveiled aggression toward their children, some people might come to the private conclusion that such behavior is "uncontrollable" as well as "natural." It could be employed as an excuse to self and society in situations in which women might otherwise have found the strength to control themselves. Our society already provides too many excuses and provocations.

This approach also fails to come to terms with the effects of social mores and value systems upon child-rearing practices, at least in any direct and systematic manner. It is unfortunate that a recent approach, such as Rheingold's, should "regress" in this way to earlier stages of psychoanalytic thought when the social context of personality development was not fully appreciated. It is likely that most contemporary students of suicide and homicide (including many with psychoanalytic orientations) would prefer an approach that explicates the specific role of child-rearing practices upon destructive tendencies in both the mother and child. What is it about the socializing process that either inhibits or facilitates the *lethal expression* of (presumed) hostile psychic impulses? That question remains unanswered here.

The question of whether the filicidal impulse is truly universal can be seen to be somewhat irrelevant. The sex impulse is virtually universal in adults, if we are going to talk about impulses. Yet the existence of this impulse does not explain or excuse rape, any more than it completely elucidates the vast range of human sexual behavior. It is the sociocultural environment that should be emphasized— first, because it defines appropriate behavior, provides channels for impulse expression, and determines management of transgressors, and second, *because it can be changed.*

Although we have disagreed with some basic tenets of Rheingold's theory, it is easy to concur with him that maternal hostility can contribute importantly to suicidal or homicidal tendencies in some people. It is a variable to be kept in mind.

HOMICIDE, SUICIDE, AND SOCIOLOGICAL VARIABLES

Let us now consider a very different approach to the relationship between homicide and suicide. Henry and Short based their judgments upon inspection of a considerable range of statistical information (16). In particular, they were interested in determining the possible relationship between these two forms of lethal behavior and a variety of sociological vari-

ables. Perhaps their most significant finding was that both suicide and homicide correlate with the business cycle, but in different ways. The suicide rate increases in times of economic depression and slackens during prosperous times. When suicide rates soar, murder tends to be on the decline, and vice versa. These are the general trends.

Henry and Short advance several interesting hypotheses pertaining to this observation, including:

1. Suicide and homicide are "acts of aggression undifferentiated with respect to their common source in frustrations generated by business cycles" (17).

2. Suicide tends to be concentrated in high status groupings "because high status categories are subject to fewer external restrictions than low status categories," in which homicide is more common (18).

This second point deserves immediate comment. Women have a lower suicide rate than men; they are also considered to comprise a relatively lower status group. As members of a low status group, women are subject to more external restraint than men. One might expect, then, in accord with the Henry and Short hypotheses, that mothers would display a higher murder than suicide rate. We have already suggested above that external restrictions might be the basis for "filicidal impulses." Of course, women commit far fewer murders than do men: but they commit more murders than other crimes (19). And who is more available to them as an object of homicidal impulses than the child?

3. There is a positive correlation between homicide and external restraint. For example: a) areas of high social status (low external restraint) have high suicide but low crime rates (20), and b) marriage is associated with lower suicide but higher homicide rates than the single life (21).

4. "When behavior is subject to strong external· restraint, the restraining

objects can be blamed for frustration, thereby legitimizing outward expression of the resultant aggression. When behavior is freed from external restraint, the self must bear the responsibility for frustration" (22).

5. " 'Love oriented' techniques of discipline are associated with strong superego formation and high guilt while techniques of punishment not threatening loss of love are associated with inadequate superego formation and low guilt" (23).

6. Homicide is followed by suicide when the homicide "destroys a primary source of nurturance and love" (24).

7. Internalized . . . demands or behavior are often projected onto the victim. . . . If through the mechanism of the projection of guilt, the harsh discipline imposed by the superego is externalized . . . the projection would at the same time weaken the internalized prohibition against the outward expression of aggression and provide an effective (though imagined) source of frustration in the external world" (25). "Internalization of harsh parental demands and discipline produces a high psychological 'probability' of homicide" (26).

Henry and Short's work is of particular interest to us here because it attempts to integrate social, psychological, and economic phenomena en route to establishing relationships between suicide and homicide. Their hypotheses concerning the possible relationship between disciplinary techniques and the propensity to lethal behavior are most provocative. Theoretically, there is much in common between their formulations and the approach we presented in Chapters 11 and 12. But are their hypotheses valid?

Lester recently attempted to test one important aspect of Henry and Short's contribution. He was particularly interested in determining whether or not "love oriented" and "punishment oriented" child-rearing practices would be associated with different directions of aggressive behavior (27). One would expect that chil-

dren who were socialized primarily by affection would express more aggression inwardly than outwardly, while the opposite would be true of children who had experienced more physical punishment. Lester related homicide and suicide rates in 33 preliterate societies to the type of child-rearing practices employed in each (based upon the well-known research of Whiting and Child) (28). This study was literally an A through Z survey of socialization and lethality—from the Ainu to the Zuni.

Lester's cross-cultural study failed to confirm Henry and Short's hypotheses. Why? Lester notes that several previous investigators had found relationships between the type of discipline administered to the child and the direction of the child's aggressive behavior (29). He suggests that suicide and homicide might follow different principles than do the less extreme forms of aggressive behavior that the previous investigators had studied.

Lester's negative findings do not necessarily rule out the general hypothesis that child-rearing practices influence the frequency and directionality of lethal behavior. Remember that both Lester and Henry and Short focused upon disciplinary techniques. While this aspect of parent-child interactions is an important one, it is far from the whole story. A broader and more intensive inquiry into the entire pattern of parent-child relationships is necessary to test the general hypothesis, or so it seems to us. It is easy for the cultural outsider to be misled about the significance of a particular type of behavior when he does not take the entire social context into account. We might revise our notions of what constitutes "love-oriented" or "punishment-oriented" parental behavior when we have the opportunity to view these within the larger pattern of cultural values and practices. At the moment we are inclined to think that Lester's study did not provide an adequate test of the hypotheses, and that Henry and Short did not take their hypotheses far enough. Nevertheless, it is clear that important formulations have been offered by Henry and Short, and that Lester has demonstrated the feasibility of evaluating these hypotheses by empirical means.

TOWARD A THEORETICAL APPROACH

Throughout this discussion we have emphasized the role of the environment, particularly the social milieu, in generating destructive behavior. This is not because we believe that other factors are trivial, but because:

1. Psychologists may have more opportunity to alter the social milieu than to reorganize the individual's biochemical makeup.

2. Murder is directly and suicide indirectly a social act. In every homicide there are at least two people objectively involved. In suicide the critical "interaction" may be taking place largely within the victim's psyche. But we are gradually learning that the social context exerts strong influence over the probabilities both of a suicidal attempt and its "success."

3. Both types of lethal behavior arouse widespread and occasionally catastrophic reactions in the community. Murder often seems to elicit a stronger, more obvious reaction than self-destruction. At times it appears as though the ancient law of the talion is activated by murder: Somebody must die by violence to compensate for the original death.

None of this means that biological factors are irrelevant and should be ignored in developing theories of lethal behavior. Biochemical aberrations may contribute to some homicidal actions, and perhaps to some suicides as well. But we have some doubt that organic factors or psychoses "cause" destructive actions per se. One

possible way in which organic factors might influence lethal behavior is by their effect upon the strength of aggressive impulses. Bromberg has suggested that "excessive quanta of aggressive energy exist in certain persons that cannot solely be accounted for by the learning process" (30). It is possible to attribute such "excessive quanta" to hereditary patterns of glandular activity that are basic to the temperamental differences that some investigators believe accompany different somatotypes. Other interpretations are also possible. In any case, the implication is likely to be that some people are born with a greater than average *potential* for aggressive behavior. The fate of this potential—how it expresses itself—would still depend largely upon environmental influences.

Relevant here is Megargee's summary of the three elements which he believes must be considered "in plotting the dynamics of an aggressive act" (31). He cites: a) "the aggressive drive level"; b) "the inhibition level—the internal forces which lessen the likelihood that an aggressive act will occur"; and c) "the stimulus situation—the degree to which external factors facilitate or impede aggressive behavior" (32).

The first of these is a combination of what might loosely be termed biological and environmental factors. The second may or may not include biological factors, but it would certainly be affected by the child-rearing practices and early experiences which influence crucial aspects of psychic development. Reality testing, superego formation (regulating inner vs outer direction of aggressivity), and affective orientation (positive or negative) to the world are primary among these factors. The third element, the external stimulus situation, refers to environmental conditions which we have already considered in detail.

One could exchange the psychoanalytic terms used in this model for the language of the learning or developmental psychologist and still be talking about substantially the same approach.

We would like now to sketch out briefly one way in which some of our notions about murder can be integrated into the conceptual framework we proposed earlier for suicide. Important elements are being excluded from this presentation. In contrast to our view of suicide, we do not believe that there is a "basically homicidal personality." We *did* recognize earlier that there is a basically suicidal personality which is possessed of certain potentials for lethality. The possible origins of these characteristics have been discussed elsewhere (Chapter 11). We *did not* accept the view that under sufficient external pressure anyone would commit suicide.

Our approach to homicide is somewhat the reverse. We *do* believe that under sufficiently intense external pressure *anyone* could be goaded into taking the life of another person. Probably the only people who would not kill in self-defense, for example, are those who do not comprehend the threat to their lives, those who are too sick or weak to protect themselves, and those who are basically suicidal. Even the latter might be prompted to homicide if they felt that the life of another person or some other core value was at stake. (This discussion centers around the act of killing another person, whether or not a court would find the slayer guilty of homicide in the legal sense.)

Are our positions on suicide and murder that inconsistent or irreconcilable? We do not think so. The acceptance of a universal *potential* for murder and the rejection of a universal *impulse* to suicide derive ultimately from our views concerning two other concepts. We tend to accept the concept of a universal impulse of self-preservation; we tend to reject the concept of a universal death instinct. (These two general concepts will be discussed in later chapters.)

Both suicide and homicide seem to have common roots in what, for want of a better term, we continue to label "aggressive impulses." Certainly, the presence of some aggressive potential in human beings is universal. But the likelihood that we all have a potential for aggressive behavior cannot be taken as evidence that a) this potential is always of lethal strength, or b) that anyone with external provocation will direct the aggression against the self. We hold that Everyman's aggressive impulses could be directed against another person a) in the presence of intense provocation—if life is threatened; b) in the case of less intense provocation, when inner controls are weak; or c) in the presence of external provocation and social permission or encouragement, unless internal restraints are unusually strong.

The last factor mentioned may be the one that is primarily responsible for the excessive display of violence seen in our society today. That both developmental and biological factors play some role in this phenomenon is exemplified in the statistics that show increasing violence on the part of 15- and 16-year-old males. People in this age group are subjected to the heightened pressure of sexual impulses. They are also ready in many other ways to participate in the full range of adult activities. Yet both sexual and general realms of action are still considered by many adults to be beyond the proper scope of the adolescent's activity. Our society, which focuses on violence as entertainment, does little to interfere with the expression of violence, and provides no authentic and rewarding role for many of its adolescents. Is it any wonder that crime rates soar in this age bracket?

We have touched on some theoretical issues related to both homicide and suicide, and have presented a few ideas of our own. We have suggested that killing takes at least two forms—deliberate homicide and deliberate suicide. We have yet to determine whether or not it can be "deliberately accidental."

REFERENCES

1. Dublin, L. *Suicide: A sociological and statistical study.* New York: Ronald Press, 1963. P. 101.
2. Mead, M. *Redbook*, June, 1967, p. 38.
3. *Ibid.*
4. Fenichel, O. *The psychoanalytic theory of neurosis.* Washington, D.C.: W. W. Norton, 1945. P. 400.
5. Bergler, E. *The basic neurosis: Oral regression and psychic masochism.* New York: Grune & Stratton, 1949.
6. Dorpat, T. L., Jackson, J. S., & Ripley, H. S. Broken homes and attempted and completed suicide. *Archives of General Psychiatry,* 1965, *12*, 213-216.
7. Rheingold, J. C. *The mother, anxiety, and death.* Boston: Little, Brown, 1967.
8. *Ibid.*, p. 149.
9. *Ibid.*, p. 150.
10. *Ibid.*
11. *Ibid.*
12. *Ibid.*, pp. 104-105.
13. *Ibid.*, p. 106.
14. *Ibid.*
15. *Ibid.*, p. 109.
16. Henry, Andrew F. & Short, James F. *Suicide and homicide.* New York: The Free Press, 1954.
17. *Ibid.*, p. 64.
18. *Ibid.*, p. 72.
19. *Ibid.*, p. 94.
20. *Ibid.*, p. 85
21. *Ibid.*, p. 95.
22. *Ibid.*, p. 103.
23. *Ibid.*, p. 110.
24. *Ibid.*, p. 117.
25. *Ibid.*, p. 118.
26. *Ibid.*
27. Lester, D. Suicide, homicide, and the effects of socialization. *Journal of Social Psychology,* 1967, *5*, pp. 466-468.
28. Whiting, J. W., & Child, I. L. *Child training and personality.* New Haven: Yale University Press, 1953.
29. Lester, *op. cit.*
30. Bromberg, W. *Crime and the mind.* New York: Macmillan, 1965.
31. Megargee, E. I. Matricide, patricide and the dynamics of aggression. Paper delivered at American Psychological Association meetings, Washington, D.C., September 2, 1967. P. 1.
32. *Ibid.*

14

Accidents

Accident: 1) Something that did not have to happen, but did; 2) something that had to happen because it did happen.

These contrasting definitions share one underlying sentiment: nothing much can be done about those events we call "accidents." The first definition is likely to be based upon the conviction that "luck" or "chance" plays the most important role in our lives. "Bad luck" strikes here and there indiscriminately. We cannot predict who will be victimized, where, or when. Therefore, we might as well just go about our daily business and forget about the prospect of accidents. The second definition is more likely to have its roots in the notion that there is a "hidden purpose" behind the major events in our lives. A fatal accident is an "act of God" or a manifestation of the inscrutable will of the universe.

The second view appeals more to the person who prefers to regard the universe as a *system* whose workings must remain forever beyond our understanding and control. The other view appeals more to the person who has been impressed by the discontinuities, incongruities, and shocks often encountered in the life experience. In either case, one's implicit definition of

"accident" tends to encourage a personal policy of nonpreparation and nonintervention.

We believe these views are inadequate; what is worse, they are likely to increase the accident rate through the failure to take appropriate precautions. Students of developmental psychology, cognition, and attitudes could make important contributions to the psychology of life and death if they were to focus their attention upon the conditions which lead to the establishment and perpetuation of these outlooks.

Here, we shall attempt simply to show that most "accidents" have identifiable causes and are preventable. By "accident" we mean simply a disastrous event that occurs suddenly, unexpectedly, without (conscious) planning or intention. Closer analyses of accidents and their contexts will modify this preliminary definition. The accident victim (if he survives), or the accident accomplice, may indeed continue to look upon the event as a sudden, unexpected disaster that was unrelated to his general life pattern. Yet it is usually possible to learn how the interaction between extrinsic and intrinsic factors operated in such a way that it clearly increased the *probability* of an accident. A quick illustration for the moment: the probability of someone dying of a bullet wound is raised enormously when a gun and ammunition are brought into a household. It would truly be an "act of God" if a gun accident occurred minus a gun. Secondly, loading the gun and keeping it in the household again greatly increase the probabilities in favor of a lethal happening. In many other ways, some obvious, and some subtle, we act upon our environments either in the direction of increasing or reducing the probabilities of "accidental" death.

Why should a book about thanatology, especially the psychology of death, devote an entire chapter to such events? For some of the same reasons that we have already considered suicide and murder in detail: a) because accidents so frequently cause death; and b) because the basic reasons for the occurrence of fatal accidents are intimately bound up with all manner of psychological and social-psychological phenomena. Such phenomena may appear to exert a lesser influence on accidents than on suicide and murder, but this is not the case. It is one of our goals here to bring to light the subtle and complex role which psychological variables often play in shaping the more concrete, so-called "objective factors" which ultimately result in, or are proximate to, accidental death. We have two additional goals: a) to demonstrate that it is not always possible to determine where an accident leaves off and homicide or suicide begins; and b) to suggest not only that thanatologists should be concerned about accidents, but that accident specialists should be interested in thanatology.

THE SCOPE OF THE ACCIDENT PROBLEM

It is scarcely necessary to remind any literate American that, in our country, accidents have become a major cause of death. The daily news media carry account after depressing account of lives lost to accidental causes. Indeed, the National Safety Council's estimates of expected highway deaths have become a traditional holiday harbinger. Our preoccupation with the automobile and the mishaps related thereto may make us forget that there are many other vehicles of death. Misadventures with guns, staircases, airplanes, poisons, knives, ropes, toys, boats, fire, and innumerable other agents have long since combined to make accidents the third most common cause of death in this country (1). Over 108,000 people lost their lives in accidents in 1965 alone (2). This toll is all the more appalling when one considers that during the same year, an additional *45.1 million* people were involved in accidents sufficiently serious to require restricted activity and/or medical attention (3). When we survey the accident literature in an effort to determine how and why all of this takes place, we are confronted by a vast panorama of statistics and frequently conflicting hypotheses. We note, for example, that men have more accidents than women, but fewer accidents at home (4); that falls are the only type of accident more frequent among women than men (5); that incidence and type of accident are often highly correlated with age (6,7); and that drinking plays an important role in accidents (8). However, we also find that the decision as to whether a behavioral event is labeled "accident," "suicide," or "homicide" is often based more on arbitrary convention than on firm data and that, finally, who lives and who dies is often predetermined from without by broad social decisions, or from within by idiosyncratic personal attributes.

The search for whom or what to blame has led to the study of many different but not always mutually exclusive variables. If we seek to dichotomize, we may divide these variables roughly into those that are intrinsic and those that are extrinsic to the human organism. Under the heading of extrinsic variables we might include such factors as motor vehicle design, level of illumination in a given area, maintenance and repair of staircases or fire escapes, electric shock hazards, structural defects in buildings, physical properties of aircraft materials, and so on. One can see at the outset that such factors and the question of how and why they contribute to the occurrence of an accident cannot be clearly divorced from intrinsic organismic variables: Who and what determines motor vehicle design? Why is building maintenance often inadequate? How do so-called structural defects originate and why do they often go unnoticed or unchanged? The answers to such questions are often to be found in people and the situations of which they are a part rather than in the objective physical characteristics of the external world.

Under the heading of intrinsic variables we might include such phenomena as an individual's mental state, attitudes toward self and others, and his system of values. Many of these variables are inferred rather than directly observed and are, therefore, open to misinterpretation. Moreover, even if our inferences are essentially correct, at a given point in time all such intrinsic covert factors are in a constant state of flux. Any attempt to treat extrinsic and intrinsic variables as separate and permanent is foredoomed to at least partial failure. We realize this. However, we must begin somewhere. Although we propose to treat intrinsic and extrinsic variables more or less separately, we shall point out their interrelationships, where appropriate, as we proceed. This may serve to reduce the amount of confusion for those new to the field and, at the same time, afford the more knowledgeable reader an opportunity to gain a somewhat different perspective on the problem of causality as it applies to accidents. We shall discuss intrinsic variables first for three reasons:

1. Because the primary focus of this book is the *psychology* of death.
2. Because extrinsic factors fre-

quently turn out to be meaningless unless intrinsic variables are understood.

3. Because the one theoretical approach which attempts to cut across and explain all types of accidents and their causes depends almost entirely upon hypotheses concerning intrinsic variables.

ACCIDENT-RELEVANT FACTORS

Intrinsic Variables

Before we can even begin to approach realistically the question of how psychological and other intrinsic variables are related to the occurrence of accidents, we must be willing to admit that we do not have the answer, an admission that many people have as yet been unwilling to make. It is appropriate, then, to begin our discussion by reviewing the *hypothesis* that is so often utilized as a ready *explanation* of many accident-related phenomena. That hypothesis—and we hasten to emphasize that it is still no more than an hypothesis—holds that there exists a group of individuals who share certain psychodynamic patterns and/or personality traits that prompt them to arrange or seek out situations that predispose to accidents. These people have been labeled "accident-prone." The validity of this hypothesis has yet to be demonstrated definitively—a fact that appears to have escaped the attention of many who espouse it. Premature acceptance of an hypothesis (or failure to distinguish between hypotheses and documented fact) is likely to obstruct progress toward true understanding of why accidents occur and how psychological factors help to determine them. Attempts to discuss accident-proneness rationally are often undermined by the tendency in some quarters to assume that this concept is an integral part of psychoanalytic theory. Analytically oriented authors have often cited case histories of the "accident-prone" to illustrate hypotheses of suicidal impulses and the death instinct. This often creates the impression that accident-proneness is a fact and that propositions concerning it will endure as long as the basic tenets of psychoanalytic theory endure. Even ostensibly empirical studies of accident-proneness often appear to be directed toward studying an established phenomenon, or even a specific diagnostic entity rather than toward discovering if, in fact, there is any such thing. The data are not all in. We simply do not know if accident-proneness, as it is usually defined, really exists. We review this concept in order to set to rest the notion that those of us who are psychologically "in the know" already have the answer to the accident problem.

Accident-Proneness and How It Grew. "The existence of the accident-prone individual is today a rather widely accepted fact" (9).

This statement is probably true; but should it be? Let us heed first the words of several noted authorities. According to the late Franz Alexander:

> The contention of modern psychiatry that most accidents are not accidents at all but are caused largely by the victim's own disposition is but a confirmation of common observation. . . . The sufferer from the accident has some active part in its causation. It is popularly assumed that he was clumsy, tired, or absentminded; otherwise, he might have avoided the accident. Scientific scrutiny, however, has established that most accidents are not due to such simple human qualities. Certain people are prone to have more accidents than others, not because they are clumsy or absentminded, but *because of the total structure of their personalities* (10) [italics ours].

Alexander held that *most* accidents are caused by unconscious motivations (11). These motives include "a sense of guilt which the victim tries to expiate by self imposed punishment" (12), and less common motives such as "the wish to avoid responsibility, the wish to be taken care of, even the desire for monetary compensation" (13).

Like many other writers in the field, Alexander based his description of the personality attributes of accident victims at least partially on the writings of Flanders Dunbar. Dunbar summarized the characteristics of those she designated accident-prone as "decisive to the point of giving an impression of impulsiveness" (14). She states that they are concerned with daily pleasures, have little interest in long-term goals and manifest a cavalier attitude toward sex and family. Their illness rates are said to be lower than average, and they have low rates of venereal disease and of pregnancy in extramarital affairs. They tend to be resentful of authority and describe their upbringing as having been "strict." In Dunbar's study the accident-prone were given to sleepwalking and sleeptalking in childhood and showed a propensity for lying, stealing, and truancy. Later this behavior disappeared, "apparently replaced by the accident habit" (15). Dunbar likened the overall pattern of accident-prone people to that of juvenile delinquents and adult criminals: "The behavior characteristic of the persistent breaker of laws is virtually identical with that of the persistent breaker of bones right up to the point where one commits a crime and the other has an accident" (16). She adds, "It is a fact that few criminals get sick. They find the release from their emotional conflict in what society has chosen to regard as an unsocial act, just as their counterparts in the accident wards of hospitals find their release in the accident habit" (17).

Dunbar's writings have been widely quoted, paraphrased, and enlarged upon by many authorities who appear to accept most of her basic tenets and/or Alexander's comments almost unquestioningly. Weiss and English in their classic text, *Psychosomatic Medicine*, state: "The decisiveness of the accident-prone person *is* part of a drive for independence and self-reliance in a situation of the moment rather than as part of a planned career or program" (18) [italics ours]. In regard to Dunbar's remarks, some of which we have quoted above, these authors remark: "Treatment for patients with the accident habit involves a deep understanding of all the factors which enter into their accident-proneness" (19). Laughlin, in his widely used book, *The Neuroses in Clinical Practice*, also makes reference to Dunbar's work. He discusses accident-proneness under the heading of "Partial Suicide" (20). In considering the psychodynamics of the accident-prone driver, Laughlin holds that we are well aware of the general factors involved: impulsiveness, immaturity and, frequently, resentment of authority (21).

One example is provided by the recent, but already ubiquitous, *Handbook of Clinical Psychology* in which Alexander and coauthor Glenn Flagg reiterate the essentials of the accident-proneness formula:

The *great majority* of accidents are not really accidents but are the result of the individual's "acting out" and discharge of a forbidden and unconscious impulse [italics ours]. Usually the sufferer from an accident has some active part in its causation, and thus it is not a true accident. . . . Most accidents are not simply due to fatigue or chance but are caused by repressed emotions (22).

Or, see Maxcy (Ed.) in *Preventive Medicine and Public Health:*

It has been shown that the majority of accidents occur among a relatively small group of people. . . . Psychiatrists have studied this problem and have described the personality structure of the *accident-prone type.* . . (23) [italics ours].

Because works such as these are in widespread use, have been written by authorities, and are generally thought to be scholarly, the impression created is that accident-proneness as it is variously defined is a clearly delineated, well understood phenomenon—or even syndrome—

and that our information about accidents is well-grounded in extensive research. Yet neither of these impressions is wholly valid. A review of even the brief excerpts cited above reveals uncertainty about what accident-proneness *is*. Alexander contended that certain people are accident-prone "because of the total structure of their personalities" and that most accidents are caused by the victim's "disposition," a term left undefined. Dunbar, too, spelled out the traits of the accident-prone and referred to the characteristics common to their upbringing and behavior patterns in early life. This certainly creates the impression that accident-proneness and the traits associated with it are more or less enduring aspects of the personality. But Weiss and English, as well as Laughlin, seem to imply only that certain traits characterize the accident repeater. Both Alexander and Gregg see repressed emotions as the cause of accidents. Hence, what is meant by "accident-proneness" or the "accident-prone personality" varies from writer to writer. In addition, and more importantly, the extensive, thorough research that one may at first be led to conclude formed the basis for the concept of accident-proneness, turns out upon closer examination to leave much to be desired:

1. Maxcy was one of the first to note that once a person has had an accident he is more likely to have another than is the individual who has never had an accident. Of course, this observation says nothing of *why* the probability seems to increase.

2. Dunbar's conclusions concerning the personality traits of the accident-prone were strongly influenced by her study of fracture patients. She noted that such patients were 14 times more likely to have disabling mishaps than the average of all other groups of hospitalized patients studied (24). Yet conclusions based on this type of patient have tended to become generalized to *all* accident repeaters.

In addition, one should raise the question of whether so-called traits identified after an accident has taken place may not, at least partially, constitute a *reaction* to the injury, the disability, and to those conducting the psychiatric investigation. Moreover, the traits found to characterize the childhood behavior of accident repeaters may have nothing whatever to do with their later accidents. We do not know because of the inadequacy of experimental control. It will be recalled that sleepwalking, sleeptalking, lying, stealing, and truancy were common in the early histories of accident repeaters. Dunbar concluded that such behavior was later replaced by the accident habit (25). This appears to support the contention that accident-proneness is an enduring personality characteristic. However, we have no control data available for comparison. How common is such behavior in childhood? What proportion of the children who manifest it develop into well-adjusted adults who do not have frequent accidents? How many give later indications of aberration, but are relatively accident-free? These are among the questions that should be explored. Haddon, Suchman, and Klein, discussing this problem in their excellent compendium of accident research, make several salient points: "It should be obvious that so indiscriminate a listing of personality traits could hardly be expected to define a *single* type of individual. The list of distinguishing characteristics changes from study to study; the results concerning any single characteristic are inconsistent; and, in general, the correlations between personality characteristics and, hence, their predictive value, are extremely low" (26).

3. Haddon, Suchman, and Klein also present an excellent summary and critique of the early, and influential papers on accident proneness. For our purposes here, the following summary of their comments will suffice:

a. The original study in the field, conducted by Major Greenwood and Hilda M. Woods, dealt with the widely discrepant accident rates among workers in a wartime munitions factory. They noted that a small proportion of the workers had the majority of the accidents. After carefully considering alternative explanations, the authors hypothesized that "some individuals are inherently more likely to have accidents than others" (27).

b. Following this study, Newbold conducted an investigation which tended to confirm the earlier findings. Newbold concluded that although it was not possible to specify to what degree the results were attributable to different work conditions or personal tendency, "there are many indications that *some* part . . . is due to personal tendency" (28). For example, "accident occurrence for given individuals was consistent 1) in different time periods, 2) for accidents of different types, and 3) in the factory and at home" (29). Haddon *et al* point out that despite Newbold's laudably conservative phrasing, "her work has been widely cited as offering proof of the existence of individuals who are *psychologically* prone to accidents" (30). Since the publication of these studies, most writers have assumed that accident-proneness does exist and is some kind of permanent tendency, trait, or behavior pattern.

However, our main purpose is not to review the literature but to stress the point that accident-proneness as it is usually defined is not an established fact and that, even if it were, it could not explain all accidents. Indeed, it is not even an adequate explanation of just the psychological aspects of accidents. One example will illustrate how uncritical acceptance of the accident-prone hypothesis and the over-generalizations derived therefrom can be misused to the public's detriment. The

Home Medical Encyclopedia, a paperback edition intended to provide commonly known medical information and guidance for laymen, states categorically:

There are people who are more prone to accidents than others.... They are very impulsive and often act before they think.... There is usually some form of rebellion against any kind of authority, so that even their own reason sometimes constitutes this sort of authority. But in practice the tendency towards accidents in a person can only be recognized by the fact that he or she has more little or big accidents than other people. This is apparent at an early age, so that one should bear this in mind when choosing a profession for the person concerned. Adolescents who have had a lot of accidents in their youth (regardless of whether or not they were to blame), should be discouraged from taking up dangerous occupations. In particular everything should be done to prevent them from becoming chauffeurs or truck drivers (31).

It is certainly reasonable to suppose that there is a relationship between one's occupation and his liability to accidents. However, to make one's apparent liability to accidents the basis for occupational choice or, more especially, to make it the basis for selection of an occupation for someone else would seem presumptuous, to say the least.

•

Alternative Explanations

Some people certainly do have more accidents than other people. If the hypothesis of accident-proneness cannot be shown to provide an entirely adequate explanation for this fact, then what can? Probably some small part of the total number of accident repeaters can be explained by the *statistical* concept of "chance" alone. Suchman and Scherzer remind us that "During any given period a certain proportion of the population would suffer an inordinately high number of accidents by chance alone" (32). It is also likely that another very small number of people, bent on self-destruction or de-

siring retribution for sin, may perennially seek out or cause accidents to themselves. These individuals have been made much of in the literature. Menninger and many other writers with a psychoanalytic orientation have long contended that accidents are partial suicides (33). Their data, however, consist of relatively few case histories of individuals already determined by other criteria to be atypical. Even if it could be shown that all basically suicidal individuals have a high accident rate, it would not follow that all individuals with a high accident rate are basically suicidal. To what other factors can we attribute the behavior of the bulk of accident repeaters? Possible clues are presented in Morris Schulzinger's interesting book (34), *The Accident Syndrome*. Schulzinger studied 35,000 cases of accidental injury which he himself treated over a 20-year period. Since this undoubtedly represents one of the largest samples of accident patients ever to be subjected to systematic investigation, the findings should be of special value. Some of Schulzinger's major conclusions can be summarized as follows:

1. "Most accidents are due to infrequent solitary experiences of large numbers of individuals" (35).
2. "The tendency to have repeated accidents is a phenomenon that usually passes with age and is not a fixed trait of the individual" (36).
3. "The frequently reported observation that most accidents are due to a small fixed group of accident repeaters holds true only when the period of observation is relatively short or when the numerical strength of the observed population greatly exceeds the numerical strength of the accidents" (37).

Schulzinger feels that susceptibility to accidents, like that to illness, varies in degree rather than kind. Thus, it is not that some people are prone to accidents and others "unprone," but rather that individuals differ in their susceptibility to accidents. Moreover, insofar as can be determined, *one's degree of susceptibility is not a constant throughout life.* Schulzinger declares that "the concept of accident-proneness as a fixed personality factor which compels or generates accidental injury throughout life or long periods of time is incompatible" with his findings (38). He notes, for example, that most of the supposedly accident-prone patients in his study dropped out of the high-accident group after various periods of time (39). He found the highest incidence of accidents to be at ages 21 and 22 years. "Precipitous increments . . . began at age 17, continued to the peak, then decreased with each year until 29" (40).

Is there a single alternative explanation of how psychological factors influence accidents? We think not. Probably, there is no way to reduce the interrelationships between psychological variables and accidents to a simple formula. Thoroughgoing library research yields only a patchwork of statistical facts, hypotheses, old wives' tales, and equivocal or contradictory experimental results. In some respects, it is more difficult to discuss the psychology of accidents than that of murder. At least in the case of murder we are usually willing to admit that someone (not us, of course) is responsible, and that someone (not us, of course) should do something about it. Society's approach to the problem of accidents often lacks even these meager assets. Nevertheless, we shall attempt to dissect out from their social matrices some of the psychological variables that appear to play a role in causing, or allowing, accidents to occur. Whenever possible, we shall refer to the direct testament of everyday life, instead of limiting our attention to theoretical interpretations. In fact, we shall take much of our information from press and magazine reports which are readily accessible to anyone. Perhaps we all know much more about the causes of accidents than we would like to admit.

SETTING THE STAGE FOR ACCIDENTS

The elements that predispose, or actually lead, to an accident or "accidental" death may be: a) inherited or acquired characteristics of the organism itself; b) latent in the objects involved in the accident; or c) manifestations of trends and values of the social milieu.

Inherited or Acquired Characteristics: Predisposing Organismic Factors

• *Body Build.* We noted in Chapter 12 that people can be more or less differentiated on the basis of what Sheldon has described as somatotype, or type of body build, and that each of three somatotypes is associated with rather different temperamental characteristics. The cerebrotonic traits associated with ectomorphy include great sensitivity, caution and a general tendency to be anxious and inhibited, especially in social situations. Somatonia, associated with mesomorphy, is characterized by a strong drive for physical activity, self-assertiveness, and rather "pushy" and frequently domineering behavior toward others. Viscerotonia, associated with endomorphy, includes a tendency to be openly affectionate, comfort-loving, sociable and concerned with food (41). Few of us exemplify any one of these types in pure form. Nevertheless, in most people, one or another of these three characteristic types of behavior tends to predominate. There is probably some kind of general relationship between one's somatotype (and its corresponding temperamental traits) and the tendency to have certain kinds of accidents.

Let us first look at the mesomorph. In Chapter 12, we noted that Gleuck and Gleuck found that the juvenile delinquents they studied tended to be mesomorphs (42). Earlier in this chapter we spoke of Dunbar's finding that the overall behavior of the fracture patients she studied had much in common with that of juvenile delinquents and criminals. It is possible that the incidence of fractures and other kinds of accidental injuries would be highest among mesomorphs. Certainly the well-muscled, athletic, assertive, action-oriented person would be likely to participate in the kinds of activities that would maximize his exposure to certain kinds of injuries. Consider, for example, such competitive sports as auto-racing, such body-contact sports as football, and such outdoor activities as hunting, camping, and swimming. However, the somatotonic individual might also be given to accidents because of his natural inclination to take action quickly—sometimes before thinking. The fact that he might quickly do something which might better have been left undone could cost him a trip to the emergency room. The ectomorph, by contrast, may be predisposed to fewer and different accidents. He is certainly less likely to act first and think later. Yet simply because he is not so used to vigorous, athletic endeavors and not nearly so well-coordinated he may be guilty of self-injury through sheer clumsiness and inexperience. There is no need to labor these points. Suffice it to say that, individual psychodynamics notwithstanding, one's body build and corresponding temperament probably do play some part both in exposing him to accidents and in increasing the likelihood that an accident will occur once he is in certain kinds of situations. Here, we should like to make one additional point. Although it is not a function of body build per se, there is a possibility that some accidents are caused by clumsiness which is congenital. Dr. John Whiting has expressed the belief that some people are born clumsy (43) and he attributes this to birth injuries which often go undetected. "Classmates stop choosing the clumsy child or stop playing with him." This could serve to increase his awkwardness through emotional discomfort and lack of

practice and thus render him more susceptible to accidents.

• *Developmental Level.* As we all know, certain kinds of accidents are more common at some stages of life than at others. Understandably, this phenomenon is most clearly manifested at the extremes of the developmental continuum. The helpless neonate is subject to falls, poisoning, suffocation, crushing, and drowning, not through any direct fault of its own, but usually because of parental ignorance, neglect, malice, or inexperience. At a later stage the infant becomes more curious about the external world and is capable of some independent mobility; at this time accidental deaths are most commonly due to "inhalation or ingestion of foreign materials" (44). This danger remains the most serious threat to life throughout the early years. In fact, accidental poisoning has been described as the most common non-surgical emergency in childhood in the United States today (45). One study reported that nearly 12 percent of two-year-old children in Syracuse, New York, had experienced an episode of poisoning in one 12-month period (46). Over three million children took poison accidentally in 1966 alone, and more than six hundred died (47). *"Substances that seem harmless to an adult can be deadly to a small child,"* as the following tragic episode illustrates [italics ours]:

We had a case of a father who dropped his can of shaving talcum powder in the bathroom. His two-year-old son was crawling around on the floor. The little boy got the cap off the can and started breathing in the sweet-smelling powder. We got a call he was gasping for breath. We did all we could and so did the hospital they rushed him to, but it was too late. The talcum powder had clogged up his lung passages, and they lost him (48).

Of course, parental ignorance and the appealing fragrance of the powder were relevant factors. However, the characteristics of the incompletely developed organism—his curiosity, mobility, and ability to open the can—coupled with his parents' ignorance and poor judgment, were important contributing factors in this tragedy.

The preschooler, next in line in the developmental sequence, is known to be at greatest risk from motor vehicles, fire, and drowning (49). Thereafter, motor vehicle accidents lead all other types by increasingly larger margins until the teen years during which one of every four deaths is attributable to this single cause (50).

One may question the extent to which purely developmental phenomena can be held accountable for fluctuations in the type and incidence of accidents such as those specified. Certainly if organismic factors are defined in the narrowest, physical sense, their liability in the middle years (even of childhood) is strictly limited. However, when more broadly defined, the organismic changes which are a function of developmental level can be seen to be the major determinants of increasing *exposure* to certain kinds of injury. Thus, developmental level sets limits not only on physical strength, size, stamina, ability to conceptualize, and experience but it also indirectly influences opportunities and ability to interact with others, and to be allowed to function without supervision in potentially dangerous situations. In short, it is a major, sometimes rather arbitrary, determinant of when a society will permit the individual to be exposed to certain dangers. Think, for example, of the ages at which different states allow children to ride bicycles in the street, drive a car, obtain working permits. Examples of less formal restrictions associated with developmental stage or chronological age would be parents' insistence that Junior not cross the street alone until he is five; or play outside independently before he can talk; or go farther than one block from his home until he starts to go to school. Thus, for example, not only does the amount of exposure to vehicle death change with

increasing age, but the manner of exposure changes also. Initially, a toddler may be at greatest risk as a pedestrian, running heedlessly into the street, or as a passenger in his parents' car. Later, as he attends school and social functions, his liability to injury in a school bus or another family's private car increases. In the adolescent years, the likelihood of being the driver of a vehicle involved in an accident increases appreciably.

It is likely that some of our ideas concerning the role of psychological variables in accidents would have to be altered if we could equate the exposure times (to various types of injury) of people in different age groups and correlate these with number and severity of accidents at these ages.

Thus far we have devoted most of our attention to the young, immature organism. Let us look now at the opposite end of the developmental continuum. It is a striking fact that motor vehicle accidents are still the most common cause of death in old age (65-74 years of age) (51), but for different reasons: "Older people are less able to perceive danger, to interpret warnings rapidly, to move quickly and with coordination, or to compensate for physical impairments. . . . Muscular skills decline, and chronic diseases increase their susceptibility to accidents. Loss of mental alertness diminishes their ability to respond to emergencies" (52).

Age also influences the individual's ability to withstand certain types of accidental injury. For example, the results of a study of 570 burn patients indicate that "age of the patient exerts a curvilinear effect on the chance of survival. The ability of a patient to tolerate a burn increases up to age 40 and then begins to fall; this decline in tolerance drops quite rapidly at age 60" (53). This fact makes all the more deplorable society's negligence in providing truly appropriate facilities for housing and caring for the elderly. It undoubtedly explains many of the tragic deaths resulting from nursing home fires.

The sensory deficits which go with advancing age also increase vulnerability to accidents. According to Dr. A. J. Mirkin, the high incidence of vehicular accidents among the elderly is at least partly attributable to a decrease in visual acuity and in the field of vision. The "intensity of light necessary to maintain threshold vision during adaptation to the dark is doubled every thirteen years..." (54). Mirkin reports: "Older drivers usually have more difficulty seeing at dawn and dusk, and recovery from glare decreases with age" (55).

Finally, a combination of many changes associated with age—musculoskeletal, sensory, neurological and judgmental—act together to make falls the chief cause of accidental death after age 74. (Falls caused 11,120 of the 17,145 accidental deaths in this age group just in 1963.) (56) Although physical changes are of primary importance in determining the high incidence of falls among the elderly, certain environmental factors are undoubtedly relevant, and we shall discuss these later.

Despite the foregoing statements, it is not only at the extremes of the continuum that chronological age and developmental stage are closely, often causally, related to the kind and incidence of accidents. As noted earlier, Schulzinger found that people 21 and 22 years of age have the highest accident rate. This is by no means an isolated finding. "Of 38,702 motor vehicle deaths in 1957, nearly one-fourth (8,667) were persons between 15 and 24 years of age" (57). Approximately 27,000 others in this age group were permanently impaired in some way by automobile accidents (58). McFarland and Moore cite two studies which show that in Massachusetts and Connecticut (during the periods studied) the youngest drivers had the highest accident rates (59): "The rate decreases with succeeding years of age, rapidly at first, and then more slowly, so that at about age 25-30 the involvement rate becomes lower than would be expected if age were of no

significance" (60). Yet another study showed that drivers under 25 and over 65 had the highest accident *rates;* of these, the younger group had the greatest *number* of accidents since they drive more (61). In addition, of the 1,600 Americans killed and 60,000 injured in motorcycle accidents in 1965, "most of the fatalities are of high-school and college age" (62). (This phenomenon is not confined to the United States. In Britain, for example, "one of every twelve boys who gets a motorcycle at the age of 16 is killed or seriously injured by the time he is 19") (63). In fact, "traffic accidents are the leading cause of death for young men between 16 and 24" in the United States (64). "Although young male drivers amount to only one-eighth of all registered drivers, they are responsible for one-third of all fatal accidents" (65). In 1966, more than twice as many men between the ages of 16 and 24 were killed in highway accidents as in the war in Vietnam (66).

We have seen that motor vehicle fatalities are particularly common among the very young and the very old drivers. There are, however, certain types of accidental death that are peculiar to the young male. Let us consider one of these in some detail, for, despite its relatively low incidence, it may help us to identify relevant organismic factors.

In a 33-year period during which records were kept, 682 young men have lost their lives in football games (67). Twenty-seven players died in 1964 alone, and an additional 53 in 1965 (68). Is it purely fortuitous that football and automobile fatalities frequently involve young men in the same age group? If not, what characteristics associated with this period of development and/or one's life style are primarily to blame? We cannot answer these questions directly but some data are certainly suggestive. Let us consider a report concerning three separate football fatalities that took place during a single autumn weekend in 1965: "All three (victims) stoically minimized their injuries. Surely this is proof that a boy's judgment as to whether he is fit to play is unreliable" (69). According to Dr. Frank Smith, a neurosurgeon, "high-school football is dangerous;" and deaths due to head and spinal injuries have increased (70). Some physicians think this is "because a teenage boy's neck may not be muscular and well developed enough to withstand the repeated shock of football contact" (71). Smith adds that the high school boy "isn't fully developed, he is highly suggestible and exposes himself to injury. In some cases he is trying to match the performance of the professional he sees on television" (72). This desire to prove himself brave and masculine and to avoid being labeled a "sissy" or "quitter" undoubtedly plays an important part in the minimization of injuries and taking of unnecessary risks. An incompletely developed physique is also a contributing factor. Do such characteristics really play an important part in causing accidental fatalities in these early years or are motor vehicle accidents and football deaths special cases? It is hard to escape the conclusion that the traits illustrated above are typical of many 16- to 24-year-olds and are often manifested in their accident-producing behavior. Examples are unfortunately ubiquitous:

1. Parachuting and skydiving for fun, sports confined primarily to the young, have a death rate 80 times that of football (73). "The great majority of parachuting deaths result from inexperience, carelessness and failure to comply with regulations (74).
2. Four inadequately equipped scuba divers, ranging from 19 to 22 years of age, voluntarily entered a deep cavernous spring, well known to be dangerous. They disappeared (75). "I don't know why they do it," said Alachua County Deputy Sheriff Shellie Downs. "It seems like they would read what happens to people who go down there without proper training."

Lacking sufficient gear for the eight people present, the boys drew straws to see who would dive (76). Since the spring involved had been sought out for exploration, it is likely that the eight boys had heard that it was dangerous *and that is why they went there.*

3. Despite the fact that it is generally acknowledged that wearing helments can often prevent motorcycle deaths (an estimated 150 could be saved each year in California alone) (77) many cyclists refuse to wear them. "They claim that helmets reduce their peripheral vision, or cut down on hearing acuity, or that they are too expensive, or *'the other kids will think I'm chicken'* " (78). [Italics ours.]

4. Risk-taking appears to be characteristic of modern teenagers and young adults the world over. It is certainly not confined to the American, or even to Western culture. Consider the headline of a recent news item: *"Jakarta Teens so Wild They Outdo the West"* (79). The story reported: "Every day the papers are filled with reports on adolescent antics. . . . The drag racing problem has grown into a public hazard on weekends. . . . These children get in their fathers' big cars and make a weekly habit of racing around the big fountain in front of the Hotel Indonesia or on the city's main streets. It's a hazard to other drivers and people attempting to cross the street" (80).

One can always debate the relative roles of nature and nuture in determining any pattern of behavior. Regardless of one's theoretical position in this controversy, the fact remains that several characteristics associated with adolescence and early adulthood undoubtedly tend to predispose this group to accidents. These include inexperience, poor judgment, the need to rebel against authority and to test limits, the desire to prove one's masculinity and competence—frequently by risk-taking, and general emotional, and possibly physical, immaturity. If we add to these the likelihood that young people will use defective and unreliable equipment and vehicles, then the accident statistics are easier to understand.

In light of the foregoing, one might suppose that adults in general, and parents in particular, would devote great efforts toward discouraging reckless driving and other hazardous behavior. Yet, this is clearly not so. We not only do not prohibit such behavior; we both tacitly and explicitly encourage it. Listen to some remarks concerning football fatalities. A physician in a town where a football death had occurred said: "All my training has been to save life. . . . Yet the arguments I hear in favor of this game show little regard for life. People say, 'I would rather my boy was killed playing football than running around in a car' " (81). The father of a dead football player said:

I think you'd make a mistake banning football. . . . I think these boys are entitled to play. I played for nine years, and I couldn't tell my boy not to and make it stick. It isn't up to you to cushion the shocks. These kids can take it. My boy did, and I'm proud of him. Don't blame football. These things, I think, are predestined. There's no shame in dying. It's how you die. If you die like a man, there's nothing wrong with that . . . (82).

These remarks reveal two basic attitudes that tend to increase accidental fatalities. The first is that *accidental death is unavoidable—it is predestined.* Hence there is no point in taking special precautions to avoid it. This attitude is implied in the statement that "I would rather my boy was killed playing football than running around in a car." The assumption seems to be that he is going to get killed by accident one way or another. The other is that *risking death, even when this is unnecessary, is honorable because it demonstrates masculinity.* "If you die like a man, there's nothing wrong with that." This "man" was a schoolboy. He had been injured previously and should probably not have been allowed to play in the game in which he died. "It isn't up to

you to cushion the shocks. These kids can take it." If it isn't up to the adults to protect the young, then who is it up to? The kid's can't always take it. If they could, the boy about whom this was said would still be alive.

These attitudes are encouraged in our culture. Our children's television and folk heroes race their cars recklessly around sharp corners, tires squealing. They leap onto their horses from the tops of buildings. This is "masculine." We promote sales by pointing out that our cars will go over 100 miles per hour, despite the fact that on no public highway in the United States is the speed limit anywhere near that high.

Unnecessary risk-taking is not "masculine"; it is dangerous and foolhardy. And most accidents are not inevitable. If they are "predestined" it is usually by our own inaction and lack of foresight. Adolescents may need to rebel and take risks but we don't need to let them kill themselves. Inertia, distorted values, and the desire to live vicarious, exciting lives through their children undoubtedly contribute to adults' unwillingness or inability to act to prevent accidents. When we view the facts in this light, how can we ignore the potential usefulness of psychological principles and techniques in the avoidance of premature, unnecessary death?

• *Sex.* The relationship of the third organismic factor, sex, to accidents is no less perplexing than is the relationship of sex to suicide, and for the same reason (See Chapter 11). Given our present state of knowledge, we cannot be certain whether it is genetic and biochemical factors or the influence of culture and experience that is primarily responsible for the differences in the male and female accident rates. However, that there are differences and rather striking ones, is not to be doubted. Generally speaking, males have more accidents than females at all ages (83). They also seem to have more of most kinds of accidents, although there are some exceptions. In one study the ratio of females to males accidentally poisoned was 63:51 (84), and over 92 percent of these victims were under the age of four years. Another study showed that females sustained a disproportionate share of the injuries in a group of beginning skiers (85). Many studies and statistical compilations show quite clearly that elderly women have more falls than elderly men (86). Whether the sex difference noted in the study of poisonings will prove upon further investigation to be reliable, is unknown. The reasons for such a difference in the age groups involved is anybody's guess. Ours is that since females' developmental timetables may be a little faster than males' (witness the fact that females on the average become pubescent sooner), toddler girls may be somewhat more capable of getting to the containers in which poisons are kept, and of opening them.

The investigators in the skiing study speculated about the sex difference and suggested as possible causes: less experience, poorer neuromuscular coordination, poorer physical condition, lower injury thresholds, inappropriate equipment, or "beginners' slopes of too great difficulty" (87). A possibly relevant factor the authors fail to mention is the women's lower motivation for or attention to skiing per se. Many young women who "go skiing" are more interested in the social aspects of the sport than they are in learning to ski. Consequently, their minds and eyes may not always be on what they are doing. In addition, they may attempt maneuvers for which they are really insufficiently trained merely so that they can keep up with male skiers whom they wish to impress. Still another factor may have been at work in the higher female ski accident rate reported, that is, the complex of changes associated with menstrual cycle. For example, Dalton found that menstruation apparently predisposes to accidents (88). (It has also been found that children are more likely to have accidents

when their mothers are menstruating) (89). The associated psychological factors appear to be feelings of lethargy and tension with consequent poorer judgment and less careful attention to detail (90).

Several factors may be involved in the finding that falls occur with greater frequency among females than males. As a group, women tend to live longer than men. If all falls after a given age (e.g., 65) are lumped together without further subdivision, and if this total is averaged for the two sexes, one would expect a greater number of falls for the females. Why? Because, since women live longer than men, a larger proportion of the women would be in the older age categories; falls are positively correlated with increasing age in the later years of life. There is another, possibly relevant factor, i.e., decalcification of bones is fairly common in post-menopausal women (91, 92). Hence it is likely that a fall that would cause little damage to a male and would, therefore, remain unreported, might, in a female, cause the fracture of a demineralized bone; therefore, her fracture and the fall which caused it would, of course, be recorded.

As to the reasons why, on the whole, men have more accidents than women, one important factor is that our culture tends to define "masculinity" in terms of physical bravery (that is, risk-taking), strength, self-assertiveness, competetiveness, and generally aggressive behavior. Quite obviously, many psychological aspects of "masculinity" as defined above are physically sex-linked. The male's structure and function in coitus determine that he must, for the most part, be the forceful initiator in this very specific type of masculine behavior. Moreover, the male's general body structure—the broader shoulders, the more highly developed musculature—better equip him for participation in many sports and in direct physical combat. Hence, there is a greater likelihood that male impulses will be expressed directly through physical channels. Intense motor activity, competitiveness, risk-taking, and aggressiveness are certainly all characteristics that increase the likelihood of accidents. However, it is reasonable to raise the question of whether the higher male accident rate is directly attributable to masculine traits per se or whether it is simply a statistical function of the increased exposure to which such traits lead. In other words, if women played football and basketball as much as men do, or if they drove motorcycles the same number of miles, and so on, would they have the same accident rate that men do? Or is the relatively high male accident rate partly an expression of a need to excel, conquer, or destroy? We cannot answer this question but we would like to explore some of the problems inherent in attempting to answer it. Let us focus on risk-taking.

Whether primarily an inborn attribute or a function of child-rearing practices, there is no doubt that there are great individual variations in the willingness to take risks. Obviously, such variations are related to the liability to accidents; but the relationship might be more complex than we yet imagine. In some situations, for example, the willingness to take a risk could save lives which might otherwise be lost. Additionally, we cannot be certain that risk-taking is a generalized personality trait manifested in a wide variety of situations. It may be that people who are quite willing to take great risks of certain kinds (e.g., with their reputations) are very unlikely to take certain other kinds of risks (e.g., passing a car on a steep upgrade.) The Character Education Inquiry's classic study of another kind of "trait" indicated that honesty is not a general trait at all. Children who were honest in one type of situation were often less trustworthy in another (93).

Furthermore, willingness to take risks may have little to do with the kind or amount of danger. Some people who might not take a particular risk when alone might do so in a group for the sake of peer approval or acceptance. Some would take risks when unobserved, but the presence of others might exert an inhibiting influence. More confusing still, the presence of certain individuals may at some times inhibit and at other times facilitate risk-taking. For example, the child who fears punishment and desires parental approval may not climb a forbidden tree today. But tomorrow, the same child desiring peer admiration, parental attention, and the chance to demonstrate that he is "his own man," may boldly climb that same tree in full view of his parents. The point we wish to make is that, whether or not risk-taking is a general trait, it is still bound to vary according to the individual's transitory needs, the external milieu, and the interaction between the two. Therefore, the person who has not previously been given to taking risks may at some point in time be *more* willing to place his life or possessions in jeopardy than the individual who has often been thought a great risk-taker. Hence, a study of the risk-taking propensities of a group in a particular situation may be of little value in enabling us to predict or prevent accidents in any other situation even if the same people are involved. For this reason, it is no more sensible to attempt to predict accidents solely on the basis of risk-taking behavior than it is to conclude that individuals who have had several accidents are necessarily and intrinsically accident-prone. (This illustrates, among other things, the fallacy of the application of a trait approach to the psychology of accidents.)

The willingness to take risks is not, as some may assume, ipso facto evidence of suicidal impulses. Take, for example, the case of three risk-takers who lost. On January 27, 1967, astronauts Virgil Grissom, Edward White, and Roger Chaffee died in a flash fire inside of their Apollo spacecraft during a launching pad test (94). In a sense, one could consider these men "test pilots"; and test pilots are often popularly thought to be happy-go-lucky, somewhat irresponsible people who flirt with death. Yet there was little about these men that could be made to fit this stereotype. All had undergone extensive previous screening to determine their stability and endurance. All had completed long periods of formal education and special training, and had planned in advance and in meticulous detail all of the moves to be executed in the space capsule. They were cognizant of the risks they took and sought to keep these to a minimum (95). They measured the risks against what they sought to gain by taking them. There is nothing to suggest that the astronauts were in any way responsible for their own deaths or could have done anything to prevent them. It is likely that some people who must take great risks in their work are so much more cautious on this account that they may actually sustain fewer injuries than others in safer occupations. Let us not forget that the real life Eliot Ness, a federal agent in the "roaring 20's" whose life was fictionalized in the television series, "The Untouchables," died a commonplace death in old age.

We have been emphasizing the need for caution in attributing accidents to any one trait or personal characteristic of the organism. There are, however, some few, often transitory organismic factors which can, of themselves, be sufficient cause for mishaps. Among these are altered states of consciousness, physical illness, and mental illness, all of which undoubtedly exert a disproportionate influence on accidental death statistics.

• *Altered States of Consciousness.* The phrase, "altered states of consciousness" covers a wide variety of phenomena although recently it has been used most often in discussing the effects of the ingestion of alcohol and other drugs.

The relationship between alcohol and accidents is hardly hypothetical. In one study, drivers killed in automobile accidents in New York City "were compared with non-involved drivers passing the accident sites at the same time of day and on the same days of the week. The greatest difference between the two groups was in the prior use of alcohol. Among drivers rated as probably responsible for their accidents, 73 percent had been drinking to some extent, whereas only 26 percent of the similarly exposed, but non-involved drivers had been drinking" (96). In addition, 46 percent of the accident-responsible group had very high concentrations of alcohol in the blood but none in the control group had (97). A second study of 83 single vehicle accidents in which the driver was killed revealed that fully 69 percent of the victims had high blood alcohol concentrations (98). In yet another research project it was noted that approximately two-thirds of the drivers who had accidents had been drinking beforehand, most of them heavily (99). One-third of these had had one or more previous court convictions in connection with accidents in which alcohol had been implicated (100). There is also some evidence that drinking is associated with pedestrian fatalities. One study showed that fatally injured pedestrians tended to be either elderly people who had not been drinking or middle-aged people who had been drinking heavily (101).

How does alcohol alter consciousness so as to predispose to accidents? Cohen, Dearnaley, and Hansel conducted a controlled experimental study of risk-taking while their subjects were under the influence of alcohol, (102) and their findings may provide an answer:

1. Drivers who consumed alcohol were willing to take greater risks than drivers who did not.

2. "As the amount of alcohol taken was increased, the drivers were prepared to drive their vehicles through narrower gaps," thus alcohol "adversely affected their judgment" (103).

3. The drivers' performance and

judgment "progressively deteriorated as they consumed more alcohol" (104).

4. "Alcohol intensified any driver tendency to overrate his ability in relation to his performance" (105).

All the studies of real accidental fatalities cited here indicate that accidents associated with alcohol tend to involve not the "one-drink-before-driving" type, but the "serious" or "problem" drinker. Thus, an attack on the auto accident problem must include an effort to discover what leads whom to drink heavily and how the number of people who do this can be reduced. Unfortunately, our approach to alcoholism in relation to accident prevention has been something less than enlightened. Rather than considering the alcoholic as an individual with a serious problem with which he needs help, society most often considers him a nuisance, a degenerate, or a criminal—and mishandles him accordingly. By so doing, we not only miss the opportunity to learn from him, but we also often contribute to his untimely death and to the death of some of those with whom he has contact. We are not even content to commit this sin of omission. Sometimes we commit actions to block constructive programs. In the same edition of the newspaper in which the problem of drinking and driving was prominently discussed, another story appeared under the following headline: "Alcoholics Center Minus Funds Faces Shutdown" (106). It detailed the plight of a center for alcoholics and unattached people which had already served 1600 individuals. Apparently a society that in one year spent over 150 million dollars on newspaper and magazine advertisements for alcoholic beverages (107) was unwilling to spend anything for food and services needed for the rehabilitation of alcoholics.

A third error in the management of the alcohol-related accident problem concerns our society's failure to implement recommendations based on objective research data, or to implement these recommendations in a thoroughgoing way. For example, it has been found that "the threshold of impairment of driving ability in expert drivers accustomed to consuming moderate amounts of alcohol is an alcohol concentration of 0.035 to 0.04 percent . . . in the blood." (108). Yet no driver, regardless of skill or usual drinking habits, is legally considered to be "under the influence of alcohol" until his blood alcohol level is, for example, 0.10 percent in Rhode Island or 0.15 percent in Massachusetts (109). At this latter level, one would be staggering drunk. A reporter who volunteered to be tested at blood alcohol level 0.15 percent was unable to touch his nose with his finger when directed to do so and had difficulty picking up coins from the floor (110). In light of the fact that national experts report an estimated 50 percent of drivers in serious accidents are under the influence of alcohol, efforts to remove the high-risk group from the road are hardly realistic.

Despite the fact that alcohol seems to play a major role in accidents, other types of drugs have also been implicated. For example, it has long been known that truck drivers and others required to drive long periods with insufficient rest sometimes employ stimulating amphetamines ("bennies") to keep them awake. Apparently many drivers believe that such drugs serve two useful purposes: a) they prevent accidents by keeping the drivers awake; and b) consequently they enable drivers to earn more money since less sleeping time is required. Unfortunately, neither drugs nor people are that uncomplicated.

When amphetamine stimulation wears off, it may do so abruptly and put the driver to sleep at 60 miles per hour. In several fatal accidents, highway police have found a half emptied bag of "bennies" in the driver's pocket, and autopsies have revealed as many as a dozen in a driver's stomach. With severe overdosage, though the driver stays awake, he may have hallucinations and see "ghosts" on the highway, with equally fatal results (111).

It would be easy to suggest that personality variables are totally responsible for this death-dealing behavior—that the dead drivers were really suicidal or perhaps sociopathic individuals, unconcerned with the consequences and their behavior or unable to look ahead. Certainly there must be some factors which separate the dead amphetamine user from the more prudent, living drivers. Nevertheless, before we assume that personality variables are solely to blame, two more parsimonious explanations will have to be considered: a) many drivers are simply ignorant concerning possible drug effects, and b) amphetamines are so universally employed and so easy to obtain that drivers cannot really believe they are dangerous, even when they have been warned. The people who inform new drivers about "bennies" are, after all, still alive. Furthermore, many naive people still believe that if products were really dangerous, they would not be available. Therefore, it would seem to be only elementary common sense both to make greater efforts to inform the public of specific dangers of "pep" pills and to increase zeal in eliminating sources of supply. Despite any such program, we would undoubtedly still be left with a certain number of drivers who would continue to seek out illegal sources of supply and hence contribute to the toll of "accidental" death. Research into the reasons for their behavior could focus on a number of different questions:

1. Are drivers who take bennies likely to take alcohol and other drugs also?

2. Do they tend to rely excessively on external sources of stimulation and upon external "props" for solutions to their problems? That is, can they be considered deficient in internal resources?

3. Is there a relationship between drivers' willingness to take the risks implicit in amphetamine use and their risk-taking behavior in any other kind of situation?

4. Do any drivers take "pep" pills simply because it is forbidden and they like to feel they're getting away with something?

5. Do most amphetamine users fall into a particular age group?

6. Are drug-taking drivers reacting to economic or other environmental pressures that lead them to push their physical endurance beyond normal limits?

It will certainly be difficult to reduce the toll of accidents due to illegal drug usage until we can learn more about peoples' motivations. However, legally prescribed drugs and over-the-counter preparations employed for perfectly legitimate purposes can nevertheless have lethal effects. And the victim is not always solely to blame. The busy physician may not emphasize sufficiently, or mention at all, the possible side effects which preclude driving or operating machinery. Only too often, drug companies list health and safety hazards in fine print or in inconspicuous places on their patent medicine labels. The user, to be sure, is often guilty of negligence. How seriously do most of us take warning labels when we read them? Does the average user of antihistamines take extra precautions while operating machinery? Does he give up driving when such preparations produce drowsiness? Drugged or not, it is probable that most people overestimate their ability to judge whether they are competent to drive—if the question ever enters their minds at all. While it is true that all states have formal licensing requirements and procedures, our society's general attitude toward driving tends to militate against our considering most attributes and mental states sufficient cause for withholding licensure. We often think of driving as a *right*, not a privilege. Thus, revocation of a driver's license is tantamount to infringement of the personal liberty which the Constitution guarantees. The fact that the driver's license is for some people no less than a license to kill does not seem to dawn on the individual who is willing to allow the drugged, the inebriated, and the near-blind to continue to use the highways, so long as his own right to drive is not challenged. The debt for convenient irresponsibility is eventually paid with someone's life.

Fatigue, although less dramatic, is undoubtedly the most universal cause of alteration in one's state of consciousness. Because of its lack of drama, its effects in accident causation are probably underestimated. Yet the manifestations of fatigue are tailor-made to produce accidents. It is well known that when one is falling asleep his reaction time increases and his reflexes are more difficult to elicit (112). The behavior of people subjected to long periods of sleep deprivation is generally characterized by "loss of efficiency in mental and physical functioning, irritability, and tendencies toward perceptual distortions and ideational confusion" (113). That such changes are not subject to conscious control, that one cannot exert "will power" and counteract such effects, is strongly suggested by data from animal studies. Some animals actually died following ten or more sleepless days (114). In some cases, postmortem examinations have revealed degeneration of brain tissue and other organs following sleep deprivation (115). Obviously, most humans will never be forced to go without sleep for very lengthy periods and thus will hardly be subject to such catastrophic effects. The chief value of these studies from our standpoint is that they emphasize that the need for sleep is a physiological need that cannot be denied indefinitely without deleterious effects: Most of these effects render one especially vulnerable to accidents.

In addition to the fatigue which signals the physical need for sleep, there is also a kind of fatigue which is, apparently, primarily a function of monotony. Some of the conditions under which we work, play, and commute seem calculated to promote this fatigue and its consequent

inefficiency. Long ago, Pavlov observed that monotonous conditions are likely to produce a drowsy, hypnotic-like state in dogs (116). More recently it has proven possible to create what appears to be the same phenomenon in humans under controlled experimental conditions (117). Eysenck has pointed out that many accidents occur because people drive off straight, monotonous roads. His explanation of this is Hull's law of reactive inhibition, according to which

> . . . any kind of mental activity sets up a fatigue-like neural state ("reactive inhibition") which becomes increasingly severe until it enforces an involuntary rest pause during which the person in question ceases to pay attention to the task in hand (118). . . . The condition best suited for the production of reactive inhibition and involuntary rest pauses is one of massed practice, that is, repetition of identical stimulus response sequences (119).

According to Eysenck, "involuntary rest pauses" can explain many otherwise inexplicable accidents, such as those in which the train engineers seem to ignore danger signals. He adds two other points that are important for our discussion: a) depressant drugs, including alcohol, increase the number and length of involuntary rest pauses, and b) extroverts "tend to develop inhibition more quickly and more strongly than do . . . introverts. . . . This would make an extrovert more liable to accidents arising from the occurrence of involuntary rest pauses during his driving . . ." (120). Eysenck feels that the elderly and the brain-damaged may also be more prone to such pauses. This kind of hypothesis could be of importance in reevaluating some of the common notions concerning the extroversive, young male accident repeaters who are sometimes described as sociopathic. These young men are not only frequently exposed to injury by virtue of their activities but also because they are extroversive and likely to ingest alcohol, they would be subject to lengthy, involuntary rest pauses, as well.

Might this factor be significant in explaining the so-called accident-proneness of this group?

Many people who are not able to countenance this type of explanation (the validity of which should certainly be investigated experimentally) will nevertheless concede that extrinsic factors can adversely influence one's vigilance and thus help to cause accidents. It is known, for example, that fatigue is not only attendant upon repetitive tasks but can be induced by monotonous sounds and rhythms. This is undoubtedly part of the reason for the age-old custom of rocking and singing the baby to sleep. (We have heard about a device that simulates the human mother's heart beat being used in putting babies to sleep. It's been suggested that the device works because the baby feels more secure when he hears this familiar, rhythmic beat. However, it is not implausible that any steady rhythmic beat, if not too loud or rapid, might induce sleep.) Such hypotheses become relevant to accident prevention wherever monotonous sounds or steady rhythmic pulsations are part and parcel of the work situation. Other factors, such as high temperature and humidity, low illumination and, possibly drab ("monotonous") decor may also sate the senses and increase reaction time—in short, induce fatigue.

• *Physical Illness.* Undoubtedly, there is a relationship between one's state of health and the kind and number of accidents he sustains. However, because "health" and accidents are so complexly intertwined with numerous other variables, we will not delve into the psychological aspects of physical ills but will simply introduce the reader to some of the material and problems involved in this relationship.

It is a truism that the state of the body affects the state of the mind and vice versa. One certainly cannot function at the peak of mental efficiency if he is actively ill. A few diseases tend to be associated with certain mental symptoms (121). In general, however, the psychological response to physical disease is less specific. Any or all of the following symptoms may occur: irritability, dysphoria, fatigue, distractibility, vague free-floating anxiety. Quite obviously, such symptoms, singly or in combination, can reduce one's effectiveness in avoiding or coping with a potentially dangerous situation.

In addition to contributing to the likelihood of self-injury, symptoms of tension and ill health may prepare the way for accidents to others. An interdisciplinary study conducted at the Childrens' Hospital Medical Center in Boston, Massachusetts, revealed, among other things, that children's accidents often occur when their mothers are ill or pregnant, or when adults in the family are under emotional stress for other reasons (122). This news may be scarcely revolutionary; yet it is precisely such long-suspected but little investigated phenomena which may set the stage for disaster. It would certainly be useful to know more precisely in what ways judgment and performance are impaired by ill health in general, and by some ills in particular, so that preventive measures might be taken.

Simply gathering information concerning the frequency and kind of accidents apparently caused by certain illnesses would be of value. Some of the basic premises on which we have been operating may prove to be false. For example, we now seek to prevent anyone labeled "epileptic" from operating motor vehicles or machinery. We hear with ever increasing frequency the suggestion that former coronary patients never drive again. We are not suggesting that all such patients be encouraged to begin driving tomorrow. We would simply like to point out that we have little data on the incidence of accidents incurred by people successfully treated for these physical problems. Perhaps studies would reveal that post-coronary patients who have been asymptomatic for X number of months or years are no more likely to have a heart attack at the wheel than apparently healthy individuals of the same age, sex, background, and socioeconomic level. Conceivably, the physical and psychological effects of a gastrointestinal upset or a severe toothache may render one more susceptible to an accident than many more serious or esoteric disorders would.

• *Mental Illness.* The role of mental or emotional illness is even more difficult to assess than that of physical illness. Much has been made of supposed "suicidal" impulses in what are otherwise described as "accidents" (see Chapter 11). Menninger, for example, in summarizing his discussion of purposive accidents, states that the same motives are operative in such accidents as in other forms of self-destruction. "These motives include the elements of aggression, punition, and propitiation. . . " (123). He suspects "that the principle of sacrifice is operative . . . so that in a sense the individual submits himself to the possibility or certainty of accidents in which he has at least a chance of escape rather than face a destruction which he fears even though it may threaten only in his imagination. In this way a partial neutralization of the destructive impulses is achieved" (124).

Although we are not ready to subscribe to the view that any sizable proportion of accidents derive primarily from suicidal impulses, it is no doubt true that some emotionally sick individuals do deliberately cause "accidents." This may be done consciously to disguise suicide so that the victim's family may escape the social stigma of suicide or collect the survivor's insurance. This may also, and perhaps more frequently, be done unconsciously so that the accident, a suicide equivalent, is not acknowledged as a self-destructive act. One of the reasons that it is so difficult to assess accurately the presence of suicidal intent in accident victims is that motivational systems, or any other aspects of the personality, are not explored when people are treated for acci-

dental injuries. Of course, because of the victim's physical condition, it is often not appropriate nor possible to conduct a probing interview. Frequently, however, hospital and police personnel do not even entertain the possibility of deliberate intent in accidents. As a result, an opportunity for future preventive work is lost and, perhaps, another life along with it.

Another reason for the dearth of firm data in this area is more obvious in suicides which successfully masquerade as accidents. The victims cannot be questioned. Occasionally, however, there is strong presumptive evidence; for example, a cook known to be depressed over his divorce and failure to get a song published, began to drink heavily and drive recklessly. His employer later reported that the cook came to see him one afternoon and asked for his pay. "He said that he couldn't straighten out and that he was no good to himself or anyone" (125). He was later reported to have been drinking and to have been talking about "driving between 90 and 100 miles an hour" (126). Twenty-five minutes thereafter, the cook, driving 70 miles per hour in the wrong direction on a divided highway, crashed head-on into a Greyhound bus. He and 19 bus passengers were killed (127). No one wishes to appear an alarmist, to be labeled the sort who interferes in other peoples' affairs. However, in a society which purports to be civilized, people certainly do have some responsibility to each other. We should make efforts to develop some way of securing help in a situation such as that illustrated above, in which there is a strong likelihood that injury to self or others is being contemplated.

Questions are sometimes raised about the possible suicidal motivations of individuals who are killed or injured while participating in highly dangerous sports or hobbies. The situation in such cases is generally complex, and unclear. Let us use the Indianapolis "500" as an example; it is a notoriously dangerous race. This event never lacks for contestants despite (or perhaps because of?) the fact that injury and death are often the driver's lot. During the fiftieth anniversary run of the "500," accidents and mechanical failures were so common that only seven of the original 33 cars were still on the track at the close of the race (128). (In addition 17 spectators were injured, one seriously.) Over the first 50 years of the "500," 32 drivers, 14 mechanics, and at least ten spectators have died. The contestant's risk-taking behavior cannot be justified as in the case of the astronauts (cited above) on the basis of potential, objective scientific gains. It might be argued that the race serves a useful technological function by stimulating and testing out new automotive developments. The cogency of this argument suffers when we note that the turbine engine, a highly significant technological development, was quickly banned from the "500" when it seemed to interfere with the glow of competition. We are also entitled to wonder if the "improvement of the breed" really has to depend upon this sort of high-risk operation. Ostensibly, one of the major reasons for racing, apart from the gratification of being first, is the prize money. This can be a considerable amount; one winner received a total of $156,297 (129). However, other less concrete motives undoubtedly play a part. Henry Lee quotes sports columnist Gene Ward: "Perhaps in some half mystical way, it is the challenge itself; the lure of an idea rather than any human motivation" (130). Ward cited a happily married, 37-year-old driver as an example. This driver raced eight times, finishing among the first three on several occasions. Yet he never actually won. When asked what he would do if he ever did come in first, he replied: "Then I'll never drive again as long as I live" (131). Unfortunately, he never won. He was killed in the 1964 race. No one can be certain what point this illustrates. However, it is possible that this driver sought to challenge death. He would either prove

that he could face death, win (i.e., come in first) and survive and, therefore, never need to drive again, or he would die in the attempt.

The puzzle of why some people indulge in certain hazardous activities is extremely difficult to unravel. Yet this is just one dimension of the overall problem to which society must address itself if certain types of accidental deaths are to be avoided. When can risk-taking be considered a manifestation of illness? Will we ever be able to develop a socially acceptable program to identify potentially suicidal individuals? Will we be able to predict which of these will be most likely to manifest self-destructive impulses in accidents? Have we the right to interfere with the individual's attempt to challenge death, if he is not psychotic? Is this not, in a sense, what we all do? Even if we had such a right, as is the case when an innocent bystander is placed in jeopardy, how could we do it? These are but a few of the technical and philosophical problems confronting us.

The mentally or emotionally sick person, or the individual with sociopathic traits, need not be suicidal to constitute an accident hazard. People can be so preoccupied with their internal states that they focus most of their attention inward, thus ignoring external signs of danger. Some may be so overly cautious and fearful that they drive too slowly for conditions or ambivalently try to pass another car, first accelerating, and then unexpectedly dropping back. Others, whose psychopathological traits incude a "let-George-do it" attitude toward life and work, may always expect someone else to tighten the last nuts and bolts, to check the fire, to turn off the power—even to remove the cleaning fluid or scissors from baby's easy reach.

The foregoing represent but a miniscule sample of the intrinsic organismic factors, some permanent, some temporary, that influence the frequency and type of accidents. As we have seen, our knowledge concerning many of these variables is at best rudimentary. In addition, our attempts to apply constructively that data which we do possess leave much to be desired. Consequently, the rate of deaths due to accidents remains appallingly high. How can we alter this? Of course, new research should be undertaken. It must be not only well controlled but *relevant* research. Perhaps more research should be directed toward discovering why we do not implement what is already known. Some of the reasons for this may emerge as we consider the role of extrinsic social and environmental factors in causing accidental death.

Extrinsic Factors

The conditions and situations that concern us here are extrinsic to the human organism in the most literal sense; that is, they concern what is physically outside of the body. They are the outward expression of the value systems, attitudes, and feelings of individuals or groups of individuals. A broken staircase lies within the province of psychology if it was broken willfully or allowed to go unrepaired because its owner hated or didn't care about the people who must use it. Seen in this light, extrinsic factors are in many ways more relevant to the psychology of death than are intrinsic ones.

• *Poor Planning.* A sizeable number of the extrinsic factors that promote the occurrence of accidents appear to be the result of poor or no advance planning. These bear careful scrutiny; perhaps we can learn from them why we do not

Plan Ahea~d~ (132)

An excerpt from the medical literature neatly summarizes one of the points we wish to illustrate. In discussing a type of lesion produced by improper use of equipment, Dr. George Milles stated: "The increasing use of ancillary personnel, not always knowledgeable in the hazards in the procedures they are called upon to perform, makes this *an accident waiting to happen*" (133) [italics ours]. Much of what we shall say in the following paragraphs concerns "accidents waiting to happen." Therefore, we shall now discuss at some length several questions that are implicit in the foregoing statement: What booby traps await us all in everyday life? Why do we fail to recognize a hazard which objectively is obvious? Why does a danger, once perceived and pointed out to others, continue to be disregarded? When such hazards are disregarded and injury or death ensue, can we legitimately consider this result an "accident?"

There are 225,000 school buses in use in the United States. A child's life and limb is in jeopardy in almost all of them. The results of a Public Health Service research project (conducted at the University of California at Los Angeles) indicated that "most school bus seats are 'grossly inadequate' for protecting children from injury and death in a collision. . . (134). The greatest single contribution to school bus passenger collision safety is the high strength, high back safety seat . . ." yet "school bus seats have backs so low that they can cause serious injury when the bus is struck head-on from the rear" (135). "There is no 'safe seat' in use in school buses today" (136). The research report also noted that:

1. School buses lack sufficient emergency exits. Children can be trapped in a burning vehicle, or be unable to escape to get help.

2. Drivers are inadequately protected; they are likely to lose control of the bus upon impact.

3. "Standees are doubly vulnerable to injury or death," as are children "seated on improvised aisle seats. . . ."

4. Used in conjunction with the poorly designed seats, seat belts *increase* the risk of injury.

5. "Many school buses are structurally unsound." Compared with the 1965

model, the *1944* model "withstood crashes better" (137).

Thirty-seven hundred children were injured in school bus accidents in 1965 (138); 3,800 were injured in 1966 (139). Fifty were actually killed in 1966, "fifteen while riding, thirty-five while leaving or entering" (140). It seems only reasonable to raise two questions:

1. Why do we not *first* investigate to see what type of vehicular design is safest and thereafter build and utilize only this kind of vehicle? At present we are, in effect, "testing" school buses in uncontrolled studies in which schoolchildren are the unwitting subjects.

2. Since it has long been suspected and now has been shown that school buses are dangerous, why have not emergency steps been taken to prevent further tragedies?

We cannot give one factual answer to the first question; but many things are relevant. When a need arises, we seek to meet it as quickly and directly as possible. Since our focus is on the goal of getting children to school, we tend to ignore "peripheral" issues—such as safety. When school buses were first introduced, there was, of course, no past experience to cause us to attend to the dangers inherent in their use. One might think that common sense would have alerted us to certain hazards. Why is safety considered only peripherally, if at all, in many situations? We have already touched upon part of the answer. Many people still think that accidents simply "happen" and therefore can neither be predicted nor prevented. Moreover, most of us indulge in magical thinking about our own "charmed" lives. Accidents are something that happen to other people, not to us or our extended selves—our children. This notion of our personal immunity can become generalized to include "my" school bus, "my" town, etc. They may have a

tragic accident over in Centerville; but things like that don't happen in my town. They not only *don't*; they *can't*. It is difficult to accept that we are mortal and that the physical laws of the universe will not be altered for us and ours.

In the course of attempting to answer the second question (why we don't quickly attempt to remedy the dangerous situation which we know exists), we must consider some disheartening information: "Thirty-two states still permit bus standees. They claim that eliminating them would require more buses, hiking beyond reasonable limits the already high cost of school transportation" (141). What are "reasonable limits"? Does it make sense to appropriate enough funds to build a school for the children, but insufficient funds to enable them all to get there alive? How much is a child's life worth? This issue was brought into sharp, but temporary, focus in a hearing before the Massachusetts Legislative Committee on Public Safety in March, 1968. An inquiry was held concerning the deaths of four children killed (in separate accidents) after alighting from school buses. A simple way to prevent such accidents from occurring in the future was suggested. A second adult could be hired to accompany children on the bus, to walk children across the street and to see to it that the bus did not proceed until all children were safe and accounted for. Additional safety devices were also proposed. One such was a mirror which would enable the driver to see children who had alighted from the bus, something which is now impossible. The Registrar of Motor Vehicles indicated that he was not opposed to the bill being introduced to provide more safeguards. However, he made the point that both "school officials and bus company owners have been against such regulations in the past." These officials and owners had contended that adding safety devices such as mirrors, or putting a second adult on each bus would increase the cost of operation for the companies and consequently for the taxpaper. "The Registry has supported stiffer school bus regulations in the past, such as the elimination of all standees (the law now allows 25 percent of seating capacity), but these have been rejected or referred to the next annual session" (142).

It would seem that the financial interest of the bus companies or of anonymous taxpapers, many of whom have children who ride the buses, are to take precedence over children's lives. How can this be? Again, partly because we cannot really believe that anything could happen to *our* child who is special and different. We are much more willing to take risks with someone else's child. We don't wish to face the fact that to others, our child is the "someone else's" being risked. It is also difficult to become upset about statistics. The 50 children killed in school bus accidents in 1966 do not really seem like people to the reader who sees the number "50" and proceeds to the next news item. Yet if we know just one of these victims, it becomes tragically real and vivid.

One of the authors was acquainted with one of the four children killed (in Massachusetts in 1967) after alighting from a school bus. It happened very swiftly. It was obvious that there was little point in taking the boy to a physician. The fire department was summoned to clean up the street. One such experience can forever alter the meaning of statistics. Unfortunately, however, a large number of such experiences may eventually serve only to blunt rather than increase one's sensitivity to death and injury. It is hard to picture the 3,800 children injured in bus accidents in one year (a total that is likely to increase as a by-product of busing to achieve racial balance in schools—this problem is seldom explored either by proponents or opponents of busing). Most people are more fully stirred by a single example, fully described. Until we can be made to realize, among other things, that the statistics were real people and that we

have no special immunity to the same fate, society will continue to value material considerations over lives. Lest the reader conclude that school bus accidents and the factors which allow them to occur comprise a highly peculiar, atypical example, we shall now focus our attention on another type of accident in which some of the same factors are at work.

Financial considerations and the reliance upon familiar, but inefficient, techniques can combine to block the amelioration of existing hazardous conditions and foster the creation of new ones. For example, railroad grade crossings are notoriously unsafe. Accident reports demonstrate this with horrifying regularity. Yet when the possibility of financial gain is pitted against the safety needs of the citizens, a whole town may opt for the former. During the period of 1966-1967, a New England town sought to attract a plant of the Gillette Company. The local paper reported: "The acquisition of the Gillette Company to Natick [sic] is looked upon by most of the town officials as one of the finest organizations possible [sic] and would supply the town with a substantial tax return" (143). Alone among town officials, and almost alone among residents, one representative persistently reiterated his objections to the grade crossing proposed to serve the Gillette Company, a crossing without which the company would not locate its plant in Natick. This representative stood to gain nothing from his position save the animosity of the electorate which wanted a lower tax rate. He pointed out that "regardless of what safety precautions may be suggested, freight cars going across West Central Street would still be most hazardous and completely against the public interest" (144). Nevertheless, both town newspapers continued to press for construction of the grade crossing and urged their readers to press for united action by the governor and the State Department of Public Works to this effect. (An underpass could have been constructed instead of a grade crossing, but the cost of this was described as "excessive") (145). The Public Works Department, surveying the situation, agreed with the maverick representative that a grade crossing would be unduly hazardous, and refused to allow its construction. Following this, "protests were registered by Natick civic groups and individual citizens" (146). However, the Department of Public Works stood firm, issued a second denial and thereby undoubtedly saved many a life and limb. Town residents and officials were, on the whole, very upset by this decision because of the loss in potential tax revenue.

Other towns have been "luckier." Everett, Massachusetts, has a grade crossing at which 13 people were killed on December 28, 1966 when a Buddcar collided with an oil truck (147). On December 26, 1967 a woman and her 13-year-old daughter were killed at a grade crossing 20 miles from Churchville, New York, when a mail train struck their car (148). That same day a man was killed at a grade crossing in Gloucester, Massachusetts, when his station wagon was struck by a Boston & Maine rail car (149). Less than two weeks later 13 people died and 50 were injured at a rail crossing in Hixon, England; an express train plowed into a truck (150).

There is no escaping the fact that grade crossings are dangerous; but what is done about it? Precious little. Although there was a functioning warning bell at the Gloucester crossing mentioned above, there was neither a warning gate nor a light (151). Of how much use to a driver in a closed car is a warning bell which must compete with the sound of an onrushing train? In 1967 the Department of Public Works and the railroads were both accused of foot-dragging: "All the conditions that permitted a major tragedy to occur at the Everett Grade Crossing a year ago remain unabated. Similar situations prevail at every railroad and highway crossing in the United States" (152). A spokesman for the Department of Public Utilities objected to some of the criticism on the grounds that the critic had something to sell (safety devices). Yet this does nothing to obviate the need for reform. Then why is nothing done?

1. It would cost a great deal to install proper safety devices at all grade crossings.

2. Spending money does not make legislators popular with taxpayers.

3. Human inertia is aided and abetted by legislative red tape. It is not easy to force oneself to face unpleasant facts and, perhaps, hostile individuals with a vested interest in the status quo. It is often even harder to make legislators enact protective laws. This takes more time and effort than most people are willing to invest. Why?

4. Many people do not, or think they do not, use grade crossings very often. Even if they do, they are not using them at the moment they read of an accident. The whole question of the determinants of "psychological distance" has a bearing on our response to safety needs. It is hard to remain upset for long about a hazard we rarely confront. If someone else must face it daily, well—that's his problem. The same factors which isolate human beings from each other and deprive them of the feeling of common cause (see Chapter 12) make it possible for us to ignore hazards to someone else's life, and for him to ignore hazards to ours.

5. Contempt is not all that familiarity can breed. It can also lead to indifference and hopelessness. The dangerous situation, confronted and overcome daily, can eventually cease to be regarded as dangerous at all. At this point one's guard drops. Conversely, one may remain cognizant of a danger for so long that he comes to think of it as necessary and permanent. He thus develops a fatalistic attitude which precludes correcting the situation: It is inevitable that sooner or

later someone will be killed at that crossing. But there are few accidents that are really inevitable.

• *The Cultivation of Hazards—Fire.* If we would but look, we would find that the same psychological and social forces contribute to a wide variety of seemingly very different types of accidents. For example, one of the life-threatening hazards that is very much bound up with both social and psychological variables is fire. Man has been fascinated by fire since early times. Fire has been revered as a god and feared as one of Hell's tortures. Death by fire is especially horrible and, more horrible still, it is often totally unnecessary.

In considering how psychological factors may be related to death by fire, one's mind may turn first to the problem of fire setting. Yet those killed by the sick few, acting alone, are as nothing compared with the number burned by the negligent, ignorant many, acting in concert. Our focus is on psychology and death. We need dwell for but a moment on the phenomenon of pyromania. Psychoanalytic theory suggests a relationship between pyromania and urethral eroticism. Fenichel (to whose work the reader is referred for a fuller discussion) states: "In an incendiary perversion, intense sadistic strivings govern the sexual life, the destructive force of the fire serving as a symbol for the intensity of the sexual urge. The patients are full of vindictive impulses, which receive their specific form from their urethral-erotic fixation" (153). If it can be shown that one deliberately sets fires to fulfill perverted impulses, which may or may not have physiological foundations, then one could argue that his proper management should include incarceration and psychotherapy, perhaps medical treatment as well. However, even if if were possible to identify most pyromanics and treat them in this manner, we would still be left with the serious problem of demonstrating something that is probably untrue—that most fires are "set." We would find, instead, that a combination of ignorance, negligence, selfishness, and poor planning and judgment are the usual culprits.

It is hard to know where to begin a discussion of the origin and prevention of fires; and it is easy to be overwhelmed by the sheer magnitude of the problem. Every 44 minutes someone in the United States dies in a fire (154). Over 12,000 people in this country perished in fires in 1966 alone (155). Repeat—12,000 people dead by fire in one year. This was not atypical. In 1965, the United States per capita fire death rate was four times as great as that of the United Kingdom and six times as great as that of Japan, a very heavily populated, overcrowded country. We cannot attribute this difference to population differences since this factor has been taken into account statistically. Nor, obviously, can we maintain that these other countries are not industrialized and lack access to incendiary materials. In fact, Japan should be particularly vulnerable to fire, since it commonly employs highly flammable materials like bamboo and paper in construction. Presumably, these countries have been more efficient than we in fire prevention, fire fighting, or both. To illustrate the kinds of factors that may be at work in condemning civilized man to ordeal by fire we will briefly review a) one of the worst fires in the history of the United States, and b) the present state of our fire protection.

On the night of November 28, 1942, the Cocoanut Grove Supper Club in Boston, Massachusetts, was the scene of a veritable holocaust. Four hundred people died within 13 minutes. One hundred more sustained burns, which would later kill them; and 250 were seriously injured (156). The fire began when a bus boy lighting a match inadvertently ignited an artificial palm frond. Thereafter, the flame spread rapidly to the draperies and other decorations. What was responsible for the horrendous toll in human life?

1. Poor design and planning. The building housing the Cocoanut Grove had originally been constructed as a garage. "Renovation had left the place with twelve smaller doors. One was blocked up. Nine others were locked. This left only two smoke filled corridors to safety" (157). One of the exits was served by a revolving door which, in the press of fleeing patrons, became dislodged from its axis and jammed. "There was really no place to go" (158).

2. The presence and wide distribution of large quantities of highly flammable materials. The nightclub decorations and synthetic upholstery were not made of flame-proof materials, nor had they been treated in any way to retard burning. The entire building became a blazing inferno within a few minutes.

3. Use of materials which when burned released lethal fumes. A physician who examined the Cocoanut Grove victims said of most: "They didn't burn to death.... These people died of fumes" (159).

4. Delay in summoning aid. About ten minutes elapsed before the fire department was called because "nobody was alarmed. If anything ... the crowd was amused. They made light of the discomfiture of waiters, who squirted water on the tiny blaze" (160).

What psychological phenomena underlie the factors listed above?

1. *Denial.* As we have already pointed out, people do not like to accept the fact that they are vulnerable to death and injury. Even when confronted by a potentially dangerous situation, we often seek to make light of it, thereby denying to ourselves and others that we are fearful. We affect a carefree facade and delay taking such appropriate action as calling the fire department. Then when we are forced finally to acknowledge that we are in desperate straits, we have no plan of action and may give way to panic.

2. *The path of least resistance.* We often act to meet present needs, and give little thought to future consequences. When remodelling an old structure for a new purpose it is cheaper and easier to make as few changes as possible. That this makes the structure inappropriate to its new purpose is often overlooked. Doors may be blocked as an easy way to keep out gate-crashers and thieves. Little thought may be given to the fact that this may make it impossible for those inside to escape.

3. *The profit motive comes first.* This is too often true, even at the cost of safety. Every nook and cranny may be overcrowded with patrons to maximize profits despite the fact that this maximizes dangers as well.

4. *Ignorance and inadequate regard for others.* Consumers are sometimes the manufacturer's "experimental animals." Even today materials for construction, decoration, and wearing apparel are often tested and labeled only inadequately or not all before they are marketed. Only when they are found to be lacking in safety features, or downright lethal, do we take action to eliminate them. In part this may be due to the Western propensity to "act now and think later"; but in part it undoubtedly derives from the desire to *cash in* now. It never occurs to many people that someone will have to pay later.

The Cocoanut Grove disaster shocked the public into painful awareness of the vital import of fire preventives. Regulations concerning fire exits, total number of people allowed on the premises, and type of materials utilized in decorations were proposed and came under careful scrutiny. One might conclude on this account that society had learned its lesson—that fire protection today is more than adequate. Unfortunately, such a conclusion would be both dangerous and false. Consider some of the facts and ask yourself "Why?" The answer to the problems of extrinsic dangers ultimately lies within all of us.

The National Fire Protection Association estimated in 1966 that more than 2,500 children would die in that one year because their clothing would catch fire. An additional 300,000 children were expected to be maimed or crippled for the same reason (161). Was this inevitable, and must it continue to be? Definitely not. Chemicals that can make clothing and bedding fire resistant are available. Then why aren't they being used more extensively? According to some manufacturers, it is the fault of "the public," from which they apparently exclude themselves. They point out that when a large department store offered nonflammable play-suits for sale, people would not buy them. They concluded that this was because customers were unwilling to pay the extra half-dollar that such suits cost. It is impossible to evaluate the validity of this conclusion in the absence of additional information. We do not know whether the safe clothes were widely advertised as such, if they were comparable in other ways with other playsuits, were available in the full range of sizes, etc. However, these facts are actually irrelevant in the face of what we are told by the manufacturers, namely that they cannot be blamed for marketing materials they know to be dangerous: "Retailers and manufacturers can hardly be blamed for not using the (fire retardant) chemicals when making their products. "The textile business is a dog-eat-dog business. Can you blame us for losing interest in retardants when we know darn well that if we make one of our items fire resistant and it sells for maybe half a buck more than our competitor's, the consumer won't buy our line. Why should I stick my neck out?... We'd all be using the new chemicals available today—if the mothers demanded we use them!" (162).

The passages quoted above illustrate the typical "pass-the-buck" rationalizations that allow us to postpone taking appropriate preventive action in many types of dangerous situations. These specific rationalizations could be refuted as follows:

1. Mothers cannot demand the use of products they have not been informed exist.

2. People have been taught through sad experience that they must view the promises of retailers and manufacturers with a jaundiced eye.

3. Retailers and manufacturers *can* and *should* be blamed for promoting the sale of items they know to be unsafe. They seem to forget that if everyone would agree to use only flame-retarding materials, no one would be at a financial disadvantage.

4. Blaming other people—the public, for example, or mothers—may make producers and retailers feel better subjectively; but objectively, this in no way frees them from the moral responsibility for knowingly exposing others to death and injury.

5. People should be willing to "stick their necks out" because they are members of the human race. If they expect others to give them a reasonable chance to survive, then they should give that same chance to others.

The basic problem in the prevention of accidents is simply how to get people to develop a sense of responsibility for others. Unfortunately, there is no "snap course" available for this. Since people tend to internalize much of what is experienced in early life, we must emphasize again the import of child-rearing practices. (See Chapters 11 and 12.) Obviously, however, such a statement is of little value in providing concrete suggestions. Until something can be done to induce people to protect each other voluntarily, it may be necessary to legally require that they do so. For example, in England all sleeping garments for children under the age of 13 must, by law, be made of fire-retardant materials (163). What is to be done about clothing for older children or that to be worn by any children who are exposed to fire during their waking hours is not mentioned in the law. Nevertheless, this statute is far better than nothing. However, even the force of law is not always sufficient. People not only passively evade laws for reasons of inertia and financial gain, but they sometimes actively seek to circumvent them for financial gain alone. We do have one flammable fabrics act, passed in 1953, "after six small boys burned to death when their cowboy suits caught fire" (164). Despite this, clothing manufacturers have continued to make apparel out of flammable materials. They must be caught by the Federal Trade Commission, which has many other duties to perform, and proven guilty, before they can be forced to discontinue this practice (165). It has been pointed out that the law as it now stands is too weak even if strictly enforced; it does not cover "hula skirts, false whiskers, masks, children's costumes of shredded paper" or highly flammable *baby blankets* (166). It should be noted that there has been no rush to improve this situation.

It may not be possible to legislate all aspects of personal morality but we certainly could legislate many aspects of safety. Why don't we? Oh well, we have too much to do already. This is somebody else's job. Then how well is "somebody else" performing?

1. We often read about a fire that has swept through a nursing home with a consequent tragic loss of life. Since the elderly are especially vulnerable to burns, it would seem only prudent to protect them all the more carefully with the safest of buildings and a well-organized system of precautionary measures. Yet we tend to do exactly the opposite. This is largely a function of our disparaging attitude toward the elderly (167, 168). Many

nursing homes are nothing more than ramshackle firetraps to which we consign society's aged rejects. We do not really want them and we will not waste our hard-earned money to protect them. One might think that they, and all patients, would somehow be protected automatically by law, but he would be mistaken. Armand Burgun, an architect, points out that some building codes are "woefully lacking in provisions for safety" (169). He states, among other things, that "hospitals should not be lulled into complacency about building codes by the thought that contemporary construction is fireproof; quite frankly, there is no such thing as a fireproof building" (170).

2. Since fire is a lethal and ever-present hazard, one might imagine that fire protection would be high on any community's list of priorities. The reverse appears to be true. Writers Ross and Kiseda, surveying the nation's fire protection, found that of the approximately 25,000 fire departments in the United States, only 1,600 are staffed by fully paid professionals (171). "That leaves most of the country's geography and much of its population in the hands of a hodgepodge of volunteers..." (172). Warren Kimball, manager of the National Fire Protection Associations' Fire Service Department has been quoted as saying: "Fewer than half of 1 percent [of the fire departments in the United States] can provide the proper measure of fire fighting capability for successful performance at potentially serious fires in major structures" (173). Ross and Kiseda found that in one community of $100,000 homes, the town spends only $4.00 per person per year on fire protection (174). It costs too much; and it can't happen to us.

3. We do not even protect the firemen who are supposed to protect us. Most fire departments in the United States use an all-service mask; this is supposed to remove noxious gases so that firefighters can breathe while they extinguish flames and save victims. In Decem-

ber, 1967, the city of New York banned this mask. One month thereafter, Boston, Massachusetts followed suit (175). *After more than 25 years of use*, the mask was finally declared unsafe. Was this the result of a sudden, albeit belated, new insight? Not at all. Questions concerning the mask's safety were raised as early as 1946, again in 1950, and twice in 1967 (176). Yet these masks were not banned until the very end of 1967 and the beginning of 1968, and then in only two cities. How was even this partial reform effected? Families of six dead firemen sued the masks' manufacturers (177). Is this what it takes to get equipment adequately inspected? Apparently. Would it not have been more practical and humane to test the masks properly *before* we required people to entrust their lives to them?

So far in this chapter we have been discussing some of the intrinsic and apparently extrinsic factors which can be responsible for accidental deaths. We have seen that the extrinsic factors are often but a manifestation of the attitudes and value systems of individuals per se and of our society as a whole. Now we should like to turn our attention to another group of factors and consider the following question: How negligent must a society be before its "accidental" deaths are tantamount to homicide?

OUR HOMICIDOGENIC SOCIETY AND ACCIDENTS

It is no accident that there are more accidents, murders, and diseases in poor than in well-to-do neighborhoods. It is no "accident" that accident death rates are highest among the very old, the very young, and minority groups. When the probabilities are stacked against an individual or a group, then we are being either obtuse or callous when we dismiss predictable deaths as mere "accidents." It is true that organic variables play an important role in many such deaths. But other factors are also of crucial importance. The helpless, by definition, cannot protect themselves. Therefore, when they die because we do not protect them, can it be their fault? Or no one's? Why is it that we expect the defenseless to have a high accident death rate? Isn't it partly because we know that we will not protect them?

• *"Seventeen to 20 children burn to death in Maine every year of faulty housing."* One-fifth of the families "receiving Aid to Dependent Children in Maine have no central heating; 48 percent have running water but no baths, and 18 percent have no running water at all" (178). Where there is no central heating, families are likely to use space heaters or to burn wood. Both of these systems are known to create fire hazards. In addition, it is rather difficult to put out a fire without water.

• *"Twenty-one miners died in an American salt mine when they were trapped by a fire that erupted in an elevator shaft.* Eight months earlier the "Federal Bureau of Mines recommended that the men sink a second shaft as an escape route and for ventilation, and install various fire controls" (179). The recommendations did not have the force of law (180). After the tragedy, a company official said that he was not aware of any such recommendation. If a study had been made and the mine owners were not informed of the findings, this was negligence. If the owners were informed and failed to act, this was negligence. In either case, 21 men are dead.

• *"Two boys were killed and six seriously injured in the Flatbush section of Brooklyn in the Spring of 1967 because 'we didn't have enough to go anywhere and we just wanted to have fun'"* (181). When a city bus rolled by, the eight boys ran after it and "found handholds on its open rear windows. . . . The driver, unaware of his extra passengers, scraped alongside a truck on the narrow street. . . . . The boys . . . were smeared off the bus like butter. . . . Police and parents saw a tragic *inevitability* in the accident." [Italics ours.] Said one father: "Orlando is a good boy but it is hard. I do not have a job and there is not much for him to play." A policeman stated: "In these neighborhoods on nice days, there's not much you can do" (182). But there could be, if society deemed it important enough to provide something better to do. Labelling accidents "inevitable" serves many, not always laudable, purposes. It temporarily shields the victim's families and friends from the hostility that would otherwise be directed at those who are to blame. This was inevitable. No one could have prevented it. It thus makes the loss easier to bear and may free the families from a sense of responsibility. The cost, in addition to more lives lost, is an intensified feeling of impotence and frustration in the survivors. These, too, can ultimately lead to hostility and the attitude that any change, however disorganizing and destructive, may be an improvement. The smug, seemingly insulated individuals who have the power but not the inclination to improve the lot of the poor should keep this in mind. For the uninvolved majority the word "inevitable" can only serve to undermine what little inclination they do have to change the negative aspects of the status quo.

Who Is to Blame?

If we know that a lethal hazard exists and we do nothing to eliminate it, are we blameless when someone falls victim to that hazard? If we move slowly to counteract a danger that could be dealt with quickly, is not the ensuing accident partly our fault?

According to Senator Warren Magnuson, a report prepared by Consumers' *Union showed that 376 household products sold to American families were (and many continue to be) "too dangerous for home use"* (183). Dangers specified included "electrical hazards in television sets, clock radios, toasters and toys; mechanical hazards in blankets, carpets, and portable heaters" (184). The senator proposed formation of a product safety commission which would eventually recommend remedies appropriate to ensure safer products. "Similar legislation was passed by the Senate last year, but died in the House Commerce Committee" (185). No one wants restrictive legislation; but few seem willing to police themselves either.

Twelve people died within six months on a 12-mile strip of one highway known as a death trap (186). Nineteen people died in the first four years after the road was opened. The State Registrar of Motor Vehicles said: "I have always maintained the road to be one of the most substandard and deficient in our highway network" (187). A local funeral director commented: "It's too bad all the state officials don't have to come down here and see the grieving people who come to visit the dead. If they did, we'd probably get something done to correct Route 140 a lot faster" (188). Seven lives were lost on this route in just one accident. "This latest accident is one of those things I've been very much afraid would eventually happen" the Mayor said. He took the case to the Governor who initiated corrective steps. Because it would take at least two years before the state could finish converting the two-lane stretch into a safe, four-lane divided highway, people were wondering how many more would be killed before the work was finished (189). If everyone knew the road to be unsafe, why weren't corrective steps taken earlier? Surely saving human lives should take precedence over business and legislative matters? Must it inevitably require two or more years to alter a 12-mile stretch of highway?

Recently, the topic of automobile safety has figured prominently in the news. One of the many reasons for this is Ralph Nader's book, *Unsafe at Any Speed*, which focuses attention on faulty automotive design. Quiet behind-the-scenes work by people like William Haddon, Director of the National Safety Bureau, has gradually brought about some favorable changes in attitude as well as vehicle design. The work of nonprofit organizations like Consumers' Union has been helpful in pinpointing automotive as well as other hazards, and in informing the public about them. The mounting highway toll, documented in each day's news, and the consequent increases in car insurance, have also called the public's attention to the problem.

What kinds of stumbling blocks, other than inertia, and possibly additional costs, lie in the path of safer automotive design? One of these blocks haunts us—the attitude of people in all walks of life who do not take safety problems seriously. The current concern over unsafe cars was described as a fad by W. B. Murphy, president of the Campbell Soup Company. "It's of the same order as the hula hoop—a fad. Six months from now we'll probably be on another kick," Mr. Murphy said (190). Undoubtedly, many people feel this way. Perhaps concern with automobile safety will no longer make the front pages six months from now; but deaths on the highway will continue to do so—unless and until society eschews this pseudo-sophisticated attitude toward other people's lives.

In discussing the intrinsic and extrinsic factors of relevance to accidents we have stressed the point that many so-called extrinsic factors are manifestations of intrinsic variables. Some readers may feel that this is an unfair generalization, especially when a certain class of accidents is considered. That class has often been labeled "natural disasters" that are "beyond human control." Some deaths are inevitable in the wake of floods, tornadoes, etc., but are all of them?

In December, 1967, a tornado spun into Alabama; four deaths were attributed to this twister (191). Two men were killed when the wind destroyed their homes. It would be hard to imagine how either man, in the absence of advance warning, could have avoided this fate. One cannot state with certainty, however, that this was equally true of the other two victims. One drowned when his car plunged into the water "where a bridge had been washed out over a creek" (192). Couldn't this victim see that the bridge was gone? Was no sign posted to warn of the bridge's vulnerability during periods of high water? We do not really know how this accident took place, but it cannot be blamed solely upon God and Nature. The fourth victim was a little boy who drowned when he slipped into a swollen creek. Was it necessary that the boy be near the creek during a flood? Would he have drowned if the creek had not been swollen? Was anyone supervising him at this period and place of danger? We do not know. These questions simply illustrate the pitfalls inherent in attributing accidents even remotely associated with a natural disaster to the disaster itself (instead of concentrating on aspects that might be altered to prevent future deaths). Were we to take this approach, then all automotive deaths would be blamed on the invention of the automobile.

There is painfully abundant material in the literature on natural disasters to indicate that many lives have been lost needlessly. Martha Wolfenstein, for example, points out that warnings often fail to register effectively upon potential disaster victims (193). Inappropriate or questionable behavior on the part of government officials and the general public may increase the toll. The interested reader will find useful explorations of this topic in Wolfenstein's book, *Disaster: A Psychological Essay*, and in contributions by Moore (194), Danzig, et al (195), and Baker and Chapman (196), among others.

Consider this second example. On October 21, 1966, the village of Aberfan, South Wales became the scene of "an act of God," a natural disaster, or whatever euphemism you choose to adopt. A slag tip (heap of coal-mine debris) slipped and, in a veritable avalanche, crashed down upon the village school and eight houses (197). One hundred and sixteen children, most of the village's younger generation, and 28 adults were killed. Some might regard this as an act of God or Nature but Wendy Danforth echoes the words of many realists who called it instead "an act of unquestioned negligence" (198). One might go even further and ask whether such monumental negligence can be termed "accidental." How did this tragedy occur? For 91 years the slag heap had grown. "The villagers had complained for years, begging to have the tip removed; but in 1947 the National Coal Board had decided it *would be far too expensive.*" [Italics ours.] W.J. Williams, former headmaster of the Pantaglas School, had said repeatedly that someday the tip would collapse, engulfing the school. "The Coal Board was very busy and inquiries were quickly squashed" (199). A tribunal meeting to enquire into the disaster fixed blame on the National Coal Board. They found "not wickedness," but . . . "ignorance, ineptitude, and a failure of communications" (200). Is saving money more important than 144 lives? Isn't such an attitude "wicked?" The head of the National Coal Board visited Aberfan after the tragedy and said: "There will be money for all" (201). Money cannot bring back life. Why do we act as if we'd never heard of an ounce of prevention?

We have now reviewed, illustrated, and discussed some of the variables causally related to accidents. However, the fate of the accident victim is not always definitively sealed at the moment the accident occurs. Often the outcome is as much, if not more, dependent upon what takes place *after* the accident as it is on the nature of the accident itself. Let us shift focus for a moment to the time and scene of the accident.

Picking Up the Pieces

An accident has taken place. What happens now? Quite possibly, nothing—for a while. It is not uncommon for people simply to stand by and watch while others suffer. It is less uncommon still for people to walk or drive away lest they become "involved" in something which is "not my business." How many accidental injuries have become fatalities because of this, we cannot know. What we do know is that failure to help the helpless when we are well able to do so makes us partially responsible for what befalls them. If we allow someone to bleed to death at our feet, can we call his death "accidental"?

Of course, *you* would not do that. If you were to come upon the scene of an accident, you would want to help. You would know enough not to move the victim so as to aggravate his injuries. But you might not know what to do *for* him. How would you reach expert help? Anyone can tell you that. Call an ambulance! But can you get one? If you can, will the attendant be of any help? Will the victims be safely transported to the hospital? If they arrive alive, will the hospital be prepared to keep them that way?

A 1963 survey conducted by the National Safety Council revealed that of 900 cities studied, only 204 had ordinances specifying service standards to be required for ambulances. Of these, only 162 stipulated that anyone in addition to the driver must respond to emergency calls (202). In fact, with the exceptions of California, Louisiana, Massachusetts, Nevada, Oregon, Texas, and Washington there are no state regulating laws controlling ambulance service (203). This means, in effect, that in most places almost anything—or nothing—can "serve as an ambulance. . . . The predominant pattern in rural America and in small cities is for the funeral homes to run the ambulances" (204). Apart from the potential for psychological damage inherent in being carted off in a hearse, the fact is that funeral home "ambulances" are generally inadequate. Dr. Robert H. Kennedy, who conducted an intensive investigation for the American College of Surgeons, concluded that ambulances run by funeral directors provide some of the worst service (205). However, most ambulances have poor or no equipment, and poorly or totally untrained attendants—if they have an attendant. A 1965 survey in North Carolina revealed that half the state's ambulances had no splints, bandages, oxygen tanks, or portable resuscitators (206). Little could be expected of ambulance personnel. Twenty-nine percent "provided no first aid at the scene of an accident . . . ; twenty percent could not splint fractures; almost half could not handle emergency births"; thirty percent knew nothing of how to handle a heart attack victim (207). Unfortunately, the situation in North Carolina is not atypical. Moreover, it has been found that recklessness and speeding characterize the driving habits of many ambulance drivers. Yet, "in an analysis of 2,500 emergency trips in Flint, Michigan, Dr. George J. Curry and Sydney N. Lyttle reported that speed would not have benefited a single patient" (208). The ambulance problem could be dramatically ameliorated by the enactment of legislation to set minimum standards for ambulances throughout the country. As of the summer of 1968, long after the dangerous situation described above had been documented, no such legislation had been proposed or enacted (209).

The conditions encountered by the accident victim when he reaches the hospital may or may not be any better than those of his ambulance trip. According to the National Academy of Sciences, 65,000 hospital beds were needed to care for accident victims in 1966 alone; and the care they provided was often inadequate (210). "In most hospitals the emergency care facilities 'have consisted only of accident rooms, poorly equipped, inadequately manned, and ordinarily used for limited numbers of seriously ill persons!' " (211). "In Germany and Austria . . . special accident hospitals are spaced every 15 or 20 miles along major highways . . ." (212). Dr. Robert Baker, the Director of Cook County Hospital Trauma Center, one place which is prepared to treat the accident victim, feels that the United States will eventually establish such a system, too (213). But when? Meanwhile people continue to die. "Accidentally"?

SUMMING UP

We have covered considerable territory in this discussion of accidents but the major points that have been presented can be summarized quite succinctly:

Accidents are one of the most common causes of death in America today. Both because of this and the fact that they can be shown to be intimately related to a broad spectrum of psychological phenomena, accidents merit serious consideration in the psychology of death. Most accidents have identifiable causes, consequently, future accidents are predictable and, if proper measures were taken, many could be prevented; thus, the validity of considering accidents as "acts of God," or fatalistically inevitable, is highly questionable.

The many kinds of variables that interact to produce an accident may be divided, for purposes of discussion, according to whether they are extrinsic or intrinsic to the human organism. Some theorists hold that a constellation of intrinsic personality traits and/or behavior patterns which characterize some individuals is primarily responsible for the majority of their accidents, and have applied the term "accident-prone" to these people. But, for many reasons, we do not believe that the hypotheses of accident-proneness is valid. Even if accident-proneness is characteristic of a few individuals, it certainly cannot explain all accidents because it appears to be but a passing phase in the lives of most individuals rather than a fixed personality trait.

Among the several organismic factors that may help set the stage for an accident are body build and the traits of temperament often associated therewith, age and developmental level and the physical and social changes which accompany them, attitudes toward accidents, attitudes toward safety, sex differences, risk-taking propensity, altered states of consciousness, illness, and various combinations of these.

Extrinsic factors that may contribute to accidents include society's failure to plan ahead to prevent school bus accidents, accidents at grade crossings, and fires; society's homicidogenic tendencies—its lack of concern about the consumer in general and in particular, and its greater concern for money than people.

Finally, our inadequate, often lethal arrangements for post-accident transportation and care of victims must be considered as factors leading to many deaths following accidents.

What Can We Conclude?

Some readers may classify the following propositions as hypotheses rather than conclusions. Granted that additional research is needed on all aspects of accidents, there is, nevertheless, considerable support for the following statements:

There is no one cause, intrinsic or extrinsic, for all accidents and no one easy path to prevention.

Although a limited number of individuals may for highly personal, pathological reasons deliberately seek out accidental injury, accidents in general cannot be attributed to a fixed group of individuals or a fixed group of personality traits.

The tendency to have accidents, as well as the number and types of accidents, vary with age and developmental level and the psychological concomitants thereof. These variations are a function not only of physical and psychological variables, but also of the social milieu which helps determine the amount and type of exposure to accidents that occur at different developmental levels.

It is frequently difficult to distinguish between suicide, homicide and accidents. What to name as the cause of death in a given situation is often largely socially and circumstantially determined unless there is blatant evidence of individual motivation. Covert attitudes toward the poor, toward minorities, toward the anonymous consumer, coupled with self-interest, enable us to overlook evidence of homicide and suicide. This leads to inflation of accident statistics and underestimation of the incidence of murder and suicide.

In our society, wealth, power, and prestige are too often given priority over human life.

Objective factors are not the sole or even the major determinants of accidents, but many lifesaving measures that would counteract these factors could be taken almost at once. But this we do not do. Neither do we implement programs that we already have or that we can envision.

We cannot really proceed efficiently to reduce the tremendous numbers of Americans who die annually as the result of accidents until we honestly face up to and attempt to alter our society's attitudes and sense of values.

REFERENCES

1. *U.S. book of facts, statistics, and information for 1968.* (Officially published as *Statistical Abstracts of the U.S.).* Washington, D.C.: Dept. of Commerce, Bureau of the Census. (88th ed.), 1967.
2. *Ibid.*, p. 59.
3. *Ibid.*, p. 86.
4. *Ibid.*, p. 87.
5. *Ibid.*
6. Lauer, A. H. Age and sex in relation to accidents. In W. Haddon, E. Suchman, & D. Klein (Eds.), *Accident research.* New York: Harper & Row, 1964. Pp. 137-138.
7. Rowntree, G. Accidents among children under two years of age in Great Britain. In Hadden, Suchman, & Klein, *op. cit.*, pp. 161-167.
8. Haddon, W., Valien, P., McCarroll, J., & Umberger, C. A controlled investigation of the characteristics of adult pedestrians fatally injured by motor vehicles in Manhattan. In Haddon, Suchman, & Klein, *op. cit.*, pp. 240-249.
9. Laughlin, H. P. *The neuroses in clinical practice.* Philadelphia: Saunders, 1956. P. 427.
10. Alexander, F. *Psychosomatic medicine.* New York: W. W. Norton, 1950. P. 209.
11. *Ibid.*, pp. 211-212.
12. *Ibid.*, p. 212.
13. *Ibid.*, p. 214.
14. Dunbar, F. *Mind and body—psychosomatic medicine.* New York: Random House, 1955. P. 109.
15. *Ibid.*
16. *Ibid.*, p. 110.
17. *Ibid.*
18. Weiss, E. & English, G. S. *Psychosomatic medicine.* (3rd ed.) Philadelphia: Saunders, 1957. P. 530.
19. *Ibid.*
20. Laughlin, *op. cit.*, p. 427.
21. *Ibid.*, p. 428.
22. Cited by B. Wolman, *Handbook of clinical psychology.* New York: McGraw-Hill, 1965. P. 910.
23. K. Maxcy (Ed.) *Preventive medicine and public health.* (8th ed.) New York: Appleton-Century-Crofts, 1956. P. 1106.
24. Cited in Alexander, *op. cit.*, p. 210.
25. Dunbar, *op. cit.*, p. 108.
26. Haddon, W., Suchman, E., & Klein, D. (Eds.). *Accident research.* New York: Harper & Row, 1964. P. 387.
27. *Ibid.*, p. 398.
28. *Ibid.*, p. 397.
29. *Ibid.*
30. *Ibid.*

31. Kiihne, P. *Home medical encyclopedia.* Greenwich, Conn.: Fawcett Publications, Inc., 1960. P. 395.
32. Suchman, E. & Scherzer, A. Accident proneness. In Haddon, Suchman, & Klein, *op. cit.*, p. 388.
33. Menninger, K. *Man against himself.* New York: Harcourt, World & Brace, 1970.
34. Schulzinger, M. *The accident syndrome.* Springfield, Ill.: Charles C Thomas, 1956.
35. *Ibid.*, p. 13.
36. *Ibid.*
37. *Ibid.*
38. *Ibid.*
39. *Ibid.*
40. *Ibid.*, p. 18.
41. Sheldon, W., & Stevens, S. S. *The varieties of temperament.* New York: Harper & Row, 1942.
42. Gleuck, S., & Gleuck, E. T. *Physique and delinquency.* New York: Harper & Row, 1956.
43. Whiting, J., M.D., quoted in *Parade (Boston Sunday Globe)*, April 7, 1968. P. 16.
44. Jeans, P., Wright, F. H., & Blake, F. *Essentials of pediatrics.* (6th ed.) Philadelphia: Lippincott, 1958. P. 119.
45. Wylie, E. Help! My child has taken poison. *Good Housekeeping*, June, 1967. P. 77.
46. P. Sartwell (Ed.) Maxcy-Rosenau, *Preventive medicine and public health.* (9th ed.) New York: Meredith, 1965. P. 681.
47. Alpert, J., director, Poison Information and Control Center, Boston, Mass. Reported by C. Cobb, *The Boston Globe*, March 19, 1967.
48. Wylie, *op. cit.*, p. 174.
49. Jeans, Wright, & Blake, *op. cit.*, p. 119.
50. *Ibid.*
51. Recht, J. L. Presentation at A.M.A. Congress on Environmental Health Problems, Chicago, Ill., 1967. Reported in *Geriatric Focus*, 1967, 5, No. 10, p. 1.
52. *Ibid.*, p. 6.
53. McCoy, J., Micks, D., & Lynch, J. Discriminant function probability model for predicting survival in burned patients. *Journal of the American Medical Association*, 1968, 203, p. 646.
54. Recht, *op. cit.*, p. 6.
55. *Ibid.*
56. *Ibid.*
57. McFarland, R., & Moore, R. Youth and the automobile. In Haddon, Suchman, & Klein, *op cit.*, p. 468.
58. *Ibid.*
59. *Ibid.*

60. *Ibid.*
61. Ingraham, J. The driver most likely to kill on the highway. *Coronet*, August, 1965.
62. Reported in *Parade (Boston Sunday Globe)*, January 29, 1967.
63. Warshofsky, F. Death rides on two wheels. *Reader's Digest*, December, 1967. P. 156.
64. *Time*, Sept. 8, 1967. P. 46.
65. *Ibid.*
66. *Ibid.*
67. Reported in *Parade (Boston Sunday Globe)*, April 4, 1965.
68. *Ibid.*
69. Lindeman, B. The slaughter of our schoolboys. *Good Housekeeping*, October, 1966. P. 95.
70. *Ibid.*, p. 162.
71. *Ibid.*
72. *Ibid.*
73. *Science News Letter*, October 30, 1965. P. 287.
74. *Ibid.*
75. *Boston Globe*, December 22, 1967.
76. *Ibid.*
77. Warshofsky, *op. cit.*, p. 154.
78. *Ibid.*
79. R. Stone, reporting in the *Boston Globe*, May 23, 1967. P. 10.
80. *Ibid.*
81. Lindeman, *op. cit.*, p. 155.
82. *Ibid.*
83. Marcus, I., Wilson, W., Kraft, I., Serander, D., Sutherland, F., & Schulhafer, E. An interdisciplinary approach to accident patterns in children. In Haddon, Suchman, & Klein, *op. cit.*, p. 324.
84. Jacobziner, H. Causation, prevention and control of accidental poisoning. In Haddon, Suchman, & Klein, *op. cit.*, p. 122.
85. Haddon, W., Ellison, A., & Carroll, R. Skiing injuries: Epidemiological study. In Haddon, Suchman & Klein, *op. cit.*, pp. 605-606.
86. See, for example, *U.S. book of facts, op. cit.*
87. Haddon, Ellison & Carrol, *op. cit.*, p. 606.
88. Dalton, K. Menstruation and accidents. In Haddon, Suchman, & Klein, *op. cit.*, pp. 201-205.
89. Boston Children's Hospital Medical Center Staff, *Accident handbook.* New York: Dell, 1966. P. 9.
90. Dalton, K. In Children's Hospital Medical Center Staff, *ibid.*, p. 10.
91. Hutaff, L. Contribution of hernatology to diagnosis and treatment in geriatrics. In W. Johnson (Ed.), *The older patient.* New York: Paul B. Hoeber, 1960. P. 457.
92. Schraer, H. Bone density changes with age and metabolic disease. In H. Blumenthal (Ed.), *Medical and clinical aspects of aging.* New York: Columbia University Press, 1962. Pp. 234-242.

93. Hartshrone, H. & May, M. S. *Studies in the nature of character: Volume 1, Studies in deceit.* New York: Macmillan, 1928.
94. *Time*, February 3, 1967. Pp. 13-16.
95. *Ibid.*
96. McCarroll, J. R., & Haddon, W. A controlled study of fatal automobile accidents in New York City. In Haddon, Suchman, & Klein, *op. cit.*, p. 183.
97. *Ibid.*
98. Haddon, W., & Bradess, V. Alcohol in the single vehicle fatal accident experience of Westchester County, New York. In Haddon, Suchman, & Klein, *op. cit.*, pp. 208-216.
99. Barmock, J., & Payne, D. The Lackland accident countermeasure experiment. In Haddon, Suchman, & Klein, *op. cit.*, p. 666.
100. *Ibid.*
101. Haddon, W., Volien, P., McCarroll, J., & Umberger, C. A controlled investigation of the characteristics of adult pedestrians fatally injured by motor vehicles in Manhattan. In Haddon, Suchman, & Klein, *op. cit.*, pp. 232-249.
102. Cohen, J., Dearnaley, E. J., & Hansel, C. E. M. The risk taken in driving under the influence of alcohol. In Haddon, Suchman, & Klein, *op. cit.*, pp. 351-358.
103. *Ibid.*, p. 357.
104. *Ibid.*
105. *Ibid.*
106. F. B. Taylor in *Boston Sunday Globe*, December 3, 1967. P. 59.
107. *U.S. book of facts, op. cit.*, pp. 807-808.
108. Bjerven, K., & Goldberg, L. Effect of alcohol ingestion on driving ability. In Haddon, Suchman, & Klein, *op. cit.*, p. 106.
109. C. M. Cobb, *Boston Sunday Globe*, December 3, 1967. Pp. 1 and 78.
110. *Ibid.*
111. *Time*, May 5, 1967. P. 69.
112. Morgan, C., & Stellar, E. *Physiological psychology.* (2nd ed.) New York: McGraw-Hill, 1950. P. 358.
113. Foukes, D. *The psychology of sleep.* New York: Scribner's Sons, 1966. P. 10.
114. *Ibid.*
115. *Ibid.*
116. Eysenck, H. The personality of drivers and pedestrians. In Haddon, Suchman, & Klein, *op. cit.*, p. 336.
117. *Ibid.*
118. *Ibid.*
119. *Ibid.*, p. 337.
120. *Ibid.*
121. Boston Children's Hospital Medical Center Staff, *op. cit.*, p. 9.
122. *Ibid.*
123. Menninger, K., *op. cit.*, p. 335.
124. *Ibid.*, p. 336.
125. *The Boston Globe*, March 9, 1968.

126. *Ibid.*
127. *Ibid.*
128. Lee, H. Fame, riches and death ride the 500. *Coronet,* May, 1967. Pp. 58-63.
129. *Ibid.*
130. *Ibid.*, p. 61.
131. *Ibid.*
132. Sign in window of a store, "The Cigar Box," North Clinton Ave., Rochester, N. Y.
133. Milles, G. Communciation in *Journal of the American Medical Association,* 1967, *202* (10,) 165.
134. *The Boston Globe,* March 15, 1967.
135. *Ibid.*
136. *Parade (Boston Sunday Globe),* September 10, 1967.
137. *Ibid.*
138. *The Boston Globe,* March 15, 1967.
139. *Parade (Boston Sunday Globe),* September 10, 1967.
140. *Ibid.*
141. *Ibid.*
142. *The Boston Globe,* March 5, 1968. Pp. 1 and 31.
143. *The Natick Herald,* (Mass.), February 28, 1967. P. 1.
144. *Ibid.*
145. *Ibid.*
146. *The Boston Globe,* April 14, 1967.
147. *The Boston Globe,* December 29, 1966. P. 1.
148. *The Boston Globe,* December 27, 1967.
149. *Ibid.*
150. *The Boston Globe,* January 7, 1968.
151. *The Boston Globe,* December 27, 1967.
152. D. Ellis, reporting in *The Boston Globe,* December 27, 1967. P. 7.
153. Fenichel, O. *The psychoanalytic theory of neurosis.* New York: W. W. Norton, 1945. P. 371.
154. Ross, S., & Kiseda, G. The shocking state of our fire protection. *Parade (Boston Sunday Globe),* April 16, 1967. P. 4.
155. *Ibid.*
156. J. Stack in *The Boston Globe,* November 26, 1967. P. 1.
157. *Ibid.*, p. 87.
158. *Ibid.*
159. *Ibid.*, p. 89.
160. *Ibid.*
161. Jaffe, G. Is your child's life worth 98¢? *Pageant,* November, 1966, Pp. 71-75.
162. *Ibid.*, pp. 73-74.
163. *Ibid.*
164. *Ibid.*, p. 74.
165. *Ibid.*
166. *Ibid.*
167. Aisenberg, R. B., & Kastenbaum, R. Value problems in geriatric psychopharmacology, *Gerontologist,* 1964, *4,* 75-77.
168. Rosenfelt, R. The elderly mystique. *Journal of Social Issues,* 1965, *21,* 190, 37-43.
169. Burgyn, J. A. Life safety code protects lives, not just buildings. *Journal of the American Hospital Ass'n.,* 1968, *42* (1), p. 45.
170. *Ibid.*
171. Ross, S., & Kiseda, G. *op. cit.,* pp. 4-5.
172. *Ibid.*, p. 4-5.
173. *Ibid.*
174. *Ibid.*
175. Mahoney, F. *The Boston Globe,* January 15, 1968.
176. *Ibid.*
177. *Ibid.*
178. *The Boston Globe,* October 6, 1967, p. 38.
179. *The Boston Globe,* March 9, 1968.
180. *Ibid.*
181. *The Boston Globe,* May 1, 1967.
182. *Ibid.*
183. Lardner, G., *The Boston Globe,* February 9, 1967.
184. *Ibid.*
185. *Ibid.*
186. Stack, J., *The Boston Globe,* February 9, 1967.
187. *Ibid.*
188. *Ibid.*
189. *Ibid.*
190. Quote from the *New York Times* reprinted in *Consumer Reports,* 1966, *31* (9), p. 426.
191. *The Boston Globe,* December 19, 1967. P. 14.
192. *Ibid.*
193. Wolfenstein, M. *Disaster: A psychological essay.* New York: The Free Press, 1959.
194. Moore, H. E. *Tornadoes over Texas.* Austin, Texas: Univ. Texas Press, 1958.
195. Danzig, E. R., Thayer, P. W., & Galanter, L. R. *The effects of a threatening rumor on a disaster-stricken community.* Washington, D.C.: National Academy of Sciences—National Research Council, Disaster Study No. 10, 1958.
196. Baker, G. W., & Chapman, D. W. (Eds.) *Man and society in disaster.* New York: Basic Books, 1962.
197. Danforth, W. The ghosts of Aberfan. *McCalls,* November, 1967.
198. *Ibid.*
199. *Ibid.*, p. 145.
200. *Ibid.*
201. *Ibid.*
202. Ross, I. Needed, first aid for ambulance service. *Reader's Digest,* February, 1967. P. 100.
203. *Ibid.*, p. 101.
204. *Ibid.*
205. *Ibid.*
206. *Ibid.* p. 99.
207. *Ibid.*
208. *Ibid.*
209. Reported in *Good Housekeeping,* June, 1967.
210. E. Edelson in *Coronet,* May, 1967. P. 56.
211. *Ibid.*
212. *Ibid.*
213. *Ibid.*

15

Illness

I'm sick to death of him.
They're getting under my skin.
He was scared to death.
She's a pain in the neck.
You're a sight for sore eyes.
She left me broken-hearted.

In the four preceding chapters we have considered three general "causes" of death. Perhaps the reader will not complain that the material has lacked in variety, but he might be distressed by a certain monotony in the conclusions. Whether the topic was suicide, homicide, or fatal accident, we came repeatedly to the same conclusion: the time and mode of death is an outcome of the individual's life style within his particular social context. Death does not simply befall one. The probability of being killed must be sought in variables that are at least potentially within our control. Any particular person did not "have to" die by suicide, homicide, or accident at any particular time. Not only did psychosocial factors play an important role in establishing the

probabilities of his death, but intervention on the psychosocial level might well have prevented it. Illness, however, might be a different story. The person who escapes violent or unnecessary death will eventually die of so-called "natural causes," i.e., disease and deterioration. Neither the individual nor his society need to take an active role in bringing about death by illness. In fact, even the most dedicated efforts to eradicate or cure a particular illness simply saves lives that will be claimed by another illness at another time.

There are probably few people who would argue that psychosocial factors have *nothing* to do with illness, fatal or otherwise. But there is a great deal of controversy and confusion regarding the significance of psychological variables in vulnerability to and recovery from disease. The positions taken on this subject are usually implicit rather than openly stated. It seems to us, however, that the major alternatives can be stated as follows:

1. Illness (including fatal illness) is always to be understood fundamentally in the technical terms of medicine and re-

lated biochemical disciplines. Psychological variables are secondary. On occasion they may be important—as when recovery is partially dependent upon one's being "a good patient."

2. Illness is always to be understood in medical-biological terms; but psychosocial factors are of great importance in *some* conditions. In other words, there are illnesses in which psychological aspects may be regarded as peripheral, and other illnesses in which the psychological aspects are central.

3. Illness is always to be understood in both medical-biological and psychosocial terms. There is no such phenomenon as a "purely medical" or "purely psychological" condition. To be consistent, this position should also aver that "health," "absence of illness," or "well-being" must be understood in both medical and psychosocial terms.

What is the layman's position? For centuries, there has been general recognition that factors in the psychological realm affect one's physical well-being. Familiar expressions such as those cited at the beginning of this chapter attest to the public's awareness that the biological and psychological realms are not mutually impermeable. We speak of people who "worry themselves sick." Sometimes we fear that a person has "lost his will to live" (the implication being that attentuation of purpose will somehow "cause" his death or at least "permit" it to take place). Most laymen are willing to accept the possibility that illness has strong psychological components. More precisely (but without a shred of real evidence), we suggest that the lay view might be stated somewhat as follows:

Just about *any* illness can be made worse by what the person does, what he thinks about, how he's treated by others. The illness can be made less severe, or more bearable oftentimes, by the same factors. Some illnesses can be caused psychologically, but some cannot. *My* illnesses are real, that is, they are caused by authentic biological factors; however, *your* illnesses may have been brought about or intensified by your emotional problems. In any case, when you get right down to it, it's all a matter of fate. Whatever is meant to happen will happen. But I'm thinking of changing my doctor.

We are suggesting, then, that the layman has a certain freedom in explaining illness to himself and others. His own observations and the Sunday supplements have acquainted him with many of the tenets of "psychosomatic medicine." He is therefore equipped to look upon illness from this relatively sophisticated viewpoint when he chooses. But he is under little pressure to be consistent at all times, at all costs. When it is appropriate in the situation to deny psychological factors in illness, why not deny them? When there does not seem to be much that one can do in the situation, why not invoke a fatalistic attitude?

We are not ridiculing or criticizing this flexible attitude. The layman, at least, can vary his explanation with the nature of the situation in which he finds himself. Many of the "pros" seem to have become hardened into positions which either accept a certain form of the "psychosomatic" explanation for all that it is worth, or reject the whole idea completely. It is possible that glib psychologizing, on the one hand, and the exasperated counterreaction to it on the other, may be obstructing our comprehension of the relationship between psychological variables and what is generally labelled "physical" illness. Just as the enlightened modern "knows" that accident-proneness is a validated explanatory principle, so the cognoscenti are convinced that the problem of psychological factors in illness can be resolved by the almost mystical phrase, "psychosomatic medicine." Meanwhile, the tough-minded contemporary may have talked himself into believing that the only alternative is a steadfast insistence upon exclusively physicalistic explanations. The underlying assumption is either that the mental life is epiphenomenal (related to bodily functions, but only as relatively inconsequential effects of the former), or that mental illness exists in something approximating a disembodied state. It is ironical that "hard" thinkers so often espouse this approach. They are the very ones who profess to believe in a totally physical, even mechanistic basis for human behavior. Accordingly, they should be numbered among the psychosomaticist's strongest allies. In another way, perhaps, their confusion or inconsistency is not so surprising, as we shall see in the following paragraphs.

PSYCHOSOMATIC AND SOMATOPSYCHIC

"Psychosomatic medicine" is a term that leaves much to be desired. Even those who believe "there is something in it" may be reluctant, for the following reasons, to embrace the term and all it implies:

1. The term tends to subtly direct attention toward the influence of what it considers to be psychological factors on what it considers to be bodily functions. Accordingly, it directs attention away from the possible influence of bodily functions on mental and emotional life.

2. It perpetuates the arbitrary—and archaic—dichotomy between mind and body. As a field of specialization, psychosomatic medicine purports to be interested in eradicating the mind-body distinction. Yet the very term, "psychosomatic," and many of the materials presented in its name seem to have had the opposite effect.

3. It defines the mind-body problem narrowly, as a medical specialty.

4. It focuses attention on pathological phenomena.

5. It emphasizes the role of the individual's problems and his psychodynamics in determining health. Hence, it stresses also individual treatment. This is not to say that the patient's immediate environment and the significant people in his life do not often figure prominently in the writings of most psychosomaticists. What it does mean is that overemphasis on the individual host as the prime factor in illness can lead us to ignore the often intensely pathogenic aspects of the host's environment, and, consequently, to deter action that could mitigate their influence.

Have we oversold ourselves on the theory of psychosomatic medicine? Does not psychosomatic medicine *as a specialty* actually do violence to the philosophy of a truly holistic approach? Before we can explore these questions usefully we must first take stock of what psychosomatic theory has contributed to our thinking about illness. We must learn what the field of psychosomatic medicine has become.

The relevance of this discussion to the major topic of this book becomes unmistakably clear if we but bear in mind that, for most of us, illness is the final common pathway to death.

Contributions That Shaped Psychosomatic Medicine

The roots of the psychosomatic approach are, along with most of our modern ideas, buried deep in antiquity. Its more recent history and basic philosophy are, of course, closely related to that of the mind-body problem (1). However, according to Grinker (2), the publication of Flanders Dunbar's monumental work, *Emotions and Bodily Changes* (3), may be regarded as the first modern and major contribution to psychosomatics. Dunbar brought together a large sampling of the available research material concerning psychosomatic problems. She herself noted that patients with certain organic ills often displayed similar behavioral characteristics. She based her personality profiles on such similarities. (One of these profiles, the "accident-prone," has been discussed in Chapter 14.) Whether or not one agrees with her approach, the fact remains that since the publication of Dunbar's first major work, most thinking people concede that some relationship does exist between mental and emotional states and alterations in bodily organs and systems.

Many investigators have tried to construct theories that would explain the nature of the relationship between psychological variables and pathological changes in the structure or function of organs. Two of these approaches have been particularly influential.

Felix Deutsch, an eminent psychoanalyst, held that physical symptoms are symbolic expressions of specific, repressed emotions and conflicts (4). Franz Alexander and his collaborators at the Chicago Psychoanalytic Institute developed alternative hypotheses. Their findings, based on studies of patients with gastrointestinal disturbances, laid the foundation upon which much present-day thinking about psychosomatic medicine in general (and some diseases in particular) is based. For this reason, we will present their findings in some detail.

These researchers hypothesized that certain patterns of conflict characterize the mental life of patients with certain physical diseases. Therefore, they "formulated a vector theory, based on the general direction of the conflicting impulses in the disturbances" (5). Three vectors were distinguished: "a) the wish to incorporate, receive or take in; b) the wish to eliminate, to give, to expend energy for attacking, for accomplishing something; c) the wish to retain or accumulate." Psychological factors found in the various gastrointestinal disturbances were seen in terms of conflicts among these three vectors. "Stomach functions, for example, seemed to be disturbed in some patients

who reacted with shame to their wish to receive help or love or to lean on another person . . . " (6).

These researchers hypothesized that stomach functions are vulnerable to this kind of conflict because:

Eating constitutes the first gratification of the receptive incorporating urge. In the child's mind the wish to be loved and the wish to be fed become deeply linked. When in later life the wish to be helped by another person provokes shame, which is not an unusual reaction in a society that places a premium on the self-made man, the wish to be helped finds regressive gratification by an increased urge toward oral incorporation. This urge stimulates stomach secretions, and chronic hypersecretion. In disposed individuals it may eventually lead to ulcer formation (7).

Different conflictual patterns for other gastrointestinal diseases were also noted. Patients with psychogenic diarrhea and colitis were preoccupied with problems concerning accomplishment. Among asthma patients, by contrast, the conflict often centered on communicating with important figures. This disturbance expresses itself in the small child in the suppression of the impulse to cry. "Later on, the small child is unable to establish frank, trusting verbal communication with the mother or mother substitutes" (8).

Alexander and his associates were able to answer in advance, as it were, some criticisms which their theory must inevitably raise. For example, they readily conceded that not everyone with a particular conflict or constellation of traits develops the organic problems that were manifested by their research patients. They concluded that psychological characteristics cannot, of themselves, explain psychosomatic illness, and that the vulnerability of the organ system in question—whether determined by constitution, or acquired early in life—is also a necessary prerequisite. Additionally, they hypothesized that these two variables are not necessarily independent. Finally, the investigators proposed:

A third condition, the onset situation, which is defined as the precipitating life situation as it affects the patient. . . . With some luck, and if the proper situation never occurs, despite a physiological vulnerability and psychological pattern, an individual may never develop the disease to which he is both psychologically and organically susceptible (9).

Despite the near impossibility of determining, in each case, the degree of vulnerability of every organ system, Alexander's approach is not only plausible, it is also fairly straightforward. But the approach does have its complicated and complicating aspects. To apply this approach one must accept the basic tenets of Freud's theory of psychosexual development. One must also be able to devote a great deal of time exploring the individual's life history as well as his present symptoms and situation. Even so, it is doubtful that Alexander's approach can encompass the full range of psychosomatic problems, whether one is concerned with this topic in its broadest aspects or just as a medical specialty. Let us look, for example, at the problems illustrated in a particularly interesting article.

Otto Ehrentheil investigated common medical disorders that are found only rarely in patients who are psychotic (10). Based on a literature survey and his own observations, Ehrentheil made the following points:

1. The incidence of "psychosomatic" disorders such as headache, hypertension, dermatitis, mucous colitis, peptic ulcer, epilepsy—and, especially, respiratory allergies—appear to be unusually low among psychotics.

2. Psychosomatic illness and psychosis often alternate in the same patient. There is at least one report of a patient in whom ulcerative colitis was replaced by dermatitis which, in turn, was replaced by migraine (11).

3. Although most papers report a low incidence of hay fever and asthma in psychiatric hospitals, some writers "have reported that asthmatic attacks either were not influenced, or were aggravated, by a psychotic state" (12). Ehrentheil's own data reveals only a negligible incidence of asthma.

4. Gastric ulcers usually are considered to be "psychosomatic." But West and Hecker's data support the hypothesis that "frequency of peptic ulcers in hospital populations of mental and general hospitals is within comparable statistical range, and that the reported low incidence is based on increased difficulties of diagnosis in the psychotic rather than on actual evidence" (13). Ehrentheil's experience corroborates the relatively frequent occurrence of both gastric and duodenal ulcers in a neuropsychiatric population (14).

Ehrentheil attempted to resolve some of the apparent inconsistencies between data regarding so-called psychosomatic ills and the theories which are intended to explain them. It is worthwhile to review these considerations briefly here since neither the status of the problems nor the theories have changed markedly since the publication, more than a decade ago, of Ehrentheil's article in which he pointed out the following:

1. Psychosomatic disorders sometimes have been considered to serve as *defenses against psychosis*. Under stress, the individual may regress from psychosomatic illness to the less mature psychotic disorder (15). This theory could explain the low incidence of certain psychosomatic conditions among psychotics. However, as indicated above, psychosomatic ills and psychoses are not necessarily mutually exclusive categories. Hence, this regression theory will hardly suffice for even the most narrowly defined types of psychosomatic disorders.

2. Another possible explanation holds that "whether a patient retains or loses his asthma attacks appears to be

directly related to the extent of his break with reality and, hence, to the depth or level of psychosis" (16). When the break with reality is not complete, then, physical symptoms may persist.

3. Can the inconsistencies between such theories and the available data be resolved? Ehrentheil attempts to explain why some psychosomatic ills are common and others rare in psychotics (17). He utilizes Alexander's distinction between conversion symptoms and vegetative neurosis. The former is considered to be a symbolic expression and, therefore, an outlet for a particular emotional content. The latter is the psychological accompaniment of an emotional state. It can be seen that a conversion symptom, so defined, may well alternate with or substitute for psychosis, since it releases a specific emotional content. By contrast, a vegetative neurosis could coexist with psychosis.

This brief review does some violence both to Alexander's original conceptions and Ehrentheil's discussion of their pros and cons. Nevertheless, it should serve to illustrate some of the problems inherent in trying to understand the most common of the so-called psychosomatic disorders. It should be pointed out that most writers do not provide us with a clear explanation as to why they consider some illnesses to be "psychosomatic" and others not. If *all* illnesses were investigated from a psychological standpoint as thoroughly as has been the case with, for example, duodenal ulcers, then we might no longer find it tenable to distinguish between "psychosomatic" and "unpsychosomatic" disorders.

This, in fact, is our contention: *The adjective "psychosomatic" should modify the word "approach" or "attitude." It should not be regarded as a specific specialty in the field of medicine or as a limited group of illnesses.*

This position is not identical with a "profile" approach to disease. We do not mean that each specific diagnostic category can be correlated with a particular constellation of personality traits. Such an approach is naively mechanistic and rigid. Rather, we believe that psychological variables are involved in *all* disorders. Moreover, their influence is not limited to any one stage of disease. Psychological factors contribute in various ways to the genesis, course, and outcome of every illness.

Perhaps it is difficult to understand how psychological variables can play a role in any disease which is not generally considered to involve either a conversion symptom or a vegetative neurosis. For that reason, we would like to discuss in some detail a few aspects of a condition that is not typically regarded as psychosomatic.

Cardiovascular Disease

In its various forms, cardiovascular disease is acknowledged to be the most common cause of death in the United States today (18). This rubric includes many different types of disease, some of which are both poorly understood and of relatively low incidence. Therefore, we will confine our discussion to coronary heart disease, a condition that has become increasingly common in recent years. We will follow Paul Dudley White's definition that coronary heart disease (CHD) refers to "myocardial ischemia with angina pectoris or electrocardiographic abnormalities due to coronary disease, acute myocardial infarction, and old scars of similar origin ... [in short] the various effects of coronary arterial disease in the heart deleterious enough to cause symptoms or signs or postmortem evidence of more than trivial damage to the heart itself" (19).

Although few dispute that CHD is one of our nation's most serious health problems, there is less unanimity of opinion concerning some aspects of its genesis. Let us consider first the data on which most authorities agree:

1. There seems to be an hereditary

predisposition to coronary disease in some families (20, 21).

2. The rate of CHD in North America is rising (22).

3. On the average, more people are suffering "heart attacks" at earlier ages today than they did in previous generations (23).

4. CHD is more common in males than in premenopausal females (24). However, the rate of myocardial infarction rises in females after the menopause (25, 26). Additionally, one study indicates than eunuchs have a low incidence of CHD accompanied by low blood cholesterol levels (27).

5. CHD is more common in some nations and some subcultures than in others (28). It is very uncommon among Chinese (in mainland China) (29).

6. Similarly, data on South African Bantus, Italians, and Japanese (in their homelands) indicate low incidence of CHD, and *no sex differential* in rate of attack (30).

These are some of the facts concerning which there is relatively little dispute at present. At first glance, they may appear to preclude the influences of psychological variables. Yet a brief inspection of each of the points summarized above will reveal that this is not the case:

Both North American and western European CHD rates have risen appreciably over the past quarter-century. If heredity were the sole or main "cause" of CHD, why would all of the "bad genes" suddenly have become dominant at this period in history? It should be recalled that Western man's increased (or supposedly increased) longevity cannot be invoked to explain this phenomenon. The greatest increase in CHD has occurred in the young and middle-aged. It is difficult to escape the conclusion that environmental factors are involved, and substantially so, in the development of this disorder. And it is relatively easy to see that

what transpires in one's environment is often a function of psychological variables (for examples, see Chapter 14).

The differential incidence in CHD between the sexes suggests that organic (probably hormonal) factors are responsible for the pathological changes basic to CHD. Yet this line of evidence in no way precludes the influence of psychological variables on the rate of heart disease—in either or both sexes. Consider, for example, Paul Dudley White's observation that the majority of young male coronary patients in his series of studies were mesomorphs. None were pure ectomorphs (31). We have already seen (in Chapter 12 and 14) that certain traits of temperament seem to be associated with certain types of body build. Could not the personality traits that go with mesomorphy induce males to seek out certain types of situations or to manifest certain patterns of behavior that could contribute to the development of CHD? White questioned whether the metabolism of the robust mesomorph plays a part in the development of early atherosclerosis (a condition closely associated with CHD). He wondered if this would be especially true when the mesomorph lacks sufficient exercise. The determinants of exercise (which is a behavior, of course) are multiple and complex; at least some of these lie within the psychological realm.

Especially relevant to this discussion is the experimental work of Jeremiah Stamler who has explored the relationships between certain sex hormones and development of atherosclerosis (32). Stamler administered estrogen (one of the female hormones) to a sample of cockerels. These estrogenized cockerels and another group that was not given the hormone were both fed a diet that was likely to result in atherosclerosis. After several weeks, the cockerels were killed and subjected to postmortem examinations. It was found that extensive atherosclerotic change had occurred in the aortas of both groups. However, in contrast to the control group, the cockerels which had received estrogens were "practically free of lesions in the coronary arterial tree" (33). Stamler reported further that several synthetic estrogens which cause feminization in cockerels also prevented coronary atherogenesis in birds on the experimental diet. Compounds which failed to feminize when given in large doses also failed to prevent coronary lesions. The important point is that:

Inhibition of coronary atherogenesis was closely linked to basic biological actions of the estrogens in avian species (34). It was also demonstrated that estrogen was capable of acting "therapeutically" in chicks: it reversed atherogenic changes. No sex differences in degree of distribution of atherogenesis were found in sexually immature chicks who were fed the atherogenic diet. However, it was a different story when mature, egg-laying hens were compared with roosters. The hens resisted atherogenesis; the roosters did not. Finally, ovariectomy (removal of ovaries) has been shown to eliminate hens' resistance to cholesterol-induced coronary atherosclerosis (35).

Certainly, the findings summarized above suggest very strongly that there is a biological base for the sex differential in coronary atherosclerosis (and, therefore, in CHD). One might be tempted to conclude that a) CHD is inevitable in males, and b) psychological factors have little or nothing to do with it. We can accept neither of these propositions. With regard to the first point, it will be recalled that the coronary rate among males is rising fastest in the younger age brackets. Are we to conclude, therefore, that young men today have more male (or fewer female) hormones than young men in previous eras? We are not familiar with any evidence to support such a contention. It may well be that there are marked variations in the amount of male sex hormones secreted in different individuals, or in the same individual from time to time. But might not psychological vari-

ables play some influential role here? Hormonal functioning is unlikely to remain isolated from the individual's general psychological disposition and the situational stresses that he encounters from time to time. Hans Selye, for example, has made a well-documented case for the proposition that "many diseases are not caused by any one thing in particular; they result from the body's own response to some unusual situation" (36). Selye's own research has been conducted on a variety of animal species, but there is reason to believe that his general conclusions apply as well to our own species. How the individual helps to create the situations in which he finds himself, and how he interprets and copes with the situations on a psychological level, should be expected to influence his bodily response, including (but not limited to) the production of sex-specific hormones.

There is another reason why we cannot agree that hormonal factors are of paramount import and psychological factors irrelevant in CHD. As already mentioned, in parts of the world where the coronary rate is very low, there is no sex differential in rate of attack. Furthermore, in Stamler's experiments, even the mature males did not develop atherosclerosis spontaneously. They had to be fed a special diet—one that was presumably not wholly "natural" and always available to their species. Thus, changes from the outside, in this case the availability of a particular diet only, were germane to the atherosclerotic changes within coronary vessels. To the extent that atherosclerosis in humans is exogenously induced, it is probably avoidable—at least in principle. Moreover, if exogenous factors are significantly involved in CHD, then psychological variables are likely to be intimately involved in determining exposure and vulnerability to such factors. Before we consider specific examples of this hypothesis, as we shall do later, it is necessary first to discuss a different class of hypotheses about CHD, all members of which have at least one aspect in common—they are swirled about by controversy.

Diet and CHD

Consider first the experimental variable that figured so prominently in Stamler's research—the possible role of diet in producing CHD. There has been long and heated argument about the effect of diet in developing or aggravating CHD. According to Ancel Keys, "No medical question in recent times has provoked more controversy . . . " (37). In seeking to resolve this controversy, Keys undertook a detailed survey of the literature which brings together diet, blood cholesterol levels, atherosclerosis, and CHD. He reviewed evidence derived from animal experiments, from studies of dietary changes and changes in CHD rates in several countries during and after World War II, from populations emigrating from one nation to another and changing their diets in the process, from laboratory studies of people in the United States, and from studies of special populations. These included, among others, Eskimos, Navajos, and Trappist monks. Keys also examined the relationship between obesity and atherosclerosis, nibbling vs meal-eating, and a host of other interesting characteristics and behaviors.

His conclusions? Although Keys took note of the work of those who disagreed with him, he concluded that diet *is* a major factor in the etiology of CHD. (The evidence cited in Keys' paper makes it difficult for anyone to conclude otherwise.) In summarizing, Keys stated: "All the evidence so far is consistent with the hypothesis that, in man, the fats in the habitual diet, operating largely through their effect on the blood cholesterol and related lipids, play a major role in the development of coronary artery and CHD" (38).

Many individuals and groups, however, continue to dispute Keys' conclusions.

There are both personal and socioeconomic reasons for this opposition. In exploring these reasons, we are at the same time exemplifying some of the psychological variables which can lead to illness and to death. First we will touch upon some of the personal reasons for sloughing off the hypothesis that diet influences the development of coronary disease.

It is a truism that we are creatures of habit. E. R. Guthrie developed his theory of "one-shot learning" around observations of cats who would persist in precisely the same form of behavior that first brought them success in an experimental situation, even when more "effective" behaviors could have been learned (39). Guthrie believed that by far the best basis for predicting an organism's behavior in a particular situation was to determine what this organism had done in the same or similar situation previously. But we probably have all witnessed and experienced enough routinization in our own lives to accept this premise even without the experimental documentation.

Just as we become accustomed to certain patterns of work and recreation, so we become accustomed to a particular kind and amount of food. Most of us will resist efforts to change our customary diet. We are apt to look askance at new or different foods, even at unusual combinations of familiar cuisine. Some people will be disturbed if offered for breakfast what they have become accustomed to eating for lunch, or vice versa. We are even more horrified at suggestions that we might consume plants or animals that are usually considered inedible in our own society, despite the fact that people in other societies may enjoy them and they are, objectively, no more or less esthetically appealing than our customary fare.

We are not particularly objective about our food. Pleasant events and experiences tend to be associated with certain foods. Americans consider such sweet, rich foods as ice-cream, whipped cream, pastries, and candy as rewards or consolation prizes.

We think nostalgically of Mama's home-made goodies, of Sunday dinner at Grandma's, and seek to recapture past pleasures by preparing and eating our family's traditional foods. Food (and drink) obviously have important emotional and social meanings to us.

For these reasons (which are intended to be suggestive rather than exhaustive), it is not surprising that we often seek to ignore or explain away any evidence that our dietary habits may ultimately prove lethal. Many individuals may regard the psychological benefits obtained through their eating patterns as being more than sufficient compensation for the increased risk of atherosclerosis. It is easy to understand how people can strike such a bargain if we remember that the atherogenic foods can be seen, touched, or tasted. Atherosclerosis is silent and invisible. Moreover, it is difficult to keep in mind that the cake, the French fries, the cream ingested now at age twenty can help to place one on the Cardiology Unit at age 45. Middle-age and illness, like murder and accidents, are misfortunes that befall "the other guy." Today's young American is apt to be a "here-and-now" man. He is not inclined to wait a long time to fulfill his desires, whether these be for merchandise, travel, sex, or food. Less social value is attached to the waiting game, while there is an immense variety of goodies, both culinary and other, to tempt a person. Enjoy now; pay later. Whatever one prefers to think about hedonism, moral character, and the like, it does appear to be true that dietary indulgences exact a harsh price from us.

The effect is likely to be much the same even when it is a different psychological pathway that leads to ingestion of atherogenic foods. "Wrong eating" (from the longevity viewpoint) does not necessarily represent uncontrolled passion for rich foods. For some people, eating is a behavior that is largely in service of their need for tension release. Eating, like smoking, may become a routine technique for taking some of the edge off our tensions. It does not follow that the indiscreet eater actually enjoys eating more than anyone else. Others may be on a self-administered atherosclerotic diet simply because they do not care much about food and food preparation. It is not an important element in their lives, so they eat what is most readily available. In our affluent society, what is readily available often is also atherogenic.

Food intake is also influenced substantially by socioeconomic factors. It is obvious, for example, that what food one can purchase is partly determined by the amount of money he has to spend. The relationship of socioeconomic factors to diet, and of diet to CHD is more complicated than the question of income per se. For example, there is no evidence that CHD is more common among people with low food budgets, or that atherogenic diets are always costly—or always inexpensive. Instead, we find social and economic factors interacting in many ways to influence dietary intake.

Decisions concerning what foods we eat—and serve to others—often is a function of the *status* that has become associated with them. This, in turn, may be determined in part by cost and availability. Lobster, roast beef, certain cuts of steak, cream, and butter are generally expensive and high-status food in this country. Tuna fish, peanut butter, frankfurters, and margarine are relatively inexpensive and are low in status. It is socially permissible to serve low-status foods at a picnic or barbeque, but not at a formal sit-down dinner. It is not true that all high-status foods are "bad" for people, and all low-status foods "good." Nevertheless, the high social desirability of fatty foods such as roast beef, butter, and cream is not realistic from a standpoint of health. Such an attitude is a boon only to the food producers, packers, and marketers who stand to profit from the sale of such products. And the profit motive exerts an important, although not always obvious influence on our diet.

Socioeconomic factors not only help to determine what foods are available to us, but also our ideas about them and, therefore, ultimately, our personal preferences. Food producers and retailers are in business to make money, not to educate the public. This proposition is all too obvious and elementary. Yet it may be difficult to keep in mind when we read advertisements. "Nice fat turkeys," "packed in extra heavy syrup," and similar descriptions have a way of implying that the foods so designated are superior or desirable in some significant way. Advertisements may be a major source of food information for the person who has never heard of atherosclerosis, and has only a very foggy notion of the difference between a protein and a carbohydrate. Even the preferences of the more knowledgeable person eventually may be altered by advertising.

What do such sources of information teach the public? One candy-bar has been advertised on a children's television program as being especially good for its viewers because it contains milk. The inference that a candy-bar can be used as a milk substitute is sure to be drawn by some naive parents. The advertisement neglects to mention that this same item also contains hydrogenated vegetable oil, a substance likely to be atherogenic.

The American Dairy Association seeks to instruct us also. It maintains that "You never outgrow your need for milk." Just how much milk or what kind is never discussed. Milk has been touted as "the perfect food" (especially for children) for a long time. Some mothers have been led to believe that giving their children milk is sufficient to compensate for a multitude of dietary sins. In actual fact, milk does not provide an adequate diet beyond the very early months of life. Reliance solely upon milk can lead to anemia (40). Even the pregnant woman's need for milk is usually overrated; and its caloric value at

a time when she should be weight-watching is often underrated (41). The public has been so thoroughly indoctrinated with the virtues of homogenized milk that we continue to serve it daily to school children in the face of mounting evidence that skim milk would serve the same useful purposes, and probably be a good deal safer as well. Yet many people have been led to believe that skim milk is somehow "cheap" and "inferior." Only milk with plenty of cream is good enough for our children.

It may be that we are easy to convince about such matters because of lingering memories from times when food deprivation was a reality to many of those who are now in the parental or grandparental generation. In the ranks of today's middle class there are many people whose families have struggled through "hard times"—sometimes for many generations. Once it may have been a source of pride, accomplishment, and security to have seen to it that there was rich food on the table. Sacrifices may have been made in other categories of expenditure in order to provide children with valued kinds of foods. Although food deprivation is no longer a realistic concern for these families, they may have a certain emotional vulnerability in this area that is easily engaged by advertisements and other pressures.

Almost every conceivable gimmick has been tried to convince people to eat what retailers have to sell, whether or not these items constitute a healthy diet. Even appeals to patriotic or nationalistic feelings are not infrequent. One national chain of hamburger stands refers to the meal it features as "The All American." This patriotic delight consists of a grilled hamburger on a bun, French-fried (!) potatoes, and a milk shake. Dedicated adherence to our accustomed diet, of which such a meal is but one example, may well be helping to make CHD "All American" also.

Diet is just one of the factors whose role in CHD, though increasingly obvious, is still considered to be controversial. Two other variables in this category are of at least equal interest from a psychological standpoint. One of these is stress.

Stress and CHD

Laymen have long believed that stress can cause or hasten the advent of cardiovascular disease. References to events as "heartbreaking," or to "dying of a broken heart," or to "eating one's heart out" are commonplace. So, too, is the notion that people can "work themselves to death" at sedentary occupations. Such ideas, nevertheless are often discounted by physicians. Michael DeBakey, the eminent cardiovascular surgeon, was quoted as saying: "Man was made to work, and work hard. I don't think it ever hurt anyone" (42).

Yet other professional people allow for the possibility that stress may be shown to influence cardiovascular disease, directly or indirectly (43). Quite obviously, part of the problem hinges on the definition of "stress." Hans Selye's well-known theory of stress is of relevance (44). He observes that "in a medical sense, stress is essentially the rate of wear and tear in the body." Nevertheless, according to Selye, wear and tear does not necessarily imply a pathological change; some stresses can be beneficial (45). Selye believes that there is an element of *adaptation* in every disease. In some diseases, the body's own adaptive reactions to the disease become more prominent than the direct effects produced by the disease itself. Selye refers to these conditions as "diseases of adaptation" (46). Since he was able to produce cardiovascular and kidney diseases in animals by administering large doses of certain corticoids, Selye hypothesized that too much or too little corticoid production may be partly responsible for the development of certain ailments (47). If alterations in psychological states—increments in emotional tension, for example—can be shown to effect changes in corticoid productivity, then it is reasona-

ble to suppose that psychological stress can indeed influence the development and/or course of CHD.

Selye's approach focuses on the possible physiological effects of stress, especially on the cardiovascular system. However, the whole problem of the relationship between stress as it is popularly defined (worry, work, etc.) and CHD is an unusually complicated one. A number of recent studies have attempted to illuminate some of its facets, but not always with much success. One investigation found "essentially no difference in pre-coronary artery disease personality between individuals who subsequently experienced myocardial infarction and those who did not on one of the most reliable and generally useful personality tests. . . " (48).

In many patients coronary artery disease resulted in a psychological disturbance characterized by depression, anxiety, increased hostility and concern over failure, but information given by such patients runs the risk of retrospective bias (49).

This is an especially important point to keep in mind concerning studies of *any* diagnostic entity. We say this not only because it makes explicit the danger of mislabelling reactions as "predisposing" or "causal" agents, but also because it emphasizes again that the psychology of illness includes somatopsychic as well as psychosomatic reactions. In this particular investigation, coronary artery disease in some patients appeared (not surprisingly) to result *in*, rather than *from* psychological stress.

Another study seemed to show that monks of high rank were more likely to develop CHD than lower level monks. The latter perform manual labor and are presumed to suffer less mental stress (50). One does not know, however, which is the more crucial variable—the (presumably) greater psychological stress of the higher ranking monks or the regular physical exercise of the lower level monks.

This question and others of a related nature also come to mind when considering results of a large-scale study involving 270,000 male telephone company employees. The researcher, Dr. Lawrence Hinkle, Jr., found that top executives appeared to have fewer heart attacks than did lower echelon workers (51). But he also found that the difference in risk of heart attack existed when the men were hired. Hinkle noted that men with college degrees have lower heart attack rates than do non-college men at every department level of the organization he studied. Differential rates of attack apparently are a function of selection:

Men who remain at lower working levels, tend to be shorter, fatter, eat more than top executives. . . . *Social and economic habits are involved* [italics ours]. . . . An unintentional by-product of the process of advancement in industry is selection of men who are slimmer and healthier for advancement. This . . . eliminates from the ranks of executives many who have a high risk of coronary disease (52).

As a result of this study, the role of psychological stress in CHD is, if anything, seen as more complex. The fact that differential coronary rates appear to be a function of selection does not preclude the relevance of stress. Perhaps some of the fatter, lower echelon employees are overweight because they have been under considerable tension throughout their lives, a tension to which they respond by overeating. Perhaps people who are not college-educated are more likely to use food for compensatory purposes. Nibbling may be a more salient "nervous habit" with them because they have developed fewer internal resources or external outlets for tension. Perhaps, again, the man of today who is not a college graduate is always under more tension because he is less likely to be considered an "expert" at anything in an era when the specialist is king. Both his job security and his income suffer by comparison with those of the college man. We would like

to add one more comment about Hinkle's study. Selection of the taller and thinner employees for higher echelon positions is itself obviously a psychological process. Functioning at a lower or higher echelon probably exposes an individual to different kinds as well as intensities of stress. Therefore, the interaction between heart disease risk status and the selection process may well have some effect on the subsequent health of both those accepted and those rejected for promotion. Is the man with a high risk actually benefited, protected by his restricted occupational success? Or is the opposite more likely to be true?

Yet another study illustrates the difficulties of trying to specify the relationships between personality traits, stress, and CHD. Friedman and Rosenman investigated proneness to coronary disease in a study which lasted four-and-a-half years and involved 3,182 men (53). They divided their subjects into two groups on the basis of personality characteristics. The men in Group A were characterized as ambitious, aggressive, and competitive. The Group B men were characterized as less aggressive, less ambitious, and less responsive to time pressure. The aggressive and ambitious men were found, as a group, to have a greater coronary risk than the Group B men.

The investigators did not assume that anxiety per se is directly related to CHD. The hard-driving man may thrive on challenging situations. But it is one thing to rise to a challenge (or seek one out)—which might reflect a personality trait—and another thing to be exposed continually to time pressures. Friedman and Rosenman were inclined to believe that chronic environmental factors, especially time pressure, are responsible for the exacerbation of Type A behavior. Unrelenting time pressure "may explain why a man in modern society may feel the stress more than the native in the jungle feels the stresses placed on him . . . . Although stress has always been with us, time as a chronic stress factor is relatively new, and so is the response it elicits" (54).

The situation becomes even more complex as other findings and interpretations are added. In their recent critique of the concept of a "coronary personality," Mordhoff and Parsons (55) called attention to some data that seem to be inconsistent with the Friedman-Rosenman findings. Keith, et al, attempted to replicate the earlier results, but with a different research design. They studied coronary artery disease patients, peptic ulcer patients, and control subjects. All the subjects were classified into Type A and Type B behavior patterns with "blind" ratings (i.e., the judges were not informed as to the individual's diagnostic classification). Polygraphs were also utilized. Results indicated that "ratings of the A and B behavior patterns were not related to the medical diagnosis or to serum cholesterol levels, but were found to be associated with the level of education completed. When the patients were divided into young (35-49) and old (50-55) groups, the interview ratings did differentiate the younger coronary artery disease patients from the other two groups, but the non-coronary artery disease patients were identified better than the coronary artery disease" (56). The authors concluded, among other things, that the ratings apparently were influenced by socioeconomic factors. We cannot be certain that we are learning anything about a *direct* relationship between personality and disease factors.

Mordhoff and Parsons also point out that there were no reports of interreliability in the Friedman-Rosenman study, and that there is a question as to whether the raters' knowledge of diagnostic categories was controlled in all cases. They also emphasize a point made earlier—clinical studies in general are necessarily *retrospective* and do not provide representative samples or systematic controls.

In view of the foregoing criticisms, it does not seem possible to draw firm conclusions concerning the relationship between personality characteristics and proneness to CHD. One can always raise questions, however. Consider the person who is not ambitious and aggressive, or who will not work efficiently under time pressures. Is it not likely that he is also the person who will be unable or unwilling to finish a lengthy educational program? Educational level and socioeconomic status are positively and intimately related. Hence, one would expect a disproportionate number of those at the higher socioeconomic levels to be people who are ambitious and aggressive.

Would not the educated, presumably intelligent, aggressive person be quicker to recognize the need for medical assistance and to seek and follow expert advice? If so, would this not ultimately be reflected in a higher and longer survival rate following myocardial infarction for such individuals as compared with others of lower socioeconomic status?

Subjects for the clinical type of study which Friedman and Rosenman conducted must, quite obviously, be drawn from among the living. Perhaps the personality traits of a large sample of those who did *not* survive a first myocardial infarction would not be at all like those of the Type A group described in this study. The technical problems that would be encountered in attempting to test this alternative hypothesis may be formidable, but we should remain aware of the possibility. On the other hand, if being a "Type A" is correlated with being coronary-prone, and if (as Friedman and Rosenman suggest) proneness is related to time pressure, then we have another possible explanatory hypothesis. Perhaps our increasing coronary rate should be attributed in part to our society's increasing reliance upon automation. Perhaps it is one thing to compete with another person, and quite another thing to compete against a machine, a computerized system, or that untiring, arbitrary, tyrannical taskmaster—the clock. Perhaps it is not entirely coincidental that

The Automation is beginning to emerge as a new image of death (Chapter 6). Friedman and Rosenman, then, have not so much provided definitive results as they have contributed to the formulation of further hypotheses. "More work needs to be done in this area" seems to be the appropriate statement once again.

Exercise

We have now briefly introduced two of the factors whose roles in CHD are still controversial—diet and stress. We have also attempted to note and discuss some of the data that contributes to their controversial status. Yet another controversial variable should be considered. As every jogging, cycling, swimming, hiking reader knows, that variable is exercise.

Practically every magazine one picks up these days carries articles exhorting him to exercise—or die. Few would dispute that moderate exercise for a healthy person is likely to prove beneficial. However, that exercise per se can be relied upon to prevent CHD or that lack thereof is primarily responsible for coronary failure, is still open to question.

It has been discovered, for example, that "sedentary Japanese in Japan . . . have lower serum cholesterol levels and fewer myocardial infarctions than their relatives in Hawaii and California" (57). The Japanese relatives in Hawaii and California exercise regularly, but their diets are higher in cholesterol than those of the native Japanese. It would appear, at least in this case, that type of diet may be more important than regular exercise in preventing CHD.

The problem of who exercises, when, and how much, is complexly interwoven with a number of other variables that are thought to be related to coronary disease:

A sizeable proportion of coronary victims tend to be mesomorphs. The mesomorph is ideally constructed for activity, exercise, the discharge of tension through motor channels. This tendency to favor abundant motoric activity could be related to their relatively higher rates of crime and accidents in early life (as discussed more thoroughly in Chapters 12 and 14). White has suggested that the metabolism of the mesomorph may predispose him to atherosclerosis, especially in the absence of regular exercise. We have seen that certain traits of temperament are associated with particular types of body build. Perhaps the mesomorph is "supposed" to be active and energetic. When he does not follow his natural inclination to discharge tension through motor activities, do these unreleased tensions produce internal pathological changes? If so, may not these be the manifestations of stress which Selye describes? Could they not contribute to atherogenesis and, ultimately, CHD? It is not inconceivable that undischarged psychological tension may exert a more deleterious influence on the coronary vessels of some individuals (possibly the mesomorphs) than on those of others. Once again, we see that the relation between psychological or behavioral factors and medical condition does not necessarily lend itself to simple formulation.

Why we exercise, and in what way is often less a function of our motivation to maintain good health than of our acceptance of social definitions of "appropriate" behavior. The junior executive on the way up often chooses to take his exercise in the form of golf rather than boxing or wrestling, although some experts believe golf to be of very limited value as exercise (58). (Experts, of course, do not invariably agree on the effects of specific forms of exercise.) However, golf is often used for making contact with the "right" people, being seen in the "right" places, and establishing a favorable social image. Wrestling, by contrast, has a distinctly lower-class, earthy, primitive image which up-and-coming people may prefer to avoid. We are by no means arguing against golf and for wrestling. We are merely reminding the reader that type of physical exercise often is selected on the basis of self-concept, group affiliation, social prescription, status, snob appeal, and transient fads as well as personal inclination. Potential physical benefits may receive only peripheral consideration in choice of exercise.

Some people have questioned the assumption that exercise always is beneficial. S. Suzuki, a Tokyo physician, has investigated the effects of forced exercise on animals. Postmortem examinations disclosed that exercised rats had enlarged adrenal glands and excessive fat deposits in the liver. Both of these conditions were absent in a control group of unexercised rats. "This meant that the exercised animals had undergone stress and strain beyond their powers of adaptation," Dr. Suzuki concluded (59). On the basis of these findings, the investigator raised questions about Japan's governmental policy of encouraging all young people to exercise and participate in sports. He believes that regular exercise may *not* increase health and longevity. "The taking of exercise is a stress. Worry and discontent and anger and resentment are stresses. They all call for cortisone, and the adrenal gland usually obliges by secreting the extra hormone required" (60).

It is reasonable to hypothesize that prolonged excessive demands for hormone secretion eventually will culminate in metabolic disturbances. The well-intentioned behavior of government officials (encouraging exercise) might then constitute a significant link in a chain of events that culminates in premature disability or death. Perhaps. Simply trying to decide which expert to believe under what circumstances is stressful enough without having also to consider whether or not such stress will increase one's predisposition to CHD.

We have been surveying, admittedly in a sketchy manner, the major factors thought to be relevant to the genesis and course of CHD. We have attempted to illustrate that whether our attention is directed toward heredity, sex, diet, stress, or exercise, we will find that psychological variables are intimately involved in how, why, and when they come into play.

Even if we knew beyond doubt the specific contribution of various "physical" and "psychosocial" factors to CHD, would this knowledge solve our nation's coronary problem? Hardly. It is easy to say, "Don't worry," but a worrier, by definition, cannot follow such advice. He will even begin to worry about not being able to stop worrying. Suppose that we knew for certain that given combinations of diet and genetic abnormalities constituted the sine qua non of CHD. Would this knowledge dictate a ready solution? No. Issuing prophylactic and therapeutic edicts is one thing; implementing them is something else. In other words, willingness to change one's way of life, to take prevention seriously, requires a favorable constellation of psychological forces. We may resist change in our dietary and other habits just as all sides in a major war tend to commit highly lethal blunders because of a disinclination to depart from their favorite beliefs and strategies.

The psychology of attitude and behavior change (and resistance to same) must be regarded as a significant influence in the prevention and treatment of serious illness. Whatever social scientists are able to learn about the analysis and manipulation of attitudes is of potentially great importance to life-and-death matters.

Assume for the moment that it is appropriate to work for the reduction of premature disability and death, that life-saving is a positive value. How can we educate people to select mates as carefully as pets or employees? How can we convince school committees that courses in diet and genetics are as valuable as those in sewing and shop? How can we persuade people to alter their firmly ingrained attitudes toward the kind and amount of foods they consume? What can we do to educate manufacturers and merchants to take their profit from foods that are conducive to health, not illness? How can we encourage people to take more responsibility for protecting their physical health without at the same time fostering somatic preoccupation and hypochondriasis? Why is it that some people will not or cannot follow a regimen meant to prolong their lives? And why do some of us bristle with resistance at the very thought that what we are doing to shorten our own lives or the lives of other people is anybody's business but our own?

It is doubtful that effective solutions to problems such as these can be achieved without consideration of their psychological aspects. It is equally doubtful that we will understand the role of the individual's psychological traits in his particular illness unless we improve our understanding of the role of psychosocial factors in all diseases. Just as the course of a disease often is determined largely by the characteristics of the organism upon which it impinges, so the mental and emotional life of the individual is shaped by the social milieu in which he was raised and in which he currently exists. CHD and the factors thought to affect it have been used here as but one illustration of how psychological variables may directly or indirectly influence the course of a "physical" disease. Any other disease could have served the same illustrative purpose (cancer, for an important example) (61). We have already emphasized that all diseases are "psychosomatic." It remains to be demonstrated that the psychology of any disease must include a *social* psychology.

SOCIOPSYCHOLOGICAL VARIABLES AND ILLNESS

It does not accomplish much simply to agree with the broad position that social factors are related to illness. If prevention and treatment of potentially fatal illness is our intention, then we must come down to specifics. Is there any real evidence for a relationship between social milieu, psychological characteristics, disease, and, ultimately, death? We believe that much evidence of this kind is already available. Social and psychological factors can be shown to be related to all aspects of disease.

- Who becomes ill? When? Under what conditions?
- Who receives treatment? What kinds of treatment?
- Who recovers? Under what circumstances?

We cannot encompass all aspects of these questions here, but we will discuss some relevant concrete examples.

Who Becomes Ill?
And Who Recovers?

Who gets sick? Everybody. True enough. Most of us have our episodes of colds, flu, headaches, gastrointestinal upsets, and so on. Despite this commonality, the incidence and severity of all forms of disease and defect certainly are not evenly distributed throughout the population. There are undoubtedly some people who would maintain that illnesses simply "happen." An excessive number of ills among some people is to be expected by chance probabilities alone. Consequently, there is no way to predict who will get ill with what disease.

This attitude is also fairly common with respect to suicide, murder, and accidents. Again, we are not willing to consider a prospective "cause of death"—illness, in this case—as merely the result of a capricious fate over which we have and can have no control. We are not invariably helpless victims, or bystanders, in suicide, murder, and accident situations. Some may protest that illness is a little different. There are not many specialists in the study and prevention of suicide, murder, and accidents. Perhaps Everyman, lacking a visible corps of specialists to depend upon, may be inclined to accept a share of responsibility for attempting to reduce these causes of death. But such is certainly not the case with illness. A host of specialists have devoted years to training themselves to cope with disease, so how can Everyman be expected to help predict, prevent, and treat illness?

This argument is based upon a rather limited conception of the nature of illness. Disease clearly is not an isolated, well-defined single phenomenon which "happens" to someone's body, totally unbeknownst to the victim, and set apart from his mental life and social milieu. (In olden times, by the way, the term was often spelled, *dys*ease, and used to denote a general state of *dys*comfort or *dys*phoria—i.e., a sense that something is wrong with one's *self*, not merely his body.) As difficult as it was for germ theory to gain acceptance in medicine and society, it may be almost as difficult now to free ourselves from overdependence upon it. A simple "bad little bugs" explanation, for example, hardly seems adequate to account for the chronic time pressure that may lead to stress-related disease, or the industrial-technological complex that pours pollutants into air and water. Our entire way of life is a crucial factor in such conditions; microorganisms do not deserve all the blame or credit.

We cannot, as individuals, control the microorganisms all about us (62) or the biochemical processes within us, but this does not mean that we are equally impotent to alter our own or our society's pathogenic patterns. To illustrate this point, let us begin with one of the classic examples of how symptomatology can be influenced by psychological means—the demonstration by Freud and Breuer of the efficacy of hypnotherapy in removing hysterical paralysis (63). Of course, there is no structural change attendant upon

paralysis of hysterical origin. However, there is evidence that readily visible lesions can result from psychological stimuli; e.g., blisters have been produced by hypnotic suggestion alone (64). Hypnosis is not required for symptom formation. Expectant fathers often develop symptoms during their wives' pregnancies (65).

There are many anecdotal reports of people apparently having been "suggested" or frightened to death. One case record involves a woman who died at the age of forty-three. When she was a child of five, someone had prophesied that her death would come at that age. The victim had successfully withstood minor surgery. "Suddenly, about an hour after the surgery, she went into shock and died of a massive adrenal hemorrhage." The psychosomatic explanation offered by those who investigated the case ran as follows: "When a tissue becomes more active, it needs more blood, and this is provided by a dilation of the vessels supplying it which are under nervous and hormonal control. It seems at least possible that in this case the conviction of disaster allied to the physical stress accompanying all operations had resulted in such an engorgement of the patient's adrenal glands that bleeding and destruction had occurred" (66).

The authors of this book are acquainted with several young adults who showed behavioral and physical symptoms as they approached what they feared would be the age of their death. In two instances, this was the age at which one of their parents had suffered an early death. Although none of these people died as a result of their expectations, all of them experienced substantial distress, sometimes including subintentional self-destructive actions. Several colleagues in the health professions have also reported such cases to us; apparently they are not so very uncommon. Psychiatrists Avery D. Weisman and Thomas Hackett have even observed that medical practitioners may inadvertently frighten or "hex" their patients, thereby producing further symptomatology (67). It is no secret that we sometimes behave the way we think we are expected to behave. Conformity to expectations can involve somatic as well as behavioral processes.

The incidents cited above illustrate the effect upon symptomatology of suggestions made by one person to another. There is no reason to believe that the "suggestions" embodied in the beliefs, taboos, and customs of a society will not be equally effective in influencing the symptoms of its members. Moreover, the prevalent cultural attitudes and behaviors toward illness may be indirectly responsible for preventing its ailing members from recovering, as was brought out in psychiatrist John Snell's interesting account of the so-called *hexing culture:* "This term denotes a set of beliefs having their roots in African folklore, West Indian voodoo, and American witchcraft, which ascribe the causation of disease or disability to the magical influence of a 'hex' or spell placed upon the patient by another person" (68). Apparently some entire communities in our rural South, both white and Negro, subscribe to such beliefs. Ailing people are likely to seek help first from lay practitioners who, Snell reported, are usually called "root doctors" or "root workers." These "root doctors" are said to be quite individualistic in their styles of practice, but most of them "utilize a blend of common positive signs, voodoo, fundamentalist Protestant religion, and imaginative showmanship" (69). When the symptoms involved are what we would term "hysterical," or psychogenic, such "treatment" may prove effective. However, when the symptoms involved result from severe organic disorders which are seldom if ever self-limiting, then the state is set for culturally determined attitudes to increase the probability of death by delaying or preventing appropriate diagnosis and treatment.

It is also possible that inappropriate treatment may be prescribed by a physician because of lack of information concerning his patient's beliefs. Bring together a patient from the rural South and a city-bred physician from the North. The patient begins to speak about the "hex" or "spell" that has befallen him. The physician thinks, "Psychosis!" Once the alarm flag of psychosis has been raised, it is not uncommon for attention to be directed primarily to the psychiatric rather than the organic disorder. In such a case, diagnosis and treatment of the physical symptoms might be delayed while the physician concentrates on managing the "psychosis." Snell specifically cautions against misinterpreting hex beliefs as evidence of psychosis.

Recently we have heard case reports from hospitals in a major city well outside the South. In these instances, the patients believed they were hex victims, but the medical staff worked assiduously to diagnose and treat the organic disorder. Despite medical efforts, some patients died— the organic cause of death remaining obscure. In such cases one is tempted to share the suspicions of hospital personnel that the patients' interpretation of the illness as a "hex" or "curse" played a role in their demise.

Although Snell has focused upon one constellation of hexing cultures, it is well to remind ourselves that "the evil eye" and other types of malicious sorcery have been conspicuous in folklore in many parts of the world for centuries. Studies in the folklore of death suggest that even today, and even in supposedly sophisticated urban areas, there are still people who perceive and respond to signs, omens, and portents (70). The omens vary from one cultural heritage to another, but the inclination to believe in them appears to be fairly general. It is probable that prescientific beliefs (e.g., illness and cure through magic) are most relied upon these days by people who have not been well integrated into our nation's general social, educational, and economic systems. They do not regard the physician and the hospi tal as part of their way of life. Illness and other hazards are dealt with through group processes, including the ritualistic. This is another way in which social factors enter into the outcome of illness.

We have been considering material that might seem rather extreme to some readers. Let us turn now to studies that demonstrate with more familiar topics that custom and preconceived ideas have their effect upon illness, diagnosis, and treatment.

Sociologist Irving Zola has demonstrated that "a socially conditioned selective process" operates to determine what kinds of complaints are brought to the attention of physicians by people from different cultural backgrounds. Specifically, he found different patterns of complaint among Irish-American and Italian-American patients, even when their diagnosed disorders were identical (71).

Consider now an even more general phenomenon. Many, perhaps most, Caucasians in the United States seem to be enamored of the suntan. Acquisition of a tan is thought to help one become (or, at least, appear) healthy, vigorous, and young. It also has social value in some circles as visible proof that one has rated a leisurely, basking vacation (the derivation from Thorstein Veblen would not be difficult to make) (72). The widely-promulgated belief that direct exposure to the rays of the sun is of great beautifying and therapeutic value is a profitable one to manufactures of sun-bathing accessories and proprietors of resort hotels who keep the picture of the sexy, attractive, and very suntanned young jet-setter forever in the public eye. Sunlight, in moderation, may be of some benefit in treating acne (73). But sunlight in moderation will not ensure the deep tan that is usually pictured and sought. In actual fact, exposure to the sun tends to wrinkle and age the skin. Its overall effect is most unhealthy. According to J. Walter Wilson, a U.C.L.A. dermatologist, "Thirty percent of the practice of dermatologists is treating skin

changes that have been brought about by sunlight" (74). One of these changes is skin cancer. Some people may not realize this fact; others may be willing to accept the risk in order to conform to their group's definition of "beauty" or "virility." For these reasons, some skin cancers and other sun-related ills are at least partially the result of sociopsychological factors.

Another example illustrates how seemingly innocuous culture-related misconceptions can lead to behavior which insidiously undermines health. Many Americans of foreign extraction, and some native-born, still like to see their babies looking "nice and chubby." For them, the chubby baby is a healthy baby. As we have already mentioned in another context, it is understandable that plumpness would be a positive value for those who have suffered "lean times" themselves. This value may persist and even be transmitted to others when it is no longer of adaptive significance. Many people seem to be embarrassed to have "skinny" children. They react to remarks about lack of girth as they might to an accusation of child abuse. The number of people who still utter such remarks ("He's so thin—don't you feed him?") bears witness to the prevalence of the notion that the thin child is a deprived child. Yet, scientific data fail to bear this out. It is well documented that it is *obesity* not thinness which predisposes to a variety of disorders.

Some parents proceed on the assumption that children will outgrow their obesity. This is not a very dependable assumption. Investigators at Rockefeller University suggest that there is a close relationship between the infant's eating habits and his later weight in adulthood. Preliminary work indicates that the number of fat (adipose) cells is fixed in early life, and cannot be changed later. The overfed child develops more and larger fat cells which "play a significant role in the carbohydrate and insulin abnormalities of obese persons" (75).

The pathway to obesity (and, hence, to certain ills) can also be traced at the socioeconomic level of analysis. A report from the United States Department of Health, Education, and Welfare indicates that obesity is more closely related to social standing than to either genetic endowment or glandular disorder. In general, the obese tend to be poor, single, divorced, separated, or widowed (76). In addition, a study of women in New York City revealed that "obesity is seven times more common in the lowest social class than it is in the highest" (77). There are several possible explanations, but none of them have adequate support at present. Perhaps people on the lower socioeconomic rungs cannot afford to buy proper foods. Perhaps they are ignorant of caloric values. Perhaps obesity is not regarded as an unattractive or unhealthy state. And perhaps they simply eat more.

Once obesity is established, whatever its cause, it is likely to have deleterious consequences. It is known to predispose to or aggravate physical ills. The linkage between obesity and illness can also include psychological variables. Psychiatrist Peter Knapp has pointed out that society regards the fat person as "different" and somehow undesirable (78). Certainly, many fat people see themselves this way. Such a self-image may have an adverse effect on one's expectations and level of aspiration. Studies have shown that slender women tend to ascend the socioeconomic ladder, while the obese tend to move downward (79). As one descends the socioeconomic ladder, it becomes increasingly difficult to follow a well-balanced weight-reduction diet even if one desires to do so. Protein-containing foods tend to be more expensive than those which are heavy in carbohydrates and fats. An unbalanced diet can cause deficiency diseases, and help lower resistance to other ills. Furthermore, obesity, for both physical and psychological reasons, may influence one to lead a dangerously sedentary life. Finally, obesity can increase the risks associated with surgery (80). Thus, socioeconomic, psychological, and physical factors can all operate simultaneously and successively to induce and intensify illness. The "cause of death" is likely to be far more complex than the brief entry forwarded to the coroner's office. It is, in a sense, the person's way of life that has patterned his death.

There are still other ways in which cultural factors make their impact. The United States has much too diverse a population to yield a single "basic personality" type. But if we do collectively possess some salient traits, then "orality" should probably be accorded a place of honor among them. The peculiarly American preoccupation with the female breast, as well as other manifestations of orality, has frequently excited comment. Psychologist Sonia Lazanska Robinson has remarked that American males seem preoccupied with bust dimensions, whereas males in her native Czechoslovakia appear to be more interested in the female *derriere* (81). She recalls seeing young Czech couples strolling down the street, the young man's arm draped not around his girlfriend's waist, but around her buttocks. There are more obvious manifestations of our culture's emphasis on oral gratification. The caricature of the young American as chain-smoking, gum-chewing, loquacious, and forever hungry does resemble a type of person who is familiar to many of us.

Orality is one of the major commodities offered by our mass media. Cigarettes, for example, are so widely advertised that they provide significant portions of the total revenue of many publication and, until recently, broadcasting operations. Visitors from other countries often express astonishment at the number of advertisements for products to be used in treating gastro-intestinal symptoms, for another example. Messages are relentlessly beamed to our "stomachs" (not always the correct anatomical referent). The success of such advertisements is documented by sales statistics. According to a national magazine, Americans spend approximately "90 million (dollars) each year for antacids and alkalizers" (82). Whether purchasers of such products actually have stomach symptoms that require treatment or stand to gain anything save a placebo effect has never, to our knowledge, been investigated. Such a study would not be difficult to conduct, and might prove quite informative. Among other things, we might learn to what extent mass media have contributed to creating a corps of gastric hypochondriacs, and to what extent they encourage dangerous misinterpretations of symptomatology that should be brought promptly to medical attention rather than to the patent medicine counter.

The fact remains that many people in this nation have come to interpret a wide variety of sensations as symptoms of disordered digestive processes. The pitchman's advice seems to be more insistent than ever. We are told to treat our oral excesses by further oral ingestions—specifically, patent medicines. One current series of radio and television commercials assures the listener that by swallowing a certain patent medicine he not only will recover from the distress of overindulgence, but will be able to return for additional helpings. Prevention of the symptoms by the control of orality (moderate eating) obviously has little value as a commercial message.

Geographic and economic characteristics of a culture also influence the available forms of overindulgence and its accompanying symptoms. America's wealth and agricultural productivity make it possible for most of us to indulge our oral impulses. Furthermore, it is likely that people raised here will *learn* to eat and drink to excess. Whatever our personal sources of frustration, it is easy to learn that oral gratifications are available as possible compensations, and that they are culturally sanctioned.

Excessive craving for oral gratification cannot always be attributed to early oral deprivation. It may instead be a learned pattern of behavior. Whether by social modeling (imitation) or other mechanisms, one learns that it is customary in our society to occupy one's lips and mouth with cigarettes, food, or drink almost constantly. Theories that consider only individual propensities err in neglecting the role of environmental availabilities and social customs. Individual patterns of oral gratification might be quite different if food were truly scarce in our country, or if cultural values negatively sanctioned the expenditure of money on such non-edible oral supplies as cigarettes. Such theories are also incomplete in their lack of attention to the effect of cultural preoccupations upon symptom interpretation. We have already touched upon the oral-gastric pattern in the United States. Let us briefly consider the French variation on this theme.

France has long been the world's most important winery. Every year approximately one billion gallons of wine are produced in France (83). Famous abroad for the high quality of its best wines, France also appreciates its own product. Wine is the common table beverage; even young children partake (84). It is not surprising that the incidence of both alcoholism and cirrhosis is high in France. Accordingly, Frenchmen tend to be concerned about their livers. A friend of one of the authors lived for many years in France. He reports that the French appear to be as preoccupied with their livers as Americans are with their stomachs. Minor distress and vague symptoms typically are attributed to "liver trouble," much as similar nonspecific complaints in this country are labelled as "upset stomach." Thus, our interpretation—or misinterpretation—of symptoms often is largely a function of social customs and attitudes. It does not necessarily reflect the actual incidence of a particular disease. While there is no lack of alcoholic and cirrhotic patients in France, it is the United States, with its more than five million alcoholics, that has the highest incidence of these conditions in the world today. It is known, for example, that at least 23,164 Americans died of cirrhosis in 1964, and that the number of victims rose to at least 24,715 the following year (85). Yet it is not very typical to hear Americans complain that their livers are "acting up." Without benefit of professional diagnosis, we cling to our "stomach troubles," just as the French hold fast to their "touchy livers."

The closer one inspects the drinking patterns-symptomatology relationship in France, the more respect one has for the role of sociopsychological variables. It has been shown that the choice of alcoholic beverages is heavily influenced by relative cost and by geographical factors. Farm workers and other low-income groups in Normandy and Brittany, for example, imbibe cider rather than wine, while expensive aperitifs are consumed mostly by young men with high occupational and economic status in large cities (86). The highest death rates from alcoholism and liver cirrhosis were found among the (hard) cider-drinking lower socioeconomic groups, while those geographical areas with the highest rates of wine-drinking reported the lowest death rates from alcoholism and cirrhosis.

We begin to see that, in France as in other countries, child-rearing practices, geography, economics, and related variables all have important bearing upon the citizen's relationship to his beverages and, consequently, to his health. The relationships are a good deal more complex than can be described here. And if one investigates Italian drinking-health patterns, still another sociopsychological constellation emerges (87). Studies of both French and Italian drinking patterns suggest that consuming wine as part of meals may protect against alcoholism and its attendant physical deterioration. Ullman, for example, emphasizes the importance of the first drinking experience (88). He believes that the Italian child (in Italy) learns that an

alcoholic beverage is a foodstuff in liquid form that one consumes along with solid food, and in the mutual-responsibility-and-affection environment of the family dining room.

As indicated in Chapter 14, the use of alcoholic beverages contributes to death statistics through other pathways than that of physical illness. If we were privy to the "whole story" in some of these deaths, it might prove exceedingly difficult to apply conventional labels. A Normandy fisherman, for example, sits alone in his small boat. He is cold and tired. A swig of hard cider (inexpensive) boosts his spirits a little. Later, still chilled and fatigued, he repeats the "treatment." Several swigs later, he is no longer in adequate possession of himself and his craft. If a physician were to examine him at that moment he would find the fisherman to be ailing and in need of rest and care. In this state of temporary distress, the fisherman is especially vulnerable to environmental hazards. Vision and equilibrium are affected. He topples over. If he were engaged in some other occupation, this tumble might result in slight injury, if any. But it is the ocean that receives him. Did he die because he was tired and cold? Because he imbibed an alcoholic beverage? Because he imbibed that particular high-alcoholic-content beverage, socially sanctioned and inexpensive? Did he die because of the transient psychobiological disorder occasioned by the drink? Was his death a "natural" (i.e., illness-related) death, because his disordered physical state was a proximal cause? Or was it a subintentioned suicidal act? (The experienced fisherman probably knows that he is increasing the risk to his life by imbibing heavily under the circumstances.) No matter what decision we make in this case, it is evident that the whole story of his death must be sought in sociopsychological factors fully as much as in specific biological alterations.

A society's value systems and prescribed behavior patterns influence not only its members' symptomatology, but also their responses to objective problems and to psychological stress. These, in turn, can exert a profound effect on health. Examples abound. Had we the space, we might explore the life-and-death ramifications of America's ambivalent youth-worship/youth-exploitation pattern, and our desperate need to act, think, and look young, whatever our chronological age. We could consider the relationship between this need and our nutritional, recreational, and marital patterns. And we might then trace the relationship of these to our physical and mental health.

There are several other, equally interesting possibilities. It would be useful to examine the effects upon health and treatment exerted by: a) our changing sex roles; b) our changing sexual mores; c) population growth; d) vertical and geographic mobility; and e) increasing urbanization and the changing nature of urban life.

We could not hope to encompass all of these topics, each of which merits its own book. Instead, our remarks here will be confined to our society's attitudes toward, and behavior with, drugs. The word "drugs" is used here in a general sense to indicate prescription medications, patent medicines, and various preparations which are ingested because of their reputed effects, whether or not there is any demonstrable therapeutic action. Always relevant to health, drugs are becoming relevant now in a new way.

Medication as a Solution to Life's Problems

Quick and simple solutions are tempting when we are facing individual or collective problems. As we have already seen in Chapter 12, violence sometimes becomes the preferred course of action when one is unable to cope with his problems in their full complexity. It is simpler to pull the

trigger (with the gun aimed in either direction) than it is to analyze the total situation and the possible alternative responses.

Medication can also be regarded as the easy way out. When our head aches, we take pills; when our stomach feels queasy—pills, again. More significantly, we no longer confine our use of drugs to the no longer confine our use of drugs to the treatment of physical symptoms. Many of us have reached the point of depending upon drugs to enable us to cope with personal problems. There are some who rely upon drugs in order to move through life without being open to the full range of emotional experiences. The intention, in effect, is to move through life without being moved. The use of drugs to *control* our affective state is a trend that may become even more pervasive as time goes on. There is less need to understand what is happening in the world or within myself if I can maintain a balance through the simple expedient of slipping a pill into my mouth. And when we are in positions of authority, we may be inclined to control other people's mental and affective state by the use of drugs without necessarily realizing what purposes we are serving and what consequences we are producing.

Some of us now use drugs to dull our concern about problems that require concern. We take pills to keep ourselves awake, to put ourselves to sleep, to speed us up, to slow us down, to provide sensual gratification, to benumb the senses. An increasing number of us act as though we believed sadness, grief, joy, worry—the normal accompaniments of life's vicissitudes—were pathological conditions that require therapeutic intervention. A friend of one of the authors reported an "amusing" incident. Soon after being put to bed, her seven-year-old son called out from his room, "Mother, I can't fall asleep. Give me a sleeping pill!" This boy's family is not in the habit of using sleeping pills. He had learned about them through television. He had also learned that it was bad, sick, or wrong not to fall asleep at once. And, finally, he had learned to remedy this situation by taking a pill. This is hardly surprising. Anyone who owns a television set has had ample opportunity to become similarly enlightened.

During the first quarter of 1968, five of the eight products on which the largest sums of money were spent for television commercials were health preparations (Anacin, Alka Seltzer, Bayer Aspirin, Bufferin, Listerine Antiseptic). The combined television advertising expenditures for just these five over a period of only three months was $17,052,900 (89). That is a lot of money—and obviously it was spent in the expectation of reaping an even greater sum of money in return from the viewing audience. Repeated exposure to materials promoting drug ingestion undoubtedly contributes to the development of a psychosocial climate that in turn increases the likelihood of drug dependence and abuse.

Regular drug usage is no longer confined to a small, atypical, easily-specified segment of the population. It has become part of the everyday routine of many "ordinary" people. "Some one and one-half million Americans now depend on the minor tranquilizers and other habit-forming sedatives. One out of six of us reaches for the pill bottle at the first sign of stress" (90).

Our twin propensities to self-medication and the overuse of drugs may have at least three kinds of deleterious effects relevant to our discussion of illness:

1. They can prevent our facing and coping realistically with life problems that are basically unrelated to physical ills.
2. They can expose us to serious physical and mental side effects.
3. They can delay or prevent our seeking appropriate treatment from people who are qualified to provide it.

Pills and Problem-Solving

LSD is like Ban deodorant . . .
Ban takes the worry out of being close.
LSD takes the worry out of being (91).

This epitomizes the attitude of an increasing number of our younger (and some of our older) citizens. Worries are to be ban-ished, rendered nonexistent by an act of thought strengthened, of course, by pill-borne chemistry. Aldous Huxley anticipated this development with his drug, Soma, in *Brave New World:*

Was and will make me ill.
I take a gram, and only am (92).

In Huxley's projected world of the future, the state controls its citizens from pre-birth through death by chemical means. Perhaps the external imposition of drugs upon a populace will not prove necessary. Many people today are imposing chemical control upon themselves, and attempting to impose it upon others. Those who disagree often are regarded with condescension or outrage. The condescension may stem from:

1. The need to feel superior. "We've had experiences that you haven't had and can't understand. We know a way around life that has eluded you."
2. Hostility against the older, parental generation, which keeps trying to "put us down."
3. Bravado—the need to convince one's self as well as others that one is doing the right thing, after all.

A sense of outrage may exist among those who use "drugs" that is expressed as hostility against those who have not and cannot solve the world's problems, but who nevertheless seek to deprive the drug user of the "solution" he has found. The "establishment" person may be despised as one who knows how to manage neither his own life nor the vital concerns of the world. Certainly, the "establishment" is wide open to criticisms from both without and within. Every instance of "boozing it up," every act of double-standard morality, every decision that ignores basic human values makes an inviting target. At question here is not the culpability or defensibility of the older generation, but the growing popularity of routine drug use as a preferred "solution." More basic still, a feeling of outrage may result from the user's sentiment that one of his fundamental "rights" is being challenged: *the right to take drugs.* What is the source of this attitude which has become so common today? And what does this attitude have to do with our consideration of psychological factors in illness?

Most Americans who are under 30 years of age cannot remember a time when "wonder drugs" (an already archaic term) did not figure prominently in their physician's armamentarium. The antibiotics, sulfa preparations, and antihistamines that were once truly wonders to those who are now middle-aged are taken for granted by the young. Moreover, in the childhood memories of today's adolescents and young adults, drugs usually are seen as unmixed blessings. Junior has an ear infection? The doctor prescribes penicillin, and the pain disappears. Sis has a urinary infection? She takes sulfa, and her problem is solved. Jimmy has strep? Time for penicillin again.

Not only were these treatments usually effective, but they were doled out lovingly by Mother. Undoubtedly, many children came to regard medication as a safe, relatively pleasant, quick and easy cure-all. As we noted earlier, today's young people have been subjected throughout their lives to advertisements promoting medication as a means of dealing with life's problems. (But the person who believes he is "tuning out" society and mass pressures by "turning on" actually is proving himself to be a docile receiver of the medication messages with which the very same society has been conditioning him all these years!) Finally and perhaps most significantly, whether their elders realize it or not, the young have resided in pill-consuming households for most of their lives. Stop and consider for a moment the drug behaviors in which children participate, or which are available for their observation in the average home: The children, and often their elders, too, ingest vitamins regularly—often in the absence of any sign of deficiency and without benefit of professional prescription. Many also take iron preparations regularly. Most adults use aspirin compounds for headaches and other mild pains; antacids for "nervous stomach" or sensations of discomfort after overeating; chlorophyll candy, gum, pills, or mouthwashes to mask "halitosis" (a term that in itself is the creation of merchandisers, not physicians or scientists); concoctions that promise to relieve constipation; and expensive exotically-labelled preparations to increase the beauty, pliability, and "health" of skin or hair. The promised rewards for all these activities is not just symptom relief but, often enough, such desirables as enhanced sex appeal, prolonged youthfulness, business and professional success, happiness, and peace of mind. Name it, and there is a medicinal preparation that promises to bestow that for which we yearn.

Children do not readily distinguish between prescribed medication that is used as directed for a short time to treat a specific condition and self-selected patent "medication" taken on general principles, and more or less indefinitely. If parents use some or all of the products mentioned above, then what is Junior to think? Isn't he likely to grow up with the belief that drugs have positive qualities only, that they are indispensable? Isn't he liable to suppose that happiness can be purchased in capsules and "fixes?" No wonder he bristles at any suggestion that he be deprived of unlimited access to drugs. He has been taught that he *needs* them. Therefore, it is his *right* to have all that modern pharmacology can provide. Between his momentary needs (energy, sleep, psychic escape, etc.) and their relief there is an exeedingly straight and narrow path: the magic pill. Apparently, he has *not* learned that one of the experiences modern pharmacology can provide is a one-way trip to the emergency room.

Toxic Effects

Physicians and pharmacologists recognize that drugs can be harmful as well as therapeutic. Whatever alters our internal environment to produce pleasant or beneficial effects also has the potential to induce unpleasant or dangerous changes—one of the reasons why so many preparations can be obtained by prescription only. It is also one of the reasons why some physicians prefer to manage their patients with "conservative" courses of treatment instead of reaching automatically for the needle or the prescription pad at every presenting symptom. Although the system that has evolved to protect us from unwise use of drugs is far from foolproof, it does provide some measure of safety. But when the system does not include control of potentially dangerous pharmacological agents, or when substances are used to obtain new physical sensations, then the stage is set for tragedy.

Quick-freeze aerosol sprays, marketed as cocktail-glass chillers, have been enjoying a vogue as an easy way to "turn on." An 11-year-old girl who tried this trick died of asphyxiation within three mintues. An 18-year-old high-school boy died the same way (93). At one time, at least 200 high-school students were said to be using these sprays in one Oregon town alone. Reports indicate that some Yale University students were trying them too. Although most people who inhale aerosol sprays do not die, they may suffer irreparable damage. "Doctors warned that sniff-

ers might suffer long-lasting effects, possibly brain damage, from anoxia." Yet the container in which the cocktail-glass chiller is packed bears the legend, "Harmless and non-toxic" (94).

Who is responsible for preventing deaths related to the misuse of potentially lethal products? The manufacturer of the quick-freeze spray certainly did not foresee that his product would be misued. Is he to blame for omitting appropriate warnings? Once a retailer becomes aware that a product is being purchased by minors for use in a potentially dangerous manner, does he have a responsibility to alert the manufacturer? And what responsibility do the parents have, if any? It is not easy to answer these questions. Usually we assume—or hope—that "somebody else" will take care of such problems. As we have already found in the chapters on murder and accident, "somebody else" is not very reliable.

A second and related example of misusing products for psychological "kicks" involves an incident in which one boy died and another required emergency hospital treatment as the result of sniffing glue. Reacting to this incident, a juvenile court judge reported: "I've asked every child who came to court on glue sniffing charges in the past year—and there have been forty or so—whether they knew they would die if they continued. Every one of them said, 'Yes'" (95). It is possible that children who sniff glue and engage in similar activities are basically suicidal, that they are deliberately playing a contemporary version of Russian roulette. In such cases, the lines between suicide, accident, and the toxic effects of drug-dependence become very thin indeed. Whether or not glue-sniffing youngsters are suicidal is something that would have to be determined by further investigation. There is another possibility—they might be lying about their knowledge of toxic effects. Feigned knowledge might help them to save face, and to appear courageous to their friends. It is also likely that some insecure youngsters are willing to risk their very lives to get and stay "in" with their peer group. Where self-respect and acceptance are lacking, life may not seem worth much anyway. In view of all the foregoing, it may not be sufficient merely to educate the young about toxic effects. We expect children and adolescents to seek new experiences, question their elders' authority, and rebel against prohibitions. These are not characteristics that spell "safety first." Hence, the responsibility for protecting the young from the toxic effects of product misuse must devolve upon society's elders, whatever this may cost in time or lost sales.

Our last examples of product misuse might be described as the modern classics. We refer, of course, to the abuse of LSD (lysergic acid diethylamide) and to the excessive use of alcohol. LSD has been, and is continuing to be, used in scientific research but as yet there is little concensus as to those conditions under which its effects may be therapeutic. Unfortunately, evidence of its deleterious effects is abundant and it has been known for some time that LSD can unleash psychotic reactions in predisposed individuals. One man, tried for murder he committed while under the influence of LSD, was acquitted on grounds of insanity. "He had been charged with stabbing his wife's mother 105 times. The defense claimed he was schizophrenic and that the LSD had aggravated his condition" (96).

Recent evidence indicates that LSD can have other extremely serious consequences. These include chromosome damage capable of producing malformation and mental retardation in the user's offspring, and blood cell changes similar to those seen in one form of leukemia (97, 98). There is no need to belabor the point. Data on the harmful effects of LSD are available not only in the technical literature, but in newspaper and magazine reports as well.

Understanding and controlling the use of LSD is another and more problematical

story. Individual psychodynamics are relevant, but these do not tell us why so many young people have opted to "turn on" through artificial, drug-induced means. The *social consequences* of the "tuning out" phase also require a broader focus than individual psychodynamics. Those who choose to "solve" their problems by making internal chemical alterations tend, by the same token, to lessen their grip upon the external course of events. Of such persons it can at least be said that they are unlikely to carry out certain "sins of commission," particularly those that require concentrated effort, long-range planning, or much energy outlay. Unfortunately, it is even more probable that the drug user's immersion in his own feeling-state leads to a vast range of "sins of omission." He is unusually vulnerable to a variety of health, psychologic, economic, and environmental risks, and he does little or nothing to reduce the vulnerability of others to these risks. To the outsider at least, it appears that he is surrendering his opportunity to play a creative role in changing what needs to be changed in society. If everyone were to follow his example, society's life-protecting systems would soon collapse around us. The LSD user manages to function as well as he does because most of his fellow citizens keep things from falling completely apart. One could hardly recommend the use of LSD and similar agents as a *general* solution to life's problems when it is obvious that both maintenance and improvement of vital social processes depends upon a level of clarity and energy that cannot be sustained by a person frequently under the influence of "mind-bending" agents. And we might also remind ourselves that the drug user scarcely can be said to transcend his society when he makes use of a modality (medication) that has been so highly touted and exercised in the culture that has influenced all of us.

Many people refuse to address themselves to the problem of drug and product misuse, claiming that it is confined to a lunatic fringe. Yet one form of misuse is so common that almost all of us have friends, relatives, neighbors, or colleagues for whom this is a very real problem. We refer, of course, to the excessive use of alcohol. According to one public opinion survey, 20 percent of American adults have a relative who "drinks too much" (99). We noted earlier that, as a nation, we have the world's highest rate of alcoholism and that alcohol is implicated in a sizeable proportion of our automobile accidents. Most adults are probably aware of alcohol's potentially ruinous physical and economic effects. Yet personal habit, the need for external support and props, and social custom converge to expose many of us, and to seduce the most vulnerable, into overindulgence.

Thus far, we have considered two of the three negative aspects of drug usage: the substitution of pills for problem-solving behavior, and the toxic effects of product misuse. But our irrationality with drugs also extends to the realm of self-treatment.

Drugs, Patent Medicines, and Self-Diagnosis

From the days of the covered-wagon medicine man to the present era of the television pitchman, we independent Americans have always been eager to "treat" ourselves. There is no way to discover how many deaths or prolonged periods of disease or disability could have been avoided had the victim promptly sought competent professional advice. But the number of such avoidable deaths has been anything but negligible.

What accounts for self-diagnosis and treatment? There are several possible answers. In frontier days, neither physicians nor medications were readily available. People often had to minister to themselves as best they could. Furthermore, physicians of the past had relatively few resources at their disposal. In many situations they were almost as helpless as their patients. This situation no longer prevails. But, as we have shown throughout this book, our behavior often is influenced primarily by perceptions and attitudes that are harnessed to outmoded experiences rather than by the objective characteristics of a situation. This tends to be true of behavior in general; it is no less applicable when we are considering lethal behavior.

But why do self-diagnosis and treatment persist today, when more appropriate alternatives are available? Let us consider the role that some of our attitudes play:

The Symptom Is the Disease. A physician's wife described how adroitly and amusingly her young son had answered the telephone. The call had been from a patient. Before his father could get on the line, the boy had listened for half a minute, then pronounced authoritatively: "Take two aspirin, and call me back in the morning." Just as authoritatively, he immediately hung up the receiver. Perhaps this is precisely the advice that the caller had desired, because he did not call back. For some people, the symptom *is* the disease. Once the symptom is relieved, they are "cured." Therefore, if a person knows what to take to relieve certain symptoms, he does not need a doctor.

The misconception that there is no more to a disease than its obvious symptoms may provide a partial explanation for a number of phenomena that trouble people in the medical profession. Not the least of these is the disquieting tendency of so many people to discontinue treatment before the required course is completed. The parent who discontinues the baby's ten-day course of antibiotics on the third day because the infant's ear no longer hurts, and the young man who refuses to continue penicillin therapy for venereal disease because he feels all right may both be laboring under the delusion that a cure has been effected. "I *feel* all right," the "dropout" patient tells himself and others despite the fact that, on an intellectual level, he knows he is not cured.

No Diagnosis Means No Disease. For some people the undiagnosed disease, like the unheard sound, does not exist. Psychologically, these people begin to consider themselves "sick" only after a formal diagnosis of illness has been made. It follows that if one can delay the formal diagnosis (and, therefore, the admission of illness), one can thereby postpone or circumvent the illness itself. A natural strategy in this situation is to treat the symptoms one's self, as though they represent only a minor disorder. Unfortunately, this is also good strategy for permitting a minor illness to become major, or a major illness to advance beyond the stage at which treatment would be most effective. Oncologists are particularly concerned about the psychological games people play with themselves (100). Delay in seeking diagnosis of a condition that *might* be a form of cancer is a serious delay indeed.

Another fallacy basic to this rationale for self-treatment is the assumption that minor symptoms mean minor illness and only major symptoms portend major illness. One would think that by now such notions would have been dispelled, but denial remains a potent defensive mechanism. "I'll just take some aspirin. I'm not really sick."

Only Weaklings Get Sick. Our thoughts about illness sometimes depart from logic. Sick people often are physically weak, so perhaps only "weak" people (i.e., cowards) get sick. The self-styled "he-man" may be ashamed to admit that he feels sick. It just doesn't sound very masculine. For the same reason, he may be ashamed to seek professional help. Perhaps the physician will uncover what he already suspects—that he is not so strong and masculine as he would like to be. In our

society, men are encouraged to deny their dependency feelings. We still harbor some vestiges of Puritanism: The "real man" stands on his own two feet and solves his own problems. For these reasons, males in particular may prefer to deny illness, suffer in silence, and surreptitiously swallow home remedies.

This pattern, by the way, can often be observed in elderly men. As he begins to "feel his years," the counterdependent male may redouble his efforts to appear independent, strong, healthy. But now he has to contend not only with an occasional "spell of sickness," but with a variety of ailments that threaten to become chronic. To maintain his self-image he resists any implication that he is aging, as well as any implication that he may be sick (101, 102). This attitude can have its admirable side ("Do not go gentle into that good night . . . "). But it is also likely to inhibit him from seeking appropriate treatment, and from modifying his life style in ways that would reduce his exposure to biological and environmental risks.

These are but some of the ways in which irrational attitudes toward illness and drugs can lead one to substitute self-treatment for professional help. If we add to this the fact that self-medication sometimes can *cause* physical illness and/or mask or distort symptoms of serious underlying disease, then we see anew how psychological and social factors can interact to produce or aggravate a sickness unto death.

We have been discussing at some length how suggestion, idiosyncratic subcultural characteristics, socioeconomic status, country of national origin, the mass media, and social and individual attitudes can influence our response to life problems. Specifically, we have been concerned with responses that foster illness and increase the likelihood of death. Taken together, these factors enable us to determine who comes down with what; they also exert an equally important influence on the treatment these people receive.

Who Gets Treated, and How?

Given a society as technically advanced and affluent as our own, the answers to the above question ought to be: "Everyone who is sick" and "Very well, thank you." Unfortunately, there is often a very wide discrepancy between what ought to be, or what could be, and what is. That many of our infants do not receive adequate care is reflected in statistics that show that 17 nations have lower infant mortality rates than the United States, and that our own rates vary from region to region by as much as 100 percent (103). In one American city, for example, infant mortality rates in a certain neighborhood are as high as those in the most impoverished, underdeveloped nations—this despite the fact that the blighted neighborhood is literally within the shadow of the city's most luxurious apartment buildings and modern medical facilities (104).

In one United States county, malnutrition is the major medical problem (105). In one Head Start program surveyed, 31 percent of the four-to-six-year-olds gave evidence of physical defects or emotional problems (106). It was estimated that 100,000 people who died of cancer in 1968 could have been saved by earlier and better treatment (107). These are a few illustrations that have been taken almost at random.

How can such conditions prevail? For the same reasons that have been cited above. It is often the sociopsychological facts of life, rather than one's physical condition or the state of medical knowledge, that are the major determinants of who receives what kind of care. We cannot consider every variable that influences the type, quality, amount, and efficacy of the treatment made available to or utilized by every individual or group. But we can examine certain pertinent aspects of our sociopsychological environment which affect the treatment of large segments of our population. One of the most potent of these is monetary.

Money and Health Care

Many people are highly sensitive about discussing the topic of money, its acquisition and use. This is partly a function of Western man's tendency to judge a person by what he is "worth" in cash. ("Oh, he's worth a million, easily.") In pinpointing money, or the lack thereof, as a major determinant of the quality of health care, we may upset some readers. Nevertheless, it is not possible to defer to our sensitivities about money when these same delicate feelings may be partly responsible for unnecessary suffering and deaths among those who lack funds. To avoid the discussion of economic factors in the psychology of death would be to avoid facing and coping with a realistic problem and, therefore, to cast a vote in favor of lethal circumstances.

It should be stated clearly at the outset that we do not mean to imply that all impoverished people receive inadequate medical care, or, for that matter, that all affluent people invariably receive the best care available. Quality of care is influenced by many factors. What we do maintain is that most poor people do not consistently have fair and equal access to quality health care. Some poor people have access to none. Thus, the poor are ipso facto likely to remain sick longer, suffer more, and die prematurely in disproportionate numbers. Does this picture seem overdrawn? It shouldn't. For those who doubt the existence of a close relationship between economic status and the quality and quantity of health care available, the following items may prove enlightening:

· *The report of a ground-breaking ceremony for a new radiation therapy center* concluded with the following statements: "The center will offer radio-therapeutic facilities for residents of the . . . area, with special attention to those hospitalized at . . . . Many of these patients are low-income citizens for whom such services now are very limited" (108). The implication is clear that up to then the more affluent had had access to life-prolonging treatment often denied to the poor.

• *Malnutrition (a potentially lethal condition that is readily treated with proper diet) affects thousands of men, women, and children all over the United States.* This was the conclusion of a citizens' board of inquiry following a nine-month investigation. The report said, in part: "Hunger and malnutrition take their toll in this country in the form of infant deaths, organic brain damage, retarded growth and learning rates, increased vulnerability to disease . . . " (109).

One of every five children admitted to a city hospital was found to be suffering from anemia secondary to malnutrition (110). A study of over 300 elementary pupils attending schools in poor neighborhoods showed that 64 percent received insufficient milk, 62 percent had infected gums, 93 percent had decayed teeth, and 25 percent had a skin rash (111). In another city more than three hundred children at a single elementary school were found to have "serious, unsolved medical problems," including many related to malnutrition. This school was within walking distance of a city health clinic, a Model Cities comprehensive health care project, and a federally funded children's health center. Serious health problems were also uncovered among students at the other five schools selected for study (112).

What about treatment? In the schools first mentioned, it was noted that milk was available for 15¢ a week, "but no attempt was made to provide milk for those who did not pay" (113). Additionally, most hospitals "do not keep systematic records or perform tests necessary to ascertain the presence of malnutrition" (114). Perhaps these omissions are predicated on the assumption that malnutrition is not a problem in this country. We don't know. What we do know is that adequate treatment is highly unlikely to be provided if no one bothers to diagnose the condition.

Ignorance is not the only villain. Even when apprised of the facts and provided with the means to bring about improvement, local officials in some states have been known to delay or actually oppose implementation. The availability of supplementary food programs to prevent and treat malnutrition is not sufficient; the "powers-that-be" must be of a mind to use these resources. Mississippi state authorities, for example, encourage participation in United States Department of Agriculture food programs. However, they "encounter opposition locally at times, giving rise to suspicions that racial bias may be involved" (115).

For whatever reasons, those in need of extra food and theoretically eligible for it frequently receive none. In Alabama, although 35 percent are classified as "poor enough" to qualify for governmental food supplies, only 4 percent actually receive the needed food supplement. In Arkansas, 38 percent are poor—only 6 percent receive food. In South Carolina, 37 percent are poor; less than one percent receive food (116). All of these people are especially vulnerable to illnesses. Some of the effects of these diseases are irreversible. Although theoretically help is available, it is not provided. The lethal gap between theoretical and actual is to be understood in terms of bureaucratic red tape, indolence, malevolent prejudice, and other individual and social thought-attitude-behavior patterns. One cannot help but think again of the concept of *administrative murder* that was suggested in Chapter 12.

• *Experts agree that cardiac intensive care units can reduce the mortality rate following heart attacks by about one-third* (117). A patient who is treated in one of the more than 400 hospitals that have such a unit obviously has an appreciably better chance for survival than he would have in a hospital lacking such facilities. The Boston City Hospital, whose patients come primarily from the lower socioeconomic strata, has at this writing no such unit. "Dr. Abelman and other medical directors have been petitioning the Department of Health and Hospitals for three years to establish such a unit—without results. . . . There is possibly no place in the country where the expenditure of so little money—perhaps $50,000—could save so many lives" (118). In many cases, a patient's limited funds dictates his selection of this particular hospital. And the hospital's limited funds, dictated by our society's peculiar sense of priorities, precludes lifesaving care. (After many lengthy discussions, meetings, and investigations—during which time people continued to die—the Boston City Hospital was finally promised a cardiac intensive care unit) (119).

· *Hospital treatment is getting more expensive all the time.* The estimated average hospital bill in 1968 was $566, exclusive of physicians' fees. Many patients admitted to hospitals that year (23 percent) were not covered by private health insurance, nor were they eligible for Medicare or Medicaid (120). Perhaps a certain proportion of that 23 percent could and should have purchased health insurance. Their sense of priorities may be in need of reevaluation. Perhaps part of that 23 percent is comprised of people who are so wealthy that they can afford to ignore conventional health insurance programs. More likely, however, a sizeable proportion of the uninsured group was made up of middle-income people who couldn't make ends meet, and were gambling that they'd manage to stay healthy. By 1970, the total cost of an average day in a hospital had risen to almost $78, and the

average hospital stay had soared to a total expense of $1360, according to the Guide Issue of *The American Hospital Association* for 1970. Hospital rates are expected to continue increasing at a faster rate than the general cost of living (121). Therefore, it is likely that increasing proportions of the population will be forced to take that risk.

The effect of hospitalization costs on individual treatment is indirect but potent. The person of modest income who lacks insurance coverage may be less inclined to accept hospitalization than the person whose treatment fees have been prepaid in part by insurance. He may delay or entirely avoid treatment of conditions that are never self-limiting. This is not necessarily to be understood as a subintentional self-destructive action. He may simply be putting the needs of other family members first.

This is no mere academic problem, nor can we ignore it on the grounds that it affects only a small minority. As hospital costs continue to climb, even the individual with insurance may not have adequate protection. As costs rise, so do insurance premiums. Some group comprehensive insurance rates increased 20 percent in 1967 alone, and large increases are predicted for the future. One editorial has made the point that the cost of insurance premiums may "become prohibitive even when they are paid by the employer" (122). Unless new programs are developed to meet the problem of spiraling hospital and treatment cost, the *majority* of us may find ourselves unable to afford adequate medical treatment.

We build nuclear submarines. We accomplish the enormous feat of landing man on the moon. We spend millions upon millions annually on cigarettes, cosmetics, useless patent medicines, and advertisements for all of these. Can it really be that we lack the technical and economic capability to ensure hospital care for all who require it? Why do we allot such a low priority to the protection of human lives? It is difficult to escape the conclusion, all our protestations notwithstanding, that most of us do not value human life very highly.

· *We value some lives less than others.* The poor are not only more likely to be sick, malnourished, and denied access to certain therapeutic techniques, but they may actually have to pay *more* for the treatment they do receive. A 1967 survey revealed that blacks in an urban ghetto were often charged more than white people to have identical prescriptions filled in the same drug stores. Ten pharmacies were involved in the survey—five in the ghetto and five in a white, middle-class area. White and Negro customers were charged the same amount in the white area, but three of the five drugstores in the ghetto charged Negroes a higher price (123). We do not know whether this survey reveals racial prejudice, exemplifies how some businessmen take advantage of a presumably captive audience which cannot afford to travel outside the ghetto for competitive shopping, or both. In either case, the ultimate effect is the same. The poor who are overcharged will have correspondingly less money available to meet other pressing needs—food, clothing, shelter.

If one's basic needs go unmet, he becomes more prone to illness. This reinforces the downward spiral in which he is probably already involved. Alternatively, the overcharged individual may find that he cannot afford to fill the prescription at all, or may be forced to prematurely discontinue vital treatment. Another possible outcome is that the poor individual who is ineligible for free or low-cost medical care may become increasingly disinclined to seek professional help for new symptoms, fearing that he will be unable to pay for the treatment anyway.

The ranks of the economically disadvantaged also include many aged persons (124). Research has indicated that the lives of aged people are considered to be less valuable, less worth saving than those of their younger contemporaries (125). To be both aged and poor is to hold the short stick in both hands. And to be aged, poor, and black? A recent survey revealed that zero percent of poor, black, aged persons in an urban ghetto had received needed professional dental care, and few had received medical care (126). Only very recently has some concerted attention been given to health problems of black aged Americans (127).

· *The physician in private practice is not always eager to treat the economically disadvantaged patient who may be slow or unable to pay.* Indeed, the attitude of a few (occasionally very influential) physicians is that such individuals are not "entitled" to treatment. Consider the opinion of this physician, writing not in the 19th century, but in 1968: "We all have the right to lead our own lives. All the other things currently referred to as such are not rights. They are privileges. Education, automobiles, *medical care*, color TV, good housing, etc., are all basically produced by the conscious effort of men's minds and they must be earned by the recipients.... Those people in government who feel they can 'plan' things and do better than the law of supply and demand are thoroughly evil and immoral..." (128) [italics ours].

It is interesting that this physician places medical care, often a lifesaving necessity, next to color television, an unnecessary luxury item. He seems to see no difference, stating explicitly that both must be earned. The assumption basic to this position is that life is of no *intrinsic* value; it is of *monetary* value only. The privilege of life or lifesaving treatment must be earned. This culturally-shared attitude is taken to be a hard-and-fast law of nature, on a par with the discoveries of Newton and Einstein. The physician then refers to the law of supply and demand. He decries interference with the operation of this additional fundamental economic law—even if interference might save human lives. Apparently, he does not pause to reflect that an authentic "natural law," such as those which describe gravitational or electromagnetic phenomena, simply *cannot* be eluded. One does not choose whether or not to obey the law of gravity. Clearly, this medical writer sounds as though he were primarily a businessman, and a narrow-gauge one at that. Should human life be consigned to the lowest ethics of the marketplace? What happens to the poor in this seller's market? Let the buyer beware (even though it will do him little good).

Clearly, socioeconomic status, health, and access to treatment are closely interrelated. What may be less obvious are the reasons why discussion of such material lies within the scope of psychology. Let us explore, for a moment, the possible relationship between certain psychological characteristics, attitudes toward socioeconomic status, and behavior toward the poor.

Psychological Influences that Shorten Other People's Lives

We might begin by inquiring why our society has been so slow to recognize and respond to the needs of the malnourished and medically indigent. It might be argued that until recently most people have been unaware of the problem. Initially, this explanation seems plausible enough. Most of us, possibly for reasons of self-preservation, attend first to our own and our family's needs. In our increasingly impersonalized society, psychological "blinders" seem to be gaining acceptance as part of our standard equipment.

It is questionable that this argument holds up any better than the defense of the German population which claimed that, during World War II, they were totally unaware that extermination camps were flourishing. For several years now there has been strong news coverage of malnutrition and inadequate health care

situations. Much of the material presented above was derived from news media available to anyone. Therefore, most people have been exposed to the facts. Secondly, blinders are not applied from without. They are developed from within, and utilized defensively by the individual to serve his own needs. Often one of these needs is to avoid facing unpleasant truths and the guilt and discomfort attendant thereupon. Frequently, *we don't know because we don't want to know.* This defensive maneuver, known as "selective inattention," has been observed in many contexts. Rarely have its consequences been as serious, however, as in our inattention to malnutrition and inadequate health care. To screen out this sort of information before it fully registers upon thoughts and feelings is to contribute one's assent to the continued distress and vulnerability of many of his fellow citizens. In even more contemporary psychological terms, it might be said that "cognitive dissonance" is best reduced by preventing the dissonant-arousing cognitive element (knowledge of existing facts) from entering one's mind in the first place. Whatever psychological terms one might care to invoke, it would appear that unwillingness to comprehend the facts is more likely a *cause* than an acceptable excuse for much of the prevailing misery.

At the group level, even the semblance of ignorance cannot be maintained:

1. Well-informed officials may deliberately block attempts to aid their needy constituents. How often this is done may never come to light, but it has been reported often enough to give us cause for concern.

2. Organized medicine is certainly well aware of the acute health needs of certain segments of the population. Yet the American Medical Association (AMA) has routinely gone on record as opposing progressive health legislation. Sometimes it has sought to hinder the effective implementation of programs designed to help

the indigent sick. As late as June, 1967, the president of the American Medical Association would not treat patients who wished to be billed through a Medicare agency. Attacking government programs that he considers to be threats to private practice, he declared in his inaugural address: "We must increase the effectiveness of our opposition" (129). (It is important to distinguish between the policy statements and actions of the AMA and the personal beliefs and actions of individual physicians. Many physicians have protested, both publicly and privately, that the AMA does not represent their thinking on these matters. Nevertheless, this organization does continue to exert powerful influences in many domains, including the governmental.)

3. If letters to the editor and columnists' reports are any indication, then middle-class taxpayers are becoming increasingly resentful that their "hard-earned" money is being used to meet the needs of the poor while they, themselves, receive no aid when ill.

Simple ignorance of the facts cannot explain our society's laxity—and resentment—in the face of the health needs of the poor. What can? Our natural heritage, combining rugged individualism with the Puritan ethic, has sometimes been indicted. Since it contributed heavily to our attitudes toward work and reward, this heritage bears close scrutiny. In frontier days, he who could not overcome obstacles independently was unlikely to survive. The family that had a poor breadwinner or producer simply had no bread. There was no lack of opportunities for work. The wilderness awaited any physically able individual who was willing to put forth the effort to make a place for himself. Formal education, personal references, and vehicle ownership were not prerequisities for entering most occupations. Under these conditions, it was reasonable to expect most people to learn to stand on their own two feet and take

personal responsibility for their family's needs.

The Puritan ethic is also said to permeate our thinking. One must always work for his keep. Idleness is sinful. Affluence is the reward for righteous labor, penury the just desert of the idle. These ideas have survived, and conditioned our attitudes toward the poor. Whatever case might be made in defense of these ideas in an earlier day, they seem inadequate in the present, more complex era. Physical bravery, the will to work, a desire to provide for the family often are insufficient to ensure employment, let alone material "success." The idle are not necessarily the lazy.

Just because the older attitudes are no longer adequate does not mean that we have abandoned them and replaced them with more appropriate concepts. Long-standing beliefs are highly resistant to change. We often continue to behave as if we believe the poor are indeed sinful. Their poverty truly is punishment for their inferior moral character. In short, we tend to hold them totally responsible for their plight. And if their current situation represents an appropriate form of punishment, then we certainly should not put ourselves in the position of interfering with divine retribution. Besides, if the poor are punished enough, why, perhaps they will come to see the error of their ways, reform, and join the ranks of the independently wealthy. (This pious assumption is rather at odds with a large body of psychological research which indicates that punishment, in general, is a rather undependable way of effecting behavior change.) But this self-righteous, pseudo-religious rationalization has much in common with similar attitudes we discussed in the chapters on murder and accidents. It also serves the same purposes: *It blames someone else for the problem, simultaneously relieving us of both the need to feel guilty and the responsibility for effecting reform.* It also makes us middle-class folk feel particularly righteous, since it reinforces our self-image as good, hard-working people who deserve all we have.

The unadorned truth is somewhat less flattering. Initially, children "inherit" socioeconomic class affiliation. This is not to deny the potential for vertical mobility. However, it is well to keep in mind that children start out with their parents' socioeconomic status, and with all of the associated advantages and disadvantages. There *is* a difference between growing up with a pony and growing up amidst rats and vermin.

Middle-class aspirations and the techniques for achieving them are not passed on to the lower-class child. First-rate education and health care are also absent from the heritage. All of these factors combine to make it especially difficult for the lower-class person to compete in the economic marketplace with his better educated, healthier, technically more competent middle-class counterparts. He is often imprisoned in his initial socioeconomic class status.

The superior health care which, among other things, middle- and upper-class people feel they have "earned," is most often handed to them on the proverbial silver platter. They "earned" this privilege simply by having selected the right family to be born into. Viewed in this light, the denial of necessary prophylactic and therapeutic care to entire segments of the population on the grounds that they are "inferior" or "haven't earned it" is unjustified. Ultimately, it is often only the accident of birth that separates the privileged from their sick and hungry "inferiors." We do not like to think of this. It is more pleasant to believe that our good fortune is of our own doing.

Implicitly, then, if we have ourselves to credit for what is enjoyable in our lives, we are in position to feel superior or one-up on those who are in more wretched circumstances. This commonplace observation has many more significant implications than appear at first

glance. If we provide good medical care, education, food, and housing to "them," how will anyone be able to distinguish between "them" and "us"? What proof of our superiority will remain? Precious little, we may fear. Concern for loss of our own distinction (which requires somebody over there to whom we can feel superior) can serve as a powerful force of resistance. Providing more adequate opportunities for "them" is experienced as a taking-away of something vital from "us."

Do we really expect babies, sick people, and elderly and disabled individuals to demonstrate that they "deserve" or have "earned" the care they require to recover or survive? Do we actually believe that medical care belongs alongside color TV sets—that is, a luxury to be reserved for the wealthy? Isn't human life of any intrinsic value? Our society purports to value each individual. Yet our behavior departs from this concept. Once again, the explanation and the potential means for bringing about change must be sought in the total constellation of social and psychological factors that have been occupying us on these pages.

In very recent years, some initial and ambivalent steps have been taken toward improving health care. Medicare and Medicaid legislation, as well as a variety of community programs, have aimed at assisting particular segments of the medically indigent population. Unfortunately, these programs have been hampered by a dearth of advance planning, inadequate administration, and the lack of wholehearted support by taxpayers, professional groups, and their legislative representatives. The results are frustratingly predictable. One state commissioner of public health described the Medicaid program as a "patchwork, crisis oriented and essentially uncontrolled aggregation of fragmented activities" (130). Clearly, innovative reform should be the order of the day. Just as clearly, this is unlikely to be achieved until we become more aware of our motives and begin to place human lives at the top of the priority list.

We have been discussing money, health, and a number of topics germane to both. But money is only one determinant of who receives what kind of treatment. Another determinant (which is not entirely independent of money) is the availability of adequate health care.

Our Distribution of Health Care Facilities and Personnel

Some communities in this nation still have neither a physician nor a dentist. In other communities, a multitude of practitioners compete for patients. A survey of one state revealed that fully 10 percent of the state medical society's active members were practicing in just five relatively affluent suburban towns (131). Dentists were also readily available in these communities. By contrast, there was a marked undersupply of professional people in other towns in the same state. Rural areas in most states tend to be particularly deprived. For example, in rural Maine people often wait four or five months "and in some cases as long as a year," (132) to see a dentist. Hospitals, too, are not well distributed geographically. Obviously, these facts exert an important influence upon who lives and who dies.

How do social and psychological factors relate to the distribution of health care facilities and personnel? Listen to the reasons advanced for the shortage of dentists in rural Maine:

First, young dentists have frowned upon settling in Maine because of the relatively low family income that results in low fees being charged. People just can't afford to pay as much here. . . . There is neither a dental nor a medical school in Maine. . . . Years ago, dentists and physicians sometimes moved to the country because it was cheaper to live but it certainly isn't cheap living in Maine today . . . (133).

The following reasons undoubtedly are germane to (although not totally responsi-

ble for) the entire health care distribution crisis:

1. Physicians in private practice naturally prefer to work where they can make good money. Under a system of fees-for-services-rendered, they cannot make much money in areas where people have none.

2. It is difficult to attract physicians and dentists to areas that are remote from training facilities. Conversely, medical and dental schools provide more practitioners to the communities which surround them. The schools not only graduate new practitioners who have developed ties to the area and who may wish to remain there, but they also maintain a large staff of professional people, many of whom will establish part-time practices in the community. Moreover, dental and medical schools do not exist in isolation. They are associated with hospitals where students and faculty can practice and learn. Hence, medical complexes, complete with hospitals and their paramedical services and ancillary personnel, tend to grow up around medical and dental schools. Similarly, new medical schools tend to be built and old ones expanded in areas where good facilities and personnel are already available. This is understandable. To a certain extent, it may be necessary. However, if most of the available funds are spent on a few major medical complexes, then people who do not live near any of them are likely to be disadvantaged in the quality of their medical care.

It can be argued that it is better to have a few very good, centrally located health care complexes where everything is, so to speak, under one roof, than to dissipate our limited funds and energies in duplicating second-rate services in small hospitals throughout the land. However, if this is to be the system, there must be a quick, reliable way to transport people from distant areas to the medical centers whenever they need specialized services. At this writing, we are not acquainted with any such system, nor does there seem to be any in the planning stages. Unless and until a transportation system is developed or some way found to upgrade small, local institutions, many of our sick are doomed to levels of medical care that are well below the best current standards, or to no care at all.

There is a second group of individual or personal reasons why health personnel tend to cluster around the large medical complex. It is intimately related to the reasons that have already been mentioned. Professionally and intellectually, most physicians and dentists want to be "where the action is." This desire is certainly understandable. Opportunities for research, teaching, and inter-professional consultation are among the possibilities available within the hospital-university-medical-dental-school complex. There is little of this in Centerville. But people continue to give birth, and take sick in Centerville. If there is no interest in finding a way to provide them with adequate health care, then a disproportionate number of people in Centerville may become victims of premature death.

There is still another factor that tends to restrict health care facilities in non-urban and non-affluent areas. This stems from the dual nature of professional practice. Medicine and dentistry are both professions; yet the practice of each is also a business (134, 135, 136). We have already noted the reluctance of professional people to practice in areas where ability to pay for this service is in doubt. Hence, there is a conflict of interests. Physicians and dentists are supposed to treat the sick, and treat them with the best knowledge, skill, and resources at their command. Yet professional practitioners and their families must eat and pay bills like anyone else. The net result is a lopsided distribution of health services and personnel.

It is not only individual practitioners who are subject to conflictual pressures. The government is similarly affected. On the one hand, the government is bound to support the position that a businessman in a capitalistic society has a right to practice his trade anywhere he pleases. On the other hand, neither medicine nor dentistry is solely a business. Health care personnel constitute a vital national resource, and the distribution of this resource is a matter of governmental concern. It may not be easy to resolve the conflictual interests if and when we try. But it will continue to be impossible *until* we try.

In the meantime, the American Medical Association has perennially voiced opposition to any national health plan because it allegedly would mean, among other things, that patients would lose the freedom to choose their own physicians. Yet the poor distribution of health care personnel that now exists already constitutes an effective constraint upon choice of a physician. In a community where there is only one physician or dentist, free choice is largely illusory. Moreover, there is no basic reason why a system that ensures at least the minimal care for all who need medical attention must specify exactly which practitioner must provide it to whom. The essential problem, once again, lies within the psychological realm. It is the attitude of some taxpayers, health practitioners, and legislators that stands between adequate treatment and its potential consumer who presently is deprived by reason of finances or geographical location.

If the only problem confronting us were *how* to provide good care for all, then we certainly could solve it. What we must first decide is whether or not we really want to provide this kind of care.

Up to now we have focused attention largely on the problem of *who* receives treatment. It is time to consider the nature of the treatment itself. The impact of social and psychological variables upon the quality of health care is as great as its impact upon the number and type of people who receive care. We must dismiss regretfully any lingering assumption that quality health care can be taken for granted. The range is not merely from superb to mediocre—in some instances, health care itself constitutes lethal behavior.

The Quality of Our Health Care

Let us suppose that you are a member of the upper middle class. You have health insurance and enough financial reserve to cover most medical emergencies. You live in a metropolitan area that has several teaching hospitals. Medical specialists of every type are plentiful. From a standpoint of health care, you are in an enviable position. If you fall ill you can obtain the services of a board-certified specialist and, if necessary, enter a first-rate hospital. Can you, therefore, rest assured that you will receive good care? Not necessarily.

An intensive study of the hospital experiences of 161 patients has been conducted by Raymond Duff (physician) and August Hollingshead (sociologist) (137). At first the investigators had planned to study only the social processes involved in becoming sick, and being sick enough for hospitalization. But the authors were disturbed to find the research project turning into something of an exposé. They discovered the following:

1. Patients with clear-cut diagnostic problems and a good physician often fared well, but "if the person comes in with a lot of confusion about his symptoms . . . he is usually in danger of being misdiagnosed and mismanaged" (138).

2. Private physicians who were supposedly treating a given patient often were unavailable. Treatment was then managed instead by house physicians. The orders given by the house staff often conflicted with those of the private doctors. Thus, treatments which patients had been led to expect sometimes were never administered.

3. Nurses no longer functioned in the traditional way. Frequently they played an executive role, directing someone else who actually performed the direct treatment. This "someone else" might change from day to day. There was no one person in charge. Therefore, "nobody keeps track of the course of treatment for any particular patient," and medication errors were sometimes made (139).

4. Duff and Hollingshead found "incomplete diagnoses *in more than one case out of three*—and occasionally—false ones" (140).

How can all of this happen?

Duff and Hollingshead feel that incorrect and incomplete diagnoses are partly attributable to the physicians' lack of interest in their patients. This attitude undoubtedly is basic to many other hospital errors and problems, and is implicit in the saying, "The patient has an illness; the physician has a career" (141). One investigator reported that a common attitude among doctors was: "Hospitalized patients exist to be studied." "Even those (physicians) who started out by taking a real interest in their patients" soon lost it in an atmosphere that did not consider patient care important: only the disease mattered (142). Further, "the young doctors' drive to 'save lives,' preferably in a dramatic way. . . leads them to look down on the chronic diseases" (143).

A sizeable proportion of those who require medical and hospital attention today are suffering from chronic conditions. This includes many elderly people. Age and the nature of one's ailment, then, may conspire to make one an unappealing patient—that is to say, a near-worthless person.

The treatment a patient receives is influenced by the attitudes held by the hospital staff. Duff and Hollingshead found that young doctors spoke of elderly or difficult patients as "crocks," and of ward areas as "the zoo." They longed for the opportunity to rid themselves of contact with the "crocks" and "crud." In short, the young physicians failed to identify with many of the people whose care was in their hands. Here we have another example of attempts to enhance one's own self-image by deprecating and dehumanizing others. It is not much different from the dehumanizing behavior discussed in our chapters on murder and accidents. Quite possibly, young physicians find this strategy useful as a means of controlling their own anxieties about dying and death, as several observers have suggested (144, 145). In any event, the cultivation of a dehumanizing "Us/Them" distinction cannot fail to be reflected both directly and indirectly in patient care and, consequently, in mortality statistics.

Duff and Hollingshead found other evidence that physicians sometimes serve their own needs before those of the hospitalized patients: "Doctors who want to demonstrate interesting procedures may do unnecessary tests and studies on ward patients for teaching purposes, but private physicians may do unnecessary surgery on their own patients, for even less worthy reasons" (146).

The study we have been discussing was conducted in one of this nation's *better* hospitals. There is no reason to believe that the situation is much different elsewhere:

1. The revelation that surgery is sometimes performed unnecessarily, for example, is not peculiar to Duff and Hollingshead's research. Furthermore, the rationalizations advanced for performing the surgery have additionally disturbing implications. A group in Britain appealed to the Health Ministry to investigate the high incidence of tonsillectomies in their hospitals. This operation was found to be causing between 20 and 40 deaths per year, and postoperative complications in 17 percent of the survivors. Studies "confirm that the advantages of performing the tonsillectomy may be few. . . . The operation may be performed because of parental pressure. . . " (147).

Parental pressure is hardly a valid reason for subjecting a child to the dangers and discomforts of surgery. Isn't this simply a euphemism for abdication of professional responsibility? And if parents continue to insist on unnecessary surgery for their children even after being apprised of the facts, then might it not be *they* and not the children who require treatment?

2. The persistence of self-serving attitudes among hospital personnel is certainly not confined to one institution. Moreover, there is evidence that it cannot be excused on the grounds of ignorance, or that it is all done "unconsciously." Even when deficiencies in hospital systems and techniques are brought to their attention, hospital staffs often are unwilling to trade their own convenience for improved patient care and comfort.

Take one example: A certain hospital conducted a study of 101 young children who had been admitted for tonsillectomy and adenoidectomy (148). Data revealed the incidence of both emotional and infective complications to be significantly lower among patients who were accompanied by their mothers, than among 96 controls without their mothers. D. J. Brian and Inga MacLay relayed their findings to the staff. They also pointed out that their results have been corroborated by other investigators. Despite all of this, hospital personnel elected to serve their own convenience first. "At the end of the experiment *the staff expressed unanimous preference for children to be admitted on their own*, although they conceded that the mother's presence comforted the very young child" (149). [Italics ours.]

3. The motives for actual mistakes in the treatment of hospitalized patients are not all purely selfish and conscious. Sometimes personnel are unaware both of the fact that they are committing errors, and of their reasons for doing so. Brann studied 31 medication errors made by student nurses at a state hospital. The resultant

data suggested that the errors were partly a function of the students' *feelings about the patient and the value of the medication* (150).

4. Attitude is often the major determinant of how whole groups of patients are treated. A journalist, reporting the results of his recent survey of the alcohol problem, stated: "Much of the suffering from alcoholism would be eliminated if most hospitals, doctors, and nurses accepted the findings of the American Medical Association that the alcoholic is ill. . . . The A.M.A. found thirteen years ago that a 'preponderance of evidence points to the conclusion that alcoholism is an illness.' " The A.M.A. acknowledges that for the most part most members of the medical profession "have tended to dismiss the alcoholic patient as hopeless or, at best, unpleasant and unrewarding" (151).

This illustrates the fact that special professional training does not magically nullify human irrationality. Neither does it erase the effects of previously learned attitudes, nor immunize against infection by new prejudices that may be prevalent in the larger society or one's peer group.

By now it should be evident that sociopsychological factors are implicated in much of the mismanagement of sick people. The type of mismanagement that involves dehumanization is particularly disquieting. We have seen something of what this attitude can produce at its extreme points (as in the chapters on murder and accidents), but this does not mean that past and present distortions must be perpetuated into the future. Unfavorable attitudes and potentially destructive patterns of behavior are learned; therefore, they can be unlearned. And new generations can be spared the type of "educational" experiences that have led to the formation of deleterious attitudes in the present generation. Dr. Oliver Cope has said of physician training:

Something happens to students during their four years. The educational mold distorts their vision

so they become increasingly centered on the exact sciences to the detriment of their interest in the behavioral and emotional aspects of the patient (152).

What we know of human behavior indicates that people tend to repeat responses for which they are rewarded. Hence, if the student is rewarded solely for acquiring and applying specialized information and techniques and not at all for attending to the patient as a human being, it is to be expected that he will concentrate upon the former. Moreover, since the social and behavioral sciences are given but relatively short shrift in many medical and dental school curricula, students are likely to develop the notion that the human aspects of illness and health require little attention. Again, there is no reason why all of this cannot be changed, if we all think it is important enough to warrant the effort.

At least one observer has taken this line of argument further. Dr. J. Sanbourne Bockoven (among other roles, an historian of psychiatric treatment) has expressed concern that the dehumanization trend in medicine will contaminate society in general. It is not limited to mismanagement of patients alone.

Medicine is contributing to, rather than counteracting, a growing tendency to regard human individuality and personality as superfluous, obsolete, and expendable. Medicine, thus, is not fulfilling its purpose. On the contrary, it is contributing to the undoing of its own efforts to the extent that it participates in demoralizing its patients and undermining their will to live" (153). There is a widespread evaporation of regard for the individuality of the individual as citizen, as employee, as patient. He is a nonentity among nonentities in practically all of his life settings. The experience that the physician has respect only for a component part of his bodily machine, and not for *him*, would surely confirm in the patient's mind that he stands in the same relation to his physician as to his employer who also has respect for one of his physical attributes but not for him . . . . For medicine also the individual's individuality or personality has little worthwhileness even as an object of interest, let alone as an object of respect and crucial concern (154).

We have been discussing the facts that hospital treatment often may be something less than therapeutic, and that the attitudes of professional personnel are partly responsible for this situation. Mention has also been made of some of the possible reasons for anti-therapeutic attitudes and behavior. But there is more to consider. In fact, it would be quite unfair to terminate the discussion at this point. Errors in patient treatment, whether in the hospital or the community, are not wholly the fault of physicians and nurses. The all too human tendencies considered above are not limited to any particular group. Physicians, nurses, dentists, social workers and, yes, psychologists, reflect the values and mores of their larger society.

Let us return to you in your role as an upper-middle-class reader. A few pages back you were left, rather unfairly, on the brink of hospitalization. Let us suppose that none of the factors mentioned in the intervening discussion applied to your case. You had a favorable hospital course. Under the care of your conscientious physician, you are well on the road to recovery. You now return to your doctor's office for a follow-up visit and a bit of laboratory work. Nothing can go wrong now; you feel content and relaxed. Yet it may be that you have taken the deep breath of relief a little too early. On the basis of the laboratory results, your physician may pronounce you cured, or recommend further treatment. But the two of you are somewhat at the mercy of the laboratory findings. Were the tests performed accurately? As a matter of fact, were they performed at all? Unfortunately, the answer to these questions too often is in the negative.

Dr. David Spencer of the National Communicable Disease Control Center declared that of the estimated 500 million medical laboratory tests done each year in the United States, no less than twenty-five percent or 125 million, produce defective or dangerously wrong results. (Among laboratories checked, it was found that) up to forty percent were unsatisfactory in testing for the presence of bacteria, up to eighty percent in identifying proportions of different blood cells, and up to eighteen percent in such a standard and simple procedure as blood typing (155).

This deplorable situation may stem in part from our system—or lack of system—of laboratory supervision and control. *Time* magazine has reported that half of the approximately 1400 laboratories in the United States are located in hospitals, and 400 are run by cities and states. The remaining laboratories—about 66,000 of them—are independent commerical enterprises. In 47 states, these "are under no effective control whatsoever.... In more than forty states, any high school dropout can set up a laboratory with no questions asked..." (156).

Again, our familiar question: How can this be?

1. *Greed.* Every society seems to produce its share of individuals with sociopathic tendencies. If a need exists, there will usually be someone willing to try to satisfy it—for a price—even if he cannot or will not satisfy the need adequately. It is not surprising that unscrupulous people might wander into the "laboratory business." But how do they manage to gain a strong foothold and to prosper? "Once in business, the laboratory can solicit doctors with profitable "come-ons." It may offer 'all the tests your patients require' for a flat fee of $75 a month—and subtly encourage the doctor who orders 100 tests a month to bill his patients at $3 to $10 each" (157). Thus, the laboratory can thrive, and do even more damage.

2. *Ignorance and inertia* play significant roles in the psychology of all forms of death. The fact that physicians patronize a particular inadequate laboratory does not mean that they know its work is

substandard. The physicans may know nothing of the techniques or technicians employed at a particular laboratory. Of course, it can be argued that they *should* know before they decide to utilize its services. Realistically, however, once a first decision has been made to utilize a laboratory, physicians cannot be expected to expend a great deal of time in spot checking its procedures. But shouldn't someone? If state legislatures can find the time and money to regulate bingo games and nightclub acts, then why can't they regulate medical laboratories? When people's lives are at stake, shouldn't this take priority over other matters? (It is not our desire to raise this question at every turning, but it does seem to follow us around, demanding to be heard.)

States have expended large sums of money and blocks of time in perennially rehashing arguments for and against retaining the death penalty. Then, through ignorance and inertia, they unwittingly expose thousands of people to the possibility of execution via the untrustworthy medical laboratory.

Well, what about the layman? If his physician does not know what is happening in the laboratory, how can he find out? By checking its reputation?

3. *Public attitudes toward science and medicine often preclude critical inquiry.* The layman who, in other aspects of his life may harbor few illusions about human perfection, often feels a deep respect and awe for the physician and the scientist. Moreover, the public's notions of what "science" is all about are frequently vague. The term "scientist" may be overgeneralized to include anyone who works in a "laboratory," especially if he wears a white coat. The nonscientist may feel timid or even presumptuous about questioning the accuracy of a laboratory worker. Many laboratory personnel (not to mention physicians and scientists) tend to encourage this attitude. Their reaction to having their authority questioned is generally negative, to say the least.

4. *Laboratory control, like other difficult social tasks, is somebody else's problem.* Of course, the information presented above is disquieting; but now that it has been made public, somebody, somewhere, will surely do something about it. A government agency, or a scientist, a physician, another Ralph Nader will devote time, effort, and money to correcting the situation. Therefore, *I* won't have to. (Besides, I'm not sick right now, so why should I worry?) A general attitude that control and responsibility is located outside of one's self must be counted as a major factor in the perpetuation of this and many other life-jeopardizing situations.

Suppose, however, that, as an hypothetical patient, *you* fared well in the hospital, and your physician has made use of a reliable laboratory. Are there other points of entry for psychological variables to affect your treatment?

Perhaps you require a blood transfusion. "A study done at a large Los Angeles hospital revealed that nineteen percent of all patients who received a blood transfusion subsequently developed hepatitis" (158). Alarming. But one cannot be sure who does or does not carry the liver-damaging virus in his blood, so how can sociopsychological factors be relevant to this statistic? "Circumstantial evidence shows a direct relationship between the incidence of transfusion hepatitis at a hospital and the amount of blood it purchases from a commercial blood bank source, in contrast with a voluntary blood bank such as the Red Cross." Dr. Redeker has explained part of the Los Angeles hepatitis problem as follows: "Several commercial (blood) banks are located in the Skid Row area, a region known to be frequented by addicts and hard-core alcoholics, another high-hepatitis group" (159).

Knowing this, wouldn't it be sensible to concentrate blood collecting efforts in low-hepatitis areas? Certainly, and this should be attempted. However, when donated "healthy" blood is unavailable, it may be necessary to use commercial sources. And why is low-risk blood in short supply? Because most of us neither see ourselves as being responsible for the health of our community in general, nor can we really believe that the next person who requires a transfusion might be ourselves or someone close to us. In other words, we are still within the domain of attitudes, belief systems, and the phenomenological world.

Perhaps, however, you were fortunate in receiving "good blood" when you needed it. Now your treatment merely calls for prescription medication. Federal control exists here (a positive instance of sociopsychological influence). Is there anything to worry about? Yes.

1. One group of drugs, the phenothiazines, frequently are prescribed for mental and emotional symptoms. A few years ago some investigators began to suspect that "opacities of the anterior lens capsule and corneal endothelium . . . are associated with prolonged phenothiazine administration." Their report concluded: "It appears from this preliminary study that the appearance of lens and corneal endothelial opacities is definitely related to the total amount of chlorpromazine received" (160). This is one of many possible illustrations of the fact that drug information must include knowledge of the effects of *prolonged* use. The fact that a medication is on the market does not guarantee that it can be used repeatedly or continuously without jeopardy.

2. Diphenhydramine hydrochloride is sometimes used to treat allergic conditions. It is considered to be of low toxicity. However, one report points out: "The effects of overdosage are less well known. In the small child, excitation, hallucinations, ataxia, incoordination, athetosis, convulsions, fixed dilated pupils, flushed face, fever, coma, cardiorespiratory collapse, and death have been described"

(161). Nigio reports a case in which the patient's symptoms were consistent with an acute schizophrenic reaction. The symptoms turned out instead to be related to an overdose of diphenhydramine hydrochloride (162). Thus, seemingly functional ills may be physically based or drug-induced. Specifically, any drug which can produce the wide range of serious symptoms described above should *not* be considered of "low toxity." The safe reputation of the drug is contingent upon avoidance of overdosage. Human error in establishing the dosage level for the particular person (including self-doctoring attitudes which assume that two pills will fix one up twice as fast as a single pill) can all too easily convert the "safe" drug into a dangerous one. The mental set that one is dealing with a "safe" drug can be a critical factor contributing to careless usage.

3. The combined use of several medications can produce unexpected effects. For example, in one reported case, gross hematuria (blood in the urine) was found after administration of four psychotropic drugs. Thus, knowledge of the effects of each drug used in isolation is often insufficient (163). And, of course, the admixture of drugs and alcohol can also produce complications.

4. A drug with great potential benefits may also have great potential risks. One such is chloromycetin. This antibiotic is a valuable bacteria killer. Unfortunately, it also may cause a severe anemia which can result in death. "By 1964 the American Medical Association counted 298 U.S. cases of serious reaction, approximately half of them fatal" (164). The California State Department of Public Health estimates that there have been about 666 deaths in the United States that are attributable to chloromycetin (165). In this case, the dangerous side effects are known, and have been well publicized. Why this knowledge and publicity is not sufficient to ensure caution remains to be explored.

It would be easy but hardly necessary, to cite further examples of adverse drug effects. Many of these are well documented. What is disquieting is the fact that severe side effects and fatalities continue to occur despite the availability of cautionary information. The public supposedly has three lines of defense against illness and death attendant upon the misuse or overuse of prescription medication: a) the United States Food and Drug Administration; b) research conducted by the drug manufacturing companies; and c) the knowledge and concern of the prescribing physician. Unfortunately, these combined resources are not always sufficient. Why?

When James L. Goddard resigned as chief of the U.S. Food and Drug Administration (FDA) in 1968, he recommended that we enact laws requiring drug manufacturers to demonstrate that a drug is both safe and effective *before* it is marketed. One would have thought such a regulation would have long since been in effect. One would have been mistaken. Who, then, has been charged with the responsibility of protecting the public from unsafe drugs? Well, we still have the protection that is provided by the drug companies' own research. But the fact that a group has been charged with responsibility does not guarantee that it will accept and discharge this responsibility properly. Dr. Goddard's recommendation was based in part on discoveries such as the following:

1. In October of 1965, FDA inspectors checked the files of a pharmaceutical company for information concerning an anticonvulsant drug. They discovered reports that "the drug caused serious glandular damage to rats." Although the facts were known in 1959 when the company's application for this drug was still being considered by the FDA, "the company had never reported them." It had also failed to report cases in which the drug "after it was cleared for prescription use caused sexual precocity in some children,

masculinization of young girls, and other untoward effects" (166).

2. Another drug company did not contest federal charges that important facts about one of their drugs had been "covered up by trick and scheme, including blindness and death among monkeys on which the medicine had been tested" (167). Some humans who took the drug developed cataracts on both eyes, lost hair, and experienced skin changes.

3. Sometimes drug companies employ a separate research laboratory to do their testing. One drug so tested was approved for sale in the U.S. on the basis of the research company's reports. However, later investigations prompted the FDA to charge that "some of the patients listed in the [Research Company X] data never participated in the test; that others were treated for symptoms they did not have, and that still others were being treated at the same time with other drugs (a practice that, of course, would make it impossible to tell which medication was having an effect). Some of the persons reported as being treated were actually deceased. . . " (168).

4. One of the present authors was asked to design and conduct a clinical evaluation of a psychotropic drug that had been on the market for a number of years. The purpose of this new study was to determine the drug's effectiveness on a specific type of patient population. It was decided to organize a formal scientific debate within the hospital to consider the merits of the drug before the study was actually initiated. The medical director of the hospital and the author tossed a coin to decide who would be "pro" and who would argue the "con" side. We reasoned that the involvement of the general hospital staff in the debate would serve as a useful educational experience all the way around, as well as yielding some insights that could be incorporated into the research design. Having been awarded the "con" side of the debate, the author prevailed upon several of his colleagues to

help him make a critical review of the existing research literature on this drug. We established a few basic criteria as to what would constitute a minimally adequate research report. This included such items as: the number, age, and sex of subjects is reported; rating scales and other research procedures are described; *some* kind of control group is employed; etc. In reviewing 15 studies, we were astonished to find that only *two* of these could meet minimal criteria for adequate research design and report. Unfortunately, it proved all to easy to demonstrate at the debate that the merits of this well-known pharmaceutical agent had not yet been adequately tested, despite the abundance of so-called research reports.

The pharmaceutical house had relied upon those physicians and others who had been willing to expend some time and effort to conduct clinical investigations. And, by and large, they had been let down by the inadequate research knowledge (or motivation) of their investigators. We *chanced* to come across this situation with respect to one drug (which, incidentally, impressed the author and his research staff as having some real merit, and deserving of competent, systematic evaluation). How many similar situations could be found if we applied basic research design criteria to the plethora of investigations which purport to test the effect of psychotropic drugs on humans?

5. Drug advertising is another area of concern. Exaggerated claims are only one part of the problem. False and misleading information is even more dangerous. Excluding necessary information is, perhaps, worst of all.

The drug most frequently prescribed for relief of the pain of angina pectoris has "a reputation among physicians as the best choice . . . even though the same drug is available under other brand names and generically. It owes its success to advertising campaigns that cost the manufacturer $1,600,000 . . . in 1965 alone" (169).

During that year, the company producing this drug "launched a gigantic advertising campaign in the major medical journals, strongly implying . . . [among other things, that the drug] could prolong the life of victims of myocardial infarction. The claim was based on the flimsiest of clinical evidence and was denied even by the researcher whose work was cited in the advertisement" (170).

When the FDA asked a drug company to warn on their labels against the use of a particular drug during pregnancy, the company "followed the warning with a statement designed to refute it." Another company, marketing a similar drug, "omitted information necessary for physicians and added wording leading physicians to believe that the drug is unconditionally safe" (171).

When Dr. Goddard took a strong stand in favor of protecting patients, it was predicted that "Dr. G. won't last a year" (172). Actually, he managed to last 28 months. Most people were indifferent when he stepped down (the familiar heritage of ignorance and inertia). Some were not: they were delighted. At one point, ostensibly because of a remark made by Goddard, "the 50,000 member National Association of Retail Druggists demanded his resignation" (173). Although there were individuals and groups that appreciated Dr. Goddard's efforts, one cannot say that the public as a whole recognized and protected the work of this man who was attempting to protect the public. And the most effectively organized groups who opposed him appeared to be those whose commercial interests brought them into opposition with the public safety measures he proposed.

In all of the examples given above, there are strong implications that a number of psychological defense mechanisms are at work. Isolation of self from others, with consequent dehumanization of the others, seems to be one of the most pervasive of these defenses. "Business as usual" and financial gain motives may be incompatible at times with public safety. Therefore, one proceeds as if his misleading claims, nonchalant research activities, or opposition to bothersome government standards and regulations had nothing to do with actual human lives. The vice-president of a pharmaceutical house may be one "great guy" in his personal dealings with other people. But he does not permit himself to recognize any relationship between his overzealous efforts on behalf of his company and their possible consequences for real people. Furthermore, those within the drug-producing and dispensing arena who fail to maintain the highest safety standards seem to imagine themselves and their loved ones as being somehow exempt from the illnesses which beset others. They do not regard themselves as potential patients and, thus, potential consumers of their own inadequately tested and labelled products.

If the FDA and the drug manufacturers cannot or will not protect the patient under all circumstances, then who or what can? One last line of defense remains: the knowledge of the prescribing physicians. Can they hold that line? Many can and do. Physicians, themselves, however, are painfully aware that some of their colleagues fail to hold the line.

Speakers at a national meeting of the American Society of Internal Medicine voiced concern over the failure of some physicians to keep up with new developments in their field. The AMA has estimated that only 10 to 15 percent of the physicians in this country participate in *any* formal continuing education course in any one year. It was felt that this failure to keep information current creates "a serious gap between scientific advances and patient care" (174). Despite this observation, there was opposition to the suggestion that the government periodically reexamine physicians and withdraw the licenses of those whose responses demonstrated that they had failed to keep abreast of recent developments.

This problem is neither new nor purely theoretical. Consider the following quote from *Science News Letter* in 1965: "The AMA charged doctors with prescribing drugs which might produce harmful effects in patients, even sudden death. . . . Appalling ignorance of the use of drugs was charged to physicians by two speakers, one from New York, the other from California" (175), and examples were cited.

The situation has not improved since 1965. If anything, the increased use of two or more drugs in combination has upped the risk. In the days when drugs were fewer and simpler, prescribing them was also an easier task. Those days probably will never be seen again. The physician who is intent upon protecting his patient requires all the information he can muster.

Almost any risk to life (as, in this case, faulty prescription of medication) can be intensified by the welter of social and psychological factors that have been described throughout this book. It has already been noted in several contexts that elderly people tend to be regarded as relatively unimportant patients. Many operatives in the "people professions," not physicians alone, are singularly unenthusiastic about treating elders. This situation has improved a bit since the advent of Medicare and Medicaid, but it remains true that simply by growing older one places himself ever more securely in the "why bother?" category for comprehensive health care. We would like to mention here just one recent example of the continued disinterest in elderly patients and its possible implications for medical treatment.

A major university in one of our southwestern states developed an educational program in gerontology in close cooperation with the federal government. It was recognized that virtually no formal educational or training experiences were being provided for physicians in this part of the country to familiarize them with new developments in the care of elderly men and women. It was apparent that informal educational experiences concerned with this topic were also minimal.

Accordingly, a short, intensive conference was arranged. Leading medical specialists in the field of geriatrics, top-ranking physicians eminent in other fields and several experts from related disciplines were invited to introduce southwestern physicians to current developments in diagnosis and care of the aged. To enhance the attractiveness of this program, it was arranged that formal educational credits be awarded to those who attended the conference. Approximately 8,000 invitations were sent to physicians in the area served by the geriatric educational center. The number of acceptances received? Fourteen. There were about as many specialists preparing to participate in the program as there were physicians willing to learn about geriatric care. The conference was never held. (This is not as singular an example as one might think—physicians generally make themselves very scarce at programs intended to acquaint them with geriatric care.) One cannot help but wonder about the 8,000 physicians who turned down this opportunity to up-date their knowledge in an area of increasing public and scientific concern. On what basis, with what background of knowledge, do they prescribe for their elderly patients?

Why is it that some physicians do not keep up with new developments?

1. Obviously, most physicians are extremely busy.
2. If they were to leave their practices, even for a short time, other physicians would have to cover for them.
3. Many physicians have not studied in a formal sense for years and are loathe to return to the classroom, or otherwise return to a student role.
4. Some older practitioners may fear that they can no longer learn efficiently or "compete" with younger colleagues.

5. Income would probably be reduced during the study period.

These are some of the conscious reasons. None of them presents an insurmountable problem. For example:

1. A rotating coverage system undoubtedly could be arranged so that physicians could take turns studying.
2. Every profession has some unpleasant, difficult, or tedious aspects. But if continuing education programs were required as a routine and universal matter, they eventually would come to be seen not as an unusual imposition, but simply as a necessary part of the work.
3. Appropriate orientation to and presentation of course material could dispel the fear of having one's ignorance exposed, or of being placed in the student role one associates with his medical school days. (However, if one literally *cannot* learn new information and techniques, should he be allowed to continue practicing?
4. A tax deduction or credit arrangement or some other sort of financial arrangement probably could be made to cover the study period.

There are undoubtedly many other alternatives. The point is that none of the objective problems is insurmountable if the intention to safeguard human lives is strong enough to overcome the force of inertia and convenience.

There are also some factors that are less objective and concrete which lead some physicians actually to oppose efforts at continued education. We must return again to the attitudinal realm:

· *The physician in solo practice functions more or less independently.* He is accustomed to being master of his own fate, as well as other people's. Therefore, he may resent what he considers to be interference in *his* business, and being directed from without. The fact is, of course, that if *his* business entails responsibility for the lives of other people, then it is really *everybody's* business.

• *The physician is often considered to be omniscient.* It is not surprising that some physicians themselves have become convinced of this by dint of continued exposure to "the doctor knows what should be done" attitude. People generally expect the physician to have the answers to their problems, and he "comes through" often enough to allow the public to maintain its serene view. Therefore, after being the local expert for 20 years or so, it may be difficult for him to accept the fact that he may actually have fewer of the answers than does a younger man only four or five years out of medical school. It may seem to him that a return to the classroom is a tacit admission, to himself and to others, that he is deficient in some ways. This possibility may be inconsistent with his self-concept as the wise, all-knowing counselor. For the same reasons, there are physicians who also resent what they consider to be impertinent questions from laymen. For example, a patient may seek information and clarification beyond that which the physician has seen fit to provide spontaneously. This request irks the physician for several reasons, but among these may be the fear that in providing this information he is weakening his mystique and exposing himself to potential embarrassment and disgrace should he be mistaken.

A number of factors have been mentioned: the difficulty of keeping up with new advances in medicine, physicians' attitudes toward themselves and their patients, and the patient's right to protection from ignorance and obsolescent techniques. These factors can interact in many ways to influence the quality and outcome of treatment.

Physicians were surveyed about the ways in which patients "bug" them. The second most frequent complaint concerned "patients who challenge the au-

thority of the physician" (176). It is often the case that we become most defensive and emotionally upset when challenged in areas in which we feel most insecure. What specific challenges does the physician most resent? Here is one example: "The patient who listens to friends, grandma, *Reader's Digest, Ladies Home Journal*, and *Good Housekeeping* but not to me" (177). It is understandable that the physician would rather not have to deal with the confused thinking which might result from a patient's exposure to half-truths. But patient education is one of the physician's functions and thus it is less understandable that he should object to patients' reading about health care. Articles in many popular magazines today are well researched and accurate. Could the physician be afraid that the patient will raise questions he cannot answer? Wouldn't a well-informed public be the physician's best ally?

Consider the following account which is of particular interest in light of the physicians' complaint quoted above:

A young child with celiac disease was being treated with a low fat diet by her physician. For a couple of weeks, Laurie held her own. But then her condition deteriorated markedly. As Thanksgiving neared, her "skin was shriveled, her appetite was fading, and her day was one long day of nausea" (178). Since the child had been put on a low fat, high protein and carbohydrate diet, her mother wrote to *Good Housekeeping* magazine for recipes. She also asked for any additional assistance it could provide: "Please help me if you can. I'm not expecting miracles, but I can't bear to watch her body keep wasting away and not do anything about it." Hazel Schoenberg, the dietician connected with the magazine was appalled—not merely by the letter's contents, but by one crucial omission. "Most of the progress in coping with celiac . . . has been made in the last twenty years. The breakthrough came when the disease was recognized as an enzyme defect—that is, essentially an allergy to gluten. . . . I suspected that what the child was getting was the treatment that was known twenty-five years ago." The mother reacted to this information: "I almost flipped. . . . I was killing my daughter with pretzels and ignorance" (179). What was her doctor doing? To his credit, a telephone call to the physician resulted in an appointment with a pediatrician. When seen, the child was so ill that she was given only a fifty-fifty chance to survive. But she did.

Also encouraging is the story about a small-town youngster who was born with a heart defect (180). Her parents had been told it was hopeless to consult a heart surgeon since the kind of surgery needed had never been performed on a child under three years of age. On their way out of the house on their "last" trip to the hospital ("If you want to see your child alive, you better come down right away"), the parents took a magazine out of the mailbox. The cover featured an article entitled "New Miracles of Baby Surgery." After reading this account of recent advances in cardiac surgery, the father spoke to the physician. He knew his baby was already dying. He "pleaded for surgery. . . . *He was warned against journalism's and surgery's perils.*" [Italics ours.] But the father persisted. The baby underwent surgery at a hospital some distance away where the surgeons had mastered the latest techniques, and appropriate facilities were available. The child is alive and well.

These examples argue both for an informed public, and for mandatory continuing education for physicians. Some people may balk at the latter suggestion. Physicians *could* continue to educate themselves voluntarily and individually by reading and informal discussions with colleagues and then formal courses would not be required. This method probably works for some physicians, but can it be relied upon? We doubt it. Indirect evidence supporting our skepticism is pro-

vided by the misuse of chloromycetin, mentioned above. It will be recalled that this antibiotic is an efficient bacteria killer, but sometimes causes fatal anemia. Physicians were educated about the danger of this drug informally:

In a current advertisement with one page of type, less than a quarter is devoted to recommending the drug, more than three-quarters to warnings about how not to use it. . . . Medical journals carry frequent accounts of severe anemia and deaths associated with chloromycetin. A fatality rate of fifty-eight percent has been reported among newborn infants treated for pneumonia or diarrhea—*despite the conspicuousness of the warnings, said Dr. Dameshek [a leading hematologist] there is no evidence that prescribing physicians pay much heed.* [Italics ours.] This drug is often prescribed for common colds . . . and similar viral infections [for which no drug is of any use], and against many bacterial infections for which safer drugs are just as effective. . . . Dr. Dameshek reluctantly conceded that governmental restriction might be necessary (181).

Printed warnings are of limited value if prescribing physicians fail to read or heed them. Formal requirements may be the only way. Yet, as recently as 1968 there was only one state (Oregon) in which physicians were required by the state medical society to continue their education or face expulsion (182). It goes against the grain to yield part of one's autonomy for the purpose of safeguarding someone else's life.

Throughout this chapter, it has been shown that illness has some important aspects in common with suicide, murder, and accidents. One does not arrive at any of these gateways to death by "chance" alone. Much of our suffering and sometimes death itself are within our power to prevent or postpone. We have also demonstrated that socioeconomic and sociopsychological factors play a cardinal role in determining who comes down with what and who is treated—and how. Before concluding this section, we should like to suggest one additional point.

Professional people often warn novices against becoming "over-involved" with their patients or clients. But *under*-involvement is at least as grave a danger. The failure to identify with other humans (seen also as a factor in the chapters on suicide and accidents) may be at the root of many of the destructive attitudes that have been catalogued here. After several decades of emphasizing objectivity and non-involvement in medical care, there is still little or no evidence to demonstrate that this approach either saves lives or simplifies the task of the physician, nurse, or any others who are involved in the care of the sick. Enlightened self-interest, if nothing more, should ensure the humane treatment of human beings. The fact is that the helpers are precisely as human as those they help—and their roles may be interchanged at any time. Today's physician or nurse may be tomorrow's patient; today's patient may be tomorrow's teacher; today's teacher may be tomorrow's experimental subject; today's subject may be tomorrow's psychologist or psychiatrist. As we have seen in previous chapters, negative or "uninvolved" attitudes toward the ill and vulnerable tend to create a psychological booby trap into which the person who holds such attitudes eventually stumbles.

Who Recovers, and Why?

Granted all of the material cited above, the individual himself must accept an important share of the responsibility for the course of his illness and the outcome of its treatment. Sometimes the most crucial determinant affecting recovery is the point at which one decides that he is ill. It is not an "expert" who makes this decision, but the individual himself or a member of his family. Dramatic symptomatology (acute pain, loss of consciousness, hemorrhage, etc.) increases the likelihood that help will be sought. Yet even painful and ominous symptoms are shrugged off by some people. Failure or delay in seeking treatment can constitute lethal behavior.

Consider, for example, the study conducted by psychiatrists Harry S. Olin and Thomas P. Hackett. They interviewed and followed the hospital career of 32 patients with acute myocardial infarction. Most of these people had suffered severe pain. Yet the investigators found that "these patients do not immediately respond to severe and continuous chest pain by seeking medical help. On the contrary, the initial reaction to critical chest pain is to deny its seriousness" (183). Many of the patients preferred to place more trivial interpretations upon their symptoms ("indigestion" was the most popular self-diagnosis). Almost all the patients knew people who had sustained myocardial infarctions, and many had previous histories of heart trouble themselves. Nevertheless, it was typical to delay treatment. Their prior knowledge of the dangers of myocardial infarction did not seem to be of any benefit to them. Even when the patient had recognized the nature of his attack, he remained disposed to delay the call for medical assistance.

A forty-eight-year-old fisherman was awakened at three A.M. from a sound sleep by a "red-hot-poker pain" in his chest. He immediately thought 'in the back of his mind' that he was having a "heart attack" because his sister had sustained two previous myocardial infarctions with similar symptoms. Nevertheless, he refused to allow his wife to call a physician because it was "too early to wake the doctor" and instead drank quantities of water to quiet his stomach. Throughout the remainder of the night he was restless and in increasing pain. The next morning, six hours after his symptoms had commenced, he consented to be taken to the hospital (184).

How can a person recognize that his life is in great jeopardy and yet fail to take prompt action in his own behalf? Is social tact a potentially lethal characteristic if it leads a man to delay treatment because it is "too early to wake the doctor?" Or is it the need to remain an unflinching "he-man" that persuades some heart attack victims to belittle their pain and jeopardy? Perhaps, again, it is a wish to place the responsibility in the hands of another person. One kind of wife might call the physician immediately, disregarding her husband's reluctance, while another kind of wife might feel it was not appropriate to talk him into accepting medical care—and never make the call. It is evident that psychological factors have much to do with receptivity to treatment.

The decision that one is now "sick enough" to seek medical help is a function of sociopsychological as well as intra-psychic factors. Subgroup membership is one such factor. In some circles, people do not, or cannot, maintain a continuing relationship with a physician. They seek help only when *in extremis*. The hospital is used as a final, desperate attempt to keep the undertaker at bay. "Minor" problems such as mumps, measles, headaches, cramps, and sore throats are to be expected in this life, and therefore, not regarded as illnesses at all. Such assumptions and practices may protect the sufferer from the dangers of mistreatment or over-treatment occasionally, but they are probably more likely to expose him to serious complications that could have been avoided with timely medical care.

The opposite attitude—that every physical change or twinge is a fit subject for medical consultation—can prove just as dangerous, albeit by a less direct route. The insecure physician may be tempted to treat minor self-limiting ills. This will make the patient feel that "something is being done for him," and thus persuade him to leave the physician in peace. But the patient is also being exposed to the possible side effects that are a risk with virtually any kind of medication. Similarly, if a physician has become accustomed to finding nothing amiss with a hypochondriacal patient, he may unwittingly become a participant in a tale analogous to "The Boy Who Cried 'Wolf' ": After ten fruitless investigations of insignificant symptoms he may decline to pursue a new symptom that reflects a really serious disorder.

The patient may contribute even more directly to his own demise. Most physicians are well acquainted with the diabetic who cheats on his diet, the patient who "can't remember" to take his antibiotics, and the fellow who is so "busy" that he cannot make an appointment for the follow-up examination, or has such an "unpredictable" life that he is unable to keep the appointments he does make. The values and processes revealed by this behavior, and the functions that they serve have already been discussed in another connection. However, they may warrant repetition in the present context:

1. *Denial.* "I'm not really sick. That little pain isn't important."

2. *Isolation of self from others, and cause from effect.* "Other people develop cancer and pneumonia: I don't." "Just eating this second piece of cake can't be that harmful; it certainly doesn't *look* as if it has anything to do with that remote-sounding term, "diabetic coma."

3. *Maintenance of self-image.* "A tough, independent guy like me can't tell someone that I'm worried about a little bump. What would the doctor think of me? I'm not a coward or a nut who has to go running into the examination room for every little symptom."

4. *Distorted priorities.* "I hate to leave a party early. Who cares about a few dizzy spells, anyway?" "There isn't time to renew this prescription before I leave for my vacation . . . well, that can wait until I get back."

5. *Selective perception and selective forgetting.* "No, Doc, I never noticed that this old bruise wasn't healing" "Oops, guess I forgot to take my morning pills

again. But I'm still on my feet, so it can't matter very much."

This chapter has explored some of the ways in which psychological and social variables affect the individual's vulnerability to illness and his chances for recovery. Occasionally, we touched upon possible ways in which human factors could be turned to the protection instead of the destruction of human life. But how far might we go in the direction of protecting—or even increasing—the human lifespan by psychological and social means? This is the subject of the following chapter.

REFERENCES

1. Boring, E. G. *A history of experimental psychology.* (2nd ed.) New York: Appleton-Century-Crofts, 1950. Pp. 160-168.
2. Grinker, R. *Psychosomatic research.* New York: W. W. Norton, 1953. P. 19.
3. Dunbar, F. *Emotions and bodily changes.* New York: Columbia University Press, 1935.
4. Deutsch, F. Thus speaks the body. *Acta Medica Orientalia,* 1951, *10,* 67-86.
5. Alexander, F. & Selesnick, S. *The history of psychiatry.* New York: Harper & Row, 1966. P. 393.
6. *Ibid.*
7. *Ibid.,* pp. 393-394.
8. *Ibid.*
9. *Ibid.,* p. 394.
10. Ehrentheil, O. Common medical disorders rarely found in psychotic patients. *Archives of Neurology and Psychiatry,* 1957, 77, pp. 178-186.
11. *Ibid.,* p. 178.
12. *Ibid.,* p. 179.
13. *Ibid.,* p. 180.
14. *Ibid.,* p. 181.
15. *Ibid.,* p. 181-182.
16. *Ibid.,* p. 182.
17. *Ibid.,* p. 182-183.
18. *U.S. book of facts, statistics, and information for 1968.* (Officially published as *Statistical abstracts of the U.S.*). Washington D.C.: Department of Commerce, Bureau of the Census, (88th ed.), 1967.
19. White, P. D. *Heart disease.* (4th ed.) New York: Macmillan, 1967.
20. Friedberg, C. K. *Diseases of the heart.* (2nd ed.) Philadelphia: Saunders, 1962. P. 494.
21. White, *op. cit.*
22. *Ibid.,* p. 520-522.
23. Peete, D. C. *The psychosomatic genesis of coronary artery disease.* Springfield, Ill.: Charles C Thomas, 1955. P. 121.
24. White, P. D. *Clues in the diagnosis and treatment of heart disease.* Springfield Ill.: Charles C Thomas, 1956. P. 9.
25. Friedberg, *op. cit.,* p. 494.
26. Stamler, J. The relationship of sex and gonadol hormones to atherosclerosis. In M. Sandler and G. Bourne (Eds.), *Atherosclerosis and its origin.* New York: Academic Press, 1963. Pp. 241-242.
27. White, *op. cit.,* p. 529.
28. Levine, S. *Clinical heart disease.* (5th ed.) Philadelphia: Saunders, 1958. P. 97.
29. Stamler, *op. cit.,* p. 235.
30. Keys, A. The role of the diet in human atherosclerosis and its complications. In M. Sandler and G. Bourne (Eds.), *Atherosclerosis and its origin.* New York: Academic Press, 1963. P. 263.
31. White, *op. cit.,* p. 530.
32. Stamler, *op. cit.,* pp. 235-236.
33. *Ibid.*
34. *Ibid.*
35. *Ibid.*
36. Selye, H. *The stress of life.* New York: McGraw-Hill, 1956. P. 217.
37. Keys, *op. cit.,* p. 263.
38. *Ibid.,* p. 292.
39. Guthrie, E. R. *Psychology of human conflict.* New York: Harper, 1938.
40. Nelson, W. (Ed.) *Textbook of pediatrics.* (8th ed.) Philadelphia: Saunders, 1964. Pp. 1018-1019.
41. Seidman, T. & Albert, M. H. *Becoming a mother.* New York: Fawcett, 1956. P. 115.
42. *Time,* May 28, 1965. P. 46.
43. Friedberg, *op. cit.*
44. Selye, *op. cit.*
45. *Ibid.,* p. 3.
46. *Ibid.,* p. 127.
47. *Ibid.*
48. Mordkoff, A., & Parsons, O. The coronary personality: A critique. *Psychosomatic Medicine,* 1967, *29,* 9.
49. *Ibid.*
50. *Parade* magazine, *Boston Sunday Globe,* Jan. 29, 1967.
51. Block, H. *The Boston Globe,* April 2, 1968. Pp. 1 and 33.
52. *Ibid.*

53. Block, H. *The Boston Globe*, Feb. 12, 1968. Pp. 1 and 11.

54. *Ibid.*

55. Mordkoff & Parsons, *op. cit.*, p. 8.

56. *Ibid.*, p. 9.

57. Keys, *op. cit.*, p. 276.

58. *Time*, Feb. 23, 1968. P. 45.

59. Suzuki, S. *Science Newsletter.* November 13, 1965, *88*, 313.

60. *Ibid.*

61. Weyer, E. M. (Ed.) Psychophysiological aspects of cancer. *Annals of the New York Academy of Sciences*, 1966, v. 125, art. 3. Pp. 773-1055.

62. Rosebury, T. *Life on Man.* New York: Viking Press, 1969.

63. Breuer, J., & Freud, S. *Studies in hysteria.* (Translated by A. A. Brill.) New York: Nervous and Mental Diseases Pub. Co., 1936.

64. White, R. *The abnormal personality.* New York: Ronald Press, 1948. P. 427.

65. *Parade* magazine, *Boston Sunday Globe*, Jan. 7, 1968.

66. *Science Newsletter*, Aug. 28, 1965, 88.

67. Hackett, T. P., & Weisman, A. D. "Hexing" in modern medicine. *Proceedings of Third World Congress of Psychiatry*, 1961, Vol. 2, pp. 1249-1252.

68. Snell, J. E. Hypnosis in the treatment of the hexed patient. *American Journal of Psychiatry*, 1967, *124*, 27.

69. *Ibid.*, p. 68.

70. Steckert, E. Unpublished archival materials. Urban Folklore Library. Detroit, Mich.: Wayne State University.

71. Zola, I. K. Culture and symptoms: An analysis of patients' presenting complaints. Department of Sociology, Brandeis University, Waltham, Massachusetts, mimeo.

72. Veblen, T. *The theory of the leisure class.* New York: New American Library, 1953.

73. Pillsbury, D., Shelley, W., & Kligman, A. *Dermatology.* Philadelphia: Saunders, 1956. Pp. 305, 815.

74. *Time*, May 12, 1967. P. 65.

75. *Parade* magazine, *Boston Sunday Globe*, July 9, 1967.

76. Block, H. & Cobb, C. Overweight. Part 4. *Boston Globe*, Jan. 5, 1967.

77. *Ibid.*

78. Block, H. & Cobb, C. Overweight. Part. 1. *Boston Globe*, Jan. 2, 1967.

79. *Ibid.*

80. Davis, L. (Ed.) *Christopher's textbook of surgery.* (8th ed.) Philadelphia: Saunders, 1965. Pp. 89-90.

81. Sonia Lazanska Robinson. Personal communication.

82. *Time*, Aug. 28, 1964. P. 39.

83. *The world almanac and book of facts, 1968.* New York: Newspaper Enterprise Assoc., Inc., 1968. P. 489.

84. *Boston Globe*, Sept. 22, 1968. P. 42.

85. *U. S. book of facts, op. cit.*, p. 59.

86. Sadoun, R., Lolli, G., & Silverman, M. *Drinking in French culture.* New Brunswick, N. J. Rutgers Center of Alcohol Studies, 1965. P. 42.

87. Lolli, G., Serianni, E., Golder, G., Balboni, C. & Marianni, A. Further observations on the use of wine and other alcoholic beverages by Italians and Americans of Italian extraction. *Quarterly Journal of Studies on Alcohol*, 1953, *14*, 395-405.

88. Ullman, A. D. Attitudes and drinking customs. In *Mental health aspects of alcohol education.* Washington, D.C.: USPHS, 1958. Pp. 7-13.

89. *Parade* magazine, *Boston Sunday Globe*, May 26, 1968.

90. Johnson, G. *The pill conspiracy.* New York: The New America Library, 1967. Pp. 9-10.

91. *Time*, Jan. 6. 1967. P. 22.

92. Huxley, A. *Brave new world.* New York: Harper, 1950.

93. *Time*, Oct. 13, 1967. P. 77.

94. *Ibid.*

95. *Boston Globe*, March 20, 1967.

96. *Boston Globe*, Oct. 26, 1967.

97. *U.S. News and World Report*, Oct. 9, 1967. P. 6.

98. *Time*, Aug. 11, 1967. P. 60.

99. *Parade* magazine, *Boston Sunday Globe*, Jan. 22, 1967. P. 4.

100. Henderson, J. G. Denial and repression as factors in the delay of patients with cancer presenting themselves to the physician. In: Psychophysiological aspects of cancer. *Annals of the New York Academy of Science*, 1966, *125*, pp. 856-864.

101. Kastenbaum, R. Training for work with the aged and dying. NIMH project MHO-4818. Framingham, Mass.: Cushing Hospital, 1963-1968.

102. Goldfarb, A. The psychodynamics of dependency and the search for aid. In R. A. Kalish (Ed.), *The dependencies of old people.* Ann Arbor, Mich.: Institute of Gerontology, 1969. Pp. 1-16.

103. *Boston Globe*, Dec. 3, 1967

104. *Detroit News*, Dec. 18, 1968. P. B 15.

105. *Boston Globe*, July 19, 1967. P. 9.

106. *Boston Globe*, March 31, 1968.

107. "Facts and figures." American Cancer Society, 1968.

108. *Boston Globe*, Dec. 15, 1967.

109. *Boston Globe*, April 23, 1968.

110. *Ibid.*

111. *Ibid.*

112. Katz, D. Unmet medical needs found at six schools. *Detroit Free Press*, June 6, 1971. Pp. 1 and 4.

113. *Boston Globe*, April 23, 1968.
114. *Ibid.*
115. Glaser, V. *Boston Globe*, Nov. 23, 1967. P. 41.
116. *Ibid.*
117. *Boston Globe*, Oct. 3, 1967.
118. *Ibid.*
119. *Boston Globe*, Jan. 11, 1969.
120. *Boston Globe*, Feb. 8, 1968. P. 16.
121. *Boston Globe*, Dec. 17, 1967.
122. *Boston Globe*, Feb. 8, 1968. P. 16.
123. *Boston Globe*, Nov. 13, 1967.
124. Brotman, H. *Who are the aged: A demographic view.* Ann Arbor, Mich.: Institute of Gerontology, 1968.
125. Kastenbaum, R. The interpersonal context of death in a geriatric hospital. Presentation at annual meetings of The Gerontological Society, Minneapolis, Minn., 1965.
126. Hirsch, C. & Kent, D. P. Preliminary report of research project. College Station, Penn.: Pennsylvania State University, Department of Sociology and Anthropology.
127. Black aging. Whole issue of *Aging and Human Development*, 1971, 2, No. 3. Westport, Conn.: Greenwood Periodicals, Inc.
128. *AMA News*, Oct. 28, 1968. P. 5.
129. *Time*, June 30, 1967, p. 44.
130. *Boston Globe*, Jan. 5, 1969, p. 48.
131. *Boston Globe*, Dec. 1, 1968.
132. *Boston Globe*, Nov. 24, 1968.
133. *Ibid.*
134. 99% collections with a judge's help. *Medical Economics*, Oct. 14, 1968.
135. Internists step up their economic pace. *Medical Economics*, July 22, 1968.
136. Doctors' earnings dissected. *Medical Economics*, Dec. 9, 1968.
137. Duff, R., & Hollingshead, A. *Sickness and society.* New York: Harper & Row, 1968.
138. Pines, M. Hospital—enter at your own risk. *McCall's*, May 1968, p. 138.
139. *Ibid.*, p. 141.
140. *Ibid.*, p. 79.
141. *Ibid.*, p. 139.
142. *Ibid.*
143. *Ibid.*
144. Kasper, A. M. The doctor and death. In H. Feifel (Ed.), *The meaning of death.* New York: McGraw-Hill, 1959. Pp. 259-270.
145. LeShan, L., & LeShan, E. Psychotherapy and the patient with a limited life span. *Psychiatry*, 1961, 24, pp. 318-323.
146. Pines, *op. cit.*, p. 79.
147. *Pediatric News*, Sept., 1968, p. 16.
148. *Ibid.*, p. 44.
149. *Ibid.*, p. 62.
150. Brann, B. M. Unconscious motivation in medication errors. *Mental Hospitals*, 1965, 16, pp. 348-351.
151. *Boston Globe*, Feb. 5, 1969, p. 1.
152. *Boston Globe*, March 17, 1968, p. 70.
153. Bockoven, J. S. Aspects of geriatric care and treatment: Moral, amoral and immoral. In R. Kastenbaum (Ed.), *New thoughts on old age.* New York: Springer, 1964. Pp. 213-228 (quoted, pp. 220-221).
154. *Ibid.*, p. 220.
155. *Time*, Feb. 17, 1967, p. 75.
156. *Ibid.*
157. *Ibid.*
158. *Boston Globe*, Oct. 14, 1968.
159. *Ibid.*
160. Buffaloe, W., Johnson, A., & Sandiber, M. Total dosage of chlorpromazine and ocular opacities. *American Journal of Psychiatry*, 1967, 124, p. 250.
161. Nigio, Samuel. Toxic psychosis due to diphenhydramine hydrochloride. *Journal of the American Medical Association*, 1968, 203, p. 302.
162. *Ibid.*
163. Miller, E., Harrell, E. L., & Stokes, J. B. Gross hematuria as a complication in combination use of psychotropic drugs. *American Journal of Psychiatry*, 1967, 124, pp. 133-136.
164. *Time*, Feb. 16, 1968, p. 74.
165. *Ibid.*
166. *Boston Globe*, May 22, 1968.
167. *Consumer Reports*, Aug., 1966, p. 413.
168. Bagdikian, B. The battle to make drugs safer for you. *Good Housekeeping*, Nov., 1966.
169. *Consumer Reports*, *op. cit.*
170. *Ibid.*
171. *Ibid.*, p. 415.
172. Bagdikian, *op. cit.*, p. 283.
173. *Boston Globe*, May 22, 1968.
174. Block, H. *Boston Globe*, April 1, 1968.
175. Marley, F. *Science News Letter*, July 3, 1965.
176. Marks, G. What bugs you about your patients? *Physician Management*, July, 1968.
177. *Ibid.*, p. 31.
178. Levy, A. Good Housekeeping helps save a life. *Good Housekeeping*, July, 1966.
179. *Ibid.*
180. Levy, A. We were in a mood for miracles. *Good Housekeeping* magazine, Sept. 1966, p. 10.
181. *Time*, Feb. 16, 1968, p. 74.
182. *Medical World News*, July 5, 1968, p. 14.
183. Olin, H. S., & Hackett, T. P. The denial of chest pain in 32 patients with acute myocardial infarction *Journal of the American Medical Association*, 1964, 190, 977-981.
184. *Ibid.*, p. 979.

16

Looking Ahead

And then . . . what?

The prospect of death both teases and frustrates our sense of futurity. Death is that point in time when our personal time ceases. Who could be curious about anything, and not be curious about death? The when - where - why - how draws our thoughts forward—although an instant of such contemplation may suffice to send us reeling backward in confusion and disarray. Even the most ardent non-facer of death must peek around the corner occasionally to assure himself that what "really isn't there" still really isn't there.

Beyond the attraction-repulsion dynamics of death as the terminus of futurity is the quest to understand what comes next. To say that what comes next is "nothing" or "something else" is seldom an adequate response. There are opinions, beliefs and speculations aplenty. But there is no precedent for personal death in our own experience. What does nothingness or something-elseness mean to *us* who have always been just "something" (ourselves) as long as we can remember? From a strictly logical view, perhaps, the question should not even be raised. What we call death implies the cessation of what we call time. Period.

Yet, as noted earlier in this book, the image of death seems to conjure up the image of birth, and vice versa. Finding ourselves at a starting place, we wonder about the finish line; learning about the end of a phenomenon, we wonder about its origins. Psychologically, "what comes next" will probably remain a relevant question. Having invented futurity, man also seems to have developed an urge to see beyond the limits imposed by his own logico-lingual systems.

In this final chapter we attempt to probe the future relationship between man and death. This could prove as inconclusive as the effort to see beyond our personal demise. However, it does seem worthwhile to draw selectively upon what has already been presented on these pages with the aim of stimulating and guiding our expectations. Special attention is given, wherever possible, to future contingencies over which we might exert some control. As we have all had something to do with the making of the past and present, perhaps we will also have some influence on the future.

This is not an exercise in fantasy-spinning (at least, it is not intended as such). Entertaining, provocative—and perhaps accurate—visions of the future shape of the world and its inhabitants have been contributed by a number of writers. We do not turn away completely from seemingly "far out" possibilities; some cannot be ignored even in a brief chapter. But our focus is on the possible relevance of psychological knowledge for man's future relationship to death.

THE CHANGING FACES OF DEATH

From the Inside Out

When we considered death as a thought (Chapter 2) it was necessary to concentrate upon patterns of cognitive development in the individual. Not much was said about the sociocultural context, although implications were strewn about for those who wished to find them. A special facet of the subject was explored further in our discussion of the personification of death (Chapter 6). While some attention was given to cross-cultural comparisons we did not pause to emphasize the influence of social environment upon death cognitions. Let us do so now.

It is obvious that the individual's cognitions of death are related to the world he lives in. Less obvious are the specific processes by which each person influences and is influenced by the death system in which he participates (Chapters 8 and 9). What eventually evolves as the adult's orientation toward death most likely has its origins in the infant's earliest transactions with the world. Separation experiences tutor the young child in his basic lesson: he is an individual—and that means to be alone and vulnerable. To what extent do differences in death orientation among adults show the mark of variations in child-rearing practices, including the frequency and context of separations? Separation experiences comprise only one aspect of the total process; yet this aspect is sufficient to remind us that cross-cultural differences (and generational differences within the same culture) might be related to important variations in death cognitions and attitudes. The transactional nature of the process should not be underestimated. Imagine a generation of children who grow up with a pervasive sense of insecurity, with supersensitivity to the fragility and precariousness of life, or with a very limited sense of being a human intrinsically related to other humans. Assume that these orientations developed either directly or indirectly in association with separation experiences (including emotional estrangement). Would we expect these children, on attaining adulthood, to have a similar orientation toward futurity, the value of life, and other death-relevant topics? We would be on firmer ground to anticipate that their special views of life and death would have a series of impacts upon the cultural milieu in which they function. Changelings themselves, they would change the death system.

Similar propositions could be formulated around other aspects of the total process within which death cognitions develop. We proposed earlier, for example, that perceptions of death contribute to subsequent conceptions. How many deaths does a child witness? Where do they take place? What is his relationship to these deaths? How is he expected to feel and behave? There are profound objective differences in the early death perceptions of, let us say, a child in Vietnam and one in Grosse Pointe Shores. Perhaps even less profound objective differences result in differences that are profound subjectively.

There is a reason for dwelling upon this matter. To consider the future shape of our relationship to death it is necessary to have some idea of the many dimensions along which change might take place. Whatever trends in our society affect who spends how much time with a child (and how this time is spent) may alter the coming generation's view of life and death—which, in turn, will alter the death system. The same may be said of those trends which affect the type and number of deaths that are available to be witnessed by young children. Prolonged separation of young fathers from their children, as required by military obligations or encouraged by the peculiarities of welfare regulations, are examples of the former. The violence content of television may be taken as a familiar example of the latter point.

Let us focus now upon one aspect of the total process that may be of particular value in foretelling change. We have in mind the individual's tendency to seek a relationship between his inner feelings and what passes for objective reality. External influences are at work upon us, early and continuously, as already acknowledged. But for our part, we often seem to be working from inside out. If a strong sentiment stirs within us, why, there must be something out there which confirms, endorses, or in some way bears a clear relationship to what we experience. The ancient proclivity for attributing human purposes and characteristics to celestial bodies is one testament to this tendency; indeed, the physical sciences continued to speak of "attractions" and other anthropomorphic phenomena long after the heyday of the astrologist. (The recrudescence of interest in astrology in our own times is perhaps another testament to the vigorous impulse for seeking a relatedness between inner state and external, physicalistic phenomena). This process could be dismissed smugly as a species of pathological projection, but that would close off the fresh and open exploration this tendency deserves. To attempt the leap from solipsistic ferment to man's place in the spheres is no small step. One who has the long conceptual reach of a philosopher might write a book such as *Mind and Its Place in Nature* (1); the less original mind might settle for astrology or some other readily available gospel. In either case, one is attempting to place his own urges, fears, and hopes within a more universal and consensual framework.

" 'A Face,' " You Might Say, " 'Without a Face' "

The tendency to personify or personalize death has manifested itself in many societies, including our own. We have been making faces of death—perhaps that should be, making faces *at* death—for centuries. It seems reasonable to consider personification as one of man's basic strategies for establishing a relationship between his inner state of affairs and the universe. Consideration of the process in general may help us to discern what is relatively distinctive in our contemporary image-making. This, in turn, may put us on the track to anticipating broad changes in our orientations toward life as well as death. Much of what is said on the following pages is speculative at this point in our knowledge.

Why do we personify death? We suggest that it is primarily a seeking after symmetry—a *psychobiological symmetry* with the external world. We think of death. A mass of feelings arises within us. These are intense, complex, shifting feelings, hard to fit into the verbal and conceptual categories that are made readily available by our culture. These feelings may also be difficult to integrate into our front-line personality structure.

Now it is intolerable to exist for very long in such a state of imbalance (or so we propose). How can all the pressure be within us? What is "out there" that might counterbalance our internal state? It is a situation akin to a response in search of its stimulus, or a would-be lover in quest of his potential mate. These analogies are not entirely frivolous. Death, as the absence of life, is a singularly empty stimulus. We know that death is around some place precisely because we cannot experience it as such. And the would-be lover knows a yearning that makes little sense were there not at least the possibility that the loved one exists. Forever to respond to an absent stimulus or to be in love without being in love with somebody are conditions that might be described as awkward at the least.

Objectivistic definitions of death do not invariably provide the external balance that is needed. There is not much emotional nourishment or cognitive support in biologically-oriented definitions. These austere and distant formulations do not give our feelings any place to go, except underground. What we need, at least at certain moments, is an external representation that can be visualized or actualized in an emotionally relevant form. And what could be more natural to our species than the anthropomorphic transformation of death? We can release and direct our feelings—do something with them—once symmetry has been established, once death has been cast into a humanoid form. We can try to "work on" Death by our favorite ploys and wiles, for example, or attempt to put our own feelings in order as we stand before his image.

At this point we re-introduce The Automaton (Chapter 6). This newcomer to the gallery of death images differs from his predecessors in that he himself seems to possess no emotional responsiveness, no point of view. The Automaton therefore deprives us of the opportunity for our own emotional expression. He appears to be a most unsatisfactory image. Consider, for example, his lack of sexuality. Each of the three traditional death images found in our study has his own sexual style. The Gay Deceiver does more than coat the bitter pill: he excites and lures us on with thinly veiled promises of fabulous enjoyment. Here we have the sexualization of curiosity and adventure. The Gentle Comforter offers a diffuse sensuality that makes few demands on its recipient. "There, there, child, take my hand; I will make you feel so contented and secure." It is the sexualization of dependency and surrender. Mr. Macabre exerts his own

form of sexual appeal as well—powerful, menacing, frightening because of what is demanded. One resists as though the victim of a freaky rapist, with a thrill of terror. By cold contrast, The Automaton offers no sexual relationship to his clients. Perhaps this should be modified to state that he offers no sexual relationship that is patterned after traditional human emotional exchanges.

Nevertheless, we suggest that The Automaton does have his function. He satisfies an emerging need in our cultural milieu that has made itself felt in some individuals rather in advance of the mainstream. The Automaton may be regarded as a transitional figure. Through him our society is attempting to represent, to externalize, to master the changing nature of our relationship to life and death. He represents the technology and mass processing that strips both our lives and our deaths of personal significance.

The Automaton is the funeral service that alienates both the deceased and the survivor through its routine, remote generalizations. He is the medical technology that relates to the dying man through his orifices while casting a calculating eye upon organs worth the detaching. He is the professional indoctrination that dulls our nerve endings so that human feeling gains neither entry nor exit while we remain captive within our roles. He is our scrap heap orientation toward the aged which leads a person to feel "as good as dead" while still on this side of the grave. He is the casual brutality of our cities. He is the war machine. These phenomena are within us as well as in our environment. With a growing sense of discomfort one notes that The Automaton begins to resemble that familiar face of Death who gazes back at us from the mirror.

To feel at home in our changing world it is no longer adequate to identify with angels or devils, saints, sinners, or heroes. It is becoming difficult enough to identify with men and women. *In representing Death as The Automaton we are perhaps beginning the long psychic task of identifying with the computerized robot-world that is taking shape around us.* The earliest machines were patterned after the human body and human modes of functioning. Now we are confronted with the challenge of patterning ourselves after our own creations.

Personification of Death as The Automaton may thus serve a double purpose: we discover a contemporary image that resonates with those inward feelings about death that are most in touch with the modern world of bureaucracy and technology; we translate the new and disturbing quality of life into psychic terms. Let us dwell upon the first purpose a moment longer. Some of our thoughts and feelings about death can find their target or partner in the impersonal Automaton. Have we ever become persuaded, even for a brief time, that life is meaningless? If so, then in The Automaton we may sense the external representation of meaningless death. There may be a certain stubborn element of human creativity here. To establish a relationship between two points is, in effect, to establish a relationship that has some iota of meaning. "I feel that life is not worth living. He indicates that death is not worth dying. We have something in common. My feelings do have some relationship to the external world, after all. Although I do not find the meaning I would choose to find, it is, in a sense, comforting to feel that the world goes along with my judgment. I am not totally abandoned even in abandonment."

The other purpose of The Automaton also invites further exploration. This image may serve as a symmetry-establishing relationship between ourselves and the shapes of life and death to come. We intuit, some of us more than others, that in years ahead we may be turning life and death off and on in unprecedented ways. Conception, abortion, euthanasia, suicide, murder, life-extension and life-interpolation may be selectively phased in or out

as seem to be required by the managers of our society. Life/death management (probably under some new euphemism) may become as familiar as efforts toward a planned economy, may in fact, become a phase of total socioeconomic planning. Our current "hang-ups" and conflicts on this topic could recede into history as naive, petty, and quaint.

By imaging The Automaton, then, we may be preparing ourselves for what is to come. (This proposition could apply as well to conceptions of The Automaton that are not directly related to death.) We are suggesting that mental and emotional preparations are already taking place within some of us at psychological levels that are not entirely obvious. In part, this is a task of catching up with changes and situations for which we were not well prepared in the beginning. But it is also possible that these psychic brewings eventually may take us far beyond this limited goal. Having once established some sort of emotional balance with the emerging quality of modern life, we may be in the position to modify both our own orientation and its referents in the world around us. The Automaton himself is likely to be only a transitional figure. Some of us find this image useful as an element in organizing and eventually reorganizing our relationship to the inner and outer world.

It is possible, nevertheless, that some of us will approach an emotional identification with The Automaton. Those who develop such an identification may achieve an attentuation of sorrow and anxiety. One would not feel insulted, attacked, reduced, or alienated when the death system goes to work on him. One would have no feelings about what becomes of one's remains or those of one's friends and relations, how the funeral services are conducted, what is done to one's body as one lies dying or, for that matter, what use is made of one's energies and body while still in health. Such a person would have transcended the attitude of those death professionals who conceive the cessation of life in completely objectivistic terms. He would have become himself an objectivistic servo-organism, feeling no particular attachment to a life which ends in so inconsequential a death.

Many questions come to mind. Is depersonalization and automatization a significant part of the psychological situation in some people who seem extraordinarily careless with both their own lives and the lives of others? Will the growing inclusion of robots in children's entertainment fare (television cartoons, for example) stimulate their subsequent ability to integrate the humanoid with the humane? Can the human mind so transform the image of The Automaton, given some time and the freedom for misadventures, that both the psychic and the external will change much for the better? Most of us are not automatons—yet. And it is conceivable that even The Automaton can be transformed like creative clay by his clay-footed creator, man.

In the foregoing discussion we seized upon The Automaton as a focal point largely because he is specific, heuristic, and has a basis in empirical research. It was not our intention to overemphasize the significance of personifications as such, although we may have been guilty of doing so in compensation for their relative neglect. Our more general intent was to call attention to the dynamic relationship between our psychic orientation toward death and our interpretation of the world around us. As we strive for a useful integration or balance, we may also be fashioning some of the psychosocial materials from which the future will unfurl.

DEATH: PRO OR CON?

It is only in recent times that man has acquired substantial potential mastery over both life and death. This trend is likely to continue unless our widely advertised capacity for "overkill" terminates all. For perspective on the present and future we turn first to an historical review.

The Prolongevity Tradition

The term *prolongevity* was introduced in 1966 by Gerald J. Gruman, a physician and historian. It is defined as "the significant extension of the length of life by human action" (2). Prolongevitism would be the advocacy of life-extension. Some of the results of Gruman's historical delvings are summarized in the following paragraphs.

Down through the centuries there have been people with very optimistic spirits— people willing to commit themselves to a high level of anti-death aspiration. Gruman describes one tradition as radical prolongevitism. "These thinkers were so optimistic that they foresaw a decisive solution to the problems of death and old age; they aimed at the attainment of virtual immortality and eternal youth" (3). Spread out along the time continuum, the radicals would include most Taoists of ancient China, many of the medieval Latin alchemists, and various individuals of later times.

Moderate prolongevitists have proposed the attainability of a limited increase in the length of life. The estimates range from a few additional years to several centuries. To qualify as a prolongevitist one must proclaim the possibility and advisability of an extension that goes clearly beyond what is already on the horizon. Prolongevity is thus a context-bound notion. As Gruman observes, "The average length of life has increased so strikingly during the past century that nearly anyone can foresee the possibility of a certain degree of further extension. All that is needed is something like the discovery of a more powerful drug against tuberculosis or the initiation of more effective measures to prevent automobile accidents or the extension of better medical facilities to Negro citizens, and one can envision life expectancy inching upwards. Without any radical innovation in science or philosophy, we can look forward to an increase in life expectancy beyond seventy years, gradually approaching but never reaching the life-span fixed at about one hundred ten years" (4). Today the idea of prolongevity is based on the possibility of breaking through the one-hundred-ten-year limit.

Both radical and moderate prolongevitists through the years have emphasized that the bonus time should be available to a person who still has the ability to make good use of it. Gruman denies that prolongevitists, either historically or at the present time, are indifferent to the quality of life. Few thoughtful people would argue for the increase of useless or agonized life. "The overly-competitive, sometimes-senile type who scans obituary columns in the search for a morbid feeling of superiority in out-living his contemporaries is no hero in prolongevity literature" (5). It is not incidental, therefore, that the prolongevity tradition has been linked closely with gerontology, the study of aging. A longer life is attractive only if the infirmities often associated with advanced age can be avoided or minimized.

Gruman points out that the prolongevity quest has deep roots in the myths and legends of mankind. The Sumerian civilization, circa 3000 B.C., is thought to have originated or transmitted elements of the Gilgamesh epic. The death of his comrade filled Gilgamesh, the youthful king, with the dreadful realization of his own mortality. His fruitless efforts to attain immortality are chronicled; scheme after scheme is explored in vain. Although the epic concludes with his submission to the common human destiny, Gilgamesh clearly represents a powerful determination to preserve life beyond its normal limits.

It is possible to interpret the antediluvian theme as a source of encouragement for prolongevitists. The notion that people once did enjoy much longer life-spans than what are known today is exemplified by the ages attributed, in the Book of Genesis, to patriarchs who lived before the flood. Gruman lists ten men whose ages ranged from Enoch's 365 years to the 969 years of Methuselah. But Greek and Roman historical traditions and a number of so-called primitive peoples have also promulgated the theme that their ancestors formerly had the ability to live exceptionally long lives. Gruman notes that the same "evidence," such as it is, could also be interpreted as indicating the present impossibility of prolongevity. There was a golden age when man was beloved of God, but that was long, long ago. Visions of a second golden age, a paradise on an earth where death would have no dominion, have persisted throughout the years, at times exerting much appeal. The myth of an original golden age is, of course, requisite for belief in its reinstatement.

Encouragement for the prolongevitists through the centuries has often come through the dissemination of reports that supernormal life-spans actually were in effect contemporaneously. Where? Some place else—as far away and little known as possible. This is what Gruman terms the hyperborean theme, after the Greek legend which proclaimed the existence of a fortunate people who enjoy a remarkably long life beyond the north wind. Many other examples are cited, including the "Land of Youth" *(Tir na nog)* of the ancient Celts, a realm that offered a marvelous array of sensuous amenities as well as immunity from aging and death.

Well before the present time, however, the hyporborean legends began to suffer from the inroads of geographical exploration. As fewer locales remained beyond the cartographer's and explorer's province, so fewer hiding places remained for prolongevitist fantasies. But it is interesting to be reminded by Gruman that such legends provided much of the motivating force behind geographical explorations in the first place. In our own century the hyperborean theme is still to be found in fiction (James Hilton's *Lost Horizon* (6) is a notable example.)

According to Gruman, there is one other main theme within prolongevity: the fountain. Juan Ponce de Leon's adventures may be the best known example of the fountain theme to most of us, but numerous other illustrations are provided. The legend has been traced back at least as far as the ancient Hindu Pool of Youth and the Hebrew River of Immortality. The latter seemed to offer perpetual life on earth but without the guarantee of renewed youth and vigor. The notion of a fountain or some other form of miraculous water may be the most important but is not the only manifestation of the belief in a substance with the property of conferring extended life. Gruman differentiates these into divine, magical, and empirical substances. The fruit of the "Jambu" tree has supernatural or divine powers; it is a form of sympathetic magic that transfers the rejuvenative powers of the snake by preparing a brew from its skin; and an herb that proves empirically to heal a particular illness may generate belief in an ultimate cure-all from the right combination of herbs and roots.

We cannot pursue here the account Gruman offers of historical attempts to actualize prolongevitism. But it is relevant to mention that much which later would emerge as science seemed to have its origins in the quest to extend the human life span. Proto-scientific work of the ancient Taoists encompassed such areas as nutrition, exercise, and sexual practice. It is true that "science," in the modern sense of the term, was a long time in coming. It is also true that the prolongevitist quest went far beyond the realm of knowledge-seeking, and exerted great influence on the cultural milieu in general. Yet some of the credit for developing the full range of science seems to belong to those who were motivated by the prolongevity ideal. Modern medicine and the

whole concept of experimental science obviously owe something to the medieval alchemists. Gruman avers that "alchemy contributed the major part of the techniques and materials for the beginnings of modern chemistry; the prolongevitist school was involved particularly in the development of distillation techniques and the chemical uses of alcohol and the mineral acids. In medicine, the alchemy of long life led, through the work of John of Rupescissa and Paracelsus, to the rise of iatrochemistry, which, in turn, was the early antecedent for the biochemistry and chemotherapy of our own time" (7).

The Opposition

The historical background sketched above has implications for the future. Mankind has long quested for the delay or defeat of death. Perhaps today we are on the verge of the necessary biotechnological breakthroughs; at least, this prospect is one that may deserve consideration in view of current scientific developments. But history has more to teach us before we proceed. Those who were looking after this planet before we came on the scene did not invariably advocate life-prolongation. It is not simply a case of "We have always wanted to avoid death, and now the means may be closer at hand." Ambivalence and conflict are part of our heritage.

Although himself to be numbered among contemporary prolongevitists, Gruman does justice to the historical opposition. For every prolongevity myth and legend one can come up with its antithesis, or the same tale can be so interpreted. The legend of Tithonus, for example, dates back to the seventh or eighth century before Christ. Zeus was prevailed upon to bestow immortality upon this young man who was beloved by Eos, daughter of the dawn. Unfortunately, Eos neglected to ask for her lover's perpetual youth as well. Eventually old age began to press upon Tithonus . . . and pressed, and pressed, and pressed. Depending upon which version of the legend one prefers, Tithonus remains alive today in the most pitiful situation imaginable, or was subsequently transformed into a grasshopper.

The opposition to prolongevity (termed "apologism" by Gruman) has often been found within the same ideologies that also have a life-extension component. In summarizing the various strands of apologism Gruman finds six major themes:

1. Human nature is so defective that prolongevity could not be attained or, if attained, could not be used wisely. These defects include sinful taints such as power or sexual lust, and other miscellaneous failings, e.g., forgetfulness, lack of persistence.

2. Prolongevity would violate the natural order. This position necessarily assumes that there is a natural order, that it is known, and that it should or must remain as established.

3. The divine order would be violated by prolongevity. Cited as especially influential here is the passage in the Psalms, "The years of our life are three score and ten," interpreted as a moral fixity rather than a neutral probability statement.

4. Original sin rules out the possibility of prolongevity. The emphasis is upon human guilt as the cause of aging and death. The Adam and Eve story has received influential interpretations in this vein, notably by Augustine and Aquinas.

5. Prolongevity is undesirable from the standpoint of the individual himself. This theme typically is found in conjunction with accounts of the miseries of old age. One avoids death only at the high price of unacceptable impairment.

6. Old age and death are positively desirable. Various sub-themes contribute to this contention. There is the religious valuation of death as the portal to a higher form of life, but also the arguments of Lucretius and Malthus that death is necessary to prevent over-population.

Counterpoint

We have been considering the pros and cons of death from a historical perspective that deals largely with culturally transmitted ideas and influences. However, it is hard to determine where the individual fits in. Historical perspective enables us to place the individual within his socio-intellectual context. Of itself, however, this approach does not tell us how the individual experiences his relationship to death, whether we are talking about past, present, or future epochs.

We can only guess. Our estimation is that while most people through history have sought to put distance between themselves and death, there has also been a continuing counterpoint of acceptance or welcome. Faced with the imminent prospect of death it is probable that most people will exert themselves to survive (including the man who has attempted suicide by hurling himself into the water from a high bridge). There are important exceptions (8). But when the quality of life is experienced as extremely bleak, disappointing, degrading, or threatening, then death may be viewed as an acceptable or even preferred alternative. Again, we cannot make the absolute statement just for the sake of providing a generalization. As has already been seen, stressful circumstances do not invariably lead to lethal behavior (Chapters 12-14), nor do all people who have certain life-situation dimensions in common show the same psychic orientation toward death (Chapters 2 and 3).

It is a reasonable hypothesis, but by no means a demonstrable conclusion, that whenever people were in great objective peril for their lives the desire to avoid death was heightened. We are thinking, for example, of medieval Europe with its diseases, famines, and wars as described earlier (Chapter 8). The macabre personification of death flourished in these times. One might say that Death loomed as a larger, more menacing figure than in our own times because he threatened the lives of "important" people as well as the aged and peripheral, and because his onslaught was so fierce as to jeopardize the survival of the family and the community.

It seems useful here to distinguish between prolongevity in the sense promulgated by Gruman and the urge to preserve the normal life-span from premature termination. The ploughman of fifteenth century Bohemia, for example, saw many of his loved ones die young. He may have desired a life-span for his family and himself that exceeded what was statistically probable in those days. Yet he was not necessarily asking for something incredible, something beyond the known span of years. Some people did survive to three-score-and-ten or beyond. It was the low probability of living out a full life-span that probably concerned him most. This does not mean that the ploughman necessarily would have been indifferent to the prospect of death even at the end of a reasonably long existence. He might also have been a prolongevitist in Gruman's sense.

The ploughman has already been given an opportunity to speak for himself. Johannes von Saaz, a notary and schoolteacher, authored a long prose poem around the turn of the fifteenth century that was cast in the form of a dialogue between the ploughman and Death (9). As a whole, this work illustrated what was suggested earlier about the personification of death as a means of externalizing and thus coming to grips with one's own feelings. The dialectic nature of the process is also made evident. Man and Death both have their say. Death is attacked and praised. Acceptance of Death is advocated, but so is resistance. Throughout the dialectic there is a gradual deepening or working inward. The ploughman is made to learn that it is his own character, his own soul that holds the key.

The tone of the dialogue can be illustrated from this mini-lecture by Death:

Drive the memory of love out of your heart, mind, and spirit, and you will at once be relieved of grief. As soon as you have lost something and cannot get it back, act as though it had never been yours, and at once your grief will flee away. If you will not do that, then you will have more sorrow to come. For after every child's death you suffer heartache, and so will they all, after your death, they and you, when you have to part from one another. You want their mother to be replaced for them. If you can bring back past years, and words that have been spoken and deflowered maidenheads, then you can restore their mother to your children. We have given you enough advice. Can you understand it, blockhead? (10).

The ploughman is appreciative of this advice, but not entirely swayed:

Your sayings are sweet and pleasant. I begin to see that now. But if joy, love, delight and mirth were driven from the world, then the world would be in a bad way. . . . If I were to drive from my mind the memory of my dear darling, evil memories would come back into my mind. With all the more reason will I always remember my beloved. Who can soon forget it when the heart's love is turned into a great heartache? Wicked people may do so, but dear friends think always of each other. Long roads and many years divide not love. Though she is dead to me in the body, yet she still lives on in my memory. Death, you must advise more sincerely if your advice is to be of any use. Otherwise, bat that you are, you must still endure the enmity of the birds (11).

A detailed commentary on *The Ploughman from Bohemia* would be interesting to develop. Here we will simply add a few remarks on the quoted passages.

1. The nub of the problem is in a human reaction—grief—rather than death itself. One should not be so antagonistic to death.

2. The cure for grief is available, but radical. One must excise his most precious memories. (This is consistent with advice offered in other passages to the effect that one ought not to grasp or possess.)

3. By further implication, time and development could not proceed were lives truly reversible. There must be death for life to exist as we know it.

4. Man protests that love is valuable and, in its way, immune to separation. The beloved lives on in memory. By implication: worse than the grief (which Death asserts is worse than death) would be the loss of love's memory.

In the end the ploughman finds solace and integration within his religious faith. It is fairly evident, however, that vital preparation for his new relationship to death had been accomplished through the probing dialogue.

The psychic counterpoint continues today. But there are some differences.

Boiling Point

The dialectic between prolongevity and its opposition moves forward today with new and powerful resources on each side. It might be said that the counterpoint is reaching its boiling point. Our actions and beliefs have more potent consequences for action than ever before. This includes varied levels of belief. Governmental policy and the values of the governed individuals may or may not coincide; within the individual there may be strong attitudes at more than one level of awareness. The intrapsychic dialectic is less obvious than some of the external developments, but it no longer seems appropriate to deny the close if not always predictable relationship. It might be easy to allow our attention to be drawn exclusively to large-scale problems and issues—war, overpopulation, medical breakthroughs, genetic discoveries, pollution, etc. But for those who have a psychological perspective to offer, this is a time to heighten our sensitivity to individual and group thinking. In our own minds the preparations are being made for actions that could initiate unprecedented developments for life and death.

Let us focus on the question: *Who* should be kept alive? Observations on this topic have already been made in this book (e.g., Chapter 15) and by many other writers. Our aim here is to illustrate the psychological complexities from which tomorrow's actions are likely to emerge.

The "who" question itself has many facets, although these are not usually identified as such. Those who would pursue the question thoroughly might find it useful to take the following into account:

1. *Directionality emphasis.* Is attention directed primarily to the prolongation of life or to the avoidance of death? It is by no means certain that these emphases have identical implications for action. The mixture of "pro-life"/"anti-death" sentiment deserves careful assessment and evaluation.

2. *Quantity.* In one sense, "who" can be translated into "how many." Some of us may be concerned chiefly with the number of people for whom survival should be especially safeguarded or promoted. The mirror image of this view, of course, is the specification of how many humans shall be regarded as expendable. The quantity dimension may be high or low in the hierarchy of life/death consideration for a particular individual or group. Determination of its priority value is one of the tasks awaiting future observers.

3. *Duration.* Gruman has divided the prolongevitists into "moderates" and "radicals." It may be that people who advocate a doubling of the present lifespan would be horrified at the prospect of immortality. Life-extension encompasses such a tremendous range of time (theoretically, at least) that the individual's particular view should be ascertained and understood.

4. *Fixed attributes.* Which people are "worth" keeping alive? Those who possess certain fixed attributes may be the desirable candidates (with the particular attributes varying, depending upon the belief

system of the perceiver). Fixed attributes would include family lineage, place of birth, and sex, for example. Individuals will differ with regard to which attributes they consider to be especially relevant, and which "side" of the attribute is to be certified as desirable.

5. *Contingent attributes.* Other people may give more weight to what a person has achieved or to his general circumstances apart from fixed characteristics. Educational and occupational achievement may be taken as examples here, but so may "being a good mother," "having a generous nature," etc. These attributes are contingent in that a person does not begin life with them or automatically become so endowed (although these attributes may be less contingent for some than others). Socioeconomic class is, in principle, a contingent attribute. It is a fixed attribute in the sense that one starts life within a particular stratum, but mobility is at least a possibility. If a person chooses to interpret a contingent attribute (e.g., socioeconomic status) as a fixed attribute in setting the survival priority of another person, then this is just one more factor to be taken into consideration.

6. *Transitional attributes.* Some of our characteristics change as a function of our position in life. Chronological age itself is the most powerful example of the attribute of transitivity. The person who has not yet reached a high priority developmental station may be regarded as relatively expendable. This attitude—which, in an extreme form, encompasses infanticide—is not unknown in our own culture. More familiar is the other side of the case. The person once valued as a prime candidate for continued survival may "outlive" this status. By growing old he may be seen as having "used up" the time he has coming to him. Theoretically this attitude should not extend to the more radical shores of prolongevitism. An old person should still be a reasonable candidate for long, long life or even immortality. It is questionable that the elderly are regarded

as good prospects for radical prolongevity, although they may be sound of mind and body. We will delve further into this topic in a moment.

7. *Conditionals.* Under what conditions would a person prefer continued life to death? It is not universally true that life is the preferred alternative. Homicide ("I prefer your death") and suicide ("I prefer my death") are among the more obvious examples. Surrender to hopelessness and disease have already been recognized. Although there are many scattered observations, systematic research on this topic remains to be done.

The seven sets of variables that have been enumerated and briefly described could be studied as though independent. In real life, however, they occur in combinations. How long, for example, should a lower-middle class, aged black woman live? And from whose perspective should the answer be given? Value problems aside for the moment, there is an urgent need to improve our understanding of the mental climates within which life-and-death propositions are being formed. This may become more evident if we impose a further restriction of focus.

Natural Death

Old age and "natural death" are concepts often found associated with each other. The disabilities afflicting an octogenarian may be offhanded as "just what you would expect with old age." Similarly, death is no more or less than the expected. If ever death is natural, it is in old age. And many of us do persist in using the concept of natural death, either explicitly or by implication. In our view, this is not only an outworn concept, but one fraught with danger.

The distinction between a "natural" and an "unnatural" death never was easy to defend in the face of logical analysis. One had to remain within a specialized framework to maintain this usage. These days it is increasingly tenuous to place a definitive qualifier upon "death," when this term itself is undergoing such intensive reexamination (12) (see also Chapter 4).

Despite the lack of sound logical or scientific underpinnings, a concept may still convey clear social meaning. But what does "natural death" convey? The message is obscure. Perhaps the most popular interpretation is that a "natural" death is one that is untainted by human hands ("murder most foul and unnatural"). Taking one's own life may be another example of unnatural death. But there is a growing conviction among students of suicide and related behaviors that *all* deaths involve significant psychosocial factors. In one way or another (usually in many ways) human thoughts, feelings, and actions are involved in all human deaths (13) (see also Chapters 10-15). The question has become: *how* did psychosocial factors influence the timing of death? All deaths, in this view, are equally "natural" or "unnatural." Presumably a death also would be "unnatural" if *delayed* by human intervention. The same considerations apply. Our decisions are continually changing the probabilities of death for ourselves and others, sometimes in one direction, sometimes in the other.

Yet the "natural death" concept does convey a message. We have decoded it as follows (14):

1. The death of an old person may strike us as natural in that *we* are not taken by surprise. Our own relative freedom from negative arousal is translated into the projection that the death itself was "natural." (This interpretation is consistent with the views developed regarding the logic and methodologic of death, Chapter 4.)

2. The verdict, "natural death" serves as a comforter to the survivors. There was nothing else that we might have done or should have done. And there is nothing more that really needs to be said on the subject. An aura of metaphysical or theological support hovers over the pronouncement.

3. The term comforts in another sense as well. Death of an elder is "natural" in that it bolsters our faith in the "natural order." An "inner monologue leads each of us to develop his own 'pecking order' of death. When the person with the highest death priority in our own pecking order does expire, then we experience a mixed reaction. We sorrow for his death according to the nature of our feelings toward him. But we also feel reassured. Death *is* behaving as It ought. We can depend upon Death to ignore us for a while longer. By contrast, what happens when Death reaches past the high priority entries? We are genuinely surprised, perhaps shocked, to learn that Death has come to a person whose 'turn' should have been remote. The death of a person who is as young and healthy as ourselves . . . is likely to fill us with apprehension. The facade of rationality has been pierced, and we are brought up against the realization that our insulation from death is illusory" (15).

In total, the notion that death is natural in old age comforts us through the implication that death would be quite unnatural for us.

Our readiness to accept the deaths of old people as "natural" has implications for both the present and the future. We will concentrate upon "premature" or "pre-necessary" death. The concepts of premature birth and premature death have recently been compared (16). Premature birth is, of course, the more familiar and better delineated concept. The notion of premature death is at its most obscure in the case of the elderly. We are so ready to accept death as an intrinsic part of old age that we seldom alert ourselves to the possibility that some deaths are "unnecessary" (avoidable) at any age. It has become customary to regard any death of a young person as premature ("cut off in his prime"), while philosophizing that all elders are ripe for death. Neither clinical nor research experience support these views. There are many elders who do not feel ripe for death and who, in fact, exhibit great determination and resiliency when confronting a threat to their existence.

Yet it remains difficult for some of us to take seriously the notion that old people may want to live, and may be capable of surviving medical and pycho-social crises if given a reasonable chance by the environment. The "natural death" doctrine dulls our sensitivities. Even such a highly trained observer as the physician may fail to notice or properly evaluate threats to the continued survival of an elder. Dr. Donald R. Lipsitt draws upon his clinical experience to caution:

The anguish arising from emotional starvation is profound and lingering, and it ultimately leads to despair, preoccupation with bodily functions, reliance upon others, physical and mental deterioration, hospitalization, and even death. *Before giving up* (italics added), geriatric individuals often turn pleadingly to their physician for the alleviation of their misery and pain (17).

According to Lipsitt, physicians too often reject the patient when they reject the medical significance of his symptoms, failing sometimes even to offer the tenuous support of a return appointment. The elder may become inadvertently conditioned by the medical system to develop more obvious and extensive somatic symptoms in order to be "worth the doctor's time." Or, left with his own anguish, the elder whose presenting problem cannot be neatly classified in medical terminology may turn to regressive or desperate solutions, as we point out later on.

An even more pointed indictment of attitudes and behavior among health personnel has been made by Dr. Alvin Goldfarb, a gero-psychiatrist of long experience. He asks, "Why do we see aged persons who have suffered stroke or car-diac failure admitted to long-term facilities and left without blankets in a drafty corridor, or kept sitting in a wheelchair for a long period of time before they are placed on a stretcher, and then roughly handled from stretcher to bed?" His answer: "Because attendants have heard a physician say, with seeming compassion, 'We can't do much for this poor fellow except to let him die'" (18). Goldfarb sees "rationalized hostility" and "justification of medical neglect" where others have been content to see philosophical surrender to natural death.

The elder's attempt to draw attention to his predicament can itself take hazardous forms. An exploratory study in one institution disclosed that more than 40 percent of the men and more than 20 percent of the women in a sample of geriatric medical patients engaged in at least one self-injurious behavior—within the span of a single week! The investigators wondered:

Could it be that within the institutional environment destructive behaviors may lead to *increased* survival potential because they provoke the much-wanted attention of nursing personnel . . . ? Is it possible that the same dynamics might be found in the home and the community as well as the institution? Might it be the case that the special care given an injured patient serves as a social reinforcer to increase the probability of further self-injurious behavior? In other words, the same action may have opposite effects: a) leading to higher probability of survival because of the additional care received which in turn bolsters self-esteem . . . and 'will-to-live,' but b) leading also to the strengthened tendency to repeat self-destructive acts, any of which may prove to be the one that introduces the preterminal process. This would indeed be a species of the double-bind situation. The elderly patient may feel (and be) ignored if he does not do something to draw attention to himself every week or so, yet every such action introduces a new risk factor (19).

It is probable that the actual incidence of self-injurious behavior was underestimated in the study that has been cited.

Certain types of life-threatening behaviors were not reported at all by the hospital staff members whose observations provided the basic data. In the experience of the present writers, a number of geriatric patients work against their own survival by refusing medication, failing to obey specific orders of the physician, smoking or drinking against medical advice, reducing or stopping food intake while trying to give the impression of having eaten the food, and situating themselves in hazardous environments. These behaviors are relatively passive and "untrouble-making," therefore more likely to escape notice. It is likely that observations would be more careful if we were convinced that death is not invariably a "natural" aim of the elderly.

Suicidal predispositions also may be overlooked, despite the clear evidence that elderly men have an exceptionally high suicide rate (Chapter 11). Public and professional alarm about suicide in old age hardly compares with that expressed about suicide in the young. Even though suicide may be considered an "unnatural" act by some, perhaps any act that culminates in death is regarded as proper or, at least, not excessively disturbing, in old age.

There is by now a voluminous literature on our society's failure to provide adequate life-supporting services to the elderly. Testimony given to congressional subcommittees, for example, has made it clear that many elders are placed in extra jeopardy by poverty, substandard housing, transportation difficulties, inadequate legal protection, and inconsistent health care—all conditions that could have been prevented and could have been alleviated when discovered (20). These vulnerabilities are even more pronounced for minority group elders (21). Perhaps, however, we should not speak of our society's "failure" to provide adequate life-supporting services; this statement assumes that helping elders to stay alive is an accepted and high priority goal. There are

observations which cast doubt on this assumption (22). Instead of social "failure," we may be "succeeding" in foreshortening the lives of our elders, in accordance with one of the poles of ambivalence characterizing our orientation toward death and the aged.

What are the future implications of this willingness to regard the death of elders as "natural" and not worth doing much about? The following hypothetical conversation has been reported:

INDUSTRIALIST: Die they must, to make room for younger workers. With increasing automation and the ever-present threat of peace, it will be tougher and tougher to hold unemployment down. Especially now that some of them are starting to oppose compulsory retirement. Just between us, I am concerned about older workers because they tend to know *too much*, and I don't fancy the size of the pension payments we will face if they persist in living for years after retirement.
ECONOMIST: Amen, brother. What disturbs me is the low productivity and low purchasing power of the aged. Definitely a drag on the economy. Die they must.
CONSERVATIONIST: You bet your blue skies! Here we are faced with the most crucial problem the human race has ever encountered—overpopulation—and there are all those old people using up valuable resources. They breathe. They occupy space. They persist in living their unnecessary lives while we are busting our axles to trim the birth rate. It is not enough to *prevent* birth—the prevention should be made retroactive after age, well, what do you say, Charlie . . . 70? 65? 60? Die they must!
SOCIOLOGIST: And who would miss them? Hardly anybody, according to our observations (23).

The implication is that certain major trends in our society are increasing the lethal pressures on the already low-valued, high-jeopardized aged. Sudden intensification of the pressures could result in "solutions" that amount to wholesale murder (called by some other name, in all likelihood). The mental preparation, the willingness to accept the avoidable death of others without concern is already a factor today. Organized societies have practiced infanticide and genocide—is gerontocide so improbable?

We are not predicting that any such thing will happen. We are, however, calling attention a) to the fact that attitudes and behaviors inimical to safeguarding the lives of elders are already with us b) at the same time that our power and versatility in meeting our death is on the rise, while c) grave socioecologic problems threaten to impel us into drastic courses of action. The ability to withhold life-sustaining resources or to inflict hazards on a remote, impersonalized footing is to be given special attention in this context. "The System" (i.e., you and I by another name) can alter the probability of survival for individuals without requiring individuals to experience themselves as responsible.

Indifference and hostility toward our elders is only part of the picture, of course. Strong emotional ties often continue across generations. The life-preserving and enhancing tradition is also in evidence, providing the counterpoint. However, it is the anti-life theme we wish to emphasize here. Two more facets related to aging will be noted briefly. First, it should be recognized that as individuals we may at times desire the removal, emasculation, or death of those older than ourselves—specific people who are seen as interfering with our comfort or aspirations. This attitude may generalize from its original target (e.g., parent) to other elders (e.g., employer, teacher, patient). Secondly, the anticipation of old age may lead to death-hastening behaviors. Here we are concerned with the individual's attitude to his own future self, rather than toward others who are now aged. It is not uncommon to hear young people say they would prefer to die before growing old. In one of our own series of ongoing studies we have received responses of this type. Carelessness with personal health and safety, and suicidal ideation, could well be associated with this aversion to old age.

(These are hypotheses now being explored.) We consider it unlikely that our life/death orientation toward the elderly could exist without implications for our own survival.

This discussion has focused upon the lethal side of our orientation toward the elderly. Parallel consideration could have been given to other topics. For example, what mental preparations have made it possible for the (undeclared) war in Indochina to become so extravagantly destructive and brutalizing? For the outbreaks of violence between some elements of the police and some young people in this nation? For the rising incidence of murder and crimes against the person? The patterns of connection between mental preparation and lethal behavior may be direct or indirect. It is difficult to conclude, with any confidence, exactly how previous psychosocial orientations led to some of the death-dealing phenomena we see today. To predict specific future trends is even more difficult. But we do stand to increase our ability to avoid or minimize unnecessary ("premature") deaths in the years ahead if we begin with appreciation of the fact that the makings of the future can be experienced in our own minds and hearts at this moment.

CONCEPTS: HEURISTIC AND OTHERWISE

Definitive comparisons between the present and the past are difficult to make at this time because the requisite background of research and theory has not been established. It is only within the last few years that a "death research" literature has begun to take shape. This has implications for prediction of the future as well. It is likely that from now on whatever new patterns develop in our relationship to death will be accompanied by the observations and conceptualizations of clinicians and social scientists. It is also likely that the concepts we decide to use will have some effect upon the total death system. The nature of our concepts has something to do with what we choose to observe, how we make our observations, and how we transmit our findings to others. Socio-emotional connotations of the concepts sometimes prove to be as significant as the technical properties of the concepts or their "fit" with empirical observations. Accordingly, it is worthwhile to explore at least a few of the concepts presently available, and a few more that might be proposed for consideration. This will be a selective and relatively brief discussion. We will focus upon concepts that have not yet been given much attention in this book, having been "saved" for this scan of future possibilities.

The Death Instinct

Freud's conception of the "death instinct" looms as the broadest formulation ever put forth on this topic. It is also one of the most famous conceptions—and, like many another classic statement, has taken on a wide variety of interpretations. Freud eventually came to the position that the shifting balance between two great "instincts," as he called them, are crucial both for the individual and for society (24). Eros represents the confluence of all those tendencies within us that aim to preserve life and sensibility, while Thanatos represents the impulse toward insensibility and oblivion. We should clearly understand from the outset that this is a "grand" concept which may not prove amenable to ordinary evaluation. Let us consider four interpretations and applications:

1. Saul (25) sees the death instinct as being closely related to the second law of thermodynamics. He notes that the tendency "to stability, to irreversibility, is expressed in the concept of entropy . . . (which applies) to all systems: mechanical, electrical, thermal, chemical, etc." (26).

Saul deduces that this principle must therefore operate in human life as well, for "bodies function in accordance with natural processes." Meeting objections in advance, he indicates that the law need not apply to every detail of a process. "If the entropy of a human is decreased by his taking in energy, this is a misapplication . . . because energy taken in . . . is part of the system." He concludes that "Freud's intuition was correct. The dissolution of the organism is the outcome of a physical chemical characteristic, and all life processes operate in the face of an opposite tendency to reversibility. The very intensity of the struggle of living beings to survive and reproduce can be considered evidence for what is well known analytically, namely, that battle against a counterforce, called by Freud, the death instinct."

2. Ostrow is another who accepts the concept of a death instinct. However, he views it as "not simply a manifestation of the second law of thermodynamics but . . . as . . . a response of living creatures to the demands of the second law" (27). According to Ostrow, it is because of this law that foraging and feeding take place. "The degradation processes must be compensated by the continual intake of sources of high grade (low entropy) energy." The demands of the second law cannot be met completely, but are attenuated and deferred "by hastening the disintegration of other forms of life."

The other two interpretations to be noted here direct attention to clinical rather than cosmic issues.

3. Jellife maintains that the death instinct often manifests itself in physical ills (28). He believes that irreversible malignant "conversion" symptoms can occur when the death instinct, expressed in sadism, operates to produce "a castration or partial death for an organ" and thus induce a general disharmony of function. He suggests that certain chronic disabling conditions are the result of the need for

self-punishment through the body.

4. Menninger, in his influential book, *Man Against Himself* (29), claims that human destructiveness—of self or other—is "evidence of a spiritual malignancy within us . . . an instinct." Suicide, "accidents," and other kinds of "failures" may be related to this instinct. "According to this concept, there exists from the beginning in all of us strong tendencies toward self destruction and these come to fruition as actual suicide only in exceptional cases where many circumstances and factors combine to make it possible" (30).

Homicidal behavior might also be seen as deriving from an instinct or, at least, inborn propensities. The highly complicated theoretical relationship between suicide and homicide has already been touched upon in this book (Chapter 13). Were one to accept the basic premise that there is a death instinct basic to suicidal behavior, broadly conceived, then it would follow logically that much homicidal behavior has the same ultimate source.

Not all theorists have been ready to accept the death instinct as fact. McDougall, one of the earliest and most trenchant commentators on Freud's theories, is said to have called the death instinct "the most bizarre of all Freud's gallery of monsters." (McDougall was not always that uncharitable with concepts advanced by the Viennese master.) Many others have turned away from or failed to embrace this formulation.

We would not characterize the death instinct as a bizarre monster. We see it, rather, as a not entirely untenable but probably superfluous construct. There are many reasons for this opinion. Some of these are acknowledged even by supporters of instinct theory in general. Others are criticisms which proponents have not, to our knowledge, answered satisfactorily.

Menninger himself raised the rhetorical question: "If some great impulse toward death dominates all of us . . . why do so many of us struggle against it as we do . . . ? Why does the wish to live ever, even temporarily, triumph over the wish to die?" In reply he cites another of Freud's assumptions, that the life and death instincts "are in constant conflict and interaction just as are similar forces in physics, chemistry, and biology" (31). Menninger holds that these forces which are originally "directed inward and related to the instinctive problems of the self" . . . eventually come to be directed outward toward other objects." This is conceived of as a normal aspect of development. "No one evolves so completely as to be entirely free from self-destructive tendencies; indeed the phenomena of life, the behavior peculiar to different individuals, may be said to express the resultant of the conflicting factors" (32). That there is conflict in life is perfectly obvious, just as the processes of anabolism and catabolism may be described as part of the larger process of metabolism. What is not obvious or necessarily true is that the source of the "destructive forces" is instinctive. It is not necessary to consider self- or other-destructive forces as the manifestation of instinctual drives. Numerous psychosocial factors that foster *life-threatening behavior* (to anticipate another concept) have been discussed in this book. These include characteristics of our social system as well as individual behavior. Furthermore, what is interpreted as "destructive" of "life-affirming" behavior can vary according to the framework of the perceiver. The same action (e.g., slaughtering an animal or building an expressway through a community) might be regarded in either way. Application of the death instinct construct typically involves the assumption that "destructive" behavior can be identified without significant dispute. This is a disputable proposition.

Data from individual psychoanalytic case treatments have often been cited as evidence to support the death instinct. Such support is open to serious criticism.

People undergoing analytic treatment are not a representative sample of the human race, nor is it easy to evaluate the role of the treatment process itself in shaping the instinct-relevant behavior. Further, psychoanalysts, no matter how sterling their qualities, cannot readily be considered as objective observers. It is interesting to hear what an orthodox psychoanalyst has to report about the death instinct of his patients, but one must keep in mind that he is providing treatment within a conceptual framework that endorses thanatos, not engaged in critical research.

As a hypothetical construct, the death instinct leaves much to be desired:

1. Saul acknowledges that it is "philosophical" and cannot be observed clinically (33). We agree. One either subscribes to it, as to the tenets of a religious or philosophical system, or he does not. It does not appear amenable to experimental verification in any reasonable sense of the term.

2. The fruitfulness of the death instinct construct is limited. The hypotheses it generates tend to be of the cosmic variety, well beyond the possibility of empirical evaluation. Neither does it suggest practical methods of managing its manifestations. Very little action would take place if we depended upon this construct to lead the way. (One notes that this construct is seldom invoked in contemporary efforts to predict or prevent suicide).

3. The construct is unparsimonious. There are so many other potential bases for hostile and destructive behavior that it scarcely seems economical to invent and maintain an instinct for this purpose. Theoretical elaboration seems to take the place of data-gathering behavior.

4. Most unfortunately, perhaps, the death instinct construct tends to operate as a drag upon efforts to prevent or alter destructive behavior. It provides a fatalistic rationalization, playing right into any reluctance we may have about taking ac-

tion. It is easy to be intimidated by the death instinct when it is flanked by the second law of thermodynamics on one side, and grand propositions about biology and society on the other side. It would be a pity if the marvelous scope of this construct should dissuade us from more heuristic pathways (But perhaps it would also be a pity if we should completely abandon the idea—it does merit a place in our intellectual life, if only for the boldness of its gesture.) For the moment, then, we do not see the death instinct as a major construct for future theory and research.

Will-to-Live

The will-to-live (WtL) concept has also been with us for some time. It has had a number of philosophical advocates, with Schopenhauer perhaps the most influential (34). There is a certain resemblance between it and the death instinct, and the resemblance can be either heightened or diminished.

We prefer to emphasize the differences. As we will use the term, WtL has no cosmic or biological implications (any reader may add these at his own discretion and responsibility). We see WtL as a molar construct that can receive direct application in research and practice. Numerous difficulties must be overcome, however, for the concept to prove truly helpful.

In an exploratory study we suggested that "*will* may be regarded as the organization of personality toward a specific direction of action—the 'unity of personality' that puts specific factors to work in the service of a central (temporary or enduring) orientation. The *will* concept does not imply unlimited capability of action, but simply the stance of the organism toward or against its total milieu, or some perceived force within the milieu. It has long been recognized in this concept that some things happen *willy-nilly*, i.e., regardless of our strongest desires and efforts. To speak of a will-to-live, then, does not prejudge the questions of efficacy and process; we merely enter the central state of the organism as a potential variable in its own survival" (35).

This particular study involved physician ratings of new admissions to a geriatric hospital. Among other things, it was learned that WtL ratings followed a systematic pattern and were related to other variables in a systematic manner. In other words, it held some promise as a construct to guide empirical research. There was a pronounced tendency for physicians to see their own patients as having a strong WtL, and to over-estimate their longevity. Early data suggested that patients who were rated as having a will-to-die (WtD) actually did succumb earlier than other members of the cohort who were given positive WtL ratings. It has not yet proven possible either to confirm or reject this trend. Unfortunately, we were unable to discover the specific clues employed by the physicians in arriving at their decisions. A subsequent attempt was made to provide WtL ratings that would be more informative about the processes involved. The raters in this instance were psychologists and research associates in the same geriatric hospital. This did not work out at all, and we are left with the problem of identifying what people behold when they make judgments about WtL or WtD.

Unlike the death instinct, WtL has now found several research applications that tend to strengthen its contruct validity and establish its relationship to external variables (36). Other studies are in progress throughout the country. The most abundant material still derives from clinical experience. Weisman and Hackett (37) reported several deaths that seem to have been of the WtD type in the influential article mentioned in Chapter 3. LeShan (38) has emphasized WtL as a factor in the lives of cancer patients. Kalish has transmitted the report of a radiologist who "had x-rayed numerous elderly pa-

tients in their eighties and nineties whose skin was so fragile that lying on the x-ray table would pull the skin off and leave them bleeding. The physician said that several of these persons begged him to leave them alone to die peacefully and without the indignities of medical treatment that would have little direct influence on their lives. Although these patients had no will-to-live, they were not eager to die, nor did they display undue signs of depression" (39). It might be relevant to add here that WtL and WtD were not conceptualized as being mutually exclusive or as opposite poles of the same dimension in the study cited at the beginning of this section. From our clinical experience, we agree with Kalish's physician-informant that absence of WtL is not necessarily identical with the presence of a determined WtD.

The WtL concept appears to have significant implications for future time perspective, hope, optimism, despair, and related concepts, although equivalent to none of these. Some of these implications have been explored recently (40), and others invite attention. WtL can be assessed from the individual's self-report, or from the observations of professional and scientific personnel. These latter observations can be made on either a "free" or a structured basis, by those charged with therapeutic responsibilities (e.g., nurse) or those responsible only for observing (e.g., anthropologist). Delineation of WtL probably could be improved by developing clear guidelines for taking environmental parameters into account as well. We will touch upon this approach later.

One of the most obvious and potentially valuable applications of the WtL concept would be in the prediction and possible modification of life-or-death outcomes. There is a bit of evidence to support the clinical observation that WtD can be transformed into WtL within a relatively short period of time (41). We should learn more about the factors involved. There is reason to be encouraged, however, in the hypothesis that accurate identification of a person's momentary "will orientation" can be followed by effective intervention, when indicated. (The question of when it is appropriate for somebody—who?—to intervene in another person's life-death dynamics has been discussed earlier in this book and by other authors. The problem is also relevant here, but we are letting it pass this time.)

Nothing that we have said so far was intended to imply that WtL and WtD necessarily exert decisive influence on survival—but there is strong circumstantial evidence that such influence does manifest itself at times. "How" and "when" are among the questions that remain to be answered. The WtL construct will be of more value to us in the long run if it is formulated and applied carefully.

In this connection reference should again be made to the categories proposed by Shneidman (42) (See also Chapter 5). He has offered a classification system centering upon the individual's orientation toward his own cessation—what role did the person play, if any, in bringing about his death? The basic categories proposed are "intentioned," "subintentioned," "unintentioned," and "contraintentioned." Each of these includes a number of more specific orientations. The "intentioned" person, for example, may be either a "psyde-seeker," "psyde-initiator," "psyde-ignorer," or "psyde-darer." (Read "death" for "psyde"). This classification system brings forward a number of potentially valuable concepts. It also seems to involve a set of assumptions somewhat different from those related to the WtL concept, and may imply some observational differences as well. The reader is invited to consult Shneidman's writings directly. There seems to be unrealized potential in both the WtL family of constructs and the Shneidman system.

Some Emerging Constructs

Attention now will be given to several concepts that are surfacing among clinicians and researchers who are deeply involved with the subject matter of this book, but which have not yet made a strong impact on the larger scientific and professional community. These constructs can be grouped in two sets: a) those that focus upon physical death as a possible outcome, and b) those that focus upon psychosocial variations on the theme of death. Set *a* may be divided into constructs that pertain chiefly to the individual (death instinct and WtL are examples already considered) and those that pertain chiefly to environmental factors.

Concerning the Individual. The first group of concepts that pertain to the individual is closely associated with the suicide prevention movement. There is a prevailing opinion that suicide is not a completely satisfactory term. Systematic efforts are being made to refine and standardize the manner in which this term is applied (43). Some experts have called for other terms and constructs to replace "suicide;" others believe the term should be retained but augmented by other modes of classification. It seems highly probable that in the years ahead a number of modifications will take place in our use of suicide and related terms. Here we are less concerned with nomenclature as such than with the opportunity to present a few of the emerging concepts for future reference.

From the Los Angeles Suicide Prevention Center has come the concept of *lethality* (44). Shneidman defines lethality "as the probability of the individual's killing himself in the present or immediate future. Ratings of lethality . . . permit one to cut across the usual categories of suicidal threat, attempt and commit and, in the terms of a single dimension, to signify the seriousness (and the magnitude of intention) of the individual vis-a-vis his own self-induced death" (45). This construct is synonymous with "suicidality," a term that some might prefer.

As employed by Shneidman and his

colleagues, lethality/suicidality includes the following conceptual properties:

1. Everybody has a certain level of lethality at every point in time (even if it is a "zero" level).

2. Consequently, lethality ratings can be made for any person at any time; the measurement is not restricted to those who are in crisis situations.

3. Each person has both his characteristic "lethality position" and his momentary position. One might speak then of "chronic" and "acute" suicidality.

4. Intentionality is a crucial aspect of this dimension.

5. Prodromal clues or signals are said to exist for a period of time prior to a suicidal act. These can be detected by attention to the lethality dimension, and by sensitive attention to specific indices. (This point does not appear to be logically required by the lethality construct, but it is usually accepted as part of the "package.")

The lethality/suicidality construct serves as a rationale for efforts to detect potentially suicidal behavior. It also may be of value, as Shneidman has suggested, in cutting across different forms of suicidal motion (ideation, attempt, completion). Furthermore, the concept has some appeal for research and educational as well as clinical purposes.

On the problematic side we would call attention to three possible sources of difficulty:

1. The concept leaves untouched the area of actions which jeopardize the other person. Incidents of homicide followed by suicide would not be adequately encompassed. Additionally, the term lethality itself seems general enough to refer to the intention to bring about death of any kind. Restriction of the construct to self-directed actions might be challenged.

2. Ultimate evaluation of the lethality construct must rest, in part, upon its association with the idea of intentionality. The latter concept is complex both philosophically and psychologically. Not everybody accepts intentionality as a valid concept, and not everybody who accepts the concept agrees as to its nature. Apart from the logico-philosophical problems involved, there is also the operational difficulty of obtaining appropriate observations for the dependable assessment of intentionality. If we remain in doubt about a person's intentionality, then we must also remain in doubt about his lethality/suicidality. This is an important problem in suicidology and the study of death generally. It deserves a great deal more attention than it can receive here.

3. While the lethality construct takes into account movement along the time continuum, it neglects other situational aspects. In an earlier chapter ("Facing the Thought of Death") it was pointed out that the situational context can be of decisive importance in the development of responses to the prospect of death. Situational components have also been emphasized elsewhere in this book. It is highly probable, we think, that the "situation" is also of great significance in suicidality. The lethality construct would account for variance in terms of the individual's orientation; it therefore relies upon the assumption that this orientation will be relatively consistent across situations. But is a person *generally* "high" or "low" lethal—or does the situational context itself include much of the source of variance? (This is not a criticism of those suicidologists who have developed the lethality construct; in their own clinical work they are alert to environmental factors. However, lethality, as a formal construct, lacks this sensitivity.)

In his concept of *life-threatening behavior* Weisman draws upon experiences with the chronically and terminally ill as well as the suicidal. His work in progress involves an effort "to combine our knowledge of the psychosomatic aspects of organic illnesses and death with what we know about suicide" (46). He notes that many self-destructive acts seem to occur without overt suicidal intent.

The most disturbing fact . . . is that frank suicide attempts may be only a minor example of the overall prevalence of equally destructive, life-threatening behavior. We are currently uncertain about what occurs to the potential suicide, especially during the dark interval between gathering ideation and inflicting physical damage upon himself. The dynamics of depression do not provide adequate insight into motives of suicide. Present-day psychological, biochemical, and sociological theories have remained surprisingly stationary for a number of years (47).

He suggests that we suspend our traditional assumptions and look instead at the wide variety of behavior that threatens life.

Thus, while the construct of the lethality has an organizing effect upon many observations in the domain of suicide per se, Weisman would broaden our horizons even further. More kinds of behavior would be considered death-relevant than previously, and intentionality would be only one relevant concept among many. (Those who have been with us through the whole length of this book will readily appreciate that Weisman's views are heading in the same general direction as our own). In developing his thesis, Weisman accepts the lethality construct, but as part of a larger framework, one that also includes the dimension of *terminality*. We will best be served by his own words:

We are convinced that the bipolar, self-contained, categorical concepts of organic death and self-induced death are no longer tenable and should be replaced with a concept that recognizes a more fluid ebb and flow of lethality in all people. Moreover, the disposition toward lethal behavior should be considered along with a complementary concept—the disposition to die, or terminality. Both lethality and terminality may be manifested in different types of behavior and under varying circumstances, not just in the

conventional outcome of extinction and annihilation.

Lethality and terminality should bracket a group of heterogeneous behaviors, called 'life-threatening.' In this way, we need not assume that all life-threatening behavior is necessarily equivalent to suicide or even to 'self-destructive' behavior. . . . Terminality and lethality are admittedly imprecise concepts, but at least they open the door to further investigations, not prematurely close it with false conclusions and postulates (48).

Weisman proposes that we consider as an "organic opposite" to terminality and lethality the concept of *viability*, or disposition to live. He further distinguishes three levels of viability. *Primary viability* refers to a level of biological intactness—survival for its own sake. "There is no preemptory demand to visualize a distant future, nor any need to contend unduly with a world of abstractions and symbolic relationships." Behavior that implies a measure of choice, control, and competence is found at the level of *secondary viability*. Realistic appraisal of the environment and ability to comprehend time, past and future, is necessary. *Tertiary viability* goes beyond both survival and competence. It is related to one's ego-ideal and self-esteem—the preservation of "an intact personal image."

The approach suggested by Weisman goes beyond one or two new constructs. It implies a rich theoretical network that perhaps can do more justice to the phenomena than any of the concepts and dimensions already described on these pages. It remains to be seen, however, whether or not adequate clinical and research operations can be developed to fulfill the implications of these constructs. Are we ready and able to step beyond the tradition which demands that there be "specific causes" for every death and "reasons" for every suicide? Can we actually make use of a framework that would encompass all deaths and, therefore, all lives? Will "life-threatening behavior" be useful only at a general level of discussion, or come to play an intrinsic role in our practice, research, and theory? These are questions for the future to answer.

The term *self-injurious behavior* (S-IB) has also been employed recently (49). It has a family resemblance to life-threatening behavior, but may be characterized as a scaled-down construct that has fewer theoretical associations. It may be possible, for example, actually to count "S-IBs" without making any assumptions about either the individual's intentionality or terminality. The observed S-IBs could be taken as an operational *estimate* of the level of a higher-order construct, such as life-threatening behavior, but the two constructs would remain at different rungs of the inference-generalization ladder. As the reader can see, we have much work ahead in developing a whole set of constructs that are graded into the various "sizes" necessary for theory-building and systematic hypothesis-testing.

Concerning the Environment. The environmental configuration has received less attention than the individual in the study of suicide and other death-relevant behaviors. Lacking theoretical constructs, we also lack assessment procedures, and, lacking assessment procedures, we lack systematic means of evaluating and modifying environments. It is true that all of the individually-oriented concepts already discussed here have certain environmental implications. Rather than attempting to draw these out, however, we will concentrate upon a few concepts that *begin* with environmental emphasis.

Two potentially valuable approaches will be mentioned in passing. For many years Roger Barker and his colleagues have pioneered the naturalistic observation of human behavior. By now they have developed a descriptive language and a set of techniques for which all the human sciences should be grateful (50). This body of terms and techniques has not yet been applied to our subject matter, to the best of our knowledge. The work of Barker et al would make a useful starting point for an ecology of life-and-death. Since this material is readily available, we will only note here that Barker's research has stimulated our own interest in this approach and will be represented more systematically in our future work.

Weisman has seen the relevance of adding an environmental component to his theoretical and empirical work. His contribution is the concept of a *risk/rescue ratio.* At present the term is being applied largely to suicidal attempts. Presumably it could also be generalized somewhat. The "risk" part of this formula pertains to the individual. How potentially deadly was the instrumentality he employed? How much actual damage was inflicted? What treatment was required? These are among the questions which are asked to determine the risk involved. The "rescue-ability" of the individual is determined largely by the environmental context in which he placed himself. How accessible or inaccessible did he make himself to potential rescuers? Did he, for example, make his attempt behind locked doors at a time when any chance intervention by another person would be minimal, or was the attempt made in full view of another person? The risk/rescue ratio is already seeing some application and may well prove to be a workable procedure that contributes to our understanding of life-threatening behavior by including some of the available environmental information.

We have been slowly evolving an approach that might appear rather "far out." No single term or construct quite conveys what we are attempting to formulate. The position, however, goes something like this:

1. Environments differ in their tendency to support life. This proposition consists of two distinct strands:

  a. Some environments *do* enhance survivorship, i.e., more inhabitants actually stay alive longer.

b. Some environments are organized around the goal of supporting life to a greater extent than other environments. What we have termed *the caring environment* (51) may or may not actually succeed in fostering life. (Similarly, a non-caring environment may nevertheless show a "good record" because of a fortunate match between types of hazard existing and types of inhabitants).

2. It is possible to establish for all or most environments an index of life/death expectation. This would be a quantitative estimate.

3. The death estimate could be computed on whatever time coordinate one prefers. Of particular interest, however, would be a computation that expresses the probabilities of death on a daily basis. This could be adjusted in both directions (hourly, monthly) depending upon the specific purpose at hand.

4. The basic probability estimate would be made in terms of "blind knowledge," i.e., making use of carefully obtained mortality information without inclusion of individual or process variables.

5. The estimate would be much improved by adding individual and process variables. Environments are not equally caring or hazardous for all individuals. It is important to have the "blind" or "empty" estimate separately. In this way we can establish the general characteristics of the environment, and then test out the importance of specific factors such as age, sex, and health of the inhabitants.

6. By "environment" we mean settings of action that lend themselves to useful analysis. These settings can be relatively permanent, or relatively transient. Some environments "happen" periodically or occasionally, instead of existing continuously. There can be great flexibility in establishing the environments. The intensive treatment unit in a hospital might be considered an environment for some purposes, but so might a neighborhood, or a football field on Sunday afternoon.

When strong weight is given to the environmental side of the equation, it becomes possible to evaluate individual factors more adequately. "Lethality," "WtL" and other states attributed to the individual always occur within some kind of environmental context. We could—today—exhibit environments that pose high death risks for all humans (or animals). Other environments pose high death risks, but only for certain types of living organisms. It would be inappropriate to rate each individual separately and forget to include the overriding fact that the environmental configuration itself predisposes to early death.

To develop this approach one would also take into account the modality of death. Some environments may heighten the likelihood of dying in a traffic accident, others by respiratory disease or cancer. A man who takes a job as gas station attendant at night in a major American city has entered an environment in which death by gunshot is one of the more salient possibilities. A child who lives in a ghetto runs a relatively high risk of suffering long-term and eventually fatal complications from ailments that could have been checked with prompt medical care (e.g., untreated strep throat leading to glomerular nephritis).

Although examples are easy to find and have a certain inherent interest, more valuable would be the systematic appraisal of environments in a manner that could be communicated to "people in high places" in terms that they can understand. Earlier we made reference to the case history of a city council that was willing to jeopardize the lives of its citizens by creating an admittedly dangerous railroad crossing in order to obtain additional tax revenue from a new factory (Chapter 14). The city officials in such a situation could dismiss protests as vague, emotional, and unconvincing, countering with hard facts about the anticipated tax revenue. It would be another story if there were "hard facts" on both sides when a money-versus-lives conflict comes up. Appraisal of the environment, with reference to previous railroad crossing fatalities in the area, could have led to a death probability estimate.

The probability of death for citizens of X City will be increased such-and-such percent by the installation. Thus x-many days of human life will be lost during the next 20 years. The expense involved, including survivor benefits, will come to approximately so many dollars. This expense, coupled with the subtraction of these human-days from the taxpayers' and consumers' rolls, will negate the new tax revenue that you have projected (from data no more solid than ours). And you will have played an enabling role in the avoidable death of men, women, and children.

Admittedly, this is a step toward the fantasy-side. But it is technically possible to develop "readings" of death hazard for most of the environments we inhabit. Conversion of individual lives into statistics is a process about which we have some misgivings. Yet statistical statements have political and economic as well as scientific power in our society—why not use this power on the side of life-support? Death estimates (or survivorship forecasts, if one prefers) could be made on a regular basis and included as part of the "news," along with the weather, sports, air-pollution index, and stock-market report. It perhaps would not be the most trivial of these number-ridden chants.

Theory and research implications of this systematic attention to the environment (with or without daily death probability forecasts) are numerous. We suggest here just one of the possible lines of inquiry which focuses upon the vulnerability of particular "kinds" of people to particular "kinds" of environment. We make one distinction on the environmental side—that between the proximal ("close-in") and distal (distant, abstracted) environment. The neighborhood and its various sub-components, including one's own residence, would be an example of the proximal environment. The distal environment would include the larger metropolitan area, and the whole "establishment" of public agencies and major commerical systems. First we offer three hypotheses which attempt to specify characteristics of the individual's relationship to his environment.

The developmental hypothesis: Dependence upon the proximal environment is greatest at both extremes of the life cycle. In other words, what happens "close-in" is more of a life-and-death matter to the very young and the very old than to those of intermediate ages.

The docility hypothesis: Dependence upon the proximal environment is greatest for those most deficient in organismic competence. This includes limitations in health, cognitive skills and ego strength (52).

The social echelon hypothesis: Dependence upon the proximal environment is greater for those who are in the lower social echelons. The individual is more immersed in and his behavior more predictable from the "close-in" environment than is the case for a person similar in age and competence but occupying a higher social echelon.

The same person may be deeply embedded in his proximal environment for any or all of the reasons mentioned, e.g., an impoverished aged woman with poor health and limited mobility. These sources of dependence upon the proximal environment probably interact dynamically rather than additively. Advanced age increases one's probability of serious financial concern. Age plus impecunity may conspire to reduce future optimism, social interaction, and level of health maintenance. The resulting phenomenological constriction, social isolation, and failing health can then serve to accelerate deteriorative changes with age, increase the discrepancy between funds available and those required, etc.

To find that a person is highly dependent on his proximal environment is to imply that he would be especially vulnerable to stresses or deficiencies within that sector. People may be at the mercy of their environment directly or "psychologically," but with a similar outcome in either case. It does not matter very much that potential help awaits the person in another sector if he does not know how to obtain or use the assistance, or is fearful of venturing out.

The person who occupies one or more of the proximal-imbedded positions suggested above (developmental, docility and social echelon hypotheses) suffers a double vulnerability. It is relevant to emphasize the desperate nature of his situation should his proximal environment reject or fail to nurture him. But he may also be in a different kind of jeopardy from the distal environment.

This threat is not as easily perceived—indeed, the invisibility or amorphousness of the distal environment . . . may itself constitute the primary threat. When he finds himself forced to interact with the distal environment on its terms he may blunder out of anxiety or inexperience. When the distal environment intrudes upon his own "turf" he may similarly behave in a manner that increases rather than diminishes his vulnerability. He does not really know ("care for") the outer world and it does not really know (or "care for") him. Thus, the ill or improverished person fails to obtain the benefits and opportunities that are rightfully his. He gets himself into trouble with the authorities . . . [or] finds his life disjointed and threatened by the end-effects of policies that began far away in the distal environment (e.g., the ghetto adolescent headed for Vietnam, the old man dislocated in an urban renewal project, headed . . . where?) (53).

It might be added that the person on the high end of the developmental-docility-social echelon axis may be especially vulnerable to problems generated within the distal environment. He has more freedom from or less connection with his immediate surround. But anxiety, despondency, "psychosomatic" disorders,

and heightened lethality may arise from his involvement in such abstract and symbolic activities as the fluctuations of the stock market.

Whether or not any of the specific ideas presented here prove to have merit, it is likely that future conceptualizations of death will give more attention to the environment than has been the case up to this time. In fact, we will once again consider the environment after the following brief discussion of another set of death constructs.

Variations on the Theme of Death. We come now to concepts that focus upon kinds of death other than physical cessation. This topic has already been touched upon at several points throughout the book. We saw, for example, that the young child may be influenced by metaphoric uses of death-related terms in daily conversation (e.g., "The motor is dead." Chapter 2). Phenomena that appear to be simulations of death were explored in some detail (Chapter 5); logical and methodological grounds for entertaining new and various conceptions of death have also been considered (Chapter 4), to recall some of the previous discussions. We now concentrate upon possible future applications of these constructs, starting with a review and elaboration of a simple classification system we have been trying out in recent years (54).

The term *phenomenological death* (Pheno/D) has been proposed for those conditions in which the individual himself is no longer an experiencer. Pheno/D may be judged to be total. However, there are many instances in which experiencing is completely absent only at one or more levels. It should be possible to specify the level or realm within which Pheno/D prevails. One might, for example, develop a classification system parallel to the one proposed by Weisman for levels of viability (55). Assessment of Pheno/D can be made by either physiological or psychological operations—perhaps, most usefully, a combination of both. There are problems in obtaining appropriate and reliable observations, as with any other variable that is attributed to an "inner circle" of the individual. The problems are not exceptional here, nor are they insurmountable, to judge by the encouraging results that have been obtained from our limited efforts thus far.

Social death (Soc/D) has been proposed for those conditions in which a person is no longer treated as though alive by others. As we observe how others in his environment behave, the decisions they make, the arrangements they carry out, we are led to conclude that the individual in question has the status of a deceased or even a "never-existed" person. Soc/D may occur in close temporal association with Pheno/D. On the other hand, it may also anticipate or follow the obliteration of personal experience by a considerable length of time. One may also have Soc/D in effect without any detectable relationship to the individual's phenomenological status (e.g., "cut dead" by the group). Similarly, a person may be treated as though still alive long after both Pheno/D and physical death have occurred (as in permitting deceased leaders to cast "absentee votes" in tribal conclaves). The cultural anthropologist and the social psychologist are among types of expert observers already among us who could develop useful Soc/D ratings.

Different from both of the above situations is that in which the observer develops the impression that he is in contact with a dead organism. Thanatomimesis (Than-Mim) is a state that sometimes appears to serve a defensive or survival function. At other times there may be no reason for attributing intentionality; rather, the perceiver has come to a mistaken conclusion based upon insufficient information or limitations in his own background. Phenomena falling into this classification range from Darwin's "death-feigning" spiders to premature human burials.

Collectively, these constructs may be regarded as comprising the realm of *psychological death* (Psych/D). They have several characteristics in common:

1. The states are to be judged within a specified, delimited observational framework. In other words, it is not necessary for the states to exist permanently or over an indefinitely prolonged period of time. Rationale for this position is presented in Chapter 4. By implication, then, Pheno/D, Soc/D, and Than-Mim can be reversible states. There is emphasis upon stringent observational criteria within a specified framework as opposed to a loose attribution that can be easily revoked or modified retrospectively if the situation appears to change.

2. Assessment of Psych/D, in all three of its aspects, requires careful attention to the observational framework and thus to the environment. This includes the role of the observer or participant-observer. As the social and physical environment changes, we might expect certain aspects of Psych/D to change as well, while other aspects may prove to be relatively invariant. The sensitivity of these constructs to environmental context suggests potential value for predicting and comprehending our changing relationships to death as future prospect becomes present reality.

3. The Psych/D constructs are descriptive. Explanatory constructs can be added and evaluated at any time. But the constructs themselves are not tied closely to particular theoretical frameworks.

4. All may be used in conjunction with the notion, *pragmatics of death* (Chapter 4). Our conceptions of death, including both official nomenclature and informal usages, are seen as being closely related to our existing capacity to *influence* life-and-death outcomes. As we become more versatile and powerful in manipulating death, so our constructs are likely to alter and expand.

At this point we reintroduce one other relevant construct. It is the notion of *clinical death* (Clin/D) that has become increasingly familiar during the past few years. Clin/D is better known than the other terms mentioned here. The fleeting phase of existence between cessation of vital signs and the onset of irreversible physical damage is obviously of crucial significance in such endeavors as organ transplants and experiments with artificial hypothermia.

Clin/D is also the variant on the theme of physical death that might appear most resistant to change. There must be limits, for example, to how long the complex structure of the brain can survive when oxygenation and nutrition cease. Yet it is likely that the duration of Clin/D will be altered both by new methods of observation and new methods of intervention. The prolongation of Clin/D appears to be highly desirable for some purposes. It would permit the initiation of lifesaving interventions that require more time than is currently available when Clin/D commences (especially in cases of traumatic or unexpected crisis). Extension of the Clin/D phase would also help to maintain the "health" of organs destined for transplantation. The value question—save the person or his organs?—is not to be lightly dismissed. In either case, however, it would be useful to have more time. In view of these and other reasons for desiring the extension of the Clin/D phase, it is probable that continuing improvements in medical technology will be made with this aim in mind.

Consider now a few other ways in which the constructs described here may become relevant. We will limit our attention to just one area of future development, "premature burial revisited."

Some of our ancestors were concerned about the prospect of premature burial. We may never be able to evaluate adequately how legitimate or unrealistic this fear may have been. In any case, the future is of greater interest. There is the

prospect before us of *planned* removal from the world of the living while the person himself is still "alive" in some sense of the term. To date, approximately a dozen humans are known to have been placed in "cryogenic suspension." Currently this procedure is regarded under the law as a form of burial. To the extent that the "buried" may also be regarded as "suspended," we already have precedence for planful semi-burial of the semi-dead. The scientific establishment does not appear to grant the current efforts any large chance of success ("success" being counted the reanimation of the suspended and their restoration to health). There is much room now for disputation regarding the pace at which suspension-reanimation efforts will be brought to fruition, and the methods that ultimately will prove effective. But it would be shortsighted to suppose that ten, fifty, or a hundred years from now society will have advanced no farther along these lines. The prospect of "suspended animation," "hibernation," or some analogous state deserves to be taken seriously.

A few of the possible forms might be guessed at here, if only to produce specific images for our discussion. Perhaps artificial hypothermia eventually will prove successful. People at or around the Clin/D phase will be "suspended" until treatment methods for their "fatal" conditions are discovered. Perhaps the same suspension techniques will be employed for other ends, such as the storage of citizens whose presence is not urgently required by society at the moment. Again, perhaps people (or some people) will have the opportunity to decide *when* they want to "live" and for how long. A person might, for example, choose to live five years per century. This would have the effect of extending his total adult life over more than a thousand years. It would also have the effect of consigning him to a series of semi-deaths and semi-burials.

Another possibility would be nothing

more than an extension of present efforts to control human behavior by drugs. People could be placed in carefully timed "drug-outs." The long sleep or controlled hibernation might become standard practice for commercial space passengers and others who would "be in the way" at certain periods of time. The mental climate for this type of behavior control may already be with us; if so, the technology cannot be very far behind.

A more exotic possibility is that the individual as such would be phased out at the time of his burial equivalent. "He" would subsequently reappear as part of a new "assembly." His central nervous system may be in a new body, and the "body" itself may be a manufactured or synthesized product. This type of burial shares with the others mentioned the aspect of "prematurity," i.e., something about the person remains "alive."

Let us try one more projection. The individual is not "buried" so much as he is "translated." A computer-guided scanning device creates a "double" of the person. This double (cf. the old German "doppelganger" tradition) is stored as a sort of "energy-stencil" to be activated when required. In this way an aging person may be replaced by his younger double; a deceased scientist, statesman, or "love goddess" may be re-materialized upon demand. The person with a diminished store of "life" within his original self (e.g., little time left to live, or already Pheno/D) is overshadowed, in effect, by his shadow, waiting for the opportunity to replace him.

Fantastical? Who can say? For whatever it means we, the present writers, do not feel we are dealing with phenomena any more incredible than what has already been observed on this planet—including the infliction of avoidable deaths upon so many of our own kind, and the jeopardizing of all life on earth. We have also attempted to suggest, here and elsewhere, that the most startling future developments probably will be unfurling from

psychological orientations that have been with us for a long time. Science fiction writers deserve the belated credit they are receiving these days for anticipating future events. But other components of our psychosocial tradition are also leading to the future agonies or ecstasies (e.g., the willingness to modulate our behavior and experiences through drugs, the growing technological and bureaucratic apparatus for surveillance and control of individual behavior, the tendency to devaluate the life-worthiness of certain classes of citizens, etc.)

The constructs that have been outlined here will be relevant in more ways than we can anticipate at present. We will touch upon just a few possible applications.

Soc/D may become a consequence of prolonged Clin/D or its associated controlled suspension states. ("Out of sight, out of mind.") But Soc/D may also have a causal role to play. The "partially buried" may remain suspended indefinitely because they no longer seem real as persons to the "fully activated." There may even develop programmed or ritualistic Soc/D. Instead of relying upon chance and idiosyncracy, we may develop formal patterns for behaving toward the suspended that rival or exceed any funerary practices yet seen in our society.

The distinction between the living and the dead would become more complex than we tend to make it these days. At the least, we would probably discriminate among the fully activated, the suspended, and the irretrievably dead. The distinctions may have to become more elaborate and refined as time goes on—even if there is no breakthrough in what might be called retroactive rejuvenation; (i.e.) the reanimation of persons who died before effective restoration techniques were developed.

In this new world, the determination of Pheno/D would take on an even more crucial aspect than it has today. A person considered still to be capable of high-level experiencing might be given certain priorities, or be the one whose psychosocial propensities are transferred to the matrix of a new body that is Pheno/D but physically restorable. A more sophisticated ability to distinguish Than-Mim from physical death (and from Clin/D) would also be required.

Further examples could be given, but perhaps the basic point has been made. Constructs which allow us to recognize and study states with some resemblance to physical death are apt to be of increasing significance in the coming years and centuries. One could hang back and complain about the inadequacy of present conceptions and techniques. The alternative is to accept the challenge with the best ideas at our disposal and attempt to make them progressively more adequate.

EPILOGUE

"In conclusion . . . . "

This phrase seems out of place even though we have in fact reached the conclusion of this discussion. The place of death in human life is neither simple nor stable. Our relationship to death has been changing over the centuries, but the greatest transformations probably lie ahead. We can offer no conclusion in the sense that the inquiry has ended, or that the subject-matter itself has reached a level of equilibrium. Perhaps we had best limit ourselves to practicing for a few more pages the "craft or sullen art" of asking questions. These questions all pertain, in one way or another, to future transactions among the living, the dying, and the dead.

Where Shall We Die?

Most of us were born in hospitals. Most of us will probably die in hospitals. It was not always thus. The likelihood, however, is that the "rites of passage" at both extremes of the life cycle will increasingly be enacted within the specialized confines of the hospital environment. *Should* this be the case? Is it necessary or desirable to allow the present tendency to prevail? Some of the following questions have implications for birth as well, but we will concentrate upon the dying process.

• *What are the socio-symbolic implications of dying within a hospital?* Is a satisfactory rite of passage accomplished for both the individual and the community? Most earlier societies have developed patterns that see the person through his terminal crisis all the way to "the other side." Our hospitals may succeed in detaching the dying person from his society, but that is only part of the total process. What new identity does he gain in return? Is it only a new non-identity, a reduction of self to the dimensions of his dying body? Is there an emotionally relevant transition between hospital and final resting place? In other words, do the individual and his survivors have the opportunity to move through the final phases together with appropriate symbols of passage? It might be objected that we should not expect hospitals to provide socio-symbolic comforts of the kind we are hinting at. This raises a related set of questions: Do hospitals really belong to us, the community? Are they already far beyond the power of being influenced by our values and needs? Is the dying process important enough to us to stimulate the development of more adequate and humanistic care? Or should we begin to develop environments other than the hospital, the nursing home, or other familiar contexts for dying?

Perhaps our institutions are succeeding, rather than failing, in carrying out our wishes to be physically and emotionally insulated from dying and death. (This means, of course, to be insulated from *people* who have the misfortune of reminding us that dying and death are real.) On the other hand, perhaps we are so discomforted because no adequate system of social support exists within which we can relate to the dying and the dead. We cannot question the adequacy of our institutionalized rites of passage without also inquiring into our own fears and motives.

• *Specifically, what aspects of the dying situation should be improved?* Questions that might be raised in this connection include the following:

Is it necessary for patterns of communication to be so edgy, skittery, and downright dishonest? Does this actually serve the needs of patients and their families in some way we do not yet comprehend? Or would an "open awareness context" (56) decrease the dying person's emotional isolation—and perhaps also the anxiety load of the hospital staff?

Does the situational context have to be so *different?* Medico-administrative arguments in favor of existing death places should be balanced against the effects of discontinuity and depersonalization. It has been observed, for example, that the typical context for in-hospital death involves decreased social visibility and the establishment of a relatively impermeable boundary with the rest of the community. The boundary between the death place and other components of the hospital may also be formidable. In addition, a highly regulated and formalized regime prevails. There is a lack of flexibility with respect to the characteristics of each individual patient. The dying person structurally has relatively little power in the total situation. Moreover, the milieu usually has also "been pumped out of stimuli that do not seem strictly necessary—the dying person's own clothes, almost all of his personal possessions, etc. The environment is stripped down to what is required for bare efficiency in surveillance, treatment, and housekeeping" (57).

Should we continue to tolerate the development of death places that are so specialized and discontinuous? Can alternatives be found within institutional structure, perhaps by providing relevant educa-

tion and training experiences for staff? Would health personnel—especially physicians—hold still for such training, or would it be seen as too threatening? Should physicians, in fact, be made to bear almost all of the responsibility as has become traditional? Is it best to conceptualize dying as essentially a medico-administrative problem? Or to reintegrate dying with the larger community? A more general question should also be faced: Do we consider the death place and all that it entails as an appropriate concern of our own, or are we willing to let happen what happens in the continuing course of social and technological change?

• *What are the alternatives to dying within any of the already familiar institutionalized environments?* How feasible is it to develop mobile and flexible systems to support dying at home? How much of the resistance to this concept is based upon objective difficulties, perhaps insurmountable at the present time, for certain terminal conditions, and how much is based upon lack of psychosocial preparation for the challenge? What values might be actualized by the propagation of institutions dedicated exclusively to the care of the terminally ill? Dr. Cicely Saunders has established a hospital that provides an outstanding model for this type of facility. High-level medical care is an intrinsic part of the program (hence, some "terminally ill" pull through), but emphasis is upon maintaining the patient's comfort, dignity, and self-respect. None of the characteristics mentioned above concerning the typical in-hospital death-place apply to St. Christopher's Hospice (London). Would hospitals of this type fulfill our most morbid expectations of gruesome "houses of the dead?" Or would they, rather, dispel many apprehensions by demonstrating that people can continue to function as people right up to the end, if given a reasonable opportunity to do so?

Is it possible to develop innovative

dying-death systems within a variety of sociophysical structures that already exist, but for other purposes? Consider, for example, the burgeoning of residential centers for the elderly (to be distinguished from nursing homes). Occasionally we learn of spontaneous actions on the part of the residents to provide sensitive emotional support to a dying member and then to memorialize him in some way that seems especially fitting. The dying person feels accepted and valued; the survivors strengthen their own belief that death should not be a shameful event (and hence bolster their spirits with respect to their own demise). Could the development of such "systems" be encouraged by those responsible for planning and managing residential centers? Might it then become less obligatory to isolate, transfer, or "cover up" for the dying member? Would morale improve because the group had found it possible to consolidate its unity in the face of that potentially disruptive influence, dying and death? Would some of the rituals and innovations prove useful in other contexts as well? Or must death be denied implicity in developing residential centers—whether for the peace of mind of the potential residents or the planners themselves ("You can grow old here—but don't let me catch you dying.")

These alternatives and others that might be devised could take some of the existing pressure off the hospital and the nursing home. The hospital of today has neither the time nor the perspective to be expert in the humanistics of terminal care. Dying "wastes" bed space, and death is failure. Should not the dying person be some place where he is wanted and valued?

How Shall We Relate to the Dead?

Earlier in this book it was observed that the dead have been virtually expelled from our culture's death system (Chapter 9). The dead seem less real and powerful to us than in most bygone cultures (in-

cluding our own past). This trend seems to be continuing, perhaps accelerating. Let us ask a few questions.

• *How long will the vestiges of traditional funeral/burial procedures survive in our culture?* Will increasingly scarce land continue to be made available for the unprecedented influx of bodies to be expected in this era of overpopulation? Will the epitaph and the eulogy completely disappear from the scene? Will obituary announcements also trickle into oblivion, as the trend now suggests? Will funeral processions come under more restrictive regulation and also, eventually, become defunct? In other words, will it become increasingly the case that virtually no notice will be taken of death (and the dead) except for those few individuals deemed especially prominent?

Would such a development constitute a kind of victory over death? By implication, "being dead" would not be anything very important one way or another. The visible supports for memorialization of the dead might become so attenuated that succeeding generations will grow up without learning to give "deadness" much thought.

• *What are some of the other implications of the potential eradication of the dead?* Would the processes of grief and bereavement be affected? And, if so, in what way? Perhaps grief reactions would be foreshortened. We no longer would be expected to have our feelings tied up with the deceased. Perhaps, however, grief would become interminable and exert a pervasive influence over thought and behavior. This could be a consequence of lacking palpable "proof" of death and the opportunity for survivors to traverse a vicarious rite of passage.

Would the dead, expelled from our conscious and social lives, now return as dream figures, as ghosts, or in other, unprecedented forms? Would the "generation gap" between the living and the dead become so great that we would live virtually as contemporaneous, spontaneous creatures? What would this do to our sense of history and continuity as a people? The prospect of instant oblivion might fit in well with existing attitudes. Many have observed that we are a "throwaway" culture. There is perhaps no reason to fancy that we constitute exceptions to this policy ourselves. Instant disposal of the dead—no deposit, no return—could begin each day with a fresh (blank?) mind.

· What exchanges will take place between the living and the dead? We have observed that the survivor often seems to take on some of the characteristics of the deceased. The widow, for example, may begin to show little traits and quirks that once were the exclusive property of her late husband. Some of her own characteristics, however, may seem to have perished, to have been buried along with him. This exchange between living and dead possibly can be understood in terms of the same general symmetry-seeking bias that has been mentioned at several points in this book. Exploratory research is now in progress on this topic.

We know little enough about the subtle dynamics of interchange between the living and the dead at the present time. It seems likely that this relationship will continue to change as a function of our system for disposing of the dead. Whatever we do with respect to the dead must have some impact on our own feelings. Is it possible that potential transformations of our behavior toward the dead will exceed our capacity for adaptation? Can we truly banish the dead without offending an important part of our nature? Will something within us rise to resist, reform or reshape our death system before really drastic changes take place? Or will future generations find themselves quite able to get along without the dead?

The Final Environment—Whose Responsibility?

Specific forecasts may prove accurate or mistaken. Wholly unforeseen developments may take precedence over any that we or other observers have expressed. Yet it seems fairly evident that our relationship to death is continuing to change. How much of this change can we take into our own hands? Should we want to do so? Whose responsibility is it, anyhow?

Psychologists and others who are committed to the understanding, protection, and enhancement of human behavior could find a challenging and fruitful outlet for their talents in this area. Each person will decide for himself how much he can or should interfere with the changing scene. Would it not be unfortunate, though, if we made our decision by default? Who would care to be an unthinking accomplice for future contexts of dying and death that might prove intolerable?

We might begin with the development of a conceptual framework to encompass the varied phenomena touched upon in this section. Take, for example, the notion of "the final environment" (58). Within a single framework we could organize our knowledge of the dying and funeral/burial processes, and the process of establishing a more or less stable equilibrium between living and dead. The aim would not be for rigid linkage or control of these phases. Rather, this larger unit of analysis would invite the collaborative efforts of many people who usually function in narrowly defined roles. Other people not usually consulted in any of the phases, e.g., the artist—might also find a relevant place. It might be possible to help the dying person and those close to him maintain a sense of continuity and purpose. Tolerance for intolerable invasions of human rights might be decreased. We would recognize more clearly that certain impositions on the dying person, for example, interfere with his preferred role in his own death and memorialization. We would become more aware of the criteria for an acceptable final environment, and more adept in meeting these criteria. We might also come to see more clearly the distinction between a final environment and one that "finalizes."

A conceptual framework, by itself, accomplishes nothing. But people who have an organizing framework in mind can do much. At the least, we could develop a counterpoise to the proliferation of environments on the basis of expedience and unexamined tradition, environments that are inimical to the preservation of human values.

In the broadest sense, earth is our final as well as our primal environment. Throughout our lives we act upon this environment for better or for worse. We close this dicussion of death with the simple suggestion that an additional measure of care be given to making the world a better place in which to die. Would this not also make our world a better place in which to live?

REFERENCES

1. Broad, C. D. *Mind and its place in nature.* New York: Harcourt, Brace, 1929.
2. Gruman, G. J. A history of ideas about the prolongation of life. The evolution of prolongevity hypotheses to 1800. *Transactions of the American Philosophical Society,* 1966, *56,* part 9 (separate).
3. *Ibid.,* p. 7.
4. *Ibid.,* p. 8.
5. *Ibid.*
6. Hilton, J. *Lost horizon.* New York: Morrow, 1936.
7. Gruman, *op. cit.,* pp. 49-50.
8. Richter, C. P. The phenomenon of unexplained sudden death in animals and men. In H. Feifel (Ed.), *The meaning of death.* New York: McGraw-Hill, 1959. Pp. 302-316.
9. Von Saaz, J. *The plowman from Bohemia.* New York: Ungar, 1966.
10. *Ibid.,* p. 71.
11. *Ibid.,* p. 75.
12. Cutler, D. R. (Ed.). *Updating life and death.* Boston: Beacon Press, 1969.
13. Shneidman, E. S. Orientations toward death: A vital aspect of the study of lives. In R. W. White (Ed.), *The study of lives.* New York: Atherton Press, 1963. Pp. 200-227.
14. Kastenbaum, R. While the old man dies. In A. H. Kutscher (Ed.), *Psychosocial care of the terminally ill.* New York: Columbia University Press, in press.
15. Kastenbaum, R. Death and bereavement in later life. In A. H. Kutscher (Ed.), *Death and Bereavement.* Springfield, Ill.: Charles C Thomas, 1969. Pp. 28-54.
16. Kastenbaum, R. & Mishara, B. Premature death and self-injurious behavior in old age. *Geriatrics,* 1971, 26,70-81.
17. Lipsitt, D. R. A medico-psychological approach to dependency in the aged. In R. A. Kalish (Ed.), *The dependencies of old people.* Ann Arbor, Mich.: Institute of Gerontology, 1969. Pp. 17-26.
18. Goldfarb, A. The psychodynamics of dependency and the search for aid. In R. A. Kalish (Ed.), *The dependencies of old people.* Ann Arbor, Mich.: Institute of Gerontology, 1969. Pp. 1-16.
19. Kastenbaum & Mishara, *op. cit.*
20. Martin, J. B. Testimony to United States Senate Subcommittee on Aging, September, 1969.
21. Jackson, J. J. The Blacklands of Gerontology. *Aging and human development,* 1971, *2,* no. 3, 156-171.
22. Kastenbaum, R. The interpersonal context of death in a geriatric institution. Presented at 17th annual scientific meetings, The Gerontological Society, Minneapolis, Minn., 1964.
23. Kastenbaum. *While the old man dies, op. cit.,* pp. 6-7.
24. Freud, S. *An outline of psychoanalysis.* New York: Norton, 1949.
25. Saul, L. Freud's death instinct and the second law of thermodynamics. *International Journal of Psychoanalysis,* 1958, *39,* 323-325.
26. *Ibid.,* p. 325.
27. Ostrow, M. The death instincts—a contribution to the study of instincts. *International Journal of Psychoanalysis,* 1958, *39,* 5-16.
28. Jelliffe, S. E. The death instinct in somatic

and psychopathology. *Psychoanalytic review*, 1933, *20*, 121-132.

29. Menninger, K. *Man against himself.* New York: Harcourt, Brace & World, 1938.
30. *Ibid.*, p. vii.
31. *Ibid.*, p. viii.
32. *Ibid.*, p. 5.
33. Saul, *op. cit.*
34. Schopenhauer, A. *The world as will and idea.* (Translated by T. B. Haldane & I. Kemp.) London: Routledge & Kegan Paul (1883) 1948.
35. Kastenbaum, R. The realm of death: An emerging area of psychological research. *Journal of Human Relations*, 1965, *13*, 538-552.
36. Heavenrich, R. Lethality as a function of experienced isolation, motivation to live, and social resources: An exploratory study in suicidology. Masters thesis, Wayne State University, Detroit, Mich., 1970.
37. Weisman, A. D., & Hackett, T. Predilection to death. *Psychosomatic medicine*, 1961, *23*, 232-256.
38. LeShan, L., & Gassman, M. Some observations on psychotherapy with patients suffering from neoplastic disease. *American Journal of Psychotherapy*, 1958, *12*, 723-734.
39. Kalish, R. A. Non-medical interventions in life and death. Presented to Conference on Social Science and Medicine, Aberdeen, Scotland, September, 1968.
40. Kastenbaum, R. & Kastenbaum, B. K. Hope, survival and the caring environment. In F. Jeffers and E. Palmore (Eds.), *Prediction of life span.* Lexington, Mass.: Heath, 1971.
41. Kastenbaum, R., & Weisman, A. D. The psychological autopsy method in geriatrics. In D. P. Kent, S. Sherwood & R. Kastenbaum (Eds.), *Research, planning and action for the elderly.* New York: Behavioral Publications, in press.

42. Shneidman, E. S. Orientations toward death: A vital aspect of the study of lives. In R. W. White (Ed.), *The study of lives.* New York: Atherton Press, 1963. Pp. 200-227.
43. Beck, A. T., & Greenberg, R. The nosology of suicidal phenomena: Past and future perspectives. University of Pennsylvania Medical School, Philadelphia, Penna., mimeo.
44. Shneidman, E. S. Suicide, lethality and the psychological autopsy. University of California at Los Angeles, mimeo.
45. *Ibid.*, p. 1.
46. Weisman, A. D. Suicide, death, and life-threatening behavior. Presented at "Suicide Prevention in the Seventies," Phoenix, Ariz., January 30-February 1, 1970.
47. *Ibid.*, p. 1.
48. *Ibid.*, p. 8.
49. Kastenbaum & Mishara, *op. cit.*
50. Barker, Roger. *Ecological psychology.* Stanford, Calif.: Stanford University Press, 1968.
51. Kastenbaum & Schaberg, *op. cit.*
52. Lawton, M. P. Ecology and aging. In L. A. Pastalan & D. H. Carson (Eds.), *Spacial behavior of older people.* Ann Arbor, Mich.: The University of Michigan—Wayne State University Institute of Gerontology, 1970.
53. Kastenbaum & Kastenbaum, *op. cit.*
54. Kastenbaum, R. Psychological death. In L. Pearson (Ed.), *Death and dying: Current issues in the treatment of the dying person.* Cleveland: Case Western University Press, 1969. P. 1-27.
55. Weisman, *op. cit.*
56. Glaser, B., & Strauss, A. *Awareness of dying.* Chicago: Aldine, 1966.
57. Weisman, A. D., & Kastenbaum, R. *The psychological autopsy: A study of the terminal phase of life.* New York: Behavioral Publications, 1969.
58. Kastenbaum, R. *The final environment.* In preparation.

CONSCIENTIOUS OBJECTOR

I shall die, but that is all that I shall do for Death.

I hear him leading his horse out of the stall; I hear the clatter on the barn-floor.
He is in haste; he has business in Cuba, business in the Balkans, many calls to make this morning.
But I will not hold the bridle while he cinches the girth.
And he may mount by himself: I will not give him a leg up.

Though he flick my shoulders with his whip, I will not tell him which way the fox ran.
With his hoof on my breast, I will not tell him where the black boy hides in the swamp.
I shall die, but that is all that I shall do for Death; I am not on his pay-roll.

I will not tell him the whereabouts of my friends nor of my enemies either.
Though he promise me much, I will not map him the route to any man's door.
Am I a spy in the land of the living, that I should deliver men to Death?
Brother, the password and the plans of our city are safe with me; never through me
Shall you be overcome.

Edna St. Vincent Millay

Author Index

Subject Index